Does presidentialism make it less likely that democratic governments will be able to manage political conflict, as many prominent scholars have argued? *Presidentialism and Democracy in Latin America* addresses the current debate regarding the liabilities and merits of presidential government. With the unprecedented wave of transitions to democracy since the 1970s, this question has been hotly contested in political and intellectual circles all over the globe. The contributors to this volume examine variations among different presidential systems and skeptically view claims that presidentialism has added significantly to the problems of democratic governance and stability. The contributors argue that presidential systems vary in important ways, mostly according to the constitutional powers accorded to the president to affect legislation and the degree to which presidents' parties control legislative majorities.

PRESIDENTIALISM AND DEMOCRACY IN LATIN AMERICA

CAMBRIDGE STUDIES IN COMPARATIVE POLITICS

General Editor
PETER LANGE   Duke University

Associate Editors
ELLEN COMISSO   University of California, San Diego
PETER HALL   Harvard University
JOEL MIGDAL   University of Washington
HELEN MILNER   Columbia University
RONALD ROGOWSKI   University of California, Los Angeles
SIDNEY TARROW   Cornell University

OTHER BOOKS IN THE SERIES

Catherine Boone, *Merchant Capital and the Roots of State Power in Senegal, 1930–1985*

Donatella della Porta, *Social Movements, Political Violence, and the State*

Roberto Franzosi, *The Puzzle of Strikes: Class and State Strategies in Postwar Italy*

Miriam A. Golden, *Heroic Defeats: The Politics of Job Loss*

Frances Hagopian, *Traditional Politics and Regime Change in Brazil*

Ellen Immergut, *Health Politics: Interests and Institutions in Western Europe*

Thomas Janoski and Alexander M. Hicks, eds., *The Comparative Political Economy of the Welfare State*

Robert O. Keohane and Helen B. Milner, eds., *Internationalization and Domestic Politics*

David Knoke, Franz Urban Pappi, Jeffrey Broadbent, and Yutaka Tsujinaka, eds., *Comparing Policy Networks*

Allan Kornberg and Harold D. Clarke, *Citizens and Community: Political Support in a Representative Democracy*

David D. Laitin, *Language Repertories and State Construction in Africa*

Doug McAdam, John McCarthy, and Mayer Zald, eds., *Comparative Perspectives on Social Movements*

Joel S. Migdal, Atul Kohli, and Vivienne Shue, eds., *State Power and Social Forces: Domination and Transformation in the Third World*

Paul Pierson, *Dismantling the Welfare State: Reagan, Thatcher and the Politics of Retrenchment*

Marino Regini, *Uncertain Boundaries: The Social and Political Construction of European Economies*

Yossi Shain and Juan Linz, *Interim Governments and Democratic Transitions*

Theda Skocpol, *Social Revolutions in the Modern World*

Sven Steinmo, Kathleen Thelan, and Frank Longstreth, eds., *Structuring Politics: Historical Institutionalism in Comparative Analysis*

Sidney Tarrow, *Power in Movement: Social Protest, Reform, and Revolution*

Ashutosh Varshney, *Democracy, Development, and the Countryside*

PRESIDENTIALISM AND DEMOCRACY IN LATIN AMERICA

Edited by

SCOTT MAINWARING
University of Notre Dame

MATTHEW SOBERG SHUGART
University of California, San Diego

CAMBRIDGE
UNIVERSITY PRESS

PUBLISHED BY THE PRESS SYNDICATE OF THE UNIVERSITY OF CAMBRIDGE
The Pitt Building, Trumpington Street, Cambridge, CB2 1RP, United Kingdom

CAMBRIDGE UNIVERSITY PRESS
The Edinburgh Building, Cambridge CB2 2RU, United Kingdom
40 West 20th Street, New York, NY 10011-4211, USA
10 Stamford Road, Oakleigh, Melbourne 3166, Australia

First published 1997

Printed in the United States of America

Typeset in Garamond

Library of Congress Cataloging-in-Publication Data
Presidentialism and democracy in Latin America / edited by Scott
Mainwaring, Matthew Soberg Shugart.

p.   cm. – (Cambridge studies in comparative politics)

Includes bibliographical references and index.

ISBN 0-521-57266-5. – ISBN 0-521-57614-8 (pbk.)

1. Executive power – Latin America.   2. Presidents – Latin America.
3. Latin America – Politics and government.   4. Democracy – Latin
America.   5. Political parties – Latin America.   I. Mainwaring,
Scott, 1954–   .   II. Shugart, Matthew Soberg, 1960–   .
III. Series.
JL961.P75   1997
321.8'098 – dc20   96-26086
                                                         CIP

*A catalog record for this book is available from
the British Library.*

ISBN 0 521 57266 5 hardback
ISBN 0 521 57614 8 paperback

CONTENTS

CONTRIBUTORS

Octávio Amorim Neto is a Ph.D. candidate in political science at the University of California, San Diego.

Ronald P. Archer is Assistant Professor of Political Science at Duke University. He is currently working on a manuscript tentatively titled *Paralysis of Reform: Political Stability and Social Conflict in Colombia* and is continuing a research project on the origin of party systems and how such systems are constrained by historical and social factors.

John M. Carey is Assistant Professor of Political Science at the University of Rochester. He is coauthor (with Matthew Soberg Shugart) of *Presidents and Assemblies: Constitutional Design and Electoral Dynamics* (Cambridge University Press, 1992) and author of *Term Limits and Legislative Representation* (Cambridge, 1996).

Brian F. Crisp is Assistant Professor of Political Science at the University of Arizona. He received his Ph.D. from the University of Michigan in 1992 and is completing a manuscript on interest-group participation in Venezuela. His work includes several chapters and articles about political participation, as well as a forthcoming book entitled *Control institucional de la participación en la democracia venezolana* (Editorial Jurídica Venezolana).

Julio Faundez is Professor of Law at the University of Warwick. His works include *Marxism and Democracy in Chile: From 1932 to the Fall of Allende*

(Yale University Press, 1988) and (coedited with Sol Picciotto) *The Nationalization of Multinationals in Peripheral Economies* (Holmes & Meier, 1978).

Eduardo A. Gamarra is Associate Professor of Political Science and Acting Director of the Latin American and Caribbean Center at Florida International University. He is coauthor (with James Malloy) of *Revolution and Reaction in Bolivia, 1964–1985* (Transaction Books, 1988).

Mark P. Jones is Assistant Professor of Political Science at Michigan State University. His work focuses on the comparative study of electoral systems and constitutional institutions in Latin America. In addition to *Electoral Laws and the Survival of Presidential Democracies* (University of Notre Dame Press, 1995), he has published in journals such as *Electoral Studies* and *Political Research Quarterly*.

Scott Mainwaring is Chair and Professor of Government at the University of Notre Dame. He is author or coeditor of *Building Democratic Institutions: Party Systems in Latin America* (Stanford University Press, 1995), *Issues in Democratic Consolidation: The New South American Democracies in Comparative Perspective* (University of Notre Dame Press, 1992), *The Progressive Church in Latin America* (University of Notre Dame Press, 1989), and *The Catholic Church and Politics in Brazil, 1916–1985* (Stanford University Press, 1986).

Matthew Soberg Shugart is Associate Professor of Political Science at the University of California, San Diego. He is coauthor (with Rein Taagepera) of *Seats and Votes: The Effects and Determinants of Electoral Systems* (Yale University Press, 1989) and (with John M. Carey) *Presidents and Assemblies: Constitutional Design and Electoral Dynamics* (Cambridge University Press, 1992).

Peter M. Siavelis is Assistant Professor of Political Science at Wake Forest University. He is the author of several articles on Chilean electoral and legislative politics.

Jeffrey Weldon is Assistant Professor of Political Science at the Instituto Tecnológico Autónomo de México (ITAM) in Mexico City and a Ph.D. candidate in political science at the University of California, San Diego.

ACKNOWLEDGMENTS

We are grateful to Alex Holzman and Helen Wheeler of Cambridge University Press and to the copyeditor, Robert Racine. We also thank Daniel Levine and two anonymous readers of Cambridge University Press for their helpful suggestions.

INTRODUCTION

Scott Mainwaring and Matthew Soberg Shugart

This book addresses two fundamental issues. First, it addresses the current debate regarding the liabilities and merits of presidential government. Does presidentialism make it less likely that democratic governments will be able to manage political conflict, as many prominent scholars have argued recently? Our contribution to this debate is to interject skepticism that presidentialism has *generally* contributed significantly to the problems of democratic governance and stability, although we recognize that it may have done so in specific cases. These questions about the general desirability of presidentialism have been at the core of a first generation of recent comparative studies of presidentialism that essentially began with Juan Linz's seminal critique of this regime type.

Second, we examine variations among different presidential systems, the implications of these variations for executive–legislative relations, and their consequences for democratic governance and stability. In Chapter 1 and the Conclusion, as well as the nine country chapters, we argue that presidential systems vary in important ways, above all according to (1) the constitutional powers accorded to the president and (2) the kind of parties and party system. We also explore how these variations in presidential powers and the party system affect the performance of presidential democracy. We believe that the first generation of (recent) comparative studies of presidentialism did not always pay sufficient attention to these issues. While we recognize the important contributions of this first generation of comparative studies, we believe that these questions on variations among presidential systems and their implications should form the core of a new generation of studies. These issues receive paramount attention in this book.

Presidentialism has become the subject of a lively intellectual and political debate since the mid-1980s. Politically, this debate has been fueled
by the succession of transitions to democracy that swept southern Europe,
Latin America, central Europe, Asia, and Africa. Political leaders sought
ways to design institutions so as to increase the prospects for consolidating
new democracies. Especially in Latin America, many questioned whether
presidentialism had been a significant contributing factor to past democratic
failure, given that presidential systems have overwhelmingly predominated
in a region beset by many democratic breakdowns.

The debate about presidentialism has had considerable political visibility in several Latin American countries because scholars and political
actors became convinced that formal political institutions can help or hinder
efforts to construct stable democracies. For the first time in decades there
has been serious debate about modifying presidential systems or even
switching to parliamentary government. This debate went farthest in Brazil,
where there was a realistic possibility that the Constitutional Congress of
1987–88 would vote to institute a so-called semipresidential government,
in which a prime minister elected by the legislature and a popularly elected
president would share executive power. A referendum on the system of
government was held in Brazil in 1993, again creating a real possibility of
a switch to a semipresidential format. Early surveys showed a significant
lead for the reform proposal in Brazil, though presidentialism ultimately
won easily.

Even where there has been less chance of a move away from presidentialism, concern about how it has worked and efforts to reform it have
burgeoned. Argentine President Raúl Alfonsín (1983–89) formed a high-
level commission to produce proposals on constitutional reforms, including
a switch to parliamentary government. Colombia adopted a new constitution in 1991, partly to rectify presidential–congressional disharmony. Constitutional reforms involving executive–legislative relations have also been
debated in the Chilean legislature. In Bolivia, the Congress engaged in
discussions about changing to a parliamentary system when it revised the
constitution in 1993. It is significant, however, that all of the reforms that
contemplated shifts away from presidentialism have been defeated.

Intellectually, the debate about presidentialism was sparked by the con-
viction that institutional arrangements have an autonomous impact in shaping politics and that the choice of a presidential, parliamentary, or some
other system is of fundamental importance. The landmark contribution that
fostered much of the subsequent debate was Juan Linz's seminal essay "Presidential or Parliamentary Democracy: Does It Make a Difference?" Origi-

nally written in 1984, the essay argued that presidential systems are inimical to constructing stable democracies.[1]

Linz's argument spawned an extensive debate,[2] albeit one in which in many countries' partisan opinions have often overshadowed careful research. In part because the policy implications of this debate have been so obvious and salient that careful academic work has sometimes taken a back seat, in part because of the long-standing neglect of presidentialism by comparative political scientists and sociologists, a great deal remains to be done.[3] This book addresses that lacuna.

In the academic debate, critics of presidentialism have dominated and have added to the set of problems that Linz identified with this regime type. Our volume recognizes the importance of the criticisms of presidentialism but stresses that there is no universally best form of government. Different conditions – including party system and levels of social conflict and economic development – may make one form of government fit better in one country, while another form would be more suitable elsewhere.

Three important unifying themes run throughout the volume. The first is skepticism regarding the dominant viewpoint that presidentialism is usually a problematic regime type. This theme is taken up most explicitly in Chapter 1 and the chapter by Faundez on Chile, but it runs throughout the rest of the chapters as well.

Second, the volume shows that presidentialism comes in different varieties and that these variations can be as important as the broad differences between parliamentarism and presidentialism. This theme is particularly important because of the tendency in the debate to focus on the contrast between parliamentarism and presidentialism and the concomitant tendency to pay less careful attention to differences among presidential systems. We develop this point in Chapter 1 and the Conclusion, where we attempt to conceptualize the major dimensions along which presidential systems vary, and it is at least implicit in every chapter in the volume.

The third theme is that the way presidentialism functions depends upon the broader institutional arrangements – especially the president's legisla-

---

1 The essay circulated widely in unpublished form in English for several years, though it was published in Spanish, Portuguese, and several other languages. An abridged English version appeared in Linz (1990). For the definitive English version, see Linz (1994). For significant antecedents to Linz's contribution, see Loewenstein (1949), Trigueiro (1959), Blondel and Suárez (1981), and Suárez (1982).

2 Among other contributions, see Linz and Valenzuela (1994), Mainwaring (1993), Riggs (1988), and Shugart and Carey (1992).

3 By contrast, there is an extensive literature on the U.S. presidency.

tive powers and the party system – as well as, of course, upon societal conditions. All of the authors pay close attention to how institutional combinations function in different national settings. For example, Carey insists that the constitutional lifetime prohibition against presidential reelection, the prohibition against immediate congressional reelection, and the power of presidents over patronage are fundamental factors in shaping how presidentialism functions in Costa Rica. Mainwaring argues that the combination of a fragmented party system, undisciplined parties, and federalism have shaped Brazilian presidentialism. The other authors underscore similar examples of the importance of the broader institutional setting for how presidentialism functions – and for how well it functions. The interaction between presidentialism, presidential powers, and the party system is developed more fully in this volume than in the extant literature.

Although the chapters in this book have policy implications, they are above all scholarly analyses, based on extensive research, that provide detailed examinations of presidentialism in different national settings. The essays do not generally advocate one set of institutional arrangements over another. They do, however, suggest that the choice of a system of government is important and that presidentialism has encountered some specific problems in various countries. This scholarly focus is not unique, but it is distinctive on an issue in which political interests and passions have often – and understandably – played a key role.

Chapter 1 provides an overview of the debate about presidentialism. We review the criticisms that have been launched against presidentialism. We acknowledge the poor historical record of presidentialism in sustaining democracy but argue that this is due in part to the tendency of this regime type to have been adopted in a series of countries that face numerous obstacles to democratization. Moreover, we argue that, alongside its liabilities, presidentialism also has some distinct advantages.

Chapter 1 then discusses variations in presidents' legislative powers; we argue that these variations constitute a fundamental divide among presidential systems. We distinguish between two forms of legislative powers that may be provided for in the constitution: proactive and reactive. Proactive legislative powers enable a president to enact new legislation of his or her preference without the prior consent of the legislature. Reactive powers permit the president to block legislative proposals that he or she does not like. We then show that there is significant variation among the countries covered in this volume in the presidents' constitutional powers in the legislative arena. Finally, we argue that a president's ability to accomplish a policy agenda depends on the interaction between such constitutionally accorded powers and what we term the president's *partisan powers*, that is, the extent to which the president's party holds a reliable majority in the legislature.

Chapter 1 is followed by nine country studies on eight different countries (with two chapters on Chile). Our selection of cases involved three somewhat overlapping criteria. We wanted to include the major countries of the region, and accordingly we have covered the four largest (by population) Latin American countries: Brazil, Mexico,[4] Colombia, and Argentina, as well as the sixth (Venezuela) and seventh (Chile) largest. We wanted to ensure coverage of most of the handful of countries (Chile, Colombia, Costa Rica, Uruguay, and Venezuela) with extensive democratic history in the region; among this subset, only Uruguay is not represented in the volume. Finally, we wanted to include cases that were theoretically and comparatively interesting. This accounts for the inclusion of Bolivia, which deviates rather markedly from "pure" presidentialism in the means by which presidents are selected.

To underscore our argument that presidentialism comes in different varieties, we have grouped the chapters according to dominant features of presidentialism in these Latin American countries. Our first two chapters deal with Brazil and Colombia, countries in which presidents have enormous constitutional powers to set the policy agenda or even to rule by decree but surprisingly little actual ability to accomplish their agendas, owing to low partisan powers (i.e., lack of reliable political support in congress). Presidents in these countries have consistently resorted to attempts to circumvent congress, with deleterious consequences for institution building. Then we have chapters on three countries in which presidents are not constitutionally granted the sweeping decree powers that we find in Brazil and Colombia, but in which presidents generally enjoy copartisan congressional majorities. This group of countries includes Venezuela, where parties have been very disciplined, but only some presidents have held legislative majorities; Costa Rica, perhaps the most successful presidential democracy outside the United States, and Mexico, where presidential control over the Congress has gone to its logical extreme in the form of an authoritarian regime.

Our next chapter concerns Argentina (since the return to democracy in 1983), which, besides being a large and important country, is theoretically interesting because of conflicts over presidential powers that ultimately culminated in a major revision of the constitution in 1995. We then present two chapters that capture very different constitutional orders in one of the

4 We address the inevitable question about why we are including Mexico in a book on democracy later on in this Introduction.

countries that has most animated the debate over presidentialism: Chile. Finally, we have a chapter on the unusual constitutional format that may have assisted the consolidation of democracy in Bolivia under very difficult conditions.

Focused on the case of Brazil, Scott Mainwaring's chapter argues that the combination of presidentialism and a multiparty system tends to create problems for democracy. Several features of the Brazilian electoral system have encouraged the formation of a fragmented multiparty system in which no popularly elected president since 1950 has had a majority in Congress. The situation of permanent minority presidentialism easily leads to executive–legislative stalemate. Because of the fixed electoral timetable of the presidential system, there are no institutionalized means of dealing with this situation of presidents who lack stable congressional support. This problem is exacerbated by the malleable character of the catchall parties. When presidents are popular, politicians of all stripes and colors support them, but when they lose favor, they often have difficulty retaining legislative support. As a result, presidents have problems formulating and implementing policy during difficult times, and they are forced to govern in an ad hoc fashion and to circumvent democratic institutions, especially congress and parties.

Ronald Archer and Matthew Shugart's analysis of Colombian presidentialism also focuses on fragmentation in the Congress, but in the context of a two-party system rather than a multiparty system. Although Colombian presidents have been portrayed as dominant due to their substantial formal powers, they have regularly had problems garnering enough support even within their own parties to make lasting policy changes. Each president from 1974 to 1990 had a comprehensive package of economic, political, and social reforms rejected or, in a few cases, passed in piecemeal form. The reform packages were all intended to cultivate the growing urban population by such measures as professionalizing the delivery of public services, but because Congress is disproportionately rural and tied to patronage networks, such reforms have failed. Thus, Colombia presents a paradox: expansive constitutionally granted presidential powers, reformist presidents, but little ability to accomplish reform. Furthering the paradox, a new constitution adopted in 1991 that reduces presidential powers somewhat was initiated by the president himself, using his emergency powers. Archer and Shugart argue that the great powers accorded to the president in the constitution must be understood within a framework that considers what constitutes the interests of Colombia's traditional party bosses. These powers are part of the means by which patronage-seeking politicians delegate most national policy making to the executive, but these politicians have numerous means to prevent the use of these powers against their own patronage-driven needs. The new constitution, the authors conclude, may not improve the situation, since the means by which members of Congress are elected have not been changed sufficiently to eliminate the scramble for patronage as a primary concern.

The next chapter deals with Venezuela, one of the oldest democracies in Latin America, but which has hit hard times of late. Brian Crisp notes that the constitution gives the president of Venezuela such limited powers that he or she could be marginalized from the legislative process. Nonetheless, most presidents have appeared quite powerful because they have generally had large legislative contingents and their parties are always highly disciplined. Moreover, they have made effective use of a series of nonlegislative powers, such as the ability to establish high-level consultative commissions that incorporate favored interest groups into the executive branch. Throughout most of the Venezuelan democratic regime's existence since 1958, two large parties have dominated. However, recent economic dislocations and political scandals have led to a disruption of the party system, which in turn has made governability difficult and led the president to try to accrue more powers.

John Carey's chapter deals with a case of quite weak presidential legislative powers, but one in which presidents nonetheless often appear powerful because their parties usually enjoy legislative majorities. Presidentialism has functioned in Costa Rica in such a way that it has been largely free of the usual pathologies that critics of presidentialism attribute to the regime type. The Costa Rican system is relevant not only because of its successful democratic record, but also because of an unusual institutional provision (and one that has been attracting a lot of attention in the United States in recent years): congressional term limits. Members of Congress cannot be immediately reelected; presidents are restricted to a single term. Carey argues that term limits make a party's presidential candidate enormously powerful over the party's delegation in the Costa Rican Congress once the candidate for the next term has been chosen in a primary election held near the middle of the incumbent's term. The candidate's power stems from the fact that if the party wins the next election, it is this future president who will have the ability to appoint former Congress members to political positions. Without this power of appointment, political careers would be practically impossible in Costa Rica, given the ineligibility of all incumbents for reelection. This desire of members to see their party's presidential candidate win the next election fosters a collective incentive to work on behalf of the party, but the possibility of policy differences between the incumbent and the future president and the selection of that potential next president in an open primary mean that party discipline is usually not so great that presidents can count on automatic support from deputies of their party. Thus, the Costa Rican Congress is able to make more effective use of its formal powers to act as a check on the presidency than is the case in most Latin American presidential systems.

Mexico is not normally analyzed in the context of democracies, and its inclusion in this book does not imply that we consider the regime to be democratic. We include the case for several reasons. First, for the United States, it is the most important Latin American country, and indeed one of the most important countries in the world. Second, as of the 1994 elections, Mexico appears to be moving in a democratic direction, even if it does not yet fully qualify as democratic. And finally and most importantly, for the-oretical reasons the Mexican case is fascinating: It allows us to think about the interplay between a president's constitutional powers and his or her partisan powers. As Jeffrey Weldon's chapter shows, the authoritarian dom-inance of Mexican presidents is largely rooted in the institutional incentives of Mexico's brand of presidentialism. Like Costa Rica, Mexico has term limits on its members of Congress, who cannot serve consecutive terms, as well as a lifetime one-term limit on the presidency. However, the conse-quences of this are very different from those in Costa Rica because presidents in Mexico have long been the undisputed leaders of the only party that has had a realistic chance of winning elections, given its enormous resource advantage and its ability to manipulate election outcomes. As in Costa Rica, political careers in Mexico depend not on representing a constituency, but on winning an appointment administered by the president. However, unlike in Costa Rica – where there is both intraparty competition (primary elec-tions) and interparty competition – in Mexico the president designates his or her own successor as head of the Institutional Revolutionary Party (PRI) and presidential nominee, thereby ensuring continuity from one adminis-tration to the next. Thus, no ruling-party deputy has any incentive to oppose the president. In other words, Mexican presidents derive their apparent dominance not from the presidential constitution, but from their over-whelming partisan powers. Weldon examines the early years of the Mexican Revolution to show that before the formation of a hegemonic party, presi-dents often appeared relatively weak, a situation that cannot be ruled out in the future as the PRI becomes weaker.

Argentina is a case in which presidents have substantial powers both in the constitution and within the party system. Presidents in the post-1983 period have not consistently had congressional majorities, but they have enjoyed the support of a disciplined major party. In his analysis of Argentine presidentialism, Mark Jones argues that the dominance of the two major parties, the disciplined character of these parties, and federalism helped the system achieve democratic stability even in the face of the severe economic problems weathered under President Alfonsín (1983–89). On the other hand, Jones points to other institutional features that allowed presidents – especially Menem – to adopt a sometimes cavalier attitude toward democratic institutions. President Menem (elected in 1989 and reelected in 1995) extensively used decrees of "urgent necessity" to broaden his legislative powers, leading to a situation in which he effectively bypassed the legislature to implement key parts of his program. Jones shows that this stretching of constitutional powers was possible because Peronist majorities permitted him to "pack" the Supreme Court with pliant justices. The result has been an unusually dominant executive for a democratic presidential system.

We have two chapters on Chile because of the considerable difference in constitutional design between the two widely separated democratic periods and because some of the most important theorizing about democratic breakdown and presidentialism has focused on this case. Julio Faundez's chapter deals with the period from 1933 until the military coup of 1973. Faundez argues that although presidentialism is frequently blamed for the collapse of democracy, the presidential constitution proved adaptable through several difficult decades during which Chilean democracy was considered a success story by Third World standards. When democracy collapsed, it was not because of the constitutional form, but because of extreme polarization brought about by the urgent tasks confronting Chilean society – tasks that previous governments, which were coalitions of several parties, had been unable to handle. It is questionable whether coalitions under parliamentarism would have been any more effective than the coalitions that were formed under presidentialism, especially during the 1950s when the party system was exceedingly weak and fragmented. Faundez shows that Chile's form of presidentialism, by giving the president a veto, led to more moderate policy outcomes in some instances than could have been achieved by parliamentary majorities alone and that a 1970 amendment providing for delegation of decree powers to the president actually restrained the use of decrees rather than opened the door to presidential dominance.

Peter Siavelis's chapter concerns the current democratic regime in Chile since the defeat of military leader Augusto Pinochet in his bid to extend his term via a plebiscite in 1988. Siavelis notes that the transition to democracy occurred within the context of a constitution originally drafted for Pinochet's benefit. That constitution calls for extreme concentration of powers in the president's hand, such that the legislature is marginalized from policy making. Moreover, the outgoing regime imposed an electoral system intended to reduce the number of parties and to overrepresent conservative interests allied with the military regime. Despite these obstacles, the regime functioned well during the term of its first democratically elected president and Congress. However, the smooth functioning of post-transition politics is more a result of the consensual nature of the transition itself than of any long-term trends. Despite the electoral system's incentives, the number of parties has not been reduced from the period before military rule; rather, parties have simply formed electoral coalitions while keeping their separate organizations and congressional identities. Moreover, the presidential term has been changed back to six years. Thus, the same electoral incentives that predominated before 1973, when parties seeking to maximize their chances in midterm elections would frequently desert the president, may return in the future. Unless presidential powers are reduced, future governability may be less smooth than it has been since 1989.

Our last country chapter is on a system that deviates from "pure" presidentialism. Eduardo Gamarra examines the performance of Bolivia's democracy since the military returned to the barracks in 1982. In Bolivia, presidents have tended to be selected through assembly negotiations rather than directly through the popular vote. It is this process, and the assembly coalition building it requires, that Gamarra sees as both the strength and weakness of the Bolivian system. As long as sufficient resources existed to supply coalition partners with white-collar patronage, the coalitions that supported executives in the late 1980s remained stable and disciplined. As demands for patronage have grown, however, coalitions have destabilized. Gamarra rejects the contention that parliamentary government would improve the quality of Bolivian democracy; but he does suggest that, without electoral reform, demands for patronage will overtax the means available for presidents to satisfy coalition partners.

In the Conclusion, we examine the interaction between presidentialism and the party system. We argue that two key features of the party system are fundamental to understanding how presidentialism functions in different contexts: the "effective" number of parties in the legislature and the degree of party discipline. With a high effective number of parties, no party controls a majority in the legislature, so some form of coalition government is necessary. If the president's party does not control a significant share of legislative seats, it often becomes difficult for the president to assemble a stable legislative coalition that will enable him or her to accomplish some meaningful policy goals. We also argue that a moderate degree of party discipline facilitates predictability in executive–legislative relations. We show how party and electoral legislation shape the number of parties and their degree of discipline. We argue that interbranch relations are likely to be smoother if presidents either have a large party backing them or at least have sufficient partisan support to ensure that their vetoes can be sustained, so that they are unlikely to be marginalized from the policy-making process. Finally, we develop several hypotheses about the relationship between constitutional and partisan powers, arguing that there tends to be an inverse relationship between the two forms of presidential power.

Finally, the Appendix provides summaries of the constitutional provisions in Latin America that pertain to executive–legislative relations. This Appendix is the only source that we know of to which readers can turn for quick reference on a wide range of information related to formal legislative and executive powers.

1

PRESIDENTIALISM AND DEMOCRACY IN LATIN AMERICA: RETHINKING THE TERMS OF THE DEBATE

Matthew Soberg Shugart and Scott Mainwaring

In recent years, many scholars have argued that the presidential form of government has been a major contributor to the travails of democracy in Latin America. This argument has been widely accepted, and there are few published counterarguments. However, as we hope to make clear in this chapter, the evidence in favor of the antipresidentialist position is weaker than often assumed. The empirical argument against presidentialism is based mostly on the Latin American experience. The failure of presidential democracies in this part of the world has led many scholars to assert that parliamentary regimes would fare better. There are two difficulties with this argument: (1) presidential democracy has existed mostly in Latin America, making it hard to disentangle those obstacles to democracy in Latin America that stem from the regime type and those that stem from socioeconomic or other factors; and (2) parliamentary democracy exists almost exclusively in Europe or former British colonies, which should make us suspicious of arguments that parliamentarism would perform as well outside these settings. To be sure, critics of presidentialism and advocates of parliamentarism have not made their case entirely on empirical grounds; they have developed compelling logical defenses of their positions, too. However, as we hope to

We are grateful to Robert Dix, Mark Jones, Charles Kenney, Timothy Power, and Jeffrey Weldon for helpful comments on this chapter.

show, equally compelling cases can be made in favor of presidentialism and against parliamentarism.

Where does this leave us? We shall argue that it raises doubts about whether one regime type is clearly superior to the other. We regard this as a conclusion that not only is empirically grounded, but also provides room for more political optimism for Latin America. There is little prospect that most Latin American countries would shift to parliamentarism, so if we were to accept the argument against presidentialism, we would have little basis for optimism over the future of Latin American democracy. Given our more skeptical reading of the antipresidentialist position, we see less reason to believe that Latin America is condemned to repeat its cycle of authoritarianism. Or, if it is so doomed, the regime type is a less central reason than some scholars have implied.

This chapter has three primary tasks. First, we define presidential democracy in contrast to other common regime types, in particular parliamentarism. Having a concise definition of the regime type is a crucial first step toward assessing variations among presidential regimes.

Second, we address the debate about the efficacy of presidential regimes for the survival of democracy. In doing so, we challenge the current consensus, which has focused too much on the flaws of presidentialism and not enough on the broader context where presidentialism has prevailed.

Third, we begin analyzing factors that strongly affect the functioning and performance of presidential democracies. Throughout this volume, we and our contributors assess variations within the presidential regime type. Too often, in our view, presidentialism is treated as a homogeneous type. This book shows that this assumption is mistaken. Some variations of presidentialism – for example, in their constitutional authority or the party system – are more likely to promote stable democracy than others.

We argue that the "strength" of presidents – their ability to influence legislation – rests on two categories of presidential powers: constitutional and partisan. Constitutional powers, like the ability to veto bills or issue decree-laws, allow presidents to shape the policy output of the system regardless of whether they head a party or bloc of parties that controls a legislative majority. Some presidents (e.g., post–Pinochet Chile, Colombia) have vast constitutional powers, while others (e.g., Costa Rica, Venezuela) have comparatively limited constitutional powers, as the country chapters and this chapter show. Partisan powers are abilities to shape (or, conceivably, dominate) the lawmaking process that stem from the president's standing vis-à-vis the party system. At one extreme (e.g., Mexico), the president may be the unchallenged leader of the majority party. At the other extreme (e.g., Brazil), presidents' parties fall far short of a majority in congress. The interaction of presidents' constitutional and partisan powers shapes the character of executive–legislative relations and largely determines the ability of presidents to turn a legislative program into policy.

DEFINING PRESIDENTIAL DEMOCRACY

Our first task is to define *democracy* and *presidential democracy*. We prefer a procedural definition of democracy. Specifically, a democracy must meet three criteria. First, democracies must have open, competitive elections that determine who establishes public policy. This means that election results cannot be determined by fraud, coercion, or major proscriptions. A given country may have a set of institutions that appear formally democratic but in which the democratic character of the system's actual operation is severely compromised, as in Mexico (see Weldon, this volume). Elections must in principle afford the possibility of alternation in power even if, as in Japan, actual alternation does not occur for decades. Second, in the contemporary period, there must be nearly universal adult suffrage.[1] Third, there must be basic guarantees of traditional civil rights, such as freedom of speech, freedom of organization, and due process of law.[2]

What do we mean by *presidential* democracy? There are two basic defining characteristics: (1) The chief executive (president) is popularly elected, and (2) the terms of office of both president and assembly are fixed. These characteristics may be contrasted with parliamentarism, in which (1) the chief executive (prime minister) is not popularly elected but instead is elected by parliament, and (2) terms of office are not fixed, since the tenure of the prime minister and cabinet depends on the confidence of the majority of the parliament, and sometimes, the cabinet may dissolve parliament and call early elections.[3] The fundamental characteristics of presidentialism –

1 Until quite recently, this criterion was debatable because some nations that were usually considered democracies excluded a large part of the adult population, but this is no longer the case. For example, Switzerland excluded women until 1971; Brazil and Chile excluded illiterates until 1985 and 1970, respectively.
2 Our definition of *democracy* essentially follows Dahl's (1971) definition of *polyarchy*, except with the additional criterion regarding traditional civil liberties.
3 Those who advocate parliamentarism partly on the grounds that the absence of fixed terms provides greater flexibility often imply that the prime minister by definition has discretionary authority to dissolve parliament in the event of an impasse. However, many parliamentary systems vest dissolution power not in the cabinet but in a president who, while not popularly elected, may have been elected by a different coalition from that which sustains a given cabinet in power. Some presidents in parliamentary systems are elected by extraordinary majorities and/or for longer terms than that of parliament and/or by

Table 1.1. *Conceptualizing presidentialism*

Head of government selected by	Fixed term	
	Yes	No
Voters	Presidential	Hybrid (Israel)[a]
Legislators	Hybrid (Switzerland)	Parliamentary

[a] This system will be used for the first time in 1996.
Source: Adapted from Lijphart (1984:70).

whatever variations there may be within types – are separate origin (i.e., popular executive election) and separate survival (i.e., neither the executive nor the legislature may shorten the other's term).[4] These two defining features of presidentialism generate a two-by-two matrix that is seen in Table 1.1.

A third and, outside Latin America, increasingly common type of democracy is premier-presidentialism (a form of what others have called semi-presidentialism).[5] In this regime type, the president is popularly elected and has political powers, including the authority to appoint (or at least nominate) the prime minister and usually to dissolve parliament.[6] However,

electoral colleges consisting of both regional and national politicians. Contrary to widespread assumptions, dissolution is often not an executive prerogative in many parliamentary systems, including in Germany and Italy.

4 Conceivably one could have separate origin without popular election, but there probably have never been such cases. An example would be if state legislatures selected the chief executive of a federal system with no role for voters or national legislators, but voters alone chose national legislators.

5 Shugart and Carey (1992) prefer *premier-presidential* because *semipresidential* is often applied to regimes in which the president has unilateral appointment and dismissal power, but cabinets also must maintain parliamentary confidence. Such regimes, for which Shugart and Carey prefer the term *president-parliamentary* manifest a confused, conflictual relationship between executive and legislative authority over the ministries. Examples have included the German Weimar Republic, Sri Lanka since 1977, and Russia under its 1993 constitution. None of these should be conflated with the regime type seen in Finland and France.

6 In a few countries, the president does not even have discretion over the naming of cabinet ministers and also cannot dissolve parliament. In these regimes the president is essentially just an elected head of state in a parliamentary system with no constitutionally guaranteed policy or governmental role. The Haitian constitution of 1987, as well as the Irish constitution and some new constitutions in former Communist countries (e.g., Bulgaria and

in such systems (unlike in presidential systems) the cabinet is collectively responsible to the parliament. Thus, the president does not have constitutional authority to dismiss ministers (at least when they enjoy parliamentary confidence). Because cabinets are responsible to parliament, the president may be able to function as the head of government (chief executive) only when his or her party (or bloc of parties) holds a majority of parliamentary seats, as was almost always the case in France between 1958 and 1986. At other times, the president must cede most significant powers to the prime minister and cabinet (as in France, 1986–88 and 1993–95).

Some scholars (e.g., Duverger 1980; Lijphart 1984) have suggested that these regimes would alternate between the upper-left and lower-right cells in Table 1.1, depending on whether the president or the opposition has the majority. However, because the president's ability to act as de facto head of government depends entirely on the legislative majority, the system is never meaningfully "presidential," since that would imply (by definition) that the president is head of government in all legislative situations. Moreover, as we have noted, presidentialism implies fixed terms; yet under premier-presidentialism, the head of the government may be dismissed through a vote of no confidence, and usually (as in France) the president may dissolve the assembly. Premier-presidentialism was considered in Brazil in the Constituent Assembly of 1987–88 and again in a plebiscite in 1993 and was officially proposed in Argentina under Alfonsín (1983–89), but there are no current examples in Latin America.

POPULAR ELECTION

In a presidential system, the head of government is popularly elected. Usually popular election means *direct* election, but some countries have an electoral college that does not significantly deviate from the principle of popular election. In a direct election, votes are counted in a single nationwide constituency. In an electoral college, votes are aggregated at subnational levels and the delegates so elected formally choose the president. If, as in Argentina before 1995 and in the United States, the delegates to the electoral college have no other political function besides choosing a president, we may nonetheless speak of popular (albeit not direct) presidential elections.

A potentially more significant deviation from the popular nature of presidential elections occurs where the congress makes the final selection. At the extreme, the congress might choose the president without any in-

Slovenia), grant such weak authority to the presidency that they are essentially parliamentary.

tervention of a popular election. Such a regime would obviously not be presidential. However, if there is a popular election, but a requirement that it requires an absolute majority in order to be decisive, the final selection in some systems falls to the congress, rather than to the electorate in a second round (runoff). In such a case, we have a hybrid of popular and congressional selection. Chile before 1973 and Bolivia currently are examples of procedures of this sort. In Chile, Congress was restricted to choosing from the top two popular vote winners; in every case, the winner of the popular plurality was selected in Congress.[7] In Bolivia through 1993, the Congress could select from among the top three popular vote winners, and in fact, both runners-up and third-place candidates have been selected, as Gamarra's chapter shows. A constitutional reform in Bolivia in 1994 reduced Congress's freedom of choice by requiring it to choose from among the top two candidates. This change increases the likelihood of the popular front-runner being selected, because a candidate will no longer have the option of playing for a third-place finish in the hopes of being selected by Congress.

FIXED TERMS

When we speak of a presidential regime as one in which both the assembly and the chief executive sit for fixed terms, we mean that the survival in office of one branch does not depend on the other. There are no presidential democracies in Latin America in which the president has the authority to dissolve congress when he finds it politically convenient to do so, as French and Finnish presidents may do.[8] However, the Peruvian constitutions of 1933, 1979, and 1993 have all allowed the president to dissolve Congress in response to repeated censures of cabinets. With this provision, terms are not really fixed, and the constitution deviates markedly from presidential-

---

7 This observed respect for the front-runner did not necessarily reflect a norm of supporting the electorate's choice. Rather, it was partly accidental: Between 1925 and 1970, only in 1970, in a presidential election without a majority winner, did the runner-up have as much as 30% of the vote. In 1970, the Christian Democrats chose to vote for Allende (whose margin over the runner-up was 36.6 to 35.3%) rather than their arch-rivals for control of the nonsocialist electorate, the National Party. Besides 1970, the only other really close election was in 1958, when Allende (with 28.9%) finished second to the conservative Alessandri (31.6%). It is questionable that a Congress dominated by traditional conservative and centrist parties would have honored the "voters' choice" if the popular vote percentages had been reversed.

8 There are, of course, cases of presidents dissolving congress in the absence of constitutional authority to do so – as in Peru in April 1992, when the contingency of censures had not been met. However, one must distinguish such presidential coups (*autogolpes*) from constitutional dissolution power.

ism.[9] Uruguay's constitution also allows for dissolution after censures, but the censure provision is so difficult to enact (it requires a two-thirds vote, rather than a majority, as in Peru) that the regime remains basically presidential.

There are no constitutions in the Spanish- and Portuguese-speaking countries of the Americas in which the head of government can be dismissed from office before the end of his or her term, except in extraordinary circumstances. Most constitutions allow for impeachment of the president, but only after a finding of criminal or anticonstitutional conduct, often involving a judicial ruling; usually an extraordinary majority of congress is required to remove the president from office. Such procedures have led to the ouster of only two presidents in Latin American history: Fernando Collor de Mello in Brazil in 1992 and Carlos Andrés Pérez in Venezuela in 1993.

REASSESSING THE RECORD OF PRESIDENTIALISM

As we noted at the outset, there has been much criticism in the literature of the presidential regime type. The starting point of these criticisms has been some empirical evidence indicating that presidential systems have not performed well, at least in terms of sustaining democracy for long periods of time.

Most criticisms of presidentialism start from the observation that among long-term stable democracies, few are presidential. There have been several attempts to count the number and percentage of "stable" democracies of one type or the other. Generally, the bottom line is that presidential democracy is a far less successful formula than parliamentary democracy. Rather than review this literature in detail (see Linz 1994:71–74), we shall use as our point of departure one of the most ambitious efforts of this kind, that by Stepan and Skach (1994), who marshal an array of evidence intended to demonstrate the superior record of parliamentarism. They note that among 43 consolidated democracies in the world between 1979 and 1989, there were 34 parliamentary systems, 2 semipresidential ones, and only 5 presidential regimes. They indicate that the overwhelming prevalence of parliamentary systems among democracies is suggestive of a better ability to sustain democracy. Second, they observe that parliamentary systems were

---

9 Even so, there is a basic distinction with the French system, where the president may dissolve the parliament for any reason as long as he or she has not already done so within the previous year.

much more likely than presidential systems to be "democratic over-achievers" according to Vanhanen's (1990) Index of Democratization, while presidential systems were much more likely to be democratic underachievers.[10]

Third, compared with presidential systems, parliamentary systems that were democratic for at least 1 year between 1973 and 1989 were much more likely to have been continuously democratic for at least 10 consecutive years during that period, and the parliamentary systems were much less likely to have experienced a military coup while democratic. In this exercise, Stepan and Skach exclude Organization for Economic Cooperation and Development (OECD) countries to control partially for level of development. Finally, Stepan and Skach analyze the comparative democratic record of 93 countries that became independent between 1945 and 1979. Of 36 countries that were presidential at independence, none was continuously democratic between 1980 and 1989. In contrast, of 41 countries that were parliamentary at independence, 15 were continuously democratic during the 1980s.

Taken together, these findings appear to offer compelling evidence that presidentialism makes the building of a continuous democracy more difficult. We do not attempt to address all of the points raised by Stepan and Skach, but some of these arguments against presidentialism fall prey to a selection bias and hence spurious correlation (see Shugart 1995b). For instance, if parliamentarism occurs more frequently than presidentialism in societies that have relatively better background conditions for democracy, then the correlation may result from selection bias and not from inherent strengths or weaknesses of institutional design. Given that so many presidential regimes have been located in Latin America and that parliamentarism has been nonexistent there, selection bias is a real possibility. Stepan and Skach acknowledge this fact and introduce some controls for level of development and the effect of British colonial rule, but they probably understate the impact of these noninstitutional factors.

In arguing that a breakdown of democracy may be attributed to presidentialism, one is implicitly arguing that a parliamentary regime in the same country at the same time would not have broken down. This type of counterfactual has been made for Chile (Valenzuela 1994), but for few other cases. In the Chilean case, a minority executive such as that headed by Salvador Allende would not have endured in power under a parliamentary system. However, to sustain the counterfactual argument that a parliamentary system would generally have served Chile better, one must also be able

---

10 Stepan and Skach used Vanhanen's Index of Power Resources to control for level of development and determine which countries were democratic over- and underachievers.

to claim that parliamentarism would have survived earlier crises that were weathered by the actual presidential regime. In his chapter in this book, Faundez argues that parliamentarism might well have failed to endure in Chile through the difficult conditions of the 1930s (when there was a brief breakdown of the presidential regime, but democracy was quickly restored) and the 1950s (when the traditional parties were badly weakened).

Another front on which the argument against presidentialism is vulnerable to the charge of spurious correlation concerns the time- and region-bound nature of breakdowns of democracy, presidential or otherwise. Most of the presidential failures that have attracted the attention of the critics occurred in a wave of breakdowns in the 1960s and 1970s. During this period, democratic breakdowns in presidential Argentina, Brazil, and Chile were a glaring contrast to the successful restoration of democracy in Spain under a parliamentary system. However, given the absence of parliamentary systems in South America, we cannot be sure that breakdowns resulted from presidentialism rather than from conditions afflicting South American democracy more generally. Moreover, the same period was not especially auspicious for parliamentary systems, the Spanish redemocratization notwithstanding. Between 1960 and 1980, there were breakdowns of parliamentary regimes in Greece (1967) and Turkey (1980)[11] after a series of open competitive elections. Several other shorter-lived parliamentary regimes broke down in the same period, including those in Burma, Kenya, and Somalia (Shugart and Carey 1992:40). These, for whatever reasons, have received less attention. The occurrence of so many breakdowns in such a short sweep of history (Huntington 1991) should make one cautious about attributing any one country's breakdown to its institutional type, let alone inferring that one type is universally more conducive to democratic stability than another.

The time-bound nature of the breakdowns of established presidential democracies in the 1960s and 1970s is further highlighted by consideration of a previous wave of democratic breakdowns. In the 1920s and 1930s, democracies broke down in Germany, Italy, Portugal, Spain, and the three Baltic states. Each of these regimes, except for Germany, was a parliamentary system; and in Germany, parliamentary features of the constitution such as the need to construct cabinet coalitions that could maintain majority support and a provision for dissolution were at least as responsible for demo-

---

11 Turkey is sometimes characterized as a hybrid, but this is a mistaken impression based on the relative visibility of the president, compared with presidents in other parliamentary systems. However, the Turkish president is elected by parliament and has no more authority over either cabinets or legislation than, for example, the Italian president.

cratic failure as the "rigidity" of the presidential features of the Brazilian and Chilean regimes would be decades later. In times of international economic and political crises, institutional mechanisms that may work in "normal" times can become scapegoats when democracy fails.[12]

DEMOCRACY, REGIME TYPE, AND BACKGROUND CONDITIONS SINCE THE 1970s

In this section we present additional evidence on the comparative democratic record of presidentialism and parliamentarism. Here we rely on evaluations by Freedom House, which has been rating countries on a scale of 1 to 7 (with 1 being best) on both political rights and civil rights since 1972. Table 1.2 lists all 33 countries that were continuously democratic from 1972 to 1994. We considered a country continuously democratic if it had an average score of 3.0 or better on political rights throughout the period 1972–94.[13] In addition, a country was not counted as continuously democratic if either score was ever worse than 4.0 in any annual Freedom House survey.

The countries in Table 1.2 are further sorted into three other categories: income level, population size, and British colonial heritage. These categories are added because each may play a role in a society's likelihood of sustaining democracy. It is widely recognized that a relatively high income level is an important background condition for democracy (Lipset 1960:27–63; Dahl 1971:62–80; Bollen 1979; Lipset 1994), although the exact form of the relationship remains a matter of dispute. In classifying countries by income levels, we followed the guidelines of World Bank (1994): Low is under $635 per capita Gross National Product (GNP); lower-middle is $636 to $2,555; upper-middle is $2,556 to $7,910; and upper is above $7,911. We collapsed the bottom two categories.

Very small countries may have an advantage in democratic stability

---

12 Proportional representation was a favorite institutional scapegoat for interwar breakdowns. See Hermens (1941) for an example and Taagepera and Shugart (1989:234–36) for a discussion.

13 Using an average of 3.0 on both measures would have eliminated some countries (e.g., Colombia, India, Vanuatu) that we (and most observers) consider democratic, but that have had problems with protecting civil rights, partly because of a fight against violent groups. We felt that a country that could maintain fairly open electoral competition even through periods of antigovernment violence probably deserved recognition as a democratic regime. We have supplied the Freedom House scores in the following tables, so those readers who might wish to adopt a tougher standard can see which countries would thereby be eliminated.

Table 1.2. *Independent countries that were continuously democratic, 1972–94*

Income level	Population size	Parliamentary	Presidential	Other
Low/lower-middle	Micro			
	Small	*Jamaica (1.8, 2.6)* *Mauritius (2.0, 2.3)*	Costa Rica (1.0, 1.1)	
	Medium/large		Colombia (2.1, 3.1) Dominican Republic (2.2, 2.0)	
Upper-middle	Micro	*Barbados (1.0, 1.0)* *Malta (1.4, 2.1)* *Nauru (1.7, 2.1)*		
	Small	*Botswana (1.9, 2.9)* *Trinidad and Tobago (1.4, 1.7)*		
	Medium/large		Venezuela (1.5, 2.3)	
Upper	Micro	Luxembourg (1.3, 1.0)		Iceland (1.0, 1.0)
	Small	Ireland (1.0, 1.3) New Zealand (1.0, 1.0) Norway (1.0, 1.0)	*Cyprus (1.7, 2.2)*	
	Medium/large	Australia (1.0, 1.0) Belgium (1.0, 1.0) Canada (1.0, 1.0) Denmark (1.0, 1.0) Germany (1.0, 1.7) *Israel (2.0, 2.4)* Italy (1.1, 1.6)	United States (1.0, 1.0)	Austria (1.0, 1.0) Finland (1.7, 1.8) France (1.0, 2.0) Switzerland (1.0, 1.0)

Table 1.2 (*cont.*)

Income level	Population size	Parliamentary	Presidential	Other
		Japan (1.4, 1.2) Netherlands (1.0, 1.0) Sweden (1.0, 1.0) United Kingdom (1.0, 1.2)		

Note: All regimes in the "other" column are premier-presidential, except for Switzerland. Numbers in parentheses are averages of annual Freedom House scores on political rights and civil rights, respectively. Countries that have become independent from Britain or a British Commonwealth state since 1945 are italicized.

because they typically have relatively homogeneous populations, at least in ethnic, religious, and linguistic terms, thereby attenuating potential sources of political conflict (Dahl and Tufte 1973). The other reason for sorting countries by population size is that it seems suboptimal to count a micronation and India each as one case, paying no attention to the fact that India's population dwarfs the sum total of all the countries in the world with populations under 500,000. We classified countries in the following tables as micro (population under 500,000), small (500,000 to 5,000,000), and medium to large (over 5,000,000). We used 1994 population data; of course, had we used an earlier source, the groupings would have been slightly different (e.g., Israel and Finland would have been in the small category).

The strong correlation between British colonial heritage and democracy has been widely recognized. Reasons for this association need not concern us here, but possibilities mentioned in the literature include the tendency to train civil servants (Diamond 1989; Weiner 1987), the governmental practices and institutions (which include but cannot be reduced to parliamentarism) created by the British, and the lack of control of local landed elites over the colonial state (Rueschmeyer, Stephens, and Stephens 1992). For the African cases, the level of economic development tends to be lower and the degree of ethnic pluralism tends to be higher than in other parts of the developing world, but even in Africa countries with British colonial heritage (e.g., Botswana) have tended to have better democratic records than those without. Thus, the selection of cases does not allow us to rule out the possible independent effect of British colonialism because there is a problem of linear dependence.

It is not our purpose here to analyze the contributions of these factors to democracy; rather, we are attempting to see if these factors appear to correlate with regime type. If a background condition that is conducive to democracy is correlated with parliamentarism, then any attempt to correlate parliamentarism and democracy may be spurious unless some effort is made to control for background conditions.

Table 1.3 expands Table 1.2 by showing 24 additional countries that had been continuously democratic by the same criteria used in Table 1.2, only for a shorter period (10 years). There have been many transitions to democracy in nearly all regions of the world, especially since the mid-1980s, and many countries became independent after 1972, when the Freedom House scores began. All these countries are shown in Table 1.3, which, when combined with Table 1.2, gives us a complete look at contemporary democracies that have lasted at least 10 years.

There are two striking facts about the additional countries in Table 1.3. First, a large number of microstates became independent from Britain in the 1970s or 1980s, and all of them are parliamentary. Second is the substantial increase in the number of presidential democracies, most of which are in the lower- and lower-middle-income categories, and all of which are in Latin America.[14] Thus, if the obstacles of lower income (or other factors not considered here) in Latin America continue to cause problems for the consolidation of democracy, the number of presidential breakdowns could once again be large in the future. On the other (more optimistic) hand, if Latin American democracies achieve greater success in consolidating this time around, we will have a substantial number of presidential democracies in the future.

Table 1.4 summarizes the distribution of cases from Tables 1.2 and 1.3 according to our background criteria. We see that there are far more parliamentary regimes (38) among the countries that have been continuous democracies since at least 1985 than there are other types; only 13 cases are presidential. However, 17 of the parliamentary democracies are found in Europe or other high-income countries such as Canada, Israel, and Japan. It is likely that these countries would have been democratic between 1972 and 1995 had they had presidential constitutions. So, as some advocates of

---

14 At least three more presidential democracies have been established more recently outside Latin America: Benin (1991), Korea (1987), and the Philippines (1986). In addition, there are several new democracies that have elected presidencies but are not presidential by our definition (e.g., premier-presidential systems in Bangladesh and Poland, hybrids in Namibia and Zambia).

Table 1.3. *Independent countries that were democratic for at least 10 years (but less than 23) as of 1994*

Income level	Population size	Parliamentary	Presidential	Other
Low/lower-middle	Micro	*Belize* *(1.0, 1.5, 1981)* *Dominica* *(2.0, 1.8, 1978)* *Kiribati* *(1.3, 1.9, 1979)* *Solomons* *(1.5, 1.8, 1978)* *St. Lucia* *(1.3, 2.1, 1979)* *St. Vincent* *(1.6, 1.9, 1979)* *Tuvalu* *(1.4, 1.6, 1978)* *Vanuatu* *(1.9, 3.3, 1980)[a]*		
	Small	*Papua New Guinea* *(2.1, 2.4, 1975)*		
	Medium/large	*India* *(2.4, 3.1, 1979)*	Bolivia (2.0, 3.0, 1982) Brazil (2.3, 2.9, 1985) Ecuador (2.0, 2.5, 1979) El Salvador (2.9, 3.6, 1985) Honduras (2.4, 3.0, 1980)	
Middle	Micro	*Antigua and Barbuda* *(2.5, 2.9, 1981)* *Grenada* *(1.6, 1.9, 1985)* *St. Kitts-Nevis* *(1.1, 1.4, 1983)*		

Table 1.3 (*cont.*)

Income level	Population size	Parliamentary	Presidential	Other
	Small			
	Medium/ large	Greece (1.5, 2.1, 1974)	Argentina (1.8, 2.3, 1983) Uruguay (1.6, 2.0, 1985)	Portugal (1.3, 1.8, 1976)[b]
Upper	Micro	*Bahamas (1.5, 2.2, 1973)*		
	Small			
	Medium/ large	Spain (1.3, 2.0, 1977)		

Note: Numbers in parentheses are averages of annual Freedom House scores on political rights and civil rights, respectively, and the beginning date from which these averages are computed. The date is when the transition to democracy took place (or the date of independence for former British colonies that were not independent as of 1972). Countries that have become independent from Britain or a British Commonwealth state since 1945 are italicized.
[a]Vanuatu was jointly administered by Britain and France before 1980.
[b]Portugal has a premier-presidential system.

parliamentarism have recognized but not stressed as thoroughly as we do here, some of the success of parliamentary democracy is accidental: In part because of the evolution of constitutional monarchies into democracies, the region of the world that democratized and industrialized first is overwhelmingly populated with parliamentary systems.

Clearly not all of parliamentarism's advantage stems from the advanced industrial states. Even in the lower- to upper-middle-income categories, there are more parliamentary systems (21, compared with 11 presidential systems). However, as Table 1.4 shows, *every one of the parliamentary democracies outside of the high-income category is a former British colony*. The only other democracies in these income categories are presidential, and all but Cyprus are in Latin America.

To the best of our knowledge, advocates of presidentialism have not recognized the size advantage of parliamentary systems. All 16 states (mostly island nations) in our sample with populations under one-half million are parliamentary, as are 8 of the 10 states with populations between

Table 1.4. *Distribution of continuous democracies (for at least 10 years as of 1994) by background condition and regime type (percent)*

	N	Parliamentary	Presidential	Other
Income Level				
Low/lower-middle	20	12 (60.0)	8 (40.0)	0 (0.0)
Upper-middle	13	9 (69.2)	3 (23.1)	1 (7.7)
Upper	24	17 (70.8)	2 (8.3)	5 (20.8)
British colonial heritage	23	22 (95.7)	1 (4.3)	0 (0.0)
Population				
Under 500,000	17	16 (94.1)	0 (0.0)	1 (5.9)
500,000–5,000,000	10	8 (80.0)	2 (20.0)	0 (0.0)
Over 5,000,000	30	14 (46.7)	11 (36.7)	5 (16.7)
Total	57	38 (66.7)	13 (22.8)	6 (10.5)

one-half and five million. On the other hand, there are no presidential systems among the microstates; many are exceptionally large countries, such as Argentina, Brazil, and the United States. Thus, if British colonial heritage or small population size is conducive to democracy, parliamentarism has a built-in advantage simply because Britain, a parliamentary system, happened to colonize many small island territories. As a rule, British colonies had local self-government, always on the parliamentary model, before independence.[15] Further, if there are aspects of Latin American societies – perhaps extreme inequality across classes or regions – that are inimical to stable democracy, then presidentialism has a built-in disadvantage.

Table 1.5 lists democracies that broke down between 1977 and 1995. To be counted here, a country needed before the breakdown to have been

15 Some British colonies later adopted presidential systems and did not become (or remain) democratic. However, in many cases, democracy was ended (if it ever got underway) by a coup carried out by the prime ministers and their associates. These were breakdowns not of presidential democracies, but of parliamentary protodemocracies. Typical was the case of Seychelles. That most of these countries have not evolved back into democracy cannot be attributed to presidentialism.

Table 1.5. *Democracies that broke down between 1977 and 1995*

Income level	Parliamentary	Presidential	Other
Lower/lower-middle	Turkey 1980 (2.1, 3.3)	*Gambia 1994*	Peru 1992 (2.1, 3.3)
	Turkey 1994 (2.6, 3.8)	*(2.3, 2.6)*	*Sri Lanka 1989 (2.4, 3.4)*
Upper-middle	*Fiji 1987 (2.0, 2.0)*		
	Grenada 1979 (2.0, 3.5)		
	Malaysia 1984 (2.8, 3.6)		

Note: Numbers in parentheses are averages of annual Freedom House scores on political rights and civil rights, respectively. A breakdown (indicated by the year of the coup or declaration of emergency rule) is defined as a Freedom House score of 5.0 on either political or civil rights in any year following a period of democracy. A period of democracy is defined as five previous consecutive years when the average scores were 3.0 or better and neither score in any year was 5.0 or worse. All countries in the table are in the small- to large-population categories, except for Grenada, which is a microstate. Countries that have become independent from Britain or a British Commonwealth state since 1945 are italicized.

democratic by the criteria used for countries in Tables 1.2 and 1.3 – that is, an average of 3.0 or better on the Freedom House political rights score and never worse than 4.0 on either political or civil rights – for at least the five immediately preceding years. A breakdown then occurred if a country's Freedom House score for either political rights or civil liberties fell to 5.0 or worse in one year. Using the 1977–95 period allows us to have five years of Freedom House data before the period in order to determine failures of regimes that were in fact democratic by their criteria; Freedom House began its rankings in 1972. Using a period within the "Third Wave" (Huntington 1991) of democratization also means we are considering breakdowns that went against the wave. In this way, we partially control for international factors that were propelling a great number of countries in one direction; thus, we can have somewhat more confidence that the regime type may have played a role in these cases than if we had used cases from the 1960s and early to middle 1970s, during the previous "reverse wave."

From Table 1.5, we see that the parliamentary breakdowns (five) outnumber the presidential cases (one), although there are too few cases to generalize firmly. Three of the countries, Fiji, Gambia, and Sri Lanka, had been democratic since the start of the Freedom House scores in 1972, while the others generally represent shorter-lived experiments with democracy. Except for Fiji and Gambia, all had average civil rights scores worse than 3.0 – indeed, ranging from 3.3 to 3.8 – while they were democratic. Thus, they were already experiencing erosions of their democracies despite maintaining good political rights scores up until the suspension of open electoral competition or the further constricting of civil rights. This finding underscores the importance of traditional civil rights in our definition of democracy, since, without such protections, democracy not only is hollow, but may prove fragile even in its more limited electoral sense. To emphasize the point even further, there are only 4 cases in Tables 1.2 and 1.3 with average civil rights scores worse than 3.0, even though our definition allowed for such countries to be counted as continuously democratic. Those cases are Colombia (3.1), India (3.1), Vanuatu (3.3), and El Salvador (3.6). The gap between civil rights scores in the failed democracies of Table 1.5 and the comparatively successful cases of Tables 1.2 and 1.3 is noteworthy, although some of the continuous democracies in Tables 1.2 and 1.3 have had similar brief episodes and managed to survive.[16]

In summary, presidentialism is more likely to be adopted in Latin America and Africa than in other parts of the world, and these parts of the world may have more formidable obstacles to democracy regardless of the form of government. On the other hand, parliamentarism has been the regime form of choice in most of Europe and in former British colonies (a large percentage of which are microstates), where conditions for democracy may be generally more favorable. Thus, there are reasons to be cautious about the observed correlation between constitutional form and democratic success, impressive though this correlation may at first appear.

Although our arguments here raise doubts about the claim that one regime type is clearly superior to another, this is *not* to claim that the choice of a system of government is irrelevant. A key theme throughout this book is that the way the executive is chosen, interacts with the legislature and parties, and maintains itself in power is of fundamental importance for democratic politics. Thus, we see the choice for presidentialism as highly important for the dynamics of democracy, but not necessarily as crucial in determining whether democracy will survive or break down. Moreover, specific arrangements within broad regime types may be every bit as important as whether a parliamentary or presidential government is chosen.

THE ARGUMENT AGAINST PRESIDENTIALISM

The critics of presidentialism have not based their case exclusively on correlations between regime type and the record of democratic success and failure. Starting from this correlation, they have identified several charac-

16 For example, Malta scored 4.0 on civil rights for four consecutive years (1983–86) but has always scored 1.0 or 2.0 since then.

teristic weaknesses of presidential systems. Here we offer a brief review of the basic arguments against presidentialism (Linz and Valenzuela 1994; Lowenstein 1949; Riggs 1988; Suárez 1982; Blondel and Suárez 1981; Stepan and Skach 1994; Mainwaring 1993).

First, the critics of presidentialism claim that the fixed term of the president's office introduces a rigidity that is less favorable to democracy than the flexibility offered by parliamentary mechanisms of no confidence and dissolution. They argue that the fixed presidential term causes difficulty in handling major crises. Although most presidential systems have provisions for impeachment, they offer less flexibility in crisis situations because attempts to depose the president easily endanger the regime itself. The president may be incapable of pursuing a coherent course of action because of congressional opposition, but no other actor can resolve the problem by playing within democratic rules of the game. In many cases a coup appears to be the only means of getting rid of an incompetent or unpopular president.

Not only are presidents difficult to remove from office, but also the chief executive cannot bolster his or her authority either through a vote of confidence or by dissolving the parliament to call new elections. Thus, presidential leadership can be weaker than that provided by some prime ministers. Presidential constitutions often manifest a contradiction "between the desire for a strong and stable executive and the latent suspicion of that same presidential power" (Linz 1990:55).[17] By virtue of their greater ability to promote changes in the government, parliamentary systems afford greater opportunities for resolving disputes. Such a safety valve may enhance regime stability, according to some proponents of parliamentarism.

Just as presidentialism makes it difficult to remove a democratically elected head of government who no longer has support, it usually makes it impossible to extend the term of popular presidents beyond constitutionally set limits. Although such provisions are not inherent in the regime type, most presidential constitutions bar presidents from serving successive terms. Consequently, good presidents are turned out of office even if the general population, political elites and parties, and other major actors continue to support them. Presidents therefore have relatively little time to pursue their projects and, as a result, are often tempted to try to accomplish a great deal in a short term. According to Linz, the "fear of discontinuity in policies and distrust of a potential successor encourage a sense of urgency . . . that might lead to ill-designed policies, rapid implementation, impatience with the

17 Advocates of presidentialism also recognize the tension between the need for an agile and effective executive and the need for checks and balances. But they cast this tension in a different light, perceiving it as constructive and necessary.

opposition" and other problems (Linz 1994:17). Moreover, Linz has persuasively argued that the desire to restrict reelection is itself a by-product of the concentration of executive power in the hands of one person. Such fears perforce do not emerge under parliamentarism, and as a result, term limits are not found in any parliamentary regimes.

A second criticism of presidential systems is that they are more prone to immobilism than parliamentary systems, for two primary reasons. First, compared with parliamentary systems, presidential systems are more apt to engender minority governments and weak executive power. Second, presidential systems are less capable than parliamentary systems of dealing with these problems when they arise (see Mainwaring 1993).

Presidential systems lack means of ensuring that the president will enjoy the support of a majority in congress. Because presidents are elected independently of the assembly and because personal qualities are often decisive in presidential campaigns, the winner need not come from a majority party – if one exists. In some countries, presidents' parties do not control anywhere close to a majority of the seats in congress. Presidents who enjoy little support in congress sometimes get elected, which can easily lead to bitter struggles between the executive and the legislature.

Many presidents begin their terms in strong control of their own parties, but lose this control as their situation as lame ducks becomes more apparent (Coppedge 1994; Carey, this volume). They cannot dissolve the legislature and call new elections, as prime ministers sometimes can. As a result, presidents may painfully await the end of their terms, incapable of implementing a coherent policy package because of their lack of support. Under these difficult circumstances of presidential–legislative impasse and a fixed timetable, presidents and the opposition alike are often tempted to resort to extraconstitutional mechanisms to accomplish their ends. All of this suggests that democratic presidents, despite high expectations for their leadership, sometimes have limited ability to implement their programs. Yet where executive authority is weak and there are no institutional means to fill the resulting vacuum, political stability and/or governability often suffers.

Immobilism in presidential democracies has often been a major ingredient in coups. In the context of ineffective government, pressing social and economic problems, and political mobilization encouraged by elite actors as a means of winning leverage in a stalemate situation, authoritarian leaders can easily justify and win support for coups. Moreover, immobilism can encourage radicalism, seen as a way of overcoming the inefficacy of feckless liberal democracies. Thus, it is not surprising that several analysts (Santos 1986; Gillespie and González 1994; Valenzuela 1994) have attributed coups partly to paralysis stemming from executive–legislative conflict.

In a related vein, Linz has argued that, in presidential systems, the president and assembly have competing claims to legitimacy. "Since both [the president and congress] derive their power from the vote of the people . . . a conflict is always latent and sometimes likely to erupt dramatically; there is no democratic principle to resolve it, and the mechanisms that might exist in the constitution are generally complex, highly technical, legalistic, and, therefore, of doubtful democratic legitimacy for the electorate" (Linz 1994:7). He argues that parliamentarism obviates this problem because the executive is not independent of the assembly. If the majority of the assembly favors a change in policy direction, it can replace the government by exercising its no-confidence vote.

A third criticism of presidentialism, also developed by Linz, is that presidentialism has a winner-takes-all logic that is unfavorable to democratic stability. "A parliamentary election might produce an absolute majority for a particular party, but more normally it gives representation to a number of parties . . . and some negotiations become necessary for obtaining majority support" (Linz 1994:18). In presidential systems, the direct popular election is likely to imbue presidents with a feeling that they need not undertake the tedious process of constructing coalitions and making concessions to the opposition. Moreover, "the danger that zero-sum presidential elections pose is compounded by the rigidity of the president's fixed term in office. Winners and losers are sharply defined for the entire period of the presidential mandate. . . . The losers must wait at least four or five years without any access to executive power and patronage" (Linz 1990:56).[18]

A final criticism of presidential systems results from the direct popular election of presidents, which in itself appears to be a desideratum. However, the down side of direct popular elections is that political outsiders with little experience in party and congressional politics can get elected (Suárez 1982; Rose 1981). As the victors in the presidential contests in Brazil in 1989 and Peru in 1990 showed, these individuals may create parties at the last minute in order to run for the presidency.[19] In some countries (e.g., Brazil and Ecuador), presidents do not necessarily enjoy secure support even in their own party (see Mainwaring, this volume). At worst, direct popular elections may serve as an incentive to demagoguery and populism and hence may discourage more realistic appraisals of policy alternatives.

18 In the definitive version of his article, Linz (1994) somewhat modified this argument about the winner-takes-all nature of presidential systems, recognizing that parliamentary systems do not consistently provide an advantage on this point. Here we cite the earlier version, cognizant of the change in Linz's thinking, because the earlier version of his argument was widely disseminated and accepted.

19 The sudden emergence of Silvio Berlusconi's Forza Italia in 1994 shows that parliamentary systems are not entirely invulnerable to outsiders. The difference, of course, is that in a presidential system it is possible for an outsider to win sole possession of executive power for a fixed term if he or she lacks a legislative base.

ADVANTAGES OF PRESIDENTIALISM

In this section, we make two basic points. First, we argue that presidentialism, in addition to presenting some peculiar problems, also has some specific advantages. Second, we argue that some arguments against presidentialism that we have just reviewed, while incisive and worthy of careful consideration, may be countered directly. The counterarguments may or may not add up to a defense of presidentialism – as noted, our point in this book is not to endorse one form of government over another. However, the counterarguments serve as a caution against too facile an acceptance of the criticisms of presidential democracy and remind us that parliamentarism is not free of flaws either. Then we can proceed to the principal task of the rest of the book: outlining variations in presidential powers and considering features that make some presidential systems function better than others.

Greater Choice for Voters

The competing claims to legitimacy that can lead to crises in presidential systems are also the flipside of one advantage. The direct election of the chief executive gives the voters two electoral choices instead of one – assuming unicameralism, for the sake of simplicity of argument. Having both executive and legislative elections gives voters a freer range of choices. Voters can support one party or candidate at the legislative level but another for the head of government.

Electoral Accountability and Identifiability

Presidentialism affords some advantages for accountability and identifiability. *Electoral accountability* describes the degree and means by which elected policymakers are electorally responsible to citizens,[20] while *identifiability* refers to voters' ability to make an informed choice before elections based on their ability to assess the likely range of postelection governments.

The more straightforward the connection between the choices made by the electorate at the ballot box and the expectations to which policymakers are held, the greater the electoral accountability. On the principle of maximizing direct accountability between voters and elected officials, presidentialism is superior to parliamentarism in multiparty contexts because the chief executive is directly chosen by popular vote. Presidents (if eligible for reelection) or their parties can be judged by voters in subsequent elections.

---

20 We specify electoral accountability because we do not have in mind what O'Donnell (1994) has called *horizontal accountability*. Electoral accountability takes place through elections; horizontal accountability occurs mostly between elections and involves institutions to oversee the executive, such as the legislature, the courts, and the comptroller's office.

One objection to presidentialism's claim to superior electoral account-ability is that, in most presidential systems, presidents may not be reelected immediately, if at all. Where this is the case, the electoral incentive for the president to remain responsive to voters is weakened, and electoral account-ability suffers. To this objection, advocates of presidentialism can respond that bans on reelection are deficiencies of most presidential systems, but not of presidentialism as a regime type. Direct accountability to the electorate exists in some presidential systems, and it is always possible under presi-dential government. If, as is often the case, the constitution imposes a ban on immediate reelection but allows subsequent reelection, presidents who aspire to regain their office have a strong incentive to be responsive to voters and thereby face a mechanism of electoral accountability. Only if a president (a) can never be reelected and (b) will become a secondary (or non-) player in national and party politics after his or her term are incentives for ac-countability via popular election dramatically weakened. However, even where immediate reelection is banned, voters can still directly hold the president's party accountable.[21] With parliamentarism, on the other hand, under conditions of a deeply fragmented party system the lack of direct elections for the executive inevitably weakens electoral accountability, for a citizen cannot be sure how to vote for or against a particular potential head of government.

Where presidential reelection is permitted, the need to secure re-nomination and a new term is itself a force for executive accountability. Provisions against reelection have been introduced primarily to reduce a president's incentives to use public policy or patronage for personal political aggrandizement and possibly also to allow lower-ranked leaders an oppor-tunity for the top job by mandating turnover. Despite the potential for abuse, reelection can be permitted – and we believe it should be in countries where there are reliable institutions to safeguard elections from egregious manipulation by incumbents.[22]

In multiparty parliamentary systems, even if a citizen has a clear notion of which parties should be held responsible for the shortcomings of a par-ticular government, it is often not clear whether voting for a certain party

---

21 Electoral accountability through party is more promising when the party system is rel-atively institutionalized. Brazilians could in theory have held Collor's party, the Party of National Reconstruction (PRN), accountable for the president's improprieties, but it was such a personalized electoral vehicle that it disappeared by the time of the next election.

22 An Argentine constitutional convention has recently repealed that country's ban on im-mediate reelection at the same time that the presidential term was shortened from six years to four (see Jones's chapter). In Peru, the Constituent Assembly of 1993 also re-pealed the ban on reelection, although the election that produced the assembly was tainted by the authoritarian seizure of power by the incumbent president.

will increase the likelihood of excluding another party from the governing coalition. Governments often change between elections, and even after an election parties that lose seats are not infrequently invited to join governing coalitions.

Strom (1990) used the term "identifiability" to denote the degree to which the possible alternative executive-controlling coalitions were discernible to voters before an election. Identifiability is high when voters can assess the competitors for control of the executive and can make a straightforward logical connection between their preferred candidate or party and their optimal vote. Identifiability is low when voters cannot predict easily what the effect of their vote will be in terms of the composition of the executive. This may be the case either because postelection negotiations determine the nature of the executive, as occurs in multiparty parliamentary systems, or because a large field of contenders for a single office makes it difficult to discern where a vote may be "wasted" and whether voting for a "lesser of evils" might be an optimal strategy. Under parliamentarism, voters may face a situation in which either (1) their choice is essentially restricted to two main parties, in the case of majoritarian parliamentarism, or else (2) they have such a wide range of choices that they cannot cast an effective vote at the executive level, in the case of multiparty parliamentarism when numerous possible postelection coalitions may emerge.

Strom's indicator of identifiability runs from 0 to 1, with 1 indicating that in 100% of a given nation's post–World War II elections, the resulting government was identifiable as a likely result of the election at the time voters went to the polls. The average of his sample of parliamentary nations in Western Europe from 1945 until 1987 was .39, meaning that most of the time the voters could *not* know what government they were voting for. Yet under a parliamentary regime, voting for a member of parliament (MP) or a party list is the only way voters can influence the choice of executive. In some parliamentary systems, such as in Belgium (.10), Israel (.14), and Italy (.12), a voter could rarely predict the impact of a vote in parliamentary elections on the formation of the executive. The formation of the executive is the result of parliamentary negotiations among many participants. For this reason, the calculus for the voter as to how most effectively to support a particular executive can be virtually unforeseeable.

In presidential systems with a plurality one-round format, identifiability is likely to approach 1 in most cases because voters cast ballots for the executive, and the number of significant competitors is likely to be small. Cases with majority runoff to elect the president are different, as three or more candidates may be regarded before the first round as serious contenders (Shugart and Taagepera 1994). When plurality is used to elect the president and when congressional and presidential elections are held concurrently, the norm is for "serious" competition to be restricted to two candidates even when there is multiparty competition in congressional elections (Shugart 1988, 1995a; Jones forthcoming; see also the Conclusion). Especially when the electoral method is not majority runoff, presidentialism tends to encourage coalition building *before* elections, thus clarifying the basic policy options being presented to voters for executive elections and simplifying the voting calculus somewhat.

Linz (1994:10–14) has responded to our earlier (1993) argument that presidentialism engenders greater identifiability by arguing that voters in most parliamentary systems can indeed identify the likely prime ministers and cabinet ministers. His logic is that because the parliament and cabinet are a "nursery" for leadership, by the time individuals are approaching leadership status, they are well known to voters. While his rejoinder is valid on its face, Linz is using the term *identifiability* in a different manner from Strom or us. He is speaking of voters' ability to identify personnel, rather than government teams, which, as we have noted, may not be identifiable. And although Linz has a point when he argues that what voters are identifying in a presidential election "is often based on an opinion about one individual, a personality, promises, and – let's be honest – an image a candidate projects" (Linz 1994:11), nonetheless in presidential democracies with more institutionalized party systems (Mainwaring and Scully 1995) – such as Argentina, Chile, Colombia, Costa Rica, Uruguay, and Venezuela – the major contenders have almost always been well-known leaders from the "nursery" of the legislature, previous administrations, or, in federal systems like the United States, Brazil, and Argentina, state governorships. Moreover, where party systems are moderately institutionalized, the party label conveys considerable information about what policies a candidate is likely to pursue.[23]

---

23 An institutionalized party system does not preclude the possibility that a party may seek to change its constituent base and its policy stances – or that a president may seek to change it on the party's behalf. This can lead to serious postelection surprises. However, this is hardly a feature unique to presidentialism; indeed, it should be less common in presidential systems, given their checks and balances. For example, in New Zealand, two consecutive governments of different parties in the 1980s went radically against campaign promises in the course of restructuring that country's import-substituting economy (Nagel 1994). This process of deliberately pursuing policies opposed to those that were announced in campaigns echoes similar practices in Latin American countries in the 1980s and 1990s: Argentina under Menem (1989–95), Venezuela under Pérez (1988–92), Peru under Fujimori (1990–95). During their second presidential runs, both Menem and Fujimori campaigned on policies that they had actually implemented during their first terms, thereby enhancing accountability.

Congressional Independence in Legislative Matters

Because representatives in a presidential system can act on legislation without worrying about immediate consequences for the survival of the government, issues can be considered on their merits rather than as matters of "confidence" in the leadership of the ruling party or coalition. In this specific sense, assembly members exercise independent judgment on legislative matters. Of course, it is precisely this independence of the assembly from the executive that can generate the problem of immobilism. This legislative independence is particularly problematic with highly fragmented multiparty systems, where minority presidents are the rule and legislative deadlock easily ensues. However, where presidents enjoy substantial assembly support, congressional opposition to executive initiatives can promote consensus building and can avoid the possibility of ill-considered legislation being passed simply to prevent a crisis of confidence. The immobilism feared by presidentialism's detractors is merely the flip side of the checks and balances desired by the U.S. Founding Fathers.[24]

Congressional independence can encourage broad coalition building because even a majority president is not guaranteed the unreserved support of partisans in congress. In contrast, when a prime minister's party enjoys a majority, parliamentary systems exhibit highly majoritarian characteristics. Even a party with less than a majority of votes can rule almost unchecked if the electoral system "manufactures" a majority of seats for the party. The incentive not to jeopardize the survival of the government pressures members of parliament whose parties hold executive office not to buck cabinet directives. Thus, presidentialism is arguably better able than parliamentarism to combine independence of legislators with an accountable and identifiable executive. If one desires that the consensual and often painstaking task of coalition building should be undertaken on each major legislative initiative, rather than only on the formation of a government, then presidentialism has an advantage.

Fixed Terms versus Cabinet Instability

The rigidity of presidentialism, created by the fixed term of office, can be a liability – sometimes a serious one. However, the argument about the "flexibility" of replacing cabinets in parliamentary systems is two-edged (Sartori 1994b). In a parliamentary system, the prime minister's party can replace its leader, or a coalition partner can withdraw its support and usher in a change of government short of a coup, which might be the only way to remove a president who lacks support. We agree with Linz and other

24 See especially the *Federalist*, no. 51.

critics of presidentialism that cabinet instability need not lead to regime instability and can even offer a safety valve. However, there is another side of the story: Regime-ending crises in many failed parliamentary systems, including Somalia[25] and Turkey, have come about precisely because of the difficulty of sustaining viable cabinets. Studies of cabinet durability (Dodd 1976; Powell 1982) have concluded that the presence of extremist parties and electoral volatility contributes to short-lived cabinets. As Powell (1982) has noted, both these factors are more widespread in developing countries. Thus, the compatibility of multiparty coalitions and regime stability in Europe cannot necessarily be assumed to be transferable to the less developed world.

Presidentialism raises the threshold for removing an executive; opponents must either wait out the term or else countenance undemocratic rule. There may be cases when this higher threshold for government change is desirable, since it would be expected to provide more predictability and stability to the policy-making process than the frequent dismantling and reconstructing of cabinets that afflicts some parliamentary systems – and that might especially be prevalent in the conditions of macroeconomic instability and scarcity that plague much of the less developed world.

The problem of fixed terms could be mitigated by having shorter terms (say, four or perhaps even three years, but allowing immediate reelection) rather than longer ones (say, six years); shorter terms would allow for an earlier resolution to the problems generated by the fixed term. The problems of a fixed term could theoretically be remedied without adopting parliamentarism by permitting – under certain conditions – the calling of early elections. After a failed coup attempt in February 1992, Venezuelan politicians briefly considered such a plan, which would have resembled the provision in some U.S. states, where a recall election can be held upon the collection of a sufficient number of voters' signatures. To avoid recall elections being used for purely partisan purposes, the threshold of required signatures would have to be relatively high; even so, the threat of a recall may deter executive abuses of authority.

Another possibility would be a regime that allows a majority of legislators to call early elections for both the president and the legislature. Although such a regime would not be strictly presidential, it would not be parliamentary either, because executive power could not be reconstituted without going back to the electorate. If not only the assembly has the right to dismiss the executive, but also the executive may dissolve the assembly

---

25 Recent events in the country make it easy to forget, but Somalia had a democratic system from 1960 until 1969.

– and new popular elections must be held for each branch after such action – then we have a new type of hybrid, which would appear in the upper-right cell of Table 1.1. Such a regime has been adopted in Israel (see Libai, Lynn, Rubenstein, and Tsiddon 1990, for an early proposal), was considered in the Netherlands by an official commission (Lijphart 1984), and has been discussed recently in Italy (Barbera 1990).

Presidentialism Can Inhibit Winner-Takes-All Games

We take issue with Linz's assertion that presidentialism induces more of a winner-takes-all approach to politics than does parliamentarism. As we see it, parliamentary systems do not afford an advantage on this point. In fact, parliamentary systems with a disciplined majority party offer the fewest checks on the ruling party and hence promote a winner-takes-all approach more than do presidential systems. Despite Linz's (1994:18) claim, quoted earlier, that typically no party wins a majority, outside of Europe there is little experience with coalition government. All the parliamentary systems in lower- to upper-middle-income categories (Table 1.2) are based on the British model of a two-party system and hence single-party cabinets. Under this system, even without a decisive margin in popular votes, a party can control the entire executive and the legislature for a protracted period of time. For instance, in Great Britain in the 1970s and 1980s, the Conservative Party three times won parliamentary majorities as large as 60% of the seats despite winning under 44% of the vote.

Because of the combination of disciplined parties, single-member plurality electoral districts, and the prime minister's ability to dissolve the parliament, Westminster systems provide little legislative check on the premier. In principle, the MPs of the governing party control the cabinet, but in practice they usually support their own party's legislative and policy initiatives regardless of the merits of particular proposals, because their electoral fates are so closely tied with that of the partry leadership (see Cox 1987; Palmer 1995). The norm is that a disciplined majority party leaves the executive virtually unconstrained between elections.[26] Here more than in any presidential system, the winner takes all. Given the majority of a single party in parliament, it is unlikely that a no-confidence vote would prevail, so there is little or no opposition to check the government. Early elections occur not as a flexible mechanism to rid the country of an ineffec-

---

26 Of course, this statement rests on the assumption that the party itself remains united. If it does not, it may oust its leader and thereby change the prime minister, as happened to Margaret Thatcher in Britain and Brian Mulroney in Canada. Such intraparty crises of leadership are, however, the exception rather than the rule in majoritarian (Westminster) parliamentary systems.

tive government but at the discretion of a ruling majority using its dissolution power strategically to renew its mandate for another five years by
calling a new election before its current term ends.[27]

Presidentialism, on the other hand, is predicated upon a system of
checks and balances. This was, after all, the rationale behind the adoption
of the U.S. system. While such checks and balances can be criticized from
other perspectives, they inhibit winner-takes-all tendencies. The checks and
balances are designed precisely to limit the possibility that the winner would
take all. If it loses the presidency, a party or coalition may still control
critical swing votes in congress, a situation that in most countries would
allow it to restrain the president and block presidential initiatives. If the
president's own legislative powers are reactive only (a veto, but no decree
or exclusive agenda-setting powers), an opposition-controlled congress can
even be the prime mover in legislating, as often occurs in the United States.
Controlling congress may not always be the biggest prize, but it allows the
party or coalition to establish parameters within which policy occurs and
can be a big prize in its own right if the presidency has relatively weak
legislative powers.

STRENGTH OF PRESIDENTS

In this final section, we review one of the principal institutional variations
that might lead to variations in the performance of different presidential
systems: the strength of presidents over policy. When observers classify
presidents in terms of being "strong" or "weak," they tend to mean presidents' ability to put their own stamp on policy – to get an agenda enacted.
We mean essentially the same thing. There are two principal ways that
presidents can have such influence. One is to have constitutional powers
inherent in the office of the presidency that allow incumbents to have their
preferences taken into consideration in the passage of legislation. Another
is to have control over their own party and for that party to be in control
of a majority of seats. Presumably, these two factors – which might be
termed their *constitutional* and *partisan* powers over legislation – interact to
determine the degree of influence presidents have over policy – and hence

---

27 A possible exception in Westminster systems occurs with the occasional minority government, which is more common than a coalition government in such systems (Strom
1990). But even then, early elections are as likely to be called by the government in an
attempt to convert its plurality into a majority, since elections are to be called as a result
of a vote of no confidence.

their strength. Presidents who have no independent constitutional authority over legislation would appear very weak if they lacked control over a majority party but might appear to dominate – in spite of their constitutional weakness – if they were the undisputed leaders of the majority party. On the other hand, presidents with substantial legislative powers may have significant influence over legislation even if their party lacks a legislative majority – indeed, even if their party is a minor one. Such presidents would also have independent influence over policy even if they were not the unchallenged leaders of their party. On the other hand, presidents without constitutional legislative powers might not be able to leave a stamp on policy even if their party has a majority in situations in which the party itself is divided with respect to the leadership provided by the president. Thus, we must consider the interaction of constitutional and partisan powers.

In terms of constitutional powers over legislation, presidents may have a veto – in which case no bill can become law without meeting the president's approval, unless the legislature musters whatever vote majority may be needed to override a veto – and many have decree powers – in which case it may be possible for the president to legislate without the congress. Clearly, presidential legislative powers are an important place to start in considering variations among presidential systems. After reviewing the basic features of legislative powers of Latin American presidents, we suggest ways in which these powers interact with presidents' standings vis-à-vis the party system. However, the bulk of the task of dealing with these interactions will wait until the chapters on individual countries and the Conclusion of this book.

TYPES OF LEGISLATIVE POWERS

Across presidential systems, chief executives share many powers (e.g., in foreign policy, as commanders of the armed forces, administrative appointment prerogatives). However, there is tremendous variation in presidents' legislative powers. One way to think of presidential legislative powers is the relationship of the exercise of power to the legislative status quo (Shugart n.d.). Powers that allow the president to establish – or attempt to establish – a new status quo may be termed *proactive powers*. The best example is decree power. Those that only allow the president to defend the status quo against attempts by the legislative majority to change it may be termed *reactive powers*. Most familiar here is the veto power, which we discuss first because it is the most common presidential power over legislation.

Veto (and Override)

Presidents with veto power may sign or veto a bill sent to their desks by the legislature. By signing it, presidents accept it in whatever version it was ultimately passed – assuming they cannot veto some parts of it and promulgate the rest (a possibility discussed later). If it is vetoed, the status quo prevails,[28] unless the congress successfully overrides the veto. The veto is a reactive legislative power, in that it allows the president to defend the status quo by reacting to the legislature's attempt to alter it.

As a reactive power, the veto does not permit the president to get more of whatever policy the bill addresses. It is an instrument that lets the president block change (Kiewiet and McCubbins 1988). Consider the following example. In 1986, President Ronald Reagan wanted to increase defense spending beyond an adjustment for inflation. When Congress refused, Reagan threatened to veto the appropriation and hold out for a bigger one. As Kernell (1991:103) says, "When told of this possibility, House Democratic leaders responded quizzically that perhaps they would send him an even smaller appropriation the next time. Eventually, the president backed off from his threat." The veto is not effective in inducing more spending on an item – a situation in which the president wants to change the status quo, but congress is happy with it. If, on the other hand, congress wanted to spend more on, say, welfare than current policy mandated, the president, by exercising veto power, could preserve the status quo against a congressional attempt to change it.[29] The problem, from a president's point of view, is that congress has the power of initiative because it sends the bill to the president's desk for signature or veto. The initiative in passing or rejecting legislation remains with congress even if, as is common in Latin America,

28 More precisely, what happens is that policy returns to the reversion point. In some cases, what policy reverts to in the absence of new legislation may be something other than the status quo, as when authorization for a program runs out in the absence of reauthorizing legislation or when existing legislation calls for continued increasing in spending, but new legislation may call for cuts. We will continue using the term *status quo* because it is easy to understand in a stylized model; however, readers should keep in mind that the reversionary outcome is not always whatever is happening at the time the bill is vetoed.

29 The examples involve expenditure policy, but the game works the same in areas that involve no spending by the government. Suppose the status quo is that all stores are permitted to remain open on Sundays, but congress passes a bill requiring bookstores to close on Sundays. If the president considers Sunday book shopping a fundamental right, his or her veto can prevent the change. But suppose instead that the president would prefer that not only bookstores but also flower shops close on Sundays. If he or she vetoes the bill, then he or she preserves the status quo in which even bookstores may remain open; he or she cannot be sure that congress, perhaps beholden to the flower-sellers lobby, will come back with a bill more to his or her liking. The outcome closest to the president's preference is thus to sign the bill.

the vast majority of bills considered by congress are submitted by the executive in the first place. Unless congress is not free to initiate its own legislative proposals or, more importantly, to amend those bills submitted by the executive, congress makes the final proposal, to which the president reacts. Later on we shall consider cases in which congressional power of initiative or amendment is in fact restricted, as it is in some Latin American countries.

Provisions for overriding presidential vetoes vary from a simple majority – in which case there is ultimately no veto but an opportunity for the president to delay promulgation and request a reconsideration, as in Venezuela – to the almost absolute veto of Ecuador, where no bill other than the budget can become law without presidential assent (but Congress can demand a referendum on a vetoed bill).[30] By far the most common veto override procedures are the absolute majority overrides found in Brazil and Colombia and the two-thirds-vote requirement of Argentina and Chile, as well as the United States.[31] An override requiring an absolute majority – that is, 50% plus one of the total number of members – is classified here as a "weak veto" and any higher requirement we consider "strong." However, we caution that in Brazil and some other countries, even the absolute majority standard can be difficult to reach because of low attendance rates that plague congress. As a result of the low attendance rates, the absolute majority standard can be tantamount to a qualified majority (i.e., a majority greater than 50% plus one) among those present. Still, we consider such a veto weak because a majority party (or coalition) whose members saw a given issue as crucial to their interests could override the president without enlisting the help of legislators from other parties. With a higher override requirement, even such a determined majority party (or coalition) could not override the president without such help.

Partial Veto

In a few constitutions, presidents may veto specific provisions within a bill. In a true partial veto – also known as an item veto – presidents may promulgate the items or articles of the bill with which they agree, while vetoing and returning to congress for reconsideration only the vetoed portions. This power is not as common in the constitutions of Latin America as it probably is in practice. Several Latin American constitutions refer to

30 Actually, the Ecuadorian veto provision is more complicated still. See the note to Table 1.6.
31 In Bolivia and Brazil, the override vote is made in a joint session of the two chambers. In the other bicameral systems, both houses must muster the stipulated override vote in order to require the promulgation of a law that has been vetoed.

the president's ability to object (*objetar*) to a bill "in whole or in part" but then suggest that the whole bill must be returned for reconsideration. Only the items on which the president has communicated objections may be reconsidered, but no portion of the bill may be promulgated unless the congress either passes the same bill by whatever override majority is stipulated in the constitution or else returns the bill to the president without the offending passages. The Argentine (1853), Chilean (1925), Colombian (1886 and 1991), and Ecuadorian constitutions are among those with provisions of this sort. None of these constitutions provides the president the authority to promulgate selected parts of a bill and thereby "fine tune" legislation by rejecting logrolls that may have been necessary to secure a majority in the legislature. However, numerous presidents have asserted the right of partial promulgation. Courts in some instances have affirmed this practice.[32] In Latin America, only under Argentina's 1994 and Brazil's 1988 constitutions do presidents explicitly have the prerogative of vetoing part of a bill while promulgating other parts. Outside Latin America, several U.S. state constitutions and the constitutions of the Philippines (both 1935 and 1987) explicitly permit partial veto and partial promulgation, at least on expenditure bills. However, partial vetoes with partial promulgation are contested legal matters in many countries, given various constitutional ambiguities.

Decree Power

We have discussed the logic of reactive powers such as the veto. Now let us consider their opposite, *proactive* powers. Just as a reactive power refers to the presidents' ability to preserve the status quo against a bill passed by congress that would change it, a proactive power is one that lets the president establish a new status quo. If, for example, presidents can sign a decree that becomes law the moment that it is signed, they have effectively established a new status quo. Most Latin American constitutions provide that presidents or cabinet ministers have the authority to issue decrees of a regulatory nature to implement the terms of existing law, but surprisingly few allow presidents to establish *new legislation* without first having been delegated explicit authority to do so.[33] Those that do confer this authority

---

32 See Molinelli (1991a:191–94) for a discussion of the debate over partial veto/partial promulgation in Argentina.

33 The distinction between laws and regulations is important and is made in all Latin American legal systems. Courts or comptroller general offices typically are empowered to determine whether a regulatory decree in fact exceeds the authorization of existing legislation. Obviously the extent to which this oversight power is exercised depends on the degree of independence accorded to these agencies. This is an area on which much more research needs to be done. For fuller discussion of these points, see Carey and Shugart (forthcoming).

potentially allow presidents to be very powerful; however, the constitution usually lets congress rescind or amend the decree, if it so chooses.

In Latin America, only the Argentine, Brazilian, and Colombian presidents have the ability to issue new laws by decree in practically any policy area. Brazilian presidents have the so-called provisional measures. These are decrees that lose effect if not converted into law within 30 days.[34] President Fernando Collor de Mello (1990–92) used this power extensively in his first months in office, issuing provisional measures at a rate of about one every 48 hours in 1990, most famously the "Collor Plan" of economic stabilization. Many of his decrees were enacted into law, which suggests that he was not acting against the interests of Congress as frequently as the numerous decrees might imply. However, there were also major conflicts over some of his decrees and in particular over his attempts to reenact decrees that had lapsed for lack of congressional action. He even attempted to reintroduce some provisional measures that had been rescinded by Congress, which prompted a Supreme Court ruling against the president (Power 1991, forthcoming). In Colombia, presidents have used their extensive emergency powers to legislate widely by decree, and from 1968 to 1991 they could intervene in financial and credit policy as their own constitutional prerogative. Considerable restrictions have been placed on these powers in the new constitution, but Colombian presidents still have extensive powers to change the status quo by enacting decrees (see Archer and Shugart, this volume, for details). In Argentina, the 1853 constitution (which was in effect from 1983 to 1994) did not provide for decree power, but as Jones's chapter indicates, it had become a de facto power held by presidents by the mid-1990s. The new (1994) constitution codifies this power. In the Peruvian constitutions of 1979 and 1993, the president's decree authority is restricted to fiscal matters. The provision is written in such a way that it may have been intended as a mere administrative mechanism, not as a tool for departing from the existing legislative status quo;[35] however, there is sufficient ambiguity that it has become generally accepted that this provision amounts to the authority to enact new laws by decree in fiscal matters (Schmidt n.d.).

Ecuadorian presidents may declare an economic measure urgent, and it becomes law after 15 days unless Congress votes to reject it. While still a

---

34 The reiteration of lapsed provisional measures has been tolerated (and is not explicitly banned by the constitution). From the implementation of the 1988 constitution until late May 1995, of 1,004 provisional measures, 274 had been approved, only 18 rejected, and 640 reissued. See "A explosão das MP," *Veja*, no. 1,394 (May 31, 1995):29. See also Power (forthcoming) and Figueiredo and Limongi (1995).

35 There was a similar provision for administrative and fiscal decree-laws in the Nicaraguan constitution of 1987. However, a constitutional reform in 1995 eliminated the phrase "with force of law" after the reference to the decrees and also restricted them to purely administrative matters.

form of decree power, this provision is significantly different from others that give a measure the force of law as soon as the president issues it.[36] An additional power held by Ecuadorian presidents is the right to submit almost any type of legislative matter to a referendum. This is not the same as decree power, but like decree power, it gives the president the possibility of legislating over the heads of Congress.

Even where a majority can rescind a decree, the president can still play a major role in shaping legislation for three reasons inherent in the decree process: (1) Unlike a bill passed by congress, a presidential decree (other than under the Ecuadorian provision just referred to) is already law – not a mere proposal – before the other branch has an opportunity to react to it; (2) presidents can overwhelm the congressional agenda with a flood of decrees, making it difficult for congress to consider measures before they have a possibly irreversible effect; and (3) a president can use the decree power strategically, attempting to discern a point in the policy space at which a congressional majority is indifferent between the status quo and the decree. Decree power alone does not let presidents dominate the legislative process – they cannot emit just any decree, confident that it will survive in congress – but it lets them powerfully shape it and obtain legislative outcomes that congress on its own would not have passed. Of course, with a strong veto, presidents may be able to get whatever legislative outcome they deem ideal by issuing a decree that will be invulnerable to congressional rescission.

Up to this point, we have been discussing what legislative decree authority *is*; it may also be useful to say what it *is not* – at least as we and our contributors use the term in this book. First of all, it is not *regulatory* authority. Nearly all Latin American presidents or their ministers can issue regulatory (not legislative) decrees to implement existing legislation. (In the United States, for the most part, the regulatory function falls to independent agencies established by acts of Congress – such as the Interstate Commerce Commission.) Second, *administrative* decree authority is also different from the legislative power we are referring to. For instance, nearly all presidencies – even in the United States – have certain inherent executive authority to rearrange functions within the bureaucracy, create interagency task forces or ad hoc commissions, and the like. Third, *emergency power* is also distinct, since in most countries this authority is narrowly circumscribed. Presidents may be authorized – sometimes with, sometimes without

---

36 The Uruguayan president also may declare a measure urgent, and such a measure becomes law after 45 days if Congress does not act. However, the constitution imposes numerous restrictions on the use of this power. These restrictions, coupled with the relatively long decision time for Congress (which can be extended in the event one house passes a different form of the bill than the other) lead us not to classify this as a form of decree power. However, it does give the president considerable control over the policy agenda.

congressional consent – to suspend certain constitutional rights under conditions of calamity or disorder. This is an important power and is subject to abuse (and at the extreme may entail the abrogation of the constitution itself, as in Uruguay and the Philippines in the 1970s). However, within the framework of a functioning democracy, we believe that it is important to keep such emergency powers conceptually distinct from those forms of decree authority that clearly permit the president to establish a new legislative status quo – for instance, a new tax, a new currency, or a new pension system (to take examples from various country chapters). The nature of the act is more important than what the legal instrument is called in a specific country.[37] If the power is understood as enabling the president to establish new policy departures, we call it *legislative decree* authority. If it is understood to pertain to temporary suspension of some rights, we call it *emergency power*.

Finally, there are decree-laws that – in contrast to those that we have discussed as *constitutional* prerogatives – require prior delegation by congress before they can be issued. These are termed *delegated faculties*. Many Latin American constitutions allow congress to pass an act granting the president the power to decide certain matters by decree-law. Examples of this kind of authority are given in several of the country chapters. The delegation law usually must indicate specific policy areas in which decrees may be issued and provide for a deadline after which the decree authority – although usually not the decrees themselves – expires unless it is extended by another act of congress. Sometimes delegated decree authority is very narrowly defined, as in 1993 when the Venezuelan Congress delegated authority to the interim president, Ramón José Velásquez, to establish by decree a value-added tax in the range of 5 to 15%. (The president set the tax at 10%.) Other times the authority that is delegated is much less carefully delimited, leaving open the possibility of presidential abuse of the authority. Still it is important to bear in mind that what congress delegates it can retract – or it can choose not to delegate in the first place. Thus, delegated decree power is substantially different from constitutionally entrenched legislative decree power, such as the Brazilian provisional measure, which presidents have used (and abused) on their own initiative.

Exclusive Power of Legislative Introduction

In addition to veto and decree powers, several Latin American presidents also have the right of exclusive introduction of legislative proposals in cer-

---

37 For instance, in Colombia, many of the decrees that would be considered legislative acts under our definition are issued pursuant to a so-called state of economic emergency. Their character, however, makes them more sweeping than *emergency acts*, as we use that term.

tain policy areas. Often this exclusive power extends to some critical matters, most notably budgets, but also military policy, the creation of new bureaucratic offices, and laws concerning tariff and credit policies. This power is another form of reactive power, in the following sense: If presidents prefer the status quo to any outcome they deem likely to win the support of a veto-proof majority in congress, they can prevent any changes simply by not initiating a bill. Most of the Latin American constitutions that contain exclusive-introduction authorities also have low formal thresholds for veto overrides, such as the absolute-majority override provisions in Brazil and Colombia. Exclusive-introduction prerogatives, then, become weak in shaping the outcome once a president wishes to alter the status quo – or is required to submit a bill, as in the case of the annual budget – if the congressional majority can amend the bill as it wishes and overcome a potential veto with relative ease. These provisions give a president an advantage in situations in which the congress might want to initiate some policy change, but the president prefers not to open the matter up for debate and hence does not initiate a bill.

Usually, congress's authority to amend a bill submitted by the president is not restricted. Thus, the power is simply one of gatekeeping. There are, however, some constitutions in which not only is the congress barred from considering changes in some issue area unless the president initiates a bill, but also congress's power to amend is restricted. Several systems – including those of Brazil, Chile, Colombia, and Peru since 1993 – limit congress's authority to increase the amounts allocated to items in the budget submitted by the president. In Uruguay, Congress cannot increase tax exemptions proposed by the president or lower proposed maximum prices, and the new (1993) Peruvian constitution stipulates that only the president may initiate some kinds of tax legislation.

Summary of Presidents' Constitutional Powers in Latin America

Table 1.6 provides a summary of presidential powers in all current and some important former Latin American constitutions (for details see the Appendix to this book). The constitutions are grouped by constellations of powers; the constellations that lead to the greatest overall powers are listed at the top of the table, while those with the weakest presidential authority to shape legislation are listed at the bottom. In the intermediate categories, it is somewhat more difficult to define which constellations are stronger than others. Is a president who has great proactive powers stronger than one who has great reactive powers? In conventional terms, the answer may appear to be an obvious yes, since a president with proactive powers can bypass

Table 1.6. *Summary of constellations of presidential powers over legislation in Latin American constitutions*

President's constitutional legislative authority	Configuration of powers	Examples
Potentially dominant	Decree, strong veto, exclusive introduction	Chile 1980–89[a] Colombia 1968–91
	Decree, strong veto	Argentina[b] Ecuador[c]
Proactive	Decree, weak veto, exclusive introduction	Brazil 1988[b] Colombia 1991 Peru 1993[a]
	Decree, weak veto	Peru 1979[a]
Reactive	Strong veto, exclusive introduction	Brazil 1946 Chile pre-1973 Uruguay
	Strong veto	Bolivia Dominican Republic El Salvador Panama
Potentially marginal	No veto	Costa Rica Honduras Mexico Nicaragua Paraguay Venezuela

Note: *Decree* – the president may establish new law without prior congressional authorization (therefore not including decrees of a regulatory nature); *strong veto* – override requires more than a majority of all members; *exclusive introduction* – certain important bills in addition to the budget must be initiated by the president, or congress may not increase items of expenditure in budget proposed by president (see Appendix for details).

[a]Decree restricted primarily to fiscal matters.

[b]Different veto provisions apply on different types of bills. The Colombian president has strong veto powers over the budget but weak power over other forms of legislation. No other presidents have veto power over budgets. Veto powers over other forms of legislation are strong in Costa Rica, Honduras, and Mexico, and almost absolute in Ecuador.

[c]The Ecuadorian president's veto may not be overridden if he or she vetoes the entire text, although Congress may request a referendum on the bill; if he or she objects only to specified parts of a bill, the veto (of the whole bill) may be overridden by a two-thirds vote.

congress in making law, while a president with only reactive powers can merely prevent congress from changing the status quo. It is with this logic in mind that we have grouped the constitutions.

However, there is an important caveat: If the congress is not restricted from legislating in the same areas as those in which the president may issue decrees, then the congress can pass a law overturning or modifying a presidential decree. Thus, only if the president also has a veto does decree power guarantee that the president can dominate the legislative process. A president whose decrees are constantly overturned is arguably weaker than a president who has a veto requiring an extraordinary majority, given that the latter president's views must be taken into account on every piece of legislation. Still, we have grouped the presidencies with decree powers but no veto as stronger than those who have veto power but no decree, because of the ability of presidents who use their decree powers extensively to set the agenda and force the congress constantly to react to a stream of executive decrees.

There is another reason why presidents with decree powers – even in the absence of veto power – may be seen as stronger than presidents with veto power (but no decree). As we noted earlier, veto power only lets presidents demand less of a policy than congress wants. If presidents want more than the status quo but congress passes less of an increase than presidents want, they cannot credibly threaten a veto that would make them worse off. Thus, presidents who favor the status quo vis-à-vis congress appear strong if they have veto power, but presidents who want more of a given policy appear weak (Kiewiet and McCubbins 1988). For decree power, on the other hand, presidents who want more action in a given policy area vis-à-vis congress may appear quite strong, since they can issue a decree that moves policy farther than congress would have done on its own. Even if presidents lack a veto, as long as they do not overreach and issue their decree at a point where a majority will be moved to act to return policy to the status quo, they may be able to extract successfully somewhat more of the policy.[38] In many Latin American countries, presidents' nationwide constituencies make them more representative of "progressive" forces, while congress, especially if malapportioned, is more representative of traditional rural areas (Packenham 1970, 1971). In these cases, if presidents have decree powers,

---

38 The same logic would hold if the president wanted less than the status quo; it is not that presidents who want more than the status quo are stronger than presidents who want less than the status quo when the president's only legislative power is the decree. Rather it is that presidents who want more are weaker if they have only the veto than if they have the decree, while those who want to move policy to less than the status quo can appear strong with either power.

we can expect them to prefer change away from the status quo and to be able to use their powers to move policy at least somewhat in their direction (see Archer and Shugart, this volume).

The constitutions in Table 1.6 are classified into four categories: potentially dominant, proactive, reactive, and potentially marginal. Some countries pose some difficulties in classifying because of different veto or decree provisions on different kinds of legislation. For instance, the presidents of Costa Rica, Honduras, and Mexico have strong vetoes on most types of legislation, but not on annual appropriation bills. These presidents are all classified as potentially marginal in terms of their constitutional powers over legislation because, absent legislative support, they could indeed be marginalized on one very important type of legislation. The extent to which these presidents appear strong rather than marginal depends on their partisan powers or other (nonlegislative or even nonconstitutional) powers, such as the power to make appointments, the ability to persuade, or their superior access to the mass media. The classification of constitutional legislative powers indicates no more than how powerful we could expect a president to be over some crucial policy areas even in the absence of much support in the form of like-minded legislators.

At the top of the table, presidents with both veto and decree powers would be potentially dominant: able to issue a decree and then veto any legislative attempt to amend it. These cases include Argentina, Chile since 1989, Colombia from 1968 to 1991, and Ecuador. The Chilean and Ecuadorian presidencies' potential for dominance exists mainly in fiscal matters, while the pre-1991 Colombian president's potential for dominance existed in practically all policy areas.

At the opposite end of the table, presidents in Costa Rica, Honduras, Mexico, Nicaragua, Paraguay, and Venezuela are potentially marginal. This is a surprising finding, particularly with regard to Mexico. This exercise in classifying presidents' constitutionally derived legislative powers is important not because it tells the full story about how strong presidents are – it does not – but because it allows us to make comparative-statics predictions about presidential strength under changed conditions of partisan standing. For instance, Mexican presidents have arguably been the most *actually* dominant in determining the legislative agenda; however, will a future president appear dominant if his or her party either lacks a legislative majority or is no longer disciplined? From Table 1.6, our conclusion would be no. Particularly on budgeting, we can predict that without the monolithic PRI behind them, Mexican presidents might seem downright weak in comparison with their predecessors. Weldon's chapter addresses these issues in detail.

On the other hand, Colombia's president before 1991 is classified as potentially dominant. Yet, even though most presidents in those years had copartisan legislative majorities, their dominance remained more potential than real because their own parties were so internally fragmented that they did not provide consistent legislative support. As Archer and Shugart argue, decree power only goes so far; eventually presidents have found that they must return to the legislature for long-term institutionalization of reforms enacted by decree. If Colombian presidents could rely on disciplined majorities, they could have converted their potential dominance into real dominance.

Presidents' constitutional powers over legislation come into play especially when they lack a strong partisan base of support. For instance, in the Colombian example just given, the president would not need his or her potentially dominating legislative powers to dominate policy if he or she had a PRI-type party behind him or her. Presidents whose parties reliably back them and who control a majority of seats can appear to dominate regardless of their constitutional powers. In addition to the Mexican case, some presidencies in Venezuela come to mind (see Crisp, this volume). Conversely, given party-system fragmentation and internal indiscipline, for example, Brazilian presidents have needed to rely on broad constitutional legislative powers in order to have an impact on the policy-making output of the system, as argued by Mainwaring in his chapter. Thus, constitutional legislative powers are an important source of variation in presidential systems; how those powers translate into presidential ability to shape actual policy is a matter that varies with other factors like the relationship of presidents to their own parties and to the legislative majority. These are matters taken up by the country chapters and in the Conclusion.

SUMMARY

We have focused on the historical record of presidentialism and the liabilities and advantages of this regime type. As we stated at the outset, our intent was not to argue for the intrinsic superiority of any major regime type. Although we are not advocating presidentialism, we have argued that some critics of presidentialism have overstated the degree to which this regime type is inherently flawed. We believe that there are trade-offs between presidentialism and parliamentarism, that presidentialism has some advantages that partially offset its liabilities, and that through careful attention to constitutional and institutional design, the advantages can be maximized and the liabilities reduced. (We take up this final theme in the Conclusion.)

While acknowledging the generally poor record of presidentialism in sustaining continuous democracy, we believe that the most important explanation for this phenomenon is not institutional, but rather is an effect of lower levels of development and nondemocratic political cultures. Presidentialism has sometimes contributed to problems of democracy, but the correlation between continuous democracy and parliamentarism is partly an artifact of where parliamentarism has been implemented.

It is important to indicate one implication of our arguments. We agree that presidentialism has contributed to democratic breakdowns in some cases, and we also agree that parliamentarism would sometimes work better. Nevertheless, we are less than sanguine about the effects of shifting to parliamentary government in countries with undisciplined parties. Undisciplined parties create problems in presidential democracies, but they create even more daunting problems in parliamentary systems (Sartori 1994b). There is a danger that in countries with undisciplined parties, switching to parliamentary government could exacerbate rather than ameliorate problems of governability and instability, unless party and electoral legislation were simultaneously changed to promote greater discipline and unless political behavior quickly adapted to the new rules.[39]

In parliamentary systems, the government depends on the ongoing confidence of the assembly. Where individual assembly members act as free agents, unfettered by party ties, the governmental majorities that were carefully crafted in postelection negotiations easily dissipate. Free to vote as they please, individual legislators abandon the government when it is politically expedient to do so. Under these conditions, the classic Achilles' heel of some parliamentary systems, frequent cabinet changes, is likely to be a problem. Any switch to parliamentary government, therefore, would need carefully to design a panoply of institutions to increase the likelihood that it would function well.

Regardless of the merits and shortcomings of these two generic types of systems, most Latin American countries – and many democracies outside Latin America – are likely to retain presidential constitutions, at least for the foreseeable future. From this vantage point, those interested in insti-

---

39 Moreover, a change to parliamentarism would need to address what to do with subnational units of government. In Brazil, the debate about parliamentarism largely ignored this question. Some analysts feared that the combination of parliamentarism at the national level and "presidentialism" (i.e., directly elected state governors) at the state and local level would have been problematic.

tutional reform to promote more effective governability are well advised to avoid casting the debate exclusively in terms of a presidential–parliamentary dichotomy. Such a dichotomy might put all the eggs in a basket – a switch to parliamentarism – that is politically unviable in most countries.

Finally, we began the task of assessing variations within the presidential regime type. We noted that too often presidentialism is treated in the literature as if all presidential regimes were alike. We reviewed variations in a basic constitutional characteristic of presidential systems: the legislative powers granted to the president. We introduced the notion of how these powers interact with presidents' partisan standing. These themes will be taken up in more detail in the Conclusion, as well as in the country chapters.

2

MULTIPARTISM, ROBUST FEDERALISM, AND PRESIDENTIALISM IN BRAZIL

Scott Mainwaring

In this chapter, I argue that Brazilian presidentialism has been affected by the combination of three institutional features that Shugart and I (Chapter 1 and the Conclusion, this volume) discuss and one that we do not. First, presidents have had sweeping constitutional powers, especially under the 1988 constitution. The 1988 constitution gives presidents exceptionally strong proactive and some significant reactive powers; the 1946 constitution gave presidents strong reactive powers. Second, a highly fragmented party system has also affected Brazilian presidentialism. With a highly fragmented party system, presidents are usually in a situation of informal coalition government or (exceptionally) of minority presidentialism. Because their parties control a minority of seats, presidents need to build cross-party coalitions to implement most major policies. Third, comparatively undisciplined catchall parties make it difficult for the president to rely exclusively on party channels of support. When presidents are popular, politicians of all stripes and colors support them, but when they lose favor, they often have difficulty winning support for their projects. Defections in hard times make it difficult for presidents to implement major reforms. Finally, federalism has also shaped the functioning of Brazilian

Ronald Archer, Michael Coppedge, Argelina Figueiredo, Daniel Levine, Antonio Paixão, Samuel Valenzuela, and especially Matthew Shugart offered helpful criticisms of this chapter. I am indebted to Argelina Figueiredo and Antônio Kandir for many conversations about the themes of this chapter.

presidentialism. The logic of politicians and parties in Brazil is deeply en-grained with robust federalism, which reinforces the dispersion of power created by the highly fragmented party system.

With this institutional combination, presidents have sweeping consti-tutional powers (especially under the 1988 constitution) but weak partisan powers. By *partisan powers*, Shugart and I refer to the degree to which pres-idents can rely on disciplined majorities in Congress (see Chapter 11).

After outlining this institutional combination, I then turn to how pres-idents have maneuvered within the system. Presidents employ a variety of practices to build support for their policies. Most important, they have attempted to build broad multiparty coalitions to secure support for their programs. They try to win the support of individual legislators, by offering them access to appointments and resources. Since 1985, they have frequently governed by decree, and before 1964, they tried to circumvent Congress by creating bureaucratic agencies responsible for implementing some impor-tant policies.

Even with this panoply of measures and resources at their disposal, this institutional structure presents its peculiar advantages and disadvantages. On balance, it is not an easy one from the perspective of presidents; imple-menting major reforms in Brazil is more difficult than in many presidential systems. This institutional system has frustrated several democratic presi-dents. One president (Vargas) committed suicide, another (Quadros) re-signed only seven months after winning a landslide victory, and another (Goulart) adopted erratic actions that contributed to the breakdown of de-mocracy in 1964. Between 1985 and 1994, successive presidents failed to engineer a successful stabilization plan, in part because of the obstacles posed by Brazil's institutional context.

In brief, the combination of presidentialism, a fragmented multiparty system, undisciplined parties, and robust federalism is often difficult. Pres-idents can succeed in this institutional context and several have, but the system makes it difficult for presidents to establish reliable bases of support.

TWO DEMOCRATIC PERIODS: BACKGROUND

I focus mostly on the post-1985 period in this chapter but also pay some attention to Brazil's earlier democratic period, 1946–64. Compared with Argentina, Chile, Costa Rica, or Uruguay, Brazil had an oligarchical po-litical system until 1945, and it had never experienced free open elections until that year. In October 1945, a coup forced dictator Getúlio Vargas (1930–45) from office, and two months later Brazil's first democratic elections took place. The newly elected Congress and president took office in early 1946. From then until March 31, 1964, when a coup toppled the government of João Goulart (1961–64), Brazil had a basically democratic government. During the 1946–64 period, there were three large parties: the center-left PTB (Brazilian Labor Party), the center-right PSD (Democratic Social Party), and the conservative UDN (National Democratic Union). As many as 10 other small parties also attained representation in the National Congress at any one time.

There were three limitations to democracy during this period. The military was not firmly under civilian control, and it interfered in politics in nondemocratic ways even before the 1964 coup (Stepan 1971; Skidmore 1967). Although the electorate was much broader than in previous periods in Brazilian history, the illiterate were still formally excluded, and in the hinterland, peasants were under the sway of powerful landowners. Finally, the Communist Party was proscribed from 1947 to 1964.

After the 1964 coup, the military remained in office for 21 years, relinquishing power to a civilian, José Sarney, in March 1985. During the post-1985 period, Brazilian democracy has had fewer formal limitations than it did between 1946 and 1964. The party system has been very fragmented since the late 1980s. Table 2.1 provides a thumbnail sketch of the main parties of this period.

Some institutional structures have been relatively similar during both of Brazil's (mostly) democratic periods. The elements of continuity include a presidential system with strong presidential powers, a large effective number of parties, comparatively weakly disciplined parties, and robust federalism.

While calling attention to these institutional similarities, I do not mean to downplay the very significant differences between Brazil's two democratic periods. Brazil has undergone massive social changes since the 1946–64 period. It has a vastly more urban, industrial, educated, and affluent society today than it had during its earlier democratic period. The electorate expanded greatly and became more educated. Communication and transportation facilities improved greatly. Even if formal political institutions had not changed, these massive social transformations would have created a markedly different political system than existed from 1946 to 1964. Relatively similar institutional structures need not produce similar effects at different moments.

Even though continuity in institutional structures has prevailed, some changes in formal institutions have occurred. Presidentialism has usually

Table 2.1. *Main political parties, 1946–64*

Left	
PCB	Brazilian Communist Party. Banned after 1947.
PSB	Brazilian Socialist Party. Created in 1946 by dissidents of the UDN.
Populist parties	
PTB	Brazilian Labor Party. A populist party created by Vargas, the PTB grew rapidly in the last years before the 1964 coup.
PTN	National Labor Party. Progressive populist orientation. Founded in 1945.
PSP	Progressive Social Party. Strongest in São Paulo and dominated by conservative populist Adhemar de Barros.
PST	Social Labor Party. Centrist populist orientation. Founded in 1946.
MTR	Renovative Labor Party. A dissident progressive PTB group.
Center	
PSD	Social Democratic Party. Despite its name, the PSD was a center-right party created by Getúlio Vargas and his associates. It was the largest party of the 1945–64 period.
PDC	Christian Democratic Party. A center-right party, typical expression of Christian democracy.
Conservative parties	
UDN	National Democratic Union. A conservative party that emerged in opposition to Vargas, the UDN was the second-largest party until the 1962 congressional elections.
PL	Liberator Party. A conservative party known for its commitment to parliamentary government. Strongest in Rio Grande do Sul.
PR	Republican Party. A conservative party with predominant strength in Minas Gerais.
PRP	Popular Representation Party. Conservative party headed by ex-integralists.
PPS	Popular Syndicalist Party. Conservative.
PRT	Republican Labor Party. Founded in 1950.

been the rule during both democratic periods, but during a short-lived experiment of September 1961 to January 1963, a semipresidential regime was implemented.[1] Under the 1946 constitution, presidents were elected

1 On paper, the system was parliamentary, but because a directly elected vice-president had assumed the presidential office in a proper constitutional succession (the president had resigned), it was semipresidential in practice. To the best of my knowledge, this was Latin America's only parliamentary system since the end of the Brazilian monarchy in 1889.

in a simple plurality format, concurrently with Congress in 1945 and 1950 and noncurrently thereafter. The 1988 constitution changed the format of presidential elections to an absolute majority, with a runoff election among the two top finishers if nobody wins a majority in the first round. Elections were nonconcurrent from 1985 to 1990, but in 1994 they were concurrent (and will remain so barring constitutional changes).

The 1988 constitution provides presidents with legislative decree powers, whereas the 1946 constitution did not. As I discuss in greater detail later, the 1946 constitution gave presidents slightly greater reactive legislative powers than the 1988 constitution did, but the latter has given them much greater proactive legislative powers. Presidents in the 1946–64 period usually needed active support to effect changes in the status quo; in the post-1985 period, they have merely needed acquiescence on some issues.

Whereas the 1946 constitution was somewhat restrictive in voting rights, the post-1985 regime has been very inclusive. The illiterate gained the franchise in 1985, and the 1988 constitution lowered the voting age from 18 to 16. Coupled with demographic changes, these constitutional rules have resulted in a quantitative explosion of citizenship.

There have also been changes in party system fragmentation. The electoral system of 1945–50 was more favorable to large parties than later electoral systems were, and party system fragmentation was less pronounced than it became later. Since 1990, party system fragmentation has been among the highest in the world and has been markedly higher than it was between 1946 and 1964.

Brazilian parties in both democratic periods have been comparatively undisciplined, but we lack careful empirical research on party discipline in the 1946–64 period that would indicate to what extent the two periods are similar. None of the major pre-1964 parties was as disciplined as the leftist PT (Workers' Party) in the post-1985 period. On the whole, politicians have been less loyal to their parties since 1985 than they were between 1946 and 1964. Federalism has been an important element in the logic of parties and politicians in both periods, but we need more careful research comparing those two periods on that dimension.

CONSTITUTIONAL POWERS OF THE PRESIDENCY

As Shugart and I argue in Chapter 1, constitutional norms regulate executive and legislative action. To a greater extent than analysts of Latin American politics realized until recently, constitutional powers of the president shape executive–legislative relations and are therefore a vital issue in democratic politics.[2]

Expanding on the analysis in Chapter 1, in this section I discuss three broad categories of presidents' constitutional powers: (1) reactive legislative powers, that is, those that enable presidents to block legislation – above all, vetoes and partial vetoes; (2) proactive legislative powers, that is, those that enable presidents to legislate; and (3) presidents' capacity to shape the congressional agenda. Brazil's 1946 constitution gave presidents strong reactive powers, and the 1988 constitution gives the president exceptionally strong leverage in the second and third broad categories, as well as some important reactive powers.

PRESIDENTS' REACTIVE LEGISLATIVE POWERS

When the president can veto legislation, and especially when it is difficult for congress to override a veto, the president has greater control over legislation. Both of Brazil's democratic constitutions gave the president a veto. Formally, the 1988 constitution makes it relatively easy for Congress to override a presidential veto. An absolute majority of the jointly assembled Congress suffices to override a package veto (Art. 66). By *absolute majority* is meant 50% plus one of the entire assembly (whether a member is absent or present), not 50% plus one of those present. Given the high absentee rates in Congress, the absolute majority standard usually requires more than a majority of those present.[3] Presidential veto powers in the 1946 constitution were more formidable because an override required a two-thirds majority of the jointly assembled Congress (Art. 70), making an override formally slightly easier than it is in the United States. (The U.S. Constitution requires two separate two-thirds majorities; the 1946 Brazilian constitution required only one two-thirds majority.)

Although an override is constitutionally easy to achieve under the 1988 constitution, some nonconstitutional factors have reduced the likelihood that Congress can override a presidential veto. The fragmentation of the

---

2 Before Shugart and Carey's (1992) seminal work, the differences among presidents' constitutional powers were virtually ignored.

3 High absenteeism results from the prevalence of patronage-oriented legislators whose political careers do not depend on being conscientious legislators. In turn, this phenomenon stems in part from an electoral system for deputies that encourages them to focus on service to local constituents and to spend time with them, even when doing so entails being away from Brasília. In addition, most voters have little political information in general and extremely limited information about legislators' policy positions, and they are not particularly policy oriented themselves.

party system makes it difficult for the opposition to assemble an absolute majority. The dependence of many Congress members on obtaining federal funds to sustain their political careers makes some of them co-optable. The high absentee rates of legislators can impede Congress from overriding vetoes; with many members absent, the requirement of support from a majority of all members of Congress becomes a de facto criterion of a majority above 50% plus one of those present.

Another reactive legislative power is the partial veto. If presidents can veto part of a bill, it enhances their control over the legislative process by enabling them to block whatever parts they oppose. Both Brazilian constitutions are exceptional in explicitly allowing presidents to veto parts of a bill. Article 70 of the 1946 constitution required a two-thirds majority of the jointly assembled Congress to override a partial veto. The combination of the partial presidential veto and the two-thirds majority needed to overcome it gave presidents great ability to block any bills or parts of bills they opposed. In this regard, the 1988 constitution (Art. 66, Secs. 1 and 2) slightly reduced presidential control over legislation by establishing an absolute majority override of the jointly assembled Congress. Still, even in its slightly weakened version in the 1988 constitution, the explicit partial veto is an unusual and powerful tool that enables presidents to fine-tune legislation they want.

A few constitutions grant presidents the exclusive right to initiate legislation pertaining to some matters; such provisions strengthen the presidents' reactive powers. The exclusive right of initiation over many key issue areas magnifies presidents' ability to prevent the passing of legislation they oppose. Congress has no means of enacting legislation that does not suit the president in these issue areas.

Brazil's 1946 and 1988 constitutions both gave the president the exclusive right to initiate legislation in some policy areas. The 1988 constitution (Art. 61), for example, gives presidents the exclusive right to initiate the laws that determine the size of the armed forces; that create jobs and functions or increase salaries in many parts of the public sector; that relate to the administrative and judicial organization, budgetary issues, and public-sector workers in the country's Federal Territories; that relate to the public ministries and the public defender (*defensoria pública*); and that create, structure, and determine the functions of ministries and public administration. In sum, the president retains exclusive initiative over legislation in an array of important policy areas. In a similar way, Article 67, Section 2, of the 1946 constitution gave the president the exclusive right to initiate some kinds of laws.

Few democratic constitutions give presidents such sweeping exclusive rights to initiate legislation. Only 6 other constitutions (4 of which are from one country, Chile) of the 43 that Shugart and Carey (1992) examined have any provision for exclusive presidential right to initiate legislation. Moreover, the 1988 constitution establishes this presidential prerogative for a wide variety of policy areas.

The 1988 constitution also gives presidents one reactive power over the budget. The president prepares the annual budget, budget guidelines, and multiyear budget plan. The Congress must approve the budget in a joint session, but it faces restrictions in the kinds of amendments it can propose. Congress is not permitted to initiate programs or projects not included in the president's budget (Art. 167). This gives presidents complete control in blocking resources for new programs they oppose. Congress can approve amendments to the annual budget only if they are compatible with the multiyear budget plan elaborated by the president and are compatible with the law on budgetary guidelines (Art. 166). Congress may not authorize expenditures that would exceed the budgetary revenue (Art. 167). These provisions enable the president to preserve the status quo on budgetary matters.

PRESIDENTS' PROACTIVE LEGISLATIVE POWERS

By *proactive legislative powers*, Shugart and I refer to whether or not the constitution gives the president any legislative decree powers and how extensive they are. If the constitution grants the president the right to issue legislative decrees, this enhances the executive's powers. Presidents then no longer depend completely on congressional initiative to accomplish their legislative agenda; indeed, they may not need majority backing for some initiatives.

Following the norm in most democratic constitutions, the 1946 constitution did not have a provision for presidential legislative decrees. In contrast, Article 62 of the 1988 constitution allows presidents to adopt provisional measures (*medidas provisórias*). Through Article 62, presidents can implement measures that have the force of law for a 30-day period without congressional approval. In comparative terms, Article 62 gives the Brazilian president exceptional legislative powers. This measure has changed the functioning of Brazilian democracy as compared with the 1946–64 period (Figueiredo and Limongi 1995a; Pessanha 1993; Power 1994).

Article 62 was explicitly designed for cases of "relevance and urgency" only. In practice, however, presidents have used provisional measures to push through all kinds of bills, with little concern for whether they truly apply to emergencies. Between October 5, 1988, when the new constitution went into effect, and late May 1995, the four presidents issued 1,004 provisional measures: 147 under Sarney, 160 under Collor, 505 under Franco, and 192 under Cardoso. Provisional measures have been used to legislate some of the most important bills that have passed under the 1988 constitution. For example, key provisions of President Collor's 1990 economic plan and Cardoso's Real Plan in 1994 were implemented via these decrees.

According to the constitution, provisional measures are to be rejected unless Congress passes them within 30 days. However, presidents have regularly reissued these decrees after they expired. Of the first 1,004 provisional measures under the 1988 constitution, 640 had previously been issued. Congress had approved 274 provisional measures and had rejected only 18. As of May 1995, 26 such presidential decrees had been recently issued by the Cardoso government without expiring, gaining approval, or being rejected. (The source gives no information on the remaining 46 provisional measures; presumably, they had been allowed to expire.)[4] The de facto practice, then, has been that presidential decrees can remain in effect unless Congress rejects them (Power 1994; Figueiredo and Limongi 1994a, 1995a). Article 62 was not intended to be used in such sweeping fashion, but it has given presidents considerable power to legislate. Indeed, among the 43 constitutions that Shugart and Carey analyzed, the 1988 Brazilian constitution gave presidents the most sweeping decree power (though the 1993 Russian constitution exceeds it).

Even in the unusual cases in which Congress rejects a presidential decree, the bill still goes into effect for a short time (up to 30 days) until it is explicitly rejected or amended. The provisions of an expired or rejected provisional measure in principle are null, but their actual effects are not automatically rescinded retroactively unless Congress passes a measure. In fact, the constitution does not even explicitly prohibit the reissuing of provisional measures rejected by Congress – though subsequent regulation of Article 62 did so prohibit (Pessanha 1993; Power 1994). A judicial ruling in 1991 prohibited the president from reissuing in the same legislative session a provisional measure that had been amended by Congress and vetoed by the president.

Decree powers under the 1988 constitution are still considerably weaker than under the military regime's 1967 constitution. Article 58 of the 1967 constitution enabled presidents to issue decree-laws, which became law unless Congress explicitly rejected them within 60 days. Congress was not allowed to amend a decree-law, which further reduced its ability to control the legislative process. These provisions, plus the military government's

4 "A explosão das MP," *Veja*, no. 1,394 (May 31, 1995):29.

consistent majorities in both chambers of Congress until 1983, virtually ensured that presidential decrees would become law. Power (1994) notes that Congress rejected only 33 of 2,481 decree-laws between 1964 and 1968 and none of 1,662 between 1968 and 1983. By making presidential decrees formally contingent on congressional approval and by allowing Congress to amend them, the 1988 constitution granted Congress greater power over presidential legislative decrees than the 1967 constitution. In practice, however, the possibility of reissuing a provisional measure that has not been rejected reduces the difference between the 1967 decree law and the 1988 provisional measure. Whereas the intent of the 1988 constitution was to require congressional approval of presidential decrees, the de facto practice became that congressional acquiescence was all that was needed.

The president also has some proactive budgetary powers that allow him or her to implement his or her preferred budget (Figueiredo and Limongi 1995a). If Congress fails to pass a budget on time, the president's proposed budget goes into effect on a month-by-month basis. The president can attempt to hinder Congress from approving the budget in order to have his or her own proposal in effect for some time. Moreover, as Congress deliberates over the budget, the president is allowed to withdraw his or her proposed budget and present a new one, thereby provoking a setback for Congress. Among the 41 non-Brazilian constitutions that Shugart and Carey ranked, only 4 gave presidents more power over the budget, and only 9 other constitutions had similar provisions.[5]

PRESIDENTS' ABILITY TO DICTATE THE LEGISLATIVE AGENDA

As Figueiredo and Limongi (1994a, 1995a) have argued, some constitutional provisions enable presidents to establish priorities on the congressional agenda, potentially superseding the wishes of congressional leaders. Article 62 of the 1988 constitution (provisional measures) not only gives presidents the power to legislate; it also gives them influence over the congressional agenda. If Congress fails to act on a presidential decree within 30 days, the provisional measure automatically goes to the top of the legislative agenda, displacing issues that the Congress may have been discussing for some time.

Further increasing presidents' agenda powers is Article 64 of the 1988 constitution, which gives presidents the right to declare a bill of their own initiative "urgent." Under these conditions, the two houses of Congress are

5 On the budgetary process in the 1946 constitution, see Articles 73 to 77.

obliged to vote on the bill within 45 days. If they fail to do so, the bill immediately moves to the top of the legislative agenda, pushing aside bills of congressional initiative. Presidents therefore have means of ensuring rapid treatment of bills of their initiative. The combination of Article 62 and Article 64 helps explain the vast difference between the mean time that bills introduced by the executive take (25 days for unamended provisional measures from 1989 to 1994; 56 days for budgetary bills; 11 days for amended provisional measures; 412 days for other executive bills) compared with bills introduced by the legislature (1,094 days; Figueiredo and Limongi 1995a:184). In combination with the partial veto, Articles 62 and 64 give Brazilian presidents great ability to block legislation they don't like and to impose their own legislative priorities onto the congressional agenda (though not necessarily to win approval for them).

Article 57 of the 1988 constitution allows the president to convoke a special session of Congress. During such a session, Congress is allowed to deliberate only those issues determined by presidential initiative. This provision further augments the president's influence over the congressional agenda.

Not surprisingly in the context of these sweeping constitutional powers, presidents have dominated the legislative process in the post-1988 period. Figueiredo and Limongi (1995a) indicate that of 1,259 laws passed between 1989 and 1994, 997 were initiated by the president compared with only 176 by the legislature (and 86 by the judiciary). Moreover, bills initiated by the executive were much more likely to win final approval than bills initiated by Congress.

On balance, Congress has weaker control over legislation under the 1988 constitution than it did under the 1946 constitution, and the president has greater legislative powers. This shift toward the presidency results mostly from Article 62 (provisional measures) and Article 64 (urgent initiatives). The 1946 constitution gave no such authority to the president.

Shugart and Carey (1992) ranked the 1988 constitution as providing the second most powerful presidential capacities in the legislative arena among the 43 constitutions they studied. The 1946 constitution ranked fourth, but this understates the difference between the two constitutions. The 1988 constitution, by virtue of Articles 62 and 64, endows the president with much greater capacity to legislate and dictate the legislative agenda.

In sum, the 1988 constitution in some respects approximates the often misleading portrayal of Latin American executive power – the imperial presidency. This situation exists not primarily because of cultural factors or some inherent features of presidentialism, but rather because of specific measures introduced by the 1988 constitution, which deliberately created a presidency with sweeping powers. Even so, it would be a mistake to assume that presidents can get everything they want by steamrolling Congress.

PARTY SYSTEM FRAGMENTATION AND MINORITY PRESIDENTIALISM

The parties of Brazilian presidents typically have controlled a distinct minority of seats in Congress. Table 2.2 gives results of presidential elections and shows the share of seats of presidents' parties and electoral coalitions.

Table 2.2 underscores the minority situation of the presidents' parties. Leaving aside the anomalous Dutra period (1946–50), when presidents assumed office, their parties had a distinct minority of the seats in both chambers of Congress. Itamar Franco (1992–94) did not have a party, nor was he closely identified with one; this further underscores the absence of a majority party supporting the president. José Sarney's (1985–90) party was formally the centrist PMDB (Party of the Brazilian Democratic Movement), but this was because in order to run for vice-president, Sarney was obligated in 1984 by the extant electoral legislation to join Tancredo Neves's party, the PMDB. (Elected as vice-president, Sarney became president when Neves died before assuming office.) Most of Sarney's close allies, including his own son, were in the conservative PFL (Party of the Liberal Front), which won only about 20% of the seats in the Chamber of Deputies and had only 21% of the Senate seats after the 1986 elections.

Table 2.3 gives the results of 1945–94 presidential elections. Tables 2.4 and 2.5 give the results of lower chamber and Senate elections for 1982–94.[6] Table 2.6 shows the effective number of parties for both chambers. By 1990, with 8.7 effective parties in the lower chamber, Brazil had one of the world's most fragmented party systems. In the 1994 elections, fragmentation diminished slightly, but remained easily the highest in Latin America.

The 1945 congressional results were an anomaly that do not affect the overwhelming tendency toward fragmented multipartism. The elections took place in a context of high continuity from the authoritarian Estado Novo of 1937–45 (Souza 1976), leaving the newly formed PSD, which was created by Estado Novo leaders, in a privileged position. Moreover,

6 For 1946–64 congressional results, see Hippólito (1985), Mainwaring (1995), or Nohlen (1993). Because these results are now readily available in several sources, I do not reproduce them here.

Table 2.2. *Main political parties, 1985–95*

Left	
PC do B	Communist Party of Brazil. An Albanian-oriented party until the early 1990s. The most Leninist of the leftist parties in Brazil. Created in 1962 as a schism of the Brazilian Communist Party.
PT	The Workers' Party. A heterogeneous leftist party, ranging from some revolutionary groups to social democrats. Created in 1979.
PCB/PPS	Brazilian Communist Party. Created in 1922. Renamed the Popular Socialist Party (PPS) in 1992.
PSB	Brazilian Socialist Party. An independent leftist party created in 1985.
Center-left	
PDT	Democratic Labor Party. A populist party with predominantly social democratic tendencies. Created in 1979.
PSDB	Party of Brazilian Social Democracy. Created in 1988 by a dissident group of the PMDB. Espoused a social democratic line until reaching power in 1994–95; has followed a centrist policy and line since then.
Center	
PMDB	Party of the Brazilian Democratic Movement. Its precursor, the MDB (Brazilian Democratic Movement) was created in 1966 as the official party of opposition to the military regime. Renamed the PMDB in 1979. Since its inception, the PMDB has been a heterogeneous party, but its hegemonic group is centrist. Many conservatives have flocked to the party since 1982.
Center-right	
PTB	Brazilian Labor Party. A predominantly center-right party. Created in 1979. A very markedly more conservative party than the center-left party of the same name that existed from 1945 until 1965.
PDC	Christian Democratic Party. Created in 1985. More conservative than Christian Democracy parties in many countries. Merged with the PDS in 1993 to form the PPR.
PP	Progressive Party. Created in 1993 through a merger of the Social Labor Party (PST) and Renewal Labor Party (PTR).
Right	
PL	Liberal Party. A conservative party known for its antistatist discourse. Created in 1985.
PRN	Party of National Reconstruction. Created in 1989 by Fernando Collor de Mello as a vehicle for running for president. Faded after Collor's impeachment in 1992.
PFL	Party of the Liberal Front. A conservative party created in 1984 by dissidents of the PDS.

Table 2.2 (*cont.*)

PDS	Democratic Social Party. Despite its name, a conservative party. The PDS and its predecessor, Arena (1966–79) provided the partisan support for the military regime. Merged with the PDC in 1993 to form the PPR.
PPR	Reformist Progressive Party. Created in 1993 by the merger of the PDS and the PDC.

the 1945 electoral law amply favored the largest party in a given state, in most cases the PSD.[7] This method was subsequently altered after the 1945 congressional elections, significantly reducing the advantage for the largest party. Also, in 1945 coalitions were not allowed in proportional elections, which diminished the prospects of small parties. After 1947, coalitions were allowed in proportional elections, a fact that aided the small parties.

The 1986 congressional elections were also anomalous in terms of the division of votes and seats. Two circumstances unduly favored the PMDB and limited party system fragmentation. These elections were the first in the new democratic period, and the PMDB benefited by having led the party opposition to military rule. In addition, political manipulation of economic policy led to a short-term boom in 1986, followed by a bust and rapidly escalating inflation after the election.

Several features of the electoral system allow for a highly fragmented party system and make it unlikely that the president's party would enjoy a majority in Congress. In the Chamber of Deputies, the system of proportional representation with a low threshold and a high district magnitude encourages high fragmentation. In Brazil, the formal threshold (i.e., the minimum percentage of votes a party needs to win a seat) is the electoral quotient in any state – the number of votes divided by the numbers of seats. If there were 25 seats in a state, a party or an alliance of parties would need 4% of the votes to attain one seat. There is no national threshold, so a party could obtain a seat with an extremely low percentage of the national vote. District magnitudes (the number of seats per district) are large. The states – there are now 26 – and the Federal District constitute the electoral districts for both chambers. Each state was guaranteed at least seven deputies

---

7 In each state, a party won one seat for every full multiple it reached of the electoral quotient, that is, the number of valid votes divided by the number of seats. All remaining seats in that state went to the largest party rather than being divided proportionally, as occurred after 1945 (and as is the norm in proportional systems).

under the 1946 constitution and at least eight under the 1988 constitution. The average district magnitude for the lower chamber in 1994 was 19.0. Between 1950 and 1964 and again since 1985, parties have been allowed to form alliances in proportional elections, and the threshold then applies to the whole coalition rather than to each party within it. Thus, a party need not meet the threshold on its own in order to win a seat. Consequently, a party can win a seat with an infinitesimal percentage of the vote. From 1955 until 1964 and again between 1985 and 1990, the fact that presidential and congressional elections were not concurrent also encouraged the fragmentation of congressional seats (Shugart and Carey 1992:226–58; Jones 1995a). The two-round, absolute majority format for presidential elections introduced by the 1988 constitution also favors high fragmentation.

What are the effects for presidents of significant party system fragmentation? Assuming for the moment that presidents need legislative support to accomplish their agendas, as party system fragmentation increases, one would expect the president's capacity to obtain what he or she wants to decrease. Party system fragmentation correlates extremely highly with the president's party's share of seats (Conclusion, this volume). Under normal circumstances, one would expect the president's party to be more likely than any other to support the president. Therefore, if the president's party has a small share of seats, obtaining legislative support is likely to be more difficult, effecting major reforms is likely to be more problematic, and Linzian-type impasses (see Linz 1994) between the executive and legislature are more probable. If, however, parties other than the president's have policy positions close to the president, then the difficulties associated with significant fragmentation should diminish (Amorim Neto 1995; Nicolau 1995). In fact, the difficulties of multiparty presidentialism in Brazil have been most acute under presidents (Goulart and Collor) whose policy positions differed markedly from that of the "mean" legislator.

Another consequence that logically stems from high fragmentation is that presidents need support from parties beyond their own. Presidents must either assemble a broad legislative coalition or deal with a situation of minority government.

As Abranches (1988) argues, Brazilian presidents have a long history of attempting to create majorities by forming broad governing coalitions. Before 1964, the search to form coalitions began during the precampaign phase, when presidential aspirants sought to win the endorsements of several parties. The plurality, single-round method of electing presidents served as an inducement to coalition candidacies. The main presidential candidates always enjoyed multiparty support.

Once elected, presidents form de facto coalition governments by offer-

Table 2.3. *Results of presidential elections*

Year, candidate, party	Votes	Percentage of valid votes	Percentage of seats in chamber of presidential electoral coalition	Percentage of seats in chamber of president's party
1945				
Eurico Gaspar Dutra, PSD/PTB	3,251,507	55.3	79.7	PSD, 52.8 (1945)
Eduardo Gomes, UDN	2,039,341	34.7		
Yeddo Fiuza, PCB	569,918	9.7		
1950				
Getúlio Vargas, PTB/PSP	3,849,040	48.7	24.7	PTB, 16.8 (1950)
Eduardo Gomes, UDN	2,342,384	29.7		
Cristiano Machado, PSD	1,697,193	21.5		
1955				
Juscelino Kubitschek, PSD/PTB	3,077,411	35.6	52.2	PSD, 35.0 (1954)
Juarez Távora, PDC/UDN/PL	2,610,462	30.3		
Adhemar de Barros, PSP	2,222,725	25.8		
Plínio Salgado	714,379	8.3		
1960				
Jânio Quadros,[a] UDN/PDC/PL/PTN	5,636,623	48.3	26.6	UDN, 21.5 (1958)
Henrique Teixeira Lott, PTB/PSD	3,846,825	32.9		
Adhemar de Barros, PSP	2,195,709	18.8		
1989, first round				
Fernando Collor de Mello, PRN	20,611,011	30.5	6.4	PRN, 4.2 (1989)
Luis Inácio da Silva, PT	11,622,673	17.2		

Leonel Brizola, PDT	11,168,228	16.5		
Mário Covas, PSDB	7,790,392	11.5		
Paulo Maluf, PDS	5,986,575	8.9		
Guilherme Afif Domingos, PL	3,272,462	4.8		
Ulysses Guimarães, PMDB	3,204,932	4.7		
Others	3,970,376	6.0		
1989, second round				
Fernando Collor de Mello, PRN	35,089,998	53.0	39.6	PRN, 4.2 (1989)
Luis Inácio da Silva, PT	31,076,364	47.0		
1994				
Fernando Henrique Cardoso, PSDB	34,377,198	54.3	42.4	PSDB, 12.1 (1994)
Luis Inácio da Silva, PT	17,126,291	27.0		
Eneas Carneiro, PRONA	4,672,026	7.4		
Orestes Quércia, PMDB	2,773,793	4.4		
Leonel Brizola, PDT	2,016,386	3.2		
Espiridião Amin, PPR	1,740,210	2.8		
Others	626,250	1.0		

[a]Quadros was not a member of any party.
Source: Tribunal Superior Eleitoral.

Table 2.4. *Chamber of deputies election results by party, 1982–94*
(percentage of seats)

Party	1982	1986	1990	1994
PDS/PPR[a]	49.1	6.6	8.3	10.1
PMDB	41.8	53.6	21.5	20.9
PDT	4.8	4.9	9.3	6.8
PTB	2.7	3.5	7.6	6.0
PT	1.7	3.3	7.0	9.6
PFL	—	23.8	16.7	17.3
PL	—	1.2	3.0	2.5
PDC[a]	—	1.2	4.4	—
PC do B	—	1.0	1.0	1.9
PCB[b]/PPS	—	0.6	0.6	0.4
PSB	—	0.2	2.2	2.9
PRN	—	—	8.0	0.2
PSDB	—	—	7.4	12.1
PSC	—	—	1.2	0.6
PRS	—	—	0.8	—
PST/PP[c]	—	—	0.4	7.0
PTR	—	—	0.4	—
PSD	—	—	0.2	0.6
PMN	—	—	0.2	0.8
PRP	—	—	—	0.2
PV	—	—	—	0.2
Total	100.0	100.0	100.0	100.0
No. seats	479	487	503	513

[a]The PDS and PDC merged to form the PPR in 1993.
[b]The PCB changed its name to the PPS in 1992.
[c]The PTR incorporated the PST in 1993 and became the PP.
Sources: Bolivar Lamounier, ed., *De Geisel a Collor: O Balanço da Transição* (São Paulo: Sumaré/IDESP, 1990), pp. 186–89; Robert Wesson and David Fleischer, *Brazil in Transition* (New York: Praeger, 1983), p. 119; David Fleischer, Centro de Estudos e Acompanhamento da Constituinte; *Folha de São Paulo*, October 29, 1990; *Folha de São Paulo*, November 16, 1994, and November 21, 1994.

Table 2.5. *Senate seats by party, 1982–94 (percentage of seats)*

Party	1982 Seats won	1982 Total held	1986 Seats won	1986 Total held	1990 Seats won	1990 Total held	1994 Seats won	1994 Total held
PDS/PPR[a]	60.0	66.7	4.1	6.9	7.4	3.7	3.7	7.4
PMDB	36.0	30.4	77.6	62.5	29.6	33.3	25.9	27.2
PDT	4.0	0.5	2.0	2.8	3.7	6.2	7.4	7.4
PTB	—	0.5	—	1.4	14.8	9.9	5.6	6.2
PFL	—	—	14.3	20.8	29.6	18.5	20.4	22.2
PL	—	—	—	1.4	—	—	1.9	1.2
PDC[a]	—	—	—	1.4	—	4.9	—	—
PSB	—	—	—	1.4	—	1.2	1.9	1.2
PMB	—	—	2.0	1.4	—	—	—	—
PSDB	—	—	—	—	3.7	12.3	16.7	13.6
PRN	—	—	—	—	7.4	3.7	—	—
PT	—	—	—	—	3.7	1.2	7.4	6.2
PST/PP[b]	—	—	—	—	—	1.2	7.4	6.2
PMN	—	—	—	—	—	1.2	—	—
No party	—	—	—	—	—	2.5	—	—
PCB/PPS	—	—	—	—	—	—	1.9	1.2
Total	100.0	100.0	100.0	100.0	100.0	100.0	100.0	100.0
No. seats	25	69	49	72	27	81	54	81

Note: Senate terms are eight years long. In alternate elections, two-thirds and one-third of the Senate seats are disputed. "Total held" columns refer to the composition of the Senate after the respective elections; it combines the seats of the newly elected senators with those who did not run that year. In 1982, one seat per state was contested, and the new state of Rondônia elected three senators. In 1986, two seats were disputed in 23 states, and the Federal District elected three senators. In 1990, one seat per state was disputed. In 1994, two seats per state were disputed.
[a] The PDS and PDC merged to form the PPR in 1993.
[b] The PST and PTR merged to form the PP in 1993.
Sources: Lamounier, ed., *De Geisel a Collor: O Balanço da Transição* (São Paulo: Sumaré/IDESP, 1990), pp. 187–89; *Folha de São Paulo*, October 29, 1990; International Foundation for Electoral Systems, *Newsletter* 1, 4 (1990): 5; *Folha de São Paulo*, November 16, 1994, and November 21, 1994; Jairo Marconi Nicolau, "Presidentialism, Fragmentary Multiparty Systems and Democracy," unpublished paper, 1995.

Table 2.6. *Effective number of parties in Brazilian Congress (in seats)*

Year	Chamber of Deputies	Senate
1945	2.77	2.24
1947	—	2.72
1950	4.10	3.18
1954	4.59	4.21
1958	4.50	3.58
1962	4.55	4.03
1986	2.83	2.27
1990	8.65	5.54
1994	8.13	6.08

Source: Calculated from Hippólito (1985) and Tables 2.4 and 2.5.

ing jobs and resources to different parties. This partitioning of government begins at the highest level (cabinet positions and heads of major public enterprises and executive agencies) and continues on down to minor federal appointments and resources in backward towns and remote regions. With comparatively weak party discipline and loyalty, these coalitions are loose and shifting rather than hard and fast. The boundary between minority presidentialism and coalition government in Brazil is permeable, more so than is the case in parliamentary systems with disciplined parties.

Between 1946 and 1964, presidents generally resorted to oversized cabinets to secure support from a wide range of parties. Table 2.7 provides evidence of the consistent option of presidents to form multiparty cabinets. If the parties represented in the cabinet had provided bloc support for presidents, they would usually have constituted an extremely broad alliance, and presidents would have secured sizable majorities in Congress. The last two columns give the percentage of seats obtained by the parties that had cabinet representatives. The parties that had cabinet positions often accounted for 80% of the seats in the Chamber of Deputies, and during the Quadros government this figure reached 92.7%. Cabinet formation obviously did not obey the logic predicted by some game theorists (e.g., Riker 1962) of minimal-winning coalitions. The breadth of the parties represented in the cabinet obeyed a logic closer to consociational than majoritarian democracy (Lijphart 1984).

Presidential efforts to win broad coalition support have often been successful. However, other things equal, coalition formation is probably less reliable in presidential systems than in parliamentary systems. A multiparty government in a parliamentary system differs in three ways from a multi-party presidential government. First, presidents are generally freer to dis-miss ministers and rearrange the cabinet than prime ministers are. This presidential autonomy is part of a generally looser institutional arrangement that can lead to a lack of stable congressional support, for just as presidents are less bound to the parties, so are the parties less bound to the presidents.

In Brazil, presidential autonomy in forming cabinets is reflected in the limited correlation between which parties supported presidents during cam-paigns and the number of cabinet appointments allocated to the parties. Table 2.8 makes this point clear, with Vargas's cabinet being especially notable in this regard. After opposing Vargas during the campaign, the PSD wound up with the lion's share of civilian cabinet posts (five of eight). The UDN, which trenchantly opposed Vargas, gained as many ministries (one) as Vargas's own PTB. Moreover, presidents changed the composition of cabinets with frequency. For example, having been elected with the sup-port of the PSD and PTB, Dutra later excluded the latter from his cabinet and included the UDN, which had been his foremost opponent in the 1945 election.

The second major difference between party coalitions in presidential and parliamentary systems is that, in the latter, individual legislators are more or less bound to support the government unless their party decides to drop out of the governmental alliance. Members of parliament risk losing their seats in new elections if they fail to support the government. In pres-idential systems, voting against a bill does not subject members of congress to new elections.

A few examples underscore that a party's participation in the cabinet did not ensure the bloc support of legislators for the president. As president in the 1950s, Getúlio Vargas included a cabinet member from the UDN, which attempted to undermine his government. Vargas's cabinet was dom-inated by the PSD, which maintained a dubious attitude toward the pres-ident. Quadros's cabinet included one politician from the PSD, which was ambivalent about the maverick president. Goulart's cabinet had a UDN member, notwithstanding this party's determination to undermine the pres-ident. The PSD, which was ambivalent toward Goulart, was represented in all of his cabinets. Sarney's cabinet included many representatives from the PMDB, which was ambivalent about his government. For several months, Franco's cabinet included a PT member, but the PT opposed his govern-ment. Cabinet representation does not guarantee that the legislators of that party support the government.

The third major difference between party coalitions in presidential and

Table 2.7. *Parties with cabinet positions*

Government	Parties	Percentage of seats, Lower Chamber	Percentage of seats, Senate
Dutra government			
Jan. 1946 to Oct. 1946	PSD, PTB	60.5	66.7
Oct. 1946 to Apr. 1950	PSD, UDN, PR	82.1	90.4; 87.9[a]
Apr. 1950 to Jan. 1951	PSD, UDN	79.7	86.4
Vargas government			
Jan. 1951 to Aug. 1954	PSD, PTB, UDN, PSP	88.1	87.5
Café Filho government			
Aug. 1954 to Apr. 1955	UDN, PSD, PR, PTB	83.8	85.9
Apr. 1955 to Nov. 1955	UDN, PSD, PDC, PR, PTB	81.3	85.9
Nereu Ramos government			
Nov. 1955 to Jan. 1956	PSD, PTB, PR, PSP	67.8	71.9
Kubitschek government			
Jan. 1956 to Jan. 1961	PSD, PTB, PR, PSP	67.8; 68.4[b]	71.9; 66.7[b]
Quadros government			
Jan. 1961 to Aug. 1961	UDN, PTB, PSD, PSB, PSP, PR	92.7	93.7
Goulart government			
Sept. 1961 to June 1962	PSD, PTB, UDN, PDC	79.1	90.5

June 1962 to July 1962	PSD, PTB, UDN, PDC, PR	84.3	92.1
July 1962 to Sept. 1962	PSD, PTB, UDN, PSB	79.8	90.5
Sept. 1962 to Jan. 1963	PTB, PSD, PSB	58.3	63.5
Jan. 1963 to June 1963	PTB, PSB, PSP, PSD, UDN	85.8	87.9
June 1963 to Dec. 1963	PTB, PSD, PDC	62.2	62.1
Dec. 1963 to Apr. 1964	PTB, PSD	57.3	60.6
Sarney government			
Mar. 1985	PMDB, PFL, PDS	91.6[c]	
Mar. 1985 to Feb. 1986	PMDB, PFL, PDS, PTB	94.0[c]	
Feb. 1986 to Mar. 1990	PMDB, PFL	72.1[d]; 77.4[e]; 54.0[f]	83.3[e]
Collor government			
Mar. 1990 to Apr. 1992	PMDB, PFL, PTR, PRN, PDS	54.9[g]	59.2[g]
Apr. 1992 to Oct. 1992	PFL, PDS, PTB, PSDB, PL	43.0	44.4

Table 2.7. (*cont.*)

Government	Parties	Percentage of seats, Lower Chamber	Percentage of seats, Senate
Franco government			
Oct. 1992 to Jan. 1993	PDT, PSDB, PFL, PMDB, PSB, PTB	64.7	81.3
Jan. 1993 to May 1993	PDT, PSDB, PFL, PMDB, PSB, PTB, PT	71.7	82.5
May 1993 to Aug. 1993	PDT, PSDB, PFL, PMDB, PSB, PTB	64.7	81.3
Aug. 1993 to Dec. 1994	PMDB, PFL, PP, PSDB	46.0	65.8
Cardoso government			
Jan. 1995–	PSDB, PMDB, PFL, PTB	56.3	69.2

[a]90.4% until the 1947 Senate elections; 87.9% thereafter.
[b]The second figure refers to the period after the 1958 elections.
[c]Combined figure for lower and upper chambers.
[d]Combined figure for lower and upper chambers for July 1986.
[e]February 1987.
[f]Combined figure for lower and upper chambers for January 1990.
[g]Percentage of seats after the 1990 elections.

Source: For cabinet positions, Hippólito (1985: 293–303) for 1946–64; unpublished information obtained from the Departamento de Documentação, Presidência da República, Brasília, for 1985–93; Amorim Neto (1995) for 1993–94; "Equipe à la carte," *Veja*, no. 1,372 (December 28, 1994): 32–33, for 1995. For seats: In addition to the tables above, Kinzo (1990: 108).

Table 2.8. *Presidents' electoral coalitions and cabinet composition*

President	President's electoral coalition	Initial cabinet composition[a]
1946–64		
Dutra, 1945	PSD, PTB	PSD (5), PTB (1)
Vargas, 1950	PTB, PSP	PSD (5), UDN (1), PTB (1), PSP (1)
Kubitschek, 1955	PSD, PTB	PSD (4), PTB (2), PSP (1), PR (1)
Quadros, 1960	UDN, PDC, PL, PTN	UDN (3), PTB (3), PSD (1), PSP (1), PR (1), PSB (1)
1985–95		
Collor (second round), 1989	PRN, PDS, PFL, PTB, PDC, PL	PMDB, PFL, PTR
Cardoso, 1994	PSDB, PFL, PTB, PP	PSDB (6), PFL (4), PMDB (2), PTB (2)

Note: Senate figures are based on the composition of the entire Senate, not on election returns for a particular year.

[a] The numbers in parentheses refer to the number of cabinet positions allocated to different parties.

Sources: Hippólito (1985: 293–303) for 1946–64; unpublished information obtained from the Departamento de Documentação, Presidência da República, Brasília, for 1985–93; Amorim Neto (1995) for 1993–94; "Equipe à la carte," *Veja*, no. 1,372 (December 28, 1994): 32–33, for 1995.

parliamentary systems is that, in the latter, the parties themselves are co-responsible for governing. When they cease supporting the government, there is a chance that new elections will be called in most parliamentary systems. These differences mean that, ceteris paribus, parliamentary systems are probably better at sustaining interparty governing coalitions than presidential systems are. This is not, however, to claim that presidentialist coalition governments are impossible or vastly more difficult than parliamentarist coalitions.

The difficulties of coalition formation under highly fragmented multiparty presidentialism help explain cabinet instability in Brazil. Presidents allocate cabinet positions in part to help secure bases of political support. But because their party support is not fully reliable, presidents frequently change the partisan composition of the cabinet in an effort to broaden or change support. The challenge in mounting a stable coalition is compounded because the catchall parties are comparatively undisciplined; as a result, party leaders cannot enforce agreements they make. Indeed, regardless of the system of government, party indiscipline is inimical to stable coalition building.

UNDISCIPLINED CATCHALL PARTIES AND LOW PARTY LOYALTY

Brazilian catchall parties in the two democratic periods have been comparatively undisciplined. In the post-1985 period, the leftist PT and the minor leftist parties have been very disciplined, but they are exceptions.

Figueiredo and Limongi (1995b) analyzed voting patterns in the Chamber of Deputies for the 1989–94 period. Using the 221 roll call votes in which at least 10% of the Chamber opposed the winning side, on average the following percentages defected from the majority position within their party: 15% of PTB members, 13% of the Party of Brazilian Social Democracy (PSDB) and PMDB members, 12% of the Democratic Social Party (PDS) members, 11% of PFL members, and 9% of Democratic Labor Party (PDT) members. Only the PT (2% mean defections) was highly disciplined. This shows higher discipline than one would expect on the basis of some portraits of Brazilian parties, but lower discipline than exists in most democracies.

Mainwaring and Pérez Liñán (forthcoming) show that levels of party discipline were markedly lower during the Constitutional Congress of 1987–88. They include votes only if 25% or more of those who voted opposed the winning side. Some 363 roll calls in the Constitutional Congress met this 25% opposition threshold. On average, the following percentages of a party's legislators opposed the majority position within the party: PMDB, 35%; PTB, 30%; PFL, 24%; PDS, 21%; PDT, 14%; PT, 2%.

Political elites in Brazil have shown comparatively low loyalty to their parties, especially in the post-1985 period. This fact is reflected in the commonplace practice of switching parties. In the 1987–90 legislature, there were at least 197 cases of party switching, and during the 1991–95 legislature there were 262 cases (Samuels forthcoming). This lack of party loyalty reinforces the unreliability of support for the president, although it also offers the president opportunities to induce members of Congress to join his or her party or coalition.

For presidents, limited party discipline and loyalty have an equivocal impact. Limited party discipline and loyalty make executive–legislative relations less predictable. Presidents cannot fully count on the support of their party or coalition, as they might with highly disciplined parties and loyal legislators. If a president's party had a majority in Congress, from his or her perspective, disciplined parties would be a clear asset. With fragmented multipartism, weaker discipline also has advantages for presidents; it enables presidents to entice members of other parties to support them, and presidents usually do not face disciplined majorities determined to block them.

Limited party loyalty has the same ambiguous effect. The Cardoso administration benefited from party switching to the PSDB and PFL. Sarney, however, presided over a mass migration away from his own PMDB and from the PFL toward opposition parties.

In both democratic periods, limited party discipline allowed for fluid relationships between presidents and their coalitions (Novaes 1994). During the Vargas, Quadros, Goulart, and Sarney administrations, major parties were divided in their positions vis-à-vis the government. None of the parties, including Vargas's own PTB (a center-left populist party), unequivocally supported his government, nor, on the other hand, did any of the major parties except the conservative UDN clearly oppose it. The PSD maintained a dubious attitude toward the president, neither supporting nor opposing him (Hippólito 1985:85–103).

Under Quadros (1961), the UDN, PSD, and PTB were all divided, with some factions of the parties supporting the president and others opposing him. The UDN dominated the cabinet, but a segment of the party began to oppose Quadros because of his foreign policy overtures to Cuba. The PTB, which opposed him during the campaign, began to support Quadros because of his independent foreign policy. All three of the major parties were highly factionalized, making it more difficult to establish bases of solid institutional support (Franco 1976:103–16; Ramos 1961:21–95; Benevides 1989, 1981; Hippólito 1985; Oliveira 1973).

The UDN generally opposed President João Goulart (1961–64), but a minority faction supported some of his nationalistic program. The PSD was deeply divided, as some factions supported while others opposed Goulart (Hippólito 1985:235–36). On March 10, 1964, three weeks before the coup, the PSD opted for an official break with the government. Goulart's own party, the PTB, was split because some radicalized factions, led by Leonel Brizola, considered the president too timid.

When Sarney was immensely popular in 1986 because of the success (albeit short lived) of the Cruzado Plan, an economic stabilization plan that froze prices and wages, the PMDB and PFL were sycophantic. With the failure of the Cruzado Plan, however, the PMDB became deeply divided over its relationship to the government. The progressive sectors of the PMDB tried to push the party into opposing the government, but they met invincible resistance. Conservative and clientelistic sectors continued to support the government, but in June 1988, 40 congressional representatives split off and formed a new center-left party, the PSDB (Party of Brazilian Social Democracy). Even among those who remained in the PMDB the schisms were deep. In the PFL, Marco Maciel led a splinter group critical of the government, while most of the party supported it. During the Constitutional Congress of 1987–88, supraparty blocs eclipsed parties as the means of organizing congressional debates.

Sarney and his successor, Fernando Collor de Mello (1990–92) enjoyed widespread backing in Congress at moments of peak popularity, but such backing eroded when public approval plummeted. Parties that initially were part of the governing coalition defected in hard times or as positioning for the next presidential campaign began. Toward the end of their terms, Sarney and Collor were weakened by their status as lame ducks. Governors and legislators distanced themselves from these unpopular presidents without paying a high price for defecting.

In sum, the comparative lack of party discipline and loyalty in Brazil has mixed effects. When presidents are popular, they generally dominate their parties, and parties and politicians identify themselves with the government to enjoy the influence of government prestige and to enhance their own access to patronage. When a president is unpopular, maintaining a coalition is problematic. Distancing oneself from the government is a means of avoiding the negative repercussions of identification with an unpopular lame duck president.

ROBUST FEDERALISM

Brazil has long been the case of most robust federalism in Latin America (the other federal nations in the region are Argentina, Mexico, and Venezuela). By *robust federalism*, I mean that, during democratic periods, mayors and governors have been powerful actors with significant autonomy vis-à-vis the federal government and with significant resources. The catchall parties are decentralized, and parties and politicians generally follow a logic of federalism. Many of their actions are determined more by what goes on in their own states than by what goes on in national politics. In fact, the national parties are still to a considerable extent a federation of state parties.

Federalism has advantages in a heterogeneous country of continental size, but it has also further dispersed power in a fragmented political system. State loyalties lead politicians to coalesce in support of projects that will benefit their own state, regardless of the politicians' party and ideology (and regardless of the cost-effectiveness of the project). Federalism has contributed to factionalism in the catchall parties and, by extension, to their lack of party discipline. Politicians of the catchall parties focus a lot on state and local issues, so they are less willing to toe the line of the national party leadership. State loyalties make it more difficult for presidents to pull together reliable coalitions; to retain the political support of a state's congressional delegation, presidents need to offer high-level positions and resources.

Powerful political figures with independent bases, governors, and mayors of major cities compete with the president for power and resources. They command impressive political and economic resources, especially in the larger and wealthier states. The 1988 constitution granted broad powers and resources to state and local governments, but without reassigning responsibilities from the central government to subnational governments. According to one expert, in few countries do local and state governments take such a large share of total tax revenue (Dain 1995:16).

Because of their influence over deputies and senators of their party or coalition, governors (and mayors to a lesser extent) can thwart or facilitate presidential designs (Abrúcio 1994). Presidents need the support of legislators, so governors acquire considerable power in national politics.

Party decisions and processes are influenced more by state than national issues. Following the logic of state politics, state party organizations sometimes adopt a line contrary to the dominant position of the national leaders. When a president offers a ministerial position to a party member, the national leadership may support the president, but it does not follow that the state party leaders do. Deputies and senators have strong local loyalties that often outweigh their commitments to the president. These local loyalties hinder a president from capturing the bloc support of parties.

Several studies of the 1945–64 regime have underscored the autonomy of state-level organizations vis-à-vis the national party, as well as the autonomy of individual politicians vis-à-vis both state and national party organizations (Petersen 1962:188–207; Lima 1983; Hippólito 1985: 119–33; Oliveira 1973; Benevides 1981:160–71). Although many features of Brazilian politics have changed since 1964, the importance of state and local politics in determining how politicians and parties act has remained constant (Hagopian 1996; Sarles 1982). In the catchall parties that still dominate electoral competition, politicians respond first and foremost to local and state interests, somewhat as they do in the United States (Mayhew 1974).

For presidents, robust federalism has several consequences. Presidents must pay attention to constructing not only coalitions that involve several parties, but also coalitions that satisfy regional demands. For example, presidents carefully distribute cabinet and other high-ranking positions across states and regions. They need to pay attention to the demands of governors, who powerfully wield vetoes even in national politics (Abrúcio 1994). At times governors and mayors can undercut national policy-making efforts, as occurred with state-level public banks in the 1980s and the first half of the 1990s. In this sense, robust federalism limits the degree to which presidents can implement their preferred policies; it disperses and decentralizes power, making possible the power-sharing arrangements that Lijphart (1984) favors, and it limits the winner-takes-all nature of the system. On the positive side, effective mayors and governors can sometimes achieve meaningful accomplishments despite serious problems at the national level.

PRESIDENTIAL STRATEGIES: PATRONAGE POLITICS

Faced with a situation in which their party has a minority and usually a small minority, Brazilian presidents have a complicated task. However, presidents do have means of dealing with these complex institutional arrangements. In addition to building coalition governments and to governing by decree, presidents can attempt to win the support of individual legislators, primarily through using selective incentives (appointments and resources). Because of the comparatively low degree of loyalty and discipline in the catchall parties, this strategy usually goes hand in hand with the effort to build party coalitions.

Presidents everywhere forge political support primarily through a combination of patronage and policy. In Brazil, for politicians of the catchall parties, patronage is particularly important (Ames 1995a, 1995b; Hagopian 1996; Mainwaring 1991). Presidents' control over appointments and resources is a key tool in their efforts to secure congressional support for their policies.

Presidents and ministers use patronage to build legislative support, to strengthen the positions of friendly federal deputies, and to undermine opponents. Many federal deputies perceive their primary jobs as obtaining resources for their electoral regions, and they rely on presidents and ministers to get these resources. These deputies depend on their ability to deliver goods to the regions they represent, and they win votes fundamentally on this basis. As Federal Deputy Lúcio Alcântara (PFL, Ceará) states, "A political career in Brazil is closely connected to success in bringing home material benefits. . . . Especially in the poorest regions, communities judge their deputies on what they bring home."[8] Federal Deputy Amaral Netto (PDS, Rio de Janeiro) incisively stated that "a deputy is a *despachante de luxo*. His reason for being in Brasília is to bring home resources. Otherwise, he's not doing his job."[9] Senators, too, spend much of their time attempting to obtain resources for their states. Senator Saldanha Derzi (PMDB) said that "both Deputies and Senators have an obligation to seek funds to solve the problems of their regions. Those who fail to do so are remiss."[10]

Many deputies see themselves as political brokers who mediate the linkage between the federal government and their local constituencies. Mayors, councillors, community leaders, leaders of social movements, and business leaders depend on deputies to get federal resources. In turn, deputies, especially those who win most of their votes in small and medium-sized towns, depend on the electoral support of mayors, community activists, and local political notables. The deputies of the catchall parties win this support largely on the basis of their ability to deliver resources to the *município*. In order to get federal resources, they need connections to ministers and heads

8 "Prática divide opiniões de congressistas," *Folha de São Paulo*, February 21, 1988.
9 "Dropes," *Folha de São Paulo*, February 13, 1988. *Despachante* literally means dispatcher. In Brazil, *despachantes* are people who make a livelihood out of processing demands and paperwork through the sinuous bureaucracy. Countless bureaucratic processes are either difficult and time consuming or virtually impossible without a *despachante*. *Luxo* is the word for luxury; thus, a *despachante de luxo* is a high-class *despachante*.
10 "Inclusão da família no apadrinhamento irrita Sarney," *Folha de São Paulo*, February 11, 1988.

of federal agencies. If a deputy doesn't support the president, the heads of agencies and ministers do not provide access to resources.

Presidents, ministers, and heads of governmental agencies and firms use the dependence of deputies on obtaining resources to pressure them into supporting the president. Presidents can attempt to build support by offering patronage positions and resources to legislators and governors who support them. They withhold resources and positions from congressional representatives and governors who oppose them. Since many legislators depend on such resources to win reelection, this leverage can be powerful. Unfortunately, in extreme cases such as the Sarney years, even if the president can obtain a temporary majority through distributing jobs and resources, the effects on institution building, public morality, and legitimacy can be pernicious.

PRESIDENTIAL STRATEGIES: BYPASSING CONGRESS

In dealing with the problems created by weak partisan powers, one strategy used by presidents between 1946 and 1964 was to bypass Congress by implementing policy through executive agencies and regulatory decrees.[11] These mechanisms of bypassing Congress require legislative assent. When presidents have such assent, they can use bureaucratic agencies to implement policies, thereby rescinding the normal law-making process. But if Congress actively opposes executive initiatives, it is difficult for presidents to bypass the legislature by using bureaucratic channels. For example, because of congressional opposition, Goulart could not have implemented an agrarian reform through extralegislative channels. Both Quadros and Goulart attempted to bypass Congress to implement their policies, but they largely failed at doing so.

Vargas and Kubitschek were particularly skillful at using administrative orders to govern. Some major successes of their administrations can be credited to their ability to circumvent Congress and parties without alienating them (D'Araujo 1982; Benevides 1976; Lafer 1970; Nunes 1984; Geddes 1994a). Both presidents had ambitious goals for modernizing their nation, and neither was willing to submit his agenda to the vicissitudes of a Congress notorious for slow deliberations. Both believed that an effective bureaucracy was an indispensable tool in realizing their goals and, as a result,

---

11 As Shugart and I discuss in Chapter 1, regulatory decrees differ from legislative decrees. The former are intended to regulate laws, while the latter are new laws.

attempted to promote broad civil service reform. Doing so, however, proved difficult, as clientelistic congressional representatives blocked reform, preventing presidents from implementing broader changes in the bureaucracy.

Given this situation, both presidents created dynamic new nuclei within the public administration, thereby circumventing the clientelistic vested interests that blocked administrative reform. Rather than relying on party and congressional channels, Vargas generally attempted to accomplish his program of government through state agencies. Kubitschek's most important projects largely circumvented Congress and the parties and instead were implemented through executive agencies. Although he sent the general outlines of his development plan through Congress, he carefully insulated some new bureaucracies from clientelistic pressures so as to concentrate expertise in and insulate those agencies that were crucial for plan implementation (Lafer 1970; Benevides 1976:199–244; Nunes 1984:131–77; Geddes 1986: 75–139; Mello e Souza 1968). Some privileged organs became the administrative means for implementing new programs, while the traditional bureaucracy remained a redoubt of clientelism and patronage politics. The skillful combination of allowing some clientelistic mechanisms so as to build institutional support and of finding the means of creating bureaucratic efficiency made Kubitschek's government the most successful of the 1946–64 regime.

COALITION PRESIDENTIALISM AND EXECUTIVE–LEGISLATIVE DEADLOCK, 1961–64

Despite their arsenal of resources, Brazilian presidents function in a distinctive and challenging institutional context, given the combination of a highly fragmented party system, undisciplined parties, and robust federalism. This system makes presidents dependent on support from an array of parties; Congress and governors can block or undermine presidential objectives. It has the advantage of encouraging power sharing among parties and through federalism; the disadvantage is that it can limit the president's ability to implement major reforms even when needed.

Executive immobilism and executive–legislative deadlock were not a major issue during the Dutra (1946–50) administration, in part because Dutra's political agenda was relatively modest, in part because the PSD enjoyed an absolute majority. But problems emerged during the Vargas (1950–54) administration. In 1950, Vargas, whose PTB had only 16.8% of the seats in Congress, ran against the largest two parties – and yet he came out an easy winner. Vargas never entirely renounced his past as an antiparty politician. In the 1950 campaign, he frequently reiterated that he considered himself a supraparty candidate (Vargas 1951). He relied on direct appeals to the masses rather than party channels, and only infrequently did he campaign for PTB candidates.

Once elected, Vargas continued to prefer to deal above parties. The ex-dictator never thought in party terms; rather, he relied on his broad popular appeal and on improvising to offset his lack of institutional support. His supraparty style was apparent in the fact that his cabinet included members of the PTB and PSP, which had supported him in the campaign, as well as the PSD, which opposed him, and the UDN, which tried to undermine him and even objected to letting him take office after his landslide victory (D'Araujo 1982:71). With the PTB breaking ranks on some issues, the PSD doing little to support Vargas in Congress, and the UDN trying to block many of Vargas's initiatives, the president had a difficult time with his programs in Congress (Hippólito 1985:90–103). Serious friction between the president and the parties erupted in 1954. Lacking support in Congress and under siege by the UDN, Vargas committed suicide as a coup attempt was under way. The PSD watched on the sidelines, doing nothing to save Vargas, and even the PTB failed to come to his defense (D'Araujo 1982: 125–28). D'Araujo (1982) argues that the crisis of Vargas's government was largely a product of his supraparty tendencies and the parallel lack of institutional support. Even though he included representatives of all of the major parties in his cabinet, Vargas could not rely on them for support in Congress.

The interregnum between Vargas's suicide and the inauguration of President Juscelino Kubitschek (1956–61) also made manifest the fragility of Brazil's democracy. Vice-President Café Filho assumed the presidency when Vargas killed himself in August 1954. He remained in that post until November 1955, when illness forced him to take a leave. Kubitschek won the October 1955 presidential election, but some conservatives wanted to keep him from taking office. These pressures were ultimately overcome by a coup against acting President Carlos Luz, whom democratically minded military leaders feared was conspiring to block the presidential succession (Skidmore 1967:149–58; Stepan 1971:85–121).

Except for the serious problems that emerged in 1954–55, Brazil's political institutions functioned adequately from many perspectives between 1946 and 1961. Two of three elected presidents served out their terms; legitimacy was relatively solid; policy implementation was relatively efficient; and governments were effectively governed. On the other hand, even during this period, this institutional combination gave rise to pervasive populism and to a serious crisis in 1954–55 that would most likely have resulted in the breakdown of democracy had Vargas not killed himself. This is not to argue that institutional arrangements were primarily responsible for these problems, but they arguably contributed to them.

Between 1961 and 1964, political institutions contributed to the breakdown of democracy. Quadros's victory in the 1960 presidential election again demonstrated that a popular individual could take on the major parties and win. Opposed by the PSD, the PTB, and a panoply of smaller parties, Quadros nevertheless scored a smashing victory, winning 48% of the vote. A populist, Quadros had visceral antiparty instincts. By 1960, Quadros did not belong to any of the parties, and during the 1960 campaign he tacitly supported João Goulart for vice-president, thereby undermining his own running mate. (The vice-president was elected independently from the president at that time.) During his entire political career, Quadros presented himself as a moral crusader, above party politics.

Like Vargas, Quadros employed a supraparty style once elected. One observer wrote that Quadros hoped to "demoralize all the parties, divide them, and blame the congress for the difficulties of his administration" (Dubnic 1968:47). In March 1961, his minister of justice said that Quadros was not even interested in working with Congress because doing so might suggest executive subordination to the legislature (Hippólito 1985:109). In contrast to Vargas, who respected the rules of the political game despite his personalistic style, Quadros made no effort to cultivate the support of the parties.

Quadros continued the tradition of supraparty cabinets, including politicians from the UDN, PSD, PSB, Progressive Social Party (PSP), Republican Party (PR), and PTB, but he had no intention of relying on or working through party channels. As had occurred with Vargas, this antiparty style led to institutional problems. Quadros alienated the main political parties, in part because of his invectives against Congress and the parties (Benevides 1981:113–18; Skidmore 1967:197–204). Even though Quadros's plans were not blocked by Congress, he felt frustrated by the difficulties of working with the legislature. Quadros could not secure the imperial mandate he longed for and resigned as a consequence on August 25, 1961. The president's friends and foes alike attributed the resignation to Quadros's desire to rule free of the institutional checks and balances that Congress created. Quadros had frequently stated that it was impossible to govern with Congress, and his resignation was intended to produce a fervor of popular support that would result in strengthening the executive's power at the expense of Congress.

A more flexible president might have built coalitions in Congress and accepted defeat when it came. In this sense, his frustration and resignation were not preordained, but rather represented the action of an intemperate maverick. But the institutional structure made it difficult to deal with such a problem.

Vice-President João Goulart assumed the presidenc – albeit with restricted powers – when Quadros resigned in 1961. Concerned about Goulart's leftist proclivities, the military nearly blocked him from assuming the presidency and insisted that presidential powers be curbed. Congress consented and passed a constitutional amendment that instituted a semipresidential system in September 1961. Frustrated by the limits that this system imposed, Goulart pressed for and got a plebiscite that restored full presidential powers in January 1963.

Goulart eventually became isolated, without a firm congressional base. The Congress blocked many of his reform measures, and the executive became increasingly immobilized (Flynn 1978:250–76). The PTB/PSD alliance had been a major pillar of the 1945–64 regime, but many PSD politicians became alarmed when Goulart shifted to the left. They refused to support Goulart's initiatives, leading to impasses in key policy areas, with agrarian reform being the outstanding case. Goulart's attempt to secure the nomination of San Tiago Dantas as prime minister in 1962 and his request for congressional approval of a state of siege in October 1963 were vetoed by Congress. His erratic style, indecisive action, and failure to build institutional support by working with Congress and the parties exacerbated the situation. Goulart responded with ad hoc measures and improvisation, but still failed to overcome executive paralysis.

Frustrated by the difficulties of working within the institutional system, Goulart increasingly turned to popular mobilization as a means of winning support for his policies. In 1964, he planned a series of mass demonstrations that would show support for his policies. This strategy was catastrophic, as it further alienated major actors, including the armed forces; Stepan (1978) and Skidmore (1967) considered it a decisive step in the breakdown of democracy. The military and many conservatives saw Goulart's moves as an indication of his willingness to break the constitution to achieve his goals.

Goulart's poor leadership contributed to executive immobility, but immobility also resulted from the difficult situation of a president who lacked a stable majority in Congress. As Santos (1986) has shown, congressional support became unstable during the Goulart period. Santos (1986:37–58) argued that the resulting decision-making paralysis was the central factor in the breakdown of democracy in 1964 (see also Lamounier 1994).

It would be facile to attribute the breakdown of democracy in 1964 solely or even primarily to Brazil's institutional arrangement. Brazil was a poor country, with some intransigent conservative elites and some radical leftists and with a populist president who seriously miscalculated – not a propitious combination regardless of institutions. Presidentialism contributed to the democratic breakdown by making it impossible to remove Goulart even though legislative support for him had eroded and despite the fact that by March 1964 he was perceived as a serious threat by some conservative elites. On the other hand, the semipresidential regime of 1961–63 was plagued by chronic government instability, and it quickly gave rise to broad dissatisfaction.

After the 1964 coup, the military expanded executive powers and emasculated – though it did not abolish – Congress. Having witnessed the difficulties of democratic presidents in realizing their agendas, the military regime changed the constitution so that the president could govern without checks and balances. One of the military's very first measures, Institutional Act No. 1, published only a week after the coup, greatly expanded executive power and limited congressional jurisdiction. Subsequent constitutional reforms further strengthened the executive and weakened Congress (Alves 1985:31–100; Diniz 1984:324–73; Pessanha 1993).

PRESIDENTIALISM, ECONOMIC STABILIZATION, AND STATE REFORM, 1985–94

Between 1985 and 1994, the combination of extreme party system fragmentation, weak party discipline and loyalty, presidentialism, and robust federalism hampered democratic governments from achieving stabilization and state reform. These institutional features limit the extent to which presidents can implement major reforms. This attribute may not generally be a liability, but in a context of pressing need for stabilization and state reform, it proved to be one. Because presidents lacked reliable support in Congress and with governors, it was difficult to implement major policy changes in these two areas. Sweeping presidential powers only partially offset the fragmentation created by other institutional arrangements. The difficulties of this institutional combination were reflected not so much in what measures Congress vetoed as from presidents' inability to win support for implementing their own agendas in a coherent fashion. Presidents rarely suffered crushing defeats in Congress, but Congress did not pass measures presidents sought or did so only at a high cost to presidents.

José Sarney (1985–90) became president through a mishap; President-Elect Tancredo Neves died before he could be inaugurated. Sarney had faithfully served the military regime as one of its leading civilian politicians before defecting to the newly formed PFL/PMDB coalition in 1984. A clientelistic conservative from the poor northern state of Maranhão, he governed with the 1967 constitution during his first three and one-half years in office. During his first year and one-half (March 1985 to late 1986), Sarney encountered little congressional opposition. This comfortable situation resulted partly from Congress's still emasculated legislative powers. Sarney also benefited from the usually reliable support of the PMDB/PFL coalition and from the relatively auspicious economic situation. Until the implementation of the 1988 constitution, Sarney was able to issue decree-laws, presidential decrees that went into effect unless vetoed by Congress. In his first three years in office, Sarney issued 144 decree-laws, 82 of which Congress did not even debate. During the same time, 353 ordinary laws were passed, so nearly 30% of the legislation passed between March 1985 and March 1988 came through presidential decrees.[12]

At the time of the transition to democracy in March 1985, the Brazilian economy was growing rapidly, but inflation loomed as a problem. The inflation rate hit 179% in 1983 and 209% in 1984, and it was showing signs of accelerating. In February 1986, Sarney addressed this problem with a heterodox stabilization plan, the Cruzado Plan, that met little congressional or gubernatorial resistance.

Sarney's ability to implement policy in unfettered fashion began to wane in 1987 because of the larger political/economic context and a changing institutional venue. As his popularity waned, Sarney lost a source of influence with Congress and governors. Declining popularity, increasing inflation, and an economic slowdown made legislators and governors more willing to distance themselves from the president, and they made Sarney more politically dependent on traditional elite networks. After the failure of the Cruzado Plan, he no longer enjoyed consistent support in Congress.

The negotiated nature of the transition to democracy forced Sarney to balance PMDB and PFL demands for cabinet posts, lower positions, and resources (Hagopian 1996). But governing with such a broad coalition that included those who had viscerally opposed and those who had supported authoritarian rule was difficult. Conflict among ministers was ubiquitous, often leading to a lack of coherence in policy making. To overcome this problem, Sarney attempted to forge his own supraparty political base and to use his considerable discretionary powers over federal resources to sway state governors and federal legislators to back him.

The Constitutional Congress dominated Brazilian politics from February 1987 until the promulgation of the new constitution in October 1988.

12 "A sobrevida do decreto-lei," *Senhor*, no. 364 (March 14, 1988):27.

Because of political exigencies related to the Constitutional Congress, Sarney had to be attentive to political demands from friendly governors and from his congressional supporters. If he did not maintain a strong legislative base, Sarney would not have been able to shape the new constitution and would even have risked having his own mandate cut short since the Constitutional Congress was going to determine its length.

The widespread use of patronage to maintain a legislative base undermined economic policy coherence. For example, the political costs of eliminating costly subsidies proved too high, so the president failed to do so. Rather than collecting massive state debts owed the federal government, Sarney decided, despite the huge cost of doing so, to roll them over to curry favor with the state governors. Sarney regularly caved in to political pressures for resources, undermining efforts to reduce the budget deficit and the inflation rate. These decisions to sacrifice stabilization measures for short-term political support generated free riding on the part of economic agents, further fueling the crisis.

By the first months of 1987, the length of Sarney's mandate had become the most polemical political issue in Brazilian politics and in the Constitutional Congress. Anxious to secure a five-year mandate, Sarney sacrificed policy coherence in order to buy the political support needed to attain that objective. Because of political exigencies that reflected his weak political base, Sarney frequently undermined his finance ministers' adjustment and stabilization measures. In a context in which Sarney had limited support and needed to dispense patronage to secure a five-year term, austerity measures were politically unpalatable.

Congress often approved measures that from Sarney's perspective undercut stabilization and state reform. As the government was pushing for greater openness to foreign markets, the Constitutional Congress adopted several nationalistic measures. As the government was starting to promote state shrinking, the Constitutional Congress approved statist provisions. On a wide array of issues, the Congress approved measures that Sarney opposed: a substantial increase in the tax resources transferred from the federal government to state and local governments; a sharp increase in social benefits and expenditures; expanded labor rights; several statist and nationalistic economic measures; cancellation of debts that private business owed to the federal government.

The implementation of the 1988 constitution brought about changes in presidential relations with Congress and the states, above all because it introduced a democratic character to the formal institutional relations and arrangements. It invigorated federalism, transferred substantial resources from the federal to state and local governments, curbed presidential powers, and expanded legislative powers. These changes created a different institutional context than the one Sarney had inherited in March 1985. A stronger legislature and stronger state and local governments created more demands on the system and limited Sarney's powers, making it more difficult for him to implement his policies.

The federal government faced a declining resource base because of the new transfers to state and local government, so Sarney tried more aggressively to collect loans that the subnational governments owed the federal government. But the state governors and Congress greatly diluted this initiative. Congress also rejected a bill that would have transferred some responsibilities from the federal to state and local governments.

Inflation spun out of control, hitting 395% in 1987, 993% in 1988, and 1,862% in 1989. In January 1989, with the inflation rate escalating, Finance Minister Mailson da Nóbrega announced a new economic plan that combined orthodox and heterodox measures. Because of political exigencies, however, Sarney never fully supported the plan. Congress rejected the government's proposed wage bill, the proposed privatization plan, and the reduction of public-sector employment. This latest economic plan quickly proved unviable, in good measure because the government lacked the political strength to win approval for many of its component measures.

Nearing the end of his term, Sarney became increasingly isolated and incapable of pursuing a serious stabilization plan. The fiscal deficit soared, as did the inflation rate. Sarney experienced a dramatic erosion of congressional support. After a series of government defeats on a wage bill in Congress in 1989, one member of Sarney's loyal retinue admitted, "This is the end. Whenever there is a secret vote, the government can only manage 31 votes [out of 570]."[13] The government lost control of the economy, leading to a hyperinflationary episode in early 1990. With the government crippled by immobilism, the economy deteriorated throughout 1989. The internal debt doubled between January 1988 and mid-1989 and inflation soared.

Elected in a runoff against PT leader Luis Inácio da Silva, Fernando Collor de Mello (1990–92) was a populist committed to state reform and economic stabilization. Collor began his term believing that the legitimacy earned by winning 35 million votes would enable him to govern without parties and Congress. As he had during his campaign, he initially evinced hostility toward traditional politicians (even though he came from a traditional political oligarchy). His initial cabinet reflected this disdain toward politicians; it included only three politicians who had successfully run for

13 Luis Eduardo Magalhães, federal deputy (PFL, Bahia), quoted in "Salve-se quem puder," *IstoÉ Senhor*, no. 1,033 (July 5, 1989):25.

political office out of nine civilian ministers. In contrast to what has been the normal practice with democratic presidents, Collor did not consult the parties about the formation of his cabinet.

In his first days in office, the youthful president initiated audacious measures aimed at stabilizing and liberalizing the economy. Most controversial among them was a temporary freeze on bank accounts; people were not allowed to withdraw more than 50,000 cruzeiros. Collor also announced a fiscal reform that would reduce the deficit by $11 billion a year, a comprehensive privatization program, the end to many subsidies, massive layoffs in the public sectors, and reform of public administration.

In pursuing these measures, Collor initially evinced disdain toward the legislature. He extensively used decree powers to govern during these early months rather than face the possibility of having to negotiate with Congress and risk delays and defeat. In his first 60 days in office, Collor issued 37 provisional measures; Sarney had issued 148 in his 525 days as president after the 1988 constitution went into effect.[14] His economic plan was implemented through presidential decrees. Yet even early on, when Congress voted on his economic package in April 1990, the government resorted to traditional patronage politics, offering high-level public-sector jobs to political allies. Collor won approval for most of his measures, but he was forced to compromise a bit, and his brazen attitude toward Congress cost him support among the political elite.

After his approval ratings declined in his first few months in office,[15] Collor found it difficult to implement stabilization measures and state reforms without reliable congressional support. Having announced bold unilateral measures in multiple arenas, Collor was forced to back off and negotiate with Congress. In late May 1990, the government suffered its first major defeat in Congress, related to efforts to contain wages. Despite occasional defeats and notwithstanding the need to negotiate on many issues, Collor was mostly able to implement his policies during his first year in office.

In mid-1990, inflation rekindled after an initial decline, and a deep recession set in. In response to the economic difficulties, Collor's economic team issued a second heterodox shock plan on January 31, 1991, once again relying on presidential decrees. Even government supporters trenchantly criticized the government for not consulting with Congress. Cognizant of

14 "Pés de barro," *IstoÉ Senhor*, no. 1,078 (May 16, 1990):19.
15 His approval ratings fell from 71% in March 1990 to 36% three months later, 23% by March 1991, and 15% by February 1992. Data from "Sem choro nem vela," *Veja*, no. 1,229 (April 8, 1992):20–21.

its political fragility, the government proceeded to negotiate several key aspects of the plan with Congress, coming to compromises that softened the government's policies. Congress approved most of this second shock plan, but amended it in important ways.

By early 1991, before Collor had completed even a year of his mandate, his support had eroded palpably. Many political leaders attributed Collor's inability to govern to his weak congressional base.[16] Increasingly isolated, the government relied more on distributing jobs and resources to garner legislative support. In an effort to secure support in Congress, Collor provided financing for huge public works projects that benefited the governor of Rio, Leonel Brizola, and ex-President Sarney, both of whom commanded sizable retinues in Congress.

In March 1991, the Chamber of Deputies failed by a scant 5 votes to approve a bill that would have prohibited the president from reissuing a presidential decree more than twice if Congress had not approved it. Although the opposition failed to muster the 252 votes needed to pass the bill, it garnered 247 votes to only 177 for the government (Power 1994).

Having begun with great audacity, by mid-1991 the Collor government was foundering. Its efforts to trim the state were undermined by its reliance on deputies and senators whose political careers depended on public resources. Beset by scandals, rising inflation, and a deep recession, after mid-1991 Collor rarely regained the political initiative and was no longer capable of effective policy implementation. One indication of Collor's growing policy lethargy is that after issuing well over 100 provisional measures in 1990, in 1991 he issued only 8 (Figueiredo and Limongi 1995a:183). Of these, only 2 were approved by Congress – and both with revisions.

In one of his rare major policy initiatives after the dismissal of his first economic team, in December 1991 Collor won congressional approval for a modest fiscal reform. However, Collor won congressional support only by making major patronage concessions that partially offset the legislative victory. To sway powerful governors and their congressional allies, Collor agreed to roll over an estimated $60 billion of debts that state and local governments owed the federal government. Deputy Genebaldo Correia (PMDB), the PMDB's official leader in the Chamber, stated in the aftermath of these negotiations that "nothing is approved in congress without negotiations,"[17] underscoring the legislature's ability to shape policy.

By early 1992, Collor was reduced to the game of building political

---

16 See, for example, the comments of Senator José Richa (PSDB/PR) in "Oxigênio para o governo," *IstoÉ Senhor*, no. 1,119 (March 6, 1991):12.
17 "Acordo de Natal," *IstoÉ Senhor*, no. 1,161 (December 25, 1991):16.

support through distributing public resources and high-level nominations, especially cabinet positions. Having promised that his ministers would remain in office for his entire five-year term, by the end of January 1992, Collor had replaced eight of his initial nine civilian ministers. He engaged in extensive cabinet shuffling between January and April 1992 to secure PFL support. This cabinet reshuffling confirmed that the days when Collor tried to govern above parties, Congress, and politicians were over.

As scandal after scandal erupted after April 1992, the Collor government's support in Congress eroded. It was no longer capable of accomplishing much. Increasingly, Collor sacrificed the effort to impose fiscal austerity to buy political support to stave off impeachment. One indication of his growing reliance on patronage to win political support was that one important dispenser of patronage, the Bank of Brazil Foundation, approved 750 clientelistic requests during his last three months in office, compared with 700 requests during his first 27 months.[18] Reports of outright vote buying circulated widely. Collor was forced to take a leave in October 1992 and ultimately resigned in December 1992 to avoid an impeachment trial in which his chances of absolution were dim.

Thus, a government that came into office with an ambitious agenda and high initial approval ratings ultimately failed to achieve economic stabilization and was at best moderately successful in promoting state reform. The inflation rate was 1,585% in 1990, declined to 476% the following year, but then hit 1,149% in 1992. Privatization and public-sector reform proceeded slowly.

Vice-President Itamar Franco assumed the presidency when Collor was forced out of office. A center-left politician with nationalistic predilections, Franco assumed office with broad support. Political elites were anxious to ensure governability in the aftermath of the Sarney and Collor debacles. The public and most political elites were relieved that Collor was gone and were disposed to grant Franco considerable latitude. Franco had ministers of the PMDB, PSDB, PT, and PFL vintage, so the ideological spectrum supporting him was broad. But congressional opposition to Franco increased until mid-1994, and the president had difficulties getting key legislation passed on salaries, inflation, state reform, and budget deficit reduction.

Franco went through a succession of finance ministers, none of whom was able to realize far-reaching state reform or achieve stabilization until July 1994. The government had difficulties enacting budget cuts to fight inflation, though it often announced the need to do so. Like Sarney and Collor, Franco rhetorically committed himself to cutting public expendi-

18 "Por decisão judicial," *Veja*, no. 1,253 (September 23, 1992):23.

tures, but like his predecessors, he made little headway, largely because he lacked the political support and constantly found himself using public resources to win that support. This practice generated contradictory pressures: on the one hand, the government affirmed the importance of cutting expenditures; on the other, it had to distribute resources in order to win the political support needed to carry out its programs.

On an array of issues related to stabilization and state reform, the Franco government failed to realize its objectives because of opposition from Congress and governors. It was frequently defeated in its efforts to curb wage increases and to cut public spending. Congress consistently diluted and opposed austerity and stabilization plans. The government repeatedly announced that it would cut billions of dollars in expenditures, but the pressures of governors, mayors, and legislators to secure resources were intense. In their public discourse, many politicians favored cuts – but they wanted to make sure that their own resources were not affected.

The Franco administration announced its intention of reining in state governments that spent beyond their resources and ultimately relied on the federal government to cover their deficits. The central government needed to reduce the hemorrhage of resources to fiscally irresponsible state governments. But here, too, the pressure of Congress and governors forced the government to gut its plans.

A related issue was central government control over public-sector banks owned by states. State-level banks, which are under the jurisdiction of governors, have had broad authority to make their own loans and have effectively had the autonomy to undermine national-level monetary and fiscal policy. They have had a reputation for profligate spending to bolster the political careers of the politicians who oversee them. Despite affirming a commitment to rein in these banks and prohibit the Central Bank from covering their deficits, the Franco government in practice did little in this regard.

In a similar vein, federal government efforts to impose new taxes or to bolster tax collection met resistance. Franco lacked the political base that would have enabled him to follow through on such endeavors. In February 1993, Congress approved a new tax, which the government supported, on financial transactions, but it also immediately committed an important part of the tax to new social programs, thereby diminishing the potential to cut the deficit.

Because many public firms were inefficient, were adding billions of dollars per year to the public-sector deficit, and were subjected to patrimonial manipulation, the government favored accelerating the pace of privatizations. Here, too, it encountered congressional resistance and largely failed to accomplish its objectives.

SUMMARY

Between 1985 and 1994, presidents were frequently unable to implement their preferred policies in the following nine policy areas related to the overarching objectives of achieving stabilization and state reform:

1. Although most economists and business leaders agreed that indexation contributed to inflation until 1994, governments had difficulties deindexing wages and pensions because of congressional opposition. Politicians knew that their votes on wage policy were monitored by unions and that they would have difficulties explaining votes that reduced wages in the short term. Even conservative politicians who rhetorically made combating inflation a top priority often voted to maintain indexing. In wage policy, Congress was a key reactive actor, and it continuously opposed measures that would have adversely affected wages in the short term.

2. Governments had difficulties cutting public-sector employment despite a fairly broad consensus that doing so was necessary. Politicians not only protected their constituents (and, by doing so, themselves) by voting against measures to cut public-sector employment, they also protected their ability to build their political careers by naming allies to public positions.

   Congress was a key actor in any effort to cut back public-sector employment quickly because doing so would take a constitutional amendment. (Congress would not necessarily be an actor in cutbacks effected through attrition.) The 1988 constitution guaranteed job tenure to public-sector servants with at least two years of service, provided that they had entered through a civil service exam (Art. 41). It also established (Transitory Art. 19) that all public-sector employees with five years of service as of the time of promulgation of the constitution would be guaranteed tenure, even if they had not entered the public sector through proper channels (i.e., via a civil service exam).

   Governors and mayors had autonomy to hire public-sector personnel. Presidents were not able to control the hiring practices of local and state governments, and until Cardoso, they were unwilling to push governors and mayors toward fiscal discipline by refusing to roll over loans to state-level banks.

3. Through the constitutional provisions (Arts. 20, 176, and 177) that made some economic activities the exclusive prerogative of the public sector or of national firms, presidents were limited in privatizing public enterprises. By not endorsing constitutional change, Congress limited the ability of governments to privatize public-sector firms. Sarney unsuccessfully fought against the provisions guaranteeing a state monopoly in many areas of the economy. Collor and Franco then unsuccessfully attempted to obtain constitutional amendments that overturned public-sector monopolies.

4. Congress limited the capacity of governments to increase taxes. Congressional approval is needed to create new taxes or to increase tax rates (Art. 150 of the 1988 constitution).

5. Congress and the governors defended the current share of state and local governments in federal tax revenues, despite a widespread perception that this arrangement contributed to fiscal problems and inflation. This share was constitutionally enshrined (Transitory Art. 34), so it could be modified only through a constitutional amendment.

6. Congress and the governors resisted federal government efforts to curb the autonomy of state-level public banks and enterprises, even though these banks and enterprises were not well run and contributed to the problems of economic policy at a national level.

7. Congress and the governors fought against the federal government's insistence that state governments and enterprises pay the interest on the massive loans they owed to the federal government.

8. Congress sometimes blocked the federal government from collecting debts owed by private business. For example, the 1988 constitution forgave interest payments of most private businesses on loans contracted between February 28, 1986, and February 28, 1987, and forgave interest payments on debts contracted by all but large farmers between February 28, 1986, and December 31, 1987. This amounted to a massive subsidization of private business.

9. Until March 1996, Congress refused to pass constitutional amendments providing for social security reform. Presidents sought such amendments because the 1988 constitution (Arts. 40 and 202) enshrined provisions that the social security system could not handle, including a low retirement age and benefits that were generous compared with the salary structure of active members of the labor force. The social security system was solvent, but experts projected that with the rapid increase in the number of pensioners, it soon would be in the red. Therefore, they believed that social security reform was a fiscal imperative.

These nine policy areas fundamentally affected the capacity of Brazilian presidents to undertake successful stabilization policies and reform the state. Stabilization and state reform were key problems on Brazil's agenda, for they were virtually necessary conditions for resuming steady growth, addressing poverty, and ameliorating inequalities.

ASSESSING THE IMPACT OF INSTITUTIONS

There is no way of calculating exactly what share of Brazil's governance problems between 1985 and 1994 stemmed from institutional as opposed to other causes. Nevertheless, there are some means of verifying whether the institutional argument laid out here is compelling.

First and most important, if political institutions contributed to Brazil's lag in achieving stabilization and implementing state reform, presidents should have been more easily able to implement their preferred policies in areas where Congress and governors are less central actors. In many policy areas of high visibility and impact, Congress and/or governors had at least a moderate ability to block the president, to force the president to change his initial proposal significantly or extract substantial concessions from the president in exchange for support, or to undertake policies that undermined presidential initiatives. However, in two important policy areas – exchange rates and tariffs – Congress and the governors were weak players. In contrast to the situation with the nine policy areas indicated earlier, the 1988 constitution gave Congress and governors no formal authority over exchange rates and tariffs. Indeed, the constitution (Art. 153) explicitly gives the president complete authority over tariff rates (and implicitly does so over exchange rates).

Collor's most significant success in implementing neoliberal reforms was opening markets. As was the case with the policy areas in which presidents were institutionally constrained, trade liberalization created many short-term losers; it was not an easy policy to undertake in that sense. Throughout Latin America, trade liberalization reversed decades of relatively closed markets, adversely affecting the powerful interests (business and labor alike) that had grown up around protection from international competition. But trade liberalization was easier institutionally than other neoliberal policies because Congress and governors did not hold veto power.

In a similar vein, exchange rates affect who wins and who loses in Brazilian society. An overvalued currency adversely affects exporters and most domestic producers who compete with imported goods, while it would presumably benefit importers. Altering the exchange rate is therefore not easy in terms of the impact on powerful actors in society, but Congress and governors have no control over the exchange rate. In this respect, it is telling that the exchange rate became a major peg of Cardoso's stabilization plan in 1994. In short, even when they faced societal opposition, presidents were able to implement their preferred policies when they had little institutional resistance, but they were not able to do so when Congress and/or governors were key players.

A second means of assessing the impact of institutional constraints looks at variation within a particular policy area – for example, the privatization of public enterprises. The institutional constraints to privatization were greatest in cases where the constitution enshrined a public-sector monopoly or where governors opposed privatization of state-level public enterprises. Privatization in Brazil proceeded slowly (Williamson 1990; Schneider 1992). By the Collor period, some privatizations were taking place – but none in the sectors where the constitution mandated a public-sector monopoly. Privatization in these sectors became possible only after the constitutional amendments of 1995. Despite efforts, neither Collor nor Franco was able to secure support for such amendments.

Under many circumstances, comparison across countries is the best means of assessing hypotheses. In this particular case, because it controls for noninstitutional factors by keeping them constant, the two forms of intra-country comparisons are the best way to assess the impact of institutional factors. Comparing presidents' capacity to implement stabilization and state reform policies across countries is less powerful because noninstitutional factors also affect this capacity. Nevertheless, presidents should be able to implement their preferred policies more easily if party system fragmentation is lower or if governors and mayors have fewer resources and less autonomy.

The evidence supports the hypothesis that presidents who faced weaker institutional resistance had greater ease in implementing their preferred stabilization and state reform policies (although this did not ensure positive policy results). Among the major countries of Latin America, institutional constraints to major reform were much lower in Argentina, Colombia, Mexico, and Venezuela than in Brazil. Economic stabilization and state reform occurred more quickly and earlier in all four countries (Williamson 1990; Williamson and Haggard 1994; Edwards 1995), though it got derailed in Venezuela. Brazil was the regional laggard in stabilization; its inflation rate was almost 20 times higher than that of any other Latin American country in 1992 and 40 times higher than that of the second highest in 1993. Brazil was also a regional laggard in state reform (Williamson 1990; Packenham

1994; Schneider 1992; Edwards 1995). Brazil's delay did not result simply from a lack of will, especially in stabilization policy. Presidents from Sarney on were anxious to bring inflation under control, but they failed to do so, partly because of institutional constraints. Brazil's delay in state reform can be partly attributed to Sarney's and Franco's vacillations, but even Collor, who was adamantly committed to the enterprise, was limited in how much he accomplished.

Another manner of thinking about the impact of institutions is seeing whether presidents in other countries who faced significant constraints from governors and congress also had difficulties implementing their policies. Arguably no other country in Latin America has comparable institutional constraints to those in Brazil, though the president's decree powers partially offset these constraints. Institutional constraints should be significant in Bolivia and Ecuador, given the considerable fragmentation of the party systems and the low degree of party loyalty in both countries. In Ecuador, presidents did have a hard time implementing adjustment and state reform policies. Edwards (1995) indicates that Ecuador was one of the regional laggards in state reform, as it also was in stabilization. During the 1990s, even presidents committed to state reform were not able to implement it because of congressional opposition. Bolivia, conversely, was an early case of state reform and stabilization. However, this exception does not undermine the general claim that institutional structures had some impact on presidents' capacity to implement their preferred policies in these two areas.

THE CARDOSO ADMINISTRATION: OVERCOMING INSTITUTIONAL OBSTACLES?

Beginning with the approval of a new tax (the Social Emergency Fund) in March 1994 and especially with implementation of the economic stabilization plan in mid-1994, the Franco and Cardoso administrations were able to get much of what they wanted from Congress in the areas of stabilization and state reform. In 1995, Cardoso won support for constitutional amendments to eliminate state monopolies in the gas, telecommunications, and petroleum industries. He also won a constitutional amendment to end constitutionally based discrimination against foreign investment. After years during which presidents generally seemed hamstrung after short honeymoons, Cardoso's success in obtaining qualified (at least 60% of each chamber) congressional majorities for what had previously been highly controversial issues was remarkable.

Whereas previous stabilization plans had faltered, the Real Plan finally tackled inflation. Inflation fell from 2,489% in 1993 to 22% in 1995. In contrast to the recessive effects caused by some aggressive stabilization plans, growth remained solid (4% in 1995). Cardoso's predecessors had failed to rein in state banks; Cardoso did so in one major state (Bahia). Previous efforts to deindex wages had met congressional resistance; Cardoso was able to get through a provisional measure that brought about deindexation.

These successes call into question why institutional obstacles that had prevented Sarney, Collor, and Franco from implementing key reforms had not similarly blocked Cardoso. Perhaps the most important factor was the profound sense of crisis that permeated Brazil by 1994. The country, for all its promise, was the only Latin American nation that had not stabilized its economy by 1994. Brazil lagged behind all of the other major Latin American countries in economic adjustment and state reform. The success of neighboring Argentina and Chile in curbing inflation and (at least temporarily) resuming growth through neoliberal policies eventually had profound repercussions in Brazil, causing a revision in how actors perceived the role of the state. This fact, coupled with the long period of stagnation, generated a willingness to try what increasingly appeared as the only way out. By 1994, many Brazilians feared that their society was disintegrating under the weight of rampant inflation, slow growth over the preceding 13 years, declining living standards, and escalating urban violence. The depth of the crisis lent an urgency to the effort to accept new measures. Under these conditions, legislators and governors were disposed to give Cardoso (first as finance minister and then as president) greater latitude to implement policies.

The growing ideological consensus in Brazil in the post–Cold War period also favored Cardoso. By 1995, when Cardoso assumed the presidency, the PMDB, PSDB, and the conservative parties had shifted far toward acceptance of the neoliberal agenda. The successful stabilization in Argentina, the robust growth of the Chilean economy, and the region-wide trend toward a smaller state helped generate a growing consensus toward stabilization, adjustment, and state-shrinking policies in Brazil. Whereas centrist parties in Brazil were fundamentally statist at the time of the 1987–88 Constitutional Congress and during the Collor administration, by 1994 they were prepared to accept much of Cardoso's state reform agenda. The collapse of real socialism delegitimated the leftist-statist utopia and fostered consensus about the role of the state: The most statist options were delegitimized. By 1994, the ideological dissensus that characterized Brazil in the 1980s was somewhat attenuated.

In addition, Cardoso was a better leader than his predecessors. He was articulate, had a clear vision of where he wanted to go, and chose capable ministers. His landslide victory in 1994 strengthened his hand with Congress and the state governors. He also won more leeway with Congress and governors because of the fact that the PT candidate was the easy front-runner in the 1994 campaign until after the full implementation of the stabilization plan in July. Fearful of the consequences of a leftist victory, Congress and the governors supported measures that might not otherwise have gotten through. Cardoso's successes in turn extended the honeymoon that presidents usually enjoy.

Following the Argentine example, Cardoso found a new mechanism to help bring down inflation: the exchange rate. Most previous stabilization plans in Brazil had relied on more conventional fiscal and monetary mechanisms. Fiscal policy was undermined by presidents' need to spend to retain political supports and by legislators' and governors' quest for patronage. Efforts to control the monetary supply were hindered by the autonomy of state governments and the difficulties of controlling state banks. Exchange rate policy was less subject to control by Congress and governors than monetary and fiscal policy.

It would be a mistake to imagine that these institutional constraints never existed or that they have disappeared. For a protracted time, the Cardoso government was not able to win support for constitutional amendments on administrative reform, tax reform, and social security reform – three pillars of its program. Congress and the governors may have rolled over for a time, but they did not disappear as political actors to be reckoned with.

In its victories, the government still had to negotiate with Congress and failed to obtain much of what it sought. For example, in April 1995 the Congress overrode a presidential veto of a law that postponed debt payments owed to the Banco do Brasil by landowners. The legislators linked to these rural interests threatened to boycott voting on the administration's constitutional amendments if the government tried to circumvent the override. Cardoso caved in despite the high financial cost; the government agreed to postpone payment on the debts, for two years, estimated at $1.8 to $5.0 billion, of the landowners. This negotiation was a sine qua non for the support of scores of legislators for constitutional reform.[19] The government was forced to resort to traditional patronage politics in order to win the congressional support of the large bloc that represented the landowners.

Only because of exceptional circumstances did presidents' inability to implement coherent policies have such deleterious effects between 1985 and 1994: Given the exhaustion of state-led development and the gravity of

19 "Era uma vez o monopólio da Petrobrás," *Veja*, no. 1,396 (June 14, 1995):32.

inflation, the country needed major reforms to resume development. The greatest difficulty for presidents given this institutional configuration is implementing major reforms, especially those that are constitutionally enshrined. Now that some of the reforms needed to modernize the economy are in place, it seems likely that institutional constraints will loom as less deleterious.

CONCLUSION

Some of the literature on Latin American presidentialism has emphasized how powerful presidents are. This chapter suggests that this argument is partially misleading. In Brazil, especially in the post-1985 period, a complex pattern emerges, based on the combination of strong constitutional powers, weak partisan powers, and robust federalism. Presidents have dominated proactive policy making, but because of the combination of a highly fragmented party system, comparatively undisciplined parties, and robust federalism, they often had trouble pushing through parts of their policy agenda in the areas of state reform and stabilization.

In principle, presidential systems are designed to encourage the dispersion of power. The problem, which is not unique to presidential systems but assumes some unique contours therein, is how to engender a strong yet democratically accountable executive. Excessive dispersion of power can cripple the executive; excessive concentration undermines accountability and checks and balances. Presidents in Brazil have tottered between the two poles; they dominate decision-making power, yet when their political base erodes, they cannot implement major reforms. Between 1985 and 1994, the difficulties in implementing stabilization programs and state reform because of the lack of political support led to policy formulation excessively oriented toward immediate political objectives. Serious policy mistakes of those years – the decision to postpone adjustments to the Cruzado Plan in 1986 and the mishandling of the debt moratorium in 1987 – were results of presidents' efforts to cultivate political support.

On first impression it would appear that the Brazilian presidency concentrates so much power that governing would be relatively easy. But this impression is partially misleading. Although constitutional presidential powers are impressive, this does not mean that Brazilian presidents are strong in all regards. In fact, Presidents Goulart, Sarney, Collor, and Franco were weak in important respects. Presidents have often faced difficulties in accomplishing their agendas, and Goulart, Sarney, and Collor were clear failures.

What explains the gap between sweeping presidential constitutional powers and difficulty in realizing presidential agendas? Brazilian presidents typically have weak (especially since 1985) partisan powers to go along with their strong (again, especially since 1985) constitutional powers. The combination of undisciplined parties, party system fragmentation, and federalism disperses power and makes it difficult for presidents to establish solid support in Congress. When congressional support for the president erodes, an impasse can result, with both Congress and the president typically debilitated in the process. Despite its difficulties in overturning presidential vetoes and despite its weakness as an agent of policy formulation, the Brazilian Congress matters – as should be the case in a democracy. When Congress does not support the president, the latter often faces difficulties implementing policies in a coherent fashion. This helps explain O'Donnell's (1992) observation that Brazilian presidents oscillate between omnipotence and impotence.

Given sweeping presidential powers and congressional difficulty in overriding a veto, why does Congress sometimes serve as a check? This issue is especially intriguing for the post-1985 period. Given their powers, why do presidents bother at all with obtaining congressional support? Why not just govern through decrees?

Unpopular presidents seemingly cannot govern mostly through decrees. Provisional measures can be a powerful tool for presidents when Congress is indifferent or deeply divided about a proposal. However, when Congress actively opposes a measure, decree powers have not allowed presidents to ram their agenda through. Congress can amend provisional measures in unrestricted ways; of the 229 provisional measures approved by Congress in the 1989–94 period, 113 were amended (Figueiredo and Limongi 1995a: 184).

In response to its dissatisfaction with Collor, the Chamber of Deputies almost passed a bill that would have regulated and restricted the use of presidential decrees (Power 1994; Pessanha 1993). Presidents are aware that if they abuse their decree powers, Congress could attempt to pass a bill that would severely circumscribe the use of these powers. If a president infringed on what Congress viewed as its prerogatives, Congress would react negatively, making it more difficult for the executive to win legislative support for subsequent bills.

Despite their formidable constitutional powers, presidents need congressional support to enact ordinary legislation. Even though it establishes an imbalance of powers favorable to the president, the 1988 constitution grants Congress some meaningful powers. The Congress is a key actor in the ordinary legislative process; with the partial exception of presidential decrees (which require congressional acquiescence but not approval), no bill becomes law without congressional approval.

Congress has some authority in setting the budget. It has a panoply of other powers that potentially constrain the president, including the exclusive authority to approve all international agreements with budgetary implications; to approve presidential and vice-presidential requests to leave the country for more than 15 days; to approve a state of defense, state of siege, or federal intervention in state-level political affairs; to directly oversee and control all acts of the executive; to approve presidential initiatives related to nuclear activities; to authorize and convoke plebiscites. The Chamber and the Senate, as well as any of their committees, have the right to interpelate ministers of state. The Chamber of Deputies and the Senate together have 10 of the 15 members of the Council of the Republic, which formally must issue a statement on federal interventions, states of defense, and states of siege, as well as issues related to the stability of democratic institutions. The Senate must approve nominations for certain judges (including Supreme Court judges), governors of territories, president and directors of the Central Bank, the attorney general, and the heads of diplomatic missions. It names two-thirds of the ministers of the National Accounting Court (Tribunal de Contas da União), and the presidential nominees to this body require Senate confirmation. It has broad powers to set limits on Brazil's internal and external borrowing and loans.

During exceptional periods, presidents have had a particular need for congressional support for issues around which decrees did not serve their needs. During the Constitutional Congress, President Sarney hoped to secure certain results (above all, a five-year mandate for himself and the maintenance of a presidential system). Sarney had some influence over Congress (above all, through patronage), but he was not able to impose his preferences on the Constitutional Congress. Another exceptional period occurred when Collor needed congressional support to avoid impeachment. To win such support, Collor negotiated with Congress and ultimately failed to get what he wanted.

Another exceptional circumstance that levels the playing field between Congress and the president is a constitutional amendment. Ever since the promulgation of the 1988 constitution, successive presidents have yearned for constitutional reforms that would make governing easier. For example, Collor, Franco, and Cardoso believed that several provisions of the 1988 constitution needed to be amended, and they had to bargain to obtain the votes to win approval of key amendments. A constitutional amendment requires 60% approval of both chambers of Congress, and both must pass the measure twice. Thus, *exceptional periods*, by which I mean times when presidents could not get what they needed without active congressional support, have been quite common.

Between 1985 and 1994, Brazilian presidents had difficulty achieving stabilization and state reform, partly because of the combination of a highly fragmented party system, undisciplined parties, and federalism. This combination made it difficult for presidents to secure legislative support for economic stabilization and state reform. Presidents had trouble overcoming congressional opposition and implementing major reforms when their popularity dissipated. This is why the presidents' lack of reliable majority support in Congress presented problems for effective governance. And it is why Sarney, Collor, and Franco had a hard time getting their agendas accomplished despite possessing sweeping constitutional powers. In the 1985–94 period, policy coherence often suffered as a result of presidents' efforts to win support in Congress and among governors.

The problems that presidents encountered in winning support for their programs usually did not surface because of congressional vetoes. Rather, the problems appeared mainly in the guise of a presidential need to secure broad-based congressional support before undertaking action. Congress can fail to adopt bills that the president would like to pass, it can approve bills that the president opposes (even though the president can veto a bill with a low likelihood of an override), and it can amend presidentially initiated bills in "unfriendly" ways.

Executive–legislative conflict need not be a pathology of presidentialism; it can even be a virtue, as the two branches of government can effectively check one another and prevent irresponsible action. However, when neither Congress nor the president can effectively pursue a policy agenda, some problems are likely to emerge. In Brazil, between 1985 and 1994, the difficulties presidents had in winning support for cohesive stabilization and state reform policies contributed to the country's economic travails. These difficulties illustrate in an extreme form the problems that can emerge given an institutional combination that promotes dispersion of power across parties, states, and regions, in a young democracy where an agile executive branch is often called for.

3

THE UNREALIZED POTENTIAL OF PRESIDENTIAL DOMINANCE IN COLOMBIA

Ronald P. Archer and Matthew Soberg Shugart

3.1. INTRODUCTION

On July 4, 1991, Colombians ceased to live under what had been the oldest continuously functioning constitution in Latin America. A new document, drafted and ratified by the specially elected Constituent Assembly, replaced a constitution that, while frequently amended, had served since 1886. In order to understand why Colombians undertook the process of constitutional revision, one needs to consider the various ways in which the old constitution had contributed to a crisis that most Colombian political observers believed was confronting the country by the late 1980s. A significant aspect of the Constituent Assembly's task was to remedy a perceived imbalance between an overly powerful president and a Congress that appeared incapable of addressing the nation's problems.

In this chapter we argue that Colombian presidents hold great constitutional powers over legislation yet frequently appear unable to accomplish policy agendas that are nominally endorsed by their own parties. Despite most presidents' having held copartisan legislative majorities, presidents have low partisan powers because parties are internally fragmented. Two institutional features contribute to low partisan powers: First, parties lack control over the use of their party labels (i.e., candidates do not need to have party approval to run under the party name); second, the electoral system fosters intraparty competition.

Evaluations of presidentialism in Colombia have tended to overlook the real limits to the powers of the Colombian executive. Our argument is that the partisan powers of the Colombian president have decreased since the mid-1970s as a result of increased intraparty competition. This increased competition in turn has been fueled in part by the growing difficulty of reconciling emerging urban demands with those of more traditional sectors. The result is that presidents must rely on ad hoc deals with power brokers who demand patronage in exchange for supporting policies desired by the president. So, despite vast constitutional powers since an important constitutional reform in 1968, real ability to effect change has been lower than the designation "potentially dominant" (see Chapter 1) would imply. We conceive of the presidential powers defined in the constitution in terms of principal–agent theory,[1] as a delegation from Congress to the executive in order to advance the goals of congressional majorities. We argue that such an interpretation is valid – despite the separate election and fixed terms of presidentialism – because, unique to Colombian presidentialism, legislative majorities determine the allocation of constitutional powers through control over the amendment process. Thus, to understand Colombian presidentialism it is crucial to understand the interests of Congress and how the formal Colombian political institutions shape those interests.

The Colombian Congress is structured in a way that makes it inherently difficult to confront national policy issues. Instead, members' incentives are to cultivate particularistic exchanges based on patronage. The resulting inability of the Colombian political system to generate stable majorities has made it difficult to confront Colombia's profound social problems, especially the country's infamous rural and urban violence. Members of the majority Liberal Party face a collective action problem.[2] Individual members can

1 A core component of the theory of the firm in economics holds that *principals* – usually those with power and/or wealth – can offer binding contracts to *agents,* who then perform specified services (Williamson 1975, 1985; for extensions to political science, see Kiewiet and McCubbins 1991: 239; Moe 1984). Certain features hold in virtually all principal–agent situations: (1) The principal retains mechanisms to oversee and verify that the agent is performing the specified service; (2) delegation entails a certain degree of agency loss or slack, where the agents can hide information or use the delegated powers against the principal, among other things.

2 First identified by Olson (1965), a collective action problem arises when a group of individuals attempts to coordinate to provide collective benefits, or public goods, for the welfare of the whole group. Since providing the collective good is costly and, once the good is provided, each individual can benefit from the public good given its public nature, individuals are likely to "free ride" on the work of others – doing nothing to provide the good, while still receiving the benefit.

understand the need for their party to back fundamental reforms that would address the interests of a growing urban electorate, because (as we shall argue later) this electorate is crucial to the party's ability to maintain control over the executive. Yet most members are tied by the electoral system to generally rural clientele networks that demand access to patronage. Members of Congress must participate in this scramble for patronage, or their political careers are doomed. Thus, the dominant incentive for members is to defect from reformist coalitions or to join them only after they have been watered down or laden with sufficient patronage resources. We should caution here that we do not mean to imply that Colombia's many social problems can be blamed on its political institutions, but we do claim that these institutions and the incentives they establish have seriously inhibited efforts to cope with these problems.

Seriously needed reforms become bogged down as they wend their way through the Colombian policy-making process. The irony of the process is that the reforms are needed not just from a normative perspective, but from a political one. A series of popular movements and *paros cívicos* (civic strikes) have articulated demands that are frustrated by the clientelistic political system (Coral Quintero 1988; Gallón Giraldo 1989; Pecaut 1988; Santamaría and Silva 1984). Colombia's growing urban population demands specific reforms such as building urban housing and infrastructure, creating a more professional civil service to replace citizens' need for political connections in order to receive many government services, reforming the judiciary so that it can deal with drug traffickers and official malfeasance, and cleaning up contamination of the country's water and other natural resources. Because the political system has been unable to deliver on presidential promises to initiate reforms of these types, urban voter abstention is high, and by the late 1980s, the country's political stability could no longer be taken for granted as conflict became more and more violent.

The rest of this chapter is organized as follows. In Section 3.2, we outline the series of reform efforts by Colombian presidents that have ended in defeat and we summarize our overall argument. In Section 3.3, we describe the constitutional powers of the Colombian presidency. In Section 3.4, we identify the electoral system and how it contributes to low partisan powers for the presidency. Section 3.5 then discusses how the party system affects presidential–congressional relations and why Colombia is characterized by a relatively reformist executive and a more conservative legislature. Section 3.6 considers whether the new constitution provides a solution to the dilemma of reform in Colombia. Section 3.7 concludes.

3.2. THE THWARTED REFORM EFFORTS OF COLOMBIAN PRESIDENTS, 1974–90

Each president since the end of the National Front power-sharing arrangement[3] has proposed a package of reforms intended to "open" and "modernize" the political system. These reform packages may be seen in large part as attempts by presidents to transcend the rural, clientelistic basis of representation in the Congress and the attendant "inefficiency" of a public administration that is based heavily on patronage. Each president found his reform package mostly stymied in the Congress and thus attempted to implement some programs by bypassing the legislature altogether. As we shall see in this chapter, the substantial decree powers granted to the president in the Colombian constitution generally have proved ineffective whenever a president tried to use them to step outside the rather narrow consensus established by Colombian party bosses with their ties in clientele networks. Colombian presidents have been able to push policy outcomes in a more "progressive" direction than Congress likely would have done on its own – as Chapter 1 suggested proactive presidencies could do – but the end result has usually been far less than what presidents have tried to accomplish.

President Alfonso López Michelsen (1974–78) launched a program called To Close the Gap, which was intended to redress Colombia's growing income inequality and to restructure the public administration (Gómez 1978). Most of the program was defeated in Congress (Dix 1987:190–93). His attempt to establish two redistributive institutions, the DRI (Desarrollo Rural Integrado) and PAN (Plan de Alimentación y Nutrición) were quickly passed by Congress and almost as swiftly cannibalized for patronage resources (Pecaut 1988:254–55). In fact, income distribution actually worsened under López (Pecaut 1988:304–5), and spending on health, education, and welfare remained comparatively low (Dix 1987:200–201).

Frustrated by the defeat or watering down of so many proposals in Congress, López, in what has become a familiar theme for Colombian presidents, attempted an end run around the legislature via a constituent assem-

---

3 The National Front was designed to reconcile conflicts between the country's two dominant political parties, Liberal and Conservative, which had led to civil war and then a four-year military dictatorship. The major provisions of the Front were: alternation of the presidency between the two parties every four years until 1974; guaranteed parity of representation in all national and subnational legislative bodies, courts, and in the bureaucracy; and, until 1968, the requirement of two-thirds majorities for the passage of legislation. For details, consult Berry, Hellman, and Solaún (1980), Dix (1967), and Hartlyn (1988).

bly that would pass reforms in the areas of departmental administration and the judiciary. The effort was nullified by the Supreme Court[4] as an unconstitutional usurpation of Congress's powers of amendment (Arboleda 1982: 11–31). In one of López's few successes, the Supreme Court upheld his creation of a more progressive income tax program by decree (Pecaut 1988: 250–52). This example of reform via decree is more exceptional than typical, however, as we discuss later on in this chapter.

President Julio César Turbay Ayala (1978–82), although not normally perceived as a reformist, picked up many of the failed López reform initiatives and sent his own package to Congress. Turbay, despite his reputation as a master at crafting clientele coalitions, fared no better than López. His reform package was even more ambitious and extended to reform of Congress and the nation's judicial, banking, and economic planning institutions. Again, the reform project was stymied by the Congress, and an end run effort to circumvent Congress was declared unconstitutional (Arboleda 1982:33–60).

By 1982 the clamor from public opinion and the mass media for the restructuring of local, departmental, and national governments – perceived as unresponsive to voters – allowed the minority Conservative Party to win a contested presidential election for only the second time since 1926.[5] Led by Belisario Betancur (1982–86), the new government combined the López and Turbay reform programs with an ambitious peace plan to end the armed insurgencies that were plaguing the countryside. The Betancur program, therefore, was even broader in scope, calling for (1) a redefinition of the role of opposition parties; (2) campaign finance reform, the institutionalization of the role of political parties, the right to information, and electoral reform;

4 The Colombian judiciary has one of the most politically insulated appointment procedures in the world. Since 1958, the president and Congress have not had their previous role in nominating and confirming justices. Instead, vacancies are filled by the remaining members themselves. Justices had life tenure until the new constitution limited them to a single eight-year term. The same procedures that are used for the Supreme Court are also used for the country's highest administrative court, the Council of State. The new constitution establishes the Superior Council of the Judicature, some of whose members are appointed by the Court and Council of State themselves and some of whose members are nominated by the president and confirmed by Congress. This judicature council will send to the two highest courts slates of nominees from which they will fill their own vacancies. Finally, the new constitution establishes the Constitutional Court, which will be far *less* insulated politically: It will be composed of members elected for nonrenewable eight-year terms by the Senate from slates of nominees submitted by the president and the other two high courts.

5 By *contested election* we mean (1) no boycott by one of the major parties, as in 1949 when the Liberals abstained, and (2) no restrictions on candidate entry, as under the National Front.

(3) a restructuring of the state; (4) a redefinition of executive emergency powers; and (5) the creation of new means of local and departmental popular participation in government, such as the direct election of mayors, public service user groups, and district councils (Santamaría and Silva 1984:73–187). By 1986, however, virtually all of these initiatives had fallen victim to congressional recalcitrance and the collapse of the peace talks with the guerrillas. Betancur also tried to implement a major tax reform by emergency decree, but the Supreme Court ruled it unconstitutional.

The successor to Betancur, Liberal Virgilio Barco Vargas (1986–90), was to fare little better in pursuing his reform agenda. Picking up the gauntlet from three former administrations, Barco attempted to craft a broad "coalition-of-the-whole" with the major leaders of all the parties and party factions around his proposal to repackage the López, Turbay, and Betancur reform programs and get them through Congress not as discrete pieces of legislation, but as part of a large package of constitutional amendments. When the original agreement among the parties collapsed, so too did the constitutional reform package, now containing more than a hundred amendments (*Semana*, May 31, 1988:36–44). Beyond the previous reform initiatives, Barco expanded the reform process to include treatment of church–state issues, property rights, access to education, the establishment of a procedure for holding national plebiscites, and many other reforms designed to open up a democracy still operating under multiple anachronistic restrictions from the National Front era (Cepeda 1987). In the end, Barco, like his predecessors, attempted to circumvent Congress, proposing the creation of an essentially unconstitutional constituent assembly (*constituyente*). By 1989 the pressure for change had grown so great from nearly all of the major forces in Colombian society that the Supreme Court closed its eyes to the illegality and approved the creation of the assembly.

In 1991, under the administration of President César Gaviria Trujillo (1990–94), the fifth president to attempt significant post–National Front reform, the pent-up reform initiatives were finally written into a new constitution with an impotent Congress on the sidelines, criticizing the entire process. The Constituent Assembly, elected in December 1990, included recently demobilized guerrillas such as the M-19, who won over a quarter of the votes cast. The Assembly even went so far as to dissolve the Congress elected in March 1990 and call congressional elections two and a half years early.

The country's new constitution thus is the culmination of nearly two decades of political reform efforts by presidents and leaders of both major parties. Party leaders have recognized the political necessity of responding to the mobilized constituency for change, but until President Barco's decree was upheld by the Supreme Court, each attempt had fallen prey to a congress more interested in defending a status quo on which they depended for access to patronage. The new constitution makes some important changes that appear to be weakening the old clientele networks. Some encouraging trends include the post-*Constituyente* passage of legislation that gives parties somewhat enhanced control over the use of party labels and a national senate district that allows new parties or factions of the traditional parties to attract support that transcends the old electoral districts, where traditional clientelistic brokers effectively shut them out before. Thus, the interests represented in Congress are becoming more diverse; yet the increase in intraparty competition continues apace, and in such a context the reduced powers of the presidency may make governability more difficult. Thus, the early postreform verdict must be a mixed one.

CONGRESS AND THE PROBLEM OF REFORM: THE ARGUMENT IN BRIEF

There is a certain irony in the just-reviewed attempts to reform public administration and the Congress: In nearly every case presidents have sponsored reforms that would have weakened their own powers, especially by restraining their emergency powers and by reducing the patronage resources that have long been the main "carrot" offered to members of Congress in exchange for their votes. This irony forms the core of the argument that we make in this chapter, which is that the seemingly "powerful" Colombian presidency has been crafted in such a way as to serve primarily the clientelistic interests that are represented in Congress. In other words, the potential dominance of the Colombian presidency between 1968 and 1991 often remained more potential than real, because the Congress was able to prevent presidents from effectively using their powers to move beyond what lower-ranking party leaders would tolerate.

As noted earlier, prior to the convoking of the Constituent Assembly through a state-of-siege decree in 1990, the only means for reforming the constitution was for the Congress to pass, in two consecutive regular sessions, a legislative act by absolute majorities of both houses.[6] Thus, the

---

6 The new constitution keeps this procedure, which is unusually easy compared with other presidential constitutions. It is possible to reform the new constitution by means of either a plebiscite or a constituent assembly, although neither path can be taken without prior congressional authorization. In addition, amendments to certain parts of the constitution can be overturned by a plebiscite initiated by 5% of registered voters after Congress has enacted them. See Articles 374–80.

constitutional allocation of powers among the branches was a matter *under the control of the Congress alone*; neither a referendum nor the consent of states or provinces (known as departments in Colombia), nor even a supermajority of the legislature, was needed. Only in 1990–91 was the congressional sovereignty over the constitution abrogated through the extraordinary procedure of convoking a constituent assembly.

Therefore, we need to understand why legislators have resisted reforms that would enable them – rather than a decree-mongering president – to claim credit for efforts to respond to mobilized popular clamor for reforms. And to understand this problem requires an understanding of what the interests of members of Congress are. In this chapter we demonstrate that these interests are primarily grounded in the provision of patronage to clients – that is, to a narrow subset of the voters in the constituency from which they are elected[7] – rather than being accountable to the larger electorate on the basis of policy programs. The delegation of extraordinary powers to the president, when viewed from this perspective, is merely a means of furthering these clientelistic interests by freeing members from the burdens of making policy. If, because of the way that they are elected from narrow clientele networks, members are not being held accountable for national policy anyway, then they have little incentive to invest time and effort in building and sustaining policy coalitions. Instead they can focus on extracting resources to reward supporters with jobs and other private goods. They will tend to involve themselves in policy only when the policy proposal under consideration furthers their primary interest in converting public funds into private payoffs. Indeed, the Colombian Congress has from time to time enacted significant policy reform, but the successful examples underscore our point: These reforms, such as the direct election of mayors since 1988 and administrative decentralization, have actually given members new opportunities to build their own careers via the provision of particularism. On the other hand, most of the reforms contained in the various presidential policy packages sketched earlier would have curtailed the ability of members of Congress to use national resources to cultivate the patronage networks on which their own careers depend. Therefore, the political system rarely has responded to demands for political reform.

---

7 As noted in Section 3.4, members of the lower house (and before 1991, of the Senate too) are elected from multiseat districts that are coterminous with the country's administrative units, knows as departments. Since 1991 the Senate has been elected from a nationwide district.

3.3. POWERS OF THE COLOMBIAN PRESIDENT

The concentration of formal power in the central government and the executive has led some scholars to characterize the Colombian president as a "Demi-God" (Cepeda 1985). The powers of the president were expanded by reforms during the National Front coalition governments (1958–74) and most especially with the constitutional reform of 1968. With the promulgation of the 1991 constitution, new constraints have been placed on the discretion of the executive in most policy areas.

Speaking of presidential powers from the National Front up through the 1980s, Vázquez Carrizosa (1986:15) said that "the President of Colombia is almost the totality of the state" and that his "decision powers are almost absolute." While we argue that this statement is a clear exaggeration, it is indeed true that the presidency is the source of nearly all substantive legislation, much of which is not even debated in Congress because it is enacted under emergency powers. Indeed, it is the regular use of what are supposed to be "exceptional" powers that has given Colombian presidents their ability to dominate the legislative process. Yet emergency powers amount to less than meets the eye when it comes to attempts by presidents to carry out structural reforms. Before developing this argument further, it is necessary to consider the formal powers of the president, which can be grouped into four different categories that, while interrelated, are analytically distinct. These are (1) powers of appointment, (2) legislative powers, (3) fiscal and planning powers, and (4) extraordinary powers.[8]

POWERS OF APPOINTMENT

The Colombian president freely names and may dismiss all ministers, other top- and medium-level employees of the executive branch, ambassadors, directors of top state "decentralized institutions" (such as the state petroleum company), and the directors and boards of various financial institutions that are intervened in or controlled by the state.[9] The new constitution has

8 This does not exhaust all possible presidential powers. For instance, the president is commander of all forces of public order, which gives him some discretion in opening or closing spaces for public protest. He also has, as head of state, powers in foreign policy, such as negotiating treaties. Under Article 224 of the 1991 constitution, he may even put treaties related to international trade into effect provisionally, subject to ex post veto by Congress.
9 The president continues to appoint all directors of the Central Bank, although these members now have staggered terms. The staggering of terms is not very significant, however, given that the terms are of the same length as the president's, and thus every president has the opportunity to change every member of the board of directors during

somewhat diminished the president's authority over the cabinet. He still may appoint and dismiss ministers without approval of the Congress, but Congress also may remove ministers through a motion of censure. Thus, a president's ability to maintain a cabinet to his liking has been weakened, although it still falls to the president to decide upon a replacement for a censured minister.[10]

Before 1991 the president's powers of appointment and dismissal extended to the governorships of all of Colombia's departments. Since 1991, however, these positions have become elective. Thus, an enormous patronage resource of the president has been eliminated under the new constitution,[11] while an important avenue of party and political career building has been opened up to electoral competition.

LEGISLATIVE POWERS

As noted in Chapter 1, a president's powers over legislation fall into two broad categories: reactive (such as a veto) and proactive (such as decree and emergency powers).

Reactive Powers

The veto power of the Colombian president is one of the major areas in which the 1991 constitution has reduced presidential powers compared with those of the former constitution. Under the pre-1991 constitutional order, on certain kinds of legislation the president's veto could be overridden by only a two-thirds vote of both houses of Congress. The list (Art. 88/1886)[12] of such types of legislation consisted of legal codes, the organic rules for the national budget, changes in territorial subdivisions of the country, and the

his term. The board has seven members: the director, chosen by the board and a member of that board; the minister of finance (*hacienda*); and five individuals serving four-year, renewable terms. At least two of the six nonministerial members must be replaced every four years, but the president has the prerogative of determining which members these will be (Art. 372 of the 1991 constitution).

10 For a discussion of censure in comparative perspective, see Shugart and Carey (1992).

11 Until 1988, mayors were appointed by governors, thus constituting a sort of indirect patronage resource for the president. Since 1988, however, mayors have been popularly elected.

12 We shall use the following format throughout this chapter when citing constitutional articles. The article number will be followed, where necessary, by the paragraph number after a colon. The constitution in question, either 1886 or 1991, will be indicated after a slash. Any reference to the 1886 constitution refers to the version in effect in the 1980s (Giraldo M. and Gómez Velásquez 1983), unless otherwise indicated. References to the 1991 constitution are based on Vidal Perdomo and Sáchica (1991).

National Development Plan.[13] All other types of legislation under the former constitution could be overridden by a majority of all members of each house. Thus, aside from the policy areas just listed, the veto is a relatively weak one if the interests of a majority party (or cross-party coalition) on a given bill is sufficiently compelling to overcome the chronic low attendance that plagues the Colombian Congress. The new constitution provides for such a formally weak veto in all areas of legislation.

The Colombian president under both constitutions has been able to indicate in his veto of a bill that he objects to only part of the bill. However, while the president may request that Congress reconsider parts of a bill, he does not have the power of partial promulgation; that is, he cannot enact into law those parts of the bill to which he does not object. Upon the president's partial veto the *entire bill* is returned to the chamber of origin, which can discuss only the objections raised by the president. The Congress can then either accept or reject the president's partial veto. Should it accept the president's veto, it then sends the bill in its changed form to the president's desk for promulgation. Should it muster the votes required to override a veto, it then returns the bill to the president in its original form. The power of partial veto, but without partial promulgation, gives the president somewhat greater leverage in dealing with the Congress. The president can be certain that the parts of the bill to which he does not object will not be eroded by new amendments when Congress reconsiders the bill, because only the parts that the executive wants changed can be debated again. However, this provision gives the president less leverage than if the parts of the bill he preferred could be promulgated before the Congress reconsidered the vetoed parts.

In both Colombian constitutions, the president has been granted the exclusive authority to initiate legislation in certain policy areas. Like a veto, this power is essentially reactive, in that it allows the president to prevent the Congress from changing the status quo unless the president submits a proposal to change it. The following policy areas have been reserved for presidential initiatives in both constitutions: laws on the structure of the

13 The National Development Plan (NDP) was, according to the 1968 amendments, to establish a general statement of long-term, medium-term, and immediate goals and a budget for all national public entities to carry out these goals. Article 341/1991 – a virtual copy of the corresponding article from the previous constitution – permits the president to enable the NDP by decree if the Congress has not come to agreement on it within three months of its submission. Such tremendous executive power may explain why the Congress never followed up by passing the implementing legislation to put the provisions of the NDP into effect. Thus, in the absence of enacting legislation, this element of the constitution itself remains no more than a statement of the principle that there should be an NDP.

executive ministries; laws establishing salaries for public officials; and general norms for regulating foreign exchange, external trade, the national debt, and tariffs (Arts. 79/1886 and 154/1991). In the 1886 constitution, but not in the 1991 constitution, the president also had the exclusive right to initiate legislation on the organic rules of the national budget and public works. Note that these were areas in which the 1886 constitution also gave the president a veto with a legislative two-thirds override. Thus, in these two policy domains, the president could be almost certain that his own preferences would be translated into law, because (1) Congress could consider no proposals other than those of the president, and (2) if a majority of Congress members (but less than the difficult-to-obtain two-thirds majority) amended the bill to such a degree that the president no longer considered the bill an improvement over the status quo, he could always veto it.

The 1991 constitution has granted the president the exclusive right to introduce legislation in two new areas in which Congress previously had the power of initiative.[14] However, the more important point about the 1991 constitution is that the president's powers to shape the legislative outcome have been reduced in two ways. First, important areas such as the organic rules for the budget and public works are no longer on the list of exclusive presidential initiative. Second, as noted, in all issue areas the president's veto is now weak. In those areas where the president has the exclusive initiative, he can still prevent changes to the status quo simply by choosing not to initiate a bill, but once he initiates it, Congress is free to amend it, and a determined majority could prevail.

Proactive Powers

It is in the area of proactive powers that Colombian presidents have earned their reputation as the chief legislators – as a force for changing the status quo, not merely preserving it. The decree powers of the Colombian president are extensive, especially if we include under this category emergency powers. These powers will, however, be discussed separately later. Here we speak only of the president's ordinary decree powers – that is, the ability to enact decrees even in the absence of a declared state of exception.

An important area of presidential decree authority is the pro tempore

14 These are grants of authority to negotiate contracts and loans and to establish the revenues and expenses of the administration. In addition, the president may exclusively initiate laws concerning the functioning of the Central Bank; however, previously the president had unrestricted *decree* power in this area. Thus, the new constitution, by giving the Congress any right to legislate on matters concerning the Central Bank, has reduced presidential powers. We discuss the president's fiscal and planning powers in an upcoming section.

authority (Arts. 76:12/1886 and 150:10/1991), which consists of special powers, delegated by Congress, to issue decree-laws during specified periods and on subjects defined in the legislation itself. Such an authority has existed since the 1886 constitution went into effect, although the precise ways in which it could be used have been redefined over time. For instance, since a 1936 constitutional amendment, the Colombian state has been charged with intervening in the functioning of the economy to "rationalize" production and the distribution of resources. A 1945 amendment clarified that this could not be accomplished through delegated decree authority, but only under specific legislation passed by Congress. In 1968, however, another amendment explicitly allowed the president to use decree-laws to intervene in the economy, as long as these decrees were under the authority of a law passed under Article 76:12/1886 (Findley 1980).

Although the purpose of delegated decree authority is to allow Congress, as principal, to empower the executive, as an agent of Congress, to undertake measures to further the interests of the Congress, in practice any principal–agent relationship is bound to entail some degree of agency slack or agency loss (Kiewiet and McCubbins 1991). Indeed, there are numerous examples, especially after 1968, of presidents' pushing to the limits their delegated authority under Article 76:12/1886. One of these examples, drawn from a more extensive study by Findley (1980), will suffice to demonstrate the problem. Colombia has long suffered from a shortage of urban housing, in part because of a shortage of long-term credit. President Carlos Lleras Restrepo in 1968 proposed a bill to create a National Savings Fund into which employers would be required to deposit, in advance, funds that would be equivalent to the severance pay rights (one month's pay for every year worked) of all current workers. Congress, under pressure from business interests, rejected the bill.

However, in spite of congressional rejection of this measure, the president implemented through decree a limited form of the policy for government employees only. Lleras cited Law 65 of 1967, which delegated powers under Article 76:12/1886 to reorganize the executive branch. On the basis of a clause in the law that authorized the president to "fix . . . the regime of social services" for government employees, the Supreme Court ruled the decree valid.

Thus, in this example, the president was able to enact a scaled-down version of a policy that had been explicitly rejected by Congress, because of an earlier act of delegation by Congress that could be interpreted as giving the president authority to legislate in the area. Article 76:12/1886 did not give the Congress the authority to pass legislation that would contradict a decree issued under the authority of that article, so the policy stood. Thus, under the pre-1991 constitutional order, the president could enact decrees that established a new status quo that Congress could not rescind or modify, short of a constitutional amendment.

The 1991 *Constituyente* put several important restraints on this power. The *proactiveness* of the pro tempore decree power has been reduced in that Congress now has the explicit authority to repeal or amend a decree issued pursuant to delegated faculties (Art. 150:10/1991). The same article also states that Congress may delegate such faculties for a maximum period of six months – previously there was no stated limit – and only in areas explicitly requested by the government. A bill establishing an area to be legislated by decree must pass with a majority of the whole membership of each house, rather than by just a majority of a quorum. Finally, pro tempore powers may not be used to decree codes, statutes, organic laws, or taxes. The Constituent Assembly thereby attempted to restrict Congress's propensity to delegate excessively, forcing it alone to come to terms with the most important legislative matters.

In addition to the power to enact legislative decrees, the president also has the authority to regulate bills passed by Congress. By means of a regulatory decree, the executive may define the precise areas to be affected by the legislation passed by Congress. An excellent example of the use of regulatory decrees can be found in the process of administrative decentralization (for a general discussion, see Dugas, Ocampo, Orjuela, and Ruiz 1992). In Article 13 of Law 12 of 1986, Congress gave the executive branch the power (for a period of one year from the promulgation of the law) to write a number of qualifications left unstated at the very heart of this particular piece of legislation. Law 12 of 1986 involved the devolution of proceeds of the national sales tax (VAT) from the central government to municipalities. At the same time, the national government also turned over to the municipalities various functions previously under the control of the central or departmental governments and closed down now-superseded national or departmental public service institutions. However, Article 13 of Law 12 left to the executive the right to determine *what* functions would be turned over to the municipalities and which institutions would be closed.

In Decree 77 of 1987, for instance, the president mandated a curtailment of the budgets and functions of various governmental institutions. At the same time, many functions were now expressly turned over to the municipalities, including providing potable water, basic sewerage facilities, and municipal slaughterhouses and marketplaces. A review of the original law and the subsequent enabling decrees illustrates some interesting and telling points. First, the original law was only 12 pages long, while the various executive decrees ran on for 72 pages. Second and more interesting from the perspective of this chapter, the Congress left in the hands of the executive branch the tough decisions about which institutions would be closed, which would be cut back, and which would see their budgets grow. In this particular case, while the various clientele networks composing Congress all supported the devolution of tax monies from the central government to the municipalities, they could not agree on the details of the transition process. Rather than chance the loss of the greater gain, they made use of the institutional structures established by the constitution to pass on this politically difficult task to the executive branch.[15]

In recent years the regulatory powers of the president have increased for many of the same reasons that the president's legislative powers have increased: the lack of technical capacity and political will on the part of Congress to confront many of the difficult political decisions necessary to regulate existing legislation. Reasons for this lack of will on the part of the Congress will be addressed in Section 3.4.

FISCAL AND PLANNING POWERS

One of the most important sources of presidential power in Colombia is the extensive control the executive has over the national budget and the various planning institutions of the state. These fiscal and planning powers of the president were greatly expanded by the constitutional reforms of 1968 (Vidal Perdomo 1970). According to Vázquez Carrizosa (1986:412), "The essence of the 1968 reform lay in the reduction in Congress's powers to organize the national budget and to control the planning policies guiding the economic activity of the state. With this reform, the process of overwhelming growth of presidential power reached its crowning point." According to one ex-government functionary, quoted by Vázquez Carrizosa (1986:413), "The constitutional reform of 1968 increased . . . the ordinary powers of the government; its central proposition, together with that of planning, was to offer the executive agile, and almost discretionary instruments, to deal with any imaginable situation in economic, social, and administrative policy."

The 1968 reforms initiated important changes in budgetary powers that remain essentially unchanged today (Arts. 210–11/1886 and 349–51/1991). The president, through the minister of finance (*hacienda*), prepares the na-

---

15 Because of the administrative nature of regulatory decrees, disputes over the president's use of this power are referred to the Council of State, the country's highest administrative court, rather than to the Supreme Court. The Council of State, under both constitutions, has an appointment procedure identical to that of the Supreme Court (see note 4).

tional budget and sends it to Congress. Congress left itself only the ability to reduce the amounts of various budget items; any attempt to increase the budget requires the express authorization of the president. Colombia's Congress, without an equivalent of the U.S. Congressional Budget Office, has by default ceded the president nearly total control over fiscal policy. The president also was granted in 1968 the authority to make contracts for the execution of public works projects and to borrow monies from international sources. Although Congress has a formal right to approve or reject such contracts and loans, as the 1990s commenced it had never made use of this faculty.

The 1968 reform also established Article 120:14/1886, which permitted the president to intervene in the functioning of the Central Bank as his "own constitutional prerogative." Exactly what this meant was left to judicial interpretation, and for several years, the president was able to accumulate more and more authority in the management of the economy in this way. For example, in 1972, the Supreme Court ruled unconstitutional a law passed by Congress that set up a publicly funded corporation to extend credit for agricultural development. In its ruling, the Court said that the law violated the exclusive power granted under Article 120:14/1886 for the president to exercise, revise, or terminate public control over persons managing public savings. Moreover, the Council of State (the supreme administrative tribunal) in 1974 ruled that decrees under Article 120:14/1886 could overturn previous legislation because Congress, in enacting the article, had transferred the matter of managing public savings from the arena of legislative control into the administrative (i.e., regulatory) arena (Findley 1980).

Under the terms of the new constitution, congress has regained considerable control over presidential intervention in the Central Bank. There is no equivalent of the former Article 120:14/1886, although the new constitution gives the president exclusive authority to initiate laws that determine the functions of the Central Bank (Art. 154/1991). Intervention in the management of savings and investment must take place only through framework laws (*leyes marco*) – that is, under pro tempore powers as delegated by Congress, rather than as an exclusive presidential prerogative.

EMERGENCY POWERS AS PROACTIVE LEGISLATIVE AUTHORITY

As noted in Chapter 1, many presidents in Latin America have emergency powers. Usually, such extraordinary authority is used only in genuinely extraordinary circumstances, such as insurrection, severe strikes, or natural calamities. These powers rarely include the ability to repeal laws or issue new laws. However, Colombia is a major exception, since the supposedly extraordinary powers are used as de facto proactive legislative authority. There are two forms of emergency authority that are used in Colombia to decree new laws, the State of Siege (now known as the State of Internal Commotion) and the State of Economic Emergency.

State of Siege

Article 121/1886 gave the president the right to declare all or part of the country under a state of siege, during which he holds the authority to suspend but not abolish existing laws and to emit decrees with the force of law. Unlike pro tempore or regulatory decrees, these extraordinary decrees were not limited to any particular policy area, although they were supposed to be consistent with "restoring order." Moreover, although all decrees issued under a state of siege automatically lapsed once the siege was lifted and any laws suspended were automatically reinstated at that time, Congress had little control over the substantive policies enacted during a state of siege.

The minimal oversight of, and the vague criteria for assuming, emergency powers led Colombia's presidents to make increased use of this prerogative. From the return to civilian rule in 1958 until the abrogation of the former constitution in July 1991, Colombia was under a state of siege an average of 75% of the time. The powers granted to the president under the state of siege are such that the president, if so inclined, would appear to be a virtual "constitutional dictator." Indeed, it was with the use of this power that President Barco authorized a referendum on convening a constituent assembly, thus bypassing the existing constitution's process for constitutional amendment.

The constitutional terms governing the state of siege have changed over time, usually limiting the president's freedom of action under the provision, with the most significant changes coming with the new constitution of 1991. In the original 1886 constitution, the power was truly unlimited, granting full powers of martial law to the president. In 1910, the first limitations were placed on the president's power, including clauses preventing the president from repealing laws and another establishing that the president and other executive branch officials would be held responsible for any abuses committed in the exercise of state of siege powers.[16] It is worth noting that the 1910 amendment was also the one that established the direct popular election of the president, thus opening up the possibility that the president would be a less reliable agent of the Congress than those

16 Legislative Act No. 1 of 1910. See also Gibson (1948).

elected under the pre-1910 procedure, which employed an electoral college elected on the same basis as the Congress itself.

Before the 1950s, the state of siege was generally used as intended – that is, mainly to comvil unrest, rather than as a policy-making tool to bypass congressional opposition. In 1956, however, under pressure from Colombia's only military dictatorship in the twentieth century, the Supreme Court said that it was permissible for the president to use the state of siege powers to attack economic as well as political causes of public disorder. Moreover, the court said that the decision to declare or revoke a state of siege was entirely a matter of executive discretion and was not subject to judicial review. The only limit left by that court decision was the rather vague requirement that decrees issued under the state of siege could be aimed only at restoring order and could not override acts of Congress for other purposes (Findley 1980).[17]

Given the vagueness of limitations placed on the state of siege powers by the 1956 ruling and an agreement upon the return to democracy to legalize all official acts taken under the 1953–57 dictatorship, presidents came increasingly to rely on the state of siege powers to attack long-term economic problems. In 1960 Congress amended Article 121 to provide for a permanent congressional session during a state of siege and to let either house of Congress be a plaintiff before the Supreme Court to challenge specific decrees issued pursuant to a state of siege. However, Congress repealed these provisions in 1968.[18] (Also in 1968, Congress created a separate and presumably more controllable *state of exception* to deal with economic troubles, which we discuss later.)

During and after the National Front power-sharing regime, state of siege powers were increasingly used as a means to overcome congressional inefficiency and immobilism. In a number of cases, the state of siege was continued long after the "crisis" used to justify it had receded, and many of the decrees issued during these periods had little to do with the ostensible purpose of declaring a state of siege – public order. Although all these decrees are automatically rescinded when the state of siege is declared over, in fact many have been incorporated into the legal code by the Congress.

---

17 Even this relatively favorable ruling prompted the dictator Rojas Pinilla to issue a decree reorganizing the court more to his liking.

18 One obvious reason for the decision in 1960 to make congressional sessions permanent during a state of siege is that congress members were paid per diem! While congress members were still paid per diem after 1968, sessions had become so long that the distinction was probably not so important, plus the 1968 amendments included a side agreement to expand congressional office staffs and to ensure each member special discretionary funds (*auxilios parlamentarios*).

Indeed, because it was a presidential prerogative to decide when to lift a state of siege, often presidents would refuse to declare an end to the siege until Congress had agreed to enact into permanent law those measures the president deemed essential. Examples include the the Statute of Security (Extraordinary Decree 1,923 of 1978, signed by President Turbay), which included a provision that placed civilians under military justice in certain cases. This provision was included within the revised Criminal Code.

As several scholars have noted, the president's use of state of siege powers presented serious dangers for Colombian democracy, especially given the government's power to restrict civil liberties and human rights severely (Umaña 1985). In response to abuses of the emergency powers, Article 213/1991 places new restrictions on these powers. For example, the initial declaration of what is now renamed a state of internal commotion[19] may be for no more than 90 days, although the president may extend it for another 90 days thereafter. A second 90-day extension – the last one permitted – requires the consent of the Senate. The constitution also forbids trying civilians in military courts under any circumstances and states that internationally recognized human rights must be upheld. The law passed in May 1994 to regulate emergency powers adds two new checks: The Constitutional Court may of its own right overturn emergency decrees if they usurp constitutional guarantees; and the Congress may revoke or amend any emergency decree at any time (*El Tiempo*, June 2, 1994). Even with these limitations, the state of internal commotion powers, coupled with the state of economic emergency powers (discussed next), give the Colombian presidency formidable proactive authority, comparable to the provisional measure in Brazil, as discussed in Chapter 1 and in Mainwaring's chapter.

State of Economic Emergency

As noted, presidents after 1958 came to declare states of siege to deal with structural economic problems. Also, as noted previously, the 1968 reforms to the constitution were intended to give the president discretion to intervene in the Central Bank and to make it easier for the Congress to delegate decree powers by which the president could manage the economy. However, some members of Congress, led by Senator (and future president) Alfonso López Michelsen, did not believe that the new economic powers were sufficient to prevent continued presidential reliance on Article 121/1886 for dealing with economic issues. As a result, when Congress passed the 1968 amendments it created a new extraordinary power, that concerning

---

19 Unlike in the previous constitution, there is now a separate article that deals with a state of external war (Art. 212).

states of economic emergency (Art. 122/1886), which the president could declare for periods not to exceed 90 days in any calendar year. During such time, he could issue decrees with the force of law with the intention of restoring "economic order." Unlike state of siege decrees, however, these decrees did not lapse once the state of emergency expired. Also unlike state of siege decrees (before 1991), Congress could repeal or amend the decrees at any time.

The right to declare an economic emergency, and to do so without a convincing reason, has given the president a tool that some analysts claim lets him circumvent the Congress to implement his projects (Cepeda 1985). One example was when President López Michelsen, citing erosion of incomes as a result of inflation and deficit financing, used this power to create a new sales tax and to change the income tax law in 1974 (Vázquez Carrizosa 1986:425–27). There was little reason to believe that these measures would deal with short-term emergency conditions, as Article 122/1886 intended. The Supreme Court's response to a challenge to López's actions was that its own competence to intervene in the matter was quite limited. The court majority ruled that it lacked authority to review either the reasons given to justify declaring a state of economic emergency or the substance of the decrees themselves.[20] It could review only whether or not all constitutionally mandated procedures had been followed.[21] The court therefore upheld the tax reform decrees, except for one section that conflicted with a provision of Article 122/1886 that prohibited diminishing "the social rights of workers under preexisting laws" (Findley 1980).

This episode provides grist for those who argue along the lines of Vázquez Carizossa (1986:429): "Article 122 went well beyond the intentions of its authors and supporters and was converted, *ipso facto*, into the equivalent of Article 121, giving the president a passport of free access to legislative powers through the emission of extraordinary or executive decrees." This criticism appears to have been accepted in recent years; witness the decision of the Supreme Court to overturn Betancur's attempt to use the economic emergency powers to institute a new tax reform in 1982. Again, in 1987, the court overturned Barco's decrees issued under a state of economic emergency, which, in this case, was clearly one of a severe economic emergency in the region of Urabá (Cepeda 1985).

---

20 The court voted 19 to 5, but 4 of the dissenters ruled that the court should not have heard the case at all, as it was a "political" matter rather than a legal question (Findley 1980).

21 These were, according to Article 122/1886, the prior (nonbinding) advice of the Council of State, the consent of all ministers, declaration of reasons (*motivos*), a termination date, and a summons to the Congress.

However, the logic used by the court in its various decisions on the use of emergency powers is consistent with an interpretation that Congress is the ultimate arbiter of the authority held by the president, which is the argument that we are making in this chapter. The court, in its 1974 decision on López's tax reform, said that because the Congress in 1968 left itself the power to amend or repeal decrees issued under Article 122/1886 at any time, it is up to Congress and not the court to decide on the "convenience and effectiveness" of the decrees, as long as they do not conflict with specific constitutional restrictions (Findley 1980). Thus, in the language of principal–agent theory, the Congress, despite its inaction, had not abdicated authority to the president, whose actions remained under the political control of Congress. The key question thus becomes why, in delegating so much power to the president, Congress has not summoned the will to exercise such political control directly. This question will be the subject of Section 3.5.

The question of why Colombian politicians would tolerate such sweeping presidential powers in the area of economic policy will prove to be highly relevant, since the Constituent Assembly made few changes in the provision for economic emergency powers (Art. 215/1991). Indeed, the 1991 constitution even expands the scope of these powers somewhat. It explicitly permits the president to decree new taxes during a state of economic emergency, thereby indicating that measures such as Betancur's failed attempt to decree a tax reform would in the future be constitutional. However, such taxes automatically lapse when the state of emergency ends, which is still a maximum of 90 days from its declaration, consistent with our claim that emergency powers are generally not effective for establishing long-term reforms. Also, the 1991 constitution explicitly permits the Congress at any time to initiate legislation that amends or repeals emergency economic decrees, even if these are in issue areas in which the Congress is ordinarily prevented from initiating legislation. It is striking that the *Constituyente* continued to rely on decree powers to address the nation's serious economic problems. However, the new checks on this power that we have reviewed here – principally the greater legal ability of Congress to pass legislation contravening a decree – have served to move Colombia out of the category of "potentially dominant" presidencies and into the category of proactive presidencies (see Chapter 1). These proactive powers, we argue, are a device by which political forces in Congress (or a constituent assembly) seek to accomplish tasks that they cannot accomplish effectively on their own. Such is the essence of a principal–agent relationship.

PUTTING LEGISLATIVE POWERS
IN CONTEXT

Chapters 1 and 11 suggest that presidencies with decree powers are most likely to be found in systems in which congress itself is poorly equipped to tackle policy matters because of internal fragmentation. Further, they note that in some countries, congress is likely to be more conservative than presidents. Congress may be elected in districts that overrepresent rural areas (which tend to be more conservative), while presidents are usually elected in national districts that perforce represent all regions equally. Unlike presidents whose arsenal of legislative powers consists principally of reactive powers, presidents with proactive powers can succeed in getting *more* of a policy relative to the status quo than what congress wants. Shugart and Mainwaring suggest that this is so because presidents can use their decree power strategically, such that decrees survive when they have to be turned into law by congress. In other words, presidents cannot decree just any policy they prefer; congress remains a check. But presidents, using decrees, can push policy farther from the status quo than congress would do on its own.

Two countries in Latin America clearly fit this pattern: Brazil and Colombia. These are also the two countries where traditional clientelistic brokering remains strongest in congressional elections, especially in the more traditional rural areas. Furthermore, these are also the two countries that have the most internal party competition, as various brokers compete to elect their favored candidates. The Brazilian case is discussed in detail in Mainwaring's chapter; in this chapter we have so far outlined the Colombian president's legislative powers, and in the rest of the chapter we note the problems caused by party factionalism (Section 3.4) and how this factionalism and the disjunction between the constituent bases of the presidency and of the Congress impose limits on presidential powers (Section 3.5).

To foreshadow the conclusions of these sections, let us recall that Colombian presidents before 1991 also had a veto, implying that they should indeed have been able to get whatever policy they wanted – in short, to dominate Congress. However, one of our principal points in this chapter is that such dominance remains more potential than real because Congress itself determines the allocation of powers under the constitution, and the constitution requires that most reforms, to stick over the long term, must be converted into regular law. Thus, decrees are an important policy instrument, but they are often only part of a complex negotiation with party bosses who control votes in a congress that must ultimately decide whether to let extraordinary decrees stand as permanent laws. Moreover, many reforms require constitutional amendments, and as noted, Congress alone has authority over these. Only in 1990–91 was Congress's sovereignty over the constitution broken; that is the subject of Section 3.6.

3.4. ELECTORAL INCENTIVES AND PARTY FACTIONALISM

If presidents in Colombia have been endowed with such formidable powers to issue decree-laws to tackle economic and other problems, a puzzle emerges: Why have recent Colombian presidents been unable to carry out large parts of their programs, especially programs that seek to implement the social, economic, and political changes necessary to bring the country's institutions in line with a radically changing society? In this section we provide an explanation based on the often-conflicting electoral incentives of presidents and Congress. The reason that presidents are allowed to make substantial policy by emergency measures is that the Congress is not an important arena for the creation of national policy or for the representation of different policy preferences. To understand why, we argue that one must look to the party system, which reflects clientelistic interests and patronage-maintained logrolling rather than nationally oriented programmatic representation. Because the system is structured in such a way as to provide politicians wide autonomy from congressional party leadership, there is no central legislative agent with the proper incentives and power to restrain the particularistic actions of the congressional rank and file. Therefore, Congress as a whole is often both unable and unwilling to join with the executive in national policy initiatives. On the other hand, as we discuss later, the Congress can set significant constraints on presidential action and can restructure presidential initiatives in ways that serve the interests of local politicians. This form of politicians' autonomy is maintained by an electoral system that encourages intense intraparty competition and factionalization.

Members of Congress, even if they value economic or political reform, face a collective-action problem wherein their dominant strategy is to defect from any reformist solution in order to ensure advancement of their own patronage-driven careers and those of their clients in the electorate. The delegation of strong but circumscribed presidential powers is a way of overcoming the most debilitating aspects of the collective-action problem. However, ultimately the political interests that have prevailed are those of the clientele networks that have long dominated the Colombian party system. A partial solution to this problem was found in the use of extraordinary powers to enable the convening of the Constituent Assembly that rewrote the country's constitution in 1991. Yet even this special constitutional body was unwilling to change many of the fundamental aspects of the country's party and electoral institutions. In this section we (1) look at the Colombian electoral institutions, (2) consider how they provide incentives toward particularism for politicians, and (3) review the changes in electoral incentives under the rules of the new constitution. Then in Section 3.5 we look at what effect these institutions have on the policy-making power of Colombian presidents.

THE ELECTORAL SYSTEM

The electoral system used in the Colombian Congress is based on the country's tradition of decentralized Conservative and Liberal regional elites. The most salient feature of the Colombian electoral system is that the proportional-representation seat-allocation procedure is applied in each district to *factional* lists, rather than to *party* lists. Each list stands alone for the purpose of allocating seats; party is not even a criterion used in the allocation of seats. In virtually every district in every election, more than one list representing each of the two major parties has been run. The reason for this proliferation of lists is that party organizations do not control the use of the party label. That is, candidates, as long they meet the minimum requirements for registration – presenting a sworn statement of candidacy and paying a small fee – may present lists of candidates under the party name of their choice. Thus, parties have little control over the composition of their delegation in either house of Congress.

Moreover, the procedure for allocating seats to lists – the simple quota and largest remainders rule – means that the least costly way (in terms of votes required) to win a seat is to win with a remainder rather than to aim for a quota.[22] For example, in the district of Magdalena in 1990, there were 258,996 valid votes cast, as can be seen in Table 3.1. Because the district magnitude was six, the simple quota was $258,996/6 = 43,166$. Any list achieving this total was guaranteed as many seats as the number of times the quota could be divided into its vote total. Any seats not filled by full quotas are awarded, one per list, to the lists with the most remaining votes until all seats have been filled. Two lists, both headed by Liberal candidates, each won over 52,000 votes, enough for each list to win one seat by quota. Neither list had a large enough remainder to win a second seat. The smallest

---

22 Cox and Shugart (1994) have shown that because there is no pooling or "transferring" of votes from one list to another, if no list wins enough votes to win more than one seat, the system is effectively identical to the single nontransferable vote, as used in Japan through 1993.

Table 3.1. *An example of how the Colombian electoral system works: Results from the district of Magdalena in 1990*

	Votes	Seats by quota	Remainder	Seats by remainder	Total seats
Liberal lists					
1 (Abdalá)	52,945	1	9,779	0	1
2 (Menotti)	52,552	1	9,386	0	1
3 (Ramos)	39,991	0	39,991	1	1
4 (Aduen)	33,669	0	33,669	1	1
Conservative lists					
1 (Mejica)	39,209	0	39,209	1	1
2 (Murica)	21,634	0	21,634	1	1
3 (Alzamora)	18,853	0	18,853	0	0

Note: District magnitude: 6; total valid votes: 258,996; quota: 43,166.

winning remainder was that of a Conservative list with 21,634 votes, or about half a quota. As shown in Table 3.1, each of four Liberal lists won a seat. However, two of these lists "paid" over 50,000 votes per seat, almost two and one half times the cost in votes of the "cheapest" seat. This example is from just one district in one election, but it is typical in that it demonstrates how relatively small lists can take advantage of the system and win seats rather cheaply. And because parties do not control the use of their own labels, a candidate who seeks to win a seat in this manner cannot be denied the use of a party's name whether or not his or her bid is supported by the party leadership.

PARTY FACTIONALISM

Because of the cheapness of winning seats and the lack of label control, there has been a tendency for more and more of these small lists. In elections from 1974 through 1990, there was a remarkable upward trend in the number of lists that received only enough votes to elect one deputy or senator. As shown in Figure 3.1, in the first post–National Front election in 1974, about 45% of deputies and 58% of senators were elected from lists that elected no other candidate. In subsequent elections this percentage increased dramatically, accounting for around 80% of members in each chamber in 1990. The significance of this trend is that increasingly lists are simply campaign vehicles for a single individual. Thus, even with no change in electoral rules, intraparty competition has increased substantially since

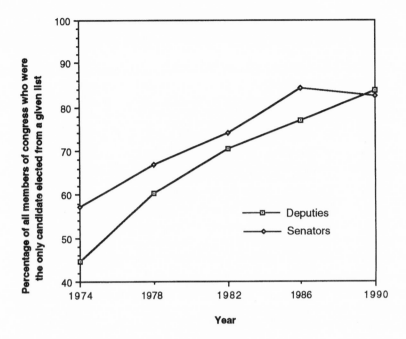

Figure 3.1. Single-winner lists in Colombian congressional elections, 1974–90.

1974. In such a competitive environment, each head of a list must construct a network of supporters who deliver votes to his or her list instead of one of the several others operating with the same party label in exchange for promised services, jobs, or cash (Archer 1990). These kinds of exchanges are the stuff of *clientelismo*, a common theme of the literature on Colombia (Díaz 1986; Leal Buitrago and Dávila Ladrón de Guevara 1990),[23] which makes voters "captive" of whichever clientele network provides them the goods.

In Colombia before 1991, candidates who were incumbents even had constitutionally guaranteed funds, known as *auxilios parlamentarios*, by

23 The tendency for the traditional parties to have multiple lists is not a new one, even if there has been growth in the number of lists electing only one member. In the 1940s and earlier, factions of one or the other party presented their own lists. The National Front contributed to an increase in party factionalization, because the requirement of parity between the parties in every district's representation made intraparty competition not just an adjunct to interparty competition, but the *only* kind of competition. Thus, it became less important for a candidate to be tied to one of the traditional party leaders of his or her region and led to the rise of more autonomous vote brokers (Archer 1990). The end of the National Front did not restore the traditional leaders' dominance because the electoral system's tendencies, reviewed earlier, make the entry of numerous lists of candidates seeking to win seats "cheaply" the norm of the system, rather than an aberration (Cox and Shugart 1994; Cox and Shugart forthcoming).

which they could fund pork-barrel projects that would win votes for them (Hartlyn 1988:171–76; Leal Buitrago and Dávila Ladrón de Guevara 1990). However, *auxilios parlamentarios* alone were insufficient to guarantee members' electoral prospects. Campaigns for office in systems such as Colombia's were so expensive and the electoral environment so competitive that funds from outside contributors were also needed.

To win and hold onto dependable blocs of voters, each candidate seeks to identify with one of several national factions within his or her party. These faction leaders, who are seeking to increase support for their own faction at the expense of others, provide funds, jobs, and other particularistic benefits to vote brokers. The local candidates receive these private goods and distribute them to their clients in exchange for votes. As Urrutia (1991: 383) has noted, "The political structure of the parties produces a congress and city councils mostly interested in distributing the budget to the largest number of potential clients." Under the 1991 constitution, the seat-allocation procedure remains the same; however, the Senate is now elected in a nationwide district rather than in regional contests. Later on, we shall discuss some of the effects of this reform; however, for now the point is that the basic incentives of members remain the same as they always were. There is great intraparty competition, and this makes the formation of reformist policy-based majorities difficult. We elaborate on these problems in the next section.

3.5. CONGRESSIONAL INTERESTS AND LIMITS ON PRESIDENTIAL POWERS

As we have noted, the constitution would appear to allow the president to dominate the Congress. Moreover, the Congress, especially since the constitutional reforms of 1968, has failed to exercise many of its own functions. The Congress is simply not a nationally focused institution and has delegated national policy agenda duties to the executive, provided that the national agenda does not impinge upon Congress members' particularistic interests.

In this section we explain the dichotomy between formal and real powers of the presidency by reference to a collective-action problem that is inherent in the composition of the traditional parties. We conclude that while the Colombian president has extensive powers, they may be used only within a relatively constrained space of prior consensus among the major political and economic players. When the president attempts to step outside these areas of consensus, his capacity to act quickly dissipates. The growing impasse between executive authority and defenders of the status quo has caused a dispersion of power and a consequent erosion of presidential authority. Moreover, this has occurred at a time in which increasingly complex problems have led to growing levels of social instability and violence.

Thus, the capacity of the president to carry out major changes in the political, social, and economic structures of the nation is truncated. Developing countries such as Colombia face massive socioeconomic challenges that place enormous pressures for change on the state. The inability of traditional mechanisms of representation, especially parties and legislatures, to face these challenges has led to growing public expectations and demands for strong executive leadership. The apparently great formal powers of the president fuel these demands, yet executive initiatives have repeatedly stumbled over the often informal limitations on the use of executive authority. Again, we are not arguing that the electoral system or the constitution have *caused* the problems of Colombian society, only that they have made tackling them *more difficult* than other arrangements probably would do.

The Congress maintains a blocking power over presidential attempts to undertake major reforms: It can simply refuse to pass the necessary legislation or constitutional amendment. When a reform desired by the president requires structural changes that cannot be addressed through the use of emergency powers, the president comes up against two obstacles in trying to win congressional passage: (1) the problems of legislative coalition building and (2) the composition of the majority party, which leads to a severe dilemma in trying to accommodate a rural-biased Congress and a president more attuned to urban interests.

PROBLEMS OF LEGISLATIVE COALITION BUILDING

Although the Colombian president has great legislative powers, when important changes are proposed to the existing social, economic, or political structure of the country, the president must have the support of at least a large part of his own party and often much of the opposition as well. The reasons are obvious. Although the president could use his extraordinary powers to carry out such transformations,[24] these changes would not survive to the next administration without the support of the important faction leaders and other relevant party bosses. Given that each president is limited

---

24 An example of such an attempt was President López Pumarejo's enactment of a labor reform in 1944 during his beleaguered second term.

to one four-year term,[25] and that his successor could simply declare an end to a state of siege and thus to any laws decreed under the state of siege, the president cannot bypass Congress if he wishes to institute important and permanent changes in the country's laws. This is especially true with respect to social and political reforms (Archer and Chernick 1989).

Problems in building legislative coalitions may be broken down into three interrelated aspects of the internal dynamics of the Congress: (1) a lack of ties between members of Congress and their constituents with respect to policy (rather than patronage), (2) low continuity in the membership of Congress, and (3) low party cohesion. All of these aspects add up to low partisan powers despite copartisan majorities for all but one president since 1974 and create important obstacles to reformist initiatives.

It is difficult – often impossible – to determine where individual members stand on questions of public policy, because very few votes on the floor are recorded. This frees members to make deals with the president over support of his programs in exchange for private goods, especially patronage, which can be provided to a Congress member's constituents. However, the limited information on voting records also means that whatever votes members cast on policy matters are not the product of voters' demands for specific policies. Neither voters nor policy-based pressure groups can assess their representative's fitness for reelection. Colombian Congress members have little or no accountability to the *broader electorate*, in the sense that that term is generally understood in the industrialized democracies (e.g., Eulau and Prewitt 1973; Fiorina 1981). Their accountability is to only that small subset of their constituents to whom they provide private goods.

Members do not seek congressional careers for the primary purpose of delivering on policy promises; indeed, few seek long-term careers in Congress at all. Turnover is very high, although the percentage of members returned to office has risen from averages of around 20–30% in both houses through the 1960s to 45–60% in the Senate and 35–45% in the House in recent elections. This is illustrated by Figure 3.2, which displays reelection rates since the restoration of the elected Congress in 1958.[26] Rather than spend a long career in the legislature, many members serve one or two terms, then either move into more lucrative bureaucratic appointive positions or use the connections gained while in Bogotá to enhance their attractiveness as a candidate for a local office. Given that mayoralties in 1988 and gov-

---

25 Under the constitution of 1886, an ex-president could run again after sitting out a term. In the constitution of 1991, there is a lifetime limit of one term.
26 The turnover rate is comparable to that in Brazil, where the reasons are probably similar to those given in this section for Colombia. See Ames (1987) for a discussion.

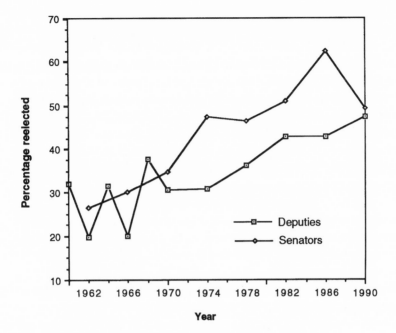

Figure 3.2. Reelection rates in the Colombian Congress, 1960–90.

ernorships in 1991 became elective positions, these executive offices offer a further source of postcongressional careers, as they do in Brazil (Ames and Nixon 1993). With over a thousand municipalities, there are plenty of these posts to go around, and the opportunities these offer for amassing power and wealth through the dispensing of patronage, the awarding of contracts, and the launching of supporters' political careers are considerable.

One immediate consequence of this nonprofessional Congress is that the president is forced to build not one coalition but a series of coalitions within Congress, sometimes beginning anew for each bill or constitutional reform he proposes. The nature of congressional alliances made up of members who demand patronage as compensation for supporting the president is that transactions are highly particularistic and likely to break down if members are unsatisfied with what they are being offered in exchange for their votes. The president, therefore, cannot assume that there is any congressional faction that will provide automatic support to his legislative priorities. Moreover, because of members' lack of accountability on national initiatives, the president's ability to deal with Congress through the mobilization of public opinion is sharply reduced and, as a consequence, so is his capacity to build reformist coalitions.

Not surprisingly, given the means by which members are elected in the first place, there is very little party unity within Congress.[27] A president cannot count on the loyalty of members from his own party because many are tied to local bosses whose own strategic calculations are determined by the logic of clientelism – how many jobs they need to reward followers – rather than by any commitment to a party program. As a result, coalition building is ad hoc and piecemeal.[28] Thus, the president's legislative task often appears nearly impossible.

THE COMPOSITION OF THE MAJORITY PARTY

We have identified a conflict between presidents seeking reforms and members of Congress seeking to preserve their perquisites and to reward constituents with patronage. We believe that this conflict between a reformist executive and an obstructionist Congress can be explained by reference to a collective-action problem within the parties, which in turn can be explained by reference to the country's political institutions. The source of the dilemma stems from the election of the president in a single nationwide constituency.[29] The successful presidential candidate thus must attract a coalition that transcends the far narrower constituencies that any individual member of Congress carves out for him- or herself. The difference between constituencies of the president and Congress is exacerbated by the over-representation of rural – and more conservative – interests in the Congress, especially as it was structured before 1991. Reapportionment of electoral districts has lagged far behind demographic changes, such that, by 1986, over half of the members of Congress were elected with primarily rural votes (Archer 1990:256–57) despite the fact that the population is more than 60% urban.[30]

27 Unfortunately for analysts, the Colombian Congress seldom records roll call votes, so we cannot provide data on the frequency of party-line votes or of deviations from leadership recommendations. Of course, legislatures set their own rules for debating and voting, and this lack of roll call voting only underscores our earlier point about the lack of accountability on policy positions to voters.
28 This creates special problems for reform proposals, which require constitutional amendments since the "reformist" coalition must be maintained over two consecutive years.
29 From the establishment of direct presidential elections in 1910 until the 1991 constitution, the president was elected by plurality (relative majority). Under the new constitution, an absolute majority is required for a one-round victory. Otherwise, a runoff is held between the top two candidates. The adoption of this new rule reflects the lack of any majority party in the Constituent Assembly (see Section 3.6) and the influence therein of the M-19.
30 The poor representation of Bogotá in the Congress is but one extreme example. With

Table 3.2. *Percentage of urban vote by party: Presidential and congressional elections*

Year	Type[a]	PL	PC	Other	PL–PC
1974	P	61.29	22.78	15.93	+38.51
	C	60.18	23.09	16.73	+37.09
1978	P	50.41	43.52	6.07	+6.89
	C	60.60	31.16	8.23	+29.44
1982	P	38.14	44.01	17.85	−5.87
	C	60.24	34.75	5.01	+25.49
1986	P	62.81	31.25	5.94	+31.56
	C	59.17	29.28	11.55	+29.89

[a] P = presidential, C = chamber
Source: For electoral data, *Resultados Electorales*. Various years. Bogotá: Departamento Administrativo Nacional de Estadística. For census data, see Colombia, *XIV and XV Censo Nacional de Población*. Bogotá: Departamento Administrativo Nacional de Estadística, 1973 and 1985.

We can also see the imperative of reaching out to urban voters by the following data. Table 3.2 shows that, from 1974 to 1986, the Liberals consistently polled around 60% of the urban vote in congressional elections. This is higher than their share of the national congressional vote, which from 1974 to 1982 (and also in 1986, if the splinter New Liberals are included) was consistently around 55% (see Table 3.3). The most striking fact about congressional votes is how stable they are from one election to the next, as we would expect in elections in which delivering particularistic goods matters so much more than policy. As long as the various clientele networks continue to have spoils to divide up, they can ensure a stable division of the electorate. In presidential elections, on the other hand, vote shares vary to a much greater degree from election to election. If we look at the urban electorate, as in Table 3.2, we find that swings there have been especially pronounced and in a way that corresponds to the varying programmatic campaigns of the candidates.

Table 3.2 shows that in the first post–National Front election in 1974,

nearly 20% of the population of the country, Bogotá together with surrounding Cundinamarca had but 14% of the congressional seats until the 1991 reforms, a difference of over 15 seats. In the new constitution, the lower house is only slightly less skewed. A separate constituency has been created for Bogotá with 18 seats, in addition to 7 for the rest of Cundinamarca, for a total of 15.5% of all the seats. The nationwide Senate district ends the underrepresentation of urban votes in that body.

the Conservative candidate, Alvaro Gómez Hurtado, carried only 22.8% of the presidential vote in urban areas. However, when the proreform Belisario Betancur ran as head of a so-called National Movement, which transcended the traditional clientelistic structures of his Conservative Party in both 1978 and 1982, the party's share of the urban vote for president was nearly twice as high as in 1974. The Liberal candidate's share in 1978 fell to just over half the urban vote, and in 1982, with a defector from the Liberal Party siphoning off a large share of the urban vote, especially in Bogotá, the official Liberal nominee carried less than 40% of the urban vote. In 1982 the Liberal Party lost the presidency when it was confronted by two candidates – Betancur and the New Liberal, Luis Carlos Galán – both of whom proved more effective at mobilizing the urban vote than the official Liberal nominee, ex-President Alfonso López Michelsen. Reunited in 1986 and confronting Gómez once again as the Conservative nominee, the Liberals returned to their 1974 levels of urban support.

If we look at the actual number of votes in the cities, rather than the percentages, we see even more strikingly why different campaign tactics must be used for presidential races in urban areas than are used for the Congress. In the 1978 congressional elections, the Conservatives won 90,910 votes in Bogotá, but later the same year their candidate Betancur won 230,563, more than two and a half times what the Conservatives won. The discrepancy was almost as great in 1982 when the Conservatives won 183,906 votes in Bogotá in the congressional election but 389,268 in the presidential elections (Latorre 1986). These numbers suggest that voters in urban areas like Bogotá are much more likely to turn out to vote in presidential elections than they are in congressional elections (Hoskin 1985).

Urban voters have become the swing vote in Colombian presidential elections. The data suggest that those urban voters who turn out only for presidential elections are less loyal to one party than are other voters. This is because, in urban as well as rural districts, congressional seats are won under the same rules of intraparty competition that require candidates to differentiate themselves not only from candidates of opposing parties but also from copartisans. As we have argued, they do so by cultivating "captive voters," those who are beholden to a given vote broker for the provision of particularistic benefits. However, as Cox (1987) has noted, the cost per voter of "buying" a vote with patronage increases as the number of voters per representative increases. Politicians may cope with this high cost of patronage politics in large electorates in one of two ways: They may shift to policy-based campaigning (which implies electoral reform, abolishing intraparty competition), or they may continue to target narrow particularistic constituencies but only within an actual electorate that is much smaller than the potential electorate. In Colombian urban areas, it is the latter tactic that has been used in congressional elections, as high urban abstention rates indicate. Without a change in the means by which seats are allocated, it is unlikely that programmatic campaigning will come to characterize congressional elections even in urban areas.

However, the dynamic of presidential elections is different, since each party has just one standard-bearer. It is thus a categoric vote – one party versus the other – and unlike in congressional elections, this creates the conditions for programmatic campaigning that can reach beyond the clientele networks. To win the presidency, then, a party has the imperative of responding to the programmatic demands of urban voters. These demands include such diverse policies as: mobilizing credit to build urban housing and infrastructure (Bagley 1989; Findley 1980); greater professionalization and efficiency in the provision of public services traditionally dominated by patronage concerns; popular representation and participation as a means to remove clientele networks as mediators between citizens and government agencies;[31] environmental protection; and liberalizing trade to favor consumers. Policy demands of this sort have been central to urban mobilization in the form of *paros cívicos* (civic strikes) over recent decades (Carrillo Bedoya 1981; de la Torre 1985; Santamaría and Silva 1984). Yet the whole system, as we have described it in preceding sections, is set up to favor the kinds of particularistic policies that benefit rural interests and clientele networks at the expense of broader public goods.

The rank-and-file members thus have a collective-action problem. They must scramble for the private goods that allow them to fulfill the demands of the clientele networks that they represent in order to ensure either their own reelection or the election of the network's next candidates in Congress and for other offices. In so doing, their dominant incentive is to defect from any coalition that provides public goods for the whole party and its national constituency, such as administrative reform that would reduce patronage (Geddes 1994). However, included among these public goods are policies that must be pursued in order to attract the urban voters who are crucial to winning presidential elections. The importance of being able to deliver on at least some of the demands of urban voters has been driven home to the Liberals by their loss of the presidency in 1982 to a Conservative who successfully campaigned on issues that went to the heart of urban voters' concerns.[32]

31 For an excellent theoretical statement of this general problem and some Mexican examples, see Fox (1994).
32 Although Betancur would not have won without the presence of the New Liberal splinter

The composition of the majority party thus accounts for the difficulties we have observed in presidential–congressional relations. Although the executive's formal legislative powers are impressive, the limits placed by Congress on the exercise of those powers are even more significant to an understanding of the Colombian political process. In fact, it is precisely this "negative power" of the Congress that has led Colombian presidents to turn to the use of their extraordinary powers.

We have painted a picture of a presidency responding to urban-centered reformist demands and parties in Congress unwilling to respond to those demands except to the minimal degree necessary to win enough swing votes in urban areas to ensure victory in presidential elections. However, it would be an overstatement of our case to argue that despite the various problems we have laid out to this point, the Colombian Congress is completely incapable of dealing with important issues raised by executives' attempts to respond to popular opinion. In fact, the various factors we pointed to earlier do not require us to assume total immobilism on all issues. Rather, the problem is that many of the policies important to urban constituents desirous of change may not be those policies most central to the head of a clientelist network deeply rooted in rural Colombia. On the other hand, in some cases, a congruence of interests may emerge, leading to a successful policy initiative. This was certainly the case with the two most successful policy initiatives of the Betancur and Barco administrations: the direct election of mayors and the process of administrative decentralization. In the case of the direct election of mayors, the process that enabled these elections required an amendment to the constitution, a two-year legislative process. And the process of administrative decentralization meant a significant reorientation in budgetary control over a large national tax from the central government to municipalities. Yet despite all of the many difficulties mentioned earlier, these two particular policy goals of a reformist president successfully ran the congressional gauntlet while many, indeed most, others failed. Why?

The essential reason is that the basic, underlying goals of the executive and the supporting congressional coalitions, while different, overlapped in crucial respects. That is, Betancur and Barco pushed these pieces of legis-

---

candidate, Luis Carlos Galán, even the share of the vote gleaned by the Liberal nominee, Alfonso López Michelsen – 41% – would have been enough to win if the Conservative candidate had been relying mainly on the traditional party base rather than explicitly cultivating urban voters, judging by Gómez's 31% in 1974 and 36% in 1986. Even without a split in the Liberal ranks in 1978, Betancur was only 3% of the total national vote behind the antireform Liberal nominee, Julio Cesar Turbay Ayala. Thus, appeals to urban voters were crucial to Betancur's ability to surpass the usual Conservative vote share and, therefore, to his defeat of the Liberals in 1982.

lation as part of a general process of re-creating democracy at the local level. For these two presidents, the direct election of mayors and the financial "shot in the arm" of the transfer of a major revenue source to municipalities were part of a broader process of democratic development. Thus, the presidents perceived these two policy initiatives as part of a package of reforms intended to stimulate democratic political development in a country where political institutions were seen as decaying morally and physically. To congressional coalitions, on the other hand,[33] the primary benefit of both of these reforms is that they transformed resources that had once been under the direct or indirect administrative control of the central government (mayoral appointments, VAT revenues) and placed them under local control. In the case of the direct election of mayors, congress members had to carefully calculate whether they would gain or lose access to mayoral positions by throwing them open to a vote. Despite some misgivings, especially from those who were most advantaged by their strong regional, as opposed to local, base, a majority of the Congress went along with the proposed change. In the case of decentralization, the calculation was relatively simple (virtually everyone gained), and the proposal moved smoothly and relatively swiftly through the congressional process.

In sum, when members perceive a particular policy prescription to be in their best interest, they are capable of moving as quickly as the basic institutional rules allow. And for most members, given the set of variables we have laid out to this point, any policy that makes it easier to convert public monies into particularistic payoffs under their control will be supported. The one calculation left to be made is whether they will be able to take advantage of the new structures and institutions being created. Thus, just as Congress helped previous presidents create new state institutions that were quickly and relatively easily converted into sources of patronage, so too did Congress operate positively in the passing of major legislation that opened a new revenue source and a major municipal institution to the direct control of congressional patronage machines.

However – and this is the crucial caveat – when presidential policy initiatives attempt to reduce or curtail the use of national resources for patronage purposes, the negative power of Congress can be insurmountable. Ironically, in the two cases mentioned earlier, presidential success was a source of further deterioration in the power of the executive. Loss of indirect control over the nation's more than one thousand mayoralties, as well as loss over a major revenue source, gave future presidents even less leverage with

---

33 These conclusions are based on 1986–87 interviews with congress members in the Chamber and Senate and functionaries of the ministry of government conducted by Ron Archer.

which to make deals with a recalcitrant Congress. And in such circumstances, often the only option left to a president trying to address urban reformist demands is recourse to emergency powers. However, as noted, these powers are an imperfect means to carry out major changes in the social and political structure of the country. Presidents who have sought to use these powers to carry out such reforms have eventually had to return to Congress for support, thus applying a brake on their initiatives. Thus, the cases in which Congress has been successfully bypassed have been rare, and the "negative power" of the Congress has been a crucial restraint on presidents' ability to achieve the kinds of policy changes they have sought as a response to unmet urban needs. We now discuss in greater detail the most important case in which the Congress was bypassed: the formation of the new constitution, which may be seen, in part, as an attempt to make the political system more responsive to the mobilized demands of urban voters.

3.6. THE NEW CONSTITUTION: A SOLUTION TO THE DILEMMA?

As we have noted, the Colombian constitution that was in effect until 1991 provided for an amendment procedure that was in the exclusive hands of the congressional majority itself. We have reviewed the powers of the presidency under this constitution, powers that were enhanced considerably over the years, especially in 1968. It is ironic – and a fact rarely noted in the literature – that a constitution over which Congress had the sole amending authority should have provided for such great powers. If that is ironic, the reform of 1991 is doubly ironic in that further checks were imposed on the presidency, yet the whole process of creating a new constitutional allocation of powers was initiated not by Congress, but by the president. That is, the president sought to reduce many of the formal powers of his own office and cede greater authority over policy making to Congress, while the Congress stood in the way of such a reallocation of power. The reforms were carried out only by abrogating formal congressional sovereignty over the constitution and creating an extracongressional constituent assembly.

The ironies in this process become less puzzling when we understand the ways in which the "powerful" Colombian presidency has been crafted to serve the clientelistic interests that are represented in Congress. We have outlined such an argument in this chapter, noting that the Congress, particularly since the National Front, has been more an arena for negotiating over patronage and other private goods than a forum for the representation and conciliation of national public policy debates.

In this section, we discuss the process by which the Constituent Assembly was established in 1990–91 to draft the new constitution and account for the outcomes that we have identified in the preceding sections on presidential powers and the electoral system.

THE PROCESS OF CONSTITUTIONAL REFORM

We reviewed early in the chapter a series of reform efforts that failed. The last one was in 1988, when the Congress rejected a package of constitutional reforms similar to what ultimately resulted from the Constituent Assembly.[34] After that defeat, President Barco changed course and relied on state of siege powers. Among the defeated provisions was one that would have allowed for a plebiscite as a means to reform the constitution. Determined to proceed, President Barco and Minister of Government Gaviria helped to promote a proreform student movement in the run-up to the 1990 elections. This movement, fueled by the assassination in August 1989 of the popular Luis Carlos Galán – who was sure to be elected president in 1990 – sponsored an unofficial plebiscite on the day of congressional elections in March 1990. More than a million voters took the initiative to deposit slips of paper advocating a constituent assembly into their ballot envelopes (Shugart 1992a).

After the student-sponsored unofficial referendum, President Barco used his state of siege powers to decree an "official" referendum in conjunction with the May 1990 presidential election. The proposal before voters, to allow for a special constituent assembly to reform the constitution, passed with over 88% of the vote. This whole process appears absolutely unconstitutional, given that the extant constitution gave Congress alone the power to reform it. Yet the Supreme Court narrowly upheld it on the grounds that the state of siege powers permitted the president in times of "abnormality" to respond to the "primary constituency" (López Villafañe 1990), as represented in the popular clamor for a constituent assembly.

Continuing the liberal use of the state of siege powers, President Gaviria, after concluding accords with the major political parties and movements, decreed that a constituent assembly would be elected in a single nationwide district of 70 seats, instead of in the regional districts used to elect the Congress. Members of the Congress or the executive were not permitted to run without first resigning their posts. By cross-party agree-

34 Gaviria was at that time minister of government, responsible for shepherding presidential initiatives through Congress.

ment at the start of the Constituent Assembly, members of the Assembly were to be prohibited from running for Congress until the second election held under the new constitution that the Assembly would enact. Thus, attempts were made to insulate the constitution writers from "normal" politics.

Barco and other party leaders also tied the constitutional reform project to the process of demobilizing the country's guerrilla insurgent groups, such as the infamous M-19 (Shugart 1992a, 1992b). The M-19 had never participated in congressional elections and could be expected to favor a political system oriented away from those particularistic, regional interests that it had defined as "corrupt" and antidemocratic. Similarly, it could be expected to seek a new constituency of consumers and other unorganized interests disaffected with the old practices. Thus, a de facto alliance resulted between the M-19 and sections of the Liberal Party tied to Gaviria (Cepeda n.d.), as well as breakaway Conservatives grouped in the so-called Movement for National Salvation. This was a natural (if ironic) result of these groups' common pursuit of a reorientation of Colombian political life away from excessive dependence upon the vote-delivering ability of relatively autonomous party rank and file.

As Table 3.3 shows, Liberals won more seats (24) than any other party or movement in the election, but a far lower share than what they normally win in congressional elections (including subsequent ones). As is obvious, the representation in the Constituent Assembly was indeed rather different from that of the Congress that had been elected earlier the same year. The list of the Democratic Alliance/M-19 was the largest single list, given the Liberals' usual fragmentation among numerous lists (none of which won more than three seats). More than half of the M-19's votes came from urban areas (Pinzón de Lewin and Rothlisberger 1991). The National Salvation Movement, an alliance of dissident Conservatives and Liberals led by Alvaro Gómez, a former Conservative presidential candidate, won 11 seats.[35] Gómez campaigned against the corrupt clientelistic "establishment," even though he was a product of it; he made the case that he was in the best position to reform the system from the inside. Most of his support came without the help of the local Conservative political machines with which he had once been associated. By contrast, the "official" Conservative list of

35 In an irony that almost qualifies for magical realism, Gómez had once been held hostage by the M-19. In 1991, he and M-19 leader Navarro shared the three-man presidency of the Constituent Assembly, along with Horacio Serpa, a Liberal. Serpa, although in many ways an old-fashioned clientelist, was widely recognized as being from a reformist wing of his party. Thus, all three copresidents can be seen as representing trends away from clientelism.

Table 3.3. *Colombian election results, 1974–91*

Election	Liberal %v	Seats	Conservative %v	Seats	New Liberal (Galán) %v	Seats	Patriotic Union %v	Seats	Democratic Alliance/ M-19 %v	Seats	National Salvation Movement %v	Seats	Others %v	Seats
April 1974														
House	55.7	113	32.0	66									12.3	20
Senate	55.8	66	32.0	37									12.2	9
President	56.3		31.4										12.3	
February 1978														
House	55.2	111	39.4	83									5.4	5
Senate	55.2	62	40.0	49									4.8	1
June 1978														
President	49.5		46.6										3.9	
March 1982														
House	56.4	115	40.3	82									3.3	2
Senate	56.3	63	40.3	49									3.4	2
May 1982														
President	41.0		46.8		10.9								1.3	

Table 3.3 (*cont.*)

Election	Liberal		Conservative		New Liberal (Galán)		Patriotic Union		Democratic Alliance/ M-19		National Salvation Movement		Others	
	%v	Seats	%v	Seats	%v	Seats	%v	Seats	%v	Seats	%v	Seats	%v	Seats
March 1986														
House	47.7	98	37.0	80	6.6	7	2.0	3					6.7	11
Senate	49.3	58	37.0	43	6.6	6	1.5	2					5.6	5
May 1986														
President	58.2		35.8				4.5						1.5	
March 1990														
House	59.1	119	31.3	62									9.2	17
Senate	58.5	66	31.2	38			0.4	1					10.3	10
May 1990														
President	48.2		12.3						12.6		23.9		3.0	
December 1990 Constituent Assembly	29.0	25	11.5	9			2.6	2	26.8	19	15.5	11	14.6	4
October 1991														
House	50.9	87	17.6	27			2.0	3	10.1	13	6.8	11	12.6	20
Senate	52.5	56	8.0	9			1.6	1	10.5	9	5.4	8	22.0	17

March 1994

	%v	seats	%v	seats	%v	seats	%v	seats	%v	seats	%v	seats
House	49.5	88	20.8	40	0.8	0	2.9	1	1.0	1	25.0	31
Senate	50.7	56	18.8	20			2.7	0	1.9	2	25.9	22

May–June 1994

	%v		%v		%v		%v		%v		%v	
President (first round)	45.2		44.9				3.8				6.1	
President (runoff)	50.4		49.1									

Note: Special seats reserved for minorities (two in the House for blacks and two in the Senate for indigenous people) in 1991 and 1994 are not included.

%v refers to the percentage of votes in the popular election. Percentages do not include blank and null votes.

151

Misael Pastrana and other "independent" Conservative lists, as well as many Liberals lists, were overwhelmingly dependent on rural vote brokers.

The decree that initiated the constitutional reform process stipulated that the Constituent Assembly would be sovereign. A new constitution would be passed by a majority of the Assembly's membership. There would be no referendum, no presidential veto, no vote on the new constitution in the Congress, and no judicial review of the outcome. Therefore, given the substantial representation of "new" forces,[36] there was an opportunity for the Constituent Assembly to produce a constitution that would represent a sharp break with the old political system.

Although the process by which the Constituent Assembly was elected would seem to have created an opportunity for radical changes, the outcome was in many ways disappointing to those who expected major change. Presidential power has been reduced, such that Colombia is now in the category of proactive (rather than potentially dominant) presidencies, along the lines of Brazil. One of the most important constitutional reforms for our purposes concerns the new Senate, as well as provisions aimed at increasing the "institutionalization" of political parties. We discuss these reforms next and assess their likely impact on the ability of Congress to sustain policy-based coalitions.

CHANGES IN CONGRESSIONAL INCENTIVES

The Senate is now elected in a single, 100-seat district.[37] Obviously the national district for the Senate means that the malapportionment of the former Congress is corrected in the upper house. With no districting, votes cast in predominantly urban departments are no longer less proportionally represented than those cast in predominantly rural departments. More important, the nationwide Senate district creates new opportunities for candidates (or, rather, the heads of lists) to exploit in attracting the votes needed to win representation. Under the prereform departmental-district system for Senate elections (and continuing in the lower house), a member necessarily represented voters in only one department. Under the new rules, it is still possible for a senator to concentrate his or her votes in just one department, but it is also possible for a candidate to pursue a dispersal strategy:

36 Besides those mentioned in the preceding paragraph, new forces included a Christian evangelical movement, indigenous groups, and a student movement.

37 Additionally, two more seats are set aside in a special district for lists representing indigenous peoples. In both 1991 and 1994, two indigenous lists were represented through the principal district as well.

garnering small shares of the votes in multiple departments that aggregate across departmental boundaries to reach the number of votes needed to win election.

The strategy of dispersed votes is most beneficial to nonclientelistic parties and movements that could not hope to break the hold of monied groups under the system of district-based allocation but that can attract minority support in many departments. For instance, the list Laicos por Colombia won a Senate seat in 1991 (with just under 50,000 votes, 0.95% of the total), despite having less than 8,500 votes in its strongest department (Boyacá). Several other lists won seats with similarly dispersed electoral constituencies. By contrast, the list of a Conservative, Fabio Valencia Cossio,[38] had an almost identical vote total, but more than three-fourths of his votes came from one department (Antioquia). Despite their similar vote totals, under the previous system only the one with the regionally concentrated votes would have been represented.

Even in the major parties, the new structure of opportunities is beginning to change how heads of lists mobilize votes. Because it is now unnecessary to concentrate one's votes in one department, sectors within the party that are not in favor with the local clientele networks can join with similarly situated groups in other localities and win seats. They can base their campaigns on "pubic goods" appeals; for instance, some major-party candidates in 1994 sought to build personal reputations for being pro-environment (*El Tiempo* 1994a). Other reputations can be built on other issues that are more consistent with programmatic coalition building than with the regional particularism that dominated both houses in the past. Dispersal strategies do not guarantee more programmatic campaigning, but the opportunity to collect votes across regions is a necessary precondition for making such appeals.

Table 3.4 presents some data on how important strategies of nonconcentrated support have been in the nationwide district thus far. The table shows the average percentage of and variance in the vote delivered to candidates (heads of lists) by whichever departmental electorate gave the candidate the plurality of his or her own votes. Under the old system, these figures were necessarily 100%, with no variance. Under the new Senate rules, it is plausible that some members would continue to be overwhelmingly dependent on one department, while others would disperse their support across many districts.

In the 1991 Senate election, the range of senators' dependence on their strongest departments was from 12.5% (the list of the Movimiento de Sal-

---

38 Running under the label Fuerza Progresista, he later rejoined the Conservatives.

Table 3.4. *Percentage of senators' votes that came from the department in which the list won most of its votes*

	1991					1994				
	Number of Senators	Lists	Percentage of list's votes that came from department where list won most of its votes			Number of Senators	Lists	Percentage of list's votes that came from department where list won most of its votes		
				Range					Range	
Party			Mean[a]	Low	High			Mean[a]	Low	High
Liberal	56	50	69.1 (19.5)	25.4	92.8	56	54	74.3 (16.0)	32.4	95.3
Conservative	27	16	60.6 (28.4)	12.5	95.3	31	30	74.7 (20.0)	39.1	97.8
MSN	5	1	12.5			2	2	59.9 (15.3)	44.6	75.2
NFD	8	1	23.9			5	5	71.5 (18.8)	41.3	97.8
AD/M-19	9	1	15.2			0				
Others	9	9	38.9 (24.0)	15.6	84.5	13	13	43.5 (26.7)	7.7	87.9
All senators	100	75	62.1 (25.1)	12.5	95.3	100	97	70.3 (21.7)	7.7	97.8

[a]Standard deviation in parentheses

vación Nacional [MSN], which elected five senators) to 95.3% (a traditional Conservative from the department of Valle). The average, as shown in Table 3.4, was 62.1% in 1991 and 70.3% in 1994.[39] The Conservatives and Liberals remain somewhat more dependent on candidates who concentrate their support than does the Senate as a whole – not surprising given that these are the parties that thrived under the old departmental-district system – but the substantial variance indicates that many members of the traditional parties have already managed to use dispersal strategies successfully.

The most important indicator of the extent to which more dispersed vote-garnering strategies matter is that there were 13 Liberal senators elected in 1991 and 21 (of 56 total) in 1994 who would not have won seats had they been dependent only on the votes they won in their strongest departments. That is, the Liberal Party would not have held a majority in the Senate had it not been for the attractiveness of some of its candidates outside their home departments. Thus, the Liberal Party has already seen that its majority aspirations depend on new kinds of constituencies.

In the Conservative Party in 1991, the effect of the Senate reform was even more dramatic. Two lists of conservatives, running under new labels, Gómez's MSN and Andrés Pastrana's New Democratic Force (NFD), each won dispersed votes across the new nationwide district and won five and eight seats, respectively. The demonstrated success of Pastrana in a nationwide election led to his being nominated as the common candidate by the reunited Conservative factions in advance of the 1994 presidential election, which the Conservatives nearly won. We can expect the national Senate district to continue serving as a useful "proving ground" to aspiring national leaders, who will seek to build national followings.

If the upper house is now more conducive to new styles of campaigning, the lower house remains traditional in its composition. New districts have been created to represent thinly populated areas that previously were absorbed within larger districts. Where before there were 199 seats divided among 26 districts, for an average district magnitude of around eight, now there are 161 seats in 33 districts,[40] for an average magnitude of around five. Reducing the magnitude of the preexisting districts works to the advantage of larger factions in the dominant parties. The reduced number of

---

39 That the figure is slightly higher in 1994 is less significant than the fact that both of these figures show that a substantial number of senators have dispersed support. The 1991 result is lower primarily because of three lists (combining for 22 seats) that each won from 5 to 9 seats. In 1994, as shown in Table 3.1, only three senators were elected who were not heads of lists.

40 There are two more seats set aside for representatives of the black community, elected from a nationwide constituency.

"serious" contenders for seats means that fewer members will be beholden
to very small personal-support groups. This was already apparent in 1991,
when the median percentage of the district-level vote won by the last candidate elected in a district was 11.7%, up from 8.8% in 1990. However,
the new thinly populated districts have the opposite effect, allowing candidates with local sway over a minuscule number of voters access to the
Congress.[41] In fact, while the Senate is no longer malapportioned because
of its single district, the House of Representatives is vastly more malapportioned than either house was previously: The ratio of most underrepresented to most overrepresented district is 39:1 (compared with around 3.5:1
before).[42] Even so, Bogotá is less underrepresented than it was before the
reform: With 14.7% of the eligible electorate (and 11.2% of actual voters
in 1994), it now has 11.2% of the seats in the House.

The outcome in terms of the structure of representation can thus be
seen as a compromise between the clientelistic and reformist tendencies,
both of which were well represented in the Constituent Assembly. The
previous system was one in which both houses were elected from districts,
with rural areas overrepresented, and in which only candidates with access
to clientelistic resources had much chance of winning. The new system
contains one house that resembles the Constituent Assembly itself and is
vastly more favorable to nonclientelistic representation than the previous
setup and another house that compensates rural clientelistic interests by
enhancing their representation. Both houses must agree to legislation, constitutional amendments, or censures of cabinet ministers, and the less clientelistic Senate has been given some new exclusive powers.[43] Therefore, those
new movements, as well as sectors of the traditional parties that seek to
break out of clientelistic practices, can no longer be ignored. They have
institutionalized veto power, and that power will grow if, as is likely, the
trend toward less concentrated constituencies for senators continues.

Besides the constituencies of senators another factor that might enhance
possibilities for greater policy focus in Colombian parties concerns public

41 In 1991, in three districts, a candidate was elected with under 1,000 votes. In the median
    district, around 12,000 votes was sufficient (compared with just over 21,500 in 1990).
    Even accounting for the lower voter turnout and the increased number of lists in 1991
    – both being factors that would depress the number of votes needed to win – many
    members of the new House represent an extremely low number of voters.
42 In comparative terms, this means that what is considered the upper house in Colombia
    would effectively be the lower house – the house that represents the population – while
    the Colombian lower house resembles other countries' upper houses, in that it over-
    represents the less populous districts.
43 The president can extend a state of internal commotion (the successor to the state of
    siege) beyond 180 days only with the prior consent of the Senate.

finance and the possibility of parties gaining some control over the use of their own labels. In March 1994, the Constitutional Court approved provisions of a law on political parties (Law 130), which makes a number of advances in the institutionalization of Colombian parties. Key provisions of the law include the establishment of a fund for the public financing of parties. Thus, it implements an idea that has been considered in Colombia for over a decade – part of Betancur's defeated reform proposal called for public campaign financing. Under Law 130, the National Electoral Court, a body given greater independence under the 1991 constitution, oversees the disbursement of funds to all political parties with legal registration or with representation in the Congress. Each such party will receive postelection compensation in proportion to its congressional representation in addition to a minimum subvention. Parties can determine on their own how to distribute funds among their candidates. These provisions greatly reduce the dependence of members of Congress on their own (or their clientele networks') fund-raising efforts and give party leaders greater sway over the activities of the rank and file; therefore, they represent important moves toward enhancing the integrity of party labels.

The law also grants parties for the first time the authority to sanction members of Congress and even expel them from the party if they deviate from party directives in matters of "ethics." In a historic turn of events, the Liberal Party in December 1994 expelled a member who as a congress member had proposed to amend a bill on education in a manner that would have benefited only one university – one that he himself had founded (*El Tiempo* 1994c). The party also used the new law to serve notice that it would not tolerate dissident candidacies by party members in gubernatorial races (*El Tiempo* 1994b). The law permits parties to bar expelled members from using the party name in future elections. Because the law also makes each party name and symbol proprietary and requires that newly registered parties have names that are clearly distinct from existent parties, dissidents can no longer launch candidacies under names that resemble that of the party that expelled them.

The new party law thus represents a delegation by the rank and file (given that it had to be passed by Congress) to party leaders of new levers with which to bring coherence to the organization. However, it is important to note that the result will not likely be the highly cohesive, disciplined parties found in some other countries, but rather more incremental changes in the direction of greater discipline on core issues. As long as intraparty competition continues, candidates will have the incentive to establish personal reputations. As a result, the public face of the party will appear anything but cohesive. Although the increasing control over finance and over the label might theoretically lead to each party's presenting one list per district – thereby eliminating intraparty competition – we expect multiple lists to continue for the foreseeable future, since individual party members and vote brokers have invested too much in rank-and-file autonomy to let go of it. Indeed, as is clear from Figure 3.1, the number of lists has risen over time, signaling increasing intraparty competition. Even if we confine ourselves to the most recent period and to the lower house, where the change in district magnitude has been less dramatic than in the Senate, the number of lists just within the Liberal Party has grown from 175 in 1990 to 237 in 1991 and 276 in 1994. Obviously the authority to deny the party label to aspiring candidates is not among the new powers delegated to the leadership. So, while the changing party system may be one in which old clientelistic bosses' power is reduced somewhat and egregious breaches of discipline are less likely than before to go unsanctioned, intraparty competition remains fierce. Thus, even if presidents continue to have copartisan legislative majorities, we can expect their effective partisan powers to remain quite low.

3.7. CONCLUSION

In this chapter we have noted that there is a dichotomy between the apparently vast powers of the presidency and the actual weakness of presidential authority in carrying out reformist policies. In spite of their powers, presidents have typically been thwarted when they attempt policy initiatives. The reason we have identified is that the powers have been crafted in such a way as to serve the interests of the clientelistic rank-and-file party members. Thus, it is Congress that seeks to preserve the status quo, and the president's proactive powers are a limited tool for attempting to take the Congress beyond the rather narrow limits that it places on policy making.

Because of the structuring by Congress of a principal–agent relationship in which the president has discretionary power only within limits set by Congress, when Liberal Presidents Barco and Gaviria sought to enable the Colombian political system to carry out long-delayed socioeconomic reforms, they attacked the very allocation of presidential powers itself. Presidents in Colombia have tended to be more liberal (i.e., in favor of social and political reforms) than Congress because of their election in a nationwide constituency in contrast to Congress's election in regional districts that overrepresent conservative rural areas. We have argued that the Colombian presidency, because of its proactive powers, is able to push policy in a reformist direction and that Congress tolerates presidents' attempts to respond to reformist pressures emanating from their more urban constituency because the majority Liberal Party needs to be able to maintain its control over the presidency in order to continue to have access to patronage. However, we have also argued that there is a distinct irony in the Colombian case. Before 1991, the Colombian presidency's powers placed the case in the "potentially dominant" category, yet presidents were seldom in fact able to dominate. The more conservative Congress and party bosses were able to keep the presidency – and social reform – in check. Moreover, when Presidents Barco and Gaviria wanted to pursue sweeping reforms in the institutional structure, they actually sought to reduce the president's decree and emergency powers. They recognized, as did even much of the rank and file, that the reforms they sought – such as sustained trade liberalization, relieving the bottleneck of urban construction, and reincorporating Colombian guerrilla groups into civil politics – could be achieved only in partnership with a congress that was equipped to tackle such weighty national issues. The existing Congress, being a place for the allocation of patronage rather than for articulating policy options, was not up to such a task.

If meaningful reform meant making members of Congress more accountable and thus reducing the temptation of presidents and congresses alike to resort to extraordinary presidential powers, does the new constitution accomplish these aims? The evidence at this early date is mixed but not highly encouraging. The reforms to the electoral process and to the Congress itself have moved in the direction of less particularism, and parties may be gradually asserting more collective control over recalcitrant members, but thus far the steps taken have been modest. As long as elections continue to be characterized by intense intraparty competition for congressional seats, the scramble for private goods will continue to be the dominant incentive of most members, and presidents will continue to be hampered by low partisan powers.

PRESIDENTIAL BEHAVIOR IN A SYSTEM WITH STRONG PARTIES: VENEZUELA, 1958–1995

Brian F. Crisp

4.1. INTRODUCTION

In Venezuela the party system has been dominated for most of the democratic era by two, highly disciplined, centrist political parties. Because parties have been so well organized and disciplined, they are important for understanding the nomination process, elections, the behavior of legislators, and even the relative success of interest groups. Scott Mainwaring's analysis of Brazil illustrates how the apparently significant, formal powers of the president can be stymied by the existence of multiple, undisciplined parties. In Venezuela, the converse is true. Presidents can overcome the relatively sparse formal powers of their office, particularly during majority governments, and interbranch immobilism is rarely a problem. Disciplined parties limit immobilism because majority presidents can almost always count on the support of their parties and because minority presidents are better able to form stable, postelection coalitions. When presidents cannot count on support in Congress, immobilism is still unlikely to result because presidents have virtually no reactive powers with which to thwart the legislature's will and clog the process. A major theme of this volume is that the interaction of constitutionally allocated powers and partisan powers is central to understanding presidentialism in Latin America. In particular, presidential strength is highly conditioned by the partisan composition of the government, which is itself the result of a number of factors including electoral regulations and timing. In Venezuela, party politics, including characteristics internal to the parties themselves and those inherent in the electoral system, affect the president's use of his or her constitutionally allocated powers in a complex and intertwining manner. Presidents' exemption from party discipline and their freedom from concerns of immediate reelection increase their license to govern as they see fit. Two of the most important incentives for being responsible – one to their party (internal regulations requiring discipline) and one to the electorate as a whole (immediate reelection) – have been removed.

Examining this interaction will reveal why some of the regime characteristics that were so important to the original consolidation of democratic rule in Venezuela are also essential for understanding its recent difficulties. Multiple, highly malleable parties may complicate democratic consolidation, while a few, highly disciplined parties may make it easier, but this strength can become rigidity. The relatively long duration of democracy in Venezuela gives us the opportunity to see what happens in a system where consensus building and protection of the democratic regime were often the primary goals taking precedence over incorporating new groups and resolving difficult conflicts. The contrast between Brazil and Venezuela further illustrates that many of these critical features are not inherent in presidential regimes but are instead characteristics of presidentialism as it developed in the two countries – and in the case of some features, elsewhere in Latin America.

The outline of this chapter is as follows. In Part 4.2, I will offer a brief overview of Venezuelan democracy. I will then analyze in Part 4.3 the party system within which politicians, including presidents and legislators, operate. I will focus on parties' relationships with interest groups, the central place for parties in electoral laws, and the discipline exercised by party elites over their congressional delegations. These characteristics not only are important for understanding the current situation, but were also critical for the consolidation of democracy after 1958. I will then briefly describe the informal powers available to the president in Part 4.4. These powers come from both the office and his position within a party. In Part 4.5, I describe the limited constitutionally allocated powers available to the president, and Part 4.6 focuses on presidents' use of their powers across administrations, paying special attention to the partisan composition of the legislature and the impact of relatively few, highly disciplined parties. In Part 4.7, I show how the combination of institutional and organizational factors in Venezuela has led to rigidity and, recently, to instability. I contrast two contradictory reform efforts that seek changes in the formal powers of the president and the party system as means to address the current crisis. I offer some general conclusions about the difference between consolidating and deepening democracy in Part 4.8.

4.2. VENEZUELAN DEMOCRACY

Democratic rule was not even attempted in Venezuela until 1945, and it lasted only until 1948 (the democratic era from 1945 to 1948 is commonly referred to as the *trienio*). Party organization had begun in the 1930s and picked up momentum after the death of General Juan Vicente Gómez, who ruled the country from 1908 until his death 27 years later. His successors, General Eleazar López Contreras and especially General Isaías Medina Angarita, were somewhat more tolerant, and as a result, both labor and party organization grew. In June 1945 a group of middle-level military officials contacted the leaders of Acción Democrática (AD), the left-of-center political party with the largest popular base (which was in fact by then nationwide), about their plans for a coup. The groups worked together to overthrow the government in October, and AD assumed power until the party overwhelmingly won elections a year later that featured five major parties, including the Comité de Organización Política Electoral Independiente (COPEI) – the Christian democratic party that would remain AD's primary rival throughout the democratic era. It was AD's overwhelming popularity and its unwillingness to compromise that eventually turned other civilian groups, the church, and the military against it. The overthrow of democratic rule and 10 more years of hard dictatorship drove home a single lesson to civilian political elites of all parties – democratic rule could not be taken for granted, and consensual support for democracy as a system had to be placed before partisan gain.

The current democratic era began in 1958, when the dictator, Lt. Col. Marcos Pérez Jiménez, was chased from the country. An interim *junta de gobierno*, initially made up of military figures but later primarily civilians, governed for an interim period until elections could be called. Again, AD won control of the presidency and both houses of Congress, but unlike during the *trienio*, this time its actions were more constrained. The transition period and early democratic rule were characterized by the signing of a number of formal pacts pledging mutual respect and support for democratic rule. The signatories to this series of agreements included not only the political parties, but also business, labor, the church, and the military. The consensual nature of the transition was then institutionalized through a decision-making style that called for consultation with civil society, primarily business and labor, through ad hoc commissions, the decentralized public administration, and other less formal contacts.

The early democratic era was characterized by leftist insurrection, occasional coup attempts, and a fragmented party system (see Table 4.1). But, by the middle to late 1960s, armed challenges to the regime had come to an end, and in the 1970s the party system consolidated around AD and COPEI. The agroexport economy of the first half of the century had been replaced by an economy dominated by petroleum exports, which quickly became the primary source of government revenue. The population became more urbanized, better educated, and employed in the service sector, and the traditional parties were capable of meeting its demands for participation. Venezuelan democracy remained stable, contradicting the trend toward bureaucratic authoritarian regimes in the region.

Venezuela began to show signs of strain in the mid-1980s, and by the late 1980s both political and economic crises were evident. Not surprisingly the two coincided, with the economic situation, after the crash in the world oil market, exacerbating political difficulties. Carlos Andrés Pérez of AD was reelected in 1988, but instead of the glory days of the oil boom that had accompanied his previous term, he brought with him a neoliberal, austerity package and plans for privatization. The freeing of consumer prices, especially bus fares, ignited public riots, and after some initial inaction the government called in the military, which responded with a heavy hand. With the legitimacy of the administration and perhaps the democratic regime more generally in decline (Crisp, Levine, and Rey 1994; Levine and Crisp 1994), two military coups were attempted in 1992. Pérez was removed from office in 1993 ostensibly on corruption charges, but his unpopular economic policies probably played a role as well. Constitutional procedures were followed to name an interim president, and regular elections were held, as scheduled, in December 1993.

Civil society had grown more complex than the classic business–labor split, but many groups found it difficult to get access to government decision making without subjugating their demands to those of one of the traditional parties (party penetration of other groups is discussed in greater detail in Part 4.3). The 1993 elections were marked by a significant drop in voter turnout and increased support for parties other than AD and COPEI. They remained the number one and number two parties, respectively, in the Chamber of Deputies and the Senate but with the smallest combined seat total ever (see Table 4.1). For the first time, the candidate of a third party won the presidency, though it was Rafael Caldera, a founding member and former president from COPEI. The parties supporting him, a coalition labeled Convergencia and the long-time number three party, Movimiento al Socialismo (MAS), also did well in congressional elections. Perhaps more lasting as an electoral phenomenon, the left-of-center La Causa Radical (LCR), or Causa R, with its origins among the industrial workers of Guaina in the eastern part of the country, also did well in presidential and congressional elections.

Even this brief overview indicates that the interaction of the president's limited, constitutionally allocated powers with his informal powers, interest-group representation, electoral laws, internal party regulations, partisan composition of the government, and the party system more broadly is important for understanding the successful transition to democracy, the stable functioning of the system for decades, and the recent crisis. Before examining presidents' use of their informal and formal powers since 1958, it is necessary to offer a more detailed analysis of the party system that has been so important in Venezuelan democratic history.

4.3. THE PARTY SYSTEM

Political parties have been very important in the history of Venezuelan democracy, and many of the existing parties in fact preceded democratic rule by decades. AD, the dominant, multiclass, center-left party, began organizing in the 1930s, though democratic rule was not attempted for the first time until 1945, and the current democratic era was not inaugurated until 1958. Its primary rival, COPEI, the center-right, Christian democratic party, was formed in 1946. While these two parties have always been important, other parties have been significant electoral forces, especially at the beginning of the democratic era and very recently (see Table 4.1). The early formation and existence of parties before democratization is important because it means that parties were able to penetrate groups that were formed after them (including labor unions, for example) and that party elites were responsible for the constitutional design of the democratic system itself. As a result, sources of party strength have become both informally and formally ensconced in the system. These sources and indicators of strength can be divided into three categories: (1) penetration of other groups, (2) position in the electoral system, and (3) discipline of members of Congress.

PENETRATION OF OTHER GROUPS

Partisan politics characterizes much of Venezuelan life, including the internal politics of many interest groups, especially labor unions. AD has typically come out on top in the heated battles for partisan control over the Confederation of Venezuelan Workers (CTV), the largest umbrella organization of labor unions in Venezuela, as well as the individual unions of which it is composed. But unions are not the only groups to have been penetrated. Incorporation or infiltration also extends to student groups, peasants, professional associations, neighborhood groups, and others. It has been notably absent in business groups like the Federation of Chambers of Commerce (FEDECAMARAS). The list of those officially "included" and those that remain autonomous is strikingly similar to the hegemonic party system in Mexico.

Party competition within these groups may originate in other ways than originally being formed by party loyalists. In addition, autonomously established groups may be "taken over" as members of a variety of parties enter the groups' membership and turn competition for their leadership position into a partisan affair. Likewise, independent leaders in interest groups may be coopted by parties offering government or party employment and other benefits available to the entire group. Finally, parties may enter an area of organizational life by founding parallel structures that have the advantage of party and possibly government spoils. Eckstein (1977) describes a very similar phenomenon in Mexico's one-party system and shows how this kind of incorporation strengthens a party's grip on the political system and serves to control demands on the government.

Venezuelan parties seek control over interest groups for a variety of reasons. First, a successful campaign within a group is often heralded as a prediction of the outcome of future, even more important races. Second, at election time groups can endorse a policy position, mobilize their membership to vote, or serve as volunteers (Coppedge 1994:31). Most importantly, party control over interest groups is critical in the policy-making process itself. Most Venezuelan legislation is drafted in the executive branch, and the government creates a number of commissions that allow interest groups to advise it and even participate in the drafting of legislation (Crisp 1994). The institutionalization of interest-group participation in the executive branch is in a sense a two-way street. On the one hand, it gives interest groups and the parties that control them an opportunity to influence policy. On the other hand, it gives the president a chance to influence the groups themselves and to strengthen his position in the policy-making process relative to the legislature. It is the president, not the legislature, that has the institutional structure capable of interacting with organized civil society. I will return to this theme in Part 4.4.

Returning to the analogy with Mexico, Weldon's chapter shows how the president's control over the nearly all-encompassing organizational

Table 4.1. *Electoral results for the executive and legislative branches (for parties receiving at least 10% of the vote for any race that year)*

President	Popular vote in the presidential race[a] (percent)	Effective no. of parties in presidential elections[b]	Seats in the Chamber of Deputies (percent)	Seats in the Senate (percent)	Effective no. of parties in congressional elections[b]
Betancourt (AD)				
1959–64				
AD	49	2.8	55	63	2.9
URD	31		26	22	
COPEI	15		14	12	
Leoni (AD)				
1964–69				
AD	33	4.7	37	47	4.8
COPEI	20		21	17	
URD	18		16	15	
IPFN	16		12	11	
Caldera (COPEI)				
1969–74				
COPEI	29	4.8	28	31	6.0
AD	27		31	37	
MEP	17		12	10	
URD	12		8	6	
CCN	—		10	8	
Pérez (AD)				
1974–79				
AD	49	2.7	51	60	3.4
COPEI	35		32	28	

Herrera (COPEI) 1979–84					
COPEI	45	2.5	42	48	3.1
AD	43		44	48	
Lusinchi (AD) 1984–89					
AD	55	2.4	56	64	2.9
COPEI	33		30	32	
Pérez (AD) 1989–93[c]					
AD	53	2.3	48	48	3.3
COPEI	40		33	43	
Caldera (Conv./MAS) 1994–99					
AD	23	5.2	27	32	5.6
COPEI	22		26	28	
Causa R	22		20	18	
Conv.	17		13	20	
MAS	11		11	2	

Note: See Appendix 4.1 for a list of acronyms and abbreviations.

[a]Individual candidates may be supported by more than one party. For example, in the 1993 elections Caldera received 30.5% of the vote – 17% from Convergencia, 11% from MAS, and another 2.5% from smaller parties.

[b]Effective number of parties is $N = \Sigma v_i^2$, where v_i is the fractional share of votes for the ith party.

[c]Pérez's second term was shortened by his indictment on charges of corruption.

Source: Rey (1994) and my own calculations based on Consejo Supremo Electoral figures.

power of the Partido Revolucionario Institucional (PRI) greatly increases his power, but, though Mexico and Venezuela share the politicization of interest groups, it must be remembered that Venezuela is not a hegemonic party system. The competition among parties within interest groups moderates the degree of cooptation that takes place. Interest-group demands are often subjugated to party interests, but the competition among parties for control of these groups in a truly democratic system means that the role of a group can change with each government or its own internal elections. For example, when AD controls both the government and the CTV, laborers may be less capable of pressing for their demands because union leaders are responsive to the party. On the other hand, if the president is from COPEI, labor unrest and conflict with the government may be exacerbated because the union is ruled by AD. Thus, co-optation of an interest group increases the power of the party that wins the internal competition for its own leadership posts, but not necessarily for the country's presidency. Unlike Mexico, where the PRI dominated both government and interest groups for so long, in Venezuela control over the government and interest groups is changeable.

THE ELECTORAL SYSTEM

The electoral rules in Venezuela greatly affect the number of major parties, the likelihood of majority governments, and the strength of the party leadership as opposed to that of individual candidates or rank-and-file members. The system of representation, relative timing of elections, pooling of votes, control over the nomination process, and control over the order in which candidates appear on the closed party list all strengthen the parties' grip on the political arena.

The president is elected for a five-year term by plurality in direct popular elections without any intervening role to be played by an electoral college. Since 1958, eight presidents have been elected without significant abnormalities in the election process, and control over the office has changed from one party to another five times (see Table 4.1). There have been five presidents from AD, two from COPEI, and one independent supported by a coalition of small parties (Rafael Caldera). Presidential elections occur simultaneously with congressional elections and thus exert a strong pull toward a two-party system, despite the use of proportional representation in congressional elections.

Until 1993 both chambers of Congress were elected by the same ballot. Voters made only two choices in national elections. The ballot for electing presidents is filled with what were known as "large cards." A color-coded card representing each party appeared on the ballot with the party's name, the party's logo, and a portrait of the candidate it was supporting (often the same candidate is supported by more than one party). A "small card" included the same color-coded rectangle for each party, and it was used to elect a party to Congress. The single ballot served to elect both the Chamber of Deputies and the Senate. The parties were responsible for preparing closed lists of candidates prior to the election, and voters chose among the parties. The nature of the ballots and the use of closed lists ensured a key role for party elites. They were responsible for determining which candidates appeared on their list and the order in which they appeared. This not only influenced the voters' perceptions but also the loyalty of members of Congress. Until 1993 (the changes instituted then are discussed later), legislators had no incentives to cater to a local constituency. In essence they had no local constituencies as districts were statewide. Instead, they were loyal to the elites who gave them access to the party label and determined the order in which they appeared on the ballot.

Senators are chosen by proportional representation, but given the district magnitude and the d'Hondt formula for representation any tendency to promote a multiparty system is overridden. Each state and federal territory elects two senators. The party that receives the highest vote total gets at least one of those seats. If it has a vote total double that of its nearest competitor it receives both seats. Otherwise, the other senate seat from that state or territory goes to the second-place party. The d'Hondt system discourages both significant fragmentation, given that there are only two seats in each district, and single-party dominance, given that capturing both seats is more difficult than achieving a plurality in two distinct races. There is, however, an additional provision that does promote minor parties. If a party receives 2.38% of the national vote total, it is given one of the "additional" seats in the Senate. This also means that the overall size of the Senate can vary from election to election. As the data in Table 4.1 indicate, AD and COPEI have on average controlled 81% of the seats in the Senate, with their combined percentage ranging from 60 to 96%.

The Chamber of Deputies is elected by proportional representation as well, and the number of seats available in each state and federal territory is large enough that the expected dispersion of representation does occur, moderated by the pull of simultaneous, plurality presidential elections. As in the Senate, a national formula is used to ensure that small parties receive some form of representation. In the case of the Chamber of Deputies the threshold is 0.55% of the national total. As one would expect given the different electoral regulations, AD and COPEI's two-party dominance has been tempered here. They have on average controlled about 73% of the seats in the Chamber of Deputies, with their combined percentage ranging from 53 to 86%.

In 1993 a system resembling the German model of compensatory member elections was adopted for the Chamber of Deputies only – Senators are still chosen by a strictly party vote. The mixed-member proportional system establishes the Chamber of Deputies from two distinct groups of elected representatives. Approximately one-half of the deputies are elected through the traditional closed-list method of proportional representation by state. The other half come from "first-past-the-post," or plurality, elections in single-member districts. A party's percentage of seats in the Chamber of Deputies is still determined solely by the proportional representation, party vote. The votes for deputies by district help influence which individuals are sent to the Chamber, but they have no effect on the percentage composition of the legislature. This connection to specific, smaller geographic districts could increase the loyalty of deputies to their constituencies, but their original nomination to run as the party representative in that district is still a highly centralized decision within the party elite.

The highly centralized internal party politics in Venezuela is a marked contrast to the possible importance of district party structures and rank-and-file membership described in Mark Jones's chapter on Argentina. In AD for example, leaders at the state level submit to the National Executive Committee (CEN) the party lists of potential candidates for the Chamber of Deputies and the Senate. These lists must contain three times the number of candidates as seats available, and the candidates must not be ranked. The CEN, a group of 20–30 leaders, chooses which candidates will run and rank orders them. What is more, it has the right to replace half the list submitted by the state-level leaders with candidates of its own choosing. That is more than enough names to fill all the available seats, let alone the number that AD is likely to win. The national leadership's control extends to the state legislative candidates through a very similar process and to the municipal level by reserving the right to intervene in the nomination process in cities with more than 40,000 inhabitants or where the process is particularly contentious (Coppedge 1994:20–21). Given the historically important role of parties, the right to the party label is a major incentive. The immediate development of pork or parochial interests is diminished by a number of other factors in addition to the nomination process. First, because single-member districts have been implemented in only one house, albeit the larger and more important one, its impact will be diluted. Second, a person's district or place of voter registration never meant anything before so many Venezuelans are registered to vote in districts other than the one in which they currently live (though this should be corrected over time). In addition, the new single-member districts are based solely on the number of inhabitants and often do not correspond to any geographic entity that might bind the voters together as a coherent unit desiring like representation.

Parties are imbedded in the electoral system in such a way that the personalistic appeal of individual candidates and promises of particularistic rewards play a minor role in voters' choices. When individuals go to the ballot box, they are faced with a clear choice among directly elected presidential candidates and among parties disciplined to pursue their respective programs. The dominance of two parties, AD and COPEI, for most of the democratic era has encouraged these parties to gravitate toward the middle of the political spectrum. They have both become multiclass parties, and the ideological distinctions between them have diminished. As the effective number of parties listed in Table 4.1 indicates, Venezuela has never had a perfect two-party system, but during the 1970s and 1980s the effective number of parties remained relatively low. Recent dissatisfaction and new electoral regulations have combined to promote a dispersion of seats in the mid-1990s.

DISCIPLINED MEMBERS OF CONGRESS

Internal party regulations mandate strict party discipline by members of the congressional delegation, and elites are able to enforce this requirement because of the incentives under their control. As outlined earlier, because votes are pooled within each state for candidates on a closed list, national-level party elites have strict control over who runs on the party label and, more particularly, the order in which candidates appear, so individual members of Congress have every incentive to promote the party line and ignore parochial interests. Unlike the situation in Costa Rica explained in John Carey's chapter, members of Congress are eligible for immediate reelection and long congressional careers are the norm, so individual members of Congress must consider the next set of elections and their standing with the party. Rare breaches of discipline are almost always met with very rancorous and public expulsion from the party. These factors work to ensure strict discipline within the legislative delegation, which in turn assures voters that programmatic promises can be met by the governing party.

Discipline among members of Congress is so well enforced that formal vote-counting procedures are rarely used. When a bill is considered, a designated spokesman for each party delegation states his or her party's position, and then a voice vote is called. For the vast majority of votes, records are not maintained of how individuals voted, but instead it is noted only whether the item passed or failed based on relative party strength in the chamber. There have been exceptions where parties were internally divided and could not agree on a common position, and parties, particularly AD in the early 1960s, have even split during a particular administration, but these are definitely exceptions to the rule.

Note that the factors that promote party discipline among legislators do not apply to the president, especially given that he must sit out two terms before running again. Directly elected presidents are rarely bound by party discipline because their separate origin and survival relative to the legislative branch, method of nomination and election, and frequent restrictions on reelection free them from many mechanisms that parties might have for inducing compliance. However, this was not always the case in Venezuela. During the *trienio* of democratic rule from 1945 to 1948, President Rómulo Gallegos of AD, which was then less centrist, was strictly bound by party discipline, which was one of the factors that contributed to the overthrow of democratic rule. Opposition forces argued that the presidency should be less partisan and more representative of the entire nation. Gallegos's obedience to party discipline made it impossible for him to moderate AD's alienation of other actors even if he had been so inclined. The discipline of presidents (which is no longer required) and other internal party regulations that promote unitary behavior (and did survive into the current democratic era) are often attributed to the clandestine formation of parties in the predemocratic era and their need to survive the repressive Pérez–Jiménez regime between 1948 and 1958.

In the current democratic era every president has been a long-time party functionary and has been nominated through relatively closed party proceedings. For example, presidential candidates from AD are chosen at a special convention attended primarily by high-ranking party officials from national and regional levels, as well as representatives of the functional organizations of the party, including labor, women's, and youth groups. Occasionally, rank-and-file members have been elected to attend the convention, but not in a number sufficient to rival high-ranking party functionaries. The Causa R has very closed internal proceedings, and its presidential candidate is simply named by a small group of party leaders. Some parties are now beginning to experiment with primary elections. For example, COPEI's candidate in 1993, Osvaldo Álvarez Paz, was chosen in a party primary that was open to all Venezuelans of voting age. Previously, COPEI had used a relatively open convention process. However, these strong party ties are balanced by official freedom from party discipline and, of course, their fixed terms. If the president were bound by party discipline, a party controlling both branches would be incredibly strong and united, but because the chief executive is freer to determine his own program, the president's own party in Congress must also react to the president's program through its legislative delegation.

TYPOLOGIES OF PARTY SYSTEMS

Parties are particularly strong in Venezuela because they have penetrated other groups, because the electoral system firmly ensconces them in voters' calculus, and because they can demand the strict loyalty of their legislative delegations. Given the efficacy of the parties, it is important to understand their goals or strategies.

Juan Carlos Rey (1991) has pointed out that the Venezuelan party system has not always fit the traditional typologies. Most scholars have conceived of parties as groups organized purely to seek power, groups designed to pursue an ideological program, or as mixed somewhere on a continuum between these two ideal types. This continuum, however, ignores one of the goals that can become primary in a Latin American democracy – preserving democratic rule. The traditional typologies were designed by scholars who focused on countries with long-standing regimes, where the stability of democracy was not an issue, but in Venezuela the need to protect the regime is often pushed to the forefront and must be accounted for when attempting to explain political behavior.

This willingness to compromise and seek consensus was important to the successful democratic transition. The continued strength of political parties and their centrality in the political system allowed them to manage sthe process of democratic consolidation:

> As understood by the political elite, then, the lessons of the *trienio* and of the subsequent decade of military rule were that conciliation, compromise and prudence were both necessary and desirable if a decent, durable political order were to be constructed. After 1958, these lessons were put into effect in five interrelated ways which can be summarized as follows: (1) pacts and coalitions; (2) inter-elite consensus; (3) program limitation; (4) encouragement of participation, but controlled and channeled; and (5) exclusion of the revolutionary left. (Levine 1985:50)

"Conciliation, compromise and prudence," as well as the specific means for operationalizing them, require a political elite that can count on the support of the masses. That support was guaranteed early in the regime through extensive party organization that sought to include the mass of Venezuelans in the democratic process, albeit with a great deal of mediation by party elites. The overriding goal of consensus or conciliation took the form of several explicit pacts, grand coalition governments, and an entire decision-making style that calls for limits to disagreements. As I will argue in Part 4.7, the conscious pursuit of consolidation can have a downside that promotes stagnation and declining legitimacy, but we must account for the tendency to protect the system if we are to understand the behavior of political elites and interbranch relations more specifically.

4.4. INFORMAL POWERS OF THE PRESIDENT

Before examining the limited, formal legislative powers of the president, it is important to look at the president's position in the policy-making process more broadly, including some of the informal powers at his discretion. Focusing solely on legislative powers makes sense in a liberal state where government action is limited to general acts that apply to the entire population equally. But government intervention in Venezuela and other Latin American countries is much more extensive than this, which means that many important government actions are particular or individualized. For example, the issuing of government concessions, the granting of import licenses, the creation of public enterprises, the naming of their directors, and the signing of government contracts are not general, legislative acts, but they are important government decisions. What is more, all of these actions can be taken by Venezuelan presidents through the normal use of their nonlegislative decree authority. The lack of oversight on how these powers are employed and the degree of discretion that is available make them very important tools for the executive branch. Not only are they important in and of themselves, but they can also have indirect consequences like gaining supporters for a particular party or for the president's program. What is more, this kind of influence can then indirectly have an impact on general, legislative outcomes.

In purely constitutional terms, as we will see, the Venezuelan presidency does not have excessive legislative powers, and in fact, this combination of powers makes the president "potentially marginal." Yet Venezuelan presidents are widely perceived to be powerful and often effective. In order to understand and evaluate this perception we must analyze the less formal powers of the president and then the interaction between these presidential powers and the party system that was described in Part 4.3.

INFORMAL CONSULTATIVE POWERS

The president's position in the policy-making process extends beyond the powers explicitly outlined in the constitution. He or she is able to interact with groups in civil society in ways that the Congress has been unable to match. Consultation between the executive branch and interest groups allows them to influence one another, but most importantly it moves the locus of decision making out of the Congress and into the executive branch. Because legislators are tightly bound by party discipline, they cannot respond individually to pressure from interest groups. The policy position of legislators is determined outside the Congress, and the importance of the institution in the policy-making process is thus diminished. Not only is the executive branch free to be influenced; it also controls significant resources – through the enormous decentralized public administration – which allow it to respond effectively. This interaction allows the president to better respond to group demands and to influence group behavior more effectively. While these activities are all perfectly constitutional, they are not formal legislative powers. Yet their impact on the policy-making process is enormous.

At the agenda-setting stage the president can use his nonlegislative decree authority to create high-profile commissions that bring executive branch authorities and the representatives of interest groups together to study issues of the president's choice. These commissions can capture media coverage and focus public attention on a particular issue. What is more, the groups the president chooses to have represented can use these opportunities to frame these issues in a particular manner and as a result structure and influence future debate.

Likewise, at the stage of policy formation, similar commissions are often charged with drafting the actual legislation that the president will then submit to Congress for adoption. The Congress has not developed a systematic structure of subcommittees that would employ technical experts and allow for consultation with interest groups. Legislators have no incentive to form such commissions because how they will vote on bills is determined by party organs. In addition, given the extreme party discipline of members of Congress, which is enforced by the national executive council of each party, lobbying individual legislators makes no sense for pressure groups. As a result, it is the president who has his finger on the pulse of the population and who is positioned to influence how interest groups stand on particular issues. This is especially the case with groups that have not been penetrated by the parties, such as private business. FEDECAMARAS, for example, has been very influential and has remained free of party infiltration.

It and other business groups interact regularly with the government through the executive branch (Crisp 1994).

Between 1958 and 1990 Venezuelan presidents created at least 330 such consultative bodies. Government officials, almost exclusively from the national level and from within the executive branch, comprised just over one-half of the participants in these commissions. More than 1,200 individuals were named to represent particular interest groups. These interest groups included businessmen, middle-class professionals, workers, neighborhood associations, students, and others. Representatives of the business class participated at a rate almost double that of any other group, with organized labor finishing a distant second. These consultative commissions give the included interest groups an institutionalized route to influence government policy making. For interbranch relations, they indicate the quasi-legislative role that the executive branch has assumed in interacting with civil society and translating its demands into policy recommendations.

Policy adoption is normally thought of as requiring congressional action through the passage of laws, but as the next section on proactive powers will illustrate in detail, the president has some ability to circumvent the Congress should he or she so desire. One sign that a great deal gets done without the involvement of the legislative branch is that the Venezuelan Congress is particularly inactive by comparative standards, approving "an average of only 27.9 laws per year from 1959 to 1982" (Coppedge 1994: 69). Given the size of the Venezuelan state and its involvement in the economy and society, the executive has under his or her control an enormous array of institutions through which to carry out his or her program. This large state apparatus and the revenue-generating ability of many state enterprises, especially the nationalized petroleum industry, diminish the importance of the legislature's budgetary power. The typical "power of the purse" is only a mild restriction on the president, since government spending has increasingly occurred through off-budget entities in the decentralized public administration. In 1960, 70% of government spending was done by on-budget ministries of the centralized public administration, but by 1980 70% of expenditures occurred through off-budget entities in the decentralized public administration (Kornblith and Maingón 1985:40).

These enterprises are important to government execution and provide another opportunity for the executive branch to work with and reward interest groups. The president has the power to name representatives of interest groups to serve on the boards of agencies in the decentralized public administration. At least 362 bureaucratic agencies were created by democratic governments through 1990. Betancourt created the fewest, 27, while Carlos Andrés Pérez, in his first term, created the most, 180. The decentralized public administration produces goods, regulates the economy, plans, lends services, and encourages private-sector efforts, among other things. It includes factories, universities, credit institutions, and regional development corporations. During the 1980s it was responsible for almost 30% of the country's gross domestic product. To the extent that it is responsible to anyone, it is responsible to the president. The governing boards of these agencies contain representatives of interest groups, with business and labor again leading the way. The president, then, has at his or her disposal an enormous bureaucracy over which he or she has a great deal of discretionary power, especially in terms of appointments, which allows for the execution of many policy decisions and which is a tremendous source of revenue.

THE PRESIDENT IN HIS OR HER PARTY

In addition to the powers that derive from the office of the presidency itself, presidential power also includes the president's role within his or her own party. No Venezuelan president has been a political outsider. Every major-party candidate has had a long history of party activism that has led to a significant following within the party. In fact, many presidents have been the official head of their party at some point prior to receiving the nomination. This internal support is necessary in order to come out on top in the nomination process. Occasionally minor parties will draft a notable figure to run, but none has come close to winning, and the tendency to draft outsiders has diminished during the democratic era. As a result, presidents have almost always been able to count on the loyal support of their parties. For one thing, they would not have risen to the top of the party had they not been compatible with the views of the majority. But when the president and the party leadership are divided, the president is usually able to get compliance from his or her party because he or she has access to information and control over resources that increase his or her ability to be persuasive. In addition the president's party recognizes his or her need to represent the nation as a whole and thus frees the president from party discipline while giving him or her party support (Coppedge 1994:65).

Much has been made of Venezuelan presidents as "lame ducks" because they must sit out two presidential terms (10 years) before seeking reelection (Coppedge 1994). Because the president's immediate reelection is forbidden, he or she is supposed to lose authority over other actors, including some in his or her own party, toward the end of the 5-year term. However, this set of incentives has rarely, if ever, caused a public rupture between a sitting president and his legislative delegation.[1] Even if some factions within his or her party were inclined to distinguish themselves from his or her program, a significant split is unlikely. First, disloyalty to the sitting president would be bad not only for his or her administration, but also for the reputation of the party, thus hurting the electoral chances of the internal faction opposing the president. Second, the president's career is far from over. Two Venezuelan presidents have waited the mandatory 10 years and been reelected, so the possibility of punishing earlier defectors is real. Finally, presidents have the ability to influence both the nomination process within their own party and the upcoming general elections. As a result, the end of the president's current official hold on power may be known, but the resources he or she wields do not expire before the end of the term. What is more, unlike the Costa Rican case described in John Carey's chapter, reelection for legislators is not restricted, so they do not have to throw themselves behind the newly identified candidate in hopes of obtaining an appointed post in the next administration. For example, since 1949 only 14% of the members of the Costa Rican National Assembly served more than one term, while 56% of the members of the Venezuelan Congress between 1963 and 1988 served two or more terms (Carey 1996).

Most presidents have remained influential party leaders after their terms, and many have exercised their position of senator-for-life to great advantage. For example, after the second coup attempt against Carlos Andrés Pérez, Caldera's chastisement of the reigning elites in AD and COPEI in a joint session of Congress catapulted him to the forefront of public attention again and launched his successful bid to regain the presidency. So, inability to be immediately reelected need not signal the end of influence, even if the individual politician never receives the nomination for president again.

Of course, it is difficult to know whether agreement between the president and the National Executive Council, which sets the party line followed by the legislative delegation, is a sign of party acquiescence to a sitting president, presidential capitulation to his or her party, or mutual agreement based on the shared beliefs that made them copartisans in the first place. For example, as support for the thesis that presidents capitulate to their parties, Michael Coppedge points out that in 1974 Carlos Andrés Pérez was forced to accept narrower delegated decree authority than he originally requested (1994:68–69). However, the "capitulation" of the president must

---

1 The most glaring exception to this rule is AD's vote to allow the trial of Carlos Andrés Pérez in 1993 and his resulting temporary removal from office. However, even then AD supported his very unpopular neoliberal program right up until he was removed from office. In addition, the party later voted against his permanent removal from office and definitive replacement for the rest of his term (Rey 1993:109).

be seen in the context of a congress that "acquiesced" to an enabling law that was drafted in the executive branch itself and that entitled the president to broad powers. Thereafter, the AD-controlled Congress failed to pass any countervailing legislation, signaling the party's agreement with Pérez's activities. As this single case illustrates, all three of these explanations for agreement between the president and his party are accurate for some points in time.

4.5. FORMAL CONSTITUTIONALLY ALLOCATED POWERS OF THE PRESIDENT

The institutional design in Venezuela is in many ways a prototypical presidential system. The directly elected president (Art. 183) is both the head of state and head of government, and he or she does have an institutionalized role in the legislative process. The terms of the chief executive and the assembly are fixed and not contingent on mutual confidence. The elected executive names and directs the composition of the government (Art. 190: 2), but a two-thirds majority in the Chamber of Deputies can censure a cabinet member (Art. 153). Relative to executives in other presidential regimes, the formal legislative powers of the Venezuelan president are fairly limited (Shugart and Carey 1992; Crisp forthcoming).

REACTIVE CONSTITUTIONALLY ALLOCATED POWERS

The Venezuelan president has virtually no veto power. He or she has only a suspensive veto, or the right to return a bill to the legislature for reconsideration within 10 days from when it was originally passed. The president does not have the right to limit revisions to a particular part of the bill, though he or she is supposed to make particular concerns known while returning it. The suspensive veto can be overridden with the same majority that passed the bill in the first place. If it is overridden by a two-thirds majority, the president must promulgate the bill within 5 days. If it is overridden by a less than a two-thirds majority, the president has the right to return it yet again if he or she so desires. However, a second override by even the barest majority (of those voting) requires that the president sign the bill into law without further recourse. Venezuelan presidents rarely exercise this authority, for a variety of reasons. First, they usually participate directly in legislative debate through the agency of their ministers, who are constitutionally given this right (Art. 170), or indirectly through the press, so their positions are often addressed. Second, their veto power is so weak that it almost certainly guarantees a public defeat. The likelihood of defeat is enhanced by the high degree of discipline among legislative delegations. It is almost impossible that a presidential veto will provoke individual members to defect from their parties' positions, and the best that the president can hope for is that an entire party might change its position. Specific instances of the president's use of the suspensive veto or the right to return legislation for reconsideration will be discussed in the analysis of majority, plurality, and minority governments in Part 4.6.

The president has no exclusive right to introduce legislation, so he or she cannot prevent the legislature from considering particular issues by refusing to introduce a related bill. It should be noted though that Venezuelan presidents have introduced the overwhelming majority of legislation since 1958. This does not mean that presidents have been able to prevent legislators from addressing certain issues by introducing their own bills, that presidents do not try to anticipate what the legislature will find acceptable, or that the legislature has been restricted in its ability to modify or reject presidents' proposals. Nonetheless, it does indicate some informal power in terms of agenda setting and the technical/political expertise necessary to draft legislation (see Part 4.4 on informal powers).

PROACTIVE CONSTITUTIONALLY ALLOCATED POWERS

Venezuelan presidents have limited decree authorities, which vary significantly based on how they are initially invoked and later brought to an end. The president has legislative power only if it is previously delegated by Congress, but he or she does have nonlegislative forms of decree authority that can be initiated without congressional consent. Article 190:8 allows the president to issue decrees related to economic and financial matters if the Congress has previously delegated him or her the authority to do so. The Congress must explicitly delegate this authority through a *ley habilitante*, or enabling law. Delegated legislative authority has been granted rather infrequently and in exceptional circumstances. Decree authority in economic and financial matters has been delegated to the president five times since 1961, and these will be discussed in greater detail in Part 4.6.

The president can assume nonlegislative decree authority without previous delegation by the Congress through a number of provisions related to "extraordinary" circumstances. For example, Article 190:11 allows the executive to create or modify public services in urgent situations when the

Congress is not in session, and Article 244 allows him or her to restrict the personal liberty of anyone threatening the public order. A more frequently used and broader provision is the president's right to suspend and restrict constitutional guarantees and to issue decrees related to these rights that have the force of law as long as the guarantees are suspended (Art. 190:6 and Art. 241). There are three rights that the president cannot curtail: the right to life (Art. 58), the right not to be held incommunicado or to be tortured (Art. 60:3), and the right not to be sentenced to cruel and unusual or permanent punishment (Art. 60:7). Otherwise, by suspending any of the individual, social, economic, and political guarantees in the constitution, the president can assume powers that are normally reserved for the Congress (Brewer-Carías 1985:521). The president must submit decrees related to the suspension or restriction of constitutional rights to the Congress within 10 days of their taking effect. The legislature does not have the right to disapprove of or modify individual decrees, but it can declare that the motivating factors for the suspension or restriction of rights has expired and thus render all decrees justified in this manner null. When a constitutional guarantee is completely suspended, the executive branch is not required to issue further decrees regulating its exercise. Instead, the government is free to act in these areas without giving any account of its activities. If the president only restricts the right, the successive decrees can determine only how the right will be exercised during the period of restriction and within previously established legal bounds. However, this distinction between the suspension and restriction of constitutional guarantees has been all but ignored recently.

Finally, the president has the right to declare a state of emergency in situations of domestic or foreign conflict or when one or the other appears imminent (Art. 240). The constitution itself does not define any additional powers that accrue to the president in a state of emergency, except the right to suspend or restrict constitutional guarantees, which can be done directly without a state of emergency. However, Venezuelan legislation has been defining additional presidential powers for states of emergency, and these powers may lead to increased use of this provision. The Organic Law of Security and Defense declares that in a state of emergency, the president along with the National Council of Security and Defense, a body created by the law with only presidential appointees and military officials as members, will have broad powers to mobilize the military and to sustain order. The Caldera government, elected in December 1993, called for and received increased emergency powers through modification of the consumer protection law, adoption of an exchange control law, and adoption of a financial emergencies law that gave the president greater rights to intervene in banks. In addition to broadening the justifications for a state of emergency, these laws defined a series of presidential powers that would result immediately from a state of emergency, rather than requiring the suspension of constitutional guarantees. Because ending a state of emergency requires action by both branches of government, the president's powers would be less subject to congressional control than they are through the suspension of constitutional guarantees. Suspended guarantees can be reinstated by either branch, but ending a state of emergency requires consensus between the branches.

4.6. PRESIDENTIAL BEHAVIOR IN MAJORITY AND MINORITY GOVERNMENTS

What relationship exists between the presidents' use of their limited powers and the size of their party's legislative delegation? Given the limited constitutionally defined powers of the office, it seems unlikely that presidents could be particularly activist without at least the tacit consent of Congress. After illustrating the partisan control of the executive and legislative branches, I will look at presidents' use of their reactive and proactive powers in majority and minority governments. When evaluating the hypothesized relationship between presidential powers and the party system, we must also keep in mind the relationship between the president and his or her party and the earlier proviso about assuming that Venezuelan parties are motivated only by the struggle for power. At times, party elites seem capable of setting their differences aside in order to work together for the stability of democracy as a whole. I will account for this possibility when looking at what might otherwise seem like paradoxical behavior by one branch or the other.

Figure 4.1 shows levels of party control over the executive and legislative branches during the current democratic era. Eight sets of concurrent national elections have been held for the presidency and Congress (though the election of Betancourt occurred while an earlier constitution was still in force). There have been three administrations that had the backing of a majority of both houses of Congress, and all three were AD governments. Despite its majority status and because of preelection agreements among competing parties, Betancourt operated with a grand-coalition-style government. His government included cabinet positions for the major opposition parties, and he was able to count on majority support in Congress despite two splits within AD itself. The first Pérez administration was notorious for its presidential activism. The AD congressional delegation provided only a limited check on the president, who was further strengthened

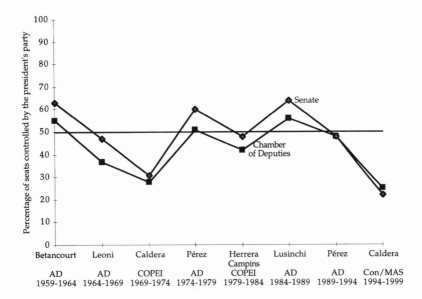

Figure 4.1. The president's party in Congress.

by his access to enormous petroleum-generated revenues. I will examine the use of constitutionally allocated powers by Betancourt, Pérez, and Lusinchi in greater detail later.

Among minority governments, the COPEI government of Herrera Campins and the second AD administration of Carlos Andrés Pérez had significant pluralities that made forming temporary legislative coalitions around individual parts of their respective programs somewhat easier. Interestingly enough, COPEI had 48% of the seats in the Senate and 42% of the seats in the Chamber of Deputies during Herrera Campins's administration, but it was still outnumbered in the Chamber of Deputies by AD. AD presented an almost insurmountable obstacle to Herrera's program, but it was unable to push through any program of its own because it did not have a majority in Congress either. COPEI had to count on the support of a number of small parties to overcome the immobilism created by the opposition of the legislative faction from AD. The second Pérez administration encountered a number of political difficulties surrounding its neoliberal package: riots, the use of military force, and two attempted coups. Despite the president's implementation of a neoliberal package that was designed by the independents with which he created his government, AD continued to support his program in Congress (Rey 1993:81–82). After the first attempted coup, in an effort to shore up his waning support, Pérez temporarily

gave COPEI minimal representation in his cabinet, and the identification
of COPEI, Eduardo Fernández in particular, with Pérez's government hurt
its electoral chances later. For most of the period, Pérez ruled without explicit accords with other parties because the major parties in Congress failed
to offer significant opposition to his major policy initiatives (Rey 1993: 82–
83).

Leoni's administration was a minority government, but AD did have a
plurality in both houses. AD and COPEI attempted to negotiate a coalition
as they had in the previous Betancourt administration, but they were unable
to reach any formal agreement. Leoni was, however, able to form a coalition
with the Unión Republicana Democrática (URD) and Frente Nacional Democrático (FND) that gave his government a majority in both houses. Both
of the minor parties received representation in Leoni's cabinet in return for
their support in the legislature. Rafael Caldera, on the other hand, has had
two minority governments where the party or parties backing him did not
have even a plurality in either house. As will be detailed later, in his first
administration Caldera and COPEI finally found it necessary to reach an
informal accord with AD to prevent continued interbranch immobilism.
This accord did not include representation of AD in Caldera's cabinet. His
second administration has been characterized by support from parties other
than his own, including AD, without the need for formal agreements. Civilian politicians of all partisan stripes are aware of the precarious position
of democracy, and thus far AD has been willing to put what it sees as the
interests of the system ahead of its own partisan policy positions.

As this brief overview points out, the relationship between the executive
and legislative branches has varied significantly. Much of this variation is
the result of whether the president's party has a majority or minority in the
legislature, but other factors are also involved. The first small twist we must
put on this relationship is the degree to which the president's party is in
the minority and what the rest of the Congress looks like. For example,
Herrera Campins nearly had a majority, but the fact that the Congress was
almost split down the middle between AD and COPEI, with AD holding
a slight advantage, meant that his coalition options were limited. Conversely, Leoni's administration had a smaller congressional delegation of its
own, but the opposition was divided as well, so the president could choose
between COPEI and URD/FND when looking for cooperative coalition
partners. A second factor that has occasionally been critical is the relationship between the president and his own party. The lame duck nature of
presidents due to their inability to immediately seek reelection does not
seem consistently to affect behavior on legislative matters. For example, AD
continued to support a very unpopular Pérez right up until a vote to remove

him from office to stand trial on corruption charges was forced. It has been rare that congressional delegations abandoned their own president, and when it has happened, as in the case of Pérez's indictment, it has been for reasons other than the identification of the party's next presidential candidate. This is not to say that intraparty factions do not form around particular leaders, only that they have not played a key role in the discipline of legislative caucuses. The final factor that bears on relative numerical strengths in Congress is the priorities of the party elites and the nature of the party system. Venezuelan elites have shown the ability to put aside their differences when it is necessary to defend the system, though in the 1990s it has not always appeared that they would be able to do so successfully. These factors are also critical for understanding presidents' use of their constitutionally allocated powers. An examination of the president's suspensive veto, delegated decree authority, and extraordinary powers will show how these variables influence specific behavior.

REACTIVE POWERS IN MAJORITY AND MINORITY GOVERNMENTS

As noted earlier, the president has virtually no reactive powers. He or she has the right to introduce legislation, but in no subject matter is this an exclusive right. The president is then left with the weak suspensive veto, which is hardly a veto at all. Probably because of its weakness, the right to return legislation for reconsideration has rarely been exercised. In most instances when it has been used, the president is returning the legislation for technical adjustments that have to do with executing the law and that are in no way efforts to seek changes in its substance.

The most widely noted use of the suspensive veto as a real expression of substantive disagreement over policy was Caldera's effort to block reform of the judicial system in 1969. COPEI, Caldera's party, did not have a plurality in either house, and in fact, the Congress was more factionalized than it had ever been in Venezuelan history (see Table 4.1 for the effective number of parties). Despite his lack of support in the legislature, Caldera attempted to forego the grand-coalition style of Betancourt and Leoni, and as a result he was often stymied by the legislative branch. Until 1969, judges were named jointly by the judicial and executive branches, but the proposed reform of the Organic Law of Judicial Power would make a new body, the National Judicial Council, responsible for naming of 2,500 to 2,800 judges below the level of the Supreme Court (Velásquez 1976:307). The National Judicial Council was to be elected by Congress with the participation of the executive and judicial branches. In practice, given its composition, the new body would have been controlled by the Congress. Originally COPEI supported the reform when it was considered in the Senate, but it then categorically opposed it when it reached the Chamber of Deputies. Why the turnaround? It appears that Caldera, as president of the country and a founding member of COPEI, convinced his partisans to change their position after the Senate had voted (Velásquez 1976:307).

Unfortunately for Caldera, and probably the autonomy of the judicial branch, convincing his own party was not enough. The opposition parties passed the reform despite Caldera's (ultimately unsuccessful) challenge before the Supreme Court and his effort to follow the previous manner of selecting judges. What is more, the opposition parties in Congress agreed to exclude COPEI completely from the newly formed National Judicial Council. Caldera exercised his suspensive veto once, and when the reform was returned to him a second time with less than a two-thirds support he exercised it again, but the reform law passed a third time and Caldera was forced to promulgate it.

In his weekly address immediately after the judicial reform appeared in the *Gaceta Oficial*, Caldera announced that despite the fact that his was not a coalition government, "my current mood does not impede the search for a cordial understanding with the most important political parties on matters of fundamental importance to the country" (Caldera in Velásquez 1976: 312). The old guard members of AD, former president Raúl Leoni in particular, who had recognized the importance of conciliation for successfully making the transition to democracy, decided that it was in the best interest of the system as a whole to strike an informal coalition with Caldera on particularly critical issues. Their unofficial understanding became known as the *Coincidencia* or Coincidence. The parties agreed to work together on a limited set of predetermined areas of common interest and to put an end to "boycotts and procedural quarrels," but AD's "legislative caucus continued to promote its own programs and modify government bills to suit its wishes" on bills that did not fall within these predetermined areas (Tugwell 1975:104). Neither party was willing to subjugate its own identity to a coalition, but the president realized that he could not govern without legislative support, and AD put concern for the system ahead of momentary partisan gains.

Caldera's situation indicates that the president's formal powers are not sufficient to stop a determined, opposition-controlled Congress. However, the resulting informal coalition illustrates the Venezuelan tendency to resort to extrainstitutional responses to potential interbranch immobilism. As Mainwaring and Shugart point out in the Conclusion, congresses controlled by highly disciplined parties can present one of two problems. If they are majority governments, they can fail to act as a significant check on the president of their own party (see the upcoming discussion of delegated decree authority), or if they are minority governments, they can become obstructionist oppositions. In Venezuela, when this situation has bordered on constitutional crisis, the parties have usually reverted to their "protect the system above all else" mode of thinking.

PROACTIVE POWERS

As was mentioned before, the Congress can delegate decree authority to the president in economic and financial matters, and it has done so five times. The pattern of when and how this authority is delegated shows a marked relationship to party politics, particularly the strength of the president's party in Congress. These five instances can be distinguished from one another by the amount of time for which the decree authority was delegated as well as the breadth of latitude granted the president. For three of the five times, authority was delegated for a full year and with a relatively broad range of activities, and in each of these cases the president's party had a majority in both chambers of the Congress. In other words, every majority president has been delegated decree authority by his legislative delegation. At the end of June 1961 decree authority was delegated for one year to President Betancourt. The president was authorized to reorganize the decentralized public administration, to reorganize public services, to defer collective contracts, to fix prices of goods of primary necessity, to modify the Property Tax Law, to modify inheritance and other national taxes, and to establish an insurance system for deposit and savings accounts (Crisp forthcoming). These powers are wide ranging and loosely defined, giving the president ample room to pursue a variety of policies. Yet given the vagueness of the enabling legislation, Betancourt was quite circumspect in his use of the authority. He issued 15 decree-laws that lowered public employee salaries, suspended their current contract, postponed their ongoing contract negotiations until 1962, revised several tax laws, made credit for building urban housing more available, intervened in the management of the Social Security Institute, created the School of Public Administration, and reorganized telecommunications services (Brewer-Carías 1980:108–11).

Betancourt might have been relatively restrained because of the particular nature of his majority government. First, despite AD's control of both houses, Betancourt formed a grand-coalition government with cabinet representation for other parties. The diversity of positions within his own cabinet then qualifies the nature of his majority. In addition, all the signatories of the pact had agreed to a common government program, which in some ways might compare with the programmatic compromises necessary to form an electoral coalition. Second, AD itself split twice during his administration, once before the delegation of decree authority and once while it was delegated, so the strength of his own party was probably less in real terms than its original electoral showing. The first split led to the formation of Movimiento de Izquierda Revolucionaria (MIR) on ideological grounds by the youngest, most radical generation of the party (commonly known as the *muchachos*), and though it would present a challenge for AD to regain support among this generation in the future, it did not have an immediate impact on the party's standing in Congress. The latter split was led by a faction of middle-generation leaders known as *Grupo Ars*,[2] who rebelled more for personal and pragmatic than ideological reasons (Martz 1966:180–92). This split was more serious in the short run because it included the majority of the party's National Executive Committee and cost AD 22 seats in the Chamber of Deputies (enough to lose its simple majority) and 4 seats in the Senate (Operations and Policy Research 1963:19–20).

Decree authority was next delegated to Carlos Andrés Pérez in 1974, again for one year. Pérez asked the Congress for the powers in order to transform the economic structure of the country in light of the tremendous increase in income from petroleum exports. The enabling law authorized reform of the national finance system and capital markets, modification of the Organic Law of the National Public Finance, creation of the Venezuelan Investment Fund, transformation of sectors of production, nationalization of the iron ore industry, payment of the Venezuelan Social Security Institute's debt, upholding the seniority and pension rights of workers, and creation of new minimum salaries, as well as salary and wage hikes. The list of areas to be addressed was long and diverse, and the enabling legislation was very vague about the particulars (Crisp forthcoming). Pérez dictated 53 decree-laws designed primarily to distribute the oil wealth to the economy through credit institutions, development plans for particular industries, or subsidies to types of producers. The large number of decree-laws, almost double the average number of laws passed by Congress in any given year, and their range of activity indicate the degree to which the executive assumed legislative authority. Pérez's majority in Congress was willing to

---

2 *Grupo Ars* was a pejorative title that referred to the slogan of a major public relations firm, *Ars Publicidades*. The firm's slogan was "Let us do your thinking for you." *Grupo Ars* was given the name because apparently they wanted to do the party's thinking for it. In the 1963 elections the group chose *AD-Oposición* as its name and received only 2.29% of the presidential vote and 3.27% of the legislative vote.

grant him significant powers, and it did not do much to enforce its own oversight provisions.

The enabling law created a congressional vigilance committee, composed of 13 members from eight parties, that was to receive all decrees before they were promulgated, but the Pérez administration ignored the commission. The opposition parties resigned from the commission in protest over what they saw as Pérez's decree mania and AD's blatant disregard for the checks and balances central to democratic rule (Fernández 1976:35–98; Karl 1982:220–21). Pérez's party, which had a majority in both houses of Congress, was either unwilling or unable to rein in Pérez. Given that Pérez was a longtime leader within the party, it is likely that the congressional delegation found his policies acceptable. Pérez remained an important figure in the party despite his supposed lame-duck status. Though he was not eligible for immediate reelection, he was a young man who could (and would) return as the party's nominee in the future. In addition, he could exert great influence in the process of selecting the next candidate and determining the future party leadership, with its strong role in the nomination process for legislators.

The other majority president, Jaime Lusinchi of AD, was also granted decree authority for a year beginning in June 1984. This time the president's request for special powers was prompted by an economic downturn rather than a boom. Lusinchi was authorized to act in 20 different areas, most of them focused on cutting government spending, raising government revenue, and refinancing public debt. The list of policy areas was even longer than that permitted Pérez, but in contrast to the earlier delegation, Lusinchi received more detailed instruction. The president issued 71 decrees, but the sheer number is tempered by the significant repetition of particular acts. More than half (36) of these decrees were used for the single purpose of selling government bonds to refinance the public debt.

When decree authority was delegated to a minority president, it was carefully circumscribed and of very limited duration. Yet one might wonder why a minority president would be delegated even this limited authority. Party elites' goal of protecting the democratic system came into play. Party elites controlling congressional delegations decided that rapid action by the unitary executive branch rather than slow progress by a divided legislature was necessary to shore up the system as a whole. This also seems to characterize the delegation of authority to the interim president, Velásquez. In his case, Pérez had finally been forced out of office after riots and military repression surrounding his neoliberal package and two attempted coups. It was in this highly volatile situation that Velásquez was delegated authority for just over four months in order to carry out tax reform, banking regulation, provision of credit for low-cost housing, the sale of a government-owned airline, and the stimulation of the agricultural sector. Compared with previous cases, the enabling law that delegated decree authority was highly detailed, including the means of congressional oversight (Crisp forthcoming). The other example of a minority president receiving delegated authority came immediately after this when the stability of the political system was further endangered by a financial crisis. The newly elected Caldera, supported for his second term by the Convergencia coalition, MAS, and other minor parties, was granted decree authority for just one month to establish a luxury tax, a wholesale sales tax, and a tax on savings accounts, all of which were accomplished with four decrees. The cases of Velásquez and Caldera show that presidents may receive legislative powers from congresses where their respective parties do not dominate, but this is not paradoxical if one takes into account the propensity in Venezuela, stemming from the earlier failed attempt at democracy, for elites of all partisan shades to band together when democracy is endangered. It is also noteworthy that the powers delegated to minority presidents were relatively circumscribed and of short duration.

A nonlegislative decree authority is that assumed by the president once he decrees a constitutional guarantee to be completely suspended or partially set aside. Decrees justified in this manner have the force of law until the executive or the Congress decides that the circumstances justifying the original suspension or restriction have ceased to exist. While this was probably meant to be a power reserved for extraordinary situations and for most constitutional guarantees it has been used only sparingly, the right to economic liberty (Art. 96) has been restricted or suspended for nearly the entire democratic era. This guarantee calls for protection against monopolies, usury, and unduly high prices. Presidents have used this power to control prices, fix currency exchange rates, offer differential rates of foreign exchange, and influence the production of "goods of basic necessity." As Figure 4.2 indicates, presidents have exercised this authority in varying amounts. The number of decrees issued that were justified in this manner (represented by the columns) are juxtaposed against the strength of the president's party in Congress (represented by the lines).

The two most avid users of this power, Pérez in his first term and Lusinchi, both enjoyed majorities in Congress. It is difficult to explain why presidents with cooperative congresses would exercise this authority rather than submitting legislation that had a high likelihood of passing. On the other hand, for some of these acts, like setting prices or intervening in foreign reserves, it would be inappropriate to legislate in normal fashion, and these two presidents may have felt freer than others to intervene re-

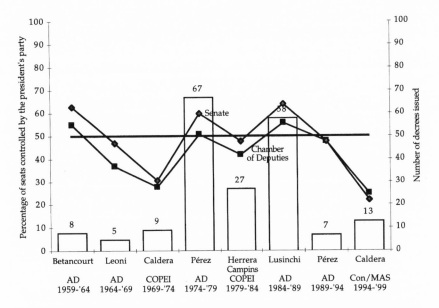

Figure 4.2. Relationship between the president's use of decree authority justified by the restriction or suspension of economic rights and the strength of his party in Congress.

peatedly in these areas because they knew that the AD-controlled Congress would not object. Betancourt seems to be an outlier in this regard in that he had a majority in Congress yet failed to issue a large number of decrees, perhaps as a result of his grand-coalition-style government.

Had a minority president been as active as Pérez and Lusinchi, it is possible that the opposition-controlled Congress would have declared the original motivating circumstances to have ceased and put the constitutional guarantee back in place – thus ending the president's decree authority in this area. As a result, minority presidents have been rather timid in the frequency with which they have invoked this power. Herrera Campins is a bit out of the norm in this regard, but his 27 decrees are not even half that issued by either of the two majority presidents. Caldera in his second term might also be an outlier given that the 13 decrees accounted for in the table were all issued during his first year in office. If he continued at this rate he would clearly have broken the pattern. But remember that Caldera, especially early in his term, was dealing with a congress controlled by elites concerned about the survivability of the regime as a whole, so he may have been acting with greater liberty from congressional oversight than the typical minority president. In fact, when Congress tried to reinstate other rights that Caldera had suspended, he openly challenged the act by immediately resuspending them, an apparently unconstitutional move. He let it be known through the press that future challenges from the Congress might force him to appeal to the people directly. With that, the original coalition of parties that had reinstated the rights broke apart, because AD was unwilling to risk a constitutional crisis in such trying times. Caldera and his supporters argued that the guarantees should remain suspended until three bills were passed strengthening the president's powers to influence exchange rates, to set prices, and to intervene in banks (these reform efforts, completed in July 1995, will be discussed further in Part 4.7).

POTENTIALLY MARGINAL PRESIDENTS

Venezuelan presidents have limited constitutionally allocated powers, but they have rarely been marginal. Why? In large part it is due to the interaction between their institutionalized powers and the party system that has developed. Majority presidents have been given enormous latitude to govern as they saw fit, especially Carlos Andrés Pérez in his first term during the oil boom. Highly disciplined parties in majority governments can lead to a breakdown in the normal set of checks and balances. Presidents are allowed to exercise great authority subject to very little oversight. Undoubtedly, minority presidents have been more restrained in their activities, but even they often exercise their limited powers to great effect. The limited number of highly disciplined parties makes the formation of stable postelection coalitions easier. The Venezuelan principle of conciliation for the sake of the system means that presidents, even minority ones, are given latitude by the parties represented in the legislature in order to stabilize the democratic system. This is particularly obvious in times of crisis, but it also characterizes Venezuelan politics in more normal times to a certain extent. As a result, extended interbranch immobilism has been rare.

In addition, interbranch immobilism has been avoided, and presidents have not become marginalized because of the extensive informal powers attributed to the office that were not intended to be particularly legislative. Presidents, including minority presidents, have an enormous bureaucratic network on which they can rely. This network is composed of everything from ad hoc committees to massive state-owned enterprises, like the nationalized petroleum industry. They are central to the political process from agenda setting and policy formation to execution and feedback. The policy-making process, as it is institutionalized in the executive branch, is designed to channel participation, control the list of potential actors, and limit the level of conflict. This set of institutions not only provides the president with the tools and resources to act with a great deal of discretion, it also gives him the opportunity to interact with organized interest groups in a meaningful way. As a result, groups in civil society see the executive branch as the place where things get done and as the political institution most capable of and willing to hear their demands.

4.7. CONTRADICTORY EFFORTS AT REFORM

Venezuelan political elites successfully managed conflict and were able to stabilize democratic rule. The ability to prevent conflict from becoming extreme and toppling the system required a significant level of control. That control was achieved by building strong parties and clear institutional channels of participation. In the electoral arena, voters were offered a variety of choices, but only choices for participating in highly disciplined parties. In institutional terms, organized groups found they had access to policy making, but only through participating in bodies created and named by the executive branch. In many ways, then, a relatively unchanging political elite put itself in key places to manage democratic participation.

While this level of control was good for consolidating democracy, it became a source of rigidity and eventually instability. Some issues were left off the agenda, like creating a more efficient and internationally competitive industrial base or establishing a tax base beyond petroleum revenues, and new groups were discouraged from forming or were frustrated once they did form. New parties found the electoral system difficult to break into because though there was a formula to ensure their participation, there was no access to the resources that the major parties use to promote themselves. Likewise, new interest groups, like neighborhood associations, found that the list of participants in the executive branch's committees and bureaucracy was rather closed.

So, the electoral system and policy-making institutions that allowed for successful negotiation of the transition to democratic rule became obstacles to its further deepening. These political sources of frustration led to a significant reform movement that was embodied by the Presidential Commission for the Reform of the State (COPRE). COPRE took decentralization as an overarching goal and sought changes within national-level government, between the national level and others, and even within the parties themselves. Its efforts met with some limited success, but the worsening political crisis combined with an economic crisis seem to have provoked a counter-movement in the area of government reform. The Caldera administration pushed for the adoption of three new laws that further centralized political authority in the hands of the president. Let me describe these contradictory reform efforts in greater detail.

COPRE

COPRE is a consultative commission created, in its present form, by President Lusinchi of AD in 1984. It concentrated its efforts in four areas: strengthening the checks and balances within the national government, moving decision-making authority to lower levels of government, decreasing the role of parties in elections, and making more transparent the internal workings of the political parties. COPRE reasoned that increasing participation, making participation more meaningful, and decentralizing authority would lead to more popular or responsive outcomes and restore legitimacy to the democratic regime. Its motto became "Democratize the democracy."

Strengthening checks and balances was dependent upon reestablishing the autonomy of the judicial branch, and though a new law reforming the Judicial Council (the body charged with naming most judges) was adopted, it was stripped of its most significant content by the time it got through Congress. Likewise, increased federalism centered on creating new elected posts at the municipal level and making governors directly elected rather than appointed by the president. While these reforms are significant, no attention was given to what authority these reformed offices would have, which ended up being very little. In addition, the expected autonomy of these posts was also diminished by party domination of candidate nomination and of electoral procedures. Efforts at electoral reform also met with some success but had less of an impact than was originally expected. The biggest change was probably the move to a compensatory-member system styled after German elections for choosing members of the Chamber of Deputies. Under this system approximately 50% of the deputies are elected from single-member districts, and the remaining 50% come from closed, blocked party lists. It is the vote for party lists that determines the partisan composition of the Chamber. Despite the greater attachment between some individual members and their respective districts, the principle of strict party discipline has not changed, and as a result parochial interests do not receive much more attention than previously.

The area in which COPRE has met with the least success is internal party reform. COPRE proposed more financial accountability, less spending, greater state financing, more internal democracy, and more open nomination procedures. Its suggested reforms have either been approved as voluntary changes to be decided upon by individual parties or not been acted upon at all. Given the historic strength of the parties and the strong grip that their central leadership bodies play, it is not surprising that they are hesitant to change.

These reform efforts seemed doomed to limited success from the start because of the nature of the reform strategy. First of all, COPRE itself is an example of how the traditional system of policy making has functioned. It is a consultative body within the executive branch created by presidential decree whose members are solely responsible to and appointed by the president. In this sense, it is the embodiment of how politics was channeled in the past. Many of its efforts have been made secondary to other interests of the executive branch. In addition, many of its members have felt "captured" or co-opted by the system. Criticism from the outside was not efficacious, but criticism from the inside had its limitations too. In the end, the substance of the proposals floundered because the very actors they were trying to change, the president and the parties that control Congress, were the ones with the power to implement the suggested changes. These elites showed a willingness to experiment with particular adjustments, but even this degree of flexibility has come to a stop in the more adverse conditions of the 1990s.

INCREASED POWERS TO THE PRESIDENT

Rafael Caldera was elected president in 1993 with the support of a coalition of small parties. The elections followed several years of crisis, including an attempted austerity package, public riots, a military crackdown, two attempted coups, legal proceedings against Pérez that removed him from office, and worsening economic conditions. Caldera positioned himself as someone with the moral force to clean up the current system, do away with corruption, and break the stranglehold of the increasingly unpopular "political class."

His proposed method for doing so has been in direct contradiction with the previous efforts at decentralization. Caldera has exercised his existing powers quite freely and has called for increased powers as well. In June 1994 he suspended a number of constitutional guarantees, including several individual rights, the right to economic liberty, and the right to property. Suspension of guarantees gives the president the right to issue decrees with the force of law regulating any activity related to these rights. Caldera argued that this power was necessary to deal with the financial crisis precipitated by the failure of several banks. Approximately a month later, Congress, with a majority composed of AD, COPEI, and Causa R, reinstated

all the constitutional guarantees, except the right to economic liberty. In
an apparently unconstitutional move, Caldera immediately resuspended the
same guarantees and threatened to appeal to the people, again an apparently
unconstitutional act, if the Congress did not back down. After this ulti-
matum AD dropped its support for reestablishing the guarantees in order
to avoid a constitutional crisis.

The constitutionality of the president's decree was challenged before
the Supreme Court by a group of law professors. A preliminary report prepared by the staff of the Court suggested that the decrees be found unconstitutional. Two days before the Court was to decide this issue, Caldera
appeared before the 11th Congress of the Confederation of Venezuelan
Workers (CTV), an AD-controlled union, and stated that factions of the
Congress and the Court were destabilizing the current equilibrium (referring to the suspension of guarantees and his increased powers), which was
essential to a transformation of government institutions. The president said
he would depend on the support of the workers if the other branches of
government continued to block his efforts. When the Supreme Court met
two days later, it rejected the recommendation of its staff and upheld the
suspension. In a unanimous message made public through a press conference, the justices did challenge Caldera's suggestion that the Court was
destabilizing democratic rule. Caldera's response was that his remarks
should be interpreted carefully and in context, and as to their veracity, he
submitted himself to the opinion of the public – again implying that he
would turn to the people in some unconstitutional manner in order to win
his disputes with the other branches of government.

Caldera and the group of parties supporting him, which by then included AD,[3] maintained that the constitutional guarantees could not be
reimplemented until three laws were passed. They would (1) give the president power to restrict and control the exchange rate, (2) allow the president
to fix maximum prices on goods of primary necessity, and (3) give him the
right to intervene in banks and other credit institutions – all without having
previously suspended or restricted constitutional guarantees. The president
can acquire these powers now by suspending guarantees, but the Congress
theoretically has the right to reestablish the guarantees, thus ending the
president's decree authority. These laws allow the president to assume these
powers without the Congress having any ability to control his actions. In

---

3 After the confrontation concerning the reestablishment and resuspension of rights in July
   1994, AD has voted with Convergencia/MAS in support of the president on a number of
   important issues. For example, in addition to the laws already mentioned, AD also opposed
   an effort by COPEI and Causa R to censure the minister of development (*fomento*).

essence, Caldera said that he would not oppose the reestablishment of constitutional guarantees once he had the authority to abrogate them at his discretion in the future. He was able to do this, despite his electoral coalition's minority status in Congress, because he had implicitly threatened legislators with an *autogolpe* legitimized by some form of appeal to the masses. With the support of AD added to that of Convergencia/MAS, all three of these bills passed Congress, though the law of financial emergencies was quite contentious and did not pass until mid-1995. On July 6, 1995, in the same meeting of his cabinet in which Caldera promulgated the last of the three laws, he reestablished the constitutional guarantees with Decree No. 739.[4]

Thus, as the crisis has deepened in Venezuela the proposed response has shifted from decentralization and increased participation to further centralization and concentration of power. Caldera augmented his discretionary powers and diminished the ability of other branches to serve as a check on his power. Of course, now in place these powers are available to all future presidents, not just Caldera. In the past, interbranch conflict has often been resolved through ad hoc coalitions or agreements to delegate authority temporarily, but Caldera's solution has been institutionalized – permanently shifting the balance of power among branches.

4.8. CONCLUSION

Venezuela's continuous experience with democracy points out a contradiction that may not be apparent in more recently established democracies. The factors that were good for the consolidation of democracy in Venezuela became sources of rigidity down the road. Venezuelan party leaders proved themselves capable of managing a difficult transition era and consolidating democracy despite insurrection by leftist guerrillas and attempted coups by the military. They did so by penetrating many other groups in civil society and incorporating important groups into the policy-making process through ad hoc and bureaucratic agencies within the executive branch. They proved themselves capable of managing interbranch conflict. Majority presidents were granted a great deal of leeway, and minority presidents were typically forced by the opposition to strike deals. However, the current economic and political crisis has called into question the continued legitimacy of this system.

---

4 Some guarantees were left suspended in border areas near Colombia where conflict with drug traffickers was a problem.

New interest groups in civil society, like neighborhood associations, are openly resisting party penetration and criticizing the current method of consultative politics. New parties like the Causa R seem less inclined to sublimate conflicts and put consensus foremost. Both of these proposed responses to the current difficulties are at the center of the topics discussed here. COPRE's frustrated reforms would have loosened the hold of the parties on the system and decreased the power of national-level officials. Caldera's efforts, on the other hand, strengthen the office of the president, who is not bound by party discipline, and increase his autonomy from the party-controlled Congress. As a result of the critical economic situation in Venezuela and the precariousness of the democratic regime, laws supported by Caldera were adopted, but they will undoubtedly face challenges to their constitutionality before the Supreme Court, which has already apparently acquiesced to Caldera on a related matter.

It should be noted that very few of the characteristics emphasized here are inherent in presidential regimes themselves. They are instead a combination of the constitutionally allocated powers particular to Venezuela, the nature of the party system, and the policy-making style and institutions that developed in an effort to protect democracy. Presidentialism in Venezuela has proved to be an institutional design suitable both for democratic consolidation and for the rebirth of instability.

APPENDIX 4.1: PARTY NAMES AND ACRONYMS

AD	Acción Democrática
CCN	Cruzada Cívica Nacionalista
Conv.	Convergencia
COPEI	Comité de Organización Política Electoral Independiente
FND	Frente Nacional Democrático
IPFN	Independiente Pro-Frente Nacional
LCR	La Causa Radical (Causa R)
MAS	Movimiento al Socialismo
MEP	Movimiento Electoral del Pueblo
MIN	Movimiento de Integración Nacional
MIR	Movimiento de Izquierda Revolucionaria
PCV	Partido Comunista de Venezuela
URD	Unión Republicana Democrática

5

STRONG CANDIDATES FOR A LIMITED OFFICE: PRESIDENTIALISM AND POLITICAL PARTIES IN COSTA RICA

John M. Carey

INTRODUCTION

Presidents are not dominant over political parties in Costa Rica, but presidential *candidates* wield tremendous influence over their copartisans. This chapter focuses attention on the rules that govern political competition and policy making: specifically, electoral laws and the constitutional division of powers between the executive and legislative branches of government. These rules endow Costa Rican presidents with some strengths in influencing partisan policy struggles, but in comparative perspective, the formal powers of Costa Rican presidents to control the actions of politicians within their parties and decisions in the Legislative Assembly are strictly limited. In short, Costa Rican institutions provide for a legislature that is largely independent of the president in debating and deciding on national policy. Nevertheless, the dependence of Costa Rican politicians on future presidential appointments implies that *prospective* presidents enjoy significant power within their parties, both inside and outside the legislature.

The chapter proceeds as follows. First, I trace the historical roots of limited presidential power in Costa Rica back to the establishment of the current regime, then review the scope of presidential power in the context of the current constitution and party system. Next, I turn attention to the nature of Costa Rican political careers, arguing that prohibitions on reelection for both legislators and presidents generate unique influence for presidential candidates over their copartisans, in both electoral politics and policy making. I then illustrate the limitations on presidential ability to affect policy making in the legislature with examples from budget and bank reform legislation and from treaty ratification. Finally, I offer some general conclusions.

THE PRESIDENCY AND THE PARTY SYSTEM

HISTORICAL ROOTS OF THE LIMITED PRESIDENCY

Costa Rica has a constitutional tradition of a relatively weak executive. A number of Costa Rica's earliest political charters provided for plural executives. Under the first postindependence pact organizing Costa Rican politics, there was even a provision that the residence of the presidency was to be shifted every three months among the four major towns: Cartago, San José, Alajuela, and Heredia (Gutiérrez Gutiérrez 1984; Seligson 1987). The idea was that the presidency should go to the people, rather than existing as a physically independent power base.

The shape of the modern Costa Rican presidency is the result of a series of events at midcentury: activist presidents, a brief civil war, and the subsequent Constituent Assembly that codified strict limitations on presidential power. Rapid social and economic reform began in the 1940s, under the administrations of Presidents Rafael Ángel Calderón Guardia and Teodoro Picado. After winning the presidency and control of Congress in 1940, Calderón and his Republican Party passed a sweeping legislative agenda, including the establishment of Costa Rica's first progressive income tax, the establishment of a Social Security pension system, and the creation of the National University (Salazar 1981; Aguílar Bulgarelli 1986). The Republicans lost their congressional majority in the 1942 midterm election, but Calderón's Republicans entered into a coalition with the Communist Party and proceeded to pass a constitutional reform providing a labor code guaranteeing a minimum wage; an eight-hour workday; the right to unionize; the right to housing, basic safety, and sanitation conditions in the workplace; and a priority for Costa Rican workers over foreigners (Salazar 1981).

From 1941 to 1944, the real expenditures of the government almost doubled, and the budget deficit in 1944 was 15 times that in 1941 (Aguílar Bulgarelli 1986). Calderón's policies drew strong opposition from economic conservatives, landowners, and employers. The opposition, moreover, charged Calderón with electoral fraud in both 1942 and 1944, when the president's hand-picked successor, Teodoro Picado Michalski, defeated the conservative, León Cortes, by a ratio of almost 2:1. By the mid-1940s, a group of intellectuals based at the University of Costa Rica's Law School joined the voices of regime opposition despite their support for the Calderón/Picado reforms. These Social Democrats objected to an alliance with the Communists on any basis, and they concurred with charges that Calderón, and later Picado, used outright fraud as well as patronage to guarantee electoral victories (Dunkerley 1988; Aguílar Bulgarelli 1986).

With the 1948 election approaching, the Social Democrats opted to forego a candidacy for their leader, José Figueres Ferrer, and coalesce with the main conservative opposition groups behind Otilio Ulate. On February 8, 1948, Ulate defeated Calderón in his effort to retake the presidency by 54,931 to 44,438 votes. However, the Republican–Communist coalition retained a majority in the Congress. Again there were charges of fraud – on both sides this time. The National Electoral Tribunal (TNE) declared Ulate the winner of the presidential election in February, but on March 1 the new Congress convened and, at Calderón's request, nullified the presidential election. After the failure of attempts by the TNE to mediate a compromise solution to the standoff, Figueres led an army of about 600 men, mostly Ulate supporters, in a civil war that overthrew the existing regime in six weeks.

In May 1948, Figueres assumed the presidency of a junta that governed the country for 18 months, while the Constituent Assembly was elected and rewrote the constitution. Figueres agreed to oversee the installation of Ulate in the presidency, but a new Legislative Assembly would be elected for the term beginning in 1949. Although Ulate's Partido Unión Nacional (PUN) held 34 of 45 seats in the Constituent Assembly, the delegates drafted a document that protected the institutional interests of the legislature and weakened the powers of the presidency, even as their own copartisan was about to assume the office. The key measures were (1) subjecting presidential emergency power to immediate Assembly approval by two-thirds majority, (2) eliminating the president's veto on the national budget, (3) mandating an eight-year intervening period before an ex-president could serve again, (4) mandating that all conventions and treaties be subject to Assembly approval, (5) explicitly prohibiting the pocket veto and any executive refusal to sign legislation passed over presidential objections, and (6) providing for the interpellation and "censure" of cabinet ministers.[1]

---

1 Censure by a majority vote in the Legislative Assembly is merely a formal expression of

THE CURRENT PRESIDENCY: CONSTITUTIONAL WEAKNESS, PARTISAN SUPPORT

The constitution of 1949 provides the Costa Rican president with complete authority over creation and maintenance of the executive, but scant formal authority to influence legislation. Presidents serve a single four-year term and are permanently prohibited from reelection.[2] Control over executive branch appointments is a principal resource of the presidency. The president names his or her cabinet without any requirement for Assembly approval and may dismiss any minister at will (Art. 139). The Assembly, in contrast, requires a prohibitive two-thirds majority vote to oust any minister (Art. 121). To the extent that executive ministers have discretion over policy, presidential influence can be considerable. Short-term decisions on an issue such as currency devaluation, for example, are controlled by the Central Bank, whose director is a presidential appointee.

On the other hand, most significant policy changes require legislative action, especially if they are to be sustained over the long term, and formal presidential authority does not extend far into the legislative sphere.[3] The Costa Rican president does not have any constitutional authority to legislate by decree; and even in cases of national emergency any presidential motion to suspend constitutional guarantees must be ratified by a two-thirds vote in the Legislative Assembly before it can take effect (Art. 140). Perhaps most notable, however, is the limitation of the president's veto authority. Across presidential systems, the veto is the most ubiquitous tool by which executives can shape legislation, generally by requiring an extraordinary legislative majority to override the president's rejection of any law. Under such conditions, lawmakers must anticipate and accommodate presidential preferences in crafting policy. The Costa Rican constitution, however, voids the president's veto power on the national budget law, leaving the Legislative Assembly sovereign over appropriations (Art. 125). Although a presidential veto requires a two-thirds override on all other legislation, it cannot

---

disapproval for ministerial conduct or policy. A two-thirds vote of impeachment is required to remove a minister.

2 The eight-year prohibition on presidential reelection imposed by the Constituent Assembly was amended, subsequent to the third presidency of José Figueres (1970–74), to a lifetime ban.

3 The importance of legislative support in sustaining a president's long-term monetary policy agenda, for example, will be illustrated later in the discussion of President Monge's (1982–86) efforts to reform the banking system.

be exercised on the annual budget – the most important single piece of legislation that must be passed each year.

A final significant authority is the power to call the Legislative Assembly into special session to consider legislation specified only by the president (Art. 118). Unlike presidential agenda-setting authorities in other systems, however, this authority in Costa Rica does not entail the ability to control procedural details, such as the number and nature of amendments that can be attached to presidential proposals. The president, then, can convene the Assembly to consider a specific issue but cannot constrain actions that the Assembly might take on that issue. The Assembly may accede to presidential proposals, but it can also simply refuse to act, or it can amend presidential proposals beyond recognition. In short, when compared with the formal authorities of other elected presidents, the constitutional powers of the Costa Rican president over legislation are remarkable mainly in the extent to which they are limited (Shugart and Carey 1992).

Apart from authorities directly endowed by the constitution, Costa Rican electoral law works to the president's advantage by fostering partisan support for the executive in the Assembly. Presidential effectiveness is severely limited and presidential regimes more frequently face constitutional crises when executives face opposition partisan majorities in the legislature (Fiorina 1992; Mainwaring 1993; Linz 1994; Valenzuela 1994). The format and timing of elections, however, strongly influence the prospects for partisan presidential support. In the Costa Rican case, two factors contribute to the tendency toward strong partisan support for the president in the Assembly. First, the Costa Rican presidency must be awarded to the candidate who wins a plurality of at least 40% of the popular vote in the first round of presidential elections. This rule discourages fragmentation of the party system, encouraging the formation of broad partisan coalitions behind fewer candidates than would be the case in a pure majority runoff system, as is used in much of Latin America (Shugart and Carey 1992). Second, Costa Rica's Assembly elections are held concurrently with the presidential election. In systems where presidential and Assembly elections are held on the same day, the parties presenting the top presidential candidates benefit in Assembly elections as well (Shugart 1995). Thus, despite proportional representation and moderately large district magnitudes (average $M = 8.1$), the Costa Rican party system since 1949 has been increasingly dominated by two major parties, and presidents have generally enjoyed majority – or at least plurality – partisan support in the Assembly.

Table 5.1 shows that 7 of 12 presidents during the current regime have enjoyed partisan majorities in the Legislative Assembly; 3 have held partisan

Table 5.1. *Partisan support in the Legislative Assembly for Costa Rican presidents (percentages)*

Year	President's party[a]	President's status	PUN	PLN	PUNIF/ UNIDAD/ PUSC[b]	Other parties
1949	PUN	Majority	71	7[c]	15	6
1953	PLN	Majority	26	67	7	
1958	PUN	Minority (plurality)[d]	22	44	24	9
1962	PLN	Majority	16	51	32	2
1966	PUNIF	Minority (opposition)		51	46	4
1970	PLN	Majority		56	39	5
1974	PLN	Minority (plurality)		47	30	23
1978	UNIDAD	Minority (plurality)		44	47	9
1982	PLN	Majority		58	34	9
1986	PLN	Majority		51	44	5
1990	PUSC	Majority		44	51	5
1994	PLN	Minority (plurality)		49	44	7

[a]The acronyms in this column represent the following parties: PUN, Partido Unión Nacional; PLN, Partido Liberación Nacional; PUNIF, Partido de Unificación; UNIDAD, Coalition of Unity; PUSC, Partido Unión Social Cristiano.
[b]This column shows the seats held by the heirs to Rafael Calderón Guardia's Republican Party. Beginning in 1982, this group has been unified in the PUSC. In earlier elections, they have run under labels including the Constitutional Party, Republicans, Unification, and UNIDAD.
[c]In 1949, before the formation of the PLN, the Social Democrats won three Assembly seats.
[d]The president's party held only 22% of Assembly seats but was part of a coalition with National Unification that had backed a single presidential candidate.

pluralities just shy of majorities, 1 headed a coalition that held a plurality, and only 1 has faced a unified opposition majority in the legislature. Costa Rican presidents generally do not confront highly fragmented legislatures with few partisan allies, as has been the case elsewhere in Latin America, especially where presidents are elected by majority runoff and/or not simultaneously with congresses (see Mainwaring, and Shugart and Mainwaring, this volume). Although partisan support is a strength of the Costa Rican presidency, it is however mitigated significantly by impediments to presidential control of copartisans in the Assembly. This partisan weakness of presidents, in turn, is attributable to Costa Rica's prohibition of reelection for both presidents and legislators, which is discussed at length later.

CAREERS, APPOINTMENTS, AND CONTROL OF PARTIES

The effectiveness of presidents or any other party leaders to shape policy is largely dependent on their ability to influence the actions of legislators. This influence, in turn, is based on the ability to control the political careers of legislators. For example, in systems where legislative careers are desirable and where party leaders control politicians' prospects for reelection, responsiveness to leadership directives is high (Duverger 1954; Epstein 1967; Coppedge 1994). Conversely, where politicians aspire to careers outside the legislature or where politicians' prospects for reelection are more directly dependent on personal support from voters than on the decisions of party leaders, responsiveness to party leaders suffers (Mayhew 1974; Ames 1995b). By the same logic, where presidents are also national party leaders, strong party discipline translates into legislative responsiveness to presidential directives.[4] But prohibitions on presidential reelection, which exist throughout most of Latin America, undermine presidential authority over legislative copartisans, because legislators know that incumbent presidents will not continue to hold their current position and so will exert less control over legislators' career prospects after a specified date.[5]

This describes the state of affairs throughout most Latin American presidential systems: Presidents generally exercise influence over the career prospects of their copartisans, via both their constitutional powers and their influence within their parties. But their constitutional powers will terminate at a known date, and their intrapartisan influence will likely diminish correspondingly. All of this holds true for Costa Rica as well. But the argument here is that the power of Costa Rican presidents over their copartisans is mitigated even further by the existence of legislative term limits. The

4 The adoption of the two-stage, majority-runoff format for presidential elections throughout much of Latin America in the 1980s and 1990s has contributed to the election of a number of "outsider" presidents – those who are not supported by major parties – for example, Fujimori in Peru, Collor in Brazil, and Serrano in Guatemala. In Costa Rica, in contrast, all presidents under the current regime have been supported by major parties or coalitions and have generally been drawn from among the most prominent party leaders.

5 Of course, former presidents may remain active in their parties' national leadership and so influential over political careers. But at the least, presidential term limits guarantee that incumbents will wield less influence after some fixed point in time.

prohibition on reelection for deputies means that legislators rely over-whelmingly on executive appointments to sustain their political careers. These appointments will be awarded exclusively at the discretion of the *next* president, whose identity is uncertain, except that he or she certainly will not be the *incumbent* president. In effect, the combination of both presi-dential and legislative term limits means that incumbent Costa Rican presidents are *constitutionally guaranteed* not to control the sources of post-Assembly patronage that are most desired among incumbent legislators. Incumbent presidents, then, have limited carrots with which to entice (or sticks with which to coerce) legislators to respond to their demands. Finally, because incumbent legislators, as well as the host of other political aspirants, are dependent on the next president for appointed posts, presidential *can-didates* exercise significant influence over their copartisans, both inside and outside the Legislative Assembly in Costa Rica.

The following discussion illustrates these arguments, by making four points. First, legislative careers are not viable in Costa Rica. Second, legis-lators are politically ambitious and are dependent on appointments by future presidents to continue their careers. Third, presidential candidates exert inordinate influence within their parties because of their expected control over appointments. More specifically, fourth, incumbent legislators have reason to expect that presidential candidates, if elected, will use appoint-ments to reward their supporters and punish their opponents, both within their party and across parties.

POLITICAL CAREERS WITHOUT REELECTION

Costa Rican legislative term limits proscribe *immediate* reelection, but do not prohibit former legislators from serving a subsequent Assembly term after having sat out at least one four-year term (Art. 107). Nevertheless, remarkably few former legislators manage to secure reelection at all. Table 5.2 shows the number of terms served in the Legislative Assembly for all those who have been elected from 1949 through the present. The columns break the data according to political parties. Of 267 politicians who have served for the PLN in the Assembly, 233 have served only one term; 29 have served two terms, and only 5 have served three terms. The prospects for multiple terms are remarkably similar across parties.

Not only are multiple Assembly terms a rarity, but there is no trend toward more reelection and increasing professionalization in the Costa Rican Assembly. Reelection rates are stable across the entire period (Carey 1996). Thus, rotation-style term limits in Costa Rica have not produced a system-

Table 5.2. *Number of terms served in Costa Rican Legislative Assembly by those who have served since 1949 (percentages)*

	Party			
Terms	All	PLN[a]	Major opposition[b]	Others
1	495 (87)[c]	233 (87)	225 (90)	59 (89)
2	60 (11)[d]	29 (11)	20 (8)	6 (9)
3	14 (3)	5 (2)	4 (2)	1 (2)
Total	569 (100)	267 (100)	249 (100)	66 (100)

Note: Service in 1949 Constituent Assembly not included.
[a]Includes Social Democrats of 1949, prior to formation of PLN.
[b]Includes PUN deputies, remnants of Calderón Guardia's Republican Party, and the various Christian democrat parties that eventually coalesced in 1982 to form PUSC.
[c]Counting across this row, and in the bottom row of the table, the sum of all deputies in the PLN, Major opposition, and Other columns exceeds the number in this column. This is because the columns broken down by party reflect the total number of terms deputies served as members of that party. Individual deputies could be counted more than once in the three right-hand columns – for example, if they switched parties during the middle of their term or if they served more than one term, but not for the same party.
[d]Counting across this row and the next, values in this column exceed the sums of the three right-hand columns. This is because this column accounts for all deputies who served multiple terms, whereas the others account only for those who served multiple terms for the same party. In sum, the All column shows the aggregate rate of reelection; the three right-hand columns reflect the same phenomenon, but within specific parties and coalitions.

atic pattern of rotation in and out of the Legislative Assembly. The bottom line is that Costa Rican politicians cannot expect Assembly careers. Although Costa Rican term limits formally allow for staggered reelection, this is the exception rather than the rule. Thus, Costa Rican legislators aspiring to build political careers need to look elsewhere besides the Assembly.

The most desirable path to a post-Assembly career is through executive appointments. Of 33 deputies asked, "If you serve your party well in the Assembly, what compensation can you expect?" fully 30 (91%) mentioned appointments to executive ministries, the foreign service, or posts as directors of the country's autonomous institutions.[6] How likely are former dep-

---

6 Appointments to these institutions are all the exclusive domain of the president, with no legislative confirmation process, as in some presidential systems. The data on the aspira-

Table 5.3. *Distribution of appointed posts among former Costa Rican deputies,*
1949–86 cohorts (percentages)

	Number of appointments per deputy					
Party[a]	0	1	2	3	4	5
All	311 (54)	172 (30)	53 (9)	19 (3)	7 (1)	9 (2)
PLN	104 (42)	97 (39)	30 (12)	9 (4)	4 (2)	4 (2)
Main opposition	174 (65)	59 (22)	18 (7)	7 (3)	3 (2)	4 (2)
Other	37 (70)	9 (17)	5 (9)	2 (4)	0 (0)	0 (0)

[a]The sum broken down by parties is greater than the figure in the All row among
deputies who received no appointments. Overcounting occurs because deputies who
served for different parties during different terms are double counted in terms of
Assembly service. In some other columns, the sum broken down by parties is less
than the figure in the All row. Undercounting occurs among some deputies who
did receive appointments because the appointments are attributed only to the party
most recently served prior to the appointment.

uties to receive such posts? The answer depends largely on how the data are
cut. Table 5.3 presents data on the rate of post-Assembly appointments
among Costa Rican deputies.[7] The columns represent the number of appointments received by politicians *after* their service in the Assembly. The
rows break down the data according to party. All those who served in the
1949 through the 1986 Assembly cohorts are included.[8] Across all parties,
54% of deputies received no appointments to ministries, the foreign service,
or autonomous institutions; 30% received one appointment; 9% received
two; and 6% received three or more appointments. The rate of appointments
is highest for former PLN deputies – not surprisingly, given that the PLN
has controlled the presidency during 6 of the 10 administrations studied
here. Deputies from the main opposition parties to the PLN have fared
somewhat worse. And deputies from minor parties are the least likely to
continue their political careers outside the Assembly.

tions of legislators are from interviews with members of the 1990–94 Assembly cohort.
During the months of January through March 1992, the author interviewed 45 of the 57
Assembly members. Because of time constraints and frequent interruptions – to go to the
chamber and vote, for example – not every deputy was asked the same set of questions.
In this case, the question was included in 33 of the 45 interviews.

7 For a more thorough discussion of how the data were accumulated and estimated, see
Carey (1996).

8 Cohorts after the 1986–90 group are not included, since they were not yet eligible for
concurrent service in the Assembly and in executive-branch-appointed positions when the
data were collected.

Table 5.4. *Estimated appointments of former deputies to executive positions during term immediately following Assembly service (percentages)*

Cohort	Party won next presidential election	Party lost next presidential election
1949	2/3 (67)	0/60 (0)
1953	4/20 (20)	1/38 (3)
1958	7/21 (33)	0/40 (0)
1962	8/25 (32)	0/33 (0)
1966	12/24 (50)	0/33 (0)
1970	7/36 (19)	0/26 (0)
1974	11/19 (58)	2/42 (5)
1978	25/29 (86)	0/33 (0)
1982	14/34 (41)	0/25 (0)
1986	18/25 (72)	0/33 (0)
Average	124/258 (48)	3/363 (1)

The aggregate data on appointments reinforce the point that political careers are possible in Costa Rica. But to explain how executive appointments affect legislative behavior, a more relevant cut on the data examines the likelihood of a deputy receiving an appointment immediately after his or her service in the Assembly. This is the critical cut for two reasons. First, term limits give Costa Rican deputies short time horizons. Deputies know exactly when their tenure in office will end and that without exception they will need to secure other employment after that date. Therefore, the prospects for appointment during the *immediately subsequent term* are the most relevant appointment data in explaining the behavior of incumbent legislators. Second, it is the promise of an immediate post-Assembly appointment that shapes the relationship between presidential candidates and their copartisans in the Assembly.

For each Assembly cohort up to 1986, I divide those deputies whose party or coalition won the next presidential election from those whose party lost. For each group, I determine the rate at which the former deputies received political appointments during the next administration. The data presented in Table 5.4 and Figure 5.1 illustrate a number of points clearly. First, for a deputy whose party or coalition wins the next presidential election, the prospects for securing a political appointment during the next administration are bright. An estimated average of 48% of this group has been able to continue national politics in the term immediately following Assembly service. Second, these prospects have grown considerably brighter

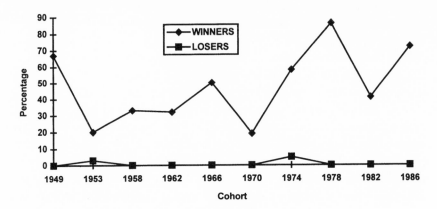

Figure 5.1. The rate of estimated appointments of former deputies to executive positions during term immediately following assembly service according to party's fortunes in the next presidential election.

over time. Whereas the estimated rate of appointment for winning partisans in the 1953 to 1974 period was 30%, the rate from 1974 to 1990 was 64%. This is largely due to the growth in the size of the Costa Rican government. There are more ministries and more autonomous institutions now than at the beginning of the current regime, and thus more appointed positions. Third, for deputies whose party loses the next presidential election, the prospects for receiving an appointment during the successive administration are close to nil, with no change in the pattern over time. In short, those deputies whose party wins the next presidency have excellent prospects for continuing their careers in politics; conversely, those whose party loses are, at least for the time being, finished.

THE INFLUENCE OF PRESIDENTIAL CANDIDATES

Incumbent legislators compose a small group and are relatively easy to keep track of. Therefore, it is possible to demonstrate thoroughly their career dependence on the subsequent president. This dependence is not limited to legislators, however, but is characteristic of all partisan political aspirants. The enormous leverage over their copartisans that is afforded presidential candidates by the prospect of control over patronage is most evident during the series of party assemblies that nominate candidates and establish lists for Assembly and local elections.

The letter of the electoral law in Costa Rica is quite specific in detailing the formal procedures by which parties can put together Assembly lists and suggests that control over Assembly nominations is strongly decentralized. The Organic Electoral Code states that each party's candidate lists for national and local elections shall be selected by majority vote of delegates to that party's national assembly, or convention. But delegates to each party's national assembly are the products of a series of lower-level assemblies. The process begins at the subcantonal level, in 510 districts nationwide.[9] Each party is to hold an assembly (effectively a primary and open to all registered partisans in the district),[10] at which 5 delegates to a canton-level assembly are selected by majority vote. These delegates then attend canton-level assemblies, where 5 delegates are likewise selected to provincial assemblies. Each provincial assembly then selects 10 delegates to the party's national assembly, where all provincial lists are drawn up and must be approved by majorities.[11]

This process appears to establish clearly the independence of those who decide nominations from control by central party leaders. Nevertheless, Costa Rican political scientists state without exception that presidential candidates tightly control the nomination process through the use of procedural tricks and manipulation, with occasional outright fraud, and, most importantly, with the promise of patronage (Sojo Obando 1992; Ventura Robles 1984; Casas Zamora and Briceño Fallas 1991).

The first important point here is that presidential nominations dominate intrapartisan elections, because presidential hopefuls take their appeals directly to partisans in the electorate, presenting lists of committed delegates even at the district-level primaries (Tribunal Supremo de Elecciones 1989, Art. 74 Trans. 3; Sojo Obando 1992). These primaries, moreover, have been pushed earlier and earlier in the electoral cycle at the behest of presidential frontrunners. District-level assemblies for the 1994 elections were held in February and March of 1992 – more than two years in advance of the general election and less than halfway through the 1990–94 term. The Costa Rican media quite reasonably pointed out that presidential candidates and national party leaders were attempting to lock in delegates to provincial and national assemblies early, before most voters began to pay attention to the campaign. Once loyal and obedient delegates are chosen by

9 Cantons are the Costa Rican equivalent of counties.
10 Registering as a partisan is a simple matter of declaring party preference when registering to vote and does not require payment of party dues.
11 *Ley Orgánica del Tribunal Supremo de Elecciones y del Registro Civil y Código Electoral y otras disposiciones conexas*, Title IV, Articles 58, 60, 61, and 63.

district and cantonal assemblies, successful presidential candidates can control subsequent decisions taken within their parties (Roverssi 1992a, 1992b).[12]

With their own nominations secured ahead of time, presidential candidates dominate their national party assemblies, which make final decisions over nominations and lists for all other candidates (Villegas Antillón 1992; Sojo Obando 1992; Asamblea Legislativa de Costa Rica 1992, Int. 93-04).[13] As Rafael Villegas Antillón, the current chairman of the Supreme Tribunal of Elections (TSE), puts it, "The national party assemblies are highly manipulable. In practice, the presidential candidate, with a look, can tell any delegate how to vote" (Casas Zamora and Briceño Fallas 1991:332n). Miguel Ángel Rodriguez, a two-term deputy and president of the Legislative Assembly, spells it out even more clearly:

> Nothing is more important in the nomination process than loyalties to the presidential candidate. All the delegates know that if their party wins the election, the future president ultimately controls all government posts. This is the source of the loyalty they profess, because they know this loyalty can be rewarded sooner or later, and all of the delegates are at the national assembly with an eye toward an ambassadorship, an advisory post, or a position in a ministry, etc. Under these circumstances, it is clear that the power of the candidate over the delegates is almost absolute. (Casas Zamora and Briceño Fallas 1992: 337)

Moreover, the president's patronage powers are not limited to the prime appointments that Rodriguez mentions by name or even those to which incumbent legislators aspire. Although some government workers are protected from the spoils system by statutory guarantees of job security and prohibitions against removing employees for political reasons, Costa Rican presidents fill posts all the way down to local police chiefs and chauffeurs

---

12 It is important to contrast the Costa Rican and Mexican cases on this point. Mexico, like Costa Rica, imposes term limits on both presidents and legislators. But Mexican presidents have proved far more influential over their copartisans in Congress than Costa Rican presidents have. The traditional ability of Mexican presidents to name their successors is the key to this difference. Rather than jockey for alliances with presidential hopefuls whose policy agendas may conflict with those of the incumbent presidents, incumbent Mexican legislators who aspire to postcongressional appointments have been best served by supporting the incumbent president, on the expectation that his handpicked successor will reward party loyalty. The critical difference between the systems is the level of competition and uncertainty surrounding presidential succession. See Weldon's chapter for a thorough discussion of the Mexican case.

13 Interviews conducted by the author with members of the 93rd Legislative Assembly (1990–94) were confidential. The deputies are identified by code numbers, for example, 93-01 through 93-57. Citations to these interviews, then, are denoted as "Asamblea Legislativa 1992, Int. 93- ," followed by the relevant deputy's code number.

for government vehicles. Scanning issues of *La Gaceta* during the early weeks of any administration, one can find literally hundreds – maybe thousands – of notices for presidential appointments to jobs at all levels of government.

REWARDS, PUNISHMENT, AND PATRONAGE

Clearly, then, presidential candidates enjoy the prospect of access to broad patronage resources, and they clearly allocate those resources on a strictly partisan basis. The next step in explaining their influence within their parties is to demonstrate that they distinguish loyal copartisans from mavericks in distributing patronage. To do this, it is necessary to identify a case in which a party was divided over the decision of a presidential candidate. The selection of the president of the Legislative Assembly in 1985, which has come to be known as the Mayo Negro, constitutes just such a case.[14]

In 1985, having already secured the PLN presidential nomination for the 1986 election, Oscar Arias Sánchez undertook to build a coalition among incumbent PLN deputies to elect Matilde Marín Chinchilla as president of the Assembly for the 1985–86 term. The Assembly had never had a woman as president, and Arias's motivation was, at least in part, to rectify this inequity (Villalobos 1992). He circulated a letter among all PLN deputies suggesting the choice of Marín Chinchilla (Asamblea Legislativa de Costa Rica 1985b). The caucus divided bitterly over this suggestion, in part because some deputies resented the interference of the presidential candidate in the selection process, but also because many strongly objected to the selection of a woman to the position of president of the Assembly (Villanueva Badilla 1992; Villalobos 1992; Asamblea Legislativa de Costa Rica 1985a:16, 30). Ultimately, the PLN caucus vote was 17 to 16 in favor of Marín Chinchilla. Arias regarded the caucus vote as binding on all PLN members, but on the Assembly floor, the 16 dissident PLN deputies joined with most of the PUSC deputies to elect an alternative PLN deputy as Assembly president.

The Mayo Negro was a widely publicized fiasco for the PLN and for Arias. For this study, however, it provides useful data, because the alliances with and against a presidential candidate were explicit (Asamblea Legislativa de Costa Rica 1985a; Villanueva Badilla 1992). Moreover, the post-

14 The Assembly presidency generally rotates among four different deputies during the four-year term. Each year, the majority-party caucus selects a candidate for president by majority vote. The entire caucus then supports that candidate in what has, in every year besides 1985, been a pro forma floor vote.

Assembly fates of those deputies involved in the Mayo Negro demonstrate that presidential candidates, if elected, use patronage to reward and punish copartisans. Of the 17 deputies who supported Arias, at least 7 received executive appointments.[15] Of the 16 who opposed Arias, only 1 received an appointment.

The main conclusion from this section is that presidential candidates hold enormous sway over their copartisans because of their expected control over patronage. In contrast, for incumbent presidents, especially late in their terms, patronage does not provide much political capital. And at no point in a president's term do patronage offers influence legislators, who uniformly are looking ahead to the next administration. The situation is described generally as follows: For any given politician, X, control over electoral prospects to the Assembly and control over post-Assembly career prospects are exercised by different principals. A presidential candidate, Y, might dominate nominations and the formation of lists that determines X's initial prospects for election to the Assembly. If Y wins the presidency, he or she serves his or her term concurrently with X's term in the Assembly. But X's post-Assembly political career is dependent on an appointment by the president who serves after Y. Thus, ex ante control over electoral prospects and ex post control over career prospects are exercised by different principals. As a result, the influence of the president over his or her copartisans wanes as the president's term progresses, whereas the influence of the party's next candidate waxes.

PRESIDENTIAL CONTROL OVER POLICY MAKING

The strength of Costa Rican presidents is derived from a constrained veto, an electoral system that encourages substantial partisan support, their control over the ministries, and, less tangibly, the electoral and institutional prominence of the office. Together these give presidents significant influence, but certainly not dominance, in Costa Rican policy making. Even when presidents enjoy partisan legislative majorities, their authority over policy making consists largely of what their Assembly copartisans choose to delegate to them. The executive frequently serves as a focal point for coordinating actions among copartisans, affording the president an informal

---

15 Seven were documented as receiving minstries, ambassadorships, or posts on the boards of directors of state-owned corporations. More may have received lower-level appointments.

agenda-setting power in selecting among various arrangements that might be acceptable to legislators. By the same token, however, presidents with such limited constitutional powers cannot compel legislators – copartisans or not – to adopt executive initiatives. Therefore, presidents are frequently left to rely on what Richard Neustadt calls "the power to persuade," especially when attempting to implement policies that are not universally embraced within their parties (Neustadt 1980). This section illustrates these aspects of presidential authority with budget-making data since the 1970s and with examples of presidential efforts to build coalitions on some critical policies in recent years.

PRESIDENTIAL EFFORTS TO CONTROL SPENDING

The discussion of budget legislation here focuses on the section of the annual budget of most direct personal concern to individual deputies, the distribution of pork-barrel projects.[16] Budgetary pork is accounted for in a distinct section of Costa Rica's annual budget bill, known as the *partidas específicas* (specific projects), where the deputy responsible for securing each individual appropriation is personally identified. *Partidas* are monopolized by the majority party or coalition, whereas the major opposition is denied pork altogether (Carey 1996). Majority-party legislators value pork highly, because the *partidas* allow deputies rare opportunities to claim personal credit for benefits delivered to their communities. Although money appropriated for *partidas* generally finds its way to its designated communities, the path is not, however, entirely certain. Despite the lack of a veto on appropriations legislation, in some years presidents have used their control over the Budget Ministry to prevent the release of some of the funds appropriated by the Assembly. Figure 5.2 shows the rate at which funds appropriated for *partidas* were ultimately disbursed over an 18-year period for which data are available.[17]

The most striking pattern is the difference between the periods of divided, as opposed to unified, government. From May 1974 through May 1982, Costa Rican presidents held partisan pluralities, but not majorities, in the Assembly – first under the PLN administration of Daniel Oduber

16 It is not intuitively apparent that budgetary pork should be of much interest to legislators who are elected from closed lists in large-magnitude districts and who cannot be reelected. See Carey (forthcoming) or Taylor (1992) for extensive explorations of this phenomenon.

17 From the *Memoria Anual*, published yearly by the Office of the Controller of Costa Rica, Part III, Tables 18 and 20.

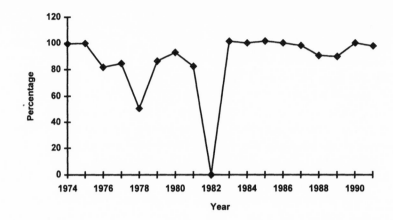

Figure 5.2. Rate at which appropriated partidas específas *funds were disbursed,*
1974–91.

Quiros, then under the Christian democratic coalition of Rodrigo Carazo
Odio. Throughout this period, the rate of disbursal of *partida* funds was
consistently lower than during the three administrations from 1982 to 1991
– when our most current data were collected – all of which have enjoyed
Assembly majorities. Presidents lacking Assembly majorities have been
more aggressive in the aggregate in impounding *partidas*. Also, 1978 and
1982, the two years in which the rate of *partida* disbursal was lowest, were
years in which new administrations hostile to the preceding Assembly plurality took office halfway through the fiscal year. In May 1978, President
Carazo inherited a budget written by an Assembly with a PLN plurality
and support from independent deputies (Volio Guevara 1988). For the year,
nearly 50% of appropriated *partida* funds were impounded. The lack of any
partida appropriations for 1982, on the other hand, was driven not by impoundments but by Assembly inaction or deadlock. The 1982 budget was
written in 1981, the last complete year of Carazo's term. Carazo's sharp
decline in popularity, as well as the deterioration of his Christian democratic
coalition throughout his term, are renowned in Costa Rica. The failure of
the Assembly to appropriate any *partidas* in the 1982 budget, then, was
likely the result of Assembly deadlock in the absence of a stable majority
coalition, as well as the anticipation that *partidas* to be appropriated could
be impounded by the next president, to be inaugurated in May.

     If partisan change in the presidency generates higher rates of impound-
ment, however, then 1990 presents a puzzle, because the *partidas* appropriated by the PLN Assembly in 1989 were disbursed in their entirety, despite

the inauguration in May of a new PUSC president, Rafael Calderón Fournier. It is possible that the outgoing PLN administration of Oscar Arias Sánchez simply disbursed all the *partidas* before May.[18] A more compelling explanation, however, is that a clarification of constitutional law has reduced the degree to which the Costa Rican president's impoundment power can be used to partisan ends. In November 1987, the Supreme Court affirmed that the prohibition on vetoes of budgetary legislation applies to supplementary items added to the annual budget throughout the year. This case reinforces 1960 and 1967 decisions in which the Court had also checked executive attempts to establish budgetary veto authority (Volio Guevara 1988; Muñoz Quesada 1981). Thus, although impoundments have not been ruled on explicitly by the Court, Assembly members have been able to secure judicial support in warding off presidential challenges to their spending prerogatives. Calderón's failure to impound PLN *partidas* in 1990, then, probably reflects a recognition, in light of the 1987 decision, that presidential tampering with the budget is possible only if it is tolerated by the Assembly.

This conclusion is supported by the results of past conflicts between the branches on budgetary issues besides impoundments. The 1966–70 presidency of Juan Joaquín Trejos Fernandes (PUNIF) is the most striking example, because Trejos is the one president to have faced a unified partisan opposition in the Assembly. The PLN majority simply ignored budgets submitted by the executive, much as the Democratic-controlled U.S. Congress of the late 1980s pronounced President Reagan's budgets "Dead on Arrival" at the steps of the Capitol. Without even a veto as bargaining leverage, moreover, Trejos was helpless to prevent the Assembly from eliminating scores of Foreign Ministry posts, which the president could have used to reward supporters with plum appointments (Muñoz Quesada 1981).

The bottom line is that the Assembly is constitutionally sovereign on government spending. Under the unified government, the Assembly majority may rely on executive budgets as starting points for negotiations over the ultimate spending bill, and impoundments are likely to reflect minor budgetary adjustments negotiated and enforced within the majority party, rather than conflicts between branches of government. When presidents lacking Assembly support have attempted to exercise authority over the budget, on the other hand, the result has been interbranch conflict. Minority presidents have at times either vetoed the budget or claimed that control over the executive entails impoundment authority. Supreme Court rulings have consistently rejected the claim of a budgetary veto, but have not yet

18 Although data on the rates of *partida* disbursals is available from the government Controller's Office, data on the timing of disbursals, unfortunately, is not.

directly addressed the impoundment issue. Nevertheless, in the wake of the most recent Court ruling on the veto, impoundments of *partidas* have been negligible.

PRESIDENTIAL INITIATIVES AND PARTY COHESION

In other policy areas as well, presidents struggle, with mixed results, to implement their policy agendas. In particular, the inability of incumbent presidents to administer important rewards and punishments to legislators implies that support from copartisans in the Assembly for presidential initiatives is far from automatic. In lieu of guaranteed partisan support, presidents frequently must stitch together policy-specific cross-partisan coalitions, inevitably requiring concessions to coalition partners in the Assembly.

Two major reforms to the national banking system in the mid-1980s illustrate the inability of presidents to elicit uniform support for legislative initiatives among their legislative copartisans and the importance of ad hoc coalition building across parties to presidential success in lieu of partisan support. The first reform was the Ley de Moneda (Currency Law), originally submitted to the Assembly in 1983 by the Monge administration. The law relaxed state regulation over international currency transactions and also allowed the deposit of public funds in private banks. The monopoly of state banks over public deposits had been established with the nationalization of banks under the Figueres junta of 1948–49 and remained an element of the PLN's party platform. Accompanying the initial reform proposal were personal letters to all PLN deputies from President Monge requesting support for the legislation.

The initiative was opposed from the outset by a group of 13 PLN deputies on the basis that the prerogatives of the national banks could not be tampered with unless the PLN party congress formally eliminated this plank from the platform. Despite the objections of these 13, however, the PLN caucus decision was to support Monge's reform.[19] The vote on final passage of the Ley de Moneda – a rare roll call – found the PLN deeply divided and dependent on votes from PUSC deputies for passage (see Table 5.5).[20] Moreover, although no PUSC deputies voted against the reform nor argued against the bill in floor debate, nearly half refused to support the

---

19 The PLN caucus was its largest ever – 33 deputies strong – during the 1982–86 term.
20 For an extensive discussion of the nature and motivations of the coalitions supporting and opposing the Ley de Moneda, see Wilson (1994).

Table 5.5. *Partisan breakdown of vote on 1984 Currency Law*

Deputy's Party	Favored	Opposed	Abstained
PLN	19	8	6
PUSC	10	0	8
Other	1	2	3
Total	30	10	17

legislation and abstained from the vote (Asamblea Legislativa de Costa Rica 1983–84; Gutiérrez and Vargas 1986).

Much of the floor debate focused on the obligations of PLN deputies to adhere to party discipline and on who, in fact, was entitled to establish the party line. Reform adherents spoke to the financial efficiency of the reform and the need to provide unified support to the president. Dissidents relied on the PLN platform and their own consciences to defend their position. Moreover, despite Monge's persistent efforts to lobby support for the bill throughout, alliance building with the party's candidates for president in 1986 was an important factor in motivating individual deputies to support or oppose the reform. Among PLN deputies, alliances behind candidates coincided with positions on bank reform. The PLN's frontrunner and eventual candidate, Carlos Manuel Castillo, strongly supported the legislation, as did PLN deputies who were openly linked to Castillo's candidacy. PLN opponents of the reform, in contrast, were also deputies who supported other presidential candidates (Gutiérrez and Vargas 1986).[21] Based on this information alone, of course, it is not possible to determine the relative extent to which support for presidential candidates was driving positions on bank reform, or vice versa. The important point here, however, is that the incumbent president's ability to implement a major policy initiative was constrained, both by the conflicting policy preferences of his copartisans in the Assembly and by the influence that competing presidential aspirants in his party exercised over deputies.

In 1988, another banking reform bill, this time at the initiative of President Arias, divided the major parties. This reform proposed to further facilitate the deposit of public funds in private banks, grant greater discretion to the directors of the Central Bank in managing state funds, end

21 Unfortunately for this study, it is impossible to determine whether PLN deputies were rewarded for their support for Castillo's position, as it was in the case of the Mayo Negro. Castillo was eventually defeated in the 1990 general election by the PUSC's Rafael Calderón Fournier and never wielded patronage power.

Table 5.6. *Partisan breakdown of vote on 1988 financial system modernization law*

Deputy's party	Favored	Opposed	Abstained
PLN	18≤23	4	2≤7
PUSC	11≤16	3	6≤11
Other	0	3	0
Total	34	10	13

Note: Reconstructed from statements made during floor debate during plenary session of the Assembly on October 20, 1988, and from newspaper accounts in *La Nación* on October 25, 1988, and in *La República* on October 25, 1988.

preferential credit from state banks for the state-owned corporations, and allow the state to underwrite international loans to private banks. Again, a minority of PLN deputies opposed the reform on the grounds that it violated the party platform, and they were joined in opposition by a handful of PUSC deputies, as well as a few deputies from minor parties. The October 1988 vote on the reform was not a roll call, so the partisan breakdown in Table 5.6, reconstructed from floor speeches and newspaper accounts, is not complete. Nevertheless, it is clear that on this critical piece of financial legislation, there was no semblance of party cohesiveness by either major party and that Arias relied on cross-partisan support to implement his policy (Asamblea Legislativa de Costa Rica 1988).

Similarly, the month before the second banking reform law was passed, a different cross-party coalition was responsible for pushing through the Assembly a reform of the law that regulated contracts between renters and tenants by relaxing rent controls that had been in place since the social reforms of President Calderón Guardia in the 1940s (see the partisan breakdown of the vote in Table 5.7). This legislation had been introduced originally by the Monge administration, but strong opposition within the PLN blocked the president's initiative. Arias likewise championed the reform and eventually relied primarily on PUSC support in the Assembly to pass it. PLN Deputy José Miguel Corrales, in his floor statement opposing the bill, directly addressed the fact that President Arias supported the bill and wanted disciplined PLN support in the Assembly:

> Needless to say, it has been said that I am undisciplined, and I have replied more than once that I would like to debate what my indisciplines consist of and who are the real undisciplined ones, but no one has accepted my challenge. This bill is an example of what I understand to be a case of

Table 5.7. *Partisan breakdown of vote on 1988 renter's law*

Deputy's party	Favored	Opposed	Abstained
PLN	9	17	3
PUSC	17	4	4
Other	0	2	1
Total	26	23	8

discipline – of that discipline that I cannot ignore. If I could, I should not have been elected for the PLN, but for some other party, as was my colleague Brenes Castillo [Agrícola Cartaginés], and here I would be as free as the wind. But I am not as free as the wind, out of respect for the voters who believed that the PLN had political ideals, and that we had to defend them. (Asamblea Legislativa de Costa Rica 1985–88:50)

Corrales Bolaños's argument was an effort to redefine the idea of party discipline on his own terms. The message his statement sends most clearly is that party discipline in Costa Rica is an ambiguous concept and that presidential support for a policy in no way guarantees support among the president's copartisans in the legislature. Indeed, when I asked whether deputies regularly vote according to a party line, the Assembly minority leader told me:

It is not at all unusual for members of the party to vote differently on a given issue. But it is hard to say exactly what it means "Voting *with* the party" or "Voting *against* the party." There is such a difference of opinion within the country over *what is the PLN* – whether it is defined by the presidential candidates (and *which* candidate), or defined by the Secretary General of the party, or by the party leadership in the Assembly, or by the individual deputies – that it is difficult to say what the party is. Therefore, it's difficult to say what constitutes a vote *with* or *against* the party. (Asamblea Legislativa de Costa Rica 1992, Int. 93-12)

In the examples cited earlier, presidents managed eventually to get their reforms passed into law despite opposition within their party. Instances of the Assembly blocking presidential initiatives, however, are common as well, although recorded debates and votes are more rare because doomed legislation is infrequently brought to the Assembly floor. In 1992, internal divisions in the PUSC Assembly majority were blocking two treaties that were supported by the incumbent PUSC president. The first, committing Costa Rica to participation in a Central American parliament, had drawn support as well as opposition from members of both the PUSC and PLN during the 1986–90 Assembly but had not been reported out of commitee

(Asamblea Legislativa de Costa Rica:Exp. no. 10,661). The second, an agreement with Colombia on rights to undersea resources, also drew support and opposition from deputies of both major parties. According to the assistant to the president's chief of staff, however, both treaties were stalled as of March 1992 due to divisions within the PUSC Assembly caucus (Madrigal 1992).

The mixed success of Costa Rican presidents in implementing policies derives from two key sources. The first is the strictly limited scope of authority over legislation granted to the presidency in the constitution of 1949 and the subsequent narrow interpretation of this authority by the Supreme Court. The second is the fact that presidents cannot depend on unconditional support from their copartisans in the legislature. The Costa Rican electoral system encourages substantial representation for the president's copartisans in the Assembly, and this is to the president's advantage. But partisanship does not guarantee discipline. Moreover, the nature of political careers in Costa Rica and the responsiveness of legislators to presidential candidates means that incumbent presidents do not command the greatest stature as leader, even of their own parties, while in office.

CONCLUSION

This chapter argues that the Costa Rican presidency is relatively weak and that the president cannot dominate policy making. The evaluation is based on examination of the constitutional authorities afforded the presidency and presidents' influence over their copartisans. Without legislative decree authority and with a limited veto, Costa Rican presidents lack the most powerful tools employed by their counterparts throughout much of Latin America to shape policy (see Archer and Shugart, this volume, for example). Moreover, despite electoral rules that encourage a strong showing by the president's copartisans in the Assembly, the combination of presidential and legislative term limits, along with open competition within parties for presidential nominations, leaves incumbent presidents with little ability to coerce cooperation among legislators. Term limits weaken party cohesion in Costa Rica and constrain presidential influence. They also generate inordinate influence for viable presidential candidates, who are likely to control future executive appointments, over their parties.

This verdict of presidential weakness should not be read as a criticism of Costa Rican presidentialism. There are really two distinct issues entailed in most discussions of presidential capacities: one is the president's constitutional authority, and the other is the president's influence over copartisans in the legislature. On both counts, there is good reason to believe that mitigating presidential power is beneficial to regime performance. In comparative perspective, the presidential regimes that limit the constitutional authorities face less frequent regime crises than those with extensive powers (Shugart and Carey 1992). This is probably because a weaker presidency allows the legislature, in which a greater diversity of political views are represented, to serve as a country's primary forum for policy debate. The impact of presidential influence within parties is not so straightforward. Certainly, systems with excessively high party fragmentation and low party discipline have been criticized for impeding the formation of stable policy coalitions (see Mainwaring, this volume, for example). On the other hand, systems in which highly disciplined national parties dominate policy making have come under criticism and pressures to reform because of their failure to allow individual legislators to respond to the interests of their own constituencies (Coppedge 1994a; Carey 1996).

I do not propose to offer here a comprehensive model of presidential influence over legislative parties. Nevertheless, the comparison of the Costa Rican case with the Mexican case, as described by Weldon (this volume), suggests a couple of observations. In both cases, legislators as well as presidents are prohibited from reelection. I have argued here that dual term limits, by shaping political career paths and the sources of access to political posts, serve to weaken the influence of incumbent presidents over the legislature. Yet the argument up to this point evidently does not hold for Mexico, where Partido Revolucionario Institucional (PRI) legislators have traditionally proved deferential to presidential initiatives. The critical difference, I would suggest, is in the nature of presidential succession. Specifically, in Mexico, where incumbent presidents have had tremendous discretion in naming their successors and have done so only very late in their terms, term-limited legislators aspiring to appointed posts have no incentive to distance themselves from the president. In Costa Rica, by contrast, multiple candidates for presidential nominations within each major party and competitiveness between parties mean that incumbent presidents are not instrumental to legislators' post-Assembly career prospects, and legislators react to them accordingly.

Elsewhere, I argue that much writing on regime types fails to distinguish sufficiently among the plethora of institutional variations in regimes described as presidential (Shugart and Carey 1992). Specifying and refining these distinctions are among the principal purposes of this book. The Costa Rican case suggests a number of institutional variables that account for a constrained presidency. The limited formal powers enumerated in the constitution are critical here. Beyond that, there is the combination of presidential term limits, legislative term limits, and open competition for presidential nominations. The combination of limited constitutional powers and loose party discipline produces a presidency with important but by no means dominant authority over policy.

6

THE POLITICAL SOURCES OF *PRESIDENCIALISMO* IN MEXICO

Jeffrey Weldon

6.1. INTRODUCTION

Mexico has been characterized as having an exceptionally strong presidency. In no country in Latin America does the president appear to wield such wide-ranging powers. The president in Mexico dominates the legislative and judicial branches of the national government and directs a highly centralized federal system in which states and municipalities ultimately appear to be subject to rule from the center.

There is no question that the president of Mexico exercises an extraordinary range of powers. He can reform the constitution by proposing amendments, which are frequently accepted by Congress with only cosmetic changes. He initiates virtually all legislation, which often is passed by Congress with dispatch. The president designates his own successor to the presidency and also nominates most of the congressional candidates of his party. He also often names the candidates of the official party for governor. He can have governors, mayors, and members of Congress removed from their posts. He designates members of his cabinet and can fire them at his leisure. The federal judicial branch is filled with his appointees, which leads to a compliant judiciary (see Garrido 1989:422–26).

This image of a powerful presidency survives despite the fact that the

The author gratefully acknowledges ITAM and the Center for U.S.–Mexican Studies for research support and thanks María Amparo Casar, Wayne Cornelius, Federico Estévez, Carolina Gómez Vinales, Alonso Lujambio, Juan Molinar, Victor Manuel Reynoso, and the editors for their comments to earlier drafts.

Mexican constitution provides for an independent congress and judiciary and insists on separation of powers. Furthermore, the 1917 constitution is explicitly federal with regard to relations between the federal government and the states, and it provides for free municipal government. How in fact is the president of Mexico so powerful? Why does *presidencialismo* flourish under a constitution that is merely *presidential?*[1]

Much of the literature on Mexican politics (by both Mexican and North American scholars) faults the centralized, authoritarian political structure on the supposed authoritarian character of political culture in Mexico (Loaeza 1989; López Villafañe 1986; Segovia 1975; Villa Aguilera 1987). This literature assumes that *presidencialismo* has been in place since at least the 1917 constitution, if not before (Meyer 1977:23–24).[2] Indeed, there is a tendency in Mexican history toward centralization, particularly the accumulation of personal power in the hands of a caudillo, a quasi-military leader. Inevitably the role of national caudillo is assumed by the president. The conventional wisdom explains the formation of the official party as a *consequence* of *presidencialismo* (Garrido 1982: 359; Segovia 1987). The Partido Revolucionario Institucional (PRI) typically has been portrayed as merely the electoral ministry of the presidency.

Other scholars credit the 1917 constitution for creating a highly presidentialist system (Carpizo 1978a:73–91, 1978b, 1988; Cosío Villegas 1978:22–30). They assume that the delegates to the 1917 constitutional convention in Querétaro endeavored to create a strong presidency in order to create greater efficiency and stability in government. These legal scholars believe the subsequent constitutional reforms that strengthened the presidency were the logical conclusion to the legal doctrine of presidentialism established in 1917. These authors rarely discuss the "metaconstitutional powers" of the president, nor broach the subject of the official party and the president's relationship with that institution.

Other researchers tend to blend the two preceding arguments, recognizing both the authoritarian nature of Mexican politics and the institutional arrangements implied in constitutional studies. According to this

---

1 Mexican scholars use the term *presidencialismo* both to define a presidential system of government and to characterize the exceptional concentration of powers, constitutional and otherwise, in the hands of the Mexican president. In this chapter, *presidencialismo* refers to the latter meaning.

2 Meyer (1992:63) places the roots of *presidencialismo* with the Aztec emperors and the concentrated executive powers of the colonial period. Cosío Villegas (1975), though he does not completely share these opinions on the origins of *presidencialismo,* does emphasize the personalistic nature of presidential rule in Mexico.

view, the 1917 constitution was written in order to limit the dictatorial aspects of the Mexican presidency by explicitly strengthening that institution. The *constituyentes* in 1917 believed that the 1857 constitution granted too much power to the Congress vis-à-vis the president, which led later-nineteenth-century presidents to resort to unconstitutional methods to strengthen their hand (Meyer 1992:58; Rabassa 1957). Therefore, they granted the president extraordinary constitutional powers. The highly centralized presidency of today is viewed as an unintended consequence (Meyer 1992:59).[3]

There is no question that the 1917 constitution is *presidencialista,* though the degree of the powers endowed to the president in that document will be questioned in this chapter. Furthermore, sociologists, political scientists, and most legal scholars who have studied the Mexican presidency mention the importance of the president's role as head of the party. However, their conclusion is inevitably that the party is weak and insignificant because it is subordinate to the president. This chapter will turn that logic on its head. The official party is *central* to Mexican politics. It is the most important determinant in establishing relationships among political actors and institutions. The president is usually the head of the party, the central mediator of intraelite disputes. This political class delegates wide-ranging authority to him.

Legal and constitutional grants of power to the president often occurred before increased delegations of power by the party to its leader: The 1917 constitution preceded the formation of the official party in 1929, which came before further legal reforms that strengthened *party* leadership. The legal authority granted to the president was insufficient in creating stability and efficiency through centralization, and it was necessary to increase the centralization within the party as well. Only then did full *presidencialismo* take hold in Mexico.

There are four necessary conditions that allow for *presidencialismo* in Mexico: (1) a presidentialist system based in the constitution; (2) unified government, where the ruling party controls the presidency and both houses of Congress; (3) discipline within the ruling party; and (4) a president who is the acknowledged leader of the ruling party.[4] If any of these four conditions cease to exist, then the equilibrium of *presidencialismo* will begin to break down. If any of the three latter conditions no longer hold true, then

3 For an analytical review of the main schools of thought on the Mexican political system, see Molinar Horcasitas (1993).
4 I thank Juan Molinar for spelling out this simple formula for *presidencialismo.*

the president of Mexico will possess only constitutional powers, and he will lose the metaconstitutional powers for which Mexican executives have been notorious.

The following section will trace a brief history of presidential–congressional relations before 1940 to demonstrate that the Mexican political system has not always been "hyperpresidential." Section 6.3 will review some of the major constitutional bases of presidential power in Mexico. Sections 6.4 through 6.6 will examine each of the three other necessary conditions for *presidencialismo*. Section 6.7 will present the case of the relationship between the president and state governments in order to explore the relative strengths of constitutional and metaconstitutional presidential powers. Finally, the conclusion will test whether the four necessary conditions apply to the current presidency of Ernesto Zedillo (1994–), where there is doubt that the fourth condition for *presidencialismo* holds.

6.2. PRESIDENTS AND CONGRESS (1857–1940)

Most studies have assumed that the Congress and the ruling party in Mexico have always been subservient to the president. In general, this assumption appears to be mostly true. There have been major exceptions to this rule, however. This section will review some of the more revealing conflicts between the Mexican president and the federal legislature between 1857 and 1940.[5] While the president was generally dominant during the whole period, Congress also at times asserted its independence.

One of the high-water marks of congressional power and prestige occurred during the presidency of Benito Juárez (1858–72). The 1857 constitution abolished the Senate, under the justification that it had been too conservative and aristocratic. Furthermore, it was thought that a unicameral congress would be better able to resist the centralizing tendencies of presidential government toward the executive (Orozco Henríquez 1988:12–16).[6] The Chamber of Deputies proved able to defeat important presidential proposals, including a treaty, and Juárez was forced to incorporate the lead-

---

5 Sordo Cedeño (1993) provides a comprehensive analysis of the Congress in the centralist period (1833–41). Costeloe (1989) traces the relationship between Santa Ana and Congress, particularly the election of 1842, when a congress was elected that was strongly opposed to his autocratic government.

6 Knapp (1953) believes that the 1857 constitution included many parliamentary characteristics, particularly with regard to the relationship between the Congress and the cabinet.

ership of the Chamber into his own cabinet (Knapp 1953:78). The Chamber of Deputies was so successful at blocking Presidents Juárez and Lerdo de Tejada (1872–76) that the Senate was reintroduced in 1874 in order to check the powers of the lower chamber.

The Congress fell into relative disuse under the *porfiriato*, after Porfirio Díaz (1876–80, 1884–1911) had placed loyalists in both chambers, though Lorenzo Meyer (1992:64) claims that full presidential control over the Congress did not really take hold until Díaz's 1888–92 term. It was said that many members attended merely to fulfill a quorum (Piccato 1991:49).

The Congress reemerged as an important actor during Madero's presidency (1911–13) at the beginning of the Mexican Revolution. The 26th Congress (1912–13) was at the time considered to be much more active than any previous legislature. Due to the chaotic political situation during the 1912 elections, and perhaps due even more to the fact that it was probably one of the cleanest elections in Mexican history, the Congress was extremely divided. This increased the frequency and importance of debates, to the point that reforms to the rules of the Chamber of Deputies were proposed to reflect the change from "an assembly that does not speak," as in the *porfiriato*, to one that "often speaks too much."[7] At the time, salaries for deputies were so low that many accepted commissions from the executive, thus limiting their independence. To correct this problem, in November 1912 the Congress passed a bill increasing their salaries, but Madero vetoed it (Piccato 1991:107).

Although the 26th Congress was considered to be *maderista*, it often took its own course. For example, in late 1912 the Congress initiated legislation to accelerate agrarian reform, over the objections of Madero, who preferred a slower approach. Out of frustration over the deliberate pace of social reforms by Madero, there were discussions in January 1913 in Congress about making the government more parliamentary, especially in matters of making cabinet secretaries more responsive to Congress (Piccato 1991:115–22).

Madero was overthrown (and assassinated) in a military coup in February 1913. The Senate, which had been more conservative than the Chamber of Deputies, played a role in his downfall. Several senators had openly lobbied for his stepping down (Piccato 1991:129–30; Knight 1990 [1986]: vol. 1, 486–87). As he took Madero prisoner, General Huerta claimed that the Senate had given him the authority to take the presidency (Piccato 1991: 130; Cumberland 1972:13). Huerta (1913–14) soon faced strong opposition from Congress, both from *maderistas* and from *anti-maderistas* who had be-

7 Piccato (1991:106), citing *Historia de la Cámara de Diputados,* vol. 2, 96–97.

come alienated when their leaders had been purged from Huerta's cabinet (Piccato 1991:141). A number of these deputies and senators had been assassinated or arrested or had disappeared by the fall of 1913. The Chamber of Deputies on October 10, 1913, threatened to impeach Huerta, charging a lack of security for members of Congress. That afternoon, Huerta sent the army to the Chamber to arrest 110 deputies; 74 were later charged (Knight 1990 [1986] vol. 2, 75). The Chamber of Deputies was dissolved by Huerta, and the Senate decided that the prudent thing to do was to dissolve itself (Piccato 1991:153). Huerta called special elections for October 26, and the new Congress was dominated by his cronies.

Even after the 1917 constitution and at least until 1935, the Congress still challenged the authority of Mexican presidents. Although presidential will often prevailed, each of the presidents from Carranza to Cárdenas faced de facto opposition majorities in at least one of the chambers at some point during his term.

President Obregón (1920–24) in the first half of his term faced a congress under the leadership of the Partido Liberal Constitucionalista (PLC), which tried to change the constitution in order to form a parliamentary system of government. These reforms were sponsored by 90 members of the Chamber of Deputies. The constitution would be altered so that the president would be elected by the Chamber. He would have the power to dissolve the Chamber of Deputies, with the consent of the Senate. There would also be ministers in the cabinet, including an office similar to that of prime minister, who would be responsible to the lower chamber (the president would submit three names for each post, from which the Congress would select the cabinet member). The leaders of the PLC were definitely opposed to some of the key supporters of Obregón, and perhaps to the president himself. They thought that a parliamentary system was the best way for them to take control of the government. Obregón and his followers responded. After much struggle, the *obregonistas* won election to the Comisión Permanente and the Comisión Instaladora (which would judge the congressional elections of 1922),[8] and the initiatives to form a parliamentary government were tabled (Piccato 1991:26; Prieto Laurens 1968:106; Dulles 1961:132).

In 1921, Obregón introduced a labor bill, which had strong support from the Confederación Regional Obrera Mexicana (CROM)[9] and the Par-

---

8 Prieto Laurens (1968:106) denies that the president intervened in the defeat of the PLC, affirming instead that it was due to the interests and efforts of a purely congressional alliance between his PNC, the PLM, and the PNA.

9 CROM was the principal labor union of the period. Through the PLM, it controlled large parts of the D.F. and several state governments in the late 1920s.

tido Laborista Mexicano (PLM). However, faced with the opposition from the Partido Nacional Cooperatista (PNC) and the Partido Nacional Agrarista (PNA), both also ostensibly pro-government parties, Obregón abandoned the labor bill, and it died in Congress (Goodspeed 1947:114–15). His budget for 1921 was delayed in Congress, and the Chamber of Deputies amended it against his wishes. Therefore, in early 1921, he asked for and received authority from Congress for extraordinary decree powers (which he kept until the end of his term). Under these decree powers, he enacted the 1921, 1922, and 1924 budgets, as well as other significant financial legislation. The 1923 budget was approved by Congress before it was introduced (Goodspeed 1947:126–29).

During the second half of his term, Obregón faced a majority in the Chamber of Deputies from the PNC, led by Prieto Laurens. This Congress elected opponents of the president to the Supreme Court, defeating the candidates for the Court that Obregón preferred; the president refused to recognize the election and called a special session of Congress, which nevertheless ratified the choices of the PNC majority (Prieto Laurens 1968: 117–20). On November 27, 1923, Prieto Laurens tried to put together a Cooperatista majority in order to elect the Comisión Permanente, hoping to put together a coalition in Congress that would support De la Huerta for president in the next term instead of Calles. He needed 128 votes and could only muster 122. Without a majority in Congress, it would be impossible for De la Huerta to win the election, and the *delahuertistas* opted for armed rebellion instead (Dulles 1961:206).

Later, during the De la Huerta rebellion (1923–24), it was necessary to call the Senate into a special session to ratify the General Claims Convention of the Bucareli agreements with the United States. Francisco Field Jurado, a PNC leader in the Senate, headed the opposition and managed to keep a quorum from forming (Dulles 1961:237). Only with the assassination of Field Jurado on January 23, 1924, the kidnapping of other senators (allegedly by members of the PLM), and the convening of their alternates, was a quorum achieved to approve the treaty (Tamayo 1987:283–86).

President Calles (1924–28) usually had a loyal majority in the national legislature, principally from his base in the PLM. However, the rest of Congress often followed the lead of Obregón, who had officially retired to his ranch in Sonora. Despite his promises to enact major labor reforms on behalf of the PLM and CROM, Calles was unable to get the comprehensive labor code through both houses of Congress.

The 1917 Constitution had not allowed the reelection of the president, but during Calles's term Congress amended Article 83 in 1927 and 1928 to permit reelection for nonconsecutive terms. These reforms were clearly written with the reelection of Obregón in mind, and his party, the PNA, introduced the reforms. In 1925, the PLM had defeated the first efforts at restoring presidential reelection, but before the 1926 elections, Obregón was able to pressure the PLM into supporting the reforms (Goodspeed 1947: 193–94). Calles's preference in this matter is not clear, but it is often thought that the president was not pleased with the prospect of the reelection of his predecessor (Loyola Díaz 1980; Zevada 1971:64–81).

Other constitutional reforms during Calles's presidency more directly affected the interests of the CROM, which was a key support group for Calles but an opponent of Obregón. For example, the municipalities of the Federal District (D.F.), which had been a stronghold for the PLM, were abolished and replaced by delegations. The heads of the delegations were appointed by the governor of the D.F., who in turn was freely appointed by the president. The reform of the appointment procedures for Supreme Court justices were also strongly criticized by the PLM leadership (see later). Furthermore, the size of the Chamber of Deputies was reduced (from one per 60,000 inhabitants to one per 100,000), which was also considered by the PLM to have been part of a package to weaken its power base. Reducing the size of the Chamber brought many incumbents together in the same districts for the 1930 election. Had he lived, this would have allowed Obregón to pick and choose among the revolutionary elite those whom he most favored. However, with Obregón's death, it was the national committee of the newly formed official party that was able to select its most favored candidates. It is likely that President Calles was opposed to some or all of these reforms, but he dared not challenge the *obregonista* majority in Congress (Loyola Díaz 1980).

The best example of a presidency that was weak with respect to the party leadership in Congress was during the *maximato* (1928–35). The *maximato* was a period when the presidents of Mexico were overpowered by the Partido Nacional Revolucionario (PNR), led informally by the so-called *jefe máximo*, former President Calles. The literature that refers to Presidents Portes Gil (1928–30), Ortiz Rubio (1930–32), and Rodríguez (1932–34) as "puppets" of Calles overlooks evidence that indicates that these presidents did maintain some autonomy from the *jefe máximo*.[10] However, the key point is that it was Calles's position as leader of the PNR that maintained the visage of puppet presidencies.[11] Many of the conflicts between the presidents

10 Portes Gil was elected by Congress as interim president to take office in the place of the assassinated president-elect Obregón. A special election held in 1929 was won by Ortiz Rubio, who took office in 1930 as substitute president. He resigned in 1932 and was replaced by Rodríguez, who was elected by Congress as substitute president to fill the rest of the six-year term that had begun in 1928.

11 For the relationship between presidents and party leaders during this period, see Meyer,

of the *maximato* and the leadership of the PNR were played out in Congress. For example, President Portes Gil presented a bill to implement the federal labor code, which was rejected by Congress after the CROM (still closely tied to Calles) intervened (Meyer 1978:149–51).

Ortiz Rubio in particular had difficulties with Calles and the Congress, including struggles over the budget. He had been a compromise candidate between the *callistas* and *obregonistas.* When he took office in 1930, he faced a congress that was 100% PNR, but divided into two major factions, *rojos (callistas)* and *blancos* (mostly*ortizrubistas*). The president's faction originally controlled both chambers. However, in January 1930, nine senators and eight deputies from the *blanco* faction were temporarily expelled from the official party (though not from Congress) for insubordination to the National Executive Committee (CEN) of the PNR. This led to a reshuffling of the factions in the Chamber, the control of both chambers by the *rojos*, and consequently the supremacy of Calles and the party leadership of Congress. After the contentious party primaries for Congress in the spring of 1930, Calles and the congressional leadership were able to replace the president of the CEN (who had had the support of Ortiz Rubio) with a loyal *callista* (Garrido 1982:111–17). The *callistas* controlled Congress through the next two elections (1930 and 1932). In the summer of 1932, loyal *callistas* were elected leader of the Chamber of Deputies and president of the Electoral College, guaranteeing control of the Congress for the rivals of Ortiz Rubio (Medín 1982:113). The struggle between Calles and the president was most dramatically played out in cabinet politics, where Calles eventually managed to gain complete control, but the president's lack of a majority in Congress made his position even more untenable. There were even rumors that Ortiz Rubio and some loyal generals would try to impede the opening of the legislature, scheduled to begin on September 1, 1932 (Lajous 1979:142). Instead, on that day he delivered his State of the Union address to a hostile Congress and on the following day resigned.

Congress replaced him with Abelardo Rodríguez, a close collaborator of Calles, to serve the last two years of the presidential term. When he became president, Rodríguez pointed out in a memorandum to his cabinet that Mexico had a presidentialist, not cabinet, government, so all members of the cabinet worked for him. He wanted all matters to be cleared with him before any action was taken (Dulles 1961:547; Gaxiola 1938; Lajous 1979:149–55). In September 1933, Rodríguez issued another directive ordering cabinet members not to consult with the *jefe máximo* on issues of the federal ex-

Segovia, and Lajous (1978), Smith (1974:25–103), Medín (1982), Dulles (1961), Lajous (1979), and Lerner de Sheinbaum and Ralsky de Cimet (1976:83–119).

ecutive, unless requested by Calles himself. Rodríguez pointed out that he consulted frequently with Calles, and it was not proper for members of the cabinet to consult with Calles without authorization (Dulles 1961:555). The lines of authority were supposed to be from Calles to Rodríguez to the cabinet, unless Calles wanted to consult with cabinet members directly. Therefore, the prohibition on initiating contact was on the cabinet, not on Calles. The president and the *jefe máximo* nonetheless had a good relationship.

Calles played a major role in the selection of Cárdenas as the candidate of the PNR for the 1934–40 term. Perhaps he believed he could continue the *maximato* through the following *sexenio*. Congress was originally dominated by *callistas*, but Cárdenas soon began to persuade deputies to his side, to the point that he commanded a majority in the Chamber. In the second half of 1935, 3 *callista* governors were deposed by the Senate. In September, there was a shootout in the Chamber of Deputies between *callistas* and *cardenistas*, and 2 deputies were killed and 2 wounded. As a result, 16 *callistas* were expelled from the Chamber of Deputies. Nevertheless, Calles believed that he could reassert control over the Congress, and he returned to Mexico City from his quasi-exile in San Diego. In retaliation, 5 *callista* senators were expelled from the Senate on December 14. Calles and his main collaborators were cast out of the PNR on December 16, and 4 more governors were removed from office by the Senate (Medín 1982:158–60). Over the next several months, Calles continued his intrigues from within Mexico against the leadership of the party, now dominated by *cardenistas*. Fearing a full-scale rebellion, President Cárdenas decided that the only recourse was to exile Calles and three of his closest allies on April 10, 1936 (see Cornelius 1973).

The *maximato* was over, but its defeat was far from preordained or overwhelming. It was not until Cárdenas restructured the party to his own preferences in the latter part of his *sexenio* that he could fully assert the role as head of the party and thus receive full compliance from the other branches of government. Ever since, the president of Mexico has had few open conflicts with Congress.

6.3. THE FORMAL POWERS OF THE PRESIDENT

The 1917 constitution grants much authority to the president of Mexico. He has great advantages over Congress in areas of legislation and appointment power. There is no doubt that the constitution confers upon the president a central role in the political system.

The president has the power to initiate legislation. Although important legislation in the United States often originates in the White House, the president must find members of Congress to introduce the legislation. The Mexican president, however, may introduce bills directly. Article 71 of the constitution allows the president, members of Congress, and state legislatures to introduce bills. Bills from the president, state legislatures, and the majority of deputies of any state delegation go directly to committees, bypassing internal rules of each chamber (and implicitly the agenda control of the chamber leadership).

In fact, most bills passed by the Mexican Congress are presidential initiatives, and most bills sent by the president are eventually passed by Congress. Before minority representation was introduced into the Chamber of Deputies, that body passed presidential initiatives with near unanimity (Carpizo 1978b:84). Most substantive legislation in Mexico since the 1917 constitution has been in the form of presidential initiatives.

However, this does not mean that presidential initiatives are not passed unamended. Almost all important bills are amended in some ways; and although these amendments are often minor, sometimes major changes are made (almost all amendments are done in committee, not on the floor, which makes the frequency of amendments – and the occasional presidential debacles – less apparent). For example, the 1931 labor law was subject to many significant changes before it was finally enacted. Some presidential initiatives are rejected. Both Calles (1924–28) and Cárdenas (1934–40) had tax bills ignored by Congress (Carpizo 1978b:84). Furthermore, bills are adjusted by the president's staff before being formally introduced in Congress to minimize the chances of legislative opposition.

The constitution does not stipulate a role for the president in proposing constitutional amendments. Article 135 merely states that a constitutional reform requires a two-thirds majority in each chamber, followed by approval by a majority of the state legislatures. In fact, however, most constitutional reforms have been introduced by the executive, using his powers from Article 71. Nevertheless, proposed reforms are often amended by Congress. This was the case with the electoral reforms of 1986, 1990, and 1993. Furthermore, it appears that Congress in 1992 was delegated the responsibility to work out the details of the reforms to Article 130, which liberalized church–state relations. Many of the details of the judicial reform of 1994–95 were also worked out in Congress. Usually a majority of states ratify the reforms in a very timely manner.[12]

12 Reforms to Article 82, approved by Congress on September 8, 1993, were not ratified by the state legislatures until the following summer (on June 22, 1994, the Senate

The president has the power to veto legislation in its entirety or in part. Article 72 states that all regular legislation that must be passed by both chambers must then be sent to the president. If he approves the bill, it becomes law when he has it published (which the constitution stipulates shall take place "immediately"). He may reject all or part of the bill and send his objections back to the chamber of origin with the whole bill. The constitution does not authorize the president to promulgate the rest of the bill. If both chambers subsequently reject the veto by a two-thirds vote, the bill is sent back to the president for its promulgation. The president may veto only legislation passed by both chambers; he does not have the right to veto resolutions that need be passed by only one chamber (Tena Ramírez 1985:263–67).[13] The president cannot veto constitutional amendments.

Mexican presidents were first authorized the veto in the 1824 constitution.[14] Vetoes under that constitution could be overturned by a two-thirds vote of both chambers. They lost the veto power in 1857 because of the experience with caudillismo and the near dictatorial powers of presidents during the centralist era (Herrera y Lasso 1964:111–14). The 1857 constitution also had only one house of Congress, the Chamber of Deputies. Under Article 70, bills passed by Congress were sent to the president for his opinion. He had seven days to veto the bill, in whole or in part. However, the Congress needed only a majority vote to overturn the president's veto. Article 71 of the constitution of 1857 allowed the Congress, with a two-thirds vote, to bypass Article 70 (and the president) entirely in the case of urgency. In the 1857 constitution, therefore, the president's veto was dilatory, meant to slow down legislation and force a reevaluation of the measure. The Senate was restored in 1874, and naturally the veto power had to be modified to reflect a bicameral system. Vetoes could still be overturned by a majority vote in both chambers, though the section that allowed the presidential veto process to be bypassed altogether was deleted. The two-thirds rule was not reestablished until 1917.

At least one veto has been overturned by a two-thirds vote by Congress. In 1935, Cárdenas vetoed a bill regarding pensions for officials and em-

---

recognized that 21 states had ratified the reform). The constitution originally restricted eligibility to the presidency to native Mexicans whose parents were native Mexicans. Now only one parent need be Mexican. The reasons behind the unusual delay are not clear (Berlín Valenzuela 1993:371–82). In contrast, the ratification process for the judicial reform of 1994 took a couple of weeks – over Christmas break.

13 The president does not have a pocket veto. He has a 10-day period in which he may veto a bill. It is considered approved if it is not returned to Congress within this period. However, if Congress adjourns within this 10-day period, the bill is returned on the first day of its next session.

14 Earlier constitutions of Mexico can be found in Tena Ramírez (1991).

ployees of the legislative branch. It was overturned by Congress, but Cárdenas subsequently refused to publish the law, and it did not take effect. The following year, Congress asked the interior minister to investigate the question, but there was no resolution (Carpizo 1978b:90–91). Therefore, the president indirectly may have an absolute veto. A law does not take effect until it is published in the *Diario Oficial,* which is an executive responsibility (Art. 89, Sect. I). This creates an ambiguous situation. The president cannot legally veto legislation a second time; he is obligated to publish or promulgate laws that are passed by Congress. However, if he refuses to publish a law, the legislation cannot be enforced (Carpizo 1978b: 93–94; Tena Ramírez 1985:461–63).

It is widely thought that the president of Mexico almost never vetoes legislation, since it is assumed that all legislation originates with the president. In fact, there have been many vetoes during this century. Carpizo (1978b:90–91) provides a list of vetoes from 1917 to 1969.[15] Between 1917 and 1976, the mean number of vetoes was around 2.6 per year. Every president before 1952, with the exceptions of Obregón (1920–24, who vetoed an average of 1.8 bills per year) and Avila Camacho (1940–46, who vetoed an average of 1.2), vetoed more bills than the post-Revolution average. For example, between 1926 and 1933, and again between 1937 and 1941, a minimum of 3 bills were vetoed every year. Eleven were vetoed by Calles in 1927 alone. The highest average belongs to Alemán (1946–52), who vetoed an average of 4.3 bills per year. Vetoes continued sporadically in the 1960s under Presidents López Mateos (1958–64) and Díaz Ordaz (1964–70), when 4 bills were vetoed in 1963, 6 in 1964, and 12 in 1965 (Carpizo 1978b:90–91). However, the last veto recorded by Carpizo was in 1969.

There were frequent vetoes of major legislation in 1932, 1933, and 1941. In 1932, the tax bill and the budget bill were both vetoed. In 1947, Alemán vetoed a major electoral reform measure (Herrera y Lasso 1964: 286–90). Often, tax bills were vetoed, especially those dealing with tariffs and taxes on particular goods, such as matches. The mining tax law was vetoed in 1933 and again in 1934 (Carpizo 1978b:90–91). Most vetoes this century have dealt with pensions, and many of those were of the nature of private bills, but the evidence shows that the president and Congress also frequently disagreed over important substantive legislation, and these differences in opinion frequently ended in vetoes until 1969.

The 1917 constitution gave the president the power to convoke Congress into special sessions. This was used in conjunction with the power to

15 Unfortunately, his list is sometimes quantitative (number of vetoes in a particular year) and sometimes qualitative (types of vetoes in a particular year).

initiate legislation. Usually, Congress would open its special session with
new presidential initiatives on its lap and would then proceed to debate the
proposed law or constitutional amendment. In 1923 the constitution was
reformed so that the president must submit a proposal to the Comisión
Permanente of the Congress,[16] explaining why a special session is necessary.
The Comisión Permanente must approve of his request before a special
session can be called. The Comisión Permanente is the only body that has
the power to call special sessions; it may also do so without the initiative
of the president, and such a declaration is not subject to a presidential veto.
This is one of the few times that a presidential prerogative has been removed
from the constitution during this century. Nonetheless, since 1923 it has
not been difficult for presidents to persuade the Comisión Permanente to
convene Congress.

One of the areas where the constitution gives the president definitive
agenda-setting powers is in the budget process. According to Article 74,
Section IV, the president must submit a budget for all government expenditures to the Chamber of Deputies every year. The Chamber of Deputies
alone considers appropriations. It is the president's responsibility to receive
funding requests from all ministries and agencies and submit their requests
to the Chamber for the authorization of expenditures. The appropriations
bill is presented to the Chamber late in its fall session (by November 15),
and it must be passed before the end of the year, when the session ends.
Since the Christmas holidays intervene, the Chamber has little time to review the budget.

The Chamber of Deputies first examines the revenue law. If it passes
the Chamber it is sent to the Senate for its approval, since the revenue law,
unlike the appropriations law, requires the approval of both chambers. Every
year a tax authorization bill must be passed. Even when the tax is meant to
have an indefinite duration, it would be null if it was not included in the
annual tax law (Tena Ramírez 1985:323–27). The tax bill can be vetoed by
the president.

The Chamber of Deputies then considers the section of the budget law
dealing with appropriations. According to Carpizo (1978b:147), the Chamber has the right to make any changes it deems necessary. Since the appropriations law is only approved by one chamber, the constitution does not

---

16 The Comisión Permanente is composed of 37 members (19 deputies and 18 senators)
named by each chamber at the closing of the regular session. The Comisión acts for
Congress when it is not in session. It decides when it is necessary to convene one or both
chambers of Congress. It performs as a gatekeeper for Congress, receiving proposed legislation and steering it to the proper committees for when the next Congress convenes.
It also has the power to confirm presidential nominees when Congress is not in session.

authorize a presidential veto, according to most constitutional scholars. Therefore, if the Chamber of Deputies amends the budget, the president technically cannot veto the bill. Nonetheless, research by the author has uncovered numerous vetoes of appropriations legislation in the first two decades following 1917. It is unclear whether these vetoes were unconstitutional, but they were accepted as legitimate by the other branches of government at the time. Supplementary appropriations must be presented to both chambers of Congress to authorize the program, appropriate funds, and sanction new sources of revenue to balance the expenditures (in this case, the president can veto the bill, because it had been passed by both chambers).

In practice, the Congress does not challenge the president's authority over the budget. In discussing the bill in 1993, a PRI deputy claimed, "It is evident that it is not up to [the legislature] to formulate the federal budget, nor generate alternative proposals."[17] Furthermore, the president usually writes into the budget bill discretionary line items for the executive branch, a slush fund for "contingencies." In the 1994 budget, for example, there was a 20 billion new peso line item for "subsidies" for the executive branch (amounting to almost 7% of the total budget).[18] Furthermore, since 1989, a large part of the budget has been administered directly by the closest aides of the president under the rubric of the National Solidarity Program (Cornelius, Craig, and Fox 1994). Social programs have been targeted at specific constituents, perhaps for partisan ends (Molinar Horcasitas and Weldon 1994). Much of the Solidarity Program's funding falls under one line item, and Congress has had little to say over how it is spent.

The president of Mexico, despite common perceptions, does not have decree powers – the power to legislate on his own, without the participation of Congress. According to Article 29, the president does not have extraordinary decree powers except during emergencies, and only then in order to suspend civil liberties. This situation requires the approval of Congress (or the Comisión Permanente when Congress is not in session). Congress may *further* authorize legislative powers to the president to expedite the resolution of the emergency, but this delegation of power is a faculty of Congress (Carpizo 1978b:100–101). By exclusion, this article denies the president extraordinary powers during peacetime.

Nevertheless, Article 29 was used by presidents to legislate outside of times of emergency. This was a common method of legislation in the nineteenth century, and it continued under the 1917 constitution. Carpizo

17 *News* (Mexico City), December 18, 1993.
18 Ibid.

(1978b:102) cites the creation of the National University and the federal electrical commission, the communications and banking laws, and various legal, commercial, and agrarian codes as examples of laws passed between 1917 and 1938. The first piece of legislation passed by Congress under the 1917 constitution gave Carranza extraordinary budgetary authority. All of the presidents from 1929 through 1937 were regularly granted decree powers between congressional sessions (Goodspeed 1947).[19]

The constitution was amended in 1938 to weaken the emergency powers of the president. Article 49, which deals with separation of powers, was reformed to add a line that states that in no circumstances, except for emergencies covered by Article 29, can the president legislate. This reform, actually just a reiteration of constitutional law previously stated in Article 29, was introduced by Cárdenas, who made it clear that he was restricting his own power in the interest of preserving the separation of powers, though he had been one of the presidents who had most benefited from delegated decree authority (Valadés 1988:263).

Despite the constitutional reforms, in June 1942, on account of World War II, President Avila Camacho asked for and received from Congress the authority to suspend civil rights and legislate by decree. This state of exception lasted until September 1945. In that time he issued decrees that legislated in areas beyond national security, and the Supreme Court declared some of those acts unconstitutional. Since then, the Congress has not authorized emergency powers to the president under Article 29 (Tena Ramírez 1985:244).

The president was granted extensive regulatory powers in 1951 through reforms to Articles 49 and 131. The latter allows Congress to authorize the president to regulate domestic and foreign commerce (including taxes, tariffs, and prohibitions of, or subsidies for, certain products), as well as anything else beneficial to the country (Valadés 1988:263–64). If the president has been authorized by law to assume these faculties, he must submit to Congress every year an account of what he has done with these powers. Congress may then approve his regulations. Rejection of the president's account of his regulatory activity does not mean that Congress vetoes the regulations; they must initiate new legislation, which can be vetoed by the president. Subsequently, however, Congress may pass new laws that restrict the regulatory powers that have been delegated to the executive.

Before 1995, the president had the constitutional right to name and

---

19 In this period, Congress met from September through December. Special sessions were often called in the interim, though these were not necessary if the president had been granted decree powers over specific areas of law for that period.

remove all of the members of his cabinet without the approval of either chamber of Congress. This included all secretaries of state, the attorney general, and the governor of the D.F. In 1993, the method of selecting the governor of the D.F. was reformed. Beginning in 1997 (after the midterm elections), the governor will be nominated by the president from the party that wins a plurality of the seats of the D.F. Asamblea de Representantes. The Asamblea must confirm his nomination.[20] It is unlikely that this reform will take effect, however, because in April 1995, the PRI proposed that the governor of the D.F. be elected by popular vote by 1997. On December 31, 1994, the constitution was amended so that the Senate would have to confirm the president's nomination of the attorney general. Despite these reforms, the president still has the right to nominate all other members of the cabinet without having to obtain congressional confirmation.

During the constitutional convention of 1917, there was a motion to require that the members of the cabinet be confirmed by the Chamber of Deputies, but this resolution failed.[21] Diplomatic officers, military officers above colonel, and treasury officials are all nominated by the president,[22] but are supposed to be confirmed by the Senate. However, treasury officials usually inform the Congress that they have taken office, without even the pretext of having their nominations ratified by the Senate. Nevertheless, the Senate has at times taken its power to veto nominations seriously. It has requested that the finance and defense ministers submit nominations of officers to the Senate for confirmation. The first nomination that was rejected by the Senate was in 1930, when the undersecretary of the treasury was not confirmed.[23] This was a year of struggle between that ministry and the

---

20 If he is rejected by the Asamblea, the president can make a second nomination to the Asamblea, and if that nominee is not confirmed, the Senate names the governor.

21 Tena Ramírez (1985:470), a consummate presidentialist, proclaims dramatically, "Thus, in a moment of disorientation, our presidential system was at the point of becoming shipwrecked."

22 This used to include all undersecretaries, the *oficial mayor,* all directors general, and other junior ministers, as well as tax collectors. The secretary himself was not included, since he was considered a member of the cabinet. Nevertheless, after 1935, the nominations of treasury officials have not been submitted to the Senate for confirmation (González Oropeza 1987b:302).

23 In 1913, the Chamber of Deputies denied by a vote of 128 to 20 a leave of absence to a deputy in order to take a position as undersecretary in the Education Ministry of the Huerta government (Piccato 1991:148). Article 58 of the 1857 constitution gave Congress the power to accept or reject leaves of absence for its members before they could take positions in the government. Article 62 of the 1917 constitution also requires members of Congress to seek a leave of absence from their chamber before taking an administrative post; the failure to receive this leave of absence leads to the member's losing his or her seat in Congress. Since this is what the member is supposedly seeking anyway, such a sanction is far from the veto that Congress held before 1917.

Congress. It also rejected the nomination of one diplomat in 1932 and postponed the confirmation of another in 1982. The Senate has refused to confirm at least 30 nominations to military appointments (González Oropeza 1987b:301–9).

Supreme Court justices are nominated by the president and confirmed by the Senate, but this has not always been the case. Early on, neither the federal executive nor Congress had any powers over naming justices. In the 1824 constitution, the Supreme Court justices were elected for life by a majority vote of the state legislatures (Fix-Zamudio 1988:274–75). The 1857 constitution established indirect popular elections for Supreme Court justices to serve six-year terms, removing the state legislatures as well as the branches of federal government from the nomination of justices. Under the *porfiriato* (1876–1911), this led to the president essentially designating the members. The Supreme Court in that period permitted President Díaz to assume legislative powers beyond the limits established by the constitution (Fix-Zamudio 1988:283–84; Meyer 1992:64).

In reaction to the complicity of the Supreme Court in the centralization of powers in the Díaz presidency, the members of the Constitutional Convention of 1917 strengthened congressional control over the Court (Orozco Henríquez 1988:28). According to the 1917 constitution, Supreme Court justices were elected by majority vote in a secret ballot by both chambers of Congress, meeting together as an electoral college. The candidates were nominated by the state legislatures in order to ensure proper geographical balance.

The election of Supreme Court justices by Congress was abandoned in 1928 by *obregonistas*, who were concerned that the nominations had become a congressional logroll and who wanted to assert control over the Court for Obregón, their candidate for president. Most of the Court at the time had been named by leaders of Congress who had in 1923 rebelled against Obregón when he had been president (Prieto Laurens 1968:117–20; González Oropeza 1987b:307). Justices were named by the president and confirmed by the Senate. The Senate had 10 days to confirm or reject the nomination. If it did not act within that period, the nominee could take office. However, if the Senate rejected the first two names that the president had submitted, the third nominee would take office on an interim basis until the next session of Congress began. Therefore, the president could name whomever he wanted to the Supreme Court, since the Senate knew that in the third round he would ultimately win.[24]

24 Vicente Lombardo Toledano, a leading opponent of Obregón, noted during the debate

In 1994, the system was reformed again to permit greater participation of the Senate in the selection of Supreme Court justices. The president will now send a *terna* (a list of three names), from which the Senate shall elect one person to the Supreme Court by a two-thirds vote. If the Senate fails to vote within 30 days, the president may chose one of the names from the *terna*. If the Senate rejects the entire list, the president sends another *terna*, and if the Senate rejects the second list, the president may choose one nominee from the second *terna* to be a member of the Court.[25]

The 1917 constitution established that Supreme Court justices would serve for life. They could be removed only by impeachment for ill conduct. In 1934, two weeks after Lázaro Cárdenas took office, the constitution was reformed so that Supreme Court justices and other federal judges were named for 6-year terms. These terms coincided with presidential terms, so courts would not reflect the interests of previous administrations. (Furthermore, in 1933, Senate terms were altered, so that all senators were elected at the same time and for the same term as the president. Therefore, a president would face a fresh Supreme Court, Senate, and Chamber of Deputies when he entered office.) Life terms for Supreme Court justices were reestablished in 1944, restoring some independence to the judicial branch. The 1994 reform institutes 15-year terms for Supreme Court justices. Justices cannot be reappointed to the Court once their term ends.

The Supreme Court of Mexico had been notorious for its lack of independence from the president, clearly due in great measure to the manner of selection. The new system is an improvement, though not foolproof: the president will win in the end if the Senate cannot agree on a candidate. The two-thirds rule should permit greater veto power to the opposition parties (although the present electoral rules permit a party to hold as many as three-quarters of the seats in the upper house), though vetoes by the Senate ultimately favor the president. The Court has been significantly depoliticized, however. Judges now cannot hold political or administrative office for one year before their appointment nor for two years after leaving the Court. The restriction on reappointment removes the likelihood that a judge near the end of his term will decide cases in favor of the incumbent president.

in 1928 that this procedure would profoundly disturb the balance of powers among the branches of government (González Oropeza 1987b:307).

25 Before 1995, federal circuit and district judges were chosen by the Supreme Court. The latest reform creates the Consejo de la Judicatura Federal, which is composed of the Supreme Court chief justice, two circuit court judges, one district court judge, two persons appointed by the Senate, and one by the president. Judges for the lower courts are now to be named by the Consejo for a period of six years. If they are renominated, or appointed to a higher post, they then serve for life under good behavior.

6.4. UNIFIED GOVERNMENT

Complete *presidencialismo* requires that the same party control the presidency and both houses of Congress. If one of the two chambers is controlled by another party, then the other two mechanisms behind *presidencialismo*, party discipline and party leadership by the president, will have diminished effect. No president can force compliance from a chamber controlled by another party.

Since it was founded in 1929, the official party has won every presidential election and has controlled a majority in both chambers of Congress. The PRI, and its predecessors, the PNR (1929–38) and the Partido de la Revolución Mexicana (PRM, 1938–46), have maintained a hegemonic party system. The official party had won every gubernatorial race until 1989, when the Partido Acción Nacional (PAN) took Baja California. The PAN took over the governor's office in Guanajuato in 1991 after allegations that the PRI's victory was tainted by electoral fraud; the PRI candidate was forced to resign before taking office, and the PRI-controlled state legislature appointed a *panista* as interim governor. The PAN then won Chihuahua in 1992 and Jalisco and Guanajuato in the first half of 1995. As of June 1996, the PAN controls four states, and the PRI the rest.

Until 1994, there were two senators per state, for a total of 64. Before 1988, the PRI had only ceded one Senate seat to the opposition. In 1988–91, four seats were held by the opposition; in 1991–94, three seats. In 1993, there was a constitutional reform to introduce minority representation in the Senate. Now, there are four senators per state. Each party nominates a slate of three candidates for senator. The three candidates on the slate that wins a plurality are elected, as is the first candidate on the slate of the second-place party. In 1994, the PRI won a plurality in all 32 states, and the PAN placed second in 24, while the Partido de la Revolución Democrática (PRD) placed second in 8. Thus, the PRI still maintains a three-quarters majority in the Senate.

The Chamber of Deputies has shown a similar pattern, maintaining a unified government for the PRI.[26] Between 1946 and 1961, the PRI won over 90% of the seats in every election to the Chamber of Deputies (average of 95.2%). Beginning in 1964, minority (but not proportional) representation was granted to the losing parties, but the PRI still held at least 82% of the seats from 1964 to 1976 and lost only 10 single-member seats in this period (average of 1.1%). In a 1977 reform, at least a quarter of the

26 The following data are from Molinar Horcasitas (1991) and Molinar Horcasitas and Weldon (1990).

seats in the Chamber were allocated to the minority parties (100 seats in multimember districts were reserved for minority parties). During the three elections under this formula (1979, 1982, and 1985), the PRI lost a total of only 16 of the 300 single-member districts. For the 1988 elections, a more proportional system was introduced, with 300 single-member seats and 200 proportional representation seats.[27] The PRI won only 260 of the 500 seats, though the opposition was highly fractionalized. In 1991, the system was modified again to guarantee that the winning party would have an extraordinary majority,[28] and the PRI won 62% of the seats. In 1994, under a semiproportional representation system, the PRI won 300 seats (60%).[29] With about the same percentage of the vote as in 1988, the PRI won an additional 40 seats in 1994 – a good cushion on which to build voting majorities in the Chamber. Nevertheless, the current electoral system puts a ceiling of 63% of the seats for any party. Constitutional reforms require a two-thirds majority, so the ruling party must obtain the support of at least one other party in the Chamber to amend the constitution.

Before the PNR was founded in 1929, most parties were ephemeral, forming for an election and disbanding at the end of the term. The few exceptions to this rule, such as the PLM and the PNA, never held majorities in the Chamber of Deputies. The presidents from Madero through Calles lacked solid partisan majorities (and when there were majorities, as under Obregón, there were tendencies toward divided government). In fact, none of the presidents in this period identified strongly with any single party; Obregón and Calles ran as common candidates for most of the major parties. Some of the obstacles that these presidents faced from Congress could be explained in part by the lack of a unified party government.

In 1988–91, the PRI held only a relatively slight majority in Congress (52%), the closest that Mexico has come to having divided government since 1929. This led to threats of blackmail from various sectors of the PRI against the congressional leadership and President Salinas (1988–94). This

27 This system closely approximated the German system, although the party with the most single-member seats was guaranteed a majority in the Chamber (the first governability clause).
28 This was the second governability clause, which gave a parliamentary majority to the party that won at least 35% of the vote and gave extra seats for every percentage point of the vote up to 60% when the system became proportional.
29 There are now two separate pools, the 300 single-member seats, and 200 multimember seats. Parties can take multimember seats in proportion to their vote total until they hit a limit of 300 seats (unless their total vote is between 60 and 63%, for which they can take the proportional amount up to an absolute limit of 315 seats). The PRI would have ended up with exactly 300 seats if they won a majority of the single-member districts with perhaps anywhere from 40 to 60% of the vote. The system is highly inelastic. See Molinar Horcasitas, Sánchez Gutiérrez, and Weldon (1994).

spooked *presidencialismo* to the degree that the electoral law was reformed to allow for greater overrepresentation of the majority party in Congress in order to make defections from the party less profitable. Some of the more controversial parts of the *salinista* project were not introduced until the 1991–94 Congress, where the PRI held a 62% majority.

If the PRI faces divided government in the future, *presidencialismo* will be fatally weakened. If no party receives a majority, then the president will have to negotiate with other parties to form a working majority in Congress. If an opposition party wins an outright majority (which is ironically more likely with the majoritarian formulas that the PRI has instituted to protect its margins in Congress), then *presidencialismo* as we know it will be dead.

6.5. RULING PARTY DISCIPLINE

A second requirement for metaconstitutional presidential powers is high discipline within the ruling party. The party of the president might also control both houses of Congress, but if it is undisciplined, then it would not be able to deliver the goods for the president in Congress. The PRI is currently a highly disciplined party. In a notorious example during the spring of 1995, only one member of the PRI in each chamber voted against a highly unpopular 50% increase in the value-added tax, while all of the opposition parties voted against. Such demonstrations of unanimity have been common in the official party since the 1940s. However, between its formation in 1929 and the mid-1930s, the official party was known for its factionalism.

There are three methods of creating discipline in the official party in the Mexican Congress: centralized party leadership, a closed-list system, and the lack of incentives for deputies to act on behalf of their local interests.

The centralization of powers in the hands of the president that were authorized by the 1917 constitution was not sufficient to create political stability in Mexico. There were major rebellions in 1920, 1923, 1927, and 1929 against the executive over presidential succession. The presidents, despite their wide-ranging authority, were unable to prevent the rebellions from occurring, and in 1920 President Carranza was in fact overthrown and assassinated. After the Revolution, Mexico was essentially ruled by numerous local and regional warlords. National parties were formed to elect (or justify the election of) presidents, but most of the political action could be found in the local political machines. During most of this period there was also a national political boss, usually with a base in the armed forces, who was able to dominate national politics, but Congress in this period tended to represent the local political machines. The local political bosses would usually align with the national caudillo or with his rivals, and factionalism would result in Congress. These factions were perhaps more important than the nominal partisan divisions in Congress in the period between 1917 and 1929, and the factions survived the formation of the PNR because the local parties survived. Even as the local parties were abolished one by one during the 1930s, the local bosses continued to dominate the PNR machines (Weldon 1994).

The structure of the PNR tended toward a centralized leadership. Calles himself was a major figure to whom many in the party were willing to delegate their authority, and the party was designed to prevent both military and electoral civil war among the "revolutionary family." The new party coordinated the candidate-selection process for most major elective posts in Mexico, and it guaranteed that the PNR candidate won, either through fraud at the voting booths or in the vote count, or by sheer majority power in the Electoral College, which was the ultimate power that assigned seats to Congress.[30] This also provided a disincentive for electoral defections from the PNR. The CEN of the party had the power to expel members and did so frequently. Since the PNR won every election, expulsion from the party was a major disincentive.

The PNR originally nominated its candidates through a decentralized mechanism that approximated a very chaotic primary election. Nonetheless, the CEN would often intervene in the vote count or in the accreditation process, which tended to close the lists more than an open primary system would. In 1937, the rules were changed to institute party conventions, which are easier to control than primaries, and the higher committees could veto nominations (Goodspeed 1947:295–96). Before the decade, this power was even more centralized, as the regional committees were suppressed (Nava 1988). The party currently has a closed-list system of nominations and has complete control over access to the ballot under the banner of the PRI. Until 1994, the national party leadership held a de facto veto over nominations for governor and Congress, even though the nominating conventions were held locally. In such a context, the leader of the PRI has had near complete control over who could hold office under the official party label.

Another contribution toward party discipline came from an unexpected

---

30 Before each session, "presumed" winners of congressional races met in the Electoral College of their respective chambers, certified their own victories, then proceeded either to certify the victories of the rest of their colleagues or to nullify adverse elections. The controversial *autocalificación* ended in 1994.

source. Ironically, the constitutional reforms of 1933, which are remembered because they restored the prohibition of reelection to the president, in fact help to explain the rise of *presidencialismo,* because these reforms also prohibited the immediate reelection of deputies and senators (as well as governors, state legislators, and mayors).[31] The subsequent weakening of the legislature was achieved not through limiting constitutional powers, but rather through the realignment of the preferences of deputies and senators that the reforms produced. Once the prohibition on reelection was placed in the constitution, deputies and senators no longer had incentives to be responsive and accountable to their local constituents (local political machines and bosses). Since national party leaders, through their control of nominating procedures, would determine the political futures of members of Congress after their terms ended, the incentives of deputies and senators were aligned with the interests of the leaders of the PNR.

According to Cosío Villegas (1978:29–30), the prohibition on immediate reelection of deputies is the key to understanding the subordination of the Mexican Congress to the executive (see also Moreno Sánchez 1970: 60–63). The leader of the PAN in the mid-1960s claimed, "The reform . . . would permit the realization, from the official party, managed by the Executive, the selective and total control of the members of Congress" (Christlieb Ibarrola 1965:31).

In 1933, it was not exactly clear who would benefit from the no-reelection reforms. The case was made at the 1932 PNR convention at Aguascalientes (called to discuss the possibility of no reelection) that the president would gain because deputies would serve less time in Congress and have less expertise.[32] Term lengths were increased as compensation. However, although the incentives of deputies and senators under the no-reelection rule would be aligned with the party leadership, in 1933 the *jefe máximo* was not the president. It was the PNR and the *jefe máximo* who would gain from the centralization. Once the president of the republic also became the head of the official party during the *sexenio* of Cárdenas (see later), the incentives of members of Congress followed the preferences of the president, since it was the president who would decide where members would go after their terms in Congress expired. It is important to note that increased *presidencialismo* was probably an unintended consequence of the no-reelection reforms. The immediate cause was probably centralization of the

31 For details on the constitutional reforms to prohibit reelection, see Garrido (1982:135–45), Alvarado Mendoza (1990:76–79), Meyer et al. (1978:184–86), Lajous (1979:155–63), Smith (1974:67, 82–84), and IIJ (1985:143–46).
32 For the debates at Aguascalientes, see ICAP (1981:251–376) and Osorio Marbán (1970: 299–336).

party, but in order to weaken local political machines and strengthen the *jefe máximo*, not to bolster the president (Weldon 1994).

As the official party has centralized over time, party discipline has become greater and factionalism has decreased. Factions remain in the PRI, though these are based more on political families within the administration or on the sectoral divisions within the party; nonetheless, they are rarely manifested in defections from the party line in Congress.

6.6. THE PRESIDENT AS HEAD OF THE RULING PARTY

The ruling party might be highly centralized, and there might be high levels of discipline among its members in Congress, but if the president is not the acknowledged leader of the party, *presidencialismo* will not necessarily result, and the president would appear relatively weak.

The political instability between the 1917 constitution and the Cárdenas presidency can be partly explained by the bifurcation of political power in Mexico between the president and the caudillo, or national political boss. The latter was the head of what Brandenburg (1964) calls the "revolutionary family." In this position, the caudillo was authorized to control presidential succession and to coordinate the business of the revolutionary family (though this authority was constantly challenged, especially before the institutionalization of party leadership via the PNR in 1929).

The norm was a dyarchy, where both the president and the leader shared power (Molinar Horcasitas 1991:17–18). In only one presidency was the leader also the president. During Carranza's term (1917–20), Obregón was a major force behind the president, enough so that he deposed Carranza when the president wanted to hand the presidency over to someone other than Obregón in 1920. Interim President De la Huerta (1920) also shared power with Obregón, who was a candidate for president at the time. Obregón remained the leader of the revolutionary coalition while president (1920–24), but even he was strongly challenged by Prieto Laurens in Congress over the leadership of the revolutionary parties (Prieto Laurens 1968:98–152). When Obregón insisted on naming Calles as his successor, De la Huerta and Prieto Laurens launched a rebellion in 1923 that nearly defeated the federal government. During the presidency of Calles (1924–28), Obregón remained a force that almost no one dared to reckon with; he was powerful enough to have the constitution changed to allow for his reelection and to eliminate the power base of the CROM.

The *obregonato* ended only with his assassination on July 17, 1928, after his election for the six-year term scheduled to begin in December 1928.[33] To fill the void left by the death of the caudillo (and to prevent imminent civil war), the PNR was formed by the revolutionary leadership immediately thereafter, with Calles recognized as the unofficial leader of the party.[34] At this point, Calles inherited the leadership of the revolutionary coalition. During the *maximato*, Calles shared power with four presidents (Portes Gil through Cárdenas). There were two partially conflicting rationalizations behind the institutionalization of the *maximato* (both the foundation of the PNR in 1929 and the no-reelection reforms of 1933). Among the possible consequences for not centralizing power was the continuation of intermittent civil wars over succession. Centralizing power in the hands of the leadership of the revolutionary party lessened the threats of anarchy and political violence. However, at the same time the party did not wish to be ruled by a dictator, so it instituted the dyarchy of *presidente/jefe máximo*. Perhaps many in the PNR thought that the most effective manner of checking presidential power was to centralize the power of the Congress in the hands of the party leadership. Congress might then have been more efficiently organized and thus more able to resist the president. Of course, this strategy backfired once the two positions of the dyarchy were held by a single person, as happened soon thereafter under Cárdenas. Then any institutional checks between the party leadership and the presidency would have been nullified, and perfect *presidencialismo* resulted.

The *maximato* lasted until Cárdenas was able to form a coalition in Congress and a cabinet that was sufficiently strong to depose Calles as *jefe máximo* and expel him from the country for good in April 1936. At that point, Cárdenas became the new *jefe*, combining the powers of the presidency and party leader. This was confirmed by the creation of a new official party, the PRM, that incorporated major *cardenista* groups into the newly corporatist structure of the party and guaranteed Cárdenas's leadership of the revolutionary coalition. By the 1937 midterm elections, the Congress was dominated by sectoral organizations (workers, peasants, and the military) from the PRM, key support groups for Cárdenas (Loyola Díaz 1990; Enríquez Perea 1988). It had taken a reformation of the party to establish firmly the president's leadership.

Through 1994, the Mexican president remained the de facto head of the PRI. The "office" of party leader was transferred along with the presidency. When the new president took office, he also acquired the powers

---

33 Another reform tailor-made for Obregón was the increase in the presidential terms of office from four to six years, beginning in 1928.
34 Knight (1992) presents the formation of the PNR as an example of an elite settlement.

belonging to the head of the party. This transfer, however, did not take place at the exact moment that the presidential sash was handed over on December 1. In other words, party leadership was *not* an attribute of the presidency. Sometimes, the presidential candidate acquired substantial powers when he was "unveiled" by the incumbent. In such cases, the candidate had the authority to draw up the candidate lists for Congress in the upcoming election. At other times, the incumbent held on to party leadership power for the first year or so of the next *sexenio*. The latter took place in 1929 and 1934; there is also evidence that Cárdenas had played an important role in the following *sexenio*, and that Alemán had been influential for one or two *sexenios* after his term. There is also some evidence that Salinas controlled much of the party machinery before becoming president in 1988 and continued to control major parts of the party after Zedillo took office in 1994.

The succession is when *presidencialismo* is at its weakest and when crises have historically been more common in Mexican politics – crises due to the lack of coordination within the political elite. Molinar Horcasitas (1994) believes that a president, both as chief executive and as party leader, who makes concessions with the various groups in the PRI coalition will consequently develop an undisciplined economic policy, leading to economic crises but a disciplined succession, where the party remains loyal (as in 1970, 1976, and 1982). On the other hand, a president who emphasizes economic discipline, to the point of ignoring the demands of other sectors of the party, will enjoy relative economic prosperity but face divisions in the party at the end of his term and suffer an undisciplined succession (as in 1988 and 1994). The party leader must endeavor to keep his party coalition together or risk electoral divisions and probable legitimacy problems in the subsequent *sexenio*. The fragility of the coalition behind the party is much more evident when it is challenged, and presidents who prefer to protect their coalition have contributed to the illusion of the *pax priísta*.

The *presidencialista* system creates a dilemma of political succession: How can the president secure commitments from deputies and senators during his term, when their political fortunes will be decided by future presidents? Since congressional terms (in the second half of a *sexenio*) end three months before the next president's term begins, there must be a way for a president to guarantee that his commitments will be honored by the new executive. Thus, it might be *necessary* that the president, as party leader, chooses his successor, who will be expected (by the party, at least) to serve as *both* the next president and the next party leader. This way, the commitments made by an incumbent president will be more credible in the eyes of the deputies, since the promises will be inherited by the next party leader, who will owe his position to his predecessor. Therefore, the *dedazo* (the president's "prerogative" to name the PRI candidate for the presidency) may be more than a result of centralization of power in the party. It may be a key element in maintaining that centralization.

The contrasts in the effects of no-reelection laws in Costa Rica and Mexico are striking (see Carey, this volume). In Costa Rica, the prohibition on reelection does not lead to party discipline in favor of the incumbent president, but rather for his successor. In Mexico, there are two legislatures per presidential term. In the first, there should be complete loyalty to the president acting as party leader. In the second term, we should expect somewhat less attention paid to the president and more toward his successor, but the *dedazo*, combined with a hegemonic party system that has traditionally guaranteed that the PRI's candidate would win, hitches the commitments of the outgoing president to the incoming one.

The same logic that created the PNR with powers delegated to Calles as the leader still operates in the Mexican political system today. The party tries to monopolize power in the fashion of a national political machine. The party also delegates extraordinary powers to party leadership to make party nominations and coordinate legislation. This guarantees party discipline and efficient law making. The party leadership gets commitments from party members in Congress to follow its lead and in return promotes them to positions in the government after their terms are up. In this case, it is especially important that federal members of Congress are not reelectable, since they cannot form their own local power bases and must depend on their party leaders for future positions in the government. When the president was not party leader, as during the *maximato*, the party leader dominates the president. The same tends to occur when there is an overlap during the succession that leads to ambiguous party leadership. Full *presidencialismo* is found only when the president is also leader of the ruling party.

The three conditions that create the metaconstitutional powers of the president are all partisan variables. It is indisputable that the party matters as an institution in Mexican politics. If the party is weakened in some way, then *presidencialismo* will fall with it.

6.7. A REEXAMINATION OF METACONSTITUTIONAL POWERS: THE RELATIONS BETWEEN THE PRESIDENT AND THE STATES

The president has extensive powers derived from the constitution and from law. However, his chief powers come from his position as the de facto head of the PRI. The PRI delegates its powers to him, and he is allowed to use these powers in what appears to be an authoritarian manner. Most of the metaconstitutional powers that are attributed to the president can best be explained by the president's relationship to his party. In this light, this section will reevaluate one of the least understood metaconstitutional powers: the right to name and remove state governors.

The president's powers over naming all members of the government has its origins both in the constitution and in the practices of the official party. The president, as head of the party, has influence over the PRI's nominations for state governors. This obviously increases the power of the federal government over the states.

The president does not have the constitutional right to remove governors, though this is widely attributed to him as a major metaconstitutional power that further increases centralism in the Mexican government. The Senate has the power to remove governors and dissolve state governments in Article 76, Section V. The upper chamber can declare that the powers of the state have disappeared (that they no longer exist) and that a provisional governor should be named.[35] The president is then invited to send a *terna* of candidates to the Senate, and the chamber then votes in a new governor to serve the rest of the term or until elections for a substitute governor are held. In fact, it is usually the president or his interior minister who submits a recommendation to the Senate that it should recognize that the powers of a state have disappeared. The Senate acts accordingly and chooses the preferred candidate of the president from the *terna*.[36]

The "disappearance of powers" of state governments has been applied relatively frequently since 1917. Forty-nine governors have been removed by the Senate, with 41 of those cases occurring before 1940, when the PRI did not yet exist or was in the process of centralization and when power within the party and between branches of government was most contested. Fifteen cases occurred during the terms of De la Huerta and Obregón (1920–24), 11 during the presidency of Calles (1924–28), and another 15 during or immediately after the *maximato* (1928–35) (González Oropeza 1987a:252).

However, since 1954, there have been only three cases of the Senate removing governors and no cases after 1975. Nevertheless, governors left office during the *sexenio* of Salinas de Gortari (1988–94) in almost record numbers. By May 1994, 17 governors (all members of the PRI) had re-

35 Technically, the Senate does not make the powers of a state *disappear*, but rather takes note that an effective government no longer exists in the state. In reality, however, the upper house deposes a state government. The constitution stipulates that *all* branches of state government must be effectively absent before the Senate can act, though in practice the action is usually against the governor.
36 The definitive resource on the disappearance of powers is González Oropeza (1987a).

signed. All of these governors resigned "voluntarily," yet certainly most would have preferred to remain in office, and some were surely forced out of office. In no case was there evidence that a case to depose a state government would have been presented to the Senate. In almost all cases, the interim governor (invariably named by the state legislature) was recognized as one preferred by the president and his inner circle. How can the president prevail so decisively over the governors?

There are two explanations: one based partly on the constitution and partly on the PRI, the other based entirely on the organization of the official party. First, assuming that all of the conditions for metaconstitutional powers hold, the president can control the Senate via his role as head of the party. Therefore, if absolutely necessary, he could persuade the Senate into using its powers under Article 76, Section V. This is a club behind the door that the president rarely needs to use. Governors can recognize that leaving voluntarily is better than being forced out by the Senate. Furthermore, in every case but one during the Salinas administration, the governors who lost their offices were compensated in some way with some office or sinecure.

The second argument is based on the assumption that governors also want to continue their future in politics after their term in office. They understand that the president, as head of the party, can influence where they end up in subsequent rounds. They know that if the party wants them to step down, and they do so quietly, there is a greater chance that they can be rehabilitated in the future.

These two complementary explanations help us understand how the president has been able to control state governments without *any* authorization from the constitution in the matter. This does not mean that federalism is weak in the Mexican constitution, nor that federalism is being undermined by authoritarian practices. Instead, party centralism overrides federalism. We find that as the internal party organization has stabilized, as the three conditions for metaconstitutional power have been guaranteed, there have been fewer cases of formal dissolution of state governments by the Senate, just as there have been fewer cases of presidential vetoes. Governors in the last *sexenio* were removed within the equilibrium of *presidencialismo*.

6.8. CONCLUSION

The metaconstitutional powers of the president of Mexico have been mistakenly attributed to *presidencialista* tendencies in Mexican society. There is an assumption that an authoritarian political culture in Mexico leads to greater centralization of powers, which in turn leads to a very strong president. Instead, this chapter argues that the metaconstitutional powers of the president are also in part due to institutional mechanisms as well as a consensus among the elite members of the party that delegation to a central authority is in their best interest. There is indeed centralization of power in the party, but this is done via delegation to the party leader, not explicitly to the president. It just so happens that this person is usually also the president.

The observed power of the Mexican president is not due to the constitutional powers of the president, but rather to the extraordinary centralization of decision making within the party. This centralization cuts across the branches of government, "violating" Article 49, which is supposed to guarantee the division of powers. Yet the writers of the constitution of 1917 did not take into account the words of Madison:

> A mere demarcation on parchment of the constitutional limits of the several departments is not a sufficient guard against those encroachments which lead to a tyrannical concentration of all the powers of government in the same hands. (*Federalist*, no. 48, 313)
>
> The ambition of one branch of government had to be set against the ambition of the other, that vetoes and checks had to be energized by different interests (such as different electoral incentives) so that the balance between the powers is preserved. (*Federalist*, no. 51, 322)

The Mexican constitution includes the basic devices to permit checks to be exercised among the various branches of government, but rules of the official party minimize the incentives to use those vetoes.

Presidencialismo in Mexico is a fragile equilibrium. It requires some considerable presidential constitutional powers on the one hand, and on the other, (1) PRI hegemony in Congress, (2) party discipline in Congress, and (3) the president as head of the party. If any of the latter requirements is relaxed, then *presidencialismo* is likely to diminish or disappear. Therefore, when *presidencialismo* is working efficiently, we should expect most of the presidents' bills to be approved by Congress, and we should not expect frequent vetoes. In fact, in several of the periods when vetoes were more frequent, the president was challenged by party leadership over control of the party (the *maximato* and the mid-1960s) or the official party did not yet exist (the presidencies of Carranza and Calles) or the party was in the process of being restructured (the presidencies of Cárdenas and Alemán).

Other factors that determine *presidencialismo* depend on internal party politics. If the party, for whatever reason, decides to delegate powers to some leader other than the president, then the powers of the president will immediately diminish. If the party suffers from lax discipline in Congress, the same result might occur. This could come about if there is increased factionalism in the party, if the party rules are changed to open up the nomination process, or if the prohibition on reelection were lifted.[37] In the latter case, the deputies would consider representing their districts, perhaps against the interests of their party. Of course, the day that a president from the official party faces a congress effectively controlled by the opposition, he will be left with only his constitutional powers. *Presidencialismo* in Mexico will definitely be through.

If another party, with different internal rules, comes to power, we should not necessarily expect *presidencialismo* to survive. In the presidential debate of May 1994, the *panista* candidate claimed that if elected he would be the first president who was not the leader of his party and asserted that he was the only one of the three candidates present who would not combine party leadership with the presidency. He emphasized that the PAN selects its candidates for all offices in democratic conventions, not by designation by the party leadership. If the PAN should win the presidency and also maintain its present methods of candidate selection, it is unlikely that *presidencialismo* will survive, even if the PAN wins a majority in Congress. *Panista* deputies will not face the same centralizing incentives that *priísta* deputies confront today, and it is has been a *panista* tradition to keep its party leader separate from its candidate. A *panista* president would not be *presidencialista*.

If the PRD were to take the presidency and Congress in 2000, under the present structure of the party it is likely that the *perredista* president would be the party leader. However, the internal rules for candidate selection in the PRD and the inherent factionalism of the left would make it very unlikely that there would be sufficient party discipline to lead to *presidencialismo*.

President Zedillo has tested the waters of how to be president without also being head of the PRI. Early in his administration, Zedillo confirmed that he was a member of the PRI, but then made it clear that he would not interfere in the business of the party. He has promised not to intervene in

---

37 The immediate reelection of senators and federal deputies is still prohibited. In 1964, the Chamber of Deputies passed a resolution in the form of a constitutional amendment to prohibit the immediate reelection of senators and the *third* consecutive reelection of deputies, thus allowing deputies to be reelected for one immediate term. The Senate rejected the amendment (Valadés 1978:56–59). As mentioned earlier, there was also talk of permitting the reelection of deputies and senators in the fall of 1991, but the proposals were quickly torpedoed. Again in the fall of 1994, there were renewed proposals to reinstitute congressional reelection. The issue has been brought up frequently in the 1995–96 interparty negotiations over the electoral reform, and the chances for its passage now appear favorable – if not in the current round of reforms, perhaps in the next.

party nominations. The reasoning behind this decision might be altruistic on Zedillo's part, or it may be more related to the unusual circumstances surrounding his accession to power.[38] A further complication is that the PRI has reformed its nominating procedures since 1994 to allow local conventions to select gubernatorial and local candidates without interference from the center. This has led to greater indiscipline among the governors.

Zedillo has been widely perceived as a weak president during the first six months of his term. It is widely believed that Salinas still controls large parts of the party apparatus (especially the groups organized around the Solidarity Program), which has caused a situation approximating that of 1935, when the *jefe máximo* challenged the president over control of the government and the party. In 1935, the president won and became *jefe máximo*. The president might win again this time, but Zedillo has made it clear that he does not want to be *jefe máximo*, so it might be perceived as a hollow victory.

One case in January 1995 revealed that Zedillo lacked traditional meta-constitutional powers over state governments. The federal government had negotiated with the PRD and the PAN over political reform in return for cooperation on the negotiations in the Chiapas conflict. The PRD had the understanding that the deal with the government would lead to the resignations of the newly elected governors of Chiapas and Tabasco (the PRD had been the principal opponent to the PRI in these elections and had alleged fraud). The governor of Chiapas soon resigned. The governor of Tabasco, however, refused to recognize the negotiations in Mexico City, and the government denied that the deal had ever been made. *Priístas* in Tabasco demonstrated violently in favor of their governor and against interference from the center. Similar cases in the previous *sexenio* led to resignations by the governors in question. However, Zedillo had not taken the role of leader of his party and was unable to enforce discipline.

Another revealing case occurred in May 1995, when the treasury minister visited with deputies to discuss another possible hike in the value-added tax (from 15% to 18 or 20%). The PRI deputies had just recently voted a raise from 10 to 15%, which had caused an uproar, and members of the PRI feared that the first hike could ruin their political careers in the future. This time they openly rebelled and went public, which effectively killed the measure. This was not technically a defeat of a presidential pro-

38 The PRI faced an unusually acute leadership crisis in the spring of 1994, after the assassination of Luis Donaldo Colosio. The death of its presidential candidate probably left the PRI without a "leader" for a few weeks, and the president of the party challenged Salinas for control over the nomination of the PRI's replacement candidate. Salinas's preferred nominee, Ernesto Zedillo, was eventually *redestapado*.

posal. It was more an attempt to test the waters. Trial balloons of this sort are not uncommon,[39] but it is unusual for them to explode in the face of the president. Some presidential bills have been significantly amended in this *sexenio*. For example, in the spring of 1996, a bill in the Chamber of Deputies to privatize social security accounts was highly modified at the last minute by the PRI-controlled committee to allow for greater participation of government agencies and the social sectors of the PRI. It appears that the *presidencialista* equilibrium is breaking down.

39 Trial balloons that insinuated a relaxation of the no-reelection clauses of the constitution (particularly for federal deputies) were shot down in late 1991 by the interior minister and congressional leaders, who were concerned that these reforms would lead to the possible reelection of the president (see Centeno 1994:1).

7

EVALUATING ARGENTINA'S PRESIDENTIAL DEMOCRACY: 1983–1995

Mark P. Jones

Despite the generally low esteem in which it is held by many academics (e.g., Linz and Valenzuela 1994), presidentialism remains quite popular throughout Latin America. Given the reality of a large number of presidential systems that show no prospects of switching to parliamentarism, what is needed is systematic analysis of arrangements and methods that can be utilized to increase the effectiveness and the probability of survival of democratic presidential government.

This chapter evaluates the functioning of the Argentine presidential system during its most recent and successful experience with democratic government, 1983–present. The chapter examines those institutional and partisan factors that have aided the success of the Argentine democratic system and those which have had an adverse impact on its functioning.

CONFRONTING CRISIS IN A PRESIDENTIAL SYSTEM

On December 10, 1983, President Raúl Alfonsín assumed office for a six-year term, thereby officially ending slightly more than seven and a half years

Gerardo Adrogué, Alejandro Corbacho, Scott Mainwaring, Guillermo Molinelli, Ana María Mustapic, and Matthew Shugart provided many helpful comments and suggestions. Any errors, however, remain my responsibility alone.

of military rule. During his administration Alfonsín faced two principal policy challenges: (1) promoting economic growth and stability and (2) normalizing relations with the military. While achieving some initial success in both areas, by the latter third of his term (1987–89) Alfonsín was confronted by growing economic difficulties (e.g., hyperinflation) and increasingly conflictive relations with the military (e.g., three serious military uprisings between April 1987 and December 1988). These problems contributed to electoral difficulties for Alfonsín's Unión Cívica Radical (UCR), which was soundly defeated by the principal opposition Partido Justicialista (PJ) in both the 1987 Chamber and gubernatorial elections and in the 1989 presidential and Chamber elections. In the May 1989 presidential election, the PJ candidate Carlos Menem handily defeated the UCR's Eduardo Angeloz.

At the time of the 1989 elections Argentina was suffering from hyperinflation, an inefficient and decaying economic system, and growing social and political instability. In light of the serious crisis that confronted the nation, Menem assumed office July 8, 1989 (five months early), after it became clear that Alfonsín was incapable of continuing to govern until the official transfer of power in December. Once in power, Menem immediately began the implementation of a dramatic neoliberal economic reform program and quickly initiated Argentina's remarkable recovery.[1] The neoliberal content of Menem's policy program was contrary to popular expectations and represented a sharp break with his Peronist party's traditional policies, which had featured a highly intrusive role for the state in the economy. Menem's economic program included a large-scale privatization of state-owned companies, a disciplined government fiscal policy that increased revenues (e.g., by a crackdown on tax evasions) and reduced expenditures (e.g., budget cuts), and a highly successful anti-inflationary policy based in large part on the 1991 Convertibility Law, which fixed the Argentine currency at a par with the U.S. dollar.

Argentina is not the only nation in the hemisphere that has recently engaged in a dramatic and successful economic liberalization program. However, along with Bolivia it has been the only nation to do so under

---

1 Of the 18 Latin American presidential democracies operating in June 1995, Argentina received the third highest (i.e., third best) composite (political, financial, and economic) risk rating (71.0) issued by Political Risk Services (1995). Only Chile and Costa Rica were considered to be in better combined political, financial, and economic shape than Argentina. This is a sharp contrast to June 1989 (the month prior to Menem's assumption of office) when Argentina's risk rating (47.5) was tied for the 13th highest out of the same 18 nations (Political Risk Services 1989). Argentina's rating increase was the third highest during this period.

democratic auspices (*Freedom Review* 1985–95; Geddes 1994). The Argentine experience contrasts with that of nations such as Brazil and Uruguay (democratic, yet constrained in their ability to implement profound structural reforms) and Chile and Mexico (capable of implementing dramatic structural reforms, but only during periods of dictatorship). Argentina's ability to respond successfully to its economic and social problems while maintaining a functioning democratic system is an example of the ability of presidential systems to confront and resolve serious policy crises.

During his first term in office Menem also successfully resolved the "military problem." This subordination of the military to the civilian government was achieved via a number of routes, but of principal importance was Menem's sweeping November 1989 pardon of 277 soldiers and civilians (the pardon covered those convicted or accused of human rights abuses during the military dictatorship, of participation in barracks uprisings during the post-1983 era, of participation in guerrilla activities during the military period, and of planning the Argentine invasion of the Malvinas Islands; Acuña and Smulovitz 1995). Also crucial to this process was Menem's successful response to a serious military uprising on December 3, 1990 (Acuña and Smulovitz 1995). Currently the military is firmly under the control of the civilian government, a sharp contrast to the situation in many other nations in the region, where the civilian government's control over the military is tenuous at best.

Three prominent partisan and institutional factors contributed to the successful functioning of the Argentine presidential system during the 1983–95 period.[2] First, a two-party-dominant system ensured that during most of this period the president possessed a sufficient number of copartisans in the legislature. Second, a moderate to high level of party discipline in the legislature meant that this large number of partisan legislators translated into real policy support for the president, yet did not turn the legislature into a mere rubber stamp of presidential wishes. Third, the nation's federal framework reduced the winner-takes-all nature of politics by providing areas of local autonomy for opposition parties as well as for the president's party.

While these partisan and constitutional traits enhanced the functioning of the nation's democratic system, other countervailing forces tarnished the political system's democratic nature. First, the national government under Presidents Raúl Alfonsín and Carlos Menem limited the power and autonomy of the provinces both through controlling the flow of resources to the

2 Success is of course a relative term. By "successful" I am here referring principally to the system's ability to survive and recover from the severe crisis it faced in the latter half of the 1980s.

provinces via the nation's federal coparticipation tax system and other financial mechanisms and through threatening use of the federal government's power of intervention. Second, the absence of adequate constitutional protections for the judicial branch allowed it to be effectively co-opted by President Menem, thereby undermining a fundamental component of the nation's checks and balances system. Third, the use of presidential decrees of urgent necessity by Menem inserted the president into the legislative process and weakened the role of Congress as a check on the executive branch.

In 1994 Argentina engaged in a partial reform of its constitution of 1853. The final section of the chapter examines the manner in which the reform affected the positive and negative factors just mentioned, and concludes with a brief discussion of the future of Argentine democracy.

THE ARGENTINE PARTY SYSTEM

Two facets of a nation's party system are of the utmost importance in assessing its impact on the functioning of the presidential system. The first is the size of the party system. That is, the relevant (i.e, effective) number of political parties in the party system. There exists a strong inverse relationship between the number of relevant parties in a party system and its tendency to provide the president with a partisan contingent in the legislature of sufficient size so that he or she may govern (Jones 1995b). As Chapter 1 and the Conclusion note, presidential systems do not work well when the president is not provided with a large partisan contingent. However, the mere presence of a large partisan legislative contingent does not necessarily imply that it is supportive of the president's policy goals. The second important facet of a nation's party system is the level of legislative party discipline and the related incentives for legislators to support/oppose the president's policy program.

ELECTORAL LAWS IN ARGENTINA

Both the effective number of parties and the level of legislative party discipline are strongly influenced by a nation's electoral laws. This section briefly reviews the electoral rules in force in Argentina from 1983 up to the 1994 constitutional reform.

President

In 1983 and 1989 the president was elected for a six-year term via an electoral college in which a majority of the electoral votes were required for election. Electors were selected from 24 multimember districts ranging in size from 4 to 144 members using the same proportional representation (PR) formula and threshold employed for the election of Chamber deputies.

Senate

Each of the nation's 22 provinces (23 after 1990) and the Capital Federal were represented by two senators.[3] Senators were elected indirectly for nine-year terms by the provincial legislatures using the plurality formula, except in the Capital Federal where they were selected via an electoral college.[4]

Chamber of Deputies

Chamber deputies were elected from 24 multimember electoral districts, corresponding to the nation's 23 provinces and the Capital Federal. In any given election these electoral districts varied in size from 2 to 35 deputies. Deputies were elected for a four-year term, with one-half of the Chamber's 257 members (130 and 127) elected every two years.[5] Seats were allocated using a PR formula (the d'Hondt divisor formula) and closed-party lists; at the same time, for parties to be eligible to receive seats, they must have received a percentage of the vote equal to at least 3% of the number of registered voters in the electoral district (voting is obligatory in Argentina and citizens are for all practical purposes automatically registered). The rules governing chamber elections remained unchanged following the 1994 reform.

No restrictions were (or presently are) placed on the reelection of deputies or senators. Prior to the 1994 constitutional reform the president could not be immediately reelected.

Each province elected (and continues to elect) a governor and legislators by rules established in its own constitution. All provinces elect their gov-

---

3 Tierra del Fuego achieved provincial status in 1990. Its two senators did not assume office until 1992. Its three additional deputies (raising the overall total from 254 to 257) assumed office in 1991.

4 By lottery, two-thirds of the Senate began in 1983 with either three- or six-year initial terms, with no province having two senators on the same cycle.

5 Each province renews one-half, or the closest approximation, of its deputies every two years. In the initiating election of 1983 all 254 deputies were elected concurrently.

ernors for four-year terms, with all but a few (three in 1983, two in 1987, three in 1991, three in 1995) employing the plurality formula for the gubernatorial election.

TWO-PARTY DOMINANCE IN ARGENTINA

The combination of the electoral college method of presidential election, a mixed executive–legislative timing cycle, senators elected by the plurality rule by the provincial legislatures, deputies elected from districts with a relatively low effective magnitude (the average for the period 1983–95 was 5.0), and the election of provincial governors (in most cases by the plurality formula) in all but a few instances concurrent with the national deputies, contributed to the maintenance of a two-party-dominant system in Argentina between 1983 and 1995. Nevertheless, it is a two-party dominant system currently in decline.

Tables 7.1 and 7.2 demonstrate the dominance of the nation's two principal parties, the PJ and UCR, between 1983 and 1995 in the Chamber of Deputies and Senate. Each controlled the presidency once during this period, with the UCR's Raúl Alfonsín governing between 1983 and 1989 and the PJ's Carlos Menem in power between 1989 and 1995. During this period the two parties combined held between 82.9 and 94.5% of the seats in the Chamber of Deputies and between 83.4 and 85.4% of the seats in the Senate. Noteworthy as well is the fact that the remaining seats were always distributed among a large number of very small parties, most of which effectively competed in only one province. Between 1983 and 1995 no "third party" ever held more than 4.7% of the seats in either of the houses.

A two-party-dominant system was crucial for providing the president sufficient legislative support. Both Alfonsín and Menem faced a Chamber in which their party held a plurality of the seats during their entire tenure in office.[6] For Alfonsín this plurality was also an absolute majority between 1983 and 1987. While Menem enjoyed a technical absolute/near-absolute majority throughout his term, two factors acted to reduce this majority slightly to a plurality. First, in a few districts a small number of deputies elected on the PJ list were members of other political parties in alliance

6 From July to December 1989 the PJ lacked a plurality of the seats in the Chamber. However, as part of his deal to assume office early Menem received the UCR's commitment not to oppose his key policies. The discussion of the issue of seat distributions thus does not incorporate seat data from this period. For more information see note 27.

Table 7.1. *Percentage of seats held in the Chamber of Deputies by party: 1983–present*

Political party	1983–85	1985–87	1987–89	1989–91	1991–93	1993–95	1995–present
Partido Justicialista (PJ)	43.7	40.6	42.9	50.0	50.2	50.2	52.1
Unión Cívica Radical (UCR)	50.8	51.2	46.1	37.0	33.1	32.7	26.9
UCeDé	0.8	1.2	2.8	4.7	4.3	2.0	1.6
Center-right provincial parties	3.2	4.3	5.9	7.1	9.3	9.3	8.2
Center-left and left parties	1.6	2.8	2.4	1.2	2.0	3.1	9.7
MODIN					1.2	2.7	1.6
Total	100	100	100	100	100.1	100	100
	(254 seats)	(254 seats)	(254 seats)	(254 seats)	(257 seats)	(257 seats)	(257 seats)
PJ and UCR	94.5	91.7	89.0	87.0	83.3	82.9	79.0
Largest "third party"	1.2	2.4	2.8	4.7	4.3	2.7	9.7
	(PI)	(PI)	(UCeDé)	(UCeDé)	(UCeDé)	(MODIN)	(FREPASO)

Table 7.2. *Percentage of seats held in the Senate by party: 1983–present*

Political party	1983–86	1986–89	1989–92[a]	1992–95	1995–present
Partido Justicialista (PJ)	45.6	45.6	54.4/54.2	62.5	55.6
Unión Cívica Radical (UCR)	39.1	39.1	30.4/29.2	22.9	29.2
Center-right provincial parties	15.2	15.2	15.2/16.7	14.6	13.9
Center-left and left parties					1.4
Total	100	100	100	100	100
	(46 seats)	(46 seats)	(46/48 seats)	(48 seats)	(72 seats)
Largest "third party"	4.4	4.4	4.4/4.2	4.2	2.8
	(3 parties)	(3 parties)	(3 parties)	(2 parties)	(3 parties)

Note: All seat totals are based on election results and do not account for minor seat changes due to defections during the congressional term of a deputy or senator. These defections are however relatively infrequent and minor in scope. For the PJ in a few instances, parties that represent PJ splinters at the provincial level are included with the PJ total. Finally, included with the PJ and UCR totals are those candidates elected on the PJ/UCR lists. In a few isolated cases members of the PI, PDC, and other parties have been elected on the PJ ticket. This phenomenon is less common for the UCR, but occurs on occasion. Center-right provincial parties effectively compete in only one province. They tend to occupy the center-right/right portion of the ideological spectrum.

[a] In 1990 the then national territory of Tierra del Fuego achieved provincial status. The province elected two senators in 1992.

Source: Elaboration by author based on data from the Dirección Nacional Electoral de la República Argentina.

with the PJ (e.g., the Partido Demócrata Cristiano [PDC] and Partido Intransigente [PI]) and thus did not consider themselves subject to PJ party discipline.[7] Second, when Menem began his neoliberal economic liberalization program a few PJ deputies broke with the party (e.g., the Grupo de los Ocho). Nevertheless, the PJ contingent easily remained in the plurality, and with the consistent support of the Unión del Centro Democrático (UCeDé) and some center-right provincial parties, Menem was able in most (although certainly not all) instances to maintain a relatively comfortable working majority in the Chamber throughout his term. When Menem did have difficulties with the Chamber, they normally stemmed from the complete opposition of the left and center-left minor parties, the UCR, and several center-right provincial parties combined with the opposition of a varying number of PJ deputies. This coalition was at times able to deny the Chamber the quorum needed to open.[8]

The Senate, while failing to supply Alfonsín with an absolute majority or plurality of the seats during his tenure, did possess a strong UCR contingent that could construct agreements from a position of relative strength with PJ senators or in certain cases broker a majority with the assistance of the four minor parties with Senate seats (three with two seats and one with one seat) and/or PJ dissidents.[9] The Senate provided solid support for Menem, with the PJ possessing 54% of the seats during the first half and 63% during the second half of his term.

This ability of the Argentine system to supply its presidents with strong legislative support has been crucial to the system's relative success. However, the fundamental basis of this support, the nation's two-party-dominant system, is currently in crisis. While the PJ remains a vibrant and electorally successful party, the UCR very recently has experienced a dramatic decline. The drop in UCR electoral support from its initial high in 1983 is not particularly surprising because in the post–World War II era the UCR has not been a majority party. However, the UCR's recent (1994–95) serious electoral difficulties threaten the survival of the nation's post-1983 bipartite arrangement. Table 7.3 details the decline of the percentage of seats won by the UCR in Chamber elections from a high of 51% in 1983 and 1985,

---

7 The PDC and PI deputies also tended to react quite negatively to Menem's neoliberal economic program.

8 Neither the Chamber nor the Senate can officially open unless a minimum of 50% plus one of the members are in attendance. Withholding a quorum is an often-used opposition mechanism to block legislation in Argentina (Molinelli 1991a).

9 In this chapter the Pacto Autonomista Liberal (PAL) is treated as a single party. It is an alliance between the Partido Autonomista and Partido Liberal in the province of Corrientes, to which smaller parties are often added.

Table 7.3. *The decline of the two-party-dominant system 1983–95: the percentage of seats won in Chamber elections by the PJ, UCR, and largest "third party"*

Party	1983	1985	1987	1989	1991	1993	1995
Partido Justicialista (PJ)	44.1	37.8	48.0	52.0	48.5	52.0	52.3
Unión Cívica Radical (UCR)	50.8	51.2	41.0	33.1	33.1	32.3	21.5
Two parties (PJ+UCR)	94.9	89.0	89.0	85.0	81.5	84.3	73.9
Largest "third party"	1.2	3.9	3.9	5.5	3.1	3.2	15.4
	(PI)	(PI)	(UCeDé)	(UCeDé)	(UCeDé)	(MODIN)	(FREPASO)

Source: Elaborated by author based on data provided by the Dirección Nacional Electoral de la República Argentina.

to a relatively stable average of 33% between 1989 and 1993, to a low of 22% in 1995. Furthermore, of equal importance is the fact that whereas previously no "third party" had been able to win more than 6% of the seats in a Chamber election, the Frente del País Solidario (FREPASO) alliance (which consists of Política Abierta para la Integridad Social [PAIS], Frente Grande, Partido Demócrata Cristiano, and Unidad Socialista) won 15% of the seats in 1995.[10] This rise of a relevant third force is also seen in the percentage of votes won in the Chamber elections. Prior to 1995 no third party had ever won more than 8% of the vote. In 1995 FREPASO won 21%, only 1% less than the UCR. Finally, in the 1995 presidential contest (won by Carlos Menem with 50% of the vote) FREPASO's José Octavio Bordón won 29% of the vote, relegating the UCR's Horacio Massacessi to third place with 17% (see Table 7.4). Bordón's 29% was 22% more than any third-party presidential candidate had won in either the 1983 or 1989 election. The combination of the UCR's recent collapse and the rise of a relevant third force signals the possibility of a significant transformation of the Argentine party system.

PARTY DISCIPLINE: PJ AND UCR INTERNAL PARTY POLITICS

To date, Argentina has provided its presidents with a large number of fellow partisans in the legislature. However, as Archer and Shugart's chapter on Colombia demonstrates, a legislature with a large number of copartisans of the president does not by itself guarantee sufficient support for the president's policies. The degree of support depends on the level of legislative party discipline and the general incentives for legislators to support the president. In Chapter 11 Mainwaring and Shugart list three key features of electoral laws that influence the level of party discipline in a nation: (1) pooling of votes among a party's candidates, (2) control over who runs on the party label, and (3) control over the order in which members are elected from the party list.

In Argentina, deputies are elected via closed-party lists, and thus for this office votes are pooled. This encourages deputies to engage in behavior that enhances the electoral prospects of their party (Molinelli 1991b). The single-member and indirect (i.e., by the provincial legislature) nature of Senate elections signifies that votes for this office are not pooled, but the

10 FREPASO is more a meta-alliance than a distinct party, although it has the potential to become one in the future. Its leadership consists of former PJ members, former UCR members, and members of small established center and center-left parties.

Table 7.4. *The decline of the two-party-dominant system, 1983–95:*
The percentage of the vote won by the PJ, UCR and largest "third party"
presidential candidates

Party	1983	1989	1995
Partido Justicialista (PJ)	40.2	49.4	49.9
Unión Cívica Radical (UCR)	51.7	37.0	17.0
Two parties (PJ+UCR)	91.9	86.4	66.9
Largest "third party"	2.3	6.9	29.3
	(PI)	(ADC)	(FREPASO)

Note: The percentage totals include votes won by the candidates on lists other than those of their respective party.

Presidential candidates in 1983–95 were Raúl Alfonsín, Eduardo Angeloz, and Horacio Massacessi for the UCR; Italo Luder, Carlos Menem (1989), and Carlos Menem (1995) for the PJ; and Oscar Alende (PI), Alvaro Alsogaray (Alianza de Centro), José Octavio Bordón (FREPASO) for the respective "third parties."

Source: Elaborated by author based on data provided by the Dirección Nacional Electoral de la República Argentina.

method of election has contributed to party control over the electoral process.

Three important party groups exercise influence over the formation of the party lists (i.e., control who runs on the party list and what order they occupy) for the election of Chamber deputies and over the selection of the party's Senate candidate: the national party organization, the district-level party organization, and district-level rank-and-file party members (i.e., party affiliates). Argentina is a federal republic with 23 provinces and a federal capital. Both the PJ and UCR are divided into 24 district-level party organizations, with central control exercised by a national party organization located in the Capital Federal. The PJ and UCR district-level organizations employ internal primaries (which, in nearly all districts, are restricted to party affiliates) to select candidates for public office.[11] The primaries range from highly competitive races to instances where strong local party leaders impose a list/candidate of unity or where local party elites agree on a single set of candidates with the result being either an uncontested primary or the avoidance of an internal election altogether.[12]

11 There is growing support within the PJ and UCR for the use of semiopen primaries (including party affiliates and independents) and open primaries (including all registered voters). FREPASO is likely to continue to employ open primaries in those instances where it decides to hold a popular election to select its candidates for public office.

12 Primaries (open only to party affiliates) were used by the UCR to select its presidential

National Party Organization

When a party's leader (de facto if not also de jure) is the president, he or she has the ability to influence local party leaders with threats of fiscal or administrative reprisal, promises of fiscal or administrative reward, or, in extreme cases, the threat or real occurrence of the direct intervention of a province governed by a copartisan (i.e., where the national government assumes direct control of the provincial government). Thus, when the leader of a party is also the president, the national party organization has a greater degree of influence than the national organization of a party out of power over who runs on the district level party lists and what order they occupy on the lists.

The national party, even when its leader is not the president, has two important powers that can be employed to influence the district-level party organizations. First, the national party can intervene in district-level party organizations and take over their governance (expelling or suspending opponents).[13] Both the PJ and (to a lesser extent) the UCR national party organizations have employed this mechanism, or the threat of it, to influence party-related events at the district level. This strategy is, however, risky because it can potentially adversely affect the party's electoral performance in the district within which it intervened.[14]

The second important national party power is its control over the use of the party label. As noted in Chapter 11, however, this control represents a power only to the extent that the party label is a valuable commodity.

candidates for the 1989 and 1995 elections (and in a more limited manner for the 1983 election) and by the PJ to select its presidential candidate for the 1989 election. The distinction between the use of a closed (party affiliates only) versus semiopen primary was a theme of important debate before the 1994–95 primary season. José Octavio Bordón demanded a semiopen PJ presidential primary. Bordón realized that in a primary restricted to party members, he had little chance of defeating Menem. When a semiopen primary was refused, Bordón defected from the PJ to form his own party (PAIS) and later became the presidential candidate for the FREPASO alliance after winning its open primary. Federico Storani, the unsuccessful candidate in the 1994 UCR closed presidential primary, also argued for a semiopen primary, which he very well might have won. The failure of the PJ and UCR to employ semiopen primaries was a key contributing factor to the emergence of the FREPASO alliance, which has attracted a large number of former PJ and UCR politicians who had become disenchanted with and/or marginalized by their respective parties.

13 It also has the power to expel or suspend individual party members.
14 For example, in 1991 the PJ intervened in its district-level party organization in the province of Catamarca to replace the province's PJ leadership. In the congressional (and provincial) elections of 1991 the displaced PJ members formed their own independent list, which competed against both a UCR list and an official PJ list. The displaced group won 37% of the vote and one congressional seat, while the official PJ list won only 14% of the vote and no seat. Furthermore, a UCR-led alliance was able to take advantage of the PJ's internal difficulties and win the race for provincial governor.

Since 1947 there have been only two relevant national political parties in Argentina: the PJ (originally the Partido Peronista) and the UCR. The PJ has been in existence since 1947 and the UCR since 1891 (Vanossi 1991). Both are highly institutionalized parties (with the UCR the more so of the two) with offices and organizations throughout the country (i.e., in all provinces and most municipalities).

Table 7.5 provides information on the percentage of registered voters in Argentina who are party affiliates. As of the most recent Chamber election for which there are accurate data (1993), 38.4% of Argentine registered voters were affiliated with a political party.[15] Even accounting for membership in more than one party (which is rare as well as prohibited by law) and the potential for the padding of membership rolls, it is safe to say that over a third of the Argentine electorate was affiliated with a political party.[16] In addition (and most importantly), 31.2% of the electorate was affiliated with either the PJ or UCR, making their respective labels particularly valuable commodities.[17]

District-Level Party Organization

The ability of the national party to influence district party officials also depends on the relative strength and unity of the district party organization. Best able to resist national party influence and defy national party authority are those district-level organizations in which the party leadership enjoys a high level of popularity with the party rank and file and strong control over the district party organization. Least able to resist national party influence and defy national party authority are those district-level organizations in which different party tendencies (one of which is often linked to the national party organization) are in conflict, with no single faction possessing secure control of the district party organization. Also, other factors held constant, the more important a district is electorally to the party, the better able its local party organization is to resist national party pressures.

In districts where prominent party leaders are highly unified (often

---

15 To become a party affiliate, eligible citizens must fill out an enrollment form that is certified and then filed with the Argentine Ministry of the Interior.

16 Analysis of public opinion data has found levels of affiliation that are similar to the official statistics provided by the Ministry of the Interior, strengthening confidence in the reliability of these data (Catterberg 1989).

17 Of course, in those few instances where a party in a district is strongly associated with a negative event, individual, or group of individuals, the party label can prove to be more of a liability than a valuable commodity. In these situations local leaders have often tended to downplay the issue of party, occasionally going so far as to form broad alliances that do not utilize the party name (e.g., the UCR-dominated Frente Cívico in Catamarca). I thank Gerardo Adrogué for bringing this point to my attention.

Table 7.5. *Party affiliates as a percentage of registered voters in Argentina, 1993*

Province	PJ (%)	UCR (%)	Others (%)	Total[a]	Registered voters
Buenos Aires	21.0	14.0	6.6	41.6	7,945,996
Capital Federal	6.6	9.3	5.3	21.2	2,457,926
Catamarca	24.3	14.7	6.9	45.8	167,500
Chaco	27.3	14.8	6.3	48.4	539,924
Chubut	14.5	8.5	5.9	28.9	210,651
Cordoba	11.1	16.4	4.0	31.4	1,927,059
Corrientes	15.9	7.4	25.4[b]	48.7	522,673
Entre Rios	20.4	11.4	2.6	34.5	705,010
Formosa	22.6	17.4	8.9	48.8	232,104
Jujuy	24.5	8.6	10.4	43.4	289,715
La Pampa	26.6	9.1	2.6	38.2	181,343
La Rioja	42.6	20.9	2.3	65.7	141,555
Mendoza	12.7	15.9	6.8	35.4	896,084
Misiones	14.6	14.1	3.9	32.7	454,200
Neuquen	8.3	7.4	24.8[b]	40.4	220,511
Rio Negro	16.1	13.7	4.0	33.7	270,859
Salta	24.0	12.1	7.8	43.9	512,538
Santa Cruz	23.7	15.1	2.7	41.6	88,658

Table 7.5. (*cont.*)

Province	PJ (%)	UCR (%)	Others (%)	Total[a]	Registered voters
Santa Fe	18.7	14.3	6.3	39.4	1,945,410
San Juan	17.0	9.8	19.7[b]	46.6	341,606
San Luis	23.3	17.5	6.4	47.2	190,121
Santiago del Estero	29.8	13.2	9.8	52.8	439,019
Tierra del Fuego	20.3	10.7	10.2[b]	41.3	45,377
Tucuman	18.9	11.1	15.5[b]	45.6	737,922
Total (number)	18.0 (3,852,402)	13.2 (2,831,833)	7.2 (1,552,881)	38.4 (8,237,116)	(21,463,761)

[a]Summing province percentage totals across may not result in the same total due to rounding.
[b]A "third party's" affiliate percentage was 5.0% or greater. The parties by province are listed next, with each party's affiliate percentage in parentheses:
Corrientes: Partido Autonomista (8.9), Partido Liberal (12.2).
Neuquen: Movimiento Popular Neuquino (22.2).
San Juan: Partido Bloquista (14.5).
Tierra del Fuego: Movimiento Popular Fueguino (6.6).
Tucuman: Fuerza Republicana (10.8).
The "third party" with the highest percentage at the national level was the UCeDé (0.7).
Source: Elaborated by author based on data provided by the Dirección Nacional Electoral de la República Argentina. Party affiliation data are from December 1993. Registered voter (*padrón electoral*) data are from the October 1993 Chamber election.

under the hegemony of one individual), the district organization has a great deal of control over who runs on its list and what order they occupy (e.g., the PJ in Buenos Aires in 1995, when Governor Eduardo Duhalde imposed a single congressional list). In districts where the local party leaders are not highly unified, the local party organization's ability to influence who is on its list and what order various candidates occupy is reduced (e.g., the PJ in the Capital Federal in 1995).

Party Members

Rank-and-file party members have an opportunity to influence who is on the party list and what order they occupy in two instances. First, when the national party and district party organizations disagree over the composition of the party list and cannot come to an agreement among themselves, the rank and file (when the national party does not intervene) is called upon to make the decision (e.g., the UCR Capital Federal primaries of 1995, when local party caudillo Fernando de la Rúa's congressional list soundly defeated the list supported by national party president Raúl Alfonsín). The other (often related) instance where the rank and file plays an important role in the list formation process is when the district party organization is divided and cannot agree on a common list (e.g., the PJ Capital Federal primaries of 1995, when two lists competed, each supported by different key Menem administration officials).

In sum, three distinct party groups influence who runs on a party's list (or as its Senate candidate) and what order they occupy. The national party's influence on candidate selection is greatest (1) when the president of the party (de facto if not also de jure) is also the president of the nation and (2) when district party elites are not unified. The district-level party organization's influence is greatest (1) when the party's president is not the president of the nation and (2) when the district party elites are unified. The rank-and-file party members' influence is greatest when there is disagreement over either the list composition or the Senate candidate (1) between the national and district party organizations and/or (2) within the district organization.

A final note should be made regarding the new FREPASO alliance, which has the prospects of becoming a third, relevant national party. As a very loose coalition of several parties, some of which are themselves coalitions (e.g., Frente Grande, Unidad Socialista), it is unclear how or if this group will consolidate as a coherent political force. If FREPASO is able to coalesce into an organized political party, it is likely to be far less disciplined than either the PJ or UCR. This is due to its use of open primaries to select its candidates, the diverse political and ideological origins of its members,

Table 7.6. *Percentage of deputies elected between*
1983 and 1991 who held office in a later term

Party	Percentage
Partido Justicialista	20.5
Unión Cívica Radical	23.3
Minor parties	30.9
Total	22.9

Note: Either via election (1985–95) or as alternates
between 1985 and 1995.

the low value of its party label, and its lack of a developed internal party
infrastructure.

PARTY DISCIPLINE:
CONGRESSIONAL BEHAVIOR

This section focuses on two important aspects of congressional behavior that
influence the degree of legislative party discipline in a nation. First, the
issue of congressional reelection is explored. Second, the relative interest of
legislators in enacting policy versus obtaining pork is examined.

Reelection

Table 7.6 provides data on Chamber reelection rates in Argentina. For
deputies elected in the 1983–91 period, an average of only 23% returned
to the Chamber between 1985 and 1995. Table 7.7 shows a similar finding
for the 1993–95 Chamber, where 78% of members were in their first term,
with only 22% of the members having previously served in the Chamber
during the 1983–93 period.[18] The PJ and UCR are quite similar in terms
of reelection rates for the 1985–95 period as well as the legislative experience
of their deputies in the 1993–95 Chamber.

The Argentine reelection rate is rather low compared with that of the
other nations reviewed in this volume, such as Brazil and Colombia. There
have been no empirical studies of legislator career pathways conducted in
Argentina. From the evidence available, however, we can deduce four prin-

18 The implementation of a gender quota law (the Ley de Cupos) has had only a marginal
   reductive effect on reelection rates in 1993 and 1995. The Ley de Cupos mandates (1)
   that a minimum of 30% of all candidates on the party lists be women and (2) that these
   women be placed in electable positions on the party lists and not, for example, only in
   decorative positions from which there would be no chance of election (Jones 1996a).

Table 7.7. *Chamber of Deputies, 1993–95: Percentage of deputies with previous (1983–93) Chamber experience*

Party	First term[a]	Second term	Third term
Partido Justicialista	77.5	17.1	5.4[b]
Unión Cívica Radical	84.5	10.7	4.8
Minor parties	70.5	20.5	9.1
Total	78.2	15.6	6.2

[a]Two first-term deputies (one from the UCR and one from a minor party) were previously national senators.
[b]One PJ deputy was in his fourth term (1983–85, 1985–89, 1989–93, 1993–97).
Source: Elaborated by author based on data provided by the Parliamentary Reference Library of the Argentine Congress.

cipal explanations for this relatively low reelection rate. First, to be reelected legislators must compete in internal party primaries. Second, even if deputies survive this first cut, they are still susceptible to the vagaries of electoral volatility. Third, many deputies opt to take positions in the national executive branch (e.g., as ministers, secretaries, assistant secretaries), provincial executive branches (e.g., as governors, provincial ministers), and the national Senate. For example, as of January 1995, four of President Menem's eight ministers previously were Chamber deputies. Fourth, a few deputies each term (particularly from the PJ) tend to defect to form their own party/bloc, as already noted. Once these legislators defect they are rarely allowed to run on their original party's list again and generally have a great deal of difficulty achieving election as the candidate of a minor party.[19]

Policy versus Pork

Between December 13, 1993, and December 12, 1994, only 14% of the bills introduced in the Argentine Chamber can be classified as having a direct and specific district-level focus, with the remainder related to more general policy topics (Jones 1996b). In addition to their drafting of legislation, legislative session attendance, and floor/committee participation, Argentine deputies engage in casework for constituents. Deputies also travel home to their districts most weekends (i.e., leave Thursday evening or Friday

19 The 1995 FREPASO experience represents a partial challenge to this latter general tendency, since three former PJ and UCR deputies (as well as two former minor party deputies who had previously been elected on a PJ list) were elected to the Chamber from FREPASO lists.

morning and return Monday evening or Tuesday morning), where they meet with constituents and engage in other district-related activities.[20]

Argentine legislators, while interested in both policy and pork, tend to focus on the former to a greater extent than the latter, particularly when compared with legislators in countries such as Brazil and Colombia. While interested in reelection, many deputies (senators less so due to their nine-year terms in the prereform era) also actively aspire to positions in the national executive branch, their province's executive branch, or the Senate. In either event, party loyalty (to either the national or district party organization) influences deputies' prospects for a political future either as a legislator or as a national or provincial government official. This factor has worked to maintain party discipline in the legislature.

PARTY DISCIPLINE IN THE LEGISLATURE

Members of Congress (see e.g., Ayala 1994; Baglini 1993; Durañona y Vedia 1993; Hernández 1993; Maqueda 1993; Rodríguez Sañudo 1993; Romero Feris 1993) and academics (see e.g., Catterberg 1993; De Riz 1993; Ferreira Rubio 1993; Gowland 1993; Molinelli 1993; Mustapic 1993; Zuleta Puceiro 1993) both consider party discipline in the Argentine Congress to be (comparatively) very high. While parties may on occasion splinter into distinct factions (more common in the PJ than the UCR), at the time of a vote either on the floor or in a legislative committee, in most instances party discipline is respected (Mustapic 1993).[21] Observers agree that legislators who do not follow party guidelines in terms of their voting in the legislature are unlikely to receive a place on the party list in the future (Ferreira Rubio 1993; Maqueda 1993; Mustapic 1993).

The scarce empirical work on the Argentine Congress supports this widely accepted conventional wisdom of highly disciplined legislative par-

20 For example, Deputy Marcela Durrieu (PJ, Buenos Aires) has worked very hard to improve the living conditions of residents of a large *villa miseria* in her district, as well as engaged in a great deal of casework for constituents (Durrieu 1994). Deputy Darci Sampietro (PJ, Entre Ríos) spends most weekends (Friday–Monday) in her province holding open houses and meeting with constituents (Sampietro 1994). Deputy Susana Ayala (PJ, Chaco) is active in constituent service efforts via her participation in training workshops for women in her province and her general role as an ombudsman for Chaco residents (Ayala 1994).

21 There is a general perception that the degree of legislative party discipline in both the PJ and UCR has declined somewhat during the latter half of Menem's first term (Mustapic and Ferretti 1995a). Exemplary of some of the discipline problems experienced at times by the PJ is the relatively high number of vetoes issued by Menem, despite the PJ's possession of an absolute majority in the Senate from December 1989 through 1995.

ties. In a study of committee votes during the Alfonsín presidency (1983–89), Mustapic and Goretti (1992) found that the political parties tended to be highly disciplined, almost always voting as a unified bloc.[22]

When a bill is introduced in either chamber it is sent to one or more committees.[23] After committee deliberation (with a combined decision if the bill was forwarded to more than one committee) one or more reports (*dictámenes*) on the bill are issued. There is always a majority report and also often one or more minority reports. Mustapic and Goretti (1992) found that in voting on these reports, the UCR committee members voted as a unified bloc (i.e., with all party committee members voting for the same *dictamen*) in 98.3% (514 of 523) of the votes in the Chamber and 99.8% (527 of 528) of the votes in the Senate, while the PJ committee members voted as a unified bloc in 97.8% (496 of 507) of the votes in the Chamber and 98.9% (519 of 525) of the votes in the Senate. These high percentages overstate the level of discipline in two respects. First, they do not identify a more modest method of expressing opposition to the party line on a committee vote: either not voting or failing to attend the committee meeting. Second, the Mustapic and Goretti analysis included only bills that subsequently became laws, and thus committee votes on some of the most controversial issues were excluded from their study. Regardless, these figures demonstrate a high level of party discipline in terms of voting in the legislature.

Party discipline is aided by two factors in addition to those electoral-law-related factors previously discussed. First, the president's party is likely to be relatively disciplined. This is due in large part to the considerable partisan and institutional powers of the president. In Argentina, if the president so desires he or she can make life very difficult for rebellious party leaders/legislators via the mechanisms of either the party or the state. Similarly the president, particularly via the mechanisms of the state, can provide important benefits to a particular party leader/legislator or to his or her province. Altogether, this gives legislators incentives not to break party discipline.

Second, in any two-party-dominant presidential system there is an incentive for the principal opposition party to challenge the national government actively, with the hope that the party will be able to win the next presidential election. This goal of obtaining future power, combined with the party's ability to discipline wayward members (e.g., by expulsion, sus-

---

22 The Argentine Congress rarely takes recorded roll call votes. Legislator support for committee reports (identified by a legislator's signature on the report), which is recorded, represents the best proxy for roll call voting.

23 With an absolute majority vote a chamber can skip sending the bill to committee and consider it with the entire chamber acting as the committee.

pension, district-party intervention), acts as a strong incentive to maintain ranks in opposition to the president's policies. The assumption is that if the party stays united, it may very well win the presidency in the next election, with all loyal members benefiting accordingly. Such an incentive does not exist for most minor parties, and as a result during both the Alfonsín and Menem administrations minor parties often supported presidential initiatives in the legislature in exchange for material and other relevant benefits.

FEDERALISM

One of the principal criticisms of presidentialism is its winner-takes-all nature (Linz 1994). While this criticism has a few debatable features (see Chapter 1), there is nevertheless merit to it. To the extent that a nation concentrates power in the single institution of the presidency, the system does take on a certain winner-takes-all nature. Federalism reduces the winner-takes-all aspect of presidentialism in two related respects. First, it provides opposition parties (i.e., those other than the president's) with important areas of local autonomy and power, thereby giving them incentives to support the democratic system. Second, the institutional distribution of power between the national and provincial governments signifies that all provinces (even those governed by the president's party) represent checks on the president's overall power.

The Argentine federal system provides both of these benefits. It supplies the opposition parties with important "bailiwicks" in which they have the opportunity to govern. Furthermore, the provinces (those governed both by the opposition and by the president's party) check and limit the scope of the president's power of action.

Table 7.8 lists the number of provinces controlled by the PJ, UCR, and provincial parties between 1983 and the present. During the Alfonsín administration the PJ governed 12 (1983–87) and 17 (1987–91) of the nation's 22 provinces. This high level of representation in the provincial governments provided the PJ with important resources while in opposition, as well as gave the party further incentives to support the democratic system. During the first Menem presidency, UCR governors held office in 2 (1987–91) and 4 (1991–95) of the nation's 22 (23 after 1991) provinces, while provincial parties held the governor's office in 3 (1987–91) and 5 (1991–95) provinces.

During Menem's first term, governors proved to be an important check on presidential power. Governors of both opposition parties (e.g., Eduardo

Table 7.8. *Governorships held by political party: 1983–95*

Party	1983–87	1987–91	1991–95	1995–96
Partido Justicialista	12	17	14	14
Unión Cívica Radical	7	2	4	6
Movimiento Popular Neuquino	1	1	1	1
Pacto Autonomista Liberal*a*	1	1	1	1
Partido Bloquista	1	1		
Acción Chaqueña			1	
Movimiento Popular Fueguino			1	1
Partido Renovador de Salta			1	
Fuerza Republicana				1
Total	22	22	23	24*b*

*a*The province of Corrientes was governed by a federal-government-appointed intervener between 1991 and 1993 and by a PAL governor between 1993 and 1997.
*b*In 1996 the mayor of the Capital Federal was elected for the first time. The mayor is the functional equivalent of a provincial governor, so the mayoralty is included.
Source: Jones (1995a).

Angeloz, UCR, Cordoba) and the PJ (e.g., Eduardo Duhalde, Buenos Aires) successfully opposed the president in several instances. Duhalde in particular has represented one of the most prominent checks on the power of President Menem.[24]

Exemplary of the importance played by the provinces in providing areas of local autonomy and power for opposition parties, as well as members of the president's party, is the fact that most presidential candidates have prior experience as governors. In 1989, the two competitors for the PJ presidential candidacy, Antonio Cafiero and Carlos Menem, were sitting governors of the provinces of Buenos Aires and La Rioja, respectively. Likewise, the UCR presidential candidate in 1989, Eduardo Angeloz, was the sitting governor of the province of Cordoba. In 1995 the same trend was present, with all three principal candidates having gubernatorial experience. In addition to Menem, UCR candidate Horacio Massacessi was the sitting governor of the province of Rio Negro, while FREPASO candidate José Octavio Bordón was a former PJ governor of the province of Mendoza (1987–91).

24 Duhalde's influence has extended into the Chamber of Deputies, where PJ deputies from the province of Buenos Aires (over whom he has a great deal of influence) have represented nearly one-third of the PJ Chamber bloc in the 1993–95 and 1995–97 congresses.

FACTORS TARNISHING
ARGENTINE DEMOCRACY

In contrast to the three partisan and institutional factors that significantly contributed to the successful functioning of the Argentine presidential democracy, three other factors were at the same time tarnishing the system's democratic nature. They were the limited level of provincial autonomy vis-à-vis the national government, the president's co-optation of the judicial branch, and the use of executive decrees of urgent necessity by the president to bypass Congress. The latter two factors were associated almost exclusively with the presidency of Carlos Menem.

LIMITED PROVINCIAL AUTONOMY

Despite the important role played by federalism in reducing the winner-takes-all nature of the presidential system, Argentine federalism generally has been classified as weak for two principal reasons.[25] First, most provinces are highly dependent on the national government for financial support (*Ambito Financiero* 1992; Frías 1993; Pírez 1986; Pontussi 1993). This dependency stems from the relatively weak economic resources of a large number of provinces, as well as from the nation's system of federal coparticipation, under which most taxes are collected by the federal government, which then redistributes the revenue to the provinces. This system has been consistently plagued by controversy, with the federal government often exercising much more discretion in the timing and size of the revenue disbursement to the provinces than is considered acceptable by many Argentine academics and politicians (Durañona y Vedia 1993; Pírez 1986; Romero Feris 1993). The combination of scarce economic resources and a relatively undefined system of coparticipation controlled by the federal government has created a situation where all but the most wealthy provinces (e.g., Buenos Aires, Cordoba, Mendoza, Santa Fe) are highly dependent on the national government for financial support (Jiménez Peña 1993; Pontussi 1993). This has the end result of placing considerable restrictions on the real political autonomy of the provinces. To the extent to which the provinces are financially dependent on the national government, the ability of federalism to provide the oppo-

---

25 This weak classification results from the comparison of the Argentine federal system both with its theoretical potential and with the world's premiere federal systems, such as Switzerland and the United States. In the Latin American context, however, despite the relatively constrained status of its federal system, Argentina reduces the winner-takes-all nature of the presidential system via the route of territorial decentralization to a greater extent than any other Latin American nation with the exception of Brazil.

sition with areas of local autonomy and power, as well as to represent a salient check on presidential power, is diminished.

Second, under Article 6 of the constitution the federal government was (and continues to be) empowered to intervene in (i.e., take over governance in) the provincial governments. This power has been used in two ways. The most common has been the president threatening intervention in order to influence provincial government behavior. The least common has been actual intervention (Molinelli 1995a). President Alfonsín never intervened in a province, whereas President Menem did so five times during his first term. The ability of the federal government to intervene or credibly threaten intervention in a specific province has an inverse effect on the level of autonomy possessed by a province and on the extent to which it represents a check on presidential power. This ability to intervene or credibly threaten intervention generally has covaried with the relative prominence of the province in question, with intervention being easiest to carry out in the nation's less populous and poorer provinces and much more difficult in the more populous and wealthier provinces (Smulovitz 1993).

CO-OPTATION OF THE
JUDICIAL BRANCH

In Latin American presidential systems the judiciary is generally inferior in terms of power to the executive and legislative branches. It can and often does, however, play the crucial role of arbiter in disputes between the two more powerful branches. President Menem's effective co-optation of the judicial branch dramatically increased the level of power held by the executive branch in two specific ways. First, it reduced the extent to which the judiciary operated as a potential check on presidential power (particularly in regard to the implementation of Menem's dramatic structural reforms). Second, Menem was able to rely on the judiciary to confirm his ability to issue decrees of urgent necessity, which in all likelihood would not have been the case had the Court been composed of a more impartial group of justices.

Argentine Supreme Court justices were formerly appointed for life. The five justices on the court at the time of Menem's inauguration had been appointed during the Alfonsín administration.[26] Soon after taking office and

---

26 In 1983 the transitional nature of the democratic system, as well as Alfonsín's lack of an absolute majority in the Senate, resulted in the appointment of a group of justices with diverse political origins and preferences (Smulovitz 1995). Four of the five justices appointed in 1983 remained in office at the time of Menem's assumption of power.

initiating his far-reaching structural reform program, Menem realized its success could be jeopardized by the rulings of what he considered to be a nonsympathetic Supreme Court. Menem thus proposed a bill (justified in the name of greater judicial efficiency) that would increase the number of Supreme Court justices from five to nine. Prior to the 1994 reform, potential justices were nominated by the President and then confirmed in the Senate by a majority vote. During the first half of Menem's term (1989–92) the PJ held 54.4% of the seats in the Senate. Since Menem could nominate and ensure the confirmation of very sympathetic justices, passage of the bill would guarantee that the Supreme Court did not interfere with his key policies (a minority on the former five-member court were considered to be pro-Menem). Attempts to pack the Court with supportive justices are relatively common in Argentine history (Garro 1993). Prior to Menem, the most recent attempt had been by Alfonsín in 1987, when he proposed (unsuccessfully) to have the number of Supreme Court justices increased from five to seven (FBIS 1990; Garro 1993).

Menem's bill to increase the number of Supreme Court justices from five to nine easily passed in the Senate and then the Chamber. In both instances the bill was vehemently opposed by the UCR (*Diario de Sesiones de la Cámara de Diputados* 1990; *Diario de Sesiones de la Cámara de Senadores* 1989; *La Nación* 1990). In the Chamber, where the PJ did not possess an absolute majority of the seats, Menem was able to rally sufficient support from the UCeDé and provincial parties to ensure that a quorum was achieved and the bill was approved (*Diario de Sesiones de la Cámara de Diputados* 1990; *La Nación* 1990). Less than three weeks after the bill passed in the Chamber (April 5, 1990), Menem's Supreme Court nominees (all with strong ties to Menem and/or the PJ) were confirmed by the Senate, and Menem possessed a secure majority on the Court (Ferreira Rubio and Goretti 1993; Garro 1993; Manzetti 1993). Menem made five nominations, four for the new posts and one to replace a justice who resigned in November 1989 to protest Menem's plan to pack the Court. As the result of a resignation following the bill's passage in the Chamber, Menem was able to appoint an additional justice. In a period of less than two months, the Supreme Court had been transformed from an institution with no Menem appointees (out of four) to one with six Menem appointees (out of nine).

While the Menem-packed Supreme Court was not completely subservient, in most cases of important policy concern to Menem (e.g., privatizations such as that of the state-owned airline Aerolineas Argentinas) the court was very supportive of the administration position (Aramouni and Colombo 1992; Ferreira Rubio and Goretti forthcoming; Garro 1993; Nino 1992). Of particular importance was the Court's ruling on the president's use of decrees of urgent necessity. In its 1990 *Peralta* decision the Supreme Court sanctioned the president's use of this constitutionally questionable device (Bianchi 1991; Ferreira Rubio and Goretti forthcoming).

PRESIDENTIAL LEGISLATIVE POWERS

Shugart and Mainwaring (this volume) identify what they consider to be the three constitutional powers that have a significant impact on the president's ability to influence legislation: (1) veto power, (2) the exclusive introduction of legislation other than the budget, (3) decree authority (see Table 1.6). A strict reading of the Argentine constitution would identify the Argentine president as comparatively weak in terms of legislative powers (i.e., "reactive"). The reality of Argentine presidentialism between 1983 and 1994, however, was a much more powerful president (i.e., "potentially dominant"), who in addition to the strong veto, possessed the power of partial veto and most importantly (principally for Menem) the ability to issue executive decrees of urgent necessity (Ferreira Rubio and Goretti 1995; Molinelli 1994).

Executive Decrees

The most commonly cited negative aspect of Argentine presidentialism between 1989 and 1994 was the extent to which President Menem was able to effectively bypass the legislative branch on many occasions through the use of decrees. When discussing decrees, an important distinction must be made among four types: regulatory, autonomous, delegated, and urgent necessity (Ferreira Rubio and Goretti forthcoming).

The Argentine constitution explicitly provided for only regulatory and autonomous decrees, which are common to virtually all presidential systems. The use of the former was a necessary component of the executive's implementation of legislation approved via the normal constitutional process. The use of the latter was in complete accord with the president carrying out his or her constitutionally mandated duties.

The delegated decree was a generally accepted mechanism by which Congress, operating under the provisions of the constitution dealing with emergency situations, could delegate to the president the authority to issue decrees of a legislative nature. The principal constitutional questions related to delegated decrees generally focused on whether or not a decree was covered by the parameters set by Congress when it delegated authority to the president (Baglini 1993).

Two of the most prominent instances of delegation took place in 1989, when Congress passed Laws 23.696 (Reform of the State) and 23.697 (Economic Emergency) in August and September, respectively. These laws provided the president with the ability to issue delegated decrees in specific areas (e.g., the privatization of state-owned companies) for a limited period of time (with some provisions for extension). These delegated powers were utilized by Menem to implement critical components of his economic liberalization program. Menem was able to obtain these substantial delegated powers due to a combination of the following factors: severe economic and social crisis, the UCR's commitment that it would not oppose the key components of Menem's policy program (part of the deal made to obtain Menem's agreement to assume power early as well as a recognition of the severe crisis facing the nation), and Menem's ability to enforce PJ party discipline (Acuña 1995).[27]

The final and most problematic type of decree was that of urgent necessity. While several Argentine provincial constitutions provide their executive with the power to issue decrees of urgent necessity (e.g., Rio Negro, Salta, San Juan), the Argentine constitution (prior to 1994) did not (Frías et al. 1989). Yet historically Argentine presidents nevertheless employed such decrees on rare occasions. Alfonsín, for example, utilized this device 10 times (Ferreira Rubio and Goretti 1993). However, whereas between 1853 and July 1989 constitutional governments issued approximately 25 decrees of urgent necessity, from July 8, 1989, through August 23, 1994, President Menem issued 336 (see Table 7.9), many in areas that were considered the exclusive domain of Congress (e.g., taxes). While the Supreme Court stated that these decrees were to be used only in emergency situations, analysis of instances where they were employed suggests that what was considered an emergency was left to the discretion of the president in most cases (Ferreira Rubio and Goretti 1996).

The Supreme Court's 1990 *Peralta* decision sanctioned the executive's use of these decrees and made them very difficult for Congress to rescind. To rescind a decree of urgent necessity Congress needed to pass a bill annulling the decree, and if the president vetoed the bill, then Congress had to override the veto, which required a two-thirds vote in each chamber. Given Menem's secure majority in the Senate and near-majority in the Chamber, such decree repeals were very rare. Of Menem's 336 decrees of urgent necessity issued through August 23, 1994, Congress only voted to wholly rescind three and partially rescind one

27 The UCR commitment was a necessity for Menem since his Chamber plurality would not be in place until the official renovation in December. As a result of this commitment the UCR provided the quorum needed to pass the two bills but, at the same time, voted nearly unanimously against them (Aramouni and Colombo 1992).

Table 7.9. *Presidential decrees of urgent necessity, vetoes, and partial vetoes: 1983–95*

President	Year	Decrees of urgent necessity	Total and partial vetoes	Vetoes overridden by Congress	Months in office
Raúl Alfonsín	1983	0	0		1
	1984	1	19		12
	1985	1	13		12
	1986	2	12		12
	1987	3	4		12
	1988	2	1		12
	1989	1	0		6
	Total	10	49[b]	1	67
Carlos Menem	1989	30	5		6
	1990	63	13		12
	1991	85	24		12
	1992	69	23		12
	1993	62	11		12
	1994	27[a]	14		12
	1995		19[c]		6
	Total	336	109[b]	10[d]	72

[a]Decrees of urgent necessity were recorded through August 23, 1994 (i.e., the last day in which the unreformed constitution was still in force).

[b]Thirty-seven (76%) of Alfonsín's vetoes were total vetoes, while 12 (24%) were partial vetoes. Forty-eight (44%) of Menem's vetoes were total vetoes, while 61 (56%) were partial vetoes.

[c]Vetoes were recorded for Menem through the last day of his first term (July 7, 1995).

[d]Two of the overrides were requested by the president.

Sources: Ferreira Rubio (1995); Ferreira Rubio and Goretti (1996); Mustapic and Ferretti (1995a); Mustapic and Ferretti (1995b).

(Ferreira Rubio and Goretti 1996). Menem successfully vetoed two of the four repeal bills.[28]

Decrees of urgent necessity provided the president with a very powerful tool with which to influence the legislative process. First, the decrees endowed the president with the ability to legislate without going through Congress. Second, the president could use the threat of a decree as a way to pressure Congress to pass a bill. That is, the president could state that if Congress did not pass a bill, then he would implement it by decree, and thus Congress would miss any opportunity to influence the content of the bill (e.g., Menem's threat in 1993 to implement legislation reforming the nation's pension system by decree if the Chamber did not approve his pension reform bill (*Clarín* 1993). In the terminology of Shugart and Mainwaring's Chapter 1, this decree power transformed the Argentine president's legislative powers from being "reactive" to being "potentially dominant."[29]

A presidential legislative majority in Argentina did not signify that a bill was guaranteed congressional passage without modifications or questions (Molinelli 1995a). To gain congressional approval of a bill the president was required to mobilize support for it among various party leaders. It was a quite different situation when the president issued a decree of urgent necessity. In contrast to the normal legislative process, for the legislature to influence policy in this latter situation it needed to mobilize itself against the wishes of the president. Furthermore, as long as Menem could demonstrate sufficient support to sustain a veto, the passage of a bill overruling a decree was not a rational action for Congress to undertake (except for publicity purposes). This was particularly the case for members of the PJ, whose support was essential to the passage of any repeal bill. In instances where a veto was forthcoming for which there did not exist sufficient support for an override, the incentives for PJ legislators to vote against Menem were quite low. The president's power to issue decrees of urgent necessity thus represented a very proactive power, putting Congress in a highly reactive situation where it needed to assemble an extraordinary majority (requiring the inclusion of a large number of PJ legislators) if it was to check the actions of the president.

---

28 In both instances he employed a partial veto to extract those portions of the bill that conflicted with his decree (Ferreira Rubio and Goretti 1996). During this same period Menem also vetoed four bills in whole and nine bills in part because they contradicted legislation contained in decrees of urgent necessity that he had issued previously (Ferreira Rubio and Goretti 1996).

29 The constitution-based classification employed in Chapter 1 correctly labels the Argentine system as "reactive."

Veto Power

Presidential veto power did not directly diminish the functioning of the Argentine democratic system. However, the employment of the veto in conjunction with the use of decrees of urgent necessity, as well as the general focus of this volume on presidential legislative powers, suggests that a brief review of the president's veto power is merited. Prior to the 1994 reform, presidents in Argentina possessed the power to veto bills passed by the legislature either in whole (full vetoes) or in part (partial vetoes). This latter power, while not explicitly mentioned in the constitution, was nevertheless a de facto power exercised by presidents, particularly since the 1960s (Molinelli 1994, 1991a; Mustapic and Ferretti 1995a). The only restriction placed on the use of the partial veto by the Supreme Court was that it not substantially alter the original intention (the "unity") of the bill (Molinelli 1994, 1991a). In practice, the ambiguous nature of this restriction allowed executives to promulgate bills that they had modified substantially.

Table 7.9 contains information on the use of vetoes by Presidents Alfonsín and Menem. Three prominent points emerge from the data. First, Menem made greater use of vetoes than did Alfonsín. Second, Menem utilized the partial veto to a much greater extent than Alfonsín, in both aggregate and proportional terms. The principal source of these two differences was the tendency of the Chamber to modify portions of bills submitted by Menem (Mustapic and Ferretti 1995a). While Menem's bills would normally be approved, they often contained modifications that the president and his advisors considered inconvenient. As a result, Menem partially vetoed 61 bills, 30 of which he had submitted. In contrast, Alfonsín partially vetoed 12 bills, only 1 of which he had submitted. Mustapic and Ferretti (1995a) attribute this difference to Menem's lack of an absolute majority in the Chamber and the PJ bloc's looser level of discipline. Given Menem's radical departure from the traditional statist Peronist policies, particularly in terms of economic policy, his greater difficulty enforcing party discipline on these matters is not surprising. Thirty-nine percent of Menem's vetoes were of bills dealing specifically (and solely) with the themes of pensions, taxes, fiscal policy, labor policy, and privatizations/transfers (Mustapic and Ferretti 1995a).

Finally, only 1 of Alfonsín's and 10 of Menem's vetoes were overridden. Menem, however, requested that Congress override 2 of his vetoes (both partial) after deciding that he preferred the original version of the bill (Mustapic and Ferretti 1995a). Thus, out of the 158 presidential vetoes issued between 1983 and 1995, Congress truly overrode only 9 (5.7%). This low percentage is not surprising since to override a veto in Argentina requires the support of two-thirds of the legislators (present) in both chambers. For both Alfonsín and Menem this meant that for an override of a veto to be successful, it needed to be supported by a significant portion of the presidential party's legislative bloc. Even assuming the extreme position that all nonpresidential party deputies and senators supported an override, for an override to succeed it required the support of a considerable number of Radicals during the Alfonsín administration and Peronists during the Menem administration. Even in Alfonsín's period of weakest legislative support (1987–89), for an override to succeed it needed the assistance of 33 UCR deputies and 3 UCR senators. During the period 1983–87 a successful override would have needed the assistance of 45 (1983–85) or 46 (1985–87) UCR deputies and 3 UCR senators. Under the same circumstances for Menem, a successful override required the assistance of 43 PJ deputies and 10 (1989–92) or 14 PJ senators (1992–95).[30]

THE 1994 CONSTITUTIONAL REFORM

Between 1983 and 1994 the combination of three (under Alfonsín) then five (under Menem) principal partisan and institutional factors made the Argentine president extremely powerful: (1) a large and relatively well-disciplined partisan legislative contingent, (2) the federal government's strong position vis-à-vis the provinces, (3) strong veto and partial veto powers, (4) the ability to issue decrees of urgent necessity (Menem), and (5) a co-opted Supreme Court (Menem). In 1994 Argentina engaged in a partial reform of its constitution that addressed many of the criticisms of the Argentine presidential system mentioned in the previous sections.

Under the prereform constitution immediate presidential reelection was prohibited. President Carlos Menem wanted to be reelected. However, to reform the constitution required (1) a call for the reform of the constitution (or as in this case specific portions of it) supported by two-thirds of the members of both chambers of Congress and (2) the election of a constituent assembly to carry out the reform. As of mid-1993 Menem found himself blocked by this first requisite. He was faced with the dilemma that the UCR controlled 33.1% (down to 32.7% after Decem-

---

30 The figure of 43 deputies listed for the PJ is based on election results. For reasons previously discussed the actual number that would have needed to have been induced to defect was somewhat lower.

ber 10, 1993) of the seats in the Chamber and thus could realistically block any attempt to reform the constitution. This was particularly the case given the strident opposition to Menem's reelection bid expressed by a few small parties (primarily of the center-left), which for ideological reasons were not likely to be susceptible to efforts by Menem to obtain their votes in exchange for material or policy benefits. The seats held by these parties along with those of the UCR totaled over 33.3% of the seats in the Chamber (see Table 7.1). Menem did, however, have several factors working to his advantage: (1) the strong victory by the PJ and the corresponding defeat suffered by the UCR in the October 1993 Chamber election, (2) the ability to call a nonbinding referendum on the reform (with a focus on the reelection amendment) which polls demonstrated would result in a clear victory for the pro-reform position, and (3) tensions within the UCR over the issue of providing support for the reform of the constitution (Acuña 1995).[31]

The UCR's poor showing in the October 1993 election, increasing difficulties in keeping the UCR united in its efforts to block Menem's reelection bid, and a growing belief that Menem would not relent in his efforts to obtain the right to seek reelection led UCR leader Raúl Alfonsín to opt to provide Menem with the reelection reform. Alfonsín, however, was determined to benefit from the constitutional reform as well (Smulovitz 1995).[32] In early November Alfonsín began secretly meeting with President Menem, and on November 14 the two signed an agreement (the Pact of Olivos) in which Menem was granted his coveted reelection reform in exchange for a number of reforms that Alfonsín felt would limit the power of the president, benefit the UCR, and restore Alfonsín to a more prominent role in Argentine politics. This agreement (and subsequent agreements derived from it) contained two principal components: (1) a set of reforms (including reelection) that would later become the Nucleus of Basic Agreements, which was to be voted on as a package in the Constituent Assembly, and (2) a list of additional portions of the constitution that would be open to reform during the Con-

---

31 Menem's threat of carrying out a nonbinding referendum (as Alfonsín had done in 1984 to demonstrate popular support for the signing of a treaty with Chile) was very credible. The Dirección Nacional Electoral had begun preparations for the referendum at the time Menem decided to cancel it.

32 During his presidency Alfonsín demonstrated considerable interest in the topic of constitutional reform. However, the sharp decline in his popularity during the last third of his term forced him to suspend his efforts to reform the constitution (Acuña 1995; Smulovitz 1995).

stituent Assembly (Jones 1996c). After a period of bitter intraparty conflict over the pact, Alfonsín was able to secure the support (or at least acquiescence) of the bulk of the UCR. He thus was able to provide Menem with the votes needed in Congress, and the law (24.309) calling for the reform of the constitution was approved in December.[33]

For Menem the goal of reelection was paramount. He therefore sacrificed some presidential powers (see the reforms discussed in the next section) as a necessary condition to gain the support of the UCR that enabled him to procure the reelection reform and at the same time provided a high degree of legitimacy to the Constituent Assembly and the reformed constitution that emerged from it (Smulovitz 1995).

The UCR's chances of winning the presidential election of 1995 were relatively low whether Menem ran or not. The reforms agreed to in the Pact of Olivos would limit the overall powers of the president and would in general provide a greater constitutional role for the political opposition in Congress, which was dominated by the UCR. The reform also would reduce the presidential term length from six to four years. Thus, from the standpoint of a general constitutional framework, the pact with Menem was not a bad deal for the UCR. From an electoral perspective, however, the pact was an unmitigated disaster. It caused severe dissent within the UCR, gave the impression that the UCR had ceased to represent an effective opposition to the PJ, and in general opened the way for the electoral rise of the Frente Grande in the 1994 Constituent Assembly election and later the emergence of the FREPASO alliance in the 1995 national and provincial elections. By signing this pact with Menem, Alfonsín and the UCR made a significant contribution to the debilitation of the nation's two-party-dominant system.

In the April 10, 1994, Constituent Assembly election, the PJ and UCR, while not making a particularly good electoral showing (especially the UCR), nevertheless won 137 and 74 of the 305 assembly seats, respectively (Dirección Nacional Electoral 1994). Thus, the Nucleus of Basic Agreements (with some minor modifications agreed to by the PJ and UCR) was approved (along with several other reforms, many related to federalism), with the reformed constitution entering into force on August 24, 1994.

---

33 Many in the UCR opposed the pact made by Alfonsín with Menem. This opposition ranged in intensity from indifference to outright rebellion. However, a significant number of key UCR politicians such as Sergio Montiel (Entre Rios), Fernando de la Rúa (Capital Federal), and Federico Storani (Buenos Aires), strongly opposed the pact.

THE INSTITUTIONAL AND PARTISAN IMPACT OF THE CONSTITUTIONAL REFORM

Presidential Legislative Powers

Overall, the reforms present something of a paradox in terms of the presidential legislative powers listed in Table 1.6.[34] A strict reading of the constitution indicates that the Argentine president's legislative powers have increased. The constitution now explicitly grants the president a limited power to issue decrees of urgent necessity, as well as the ability to issue partial vetoes.[35] At the de jure level this increase in constitutional power was countered by the creation of the post of cabinet chief along with the placement of restrictions on the congressional delegation of decree authority.[36] However, under the preceding constitution the president possessed the de facto power to issue decrees of urgent necessity and partial vetoes, powers that in many ways were strengthened due to the lack of explicit reference to them in the constitution (Espinosa-Saldaña Barrera 1995). In sum, while increasing the de jure legislative powers of the president the constitutional reform has in fact decreased the president's de facto legislative powers.

34 Many of the reforms related to presidential legislative powers were very general (i.e., vague), with the Constituent Assembly delegating to Congress the task of issuing the appropriate regulation of these reforms. With a few minor exceptions, Congress has yet (as of July 1996) to issue any of the corresponding regulation. There thus is a considerable degree of uncertainty regarding the true scope and depth of many of the reforms, particularly those related to decrees of urgent necessity and the issuing of partial vetoes.

35 The president may issue decrees of urgent necessity only in exceptional circumstances that make it impossible to utilize the normal constitutional process. Even in exceptional cases the president cannot issue these decrees in the areas of criminal law, taxes, electoral law, or political party law. Finally, the decree must be submitted to a bicameral commission within 10 days of its promulgation. This commission in turn must in 10 days bring the issue to the respective chambers to be voted on. Partial vetoes must now follow the same process as decrees of urgent necessity (be submitted to a bicameral commission, etc.).

36 Some powers formerly held by the president will henceforth be exercised by a cabinet chief (*jefe de gabinete*) who is appointed by the president but can be removed by an absolute majority vote in each of the two chambers. The actual role that the cabinet chief will play is unclear. Given the high probability of the PJ having an absolute majority in at least one of the houses during Menem's second term (1995–99), it is unlikely that the cabinet chief will be an important check on the president for the near future. Congress is prohibited from delegating congressional authority to the president, except in areas of administration and during emergencies and even then only for a fixed period of time (Molinelli 1995b).

Judicial Branch

The constitutional reform weakened the ability of the president to exert influence over the judicial branch (Sabsay and Onaindia 1994).[37] Under the reformed constitution, as before, the president submits Supreme Court nominations to the Senate for approval. However, confirmation now requires a two-thirds vote in the Senate. This check is further strengthened by a change in the rules governing the election of senators. Under the new constitution (beginning in 2001 in full, but starting in 1995 in a transitional manner), three senators will be directly elected at the same time from each province (and the Capital Federal) for six-year terms, with two seats going to the plurality winner and one going to the second-place finisher (i.e., the "first minority"). These elections will be staggered (beginning in 2003), with one-third of the provinces renewing their senators every two years.[38] Thus, to obtain the two-thirds vote of the Senate needed to confirm a justice on its own, the president's party would need to win a plurality of the vote in every province for six straight years.

Federalism

Argentine federalism has been strengthened in four principal ways by the reform. First, the system of federal coparticipation is now much more explicit. It has been included in the constitution, with the distribution of funds to the provinces now automatic, and an institution to monitor national–provincial fiscal and administrative organization has been created. Second, the provinces received a number of new powers related to the creation of regions, as well as the ability to enter into international agreements (within certain limits) that will increase their financial independence. Third, federal intervention in a province now explicitly requires congressional approval (Molinelli 1995b). Finally, the Capital Federal received a much greater degree of autonomy, including a directly elected mayor (previously appointed by the president). These four reforms increase the autonomy (both political and economic) of the provinces and capital (thereby reducing the winner-takes-all nature of the system) and at the same time bolster the check

---

37 In addition, as part of his agreement with Menem, Alfonsín obtained the guarantee that two Menem-appointed Supreme Court justices would resign (only one actually resigned, however) and that the UCR would play a prominent role in the process of naming their replacements (Acuña 1995).

38 In 1995 and 1998 (prior to full implementation) the senators will be elected by the same method as before (except in the Capital Federal), but with the stipulation that no one party can have more than two senators from a district. For example, in a province where the two current senators belong to the same party, the third (i.e., "first minority") senate seat goes to the party (other than the party to which the two senators belong) with the most seats in the provincial legislature. The Senate will renew completely in 2001.

they represent on the national government (particularly on presidential power).

The Party System

Three important changes took place in the electoral rules (in addition to the provision for immediate presidential reelection for one term). First, the president is now elected directly. Under this new arrangement (first used in May 1995), if in the first round no candidate receives either (1) over 45% of the valid vote or (2) a minimum of 40% of the valid vote and at the same time is more than 10% ahead of the second-place candidate, then a runoff is held between the top two candidates from the first round. Second, the presidential term was shortened from six to four years, signifying that every other Chamber election will now be concurrent with the election of the president. Third, senators will be elected henceforth from three-member districts, with two seats going to the plurality winner and one to the "first minority." In general these reforms are not likely to greatly brake or accelerate the recent emergence of a multiparty system in Argentina.[39] The reforms are also unlikely to have any noteworthy direct effect on party discipline.

Presidential Legislative Contingents

The recent deterioration of the two-party-dominant system, which is likely to continue in the near future, will result in a commensurate decrease in the average size of the president's legislative contingent. This decrease is likely to be offset (in the Chamber) only slightly by the increase in the percentage of concurrent presidential and Chamber elections.

In general the constitutional reforms are not likely to prevent the emergence of a multiparty system and the concomitant reduction of the average size of the president's legislative contingent. The failure of the Constituent

---

39 The decline of the nation's two-party-dominant system and the ensuing emergence of a multiparty system is the result of a convergence of several situation-specific factors. These include the tarnished UCR image resulting from its participation in the Pact of Olivos, the UCR's presentation of a relatively weak presidential candidate in 1995, and the UCR's serious intraparty conflict. These factors resulted in a severely weakened UCR. At the same time, Menem's refusal to hold a semiopen primary resulted in Bordón's defection and subsequent presentation as a candidate in the FREPASO primary. Bordón's surprising victory in this primary helped to vault FREPASO from its third-place ranking (based on the prediction of "Chacho" Alvarez as the alliance's presidential candidate) to second. The end result of the UCR's difficulties and the Bordón presidential candidacy was a strong showing for the FREPASO alliance in the 1995 presidential and legislative elections. This success has provided FREPASO with a base from which there is a potential (not yet realized) for substantial growth and the possibility of FREPASO's consolidation as a strong and relevant political force in Argentina.

Assembly to adopt concrete measures to help counteract the current decline of the nation's two-party-dominant system represents a notable flaw in an otherwise positive reform.[40]

There is a very strong inverse relationship between the level of legislative multipartism in a nation and the size of the executive party's contingent in the legislature. Furthermore, evidence from the Latin American nations as well as the Argentine provinces shows that systems with levels of multipartism greater than that of a two-party-dominant system are generally unable to consistently provide the president with sufficiently strong support in the legislature (Jones 1995b). In instances where the president is not provided with sufficient legislative support (generally a majority or near-majority of the seats in the legislature), the stability and effectiveness of the government is reduced and the democratic system is undermined, sometimes to such an extent that it collapses (e.g., Chile in 1973, Peru in 1992, and Uruguay in 1973). It is for this reason that the current trend of increasing multipartism, if it continues, bodes badly for the future functioning of the Argentine democratic system.

SUMMARY

Argentina is currently enjoying its most successful experience with democracy ever. At the same time, despite some current economic difficulties, the country's economic future is brighter than anytime in the past 50 years. Argentina's presidential system has combined the twin goals of economic growth (particularly in terms of much needed structural reforms) and stability with a highly democratic system of government. Institutional and partisan factors that contributed to this success include the two-party-dominant system's provision of strong partisan support for the president in the legislature, the moderate to high level of party discipline in the legislature, and the ability of the federal system to mitigate the winner-takes-all nature of presidentialism. At the same time, institutional and partisan factors that diminished the functioning of the Argentine democratic system include the limited autonomy of the provincial governments, a judicial branch that was co-opted by the president, and the president's use of decrees of urgent necessity to bypass the Congress.

40 Concrete measures that could have been adopted include: completely concurrent presidential and legislative elections; the direct election of senators from single-member plurality districts (i.e., the provinces); the reduction of the Chamber's effective magnitude (by creating multiple districts within the largest provinces); and presidential electoral formulas such as the plurality formula or the Costa Rican variant of the plurality formula.

The constitutional reform of 1994 addressed many of the institutional features that had been tarnishing the Argentine democratic system. Under the new constitution the president's ability to issue decrees of urgent necessity has been restricted and placed under greater congressional control. The president's ability to influence the judicial branch in general and the composition of the Supreme Court in particular has been curtailed. Finally, the role of the provinces as bailiwicks for opposition parties as well as checks on presidential power has been strengthened.

Combined, these and related institutional reforms are likely to have a positive impact on Argentine democracy by reducing the power of the president and increasing the power and autonomy of the principal checks on the president: the Congress, judicial branch, and provinces. The primary negative aspect of the reform is its failure to introduce the measures necessary to help impede the party system's transformation from a two-party-dominant to a multiparty system. Presently, the greatest institutional or partisan threat to the successful functioning of the Argentine democratic system is the decline of its two-party-dominant system.

It is difficult to predict the future structure of the Argentine party system given its present state of flux. Much depends on whether the current FREPASO alliance coalesces into a coherent political party. If the alliance survives until the 1997 Chamber election, of particular interest will be how it fares when its popular presidential and vice-presidential candidates, José Octavio Bordón (who left FREPASO in early 1996) and Carlos "Chacho" Alvarez (who headed the alliance's list in 1995), are absent from the ticket. The most likely scenario for the near-future is a growing multiparty system with the PJ remaining strong (although not unscathed) throughout the nation and possessing a majority or near-majority in the Senate and Chamber. In the near future the "opposition" (principally the UCR, FREPASO, and the center-right provincial parties) is likely to remain fragmented, with parties varying significantly in terms of their electoral support, depending on the district in question (Adrogué 1995).[41]

The composition of the legislature for the 1995–97 (Chamber) and 1995–98 (Senate) periods points to the potentially problematic future of the Argentine democratic system (see Tables 7.1 and 7.2).[42] Stripped of its

41 Two other possible (although less likely, particularly the second) party-system scenarios are as follows: one, the UCR experiences a rejuvenation while FREPASO disintegrates, with the result being a restoration of the previous two-party-dominant system; two, the UCR experiences a complete collapse, while FREPASO is able to consolidate, absorbing many former UCR leaders and voters, thereby establishing a new two-party-dominant system consisting of the PJ and FREPASO.

42 Due to defections from the PJ, the actual FREPASO contingent is slightly larger than

two-party-dominant system, and resultant tendency to provide the president
with sufficient legislative support, the system could in the near future face
a serious crisis at such time that a non-PJ candidate wins the presidency.
If, for example, either José Octavio Bordón (FREPASO) or Horacio Massacessi (UCR) had won the 1995 presidential election, each would have faced
a legislature in which his respective forces possessed less than one-eighth
and one-third of the seats in each chamber.[43] This is below even the minimum necessary for either of their respective parties to sustain a presidential
veto on its own. As the experiences of the Argentine provinces and the rest
of Latin America ably demonstrate, either a Bordón or a Massacessi presidency would have had serious negative consequences for governability in
Argentina (Shugart and Mainwaring, this volume; Mainwaring and Shugart,
this volume; Jones 1995b).

CONCLUSION

A fundamental premise of this volume is the importance of distinguishing
between the constitutional and partisan powers of the president. During the
1983–94 period the Argentine president possessed considerable constitutional powers (both de jure and particularly de facto). The president also
possessed on average a large and relatively disciplined partisan contingent
in the legislature. Combined, these factors created an extremely powerful
executive. This was particularly the case during the presidency of Carlos
Menem.

The 1994 constitutional reform attempted to reduce the power of the
president by curtailing the executive's constitutional powers. These reforms,
combined with the growing multiparty nature of the Argentine party system (and the concomitant decrease in presidential legislative support), signify that future Argentine presidents will be less powerful than their
predecessors in the 1983–95 era.

While the reduction of the president's constitutional power is a positive
occurrence for the future of Argentine democracy, the decline of its two-

---

that represented in the table. It should be remembered that in contrast to the PJ and
UCR, FREPASO remains a relatively undisciplined alliance of politicians with very
diverse political roots.

43 The percentages of valid votes won in the 1995 presidential election were as follows:
Menem (49.9), Bordón (29.3), Massacessi (17.0), Aldo Rico (1.7), and 10 other candidates
together (2.0). Had Bordón been able to force a runoff (which public opinion polls
conducted in the weeks prior to the election suggested was a very real possibility), he
would have received the support of an overwhelming majority of Massacessi voters. There
was thus an outside chance of a Bordón victory.

party-dominant system is a source of great concern. If the two-party-dominant system is replaced by a multiparty system, the result will be increased difficulties in governance and a greater likelihood of political and economic instability. As a reminder of the potential dangers of this growing multipartism, Argentina need only look to its neighbors Brazil and Uruguay, where high levels of multipartism and ensuing small presidential legislative contingents have contributed to the creation of ineffective governments, unable to address adequately key national social and economic problems.

8

IN DEFENSE OF PRESIDENTIALISM: THE CASE OF CHILE, 1932–1970

Julio Faundez

Until recently, the development of Chilean democracy between 1932 and 1970 was regarded as a success story, at least by Third World standards. For during this period there was a major expansion of political participation combined with ever more systematic attempts to deal with the root cause of economic underdevelopment. As industry became more diversified and government policy on copper and other natural resources became more coherent, there was also a serious attempt, through an agrarian reform, to tackle the problem of low productivity in the agricultural sector.

Political stability had facilitated the development of a large network of state institutions that played a prominent role in promoting economic development. Over the years, these institutions had made it possible to combine the implementation of imaginative socioeconomic reforms with a sustained process of political and electoral mobilization. This process had not only strengthened the legitimacy of the political system, but had helped generate among political leaders an unbounded confidence in the possibility of achieving socioeconomic change through the existing institutional framework.

One feature of Chile's political system that had gone largely unnoticed by specialists was its presidential system of government. However, the collapse of democracy in 1973, which prompted many scholars to reflect upon the reasons for the breakdown, also brought about a renewed interest in this feature of the political system.

This chapter is an expanded and revised version of a paper presented at the Conference on Transition to Democracy in Chile at the University of Liverpool in December 1990.

Some of the most stimulating contributions to the study of political transitions have come from scholars who, until recently, have concentrated on the study of the breakdown of democracy: in particular, Linz (1978), Linz and Stepan (1978), and Valenzuela (1978). Their systematic reflection about factors leading to the collapse of democracy sharpened their awareness of the role of institutions in determining the outcome of political processes. Thus, it is not surprising that on the eve of the transition to democracy in Chile, the views and policy recommendations of these scholars were taken into account by politicians and academics busy drafting new constitutions. The object of this chapter is to examine the academic critique of Chile's presidentialism. I start with background information about the current debate in Chile. I then examine the critiques of presidentialism in Chile in the light of an alternative interpretation of the Chilean political process between 1925 and 1973. This interpretation is based on my previous work on Chilean politics (Faundez 1988) and on my current research on law and politics under the 1925 constitution.[1] I argue that presidentialism was not the cause of regime breakdown in Chile, but to the contrary, presidentialism in Chile may have actually prevented that breakdown from occurring much earlier in the country's history. The profound socioeconomic problems that Chile faced between 1930 and 1970 were wrenching, and given those difficulties the country's institutions performed remarkably well. In fact, often during that 40-year period, presidents worked strongly to moderate partisan polarization and to draw differing factions together in negotiations. Party polarization did indeed reach the point of irreconcilability under Allende, but I argue that presidentialism was not the cause of that crisis.

THE DEBATE IN CHILE

In Chile, Linz's attack on presidentialism found a receptive audience. The constitution of 1980, designed to serve as a vehicle to legitimize Pinochet's rule until the end of the century, was not only weak concerning democracy, but also strongly presidential. Thus, not surprisingly, the democratic forces opposing Pinochet were critical of the constitution, and some, expecting that the transition to democracy would bring about a new constitution, advocated the introduction of a parliamentary form

---

1 My work in progress examines the legality debate during the Allende administration within the context of the evolution of legal doctrine and ideology. A special focus of attention is the political role of the Supreme Court.

of government. In the event, the transition took place within the framework of Pinochet's constitution, albeit amended, and the presidential regime remained in place.

The issue of parliamentarism has not, however, disappeared from the political debate. Several prominent politicians within the government coalition still favor the introduction of a parliamentary or a semipresidential system (see Siavelis, this volume, for details). In their view, this change would ensure the successful transition, as well as enhance the democratic character, of the emerging political system. While I have no reason to doubt the sincerity of the views expressed by these politicians, it should be noted that their advocacy of parliamentarism or semipresidentialism is also based on tactical considerations. The Concertación, the coalition of parties that has been in office since the return to democracy in 1990, is dominated by the Christian Democratic Party (CDP), with the Socialists as the second major group within the coalition. Owing to the unwillingness of the Christian Democrats to support a Socialist for the presidency – as demonstrated in the 1993 election – a system in which the office of head of state and the office of head of government are split might offer a convenient solution to a potentially embarrassing political conflict. The assumption is that the CDP would tolerate a Socialist prime minister, provided that it retained the presidency; likewise, the Socialists would allow the CDP to run the government from the office of the prime minister, provided one of their members occupied the presidency. In brief, while the prevailing presidential system appears to condemn the Socialists permanently to a subordinate role within the coalition, a parliamentary system would give them access to one of the two main offices of state, thus giving durability to their coalition with the CDP and making this alliance more acceptable to their supporters.

While the advocacy of parliamentarism or semipresidentialism in Chile may be prompted by short-term political calculations, arguments for it are solid and deserve careful consideration. These arguments are mostly derived from the work of several respected experts on the Chilean political system, of whom the leading one is Valenzuela (1977, 1978). Unfortunately, the academic arguments in favor of parliamentarism have been uncritically accepted by its advocates. Few have developed contrary arguments (but see Shugart and Carey 1992).

It is perhaps surprising that the arguments against presidentialism should have been so well received among Chilean academics and policymakers. After all, during this century Chile appears to have done quite well despite its presidential system. Between 1932 and 1973, the presidential system appears to have delivered a stable and relatively efficient system.

Civil and political rights were generally respected, and conflict was largely channeled through the political system. These achievements were all the more significant if one examines the poor democratic record of other countries in the region during this same period.

THE CRITIQUE OF PRESIDENTIALISM AS APPLIED TO CHILE

Presidentialism under the 1925 constitution provided that (a) the president was elected for a single six-year term by a majority of the popular votes or, failing that, by the Congress from among the two most popular candidates; (b) Congress could not remove the president or cabinet ministers on a vote of nonconfidence; (c) ministers could not be selected from among the elected members of the Congress; and (d) the president played an active role in the legislative process, having exclusive power to initiate legislation in certain areas and wide powers to participate in the drafting of bills through a veto that required a two-thirds vote in each house of the legislature to override.

The leading academic critic of presidentialism in Chile is Arturo Valenzuela, whose work on the topic has had a major impact among Chilean academics. It is interesting to note that one of Valenzuela's strongest arguments for the introduction of a parliamentary system in Chile was used against Pinochet's model for the transition to democracy and thus revealed a deep distrust for political parties generally (Valenzuela 1985, 1994). Valenzuela rightly and persuasively pointed out that the party system and its profound ideological cleavages could not be easily wished away or repressed out of existence. Instead, he proposed that the introduction of a parliamentary system would facilitate a smooth transition to democracy since it would moderate the claims of the extreme parties and would provide politicians with a valuable lesson about the virtues of a more pragmatic and less ideological approach to politics.

Presidents in Chile, according to Valenzuela, found it extraordinarily difficult to govern. They were generally elected by minority coalitions that almost invariably tended to disintegrate shortly after the election. As a consequence, they were permanently in conflict with the congressional majority, which either refused to approve legislation or subjected it to inordinate delays. Paradoxically, the main actors in the political system attempted to resolve the stalemate between the president and the Congress through a series of constitutional amendments that purported to strengthen the powers of the president and of the executive branch generally. This approach, however, failed to resolve the problem for presidents, who, despite their increased power, could not use it effectively because of the inherent weaknesses of the presidential system. Indeed, as Valenzuela (1994:138) puts it, "The stronger the president, the weaker the presidential system."

As the powers of the president were increased, the relative strength of the Congress declined. Valenzuela points out that the traditional role played by the Congress as the main organ through which particularistic interests were channeled was greatly changed as a consequence of the constitutional amendments that transferred power to the president. Because political competition had become more ideological, political groupings in the Congress became increasingly unwilling to make concessions to their adversaries. Practically everything had become a nonnegotiable point of principle.

The presidential system exacerbated existing ideological differences. A weak president who could not be reelected and was incapable of fulfilling electoral promises was a political liability. Accordingly, coalitions tended to disintegrate, since no party wanted to assume responsibility for the shortcomings of the government. Moreover, because of the winner-takes-all factor mentioned in the preceding section, politicians were often carried away by their own rhetoric, forming "high-stake" coalitions which further deepened the polarization within the system.

Following Sartori (1966), Valenzuela (1994) argues that Chile's polarized party system left little room for the emergence of a centrist consensus. The center parties did not represent a viable centrist tendency. They were made up of fragments of the extremes and were a reflection of the erosion of the system. Consequently, the centrist parties – Radicals and Christian Democrats – were not capable of forming stable coalitions. A parliamentary system with its emphasis on continuous negotiations and concessions would presumably have created more favorable conditions for a solid centrist consensus, thus stabilizing the system and moderating the ideology of the main political actors.

PRESIDENTIALISM AND CHILEAN POLITICAL DEVELOPMENT

In the following sections I discuss some aspects of Chile's political development that, in my view, provide an alternative perspective from which to evaluate the role played by presidentialism in the development of the political system. The object, as stated earlier, is to contribute toward the task of designing effective political institutions.

THE PARLIAMENTARY REPUBLIC

For just over three decades, between 1891 and 1924, Chile had a hybrid system of government sometimes described as semipresidential and sometimes as semiparliamentary. In Chilean historiography, it is known as the parliamentary republic, and it is, on the whole, regarded as a politically sterile period. It was a peculiar form of government because although Congress managed informally to become involved in the making and unmaking of cabinets, the president did not have the corresponding power to dissolve the Congress and call for a general election. The making and unmaking of cabinets prevented governments from formulating and implementing long-term policies, hence the sterility of the period.

Present-day advocates of presidentialism rightly point out that since the parliamentary republic was not a genuine parliamentary regime, it is not a valid precedent from which to assess the chances of parliamentarism in Chile. But they also make the important point that the legacy of the parliamentary republic has been underestimated. Acknowledging that during that period the state employed rather brutal methods to repress and destroy the organizations of the emerging mining and industrial proletariat, Valenzuela (1994:98) points out that "the competitive nature of the political system centered on the parliament permitted parties created outside the legislative arena to become incorporated into the political system."

It is undoubtedly true that the existence of a strong competitive party system – whose origins predate the parliamentary republic – made possible the integration of new parties into the system. However, this integration was not achieved through the parliamentary republic, but against it. Indeed, the collapse of democracy in the early 1920s was largely brought about because the parliamentary republic was unable to find a way of integrating the new political forces into the official political system.

In the 1920s, the objective of both President Arturo Alessandri Palma (1920–25) and General Ibáñez (1927–31) was to design an institutional framework to channel the new social forces that, though apparent in society, did not as yet have adequate political representation. The legislative package that Alessandri could not persuade the Congress to approve and that Ibáñez – relying on the threat of military intervention – succeeded in getting through in a matter of hours – was meant to resolve urgent social issues that the Congress had shown little or no interest in resolving.

It is interesting that, despite their ideological differences, both Alessandri and Ibáñez regarded the restoration of presidentialism as indispensable to the resolution of the political and economic crisis. This crisis, partly attributable to the shortcomings of the political system, largely resulted from the fluctuating prices of nitrate, the main export commodity, on the international market. The policy of the authoritarian government of Ibáñez was to set up a network of state institutions that significantly increased the economic powers of the executive and enabled the Chilean state to respond flexibly and efficiently to changes in the world economy. Of course, these measures could not shelter the economy from the Great Depression. However, they did provide a solid base on which to build, during the next two decades, a coherent policy of industrialization. It is no small achievement that this postdepression policy was carried out within a democratic framework.

The institutional reforms introduced by Ibáñez in the 1920s were consistent with Alessandri's conception of a strong presidency. Ibáñez, unlike Alessandri, was not a liberal democrat. His conception of the state was authoritarian, and he aspired to change the boundaries of the political system. Not unlike Pinochet, he was deeply suspicious of political parties and was convinced that the labor movement, led as it was by left-wing parties, had to be radically transformed. Ibáñez, however, unlike Pinochet, did not ban political parties altogether, although he did manipulate congressional elections. But inspired perhaps by the fascist model, which he admired, he did try to create a vertically controlled labor movement. Although Ibáñez failed to implement his authoritarian political model – popular protests forced him to resign from office and flee the country in 1931 – his greatest achievement was to strengthen the executive branch, thus facilitating the consolidation of the presidential system advocated by his arch-enemy, Arturo Alessandri.

PRESIDENTIALISM: THE FIRST TWENTY YEARS

With the return to democracy in 1932 there began more than 40 years of presidentialism. During this period, the political system underwent major changes, which naturally had an impact on the evolution of the country's presidential regime. Initially, practically all the political parties had misgivings about presidentialism: The left, as the prime target of security measures taken by the newly established democracy, regarded the new regime as a continuation of Ibáñez's authoritarianism; the Radical Party had developed a taste for coalition politics under the preceding regime; the right feared that a strong president – even one from its own ranks, such as Alessandri – would succumb to the populist temptation and attempt a major reform in the agricultural sector.

These misgivings were, however, tempered by the realization that a strong executive was necessary to succeed in revitalizing the economy. Moreover, the discredit of the parliamentary republic was such that proposals to introduce parliamentarism were not taken seriously. During this first 20 years of democracy, a flexible form of presidentialism emerged. It was based on broad coalitions in which the Radical Party played a dominant role, but which made it possible, at one time or another, for all the parties in the political spectrum, from Conservatives to Communists, to be part of the governing coalition. These coalitions were often short-lived, but – contrary to Linz and Valenzuela's model of presidentialism – the president of the day always managed to form another coalition to replace the old one. The winner-takes-all factor does not seem to have affected the capacity of political parties to make the system work in a flexible and fairly efficient manner.

Presidents during this period were not lonely figures detached from the parties and constantly moaning about political obstruction. They were very much involved in day-to-day negotiations with political parties. Their success as presidents was largely based on their negotiating skills. Although not subordinated to the wishes of the political parties, they were aware that they could not ignore their views. I argue that the ability of presidents to form new coalitions was due precisely to their special role within the constitutional framework.

These continuous negotiations neither weakened the executive nor transformed the president into a constitutional dictator. Throughout this period, successive governments implemented a remarkably coherent and, at the time, original policy of industrialization based on the import substitution model. The main instrument for the implementation of this policy was the State Development Corporation (CORFO), an autonomous state agency established in 1939 by the Popular Front government of Pedro Aguirre. Although CORFO enjoyed broad technical autonomy in the execution of its programs, it was not a bureaucratic monster unaware of the needs of the political parties. Indeed, some of the shortcomings of CORFO's work during this period – such as the failure to modernize the agricultural sector – stem from its sensitivity to the demands of the political process in which the right-wing parties played an important role.

During this period, a constitutional amendment, passed in 1943 by the required majorities in Congress, strengthened the powers of the president in financial matters so as to introduce discipline in state expenditure. Members of the Congress gave up the power to sponsor amendments to government bills as a means to finance their pet projects. But this increase in the power of the president was not one-sided. Although the amendment also allowed the president to make payments not authorized by law, it set clear limits on the use of this power. These emergency financial powers could be exercised only in certain specified cases (public calamities, internal disorder, foreign aggression, exhaustion of funds to maintain essential public services) and could not exceed, altogether, 2% of the expenditure authorized by the annual budget (Art. 72, No. 10).

Moreover, the 1943 constitutional amendment, which strengthened the financial powers of the president, also gave constitutional recognition to the Office of the comptroller general (the Contraloría) (Evans 1970a). The constitutional recognition of the Contraloría did not involve an expansion of its powers, but it made a crucial change in the appointment procedure and tenure of the comptroller general. Prior to the amendment, the comptroller was subject to removal from office, just like any other civil servant. After the passage of the amendment, the comptroller was granted life tenure, just like justices of the Supreme Court, thereby enhancing the ability of this official to act as an independent check on executive power.

The main tasks of the comptroller general were to ensure that public monies were properly spent and that presidential decrees and regulations were within the powers delegated by the Congress. The Contraloría performed its role admirably well regarding both these tasks. Also in 1945, Congress impeached and removed from office the incumbent comptroller general for failing to fulfill his duty to control the legality of government action. Thus, the Congress indeed took the Contraloría seriously and kept close watch on the activities of the president.

RESTRUCTURING THE POLITICAL SYSTEM

The coalition politics of the 1930s and 1940s came to an end with the victory of the ubiquitous General Ibáñez in the presidential elections of 1952. Running on an antiparty platform and supported by an obscure right-wing nationalist political movement, Ibáñez managed to obtain nearly 50% of the vote. The party platform was also the key for the success of the independent right-wing candidate, Jorge Alessandri, six years later in 1958.

Several factors account for the end of the period of coalition politics. Following the end of World War II, the economy was once again faced with excessive dependence on a single export commodity. The highly volatile price of copper in the international markets aggravated an already intense inflationary process. As usual, those hardest hit by inflation were the lowest paid, a fact that the left-wing-controlled unions could not afford to ignore. Hence, there began a vicious circle of strikes, which brought about mild repressive measures from the government of the day, followed by more labor unrest. The government of Gabriel González passed the draconian 1948 State Security Act, which – apart from banning the Communist Party from politics – was an antiunion law with a devastating impact on the labor movement generally.

While the labor movement was under attack, the party system – which had relied on the support of organized labor to play the game of coalition politics – was in disarray. Old political partners could no longer form alliances, and factionalism brought about a dangerous fragmentation of the party system. In the early 1950s the number of parties contesting congressional elections more than doubled, reaching nearly 32 in 1953 (Urzua 1968). Even based on the *effective* number of parties, we can see a dramatic upturn in congressional elections during the 1950s (Figure 8.1).

It is interesting to note that the end of the period during which broad coalitions could be made as easily as they could be unmade was not marked by a dramatic fall in the electoral support of the Radical Party – the party that had played a pivotal role in the 1930s and 1940s. On the contrary, it was accompanied by the disintegration of the two extreme poles of the party system. Indeed, both right- and left-wing parties lost much of their electoral strength and had to cope with factionalism and other forms of internal strife.

Thus, on the surface, it could well be argued that the stability of the political system in the 1930s and 1940s was achieved not despite but because of the existence of the two extreme political poles. While this is not an adequate explanation, there is enough truth in this statement to remind us that the alternative explanation – which regards the collapse of the political center as the source of the political malaise that plagued the country from 1950 to 1970 (Valenzuela 1994) – is equally inadequate.

It is arguable that presidentialism – despite the antiparty biases of both Ibáñez and Alessandri – played a major role in reviving the party system and, indeed, in ensuring the continuity of the democratic system altogether. Figure 8.1 shows that even at the time of maximum fragmentation of the congressional party system, the parties managed to coalesce behind presidential candidates, such that the effective number of presidential candidates was usually in the 2.0 to 2.5 range. Moreover, the election of Ibáñez in 1952 provided the political parties with a much needed breathing space to get their houses in order and to reassert their predominant role in the political system. The populist movement of Ibáñez all but disintegrated shortly after his electoral victory, and he was forced to work with rather than against the party system, thus contributing to its revival. Given the severity of the crisis affecting the party system in the late 1940s, it is very likely that democracy would not have survived had the political regime been parliamentary rather than presidential.

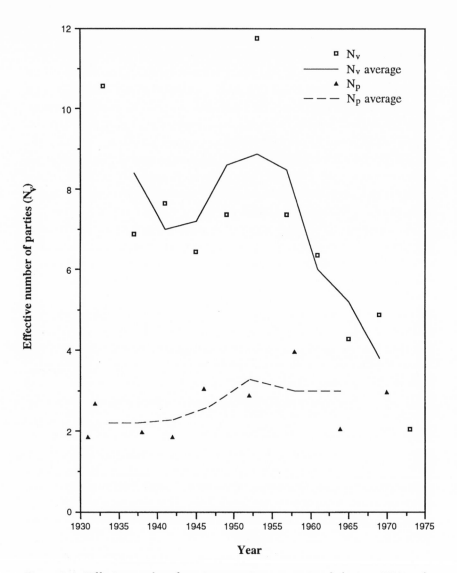

Figure 8.1. Effective number of parties contesting congressional elections (N_v) and effective number of presidential candidates (N_p), Chile, 1931–73.

Advocates of parliamentarism claim that, from the 1950s onward, presidentialism exacerbated the polarization of the party system, creating two irreconcilable extremes and a fairly weak political center. This argument is not unappealing. After all, from the mid-1950s onward, politics became more ideological in content, and the scope for alliances among the parties was greatly reduced. Communists and Socialists were no longer regarded as acceptable coalition partners by most of the parties in the political system. The emerging new force, the CDP was desperately seeking to establish its left-wing credentials; hence, backing a right-wing candidate was out of the question, and an alliance with the Radical Party was seen as useless.

The highly charged ideological battle had not, however, caused the polarization. The banning of the Communist Party, prompted by the cold war ideology prevailing in Washington, brought about the political isolation of the left-wing parties, which had hitherto played such a fundamental role in the country's political development. Attempts by a faction of the Socialists to form a durable alliance with Ibáñez failed early on during his government, thus strengthening the position of those within the Socialist and Communist parties who regarded the attempts to form alliances with bourgeois parties as both futile and politically mistaken.

The CDP was taken to task by advocates of parliamentarism for failing to form alliances with other parties and thus broaden its base of support. It is undoubtedly true that the CDP appeared quite inflexible and unwilling to make concessions to political adversaries. It is often forgotten, however, that the CDP had not always been averse to coalition politics. In the 1930s and 1940s, when it was called Falange Nacional (1938–57), it was an enthusiastic, though not electorally successful participant in various government coalitions. Hence, it is not surprising that the CDP should have found it difficult to form alliances with left- or right-wing parties.

The political polarization that indeed took place during the 1950s and 1960s was largely a consequence of urgent tasks on the political agenda. These tasks stemmed largely from problems that the coalition governments of the preceding period had been unwilling or unable to resolve. Three related economic problems called for tough measures but also created sharp divisions among the leading political parties. First, it was necessary to put forward a coherent and politically unpopular program of economic stabilization to control inflation, which by 1955 had reached 84% a year. Second, there was an urgent need to formulate a new policy on copper so as to ensure a more equitable sharing of revenue with two U.S. companies, the main investors in the area. And third, the rapid urbanization that had taken place over the preceding two decades made it impossible to delay any further the modernization of the inefficient agricultural sector.

The resolution of these three major economic problems was made all the more difficult by long-overdue changes in electoral and union laws. During the preceding two decades there had been practically no electoral mobilization, and unions were effectively banned in the public sector and in agriculture. During the 1950s and 1960s there was a massive increase in

registered voters (from 1 million to nearly 3 million), and the union movement more than doubled its membership, reaching 600,000. The broadening of the channels of political participation at a time when the political
system was confronting such major economic problems naturally had a po-
larizing effect on the political system. Presidentialism neither was the cause
of this polarization nor had a significant effect on the process of political
polarization.

The three main programs of stabilization launched during this period,
though not entirely successful, did manage to control inflation and to introduce fiscal and financial discipline. It is interesting to note that despite
the different ideological backgrounds of the three presidents who implemented the stabilization policies (Ibáñez, Alessandri, and Frei), the programs were technically quite similar, and all three presidents were strongly
resisted by forces within the Congress. The political polarization, allegedly
brought about by presidentialism, did not seem to affect the actual policies
put forward by these presidents. Likewise, in the case of copper, the policies
of these presidents were not significantly different. None called for outright
nationalization, but all three were committed to the goal of obtaining a
greater share of copper revenue for the state. The demand for ever-more
radical policies with regard to U.S.-owned copper companies stemmed
largely from the realization that the various deals that successive governments had made with the U.S. companies failed to fulfill the legitimate
expectations of both the government of the day and the political parties in
the Congress. The radical demand for outright nationalization, which by
the late 1960s was shared by most of the political parties, stemmed largely
from widespread frustration at the way the U.S. copper companies appeared
to be using their superior knowledge of the international commodity markets and financial systems. Whether this frustration was right or wrong, it
had nothing to do with presidentialism.

The modernization of the agricultural sector raises slightly different
issues. There were two agrarian reform laws that purported to achieve the
objective of bringing the agricultural sector in line with the more advanced
sectors of the economy. These two laws were, however, quite different. The
first, enacted under the administration of Alessandri, was little more than
a gesture that the government felt compelled to make in order to retain
eligibility under the foreign aid program of the United States – the Alliance
for Progress. The second, passed during the Christian Democratic administration of President Frei, was undoubtedly more radical, since it was supposed to achieve an increase in production together with a more equitable
redistribution of the land. This ambitious agrarian reform program was,
however, not a product of irresponsible politicians who, carried away by

their own rhetoric and under the influence of the winner-takes-all factor of presidentialism, had lost control over their actions and were behaving irresponsibly. In fact, the agrarian reform of the Christian Democratic government was perhaps one of the most carefully planned programs ever enacted in Chile. It was based on years of study by CDP specialists and backed by technical reports prepared by several international organizations. Although from today's prevailing free market perspective this initiative may seem both radical and foolish, at the time it was not.

I fail to see how the presidential system could have made the agrarian reform law enacted by the CDP more radical. Indeed, anyone familiar with the long congressional debates that led to the approval of the law knows that President Frei, with the threat of his veto power, played a crucial role in moderating the left-wing groups within his own party, who, together with Communists and Socialists, were demanding a more radical law.

Frei's agrarian reform proposal proved especially controversial because the right saw it as too radical and the left saw it as not radical enough. Thus, Frei's policy team poured significant energy into preparing the agrarian reform bill because they were extremely conscious of the need to get it right – both politically and technically. The technical aspects were vital because Frei envisioned serious gains from improving the productivity of the agricultural sector. In designing the reforms, Frei managed to appease the right by accepting a formulation of the compensation clauses that appeared to open the door for the Supreme Court to have the final say on the issue. However, the Supreme Court, lacking political imagination and legitimacy at the time, chose to pass over the opportunity to modify the legislation. Thus, the bill left open the question of property rights to the expropriated land.

The reform did, however, provide for the establishment of temporary *asentamientos campesinos*, or peasant-collective lots, which, at a later stage, would either be made permanent or be parceled out to the individual members of the *asentamientos*. The left accepted this provision because of the promise – which was eventually fulfilled – that peasants would be given the right to form labor unions.

The CDP had to make some concessions to the left in order to attract its support, but if the left had pushed the matter too far, the president was prepared to use his veto and then blame the lack of agreement on agrarian reform on the leftist parties. The moderating influence exercised by President Frei in the gestation of the agrarian reform law shows that broad presidential powers need not lead to paralysis or marginalization of the legislature. In particular, as noted in Chapter 1, the veto power can be used to craft a more moderate policy than could otherwise be passed. Indeed,

Frei's entire legislative program could be regarded as a balance between conservative and radical forces achieved largely through the pivotal role played by the president in the legislative process.

The implementation of the agrarian reform program was of course plagued by controversy and led to a radicalization of the position of the parties and, most important of all, agricultural workers, who were beginning to realize the extent to which they could influence political events. It is true that the 1970 presidential elections had the effect of further radicalizing political discourse not only on the agrarian issue, but on all other matters. I do not see how, if there had been a parliamentary system in place, this process would have been avoided. Indeed, without the executive veto power provided by the Chilean constitution, policy outcomes could have been more radical even before Allende's election, as shown by the example of the agrarian reform. Indeed, by the late 1960s, the political parties had been overtaken by the process of mobilization begun in the mid-1950s with the liberalization of electoral laws and the reform of trade union legislation. It is inaccurate to blame the Chilean constitutional structure for this radicalization.

THE WEAKENING OF THE CONGRESS

The advocates of parliamentarism point out that from the constitutional amendment of 1943 and another major amendment of 1970, there was a gradual but consistent erosion of the powers of the Congress in favor of the president (Valenzuela and Wilde 1979, 1984). The Congress became increasingly irrelevant, according to this argument, for resolving conflicting interests and thus could not fulfill its proper role in a democracy. This is an interesting point that, if true, raises several further questions about the nature of Chile's political system. In any event, even if it were true, it would not necessarily mean that a parliamentary regime would have fared any better.

The issue of the relative powers of the Congress and the president was a permanent item on the agenda of constitutional reform. In 1943, as discussed earlier, a constitutional amendment gave the president exclusive power to introduce bills that involved an increase in public expenditure. Hitherto, the constitution made it impossible for members of the Congress to introduce legislation creating new services in the state sector, increasing salaries for civil service, or generally increasing public expenditure. The object of the 1943 amendment was, quite reasonably, to ensure that the president, who was responsible for the administration of the state, should have the power to implement a coherent economic policy. The 1943 amendment, however, though not ineffective, left some important loopholes that enabled members of the Congress to continue this practice, thus effectively derailing government economic policy.

Dissatisfaction with this practice led both the Alessandri and the Frei governments in the 1960s to introduce constitutional amendments designed to tighten the rules on public expenditure. Eventually, in 1970 President Frei managed to persuade the Congress to approve such an amendment. He did it with support from the right, which equated a strong president with a strong state and saw the move as a positive step for the country.

It is true that as a result of these constitutional amendments, the Congress had delegated further power to the president. Members of the Congress were, accordingly, no longer able to introduce bills that benefited individuals (*pensiones de gracia*) or that promoted pet projects in their constituencies. Critics of presidentialism argue that these particularistic practices were crucial to further the democratic spirit among sections of the population that benefited from such legislation (Valenzuela 1994:127–28, 131). On the other hand, the practice had become so widespread that it was undermining the ability of the government to control public expenditure, a matter of great importance for any country, especially one plagued by inflation. Communists and Socialists opposed Frei's 1970 constitutional amendment on the ground that it was creating an imperial presidency with unlimited powers. Ironically, as it turned out, they were the main beneficiaries of this amendment, since President Allende (1970–73), who did not command a majority in the Congress, had to rely on the broad powers of the executive to implement his program of government.

DELEGATED LEGISLATION

The widespread use of delegated legislation is often seen as a symptom of the malaise of presidentialism (Lambert 1967), first, because it suggests that in a presidential system the Congress tends to abdicate its responsibilities out of apathy, frustration, or simply because it is manipulated by the president and second because presidents often tend to stretch their delegated powers beyond the limits set by the enabling act; that is, they act ultra vires.

Delegated legislation was widely used in Chile. This type of legislative enactment was known as "decrees with force of law" (DFLs). Between 1932 and 1966 some 800 DFLs were enacted (Insunza 1966). The 1925 constitution contained no provision for delegated decree authority, and hence – following strict principles of legal interpretation – it was unconstitutional. The unconstitutionality of this practice was never formally declared by the

Supreme Court, but was widely accepted by constitutional law experts and was consistently pointed out in congressional debates.

DFLs were generally used to consolidate and systematize rules in areas where the Congress had either approved legislative norms, though those norms were scattered in several instruments, or had provided fairly detailed policy guidelines. Thus, for example, DFLs were used in areas such as housing, economic regulation, social security, and industrial relations (Evans 1970b).

While there is little doubt that DFLs often exceeded the terms of the enabling acts, on the whole presidents did not abuse their power. Indeed, the fact that the practice of delegating legislative power was so widespread suggests that the parties in the Congress did not have major complaints on this score. The issue of delegated legislation was actually never a major item of public debate. Although it could be argued that the absence of public debate does not necessarily prove that political parties were satisfied with this practice, alternative explanations are no more persuasive. Such an explanation, for example, would have to cast successive presidents in the role of crafty manipulators and the members of the Congress in the role of naive politicians, who, despite their awareness of the abuses committed by presidents, would nonetheless abdicate their constitutional responsibilities. I suspect that even the most fervent advocates of parliamentarism would reject this alternative explanation.

It must be noted that the 1970 constitutional amendment, which gave constitutional status to the practice of delegated legislation, was not an initiative of frustrated opposition parties dissatisfied with the way presidents had used their powers. On the contrary, it was an initiative of the Frei government largely meant to exclude certain areas of policy from the scope of DFLs. The amendment did not permit the use of DFLs in such areas as the budget or national defense. Thus, the decision that resulted in the constitutional regulation of DFLs could well be interpreted as placing limits on an already widespread practice of delegating legislative powers to presidents. A plausible explanation for this modification is that politicians and lawyers in Chile had become increasingly aware of the practice's incongruence with the constitution. Also, Frei perhaps saw the move – restricting the domain of decree-laws constitutionally – as a way to compensate Congress for the other increased executive powers he was calling for. In any event, the delimitation of the DFLs did not appear to pose too great a sacrifice for Frei.

The proliferation of delegated legislation is not a practice found only in presidential systems. It is a widespread practice that raises important issues about the nature of democracy and state power in modern complex societies. Recent attempts to roll back the frontiers of the state through deregulation and privatization have to some extent been prompted by an awareness that excessive state regulation involves giving more and more power to state bureaucrats who enact rules – perhaps usurping the powers of the legislature – with little or no concern for the real interests and needs of individual citizens. Interestingly, however, these efforts to deregulate have not significantly reduced the powers of the state or the overall output of regulations.

The task of reducing the size and power of state bureaucracies is undoubtedly very difficult. In any event, the solution to this problem, either in industrialized countries or in less developed countries such as Chile, does not lie in transforming presidential systems into parliamentary systems.

ALLENDE'S BRAND OF PRESIDENTIALISM

The ill-fated attempt by the Popular Unity government (1970–73) to bring about socialism through the prevailing political system offers plenty of ammunition to the critics of presidentialism; for the Popular Unity, unable to secure a congressional majority in favor of its program, used every iota of power vested in the executive branch to implement its nationalization policies. While the opposition claimed that the government showed nothing but contempt for the constitution and democracy, the government responded that it was simply relying on powers that had long been vested in the executive branch and had been used before by other administrations. The government knew, of course, that it could not fully implement its program without the support of the Congress. However, its decision to begin its implementation without first seeking a congressional majority was partly a tactical decision based on the expectation that by showing determination the opposition would be more likely to compromise. The government was also aware that given the prevailing levels of popular mobilization, the failure to act immediately would have been regarded as a betrayal by most of its supporters. In the event, government and opposition did not agree, and as the political confrontation became more acute, with the government refusing to revoke its administrative orders and the opposition demanding the resignation of Allende, the military finally stepped in and staged a coup that brought down the Popular Unity government and democracy.

The collapse of Chilean democracy has been the subject of a lively and as yet inconclusive academic and political debate (see Faundez, 1980, for a review). However, some critics of presidentialism now appear to have found a simple explanation. According to Valenzuela, the collapse of democracy in Chile was largely caused by presidentialism. Had there been a parliamentary system in place, Allende would have applied more reasonable policies, making it possible for the CDP to support the government, thus securing the survival of the democratic system (Valenzuela 1994:136). This explanation could be elaborated even further: Had there been a parliamentary system in place, Allende would have been able to take office only if he had been prepared to make a deal with the CDP, which would have significantly changed the scope of his program.

This explanation is appealing because it is not altogether unfounded and because it is simple. Indeed, had Allende been required to negotiate his program before becoming prime minister he would not have been the leader of a radical government trying against all odds to implement reforms not supported by a majority in the Congress.

Following the logic of this reasoning, I would go further: *Had there been a parliamentary system in place, democracy in Chile would probably have collapsed long before 1973* – perhaps in the early 1950s, when the political system was in deep crisis, the labor movement was divided, and the party system was unable to form a viable electoral coalition. However, the fact that democracy did not collapse owes much to presidentialism. Indeed, it is arguable that the populist movement that led to the election of Ibáñez as president gave the party system a breathing space to recover its strength and become once again a leading force in the system. It must be noted that the two presidents elected in the decade of the 1950s based their popular appeal on antiparty themes, which, though not a model of democratic discourse, greatly contributed to reviving the fortunes of the ailing party system.

The view that presidentialism prevented Allende from acting more reasonably and making a deal with the opposition is deceptively simple – hence its appeal. Yet as anyone familiar with the Popular Unity period will know, Allende desperately wanted to settle his differences with the opposition and tried, on several occasions, to reach an agreement with them. Indeed, in the middle of 1972 the Popular Unity government and the CDP came very close to reaching an agreement on the thorny issue of the government's nationalization policies.[2] In the end, however, the much-awaited agreement failed to materialize. Each side attributed the breakdown of the negotiations to the other side's dogmatism and lack of flexibility. There was, of course, plenty of that around at the time. However, the main reason for the failure of these negotiations has to be found in the prevailing political context. For indeed, al-

---

2 The proposal, introduced by the Christian Democracts, would have recognized a substantial state-owned sector, as well as worker cooperatives, but also would have given sanction to private property and banned most further expropriations.

though a reasonable draft agreement had in fact been hammered out by the Popular Unity government and the CDP negotiators, neither side would have been capable of persuading its own supporters to accept it. Such was the polarization that prevailed at the time that a deal between Allende and the CDP would have satisfied neither left- nor right-wing forces, and thus it would have contributed very little to the survival of the political system.

My interpretation of the reasons accounting for Allende's failure is perhaps too pessimistic. However, it does help to highlight one of the main weaknesses of the approach of presidentialism's critics, that is, their failure to distinguish adequately between political deals struck by party leaders and effective political consensus in society at large. This distinction is perhaps not so necessary to take into account in countries either where the party system effectively represents the majority of citizens or where political deals do not impinge upon important areas of public policy. But in underdeveloped societies, including Chile during Allende's term, the channeling of severe conflicts may be no easier under parliamentarism than under presidentialism. Indeed, as I have suggested, the presidential system may deserve credit for the *survival* of democracy in Chile during previous times of social crisis.

Presidentialism as it had evolved in Chile under the 1925 constitution is not unrelated to the failure of the Popular Unity government or to the collapse of democracy. Yet presidentialism was only one of several institutional factors that had a bearing on this outcome. The judiciary, the Congress, and the state bureaucracy also played parts in the destruction of the institutional framework.

It is interesting to note that while, during the Allende administration and in the immediate aftermath of the military coup, the media and most political observers concentrated on how Allende would deal with the broader institutional questions – which in those days was generally referred to as the issue of legality and the rule of law – these questions soon disappeared from the debate on Chile. Instead, the analysis concentrated almost exclusively on economic and on noninstitutional political aspects of the period. I would hope that critics who place the blame for the collapse of democracy on the presidential system will not be discouraged from studying other institutional aspects of the Allende period in greater depth.

CONCLUDING REMARKS

The current process of democratization has made political scientists aware of the importance of political institutions and procedures. This is a positive development since until recently this aspect of political studies has been neglected. As an academic lawyer, I share this new interest and hope that it will lead to fruitful interdisciplinary research.

Critics of Chilean presidentialism have undoubtedly made a useful contribution to the study of political institutions. My concern, however, is that their analysis tends to focus too narrowly on only one institutional factor, neglecting broader institutional aspects. In this chapter, I have argued that critics of Chilean presidentialism have not yet made a persuasive case. Their excessive concern to prove that their ideal type of system – parliamentarism – is superior to their less than ideal type – presidentialism – leads them to ignore important aspects of Chile's political and institutional development. This approach unnecessarily restricts the focus of their research. More research ought to be done on the development of Chilean political institutions. Only thus would we be able to arrive at sound conclusions about the role of presidentialism under the 1925 constitution and its likely development under the new democracy of the post-Pinochet period.

9

EXECUTIVE–LEGISLATIVE RELATIONS IN POST–PINOCHET CHILE: A PRELIMINARY ASSESSMENT

Peter M. Siavelis

INTRODUCTION

With Chile's return to democracy in March 1990, the Chilean legislative branch reopened its doors for the first time in 16 years. The military coup of September 11, 1973, brought an end to one of the longest periods of democratic rule in South America. The Chilean Congress, virtually in continuous operation from 1823 to 1973, was historically one of the strongest legislative bodies on the continent. It played a key role in the development and maintenance of democracy, serving as an arena for the resolution of political conflict in a highly divided political system by channeling demands and encouraging bargaining, compromise, and consensus.

Despite this impressive record of democratic stability and longevity, military authorities attributed the democratic breakdown to the political process itself, seeing little value in the legislative regime that had helped sustain Chilean democracy for decades before the crises of the 1970s. They

Research for this project was supported by a Fulbright–Hays grant. An earlier version of this chapter was presented at the 18th International Congress of the Latin American Studies Association, Atlanta, Georgia, March 10–12, 1994. The author thankfully acknowledges the support of the Institute of Political Science at the Catholic University of Chile and the useful comments and criticisms of Scott Mainwaring, Timothy Power, Matthew Shugart, Michelle Taylor, and Arturo Valenzuela.

blamed the country's political parties and its succession of coalition governments structured in the legislature for the gradual erosion of government effectiveness and the rise of the left. In a decree-law issued on September 24, 1973, the Congress was dissolved, and all legislative functions were indefinitely transferred to the governing junta.[1]

Throughout the process of the negotiated democratic transition, military leaders utilized their considerable leverage to shape the postauthoritarian political system in order to limit the political forces that they viewed as responsible for the institutional crisis of democracy. The constitution of 1980, drafted by the authoritarian government and approved in a national plebiscite, establishes an institutional framework for a limited democracy characterized by executive domination.[2] While constitutional reforms in 1989 and 1991 limited some of the powers originally granted to the president, the Chilean presidency remains one of the most powerful in Latin America and the world, with broad powers to control the legislative process.[3]

In addition to the creation of a strong executive, military authorities also sought to devise an electoral system that would fundamentally transform the sometimes-fractious Chilean multiparty system. In order to reduce party-system fragmentation, an electoral formula with two-member districts was introduced. Nonetheless, after two democratic congressional elections it has become clear that the electoral law has simply forced political parties to negotiate elaborate pacts to provide representation for coalition partners. The party system continues to be characterized by four or five significant parties, just as it had from midcentury until the period of authoritarian rule.

Studies of the Chilean democratic breakdown and subsequent comparative work on other Latin American presidencies have demonstrated that the configuration of executive and legislative institutions is a crucial variable that determines the incentives and prospects for cooperation among political elites. Within this dialogue, parliamentarism has emerged as the preferred type of regime for multiparty systems because of its flexibility and its ability to avoid the problems of minority presidencies and the dual legitimacy produced by having two agents of the electorate (Linz 1990; Valenzuela 1990; Linz and Valenzuela 1994).[4] Fundamentally, according to this view,

---

1 Decree Law No. 27, published in the *Diario Oficial*, No. 28.658, September 24, 1973.
2 Arriagada (1984) provides an excellent analysis of the authoritarian features of the 1980 constitution.
3 For an analysis of the constitutional reforms of 1989, see Andrade Geywitz (1991).
4 Discussions of the significance of each of these problems in various presidential regimes appear in Linz and Valenzuela (1994).

parliamentary systems better produce incentives for executive–assembly co-operation within the context of multiparty systems.

Shugart and Carey (1992) question the prevailing preference for parliamentary systems and in the process make a valuable contribution to the debate on the importance of institutional arrangements by demonstrating that the treatment of parliamentary and presidential forms of government as polar opposites is incorrect. They stress that there are numerous variables that differentiate presidential systems and affect the way they function and that, in fact, some types of presidentialism may better contribute to the prospects for democratic longevity. For Shugart and Carey the issue is not the mere existence of presidentialism, but the balance of power between the president and assembly, the question of who names cabinets, and other institutional characteristics that also make a difference.

One of the most important conclusions of Shugart and Carey's study as it relates to the Chilean case is that the strengthening of presidential power especially in the legislative arena helped lead to the deterioration and ultimate overthrow of Chilean democracy. They find that political systems characterized by very powerful presidents, especially in terms of legislative prerogatives, have less successful records of democratic longevity than other types of presidential systems (Shugart and Carey 1992:148).

As the discussion of the historical evolution of presidential prerogatives in Chile in Faundez's chapter demonstrates, between the period when the 1925 Chilean constitution was promulgated and the 1973 breakdown, legislative power was systematically reduced with successive waves of constitutional reform. These reforms invested increased power in the executive branch, at the expense of the legislature. The 1980 constitution fits well within the historical evolution of presidential power in Chile outlined by Faundez, providing the framework for the strongest presidency since the 1890s.

Reforms of the constitution in 1989 and 1991 slightly narrowed the scope of presidential power by eliminating the executive's ability to dissolve the Chamber of Deputies once during his or her term, restricting the president's ability to proscribe civil rights during states of siege, and preventing the president's use of forced exile during periods of crisis. In addition, the reforms provided for an increase in the number of popularly elected senators, diluting the power and influence of senators designated by the president.[5]

5 The constitutional reforms of 1989 and 1991 discussed here deal only with the relative powers of the executive and legislative branches. A much broader range of reforms was undertaken in addition to those discussed here, including changes in the role of the

Nonetheless, the 1980 Constitution still provides for a president with the widest range of constitutional legislative powers in modern Chilean history. Thus, in theoretical terms, the current Chilean institutional structure not only is subject to the tensions that advocates of parliamentarism have identified; it is also an especially problematic variety of presidentialism.

All of these empirical realities and theoretical conclusions raise a number of intriguing questions concerning the potential longevity, stability, and quality of Chilean democracy for the future. Why has the postauthoritarian presidential system functioned so well up until now? Why have the problems that theorists associate with exaggerated presidentialism not emerged? What are the long-term consequences of exaggerated presidential power and legislative weakness for future democratic governability and longevity within the context of an entrenched multiparty system?

Despite what has been said about the consequences of constitutionally strong presidents in the theoretical literature and in this volume, this chapter will argue that during the four years of the first postauthoritarian democratic government, the Chilean presidential system has functioned relatively well. During the administration of President Patricio Aylwin, executive–assembly relations were characterized by a high degree of cooperation, consensus, and compromise. There was a willingness on the part of both branches of government to give and take and attempt to negotiate in trying to confront challenges posed by the transition to democracy, including the resurrection of political institutions, the problematic legacies inherited from the preceding regime, and the deepening of democracy to the regional and municipal levels.

However, this chapter contends that the legislative success of the Aylwin government was due to a great extent to the contextual features of the democratic transition itself, which tempered the drives associated with exaggerated presidentialism that can lead to problems of governability and executive–assembly deadlock. It argues that in the long term the emasculation of the Congress will prove inimical to the maintenance of democratic stability and will threaten the prospects for democratic longevity.

This chapter begins by outlining the features that make the Chilean presidency as powerful as it is. It examines the tensions that executive domination has already produced and shows how they may become aggravated in the future. It then outlines how some of these tensions were tempered by the contextual features of the democratic transition itself, underscoring

Constitutional Tribunal and the National Security Council, as well as the reform of laws governing the legal status of political parties. In addition, certain of the requirements that made constitutional reform almost impossible were eased.

why these features of the political system will become less important during subsequent governments. It assesses some of the long-term consequences of the particular type of presidentialism that exists in Chile. Finally, given that the adoption of a parliamentary or "premier-presidential" regime is unlikely, it outlines certain reforms that can enhance the functioning of the Chilean presidential system for the long term.

THE CHILEAN PRESIDENCY UNDER THE 1980 CONSTITUTION

The Chilean regime has both of the characteristics of presidentialism as defined in this volume, including popular election of the chief executive and fixed terms for the assembly and the president. Shugart and Carey correctly underscore the exaggerated strength of the Chilean president, calling the system "super presidential" (1992:129).[6] What is more, in Table 1.6, Shugart and Mainwaring rank it as the most constitutionally powerful presidency dealt with in this volume in terms of decree and veto powers and areas of exclusive executive initiative. However, there are a number of other constitutional and statutory prerogatives that when considered along with these, really grant the president much more legislative power than suggested by either Shugart and Carey (1992) or Shugart and Mainwaring (this volume). While individually these prerogatives are not unique to the Chilean presidential system, their combined effect makes for a formidable executive branch and transforms the president into the most important legislator in the country.

PRESIDENTIAL URGENCIES AND EXTRAORDINARY SESSIONS

One of the most important prerogatives of Chilean presidents in the 1980 constitution is the ability to control the legislative process and set the legislative agenda through the use of declared executive urgencies. The president of the republic may declare a proposal urgent in any one or all stages of its consideration, regardless of its branch of origin. Congress must then act on the measure within 30, 10, or 3 days, depending on whether the

6 Although part of the reason Shugart and Carey call the Chilean regime "super presidential" is based on the president's ability to dissolve the Chamber of Deputies once during his or her term, that prerogative was eliminated by the constitutional reforms of 1989. Nonetheless, as will be shown later, the extraordinary power of the president in other areas certainly makes the term appropriate.

proposal is designated as a *simple urgencia*, *suma urgencia* or for *discusión inmediata*, respectively (Art. 71). If a proposal is declared urgent, the consideration of all pending proposals is put on hold. The urgent proposal is then considered in accordance with its level of urgency and the amount of time remaining until it and other declared urgencies are due to expire. This applies both to proposals in committee and to those pending discussion and approval by the general assemblies of the chambers.

Though designed as a measure to be employed in extraordinary circumstances to ensure the passage of key legislation, use of the faculty has become something of a standard operating procedure in order for the president to expedite the consideration and approval of his proposals. Though during the first democratic administration President Aylwin was often willing to provide additional time to the Congress for the consideration of proposals by rescinding urgencies or by withdrawing and reiterating them, the faculty was used at some point in the approval process in 40% of the projects that have been sent to Congress.[7]

Because the designation of urgency by the president means that there must be immediate discussion of the proposal, the consideration of other pending bills is delayed. Those put on hold are most often legislative initiatives, given that members of Congress lack the ability to declare urgencies.

One deputy lamented that he had had a proposal accepted by a Chamber committee but that its discussion had been pending for three years and three consecutive legislative sessions, given that it had consistently been moved down to a lower level on the agenda as executive urgencies were moved ahead of it. He was convinced that the legislative period would end without the committee's consideration of a piece of legislation that he deemed important both for his district and for the country as a whole.[8]

The designation of urgency by the executive also upsets the rhythm of work in Congress and creates discontinuity in the consideration of individual

---

7 For the period between the initiation of the first Congress and October 8, 1992. "Diputados Pesimistas por Número de Proyectos que Alcanzarán a Tratar," *El Mercurio*, October 8, 1992:C2. Despite this 40% figure it is difficult to measure effectively the number of proposals that have passed with the use of executive urgencies, because they are sometimes withdrawn. An advisor in the Judicial/Legislative Division of the Ministry of the General Secretary of the Presidency stated that the executive branch has attempted to keep the number of pending proposals declared urgent at or under 20% of the total. Even if this 20% figure is taken into consideration, executive urgency is clearly not an "extraordinary measure." Interview with Cesar Ladrón de Guevara, advisor, Judicial/Legislative Division of the Ministry of the General Secretary of the Presidency, Santiago, April 28, 1993.
8 Off-the-record interview with Concertación deputy, Valparaíso, April 15, 1993.

proposals. While a committee is studying a particular project in depth, an urgent executive proposal often arrives without previous notice and forces delay in the discussion of the original project. By the time the original proposal is again ready for consideration, much of the initial deliberation and study must be repeated in order to refamiliarize committee members with the most important aspects of the proposed legislation.

Of course, the Congress may refuse to act on a declared presidential urgency, but even in this case the president retains the ability to continually "bottle up" the legislative agenda, thus maintaining control over the initiatives that will ultimately be considered.

The president's control of the legislative agenda is further reinforced by his or her ability to call the legislature into extraordinary session. During these sessions the Congress can consider proposals introduced only by the executive (Art. 52).[9] In each of the four congressional periods of the Aylwin administration, the Congress has been called into extraordinary session by the president.

The executive's ability to declare legislation urgent and to convoke extraordinary sessions grants the president a powerful agenda-setting ability throughout the legislative process. While, as has been noted, President Aylwin exercised his power with a relative amount of flexibility, there is nothing to ensure that future presidents will be as charitable in their use.

AREAS OF EXCLUSIVE INITIATIVE

Another source of executive strength and legislative limitation lies in areas in which the president has exclusive initiative. But unlike the other cases where presidents have areas of exclusive initiative discussed in Chapter 1, in Chile these faculties are not counterbalanced by a low threshold for veto overrides. A two-thirds majority is necessary to override a presidential veto.

Article 62 of the constitution states that the "President of the Republic holds the exclusive initiative for proposals of law related to changes in the political or administrative division of the country, or to the financial or budgetary administration of the state." However, the president's right of exclusive initiative is not limited to only these issues. Article 62 also specifies a series of areas in which the executive shall have exclusive initiative, including: "establishing, amending, granting or increasing remunerations,

9 If the president does not convoke an extraordinary session, the Congress may do so, during which time any types of proposals may be discussed. In addition, the president may also decide to allow the discussion of bills proposed by the members of Congress during an executive-declared extraordinary session.

retirement payments, pensions," and "widows' and orphans' allowances" (No. 4), "establishing the norms and procedures applicable to collective bargaining and determining the cases where bargaining is not permitted" (No. 5), and "establishing or amending the norms on or regarding social security of both the public and the private sector" (No. 6). Each of these stipulations further extends the reach of the legislative power of the president.

First, the president has almost exclusive control over the budgetary process. He or she must submit the budget at least three months before it is to become effective. The Congress may then only reduce or approve the expenditures contained in the budgetary law. It may not increase or redistribute them. If the budget law is not approved by both chambers within 60 days, the president's proposal enters into force, in effect granting the president decree power in fiscal matters. These limitations on Congress's role in the budgetary process were designed in part to prevent the proliferation of clientelistic and individualistic legislation and coterminous spending excesses. However, the measure also imposes limitations on the latitude that assembly members have on questions with a bearing on policy making at the national level.

Almost all significant legislation involves some type of expenditure or deals with a social or economic question of the type described in Article 62. When combined with the president's ability to set the legislative agenda, these features make it difficult for legislators to propose bills of any significance.

For example, during the 1993 legislative session an opposition senator sought to present a bill to Congress that would allow women to determine when state-sanctioned maternity leave would be taken. Currently, the law establishes certain periods for pre- and postpartum leave. Though not modifying the established period for maternity leave, this bill would have let women themselves decide how much time would be taken before and after the birth of their children. Nonetheless, upon review by the appropriate legislative committee the introduction of the bill was ruled unconstitutional and thus nonadmissible because it dealt with "social security," an area in which the executive has exclusive initiative.[10]

Respect for the limitations on assembly members' spheres of action is enforced through the existence of the Constitutional Tribunal, which possesses broad powers to determine the constitutionality of proposals at any point in the legislative process. Once the Tribunal rules on a particular proposal, the president of either chamber of Congress may be removed from

10 Off-the-record interview, Valparaíso, May 12, 1993.

office if he or she "permits the voting of a motion which is declared openly contrary to the Political Constitution of the State" (Art. 57). The Tribunal has in several instances declared unconstitutional initiatives of the type just discussed on the basis of Article 62 of the constitution, resulting in their immediate withdrawal.

In essence, assembly members can neither propose what is traditionally understood as "clientelistic" legislation nor sponsor bills in several areas that have a bearing on national policy making and involve no additional expenditures.

These limitations place legislators in a difficult position in regard to their constituents. Despite a 16-year closure of the National Congress, a certain public vision of the role of the legislature persists at the constituent level. Logrolling and the satisfaction of particularistic demands were a key part of the role of legislators in the preauthoritarian period.[11] Constituents often continue to expect that their deputy or senator can deliver favors or intervene in terms of jobs, benefits, pensions, streetlights, funding for a community or youth center, and the like. Though, with the reestablishment of municipal authorities in June 1992, many of these types of requests should now be referred to the municipality, there is often an expectation on the part of the electorate that a legislator should be able to satisfy these demands.[12] A staff member for a Concertación deputy estimated that only 5% of the correspondence he receives from constituents has anything to do with legislative issues at the national level. The other 95% consists of requests for jobs, scholarships, increases in pensions or concerns problems related to lighting, roads, sewage, and water.

Part of the reason for this expectation is the long preauthoritarian tradition of deputies providing pork through tacking their own particularistic initiatives onto those of the president. Given the low threshold for election and extreme competitiveness created by Chile's historic proportional representation system, personalism and the satisfaction of constituent demands were essential to reelection. Tapia Valdés (1966:42–47) cites Law No. 10.343 as an example of the extent to which legislative proposals were tacked on to presidential initiatives in the preauthoritarian period. The law,

11 Valenzuela and Wilde (1979) assert that the Congress's role in the satisfaction of particularistic demands was important to the maintenance of the institutional balance of powers that helped to maintain Chilean democracy. They argue that the gradual disintegration of congressional prerogatives, most notably the provisions of the 1970 constitutional reforms that barred particularistic legislation, was instrumental in the decline of the Congress and contributed to the polarization that led to the eventual breakdown of democracy.
12 Personal interview with Eduardo Barros González, Valparaíso, April 2, 1993.

which consists of 215 articles, deals with 28 separate issues, ranging from a municipal loan for the town of Talca, laws regulating the production of whale oil, the creation of a journalism school, and a tax exemption for firemen. He estimates that between 1938 and 1958 over 55% of legislation dealt with such particularistic issues. Given this widespread public image of what deputies are supposed to do and the lack of voice Chamber members have concerning national issues, they have a strong incentive to attempt to satisfy these demands in exchange for support in future elections. Nonetheless, contemporary constitutional proscriptions on the inclusion of articles not germane to the *idea matriz* (central concept) of legislation eliminates the ability of legislators to provide pork, which further undermines legislative strength and the capabilities of individual legislators.

Because of the limitations imposed by budget restrictions, exclusive executive initiative, and presidential urgencies, the range of possible congressional actions in satisfying these personalistic demands is limited. Members can either recommend action in the form of an *oficio* (request for information) sent to the ministry involved in the issue or directly intervene with an appeal to municipal government authorities. Neither of these avenues guarantees substantive results in resolving the issue or satisfying the demand. In this sense deputies are expected to provide pork, have incentives to provide pork, but are limited in their capacity to do so.

Because of the unlikelihood of assembly proposals being considered, let alone published as law, legislators can neither satisfy demands nor significantly affect the legislative process on the national level, undermining the legitimacy and perceived necessity of members of congress in the eyes of constituents.

OTHER SOURCES OF PRESIDENTIAL POWER

The president in Chile is also vested with some additional proactive and reactive powers. The range of implied powers of the president is quite broad in Chile. The president is granted the right to "exercise statutory authority in all those matters which are not of a legal nature, without prejudice to the power to issue other regulations, decrees or instructions which he may deem appropriate for the enforcement of the law" (Art. 32, No. 8).

In addition, as in most presidential systems, the Chilean president has a right to veto legislation. Though the executive does not have what is normally understood as a line-item veto, he can make specific comments or changes to legislation, as long as these are "related to the central or fundamental ideas of the bill" (Art. 70). Therefore, the president does have the power to change major aspects of bills before returning them to Congress. If the Congress disapproves of presidential comments, it may insist on approval of the legislation by a vote of two-thirds of the members of both chambers, in which case the proposal becomes law. However, despite the Congress's power to override presidential vetoes, during the first four annual legislative sessions, in no case has a bill become law without the president's signature.

The power of the president as a legislator is not limited to the legislative process itself, but also extends to designating a portion of the assembly and appointing other authorities, which expand the reach of executive influence. In addition to the 38 elected members of the Senate, there are also nine appointed senators. The president appoints two, one required to be a former university president and one a former minister of state. The Supreme Court names three. The National Security Council designates four senators, each of whom must be a former commander of the Army, National Police (Carabineros), Navy, and Air Force who has held that post for at least two years (Art. 70).[13] However, because the president also influences the appointment of, and in some instances names, the officials who staff the institutions that designate senators, executive influence is more far-reaching than it appears.

Finally, there are also a number of nonstatutory elements that skew the balance of power in favor of the executive branch. Though not specifically outlined in the 1980 constitution and therefore not technically "constitutional" powers of the president, they do result from the overall framework of presidentialism set out in the document and grant the president increased lawmaking capabilities. The visibility of the president, the importance of the tradition of presidential government, and the role of the president as a symbol of the nation all grant the president authority and esteem. This contrasts sharply with the public's view of assembly members, who are often seen as venal, corrupt, overpaid, and self-interested.

Survey data demonstrate that the public is not really sure exactly what the Congress or its members actually do, nor do they have a positive estimation of the performance of the institution. This contrasts markedly with respondents' approval rating of the executive branch, or "the government." In a survey interviewees were asked, "With respect to the Deputies which represent your district, which phrase best describes what you think in terms of how they are doing their work?" Then respondents were asked, "And now, in terms of the government, how would you say that it is doing its work?" Table 9.1 compares the responses.

13 In addition, according to Article 45 of the 1980 constitution, ex-presidents of the republic are granted membership for life in the Senate.

Table 9.1. *Comparative evaluation of deputies and the executive branch* *(percentages)*

	Deputies	Executive
They/it are/is doing it well.	21.9	55.1
They/it are/is doing it badly.	11.6	15.4
Not exactly sure what they/it are doing.	59.6	19.7
No response	6.9	9.8
Total	100	100

Note: N = 1,503 for both surveys.
Source: Participa, "Estudio sobre la democracia y participación política," Informe Segunda Medición 1992, Santiago, Chile, April, 1993, pp. 31–36.

Clearly, respondents are more familiar with actions of the executive branch. More significant than the high level of approval for the executive branch is the fact that 59.6% of respondents are not exactly sure what their deputy does.

In addition, according to survey data there is a growing frustration with the performance of the Congress as an institution. While approval ratings for the president were consistently high throughout the first administration, the general approval rating of Congress has decreased since the first surveys were performed in 1991. The current survey asked interviewees if they agreed with a number of statements regarding the Congress. Table 9.2 summarizes the results.

However, the most important nonstatutory source of presidential power lies in the unequal balance of staff and access to information. The executive branch can rely on a vast network of experts, attorneys, and advisors within each of the ministries charged with particular subject areas, enabling it to elaborate proposals of a much higher quality than possible for the legislative branch. Because the ministries are divided along functional lines, the staffs tend to be experts in the subject area for which they are drafting legislation and have a better understanding of the structure and day-to-day functioning of the institutions administered by the ministries, as well as the problems that proposed legislation should address.

On the other hand, most deputies and senators have relatively small staffs, each of which consists of a secretary and one or two advisors, often members of legislators' own families. While members with more resources, or those with additional outside occupations such as a partnership in a law firm, may have larger staffs, most have very little access to expert infor-

Table 9.2. *Public evaluation of the legislative branch, 1991–92 (percentages)*

	1991	1992
The Congress is functioning well.	54.7	43.0
Members of parliament only worry about people at election time.	54.8	74.7
There needs to be more contact between the people and Congress.	79.8	85.5
Laws do not help people like me.	40.9	44.4

Source: Participa, "Estudio sobre la democracia y participación política," Informe Segunda Medición 1992, Santiago, Chile, April, 1993, pp. 31–36.

mation and advisors.[14] At the same time, because assembly members are involved in such a broad range of legislative activity, they must attempt to become experts on legislation that can range from defense policy, to fishing, to issues involving social welfare. Though congressional committees are also ordered along functional lines, there is no permanent team of experts to advise committee members.

There are independent "think tanks" and an Office of Information for both chambers, but the types of materials provided by these institutions deal more with legislation from a broad perspective. They do not provide the individualized or specialized information services often needed by members with specific interests or concerns related to the effect of legislation on their districts.

In addition, unlike ministerial staff, members of the Chamber and Senate must also concern themselves with the demands of their constituency and reelection (with the exception of designated senators), both of which limit the time and resources that can be devoted to the study and formulation of legislative proposals.[15]

This imbalance in staff and access to information transfers a tremendous amount of power to the executive branch in terms of its capacities to initiate

14 Interview with Eduardo Barros González, Valparaíso, April 2, 1993. The lack of personnel was a recurrent theme in several interviews with congressional staff members. For example, because of budgetary constraints, during the 1993 legislative period five Radical Party deputies shared a single secretary, who had a corresponding number of telephones on her desk.

15 The institution of appointed senators has often been defended precisely for this reason. Proponents contend that the lack of restraints imposed by reelection and by having to deal with constituents provided appointed senators more time to study and reflect upon proposed legislation, ultimately improving its quality.

legislation. It is difficult for members of the assemblies to draft legislation approaching the quality of that produced by the executive, both in terms of substantive content and legislative technique. This makes the already limited chances for the approval for legislative initiatives even less likely.

Given these broad powers to formulate and propose legislation and control the legislative agenda, the president is not merely a "co-legislator," as students of the Chilean presidency often contend, but the most important legislator in the country.

Aylwin was quite successful in employing these powers to promote his legislative agenda. During the first four legislative periods of the democratic government, very few initiatives that originated in one of the two assemblies succeeded in being transformed into law, while the executive branch has had an impressive record of success in converting its proposals into laws of the republic.[16] Though legislators proposed 529 bills, only 69 were converted to law. Furthermore, of the congressional initiatives that have been passed, most have dealt with insignificant matters. Of the 69 approved during the first four legislative periods, many have to do with insignificant issues such as the erection of monuments to important national or provincial figures. One of the few significant bills originating in the Congress was one that lowered the legal age of adulthood. Table 9.3 summarizes all of the laws promulgated during the first four years of democratic government based on whether the bill was presented by the President or by a member of one of the two chambers of Congress.

Table 9.3 demonstrates clearly that the Congress has been less than successful in securing the approval of its members' initiatives. However, it is important to analyze these data with a great deal of caution. First, in employing these types of statistics as measures of presidential power, what really matters is the final wording of bills after they have been amended by Congress (something very difficult to measure effectively). In addition, it is probably correct to assume that when a president controls a majority coalition in at least one of the two houses, he would define the legislative program of the government, and many legislative initiatives would come from members of the opposition.[17] However, it is important to note that in the first two years of government, 63.9% of legislative initiatives originating in the Chamber were proposed by deputies of the *governing* parties (Instituto

---

16 A few congressional initiatives are in fact "hidden" within executive branch proposals because of the willingness of the president to include certain congressional proposals within his legislative packages. Nonetheless, this reality demonstrates the importance of executive sponsorship in ensuring the passage of legislation and further underscores the dominant role of the president as the country's most important legislator.

17 The author is grateful to the editors of this volume for these insights.

Table 9.3. *Laws promulgated during the first postauthoritarin government: Number and percent by origin*

Session	Total	Executive origin	Legislative origin
1990	186	151	35
1991	150	128	22
1992	122	112	10
1993	59	57	2
Total (percentage)	517	448	69
	(100)	(86.7)	(13.3)

Source: Congreso de Chile (1994:9).

Libertad y Desarrollo, 1991:7). In addition, while the president was able to rely on a legislative majority coalition, his party, the Christian Democrats, controlled a minority of seats in both houses, and coalition partners did have policy agendas distinct from those of the overall governing coalition. In this sense, while these data are not a definitive indication of presidential domination, they do at the very least suggest that Aylwin was successful in employing his legislative and partisan powers in a way to succeed in his legislative agenda, while legislators have been less successful in securing the passage of legislation not tied to the president's initiatives.

THE AYLWIN ADMINISTRATION: A PRELIMINARY ASSESSMENT OF THE CHILEAN PRESIDENTIAL SYSTEM

Unlike many of the presidential successions in recent Latin American history, President Aylwin transferred the presidential sash to his successor with exceedingly high approval ratings. The Aylwin government was quite successful in confronting the myriad complex and controversial issues that invariably arise in an immediate postauthoritarian situation. The Aylwin government, particularly the Ministry of Finance headed by Alejandro Foxley, performed exceedingly well in maintaining macroeconomic stability and continuity in economic policy making. Relations with the armed forces, though characterized by tense moments and sometimes acrimonious exchanges, were prudently managed. Though on occasions the government criticized the armed forces for meddling in civilian politics, it never threatened their fundamental institutional interests, nor were there serious threats of military incursions into politics. At the same time, the Commission for Truth and Reconciliation formed by President Aylwin has systematically investigated most instances of human rights violations that occurred during the preceding regime, though not to the extent hoped for by victims and their families, who have demanded an end to the government's policy of impunity for violators.

In terms of executive–assembly relations, during the first years of democratic rule an impressive array of initiatives were proposed, discussed, and promulgated. Returning to Table 9.3, between the initiation of the first legislative period in March 1990 and the end of the fourth session in March 1994, 517 proposals were presented, discussed, and published as law. About 87% of these initiatives originated in the executive branch, demonstrating an impressive record of interbranch cooperation, especially considering that the government did not enjoy a majority in the Senate due to the bloc of institutional senators. There were approximately 1,150 working days during the first four legislative periods, meaning that it took the Congress and the president an average of 2.2 days to dispatch a law. However, these figures take into account only the presidential messages and congressional motions that were converted into law. During this period the Congress had to consider 1,166 proposals, for an average of about 1 proposal per day (Congreso de Chile, 1994:9).

However, simply passing and debating a large number of proposals is not the only significant indicator of interbranch cooperation and the legislative success of the government. What is also important is the qualitative content of the laws passed. During the first three congressional periods the Congress and president have passed a number of major, complex, and often controversial measures into law, including:

- Modifications of the Fishing Law (Ley de Pesca – numerous laws).
- The establishment of democratic local governments (Law 19.130 and others).
- Laws on regional administration and government (Laws 19.097 and 19.175).
- Creation of the National Women's Service (SERNAM – Servicio Nacional de la Mujer) and the National Youth Institute (Instituto Nacional de la Juventud) (Laws 19.023 and 19.042, respectively).
- Reforms in the Administration of Justice, including modification of the criminal code on terrorism and issues involving political prisoners (Law 19.027).

- Tax Reform Law (Reforma Tributaria) (Law 18.985).
- Creation of the National Return Office to ease the reintegration of returning political exiles and the National Reparation and Reconciliation Commission to deal with restitution for victims of human rights abuses (Laws 18.994 and 19.123, respectively).

CONTEXTUAL VARIABLES, PRESIDENTIAL PARTISAN POWERS, AND THE LEGISLATIVE SUCCESSES OF THE AYLWIN PRESIDENCY

Given what has been said in this volume and elsewhere (Shugart and Carey 1992; Suarez 1982) in regard to the difficulties associated with constitutionally strong presidents in multiparty systems, the success of the Aylwin administration may seem surprising. What were the roots of the success of this government and, more particularly, the impressive record of executive–assembly relations? In order to answer this question one must also explicitly take into account the contextual situation in which legislative–executive relations were carried out and the partisan powers of the president.

Perhaps the most important contextual feature that allowed the Chilean presidential system to function so well in the face of all of the challenges posed to the new government was the unique circumstances of the democratic transition itself. Undoubtedly, the first democratic government benefited enormously from the fiscal health and economic policies inherited from the preceding regime. However, from a political perspective and unlike other Latin American democratic transitions, in Chile no set of actors involved was able to completely impose its will upon another. General Augusto Pinochet failed to achieve victory in the plebiscite of 1988 and stay on as president, but at the same time the leaders of the opposition were unable to defeat the constitutional straightjacket imposed by the outgoing regime, despite the constitutional reforms of 1989 and 1991. In addition, though the parties of the Concertación achieved an impressive victory in the first democratic election, they were denied a majority in the Senate because of the institution of appointed senators and had to deal with an opposition that was overrepresented in both chambers of Congress due to the characteristics of the electoral system designed by the preceding government.[18]

---

18 For a discussion of how the electoral system was designed to overrepresent the right and succeeded in doing so, as well as the long-term significance of the electoral system in terms of democratic governability, see Valenzuela and Siavelis (1991).

These exigencies forced the government into a position of having to seek majorities through negotiation and compromise in order to introduce change and reform in a gradual manner. These dynamics set the stage for the *democracia consensual*, which would be the defining principle of the first democratic government.

In particular, the context of the democratic transition helped to produce two features that were important to the success of the Aylwin government, one related to the party system and a second tied to the structure and conduct of executive–assembly relations. The following section outlines how each of these variables helped to ensure the success of the Aylwin government. It goes on to show that once the contextual features of the Chilean transition fade in importance or future governments face a severe economic or other type of crisis, the incentives for maintaining this pattern of co-operation will diminish, and the latent tensions of exaggerated presidential-ism may exert themselves more forcefully.

THE TRANSITIONAL PARTY SYSTEM AND GOVERNMENTAL SUCCESS

One of the most important moderating features of the Chilean democratic transition was the way its contextual and legal framework encouraged competition between center-left and center-right coalitions and granted the president the partisan powers necessary to accomplish his legislative goals successfully. The dynamic of bipolar competition that has characterized the political system until now is an important departure from the traditional three-bloc pattern of competition that had been the distinguishing feature of the Chilean party system since midcentury.[19] This recent bipolar pattern of competition grew out of the natural correlation of forces produced by the 1988 plebiscite and has made an important contribution to the transition by structuring competition between the government and a loyal opposition.

In the period leading up to the 1988 plebiscite the deep divisions that had characterized the Chilean democratic opposition parties throughout the authoritarian regime were eclipsed by their effort to achieve one goal: an end to the authoritarian regime. The unified front that formed out of this collective effort led to an alliance in the presidential elections of 1989 and 1993. In addition, the recognition by the democratic opposition of the political exigencies demanded by the structure of the new electoral law made

---

19 The significance of this three-bloc pattern of competition, known as the Chilean *tres tercios*, is well described by Arturo Valenzuela (1990:135–56).

it clear to opposition leaders that the only way to ensure a decent showing for their parties was to form joint congressional lists. The success of the first government, combined with similar electoral incentives, encouraged the maintenance of the Concertación alliance for the second presidential election in December 1993.

This pattern of party competition has had two major consequences. First, for the first two elections the traditional problem of Chilean presidents elected with a *doble minoría* (those who receive less than 50% of the popular vote in the presidential election and lack a majority in Congress) has been avoided. Though the constitution of 1980 provides for a presidential second-round election if the highest-polling candidate does not receive a majority of the popular vote, during the first two elections, both Patricio Aylwin and Eduardo Frei Ruiz-Tagle were elected with a level of support over 50% (55.17 and 58.01%, respectively).[20] This gave both leaders clearer mandates than most Chilean presidents have had and gave Frei the most significant majority of any president since 1931.[21] The ability of the major parties of the center-left and center-right to coalesce and each choose a single standard-bearer in both elections produced a dynamic of competition between two major candidates (despite the participation of presidential aspirants from smaller, less popular parties).

But more importantly, the two-candidate presidential race combined with the influence of the parliamentary electoral system led to the formation of joint lists for both congressional elections. This dynamic of competition provided the Concertación government a majority in the Chamber of Deputies and a near majority in the Senate. Tables 9.4 and 9.5 present the results of legislative elections for both houses, in terms of the number and percentage of seats and the percentage of popular votes for the 1989 and 1993 elections.

These results provided the president with significant partisan powers, and through negotiation with opposition and institutional senators, the government was able to ensure the passage of the most significant legislation and to avoid executive–assembly deadlock. Had these two legislative and presidential alliances not existed and the president not had the benefit of a

20 According to the 1925 constitution, presidential races in which no candidate won a majority of the vote were decided in the Chamber of Deputies. Election results for Eduardo Frei are from Ministerio del Interior de Chile, "Informativo Elecciones 1993," Computo No. 4 (99.06% of the total vote computed), and those for Patricio Aylwin are from *El Mercurio*, December 12, 1993:A12.

21 The only president since the 1930s who could claim as strong a popular mandate was the current president's father, Eduardo Frei Montalva, who received 55.67% of the vote in 1964.

Table 9.4. *Chilean House of Deputies election results (1989 and 1993): Percentage of votes and percentage of seats (only valid votes) (total seats is 120)*

1989 Elections

Party/list	Votes (%)	Seats No.	%
Concertación			
PDC	26.0	39	32.5
PR	3.9	6	5.0
PPD	11.5	7	5.8
PS[a]		18	15.0
Other & Inds.	10.1	2[b]	1.7
Total	51.5	72	60.0
Democracia y Progreso			
RN	18.3	32	26.7
UDI	9.8	14	11.7
Other & Inds.	6.1	2	1.7
Total	34.2	48	40.0
Other lists			
Left			
Unidad para la Dem.	5.3	0	0.0

1993 Elections

Party/list	Votes (%)	Seats No.	%
Concertación			
PDC	27.1	37	30.8
PR	3.0	2	1.7
PPD	11.8	15	12.5
PS	12.0	15	12.5
Other & Inds.	1.5	1	.8
Total	55.4	70	58.3
Unión por el Progreso			
RN	16.3	29	24.2
UDI	12.1	15	12.5
UCC	3.2	2	1.7
Other & Inds.	5.1	4	3.3
Total	36.7	50	41.7
Other lists			
Left			
Alt. Dem. de Izq.	6.4	0	0

				Nueva Izq.			
Right							
Al. del Cent.	2.6	0	0	1.4	0	0	0.0
Ptdo. del Sur	.7	0	0	0	0	0	0.0
Lib.-Soc. Chileno	3.1	0	0	0	0	0	0.0
PN	.8	0	0	0	0	0	0.0
Independents	1.8	0	0	1.4	0	0	0.0
Total	100	120	100	100	120	100	100

Note: Al. del Cent.: Center Alliance (Alianza del Centro); Alt. Dem. de Izq.: Democratic Alternative of the Left (Alternativa Democrática de Izquierda); Lib.-Soc. Chileno: Chilean Liberal-Socialist (Liberal-Socialista Chileno); Nueva Izq.: The New Left (Izquierda Nueva); PDC: Christian Democratic Party (Partido Demócrata Cristiano); PN: National Party (Partido Nacional); PPD: Party for Democracy (Partido por la Democracia); PR.: Radical Party (Partido Radical); PS: Socialist Party (Partido Socialista); Ptdo. del Sur: The Southern Party (Partido del Sur); RN: National Renewal (Renovación Nacional); UCC: Union of the Center-Center (Unión del Centro-Centro); UDI: Independent Democratic Union (Unión Demócrata Independiente); Unidad para la Dem.: Democratic Unity (Unidad para la Democracia).

*a*There was a great deal of fluidity in party identification during and immediately after the 1989 election due to problems with party registration and the question of whether the PPD should simply disband and join the Socialists, given that the former was created as an "instrumental" party purely in support of the return of democracy. Thus, the movement of legislators between the two parties was rather fluid. Those candidates elected who eventually assumed the PS label really initially ran under the PPD label. This explains the lack of votes for the PS in the 1989 election. Similarly, many candidates on the right characterized as "others" later joined one of the major parties of the right. While the statistics for votes received reflect what parties polled in actual elections, the statistics for the makeup of both the Chamber and the Senate reflect the genuine party composition of the assembly for the majority of the Aylwin administration after party identification had been solidified.

*b*For the 1989 Chamber of Deputies elections the Concertación had two members listed as "others" who ran

Notes to Table 9.4 (*cont.*)

as leftist candidates independent from the Concertación. Nonetheless, they have generally supported the government in Congress, so they are included here as members of the Concertación alliance.

c All elective Senate seats were up for election in the first post-authoritarian election. However, for the 1993 elections one-half of the Senators served only four instead of eight years within the transitional framework. From now on all senators will serve eight-year terms, but approximately one-half of the Senate will come up for election every four years (taking into account that there are an odd number of districts). Because the real goal here is to demonstrate whether or not the president could rely on a legislative majority, data for the new total number and percentage of seats held by each coalition and party is presented, including those senators not subject to reelection.

d Though the appointed senators are not bound to support the opposition, nor have they in every case, they did provide effective veto power for the parties of the right for major legislation and constitutional reform and are thus listed along with this sector. Only eight designated senators served during the majority of the Aylwin government, since one died while in office and was not replaced.

Sources:: Popular vote, 1989 elections – House of deputies: Servicio Electoral de Chile (modified to discount null and void votes) Senate: Nohlen (1993: 239–70). Seats, 1989, House of deputies; *El Mercurio*, December 12, p. A5, Senate: Servicio Electoral de Chile. Popular vote, 1993 elections: House of Deputies and Senate (adjusted for noninclusion of independent) Participa (1993). Seats, 1993 House of Deputies: (Godoy 1994: 334), Senate, Ministerio del Interior de Chile (1993).

Table 9.5. *Chilean Senate election results (1989 and 1993): Percentage of votes and percentage of seats (only valid votes) (Total seats is 47: 38 elected, 9 appointed)*[c]

	1989 Elections				1993 Elections (1/2 of senators)		
Party/list	Votes (%)	Seats No.	%	Party/list	Votes (%)	Seats No.	%
Concertación				*Concertación*			
PDC	31.9	13	27.7	PDC	20.3	14	29.8
PR	2.2	3	6.4	PR	6.3	1	2.1
PPD	12.1	1	2.1	PPD	14.7	2	4.2
PS[a]	*[a]	4	8.5	PS	12.7	4	8.5
Other & Inds.	8.2	1	2.1	Other & Inds.	1.5	0	0.0
Total	54.4	22	46.8	Total	55.5	21	44.7
Democracia y Progreso				*Unión por el Progreso*			
RN	10.8	13	27.6	RN	14.9	11	23.4
UDI	5.1	2	4.3	UDI	11.2	3	6.4
Other & Inds.	19.0	1	2.1	UCC	8.1	1	2.1
				Other & Inds.	5.3	2	4.2
Appointed[d]	0	9	19.1	*Appointed*[d]	0	9	19.1
Total	34.9	25	53.1	Total	39.5	26	55.3
Other lists				*Other lists*			
Left				Left			
Unidad para la Dem.	4.2	0	0.0	Alt. Dem. de Izq.	4.3	0	0.0
				Nueva Izq.	.7	0	0.0
Right							
Al. del Cent.	1.4	0	0.0				
Ptdo. del Sur	.6	0	0.0				
Lib.-Soc. Chileno	3.3	0	0.0				
PN	.6	0	0.0				
Independents	.5	0	0.0				
Total	100	47	100	Total	100	47	100

Note: See Table 9.4.
Sources: See Table 9.4.

multiparty governing coalition, not only would the government have faced a far more arduous task in terms of its legislative agenda, but some of the difficulties of exaggerated presidentialism may have more forcefully emerged.

THE PARTY SYSTEM AND POST-
TRANSITION POLITICAL COMPETITION

But is this bipolar pattern in the party system, so important to the success of the past government, a permanent feature of the political landscape? Did military electoral reformers and the almost 17-year interregnum of authoritarian rule succeed in fundamentally transforming the party system? Will the electoral system and future party system provide presidents as strong a popular mandate and the benefit of the type of congressional composition that was so important to the success of President Aylwin?

The electoral reforms undertaken by the military regime were designed with two principal goals in mind. First, reformers sought to ensure the parties of the Right a majority in the legislature, assuming they would receive approximately 40% of the vote, a figure comparable to that received by Pinochet in the 1988 plebiscite. For the longer term, the authorities sought to create a formula that would encourage the formation of a two-party system.

The electoral system ultimately adopted creates 60 legislative districts with a magnitude of two.[22] However, in order for a party or coalition to win both of the seats in a district, it must double the vote of the second highest polling party. Consequently, the cut-off point that a party must reach in order to obtain at least one seat becomes 33.4% of the votes of the two largest parties or coalitions, assuming there are two lists. Hence, the system tends to favor the *second* largest list. This is the case because in order to obtain two seats, the largest party must receive twice the vote of the second-largest party, or 66.7% of the vote of the two largest parties or coalitions. Therefore, for the largest party electoral support in excess of 33.4% is superfluous until its level of support approaches 66.7%.

In other words, if the party lists of the largest party and the second-largest party earn 66 and 34% of the vote, respectively, they will divide the district, each receiving one seat, or 50% of the seat allocation for that district. Because of this feature of the electoral system, military reformers partially succeeded in achieving their first goal. While not garnering a majority, the parties of the center-right benefited by receiving a disproportionate number of legislative seats when compared with the proportionality indices of the parties of the Concertación alliance.[23]

In regard to the second goal, military reformers believed that the low

---

22 A small portion of this section is a translation from Spanish drawn from Valenzuela and Siavelis (1991).
23 Proportionality indices for all of the major parties participating in the 1989 election appear in Valenzuela and Siavelis (1991:44).

district magnitude of the electoral system would produce party system integration and eventually a two-party system. Though an incipient bipolar configuration of competition seems to have prevailed for the first two elections, there are several indications that point to the fact that this may just be a temporary phenomenon. First, as noted earlier, just as in the preauthoritarian period, the Chilean party system is characterized by four or five parties that can be considered relevant, as well as a number of smaller parties. The average effective number of parties in the lower house in the preauthoritarian period was 5.45, very close to the 4.91 average for the period since the return of democratic government.[24] Those parties that can be considered relevant within the current center-left Concertación alliance include the main Christian Democratic Party (PDC), the Party for Democracy (PPD), and the Socialist Party (PS). In addition, both the Independent Democratic Union (UDI) and National Renovation (RN) of the center-right alliance can be considered relevant.[25] Each of these parties has its own platform, its own constituency, and its own individual partisan interests, a reality often obscured by the apparent unity of both the Concertación and the center-right alliance. Several smaller parties also influence coalition decisions and present candidates for the National Congress on one of the two larger lists. In the case of the Concertación, representatives of these smaller parties have also been considered for, and in some cases served in, ministerial positions.

Second, and on a deeper level, there is strong evidence that the tripartite division of Chilean politics continues to exist beneath the veneer of temporary bipolar competition.[26] Table 9.6 shows the returns from Chamber of Deputy elections for 1937–73, as well as the mean percentage received by parties of the right, center, and left during this period. It also presents results from the two Chamber of Deputies elections that have occurred in Chile since the return of democratic government, also disaggregated into forces representing the right, center, and left. The table demonstrates a remarkable consistency in voting patterns for the three ideological blocs.[27]

24 The figures cited here are drawn directly from Table 11.2, this volume. If only the 20 years prior to the authoritarian regime are considered, the effective number of parties is actually higher in contemporary Chile than it averaged during these years. For discussion of continued existence of Chilean multipartism and calculations of the number of effective number of parties for all elections since 1932, see Siavelis (1995).

25 Not only are these parties relevant in Sartori's (1976:121–24) terms as having "coalition" and "blackmail" potential, but each party also has representatives in Congress and polled over 10% in the 1993 elections. Arguably, certain other parties can also be considered relevant, but these five clearly are according to most criteria.

26 This analysis of continuity in the ideological orientation of the Chilean electorate is supported by the findings of Scully and J. S. Valenzuela (1993).

27 The returns for the parties of the left between 1938 and 1958 are really not representative

Table 9.6. *Percentage of vote received by parties of the right, center, and left in Chilean House of Deputy Elections 1937–93 (percentage of total vote)*

Party	1937	1941	1945	1949	1953	1957	1961	1965	1969	1973	Mean (1937–1973)	1989	1993
Right (a)	42.0	31.2	43.7	42.0	25.3	33.0	30.4	12.5	20.0	21.3	30.1	34.1	29.8
Center (b)	28.1	32.1	27.9	46.7	43.0	44.3	43.7	55.6	42.8	32.8	39.7	33.1	31.6
Left (c)	15.4	33.9	23.1	9.4	14.2	10.7	22.1	22.7	28.1	34.9	21.5	24.3	30.9
Other	14.5	2.8	5.3	1.9	17.5	12.0	3.8	9.2	9.1	11.0	8.7	8.5	7.7

Note: For 1937–73: (a) Right: Conservative, Liberal, and National parties after 1965; (Center: Radical, Falangist, Christian Democrats, Agrarian, Laborist; (c) Left: Socialist, Communist. For 1989–93: (a) Right: National Renovation, Independent Democratic Union, National, and independents on congressional lists of the right (for 1989 this also includes the Union of the Center, a center party); (b) Center: Radical, Christian Democrats, Social Democrats, Center Alliance Party; (c) Left: Party for Democracy, Socialist Party, Almeyda Socialist Party, National Democratic Party, Christian Left, Humanists, Greens, and independents of congressional lists of the left.

Sources: For 1937–73: Arturo Valenzuela, *The Breakdown of Democratic Regimes: Chile* (Baltimore: Johns Hopkins University Press, 1978), p. 6. For 1989: elections, Programa de Asesoria Legislativa, "Análisis de actualidad," No. 43 (June 1992):54–57. For 1993: *Nondefinitive* data *La Epoca,* December 13, 1993, p. B1.

The persistent reality of Chilean multipartism is based more on the convergence of a number of cultural, social, and political variables than on the potential drives that the new electoral system may exert. While there is certainly less ideological distance between the relevant parties, as platforms have become more similar across the political spectrum, this should not lead one to assume that the multiparty system has disappeared. Important differences between the parties remain, and once more controversial issues such as poverty, divorce, and abortion become more salient, many of these programmatic differences will assert themselves more forcefully.

Further, rather than encouraging the combination of party platforms and the integration of party organizations as military reformers envisioned, the electoral system has in practice encouraged divisiveness. Because there are only two seats available in each congressional district, there are a limited number of rewards for coalition participation. Each of the parties within each of the alliances is forced to engage in a frenzied and time-consuming negotiation process to determine the number of candidates each party will be allowed to present in elections and which districts they will be presented in.

However, in the future there is no guarantee that the incentives for undertaking these types of negotiations will exist or that they will be successful. The maintenance of the Concertación has been most threatened when arguments over electoral spoils and cabinet positions have emerged.[28] In a less propitious atmosphere for negotiation, or one in which coalition partners are attempting to distance themselves from an unpopular or unsuccessful government, there are fewer incentives for reaching agreements for the presentation of joint lists, and parties may be more tempted to "go it alone."

In this type of situation the electoral system has the capacity to under-

---

of that sector's full range of support, since the Communist Party was banned during this period.

28 The periods leading up to presidential, legislative, and municipal elections have uniformly been characterized by threats and rumors predicting the breakup of the Concertación, principally over disputes involving candidatures. Even after elections, disagreements persisted over cabinet assignments. Given recent experiences, a likely future source of conflict is the next presidential election. In the first two presidential elections, the parties of the left (PS–PPD bloc) have been denied the presidential candidacy of the Concertación, despite having a strong and tenable candidate in Ricardo Lagos. After Lagos served as minister of education in the Aylwin government and launched an unsuccessful primary bid to become the Concertación's presidential candidate in 1993, the administration of President Frei offered him the less than glamorous position of minister of public works, apparently to decrease his stature as a national political leader. This created a great deal of angst on the left and led to calls for an end to the coalition.

represent significantly or exclude parties and even broad coalitions from the National Congress. Despite the success of small parties gaining representation in the 1989 and 1993 elections, the fact remains that there are only two congressional seats available in each district in a country characterized by four or five parties. Coalition formation in the last two elections provided for relatively proportional representation for most parties, but without it certain parties would certainly have been significantly underrepresented in Congress. Small, nonaligned parties have already been completely barred legislative representation in these two elections. But more significantly, assuming there is a reemergence of a three-bloc pattern of competition, entire political currents can be seriously underrepresented in Congress, despite having received a significant amount of support.[29] Even if the current pattern of bipolar competition continues, a poor electoral showing by the right could have disastrous electoral consequences. It would leave a significant political sector with a limited institutional voice and perhaps signify an end to the *democracia consensual* that has characterized Chilean politics since the end of the authoritarian government.

MULTIPARTISM, EXAGGERATED PRESIDENTIALISM, AND ELECTORAL LAWS

What are the consequences of continued multipartism combined with the exaggeratedly strong Chilean presidential system and a potentially exclusionary electoral law? As Shugart and Carey have convincingly demonstrated, it is really impossible to isolate the effects of executive and assembly elections on one another. Their relative timing and sequencing has an important effect on the prospects for executive–assembly cooperation (Shugart and Carey 1992:chaps. 9–12).

In Chapter 1 of this volume (and departing from some of the conventional wisdom concerning the perils of presidentialism), Shugart and Mainwaring argue that the problems of presidentialism do not emerge as a result of minority presidents per se, but rather from situations in which a president's party lacks a "sizeable legislative contingent." While the Aylwin and Frei governments could rely on a *coalition*, it is important to bear in mind that as the highest-polling party, the Christian Democrats received only

---

29 This argument is more fully developed in Valenzuela and Siavelis (1991) and is supported by a series of electoral simulations that demonstrate the exclusionary characteristics of the electoral system. For a more complete and varied set of simulations that test the functioning of a moderate proportional representation system against that of the two-member-district system, see Siavelis (1993).

27.12% of the vote in the 1993 elections for the Chamber. What is more, it did so in a situation of unprecedented popularity for the party's retiring president. Given the current dynamic of the party system and the uncertainty of coalition formation for the future, it is quite likely that in the future presidents may not be able to rely on sizable legislative contingents of their own parties.

In this sense, then, the most important consequence of the combination of multipartism with exaggerated presidentialism in the Chilean case is that the problem of *doble minoría* presidents has not been solved. Indeed, certain features of the Chilean institutional and legal structure make their existence more likely.

A major step taken by constitutional reformers in an attempt to avoid the problem of presidents elected with a minority of the vote was the establishment of a second-round runoff election between the two highest-polling candidates in the event that one candidate does not receive a majority of the vote. The majority rule for presidents does not really solve the problem of minority presidents. Rather, it manufactures a majority where one might not exist.[30] In fact, a majority system may encourage candidates to enter a race with no possibility of winning, in an effort to force a second round.

Even if the second round helps to ameliorate the problems of legitimacy and presidential stature that the election of presidents with small pluralities can cause, it does nothing to eliminate the second component of the *doble minoría* problem: presidents without significant legislative support.

The possibility of presidents serving with legislative minorities is made more likely given the practice of second-round elections. First, second-round elections often lead to the formation of temporary alliances. However, following the presidential election there is little incentive for coalition members to continue to support the president. If a president who received only a plurality were chosen in the Congress as in the past, at least he or she would be cognizant of the political alliances that resulted in his or her election and the importance of maintaining them. By giving a presidential candidate a majority of the popular vote, election with the use of a second round may cause presidents to interpret their mandate as an expression of the support of the majority of the electorate and make them less appreciative of the importance of congressional coalitions. Second, the majority rule essentially means that in some cases presidential and legislative elections are no longer concurrent, because the second-round election takes place after the composition of Congress has already been determined. In this case, while

30 Rae (1967:74–77) uses the term "manufactured majorities" to refer to those majorities artificially produced by the electoral system.

the president may be a representative of the least-objectional party to a majority of voters, the Congress may be composed of members of the preferred parties of the electorate.

Other aspects of the Chilean presidential system also increase the probability that presidents will face a hostile Congress. In February 1994 the Chilean Congress overwhelmingly approved a reduction in the presidential term of office from 8 to 6 years. Though intended to add increased flexibility to the presidential system by allowing the early removal of an unpopular president through the electoral process, the reform creates other problems in terms of the timing and sequencing of elections. Specifically, the reform makes it even more likely that presidents will not be able to rely on a majority in Congress, because presidential and legislative elections will be held concurrently less often than they would have been with the previous 8-year formula. Instead of every 8 years, congressional and presidential elections will now be held concurrently every 12 years.[31]

What is more, all presidents will be subject to at least one congressional election during their term in office. If an unpopular president depends on a coalition of parties in addition to his or her own in the legislature, there may be an incentive for other parties of the coalition to distance themselves from the president in preparation for future elections, thus creating a minority presidency despite the fact that the president may have been elected with the support of a legislative coalition. Parties that once formed part of an unpopular president's coalition will have more to gain by presenting separate legislative lists. In this situation, the exclusionary tendencies of the legislative electoral system make it even more likely that the president will be left without legislative support following the election. This is an especially serious problem in cases in which congressional elections occur toward the end of a presidential term.

The significance of this scenario may become clearer with a purely hypothetical example employing the current government as a baseline. If the performance of Christian Democratic President Eduardo Frei, who serves until 2000, begins to falter, or if a significant economic or other type of crisis occurs, the PPD and Socialist members of the governing coalition would certainly have more to gain from presenting a separate list for the 1997 legislative elections than from aligning with the Christian Democrats. If the Christian Democrats perform poorly in the election, the exclusionary drives exerted by the electoral system may result in significant underrepresentation for the party. The president would face a legislature dominated by the left and the right with two years remaining in his term. There would

---

31 All deputies and half of the senators are elected every four years.

be few incentives for the opposition-dominated Congress to cooperate with the president, as all sights would be set on the 1999 presidential elections.[32] Because a winning candidate serves for six years in an office in which the majority of the political power in the country is concentrated, the presidential race becomes a political game with extremely high stakes.

Mainwaring and Shugart's discussion of the negative consequences created by the combination of fragmented multipartism and presidentialism, as well as that which deals with the constellation of institutional features that encourage the election of minority presidents, supports many of the contentions outlined earlier (see their Conclusion). One of their most significant findings as it relates to the Chilean case is the tendency of nonconcurrent elections to contribute to party-system fragmentation. Their theoretical conclusions suggest that it is likely that the effective number of parties will remain about the same in Chile.[33] This is especially true given that the purported reductive effects of the new electoral system have not yet materialized, nor are they likely to in the near future. Continuing fragmentation makes it less likely that presidents will be able to rely on sizable legislative contingents during future governments.

GOVERNMENT STRUCTURE, ELITE BEHAVIOR, AND THE SUCCESS OF EXECUTIVE–ASSEMBLY RELATIONS

While the current pattern of party competition described earlier helped to encourage cooperation, the impressive record of executive–assembly relations during the Aylwin government is also rooted in the structure of the executive branch and the behavior of executive and legislative actors.

In structural terms, each of the ministries during the Aylwin administration was staffed with an undersecretary who belonged to a different party of the Concertación alliance than that of the minister. In this way, the influence and interests of the various parties of the coalition were balanced through participation in ministerial decisions. This integration of the members of the coalition precluded the dominance of the main Christian Democratic Party and was important in maintaining the loyal collaboration of coalition members, both in the assembly and within the executive branch.

---

32 Both presidential and legislative elections are held in December. Elected candidates assume office in March.
33 In the Chilean case this effect may be even more powerful than Mainwaring and Shugart suggest, given that local elections in Chile are held employing a proportional representation system that further encourages fragmentation, given that parties can effectively compete at at least one electoral level.

A more vertical, Christian Democratic–centered organizational framework would have been open to charges of attempting to dominate the governing process and have been more likely to produce partisan infighting, weakening the coalition's strength and the legislative capacities of the executive branch.[34]

Much of the coordination within the executive branch and between it and Congress is centered within the Ministry of the General Secretary of the Presidency. Elevated to the ministerial level early in the Aylwin administration, this body is composed of several divisions, each of which is charged with a different area of responsibility. The Division of Interministerial Coordination is responsible for ensuring the coherence of government policy and for coordinating work and brokering negotiations between each of the ministerial commissions. It has been important in maintaining functional and harmonious relationships between each of the ministries made up of individuals from the diverse parties of the Concertación.

All proposals for legislation from each of the ministries pass through the Ministry of the General Secretary. The Division of Legislative Relations then consults each of the other ministries with potential involvement in a given issue and elaborates proposed legislation, taking into consideration input from the ministries, the goals of the president, and questions of constitutionality. This process ensures the coherence of proposed legislation within the government's program and eases the potential for conflict between ministries and between coalition members.

Equally important, the Division of Political Relations of the General Secretary maintains open and fluid communications between it and other social and political organizations, including political parties, unions, the Catholic Church, and most importantly, the legistative *jefes de bancadas* (leaders of the legislative parties). The division also has a permanent staff within Congress to maintain constant government contacts with members.

There is also a high degree of interaction of executive and assembly representatives throughout the legislative process. Interbranch relations

34 For a discussion of this point and other aspects of the organization of the presidency that helped to encourage cooperation, see Rehren (1992). Rehren suggests that the discussion in the literature concerning the desirability of parliamentary systems may be missing the point. He contends that presidential leadership styles and the organization of the presidency may be more important contributing factors to the success of presidential government. The author agrees with his analysis concerning how these variables helped to make the Aylwin presidency a success. However, leadership and organizational variables only help to overcome the tensions that the presidential system may create; they do not eliminate them. With different executives with distinct management and personal styles, the problems associated with presidentialism can easily reemerge.

have been conducted through a series of informal meetings between members of congressional committees and the representatives of the executive working in the same policy area. In addition, all of the Concertación's *jefes de bancadas* meet each Monday with ministers to determine the legislative agenda for the week. By mutual accord and negotiation they decide which projects will have priority.[35]

This pattern of cooperation has also characterized relations between parties outside of the governing coalition. The parties of the center-right have played a vital role as a loyal opposition, willing to broker negotiations between the military and the Concertación, both in regard to the reforms of the 1980 constitution and later through participation in the *democracia consensual* that characterized the first government. Indeed, the president and representatives of the executive branch have often entered into negotiations directly with the center-right in order to reach solutions to controversial legislative issues, some would say going over the heads of Concertación members of Congress. This occurred most notably during negotiations on the proposal for the Reforma Tributaria (Tax Reform). Despite the occasional criticisms of members of the governing coalition, this type of executive behavior has moderated many of the Concertación's proposals, making them more acceptable to a broader range of political parties and more likely to pass in Congress.

In addition, despite initial expectations that the institutional senators would always side with the opposition for key votes, they have also been willing to reach agreements with the government in order to pass vital legislation.

However, structural features are not the only bases of the legislative success of the first government. The decisions and behavior of members of each of the branches of government have also been crucial. First, the executive branch avoided proposing legislation that challenged the fundamental interests of the right and of the military, including prosecution for human rights violations and major constitutional reforms. The government was forced into assuming such a stance because it lacked a majority in the Senate. At the same time, however, it also understood the need to maintain the *democracia consensual*, which was fundamental in easing the tensions posed by the return of democratic politics.

Second, and as noted earlier, the president was willing to rescind urgencies to grant Congress extra time to consider proposals when necessary.

---

35 Interview with Cesar Ladrón de Guevara Pardo, advisor, Judicial/Legislative Division of the Ministry of the General Secretary of the Presidency, Santiago, April 28, 1993.

During extraordinary legislative sessions the executive was also willing to allow the debate and study of bills presented by members of the Chamber and Senate.

On the assembly side, instead of attempting to block the urgencies designated by the president, the Congress was been exceedingly cooperative in respecting the legislative agenda as determined by the executive branch, despite the fact that there are neither constitutional nor statutory penalties for ignoring presidential urgencies.

THE FUTURE OF EXECUTIVE–ASSEMBLY RELATIONS

It is clear that the success of the legislative process during the Aylwin administration was to a large extent due to the contextual and party system features of a particular moment, as well as the actions and decisions of the political actors involved. Many of the incentives that have existed for executive–assembly cooperation in the legislative process would be less influential in the future in a case where the president lacks or loses a coalitional legislative majority while in office.

Throughout the Aylwin presidency the legislative agenda was set on the basis of interbranch and interparty cooperation and negotiation. If future presidents are elected without the support of a coalition of parties or lose that support in midterm elections, the number of parties represented within the executive branch would decrease. With fewer parties represented, the mechanics of the legislative process would change. Without the guarantees provided by the representation of an array of parties within the executive branch, there is nothing to ensure that a president will have the goodwill, good judgment, or opportunity given the correlation of forces in the Congress to organize the type of informal cross-branch and cross-party legislative consultations that characterized the Aylwin government. Indeed, there is no incentive for a president to make such arrangements because the party in power will want to reap the benefits of governmental achievements and would be understandably less willing to share the credit for success with other parties.

When a president lacks significant legislative support the incentive structure created also exerts an influence on the behavior of the legislative branch and increases the probability for both interparty and interbranch conflict.

First, without a stake in the government, members of other parties do not have as much invested in the success of the legislative process. Because the locus of the legislative process is the executive branch, the executive benefits more than individual legislators from the successful passage of legislation.

But more important, the Congress is one of the few institutional arenas for the articulation of opposition demands. Therefore, the marginalization of Congress also serves to exclude the opposition. Even members of the president's own coalition may begin to feel that the interests of their own party are undermined by their subordinate role as actors within the political process. This is an especially acute problem in a multiparty system in which there are major differences in both the constituencies and platforms of the parties. As the shadow of the military fades and the overriding regime cleavage that led to the creation of *democracia consensual* becomes less important, parties may have less and less to gain from *democracia consensual* and more to gain from *democracia confrontacional*.

Second, the potential exists not only for partisan conflict but also for interbranch conflict. The actions of the assembly during the Aylwin administration were a product of the goodwill of legislators and were subject to the incentives acting upon legislators at the time. However, given a return to a more partisan pattern of political competition, the costs of cooperation may exceed the benefits gained. The Congress may become increasingly hostile toward presidential domination of the legislative process, especially if the president relies on a legislative minority. While a future president can continue to declare legislation urgent at the same rate that President Aylwin did, if some of the incentives outlined earlier begin to operate, there is no assurance that the assembly will respect those urgencies. It can either ignore them or simply vote down all presidential initiatives in favor of devoting time to the consideration of proposals originating in the legislative branch, from which individual legislators may have more to gain. In essence, without the range of "partisan" powers, so important to Aylwin's legislative success, future presidents may encounter an exceedingly difficult time in accomplishing their legislative agenda.

All of the scenarios just described are, of course, purely hypothetical. However, the point of this discussion is that constitutionally strong presidents can become *functionally* very weak given a change in contextual and party system variables.[36] In the terms discussed in this volume, while Aylwin benefited enormously from both constitutional and partisan power, a transformation in the coalitional dynamic that undermines partisan powers can produce a constitutionally strong yet moribund president. The tremendous importance of partisan powers are well demonstrated in Weldon's

36 Here the author expands on the idea of the "functional" weakness of presidential systems discussed by Suarez (1982).

chapter on Mexico. He shows that even constitutionally weak presidents can forcefully initiate their legislative agenda, given a favorable constellation of partisan powers. On the other hand, as Mainwaring's chapter on Brazil demonstrates, a strong president may face difficulties in employing his or her broad constitutional tools (beyond the use of decrees of questionable constitutionality), given the obstacles created by the consistent lack of partisan power characteristic of Brazilian presidencies.

Presidents may indeed have the right of exclusive initiatives in certain areas, the ability to declare legislation urgent, and strong veto powers. However, a simple change in the political context may leave a president with little power and influence. Presidential strength is situational and subject to majorities in Congress, social and party system contextual features, as well as the timing and sequencing of legislative and presidential elections.

In essence, the Aylwin administration had enormous success in the legislative arena. However, many of the roots of this success are not found in legal structures or institutional and constitutional arrangements. Nor are they generalizable for future governments. Rather, they are time and actor dependent. With a change in contextual variables in the future and the fading of the economic, social, and political factors that positively affected transition politics in Chile, many of the difficulties theoretically associated with exaggerated presidentialism may emerge.

Advocates of parliamentary regimes point to the tendency of presidential regimes to produce executive–assembly deadlock and military incursions into politics. There are also less dramatic but more common and likely possible results of the incentive structure created by Chile's presidential system: drifts in policy making, decreased governmental efficiency, and a dwindling confidence in political institutions.

EXAGGERATED PRESIDENTIALISM AND THE NECESSITY OF REFORM

Because of the unlikelihood of a fundamental regime change in Chile, it is important to analyze ways in which the Chilean presidential system can be improved. Bearing in mind the importance of Shugart and Carey's (1992) analysis of the significance of various types of presidentialism and the additional fruitful theoretical contributions provided by the case studies in this volume, there are a number of other reforms to the current presidential system in Chile that could help to temper some of its negative characteristics.

The point of departure for understanding the need for reform in these areas is the recognition that Chile is and will remain a country characterized by a multiparty system. What is more, unlike in Brazil, Ecuador, and some other presidential systems, Chilean parties are relatively well disciplined and characterized by strong party organizations. Both Mainwaring in his chapter on Brazil and Shugart and Mainwaring in Chapter 1 underscore the problematic consequences of combining presidentialism with fragmented multipartism characterized by malleable, undisciplined parties. While the Chilean party system remains fragmented, despite the efforts of military reforms, the moderately disciplined and institutionalized nature of Chilean parties provides a potentially more workable context for presidentialism.[37]

Given these realities, the most pressing need is to create mechanisms that encourage cooperation among Chile's numerous parties in spite of some of the disincentives that currently exist. There are two major ways this can be accomplished. The first is to reform both the timing and sequencing of elections and the electoral system for the legislature. The second is to reestablish the Chilean Congress as the arena for compromise and negotiation between parties that it once was and to adopt measures that will encourage institutionalization and maintenance of the existing pattern of *democracia consensual*.

Electoral Reform

As Chapter 1 and the Conclusion of this volume (as well as a number of case studies contained herein) make clear, presidential government is likely to be problematic in situations of high party fragmentation, given the unlikelihood that presidents will be able to rely on a sizable legislative contingent. However, presidential forms of government are also based on the principle of checks and balances and congressional oversight of executive action. The goal of reform should be to balance these two principles – that is to say, to devise an institutional structure that will be more likely to result in the election of presidents with legislative majorities but that also allows for the flexible alternation of shifting majorities.

The presidential and legislative electoral systems are extremely important variables that influence the political system's capacity to balance these principles. By shortening the presidential term and making all legislative elections concurrent with presidential elections, it would be more likely that a president would be able to rely on a majority of his or her own party

37 It is extremely difficult to arrive at measures of party discipline in Chile, given that no records are kept or published that detail how individual members vote. These conclusions are based on interviews with members of the Chamber of Deputies and Senate. Table 11.4 and the accompanying discussion in the Conclusion to this volume provide support for the proposition that the party system will remain moderately disciplined.

or coalition of parties or, at the very least, a larger legislative contingent. A presidential term of four years would allow concurrent elections without altering the existing cycle of legislative elections.[38] In addition, a four-year term would allow incompetent or unpopular presidents to be removed and replaced sooner by popular election. Though members of a coalition may still attempt to distance themselves from the president's party when approaching an election, the electorate would have the responsibility to determine whether or not this course of action was a wise one. Former coalition members would be either elected or immediately sanctioned.

The elimination of the second-round presidential election would also decrease the chances of a president serving with a legislative minority, by ensuring that the definitive presidential election is concurrent with the congressional election.

Reform of the current legislative electoral system is also a necessary element to achieve the preceding goals. While one could argue that the current electoral system is technically a proportional one with extremely small magnitudes, its operational characteristics and capacity to produce proportional outcomes more closely approximate a single-member system precisely because the magnitude is so low. A more proportional system (i.e., one increasing the district magnitude) would avoid the dramatic shifts in legislative representation and exclusionary propensities of the current two-seat-district system. However, the system adopted should be a moderate type with district magnitudes of four or five. Such a system would provide for representation of the most significant parties of the government and opposition but avoid hyperproportionality in the representation of smaller parties able to engage in legislative blackmail.[39]

Also, and just as important, a proportional system would be less likely to exclude a democratic opposition. An electoral sweep of the president's party in a legislative election can easily result in the significant underrepresentation of other parties. Single-party domination of the political process is unhealthy in a country like Chile, where no single party can come close to garnering a majority.

---

38 Another alternative would be to shorten the term of deputies to three years and that of senators to six, making half of the legislative elections concurrent with presidential elections. Nonetheless, a reform of this type is unlikely given the significant public and elite opposition to increasing the frequency of elections. In addition, despite all of these arguments advocating an additional adjustment to the electoral calendar, reform is unlikely given the already large amount of political capital expended by both the government and the opposition in order to arrive at an agreement on shortening the presidential term to six years.

39 This argument is more completely developed and supported by electoral simulations in Siavelis (1993).

Finally, any electoral reform should abolish the existence of appointed senators. The "hangover" from previous presidents' appointments in the Senate can help to prevent presidents from obtaining a majority in the upper chamber. Arguably, the appointed senators were a useful moderating element within the context of the democratic transition. However, a role for the opposition could better and more legitimately be ensured through the establishment of a more proportional electoral system rather than a series of appointments made by authorities outside the legislative branch.

Reforms to the Legislative Process

In terms of the legislative process the most urgent reform necessary is the reestablishment of equilibrium between the executive and legislative branches. From a theoretical standpoint, Shugart and Carey (1992) make the convincing though necessarily tentative argument that systems characterized by extremely strong presidents, especially in terms of legislative powers, tend to be less durable. They do not explicitly discuss the probable causes of such a phenomenon. The arguments advanced next set forth some tentative reasons why this might be the case.

First, in the years between the promulgation of the 1925 constitution and 1973, the Congress progressively lost prerogatives and influence through reforms granting the president increased powers. Given the role of the legislature as an arena for the expression of the opposition, a weakening of the Congress also meant declining influence for the opposition. If opposition forces are continually denied a voice in the national political dialogue and limited in their influence over the actions of the executive, achieving party goals through democratic means is likely to become a less attractive option. As Sartori has convincingly shown, participation within the institutions of democracy fosters their acceptance (1976:139).

Second, a strong Congress reduces the majoritarian tendencies of presidential government that have often precipitated executive–assembly conflict and in many cases led to democratic breakdown. With a stronger Congress, a president is forced to negotiate both policy and the legislative agenda. Presidents would have to allow the consideration of proposals originating in the legislative branch, both from sectors supporting the president and from opposition members. The outcome of negotiations may not be the preferred option of any one sector, but rather a middle ground that is tolerable for a greater number of sectors across the party spectrum in Congress. This reinforces the notion that the Congress also has a popular mandate that is no less legitimate than that of the president, though it is based in distinct party options. As Shugart and Carey underscore, strong legislative branches provide a mechanism for the resolution of conflict between parties by serving "as arenas for the perpetual fine tuning of conflicts" (1992:165).

There are a number of ways not requiring significant modifications to the constitution or other statutes that can reinforce the powers of the Congress. First, the faculty to set legislative urgencies in collaboration with the executive branch can be returned to the Congress, as was the case according to the constitution of 1925. If there is widespread agreement by the Congress that an initiative of its own is of significant importance, the executive cannot single-handedly delay or prevent its consideration. In addition, Congress would have more time to better debate, study, and alter presidential initiatives and ultimately to influence policy and produce higher-quality legislation. Members of Congress could induce the executive to include legislative proposals into executive policy by making the approval of a presidential urgency contingent upon their incorporation. One of the most important roles of Congress is to improve legislation through collective deliberation. It should be given the time and capacity to do so.

Another way to reinforce Congress's role in setting the legislative agenda would be to end the traditional division between ordinary and extraordinary legislative sessions, thus eliminating the presidential prerogative to determine the materials to be considered during the latter. This would give the Congress additional time to consider initiatives that its own members have proposed.

The balance of power between the branches of government can also be made more equitable by allowing the Congress an increased voice in the areas in which the executive now has exclusive initiative. In interviews with a representative sample of 43 members of the Chamber and Senate, only a single member contended that the Chamber of Deputies should have the right of exclusive initiative for the national budget.[40] Members of Congress recognize that the clientelistic logrolling policies of the past had a pernicious effect on the economic well-being of the country. Though contributing a measure of democratic stability through the satisfaction of demands, ultimately these types of expenditures led to government deficits, a bloated state sector, and the financial difficulties that characterized the early 1970s.

However, the current limitations on the Congress's areas of initiative extend beyond the realm of particularistic spending and include issues of national budgetary priorities and large-scale social questions that affect the entire country. A reform of the budgetary process could proscribe the proposal of particularistic spending while giving back to the Congress some

40 These interviews were carried out by the author in Santiago and Valparaíso between March 30 and June 3, 1993.

initiative in issues affecting social policy at the national level and allowing it to make transfers between categories of national spending.

Congress's role in the national political process can also be bolstered by eliminating limitations on the origination of bills dealing with such national issues as maternity leave, working conditions, management–labor relations, and collective bargaining. With these reforms Congress would play an enhanced role in determining national priorities without falling victim to populist temptations.

Finally, reform in all of these areas requires that the imbalance of information between the executive and assembly be eliminated. In order to initiate quality bills and perfect and influence those originating in the executive branch, the assembly must have increased access to information and expert advisors. However, there is strong political resistance to increasing the budget of individual members to provide for larger staffs. Improvements can be made without increased expenditures. There is a great deal of overlap in the services provided to individual members by the Offices of Information of the Chamber and the Senate and the Library of Congress.[41] Streamlining these three bodies and consolidating into one office the areas in which they overlap would provide additional funds for more focused and specific informational resources. A team of professional, permanent, nonpolitical appointees with subject-specific expertise for each of the legislative committees could provide the specialized information and counsel necessary for members to make informed judgments concerning the main issues and fundamental questions pertinent to each piece of legislation.

CONCLUSIONS

Much of the academic debate concerning executive–assembly relations in Latin America has focused on the issue of the distinction between presidential and parliamentary forms of government. Linz (1990), Valenzuela (1990), Linz and Valenzuela (1994), and others have shown that the institutional configuration of executive–assembly relations is an important variable affecting the prospects for democratic longevity. By bringing the issue

41 The Office of Information of the Chamber and that of the Senate both produce general reports of legislative statistics that could easily be performed by one body. Individual parties and party sectors also have access to "think tanks" that provide information identical to that of the Offices of Information. In addition, the questions that individual members submit to the Offices of Information are often referred to the Library of Congress. There is no reason that these requests cannot simply be submitted directly to the Library.

to the fore, they have induced scholars to realize that there has been insufficient focus in the literature on this important political variable. However, advocates of parliamentarism have focused almost exclusively on the distinction between parliamentary and presidential systems without sufficient differentiation between types of presidentialism. The work of Shugart and Carey (1992) and the case studies in this volume have added a valuable new dimension to this theoretical discussion by underscoring the importance of the variables that differentiate types of presidential systems and affect their functional properties. These findings are especially important where fundamental regime change is unlikely or undesirable given the political and party system context of the country. By pointing to the variables that most affect the prospects for the success of presidential government, these studies have provided a valuable blueprint for ways that presidentialism can be improved.

Though a parliamentary system may be a more workable option for Chile given the country's sociopolitical context, the prospects for fundamental institutional reform become less likely with each successive government. The task now is to remedy some of the widely recognized inadequacies of the Chilean presidential system. While for the moment the apparent success of the preceding government seems to mitigate against reform of the presidential system, the country's positive political and economic context, which has been so important in encouraging governmental success, is by no means a permanent condition. Through electoral reform, the strengthening of Congress and limiting the latitude of executive authority, Chile will be left with an institutional structure that better creates the incentives for cooperation among its diverse and multiple political parties, thus enhancing the legitimacy of both the National Congress and democratic institutions in general.

10

HYBRID PRESIDENTIALISM AND DEMOCRATIZATION: THE CASE OF BOLIVIA

Eduardo A. Gamarra

INTRODUCTION

Bolivia's democratization efforts in the past decade confirm many of the perils associated with Latin American presidentialism. Owing to the complex and hybrid nature of the Bolivian presidential system, however, generalizations to other Latin American cases are difficult to make. Because it includes certain features normally associated with parliamentarism, Bolivia's system is not strictly presidential (Shugart and Carey 1992:81–85).

The most important difference between the Bolivian system and other contemporary Latin American presidential systems lies in the selection of the Bolivian president. When no candidate achieves an absolute majority, Congress must elect the chief executive – from among the top three finishers (before the constitutional reform in 1994) or from the top two (since then). While selection of the chief executive by the legislature is often seen as a positive aspect of parliamentarism, in Bolivia it has at times served to weaken and even destabilize executives. As this chapter will show, when coalitions in the National Congress are stable, the congressional election of the head of state has also served to strengthen the executive. Although Congress elects the president, there is no dependence of the executive branch on parliamentary confidence. Thus, Bolivia's system is a hybrid that com-

I am extremely grateful to Scott Mainwaring and Matthew Shugart for their insightful and useful comments on earlier versions of this chapter. Responsibility for the shortcomings of this effort rest with me alone.

bines features of both presidentialism and parliamentarism. I shall call this form of government *hybrid presidentialism*.[1]

Owing to a congressional electoral system based on single-member districts, the full hybrid nature of the system did not manifest itself until after the 1952 Movimiento Nacionalista Revolucionario (MNR)-led revolution. Key reforms, such as the adoption of a proportional representation electoral system for the lower house of Congress, were instrumental in debilitating the capacity of presidents to control the National Congress.[2] Paradoxically, electoral reforms ran counter to the logic of the MNR to strengthen the executive power and subordinate the legislature.[3]

Following a period of military rule dating from a coup in 1964, Bolivia moved toward democratization in the late 1970s. As the nation lurched through abortive elections, coups, and countercoups it became evident that many of Bolivia's problems were rooted in the conflict between the imposition of state capitalist measures, such as economic stabilization, and the country's hybrid presidential system.

This chapter analyzes the dilemmas of Bolivia's hybrid presidential system, beginning with the transition to democracy in the late 1970s. The principal issue to be examined is how the institutions of Bolivia's hybrid presidential system have shaped policy outcomes in the context of a democratizing society. In Bolivia policy outcomes appear to hinge on the congressional election of the president. As a result, to govern Bolivia, the key has been to establish viable ruling coalitions to deepen stabilization and restructuring measures while simultaneously keeping the democratization process alive.

This approach assumes that certain structural realities are a given; thus, the fundamental issue is to understand how Bolivia's hybrid presidential system has dealt with specific problems such as economic dependence, a dependent middle class with no sources of employment other than the state,

1 There are other less salient features of Bolivia's system that differ from most presidential systems. Unlike in most presidential systems, members of Congress can serve in the cabinet. There is also a provision for the interpellation of cabinet ministers; however, a vote of censure must be passed by a two-thirds majority and even then does not force the president to accept the resignation of the minister. There is also a long tradition of malfeasance trials (*juicios de responsabilidades*), which granted the National Congress an oversight capability beyond those of other presidential systems.

2 Since 1966, the Senate has been elected from three-member districts, with the party winning the plurality getting two seats.

3 The military government of General René Barrientos, which followed the MNR's 1964 overthrow, exacerbated a specific contradiction of Bolivia's hybrid system: a state capitalist development strategy that called for a strong executive, and electoral laws that encouraged the proliferation of political parties, thereby undermining the capacity of the executive to control the National Congress.

and a political party system tied almost exclusively to state patronage. As elsewhere in Latin America, these structural realities have limited the options available to policymakers to respond to crisis situations. Thus, the principal question is how Bolivia's institutional framework has dealt with these structural problems. Bolivia's hybrid presidential system has provided some interesting mechanisms, which, for better or for worse, have ensured the continuity of the democratization experience.

In contrast to others who advocate the replacement of presidentialism with a parliamentary system, this approach argues that the key to governance in Bolivia lies in legitimately and constitutionally strengthening the capacity of executives to work with other institutions, such as the National Congress. This argument suggests that the experience of parliamentarism with democratization in other cases, such as in Spain, is not enough to propose a radical transformation of the Bolivian system. Indeed, the Spanish example has served as a model of institutional reform for officials of the current Sánchez de Lozada government. Available data suggest that parliamentarism would fare no better than and indeed might worsen Bolivia's current system if the structural realities facing this nation are taken into account.

PRESIDENTIALISM AND DEMOCRATIC TRANSITION: BOLIVIA, 1979–1985

In the late 1970s Bolivia's hybrid presidential system was one of the least prepared in Latin America to undertake the process of democratization. When the military opted to disengage from politics, Bolivia was a nation plagued by deep-seated regional, class, and political conflicts. Weak institutions and an atomized political society exacerbated tensions built into the system over years of intense political struggles. Consequently, the tumultuous round of coups, countercoups, and aborted elections that followed the military's withdrawal should not have been surprising. Between 1978 and 1982 seven military and two weak civilian governments ruled the country, as shown in Table 10.1

Numerous conflicts and contradictions arose during this period that revealed the weaknesses of Bolivia's hybrid presidential system. Every government between 1978 and 1985 demonstrated that presidents lacked the capacity to govern mainly because of structural constraints. Because no government was able to address an impending economic crisis, the country edged slowly toward a precipice of hyperinflation.

Table 10.1. *Bolivian presidents, 1971–93*

President	From	To
Gen. Hugo Banzer*a*	August 1971	August 1978
Gen. Juan Pereda*a*	August 1978	November 1978
Gen. David Padilla*a*	November 1978	August 1979
Walter Guevara Arce	August 6, 1979	November 1, 1979
Gen. Alberto Natusch*a*	November 1, 1979	November 15, 1979
Lidia Gueiler	November 15, 1979	July 17, 1980
Gen. Luis García Meza*a*	July 17, 1980	July 1981
Gen. Celso Torrelio*a*	July 1981	July 1982
Gen. Vildoso*a*	July 1982	October 12, 1982
Hernán Siles Zuazo	October 12, 1982	August 6, 1985
Víctor Paz Estenssoro	August 6, 1985	August 6, 1989
Jaime Paz Zamora	August 6, 1989	August 6, 1993
Gonzalo Sánchez de Lozada	August 6, 1993	Present

*a*De facto.

As in other deeply divided societies, democratization in Bolivia during the late 1970s faced an even greater challenge; when the military lifted proscriptions on political parties, over 70 made their appearance on the scene. The number of parties reached the extreme where Bolivians derisively referred to them as "taxi parties"; organizations so small that they could hold their national conventions in a taxi cab. At least 30 of these were identifiable factions of the MNR.

Three principal contenders emerged during the transition process. The Unidad Democrática y Popular (UDP) – a coalition of the Partido Comunista Boliviano (PCB), the Movimiento de Izquierda Revolucionaria (MIR), and Hernán Siles Zuazo's leftist MNR (MNRI) – was the front-runner in the 1978, 1979, and 1980 elections. Victor Paz Estenssoro headed the largest faction of the MNR, luring other members of Bolivia's political class. Facing an onslaught of civilian investigations into his seven-year tenure as president, General Hugo Bánzer Suárez founded Acción Democrática y Nacionalista (ADN) to help fend off charges of human rights violations and corruption. These three groups have dominated the political arena since 1978.

The proliferation of political parties in Bolivian politics exacerbated what has been described as the problem of dual legitimacy (Linz 1994). Under the terms of Article 90 of Bolivia's 1967 constitution, when no candidate achieves an absolute majority the National Congress must elect a president from the top three contenders. With as many as 27 political parties present in the Chamber of Deputies this proved to be a most difficult task. Whichever candidate was able to put together a coalition to win the presidency soon faced a chronic conflict with the legislature (Gamarra 1987; Malloy and Gamarra 1988).

The real task facing every president elected by the legislature was to maintain a coalition in place long enough to support presidential policy initiatives. By virtue of Article 90, members of Congress believed that because they elected the chief executive, they also had the power to oversee each and every activity of the president. Claiming that the National Congress was the only truly representative institution, the *fiscalización* of executive actions continued apace. It is noteworthy that, since 1978, Congress elected presidents who had obtained less than 35% of the popular vote, and in two of the last three elections, the winner of the popular plurality was not the winner of the congressional round. For example, Jaime Paz Zamora, Bolivia's current president, won less than 20% of the total vote in 1989 and placed third in the popular balloting. This situation exacerbated dual claims to legitimacy. Presidents claimed to enjoy a "popular" mandate, while congress members argued that legitimacy rested in the National Congress. The result was an intense and bitter interinstitutional dispute. In short, throughout this democratizing period, Bolivia moved gradually toward a political system characterized by a resurgent and dominant Congress and an extremely weak executive branch.

Competing claims to legitimacy were only one dimension of the governance problem faced by Bolivia's presidents. Disputes over the distribution of state patronage were an even graver issue. Political parties in the National Congress demanded patronage in exchange for their legislative support; however, because the size of the patronage pot was limited, even members of the president's own party were excluded. The result was an almost immediate assault on the executive for a greater share of the patronage pool. In Congress political parties and factions immobilized the actions of the executive branch through congressional investigations, "constitutional coups," and the like.[4]

Bolivian presidents were also incapable of asserting authority over the

4 The first constitutional coup came in November 1979, when a congressional–military plot overthrew the interim "transactional" government of Walter Guevara Arce, which had been elected by Congress in August of that same year. In brief, the plotters expected a military coup headed by Colonel Alberto Natusch Busch to be followed by a congressional vote of no confidence for President Guevara. The plotters then expected the legislature to "elect" Natusch president of Bolivia. Similar plots and variations on the same theme were common between 1982 and 1985 against the government of Hernán Siles Zuazo, which was also elected by Congress, in October 1982. For the details of constitutional coup plots, consult Gamarra (1987).

sprawling bureaucratic apparatus housed in the executive branch. As presidents handed out posts in the bureaucracy in exchange for support, the state bureaucracy became captured by a series of rival patron–client networks. Because these patron–client networks in control of state agencies and corporations consumed all surplus extracted from society, little if anything was left over to finance public policy. In short, presidents were forced to deal with assaults not only from Congress, but also from an inefficient and parasitic bureaucracy. As a result presidents were incapable of resolving even the most simple problems of governance.[5]

These conflicts illustrate another dimension of hybrid presidentialism in Bolivia. The fixed terms to which presidents are elected exacerbate tensions between branches of government. Because they elected the president, members of Congress believed they also had the right to revoke his or her mandate either through impeachment, malfeasance trials, or constitutional coups. To overcome these maneuvers and legislative inaction Bolivian presidents resorted to decree-laws, which, in turn, brought charges of unconstitutionality from the legislature. This situation was particularly evident during the 1982–85 Siles Zuazo period. Bolivian presidents were thus rendered totally ineffective in dealing with any crisis. They were particularly helpless, however, in dealing with the economic crisis. While this can be viewed as a problem of presidentialism, the problem, in my view, also lies in the nature of the party system and the form of proportional representation used to elect the Congress.[6] This problem became apparent with the explosion of parties and factions that occurred during the transition to civilian rule.

ELECTORAL LAWS AND THE
PARTY SYSTEM

In 1956 the MNR government adopted closed-list proportional representation according to the system of simple quota and largest remainders for the lower house. The average district magnitude is about 14, with five of the nine districts being very large. Because this allocation formula is favorable to smaller lists (Taagepera and Shugart 1989) and because of the large magnitude, very small parties can easily gain representation. Moreover, the

---

5 For a similar argument, see Malloy and Gamarra (1988) and Malloy (1989).
6 Elsewhere I have made the argument that by allowing the proliferation of political parties and alliances, electoral laws undermined and even directly contradicted the nature of Bolivia's presidential system as established by the 1967 constitution. See Gamarra (1987) and Gamarra and Malloy (1996).

closed-list system applies not only to Congress, but also between Congress and president. That is, voters may not split their tickets, but rather must cast a single vote for one party in both the presidential and congressional races. This means that small parties cannot endorse a major-party presidential candidate and still keep their own identity in the congressional election; they must run a presidential candidate. In turn, this proliferation then reduces the likelihood of one presidential candidate winning a majority of the votes, thereby enhancing the hybrid nature of the system.

Because of the closed lists, the MNR (and other parties) handpicked their supporters. Party factional leaders selected the individuals and the order in which they would appear on the ballot. Not surprisingly, party discipline in the legislature was tied to patron–client networks. As long as patronage was available discipline in the legislative assembly was possible. However, when the spoils were scarce, legislators often turned on the very individuals who had nominated them for the ballot in the first place.

The military government of General René Barrientos (1964–69) introduced few modifications to the 1956 electoral law. Apart from allowing a greater number of political parties to run for office the proportional representation system remained virtually intact. This was the electoral system employed in 1978 when the military convoked elections. When General Bánzer lifted proscriptions (not found in the electoral law) his government faced an uncontrollable phenomenon. Not only did dozens of parties register with the national electoral court, but the same old tired faces of Víctor Paz Estenssoro, Hernán Siles Zuazo, and Walter Guevara Arze, the old MNR titans, emerged as the front-runners.

Given this peculiar set of circumstances Bolivia's political elite recognized the problem with electoral mechanisms as early as 1979. Reforms to the electoral law aimed to prevent the proliferation of the so-called taxi parties. Under the terms of these reforms, parties that did not achieve a 50,000-vote minimum were forced to pay their share of printing the ballot. To guarantee minority representation, the electoral law allowed alliances and coalitions. A new multicolor and multisign ballot helped end the practice of ballot stuffing by political parties; until 1979 parties printed their own ballots.[7]

Because the 1979 and 1980 electoral laws allowed alliances and coalitions, smaller parties threw their support to the principal presidential can-

---

7 The 1979 reforms produced some questionable results. To get elected in La Paz, for example, a deputy required approximately 70,000 votes. In the remote department of Pando, a deputy required only 6,500. Consult Gamarra (1987:189) for a discussion of the 1979 electoral reforms.

didates in exchange for electable positions on an alliance's list. Despite controlling only a few seats in Congress, these smaller parties became the key to electing a new president. Because a single seat might be crucial to ending impasses, minority parties became important instruments to both block and oversee executive initiatives. In short, the proliferation of parties in the legislature contributed greatly to the hybrid nature of Bolivia's presidential system.

The party system, however, maintained the same characteristics: Patron–client networks were responsible for the selection of individuals to party lists. Beyond these tenuous links no guarantee of party discipline in the legislature was available. Beyond providing a seat in the legislature, party coalitions could do little else for the individuals who rode into Congress on the coattails of a conjunctural alliance. As a result party discipline in the National Congress was lax, often lasting less than a few days after the inaugural session.[8]

A basic and recurrent pattern has dominated all elections in Bolivia between 1979 and 1989. Presidential candidates have gone through three distinct coalition-forming stages. Electoral coalitions were formed to contest the elections and so secure a position for the critical second round. In Congress a round of maneuvering and coalition building took place to elect a president. When Congress finally elected a chief executive, the coalition broke down as presidents scrambled to form a governing coalition.

This hybrid presidential system is a product not only of institutional constraints. Other factors, common to several Latin American nations but present in more acute ways in Bolivia, contributed to the emergence of the current system. These factors, which were brewing beneath the surface during the military period, came to the fore during the transition period and have yet to be resolved.

SOCIAL GROUPS AND THE ECONOMIC CRISIS

One of the principal problems that Bolivian presidents faced during the transition was to respond to demands from social groups and movements

8 Party undiscipline was exacerbated by the high stakes repeated each time a president was to be elected. Individual members of minority parties cut deals with those alliances that had a greater possibility of emerging victorious. Votes were often rewarded with prominent posts in the executive branch or a high-ranking leadership position in the National Congress. Interviews with several deputies and senators over the past six years have confirmed that key swing votes are often bought and sold.

without the mediation of political parties or the National Congress. Several conflicts manifested themselves simultaneously. An intense struggle developed between the private sector, represented by the Confederación de Empresarios Privados (CEPB), and the Central Obrera Boliviana (COB) over the implementation of economic stabilization. Class conflict was complicated by inter-economic-sector tensions, which set traditional peasants against the urban sectors and the newly emerging agroindustrial interests of the eastern lowlands. Finally, a very intense process of interregional rivalry to control national policy and resources unfolded as regional "civic committees" moved to advance local interests.[9]

Political parties and Congress played little or no role in mediating the impact of these conflicts on weak presidential structures. Parties were largely disconnected from the main interests of class or regional groups. As a result, the primary organizations expressing the interests of society were the regional civic committees, peasant unions, and syndicates, the CEPB, and the COB. Each group bypassed the legislature and the political parties and pressed their demands directly on the executive. These conflicts forced presidents to avoid unpopular initiatives, especially in economic policy, or to present watered-down versions of economic stabilization programs to get over the opposition mounted by these groups. The result was an economic crisis of major proportions.

The general pattern described here revealed itself in a rather dramatic fashion during the 1982–85 Siles Zuazo government. When Siles was sworn into office, Bolivia was already experiencing the worst political and economic crisis of its history. Siles attempted to govern at the head of the UDP, the alliance that had won the most votes and seats in the most recent elections, those of 1980 (see Table 10.2). Siles never controlled his coalition, particularly in the National Congress, which almost immediately set out to conspire against him. The instability of the period was reflected by numerous cabinet crises and the recurrent interpellation and censure of cabinet ministers. Between 1982 and 1985, over 80 individuals served in the cabinet.

Led by the COB, organized labor vigorously pressed upon the weakened president to resolve the demands of the popular classes. Simultaneously, the private sector, regional civic committees, and other groups exerted untenable demands on the Siles presidency. Siles's problems with these groups were made worse by the lack of institutional mechanism to respond to crisis situations. As a result the hapless Siles government was unable to achieve

---

9 For an expansion of this analysis, consult Gamarra (1987), Malloy and Gamarra (1988), and Gamarra and Malloy (1996).

Table 10.2. *Election results in Bolivia, 1980–93*

Year	UDP	MNR^a	ADN	MIR	AP	CONDEPA	UCS	Others
1980								
Percentage of votes	38.7	20.2	16.8	—	—	—	—	24.3
Seats, Chamber	47	34	24					25
Seats, Senate	10	10	6					1
1985								
Percentage of votes	—	30.4	32.8	10.2	—	—	—	26.6
Seats, Chamber	—	43	41	15	—	—	—	31
Seats, Senate	—	16	10	1	—	—	—	0
1989								
Percentage of votes	—	25.6	25.2	21.8	—	12.3	—	15.1
Seats, Chamber	—	40	38	33	—	9	—	10
Seats, Senate	—	9	8	8	—	2	—	0
1993								
Percentage of votes	—	33.8	—	—	20.3	13.6	13.1	19.2
Seats, Chamber	—	52	—	—	34	13	20	11
Seats, Senate	—	17	—	—	8	1	1	0

Note: ADN: Acción Democrática Nacionalista; AP: Acuerdo Popular; CONDEPA: Conciencia de Patria; MIR: Movimiento de Izquierda Revolucionaria; MNR: Movimiento Nacionalista Revolucionario; UCS: Unión Cívica Solidaridad; UDP: Unidad Democrática y Popular.
^aRan as MNRH (MNR Historic) in 1985.
Source: Gamarra and Malloy (1995).

any kind of coherent economic program, and the economy plunged into a crisis of catastrophic proportions characterized by a hyperinflation rate that reached 26,000 percent in 1984–85.

By the end of 1984, politicians threatened to impeach Siles, labor took to the streets in month-long strikes, the military threatened to launch a coup, and other groups pressed for the president's resignation. Facing an imminent collapse of the economy and a derailment of Bolivian democracy, these forces came together to force Siles from office a year early and to organize another attempt to find an electoral "way out" (*salida*) to the profound political impasse.[10]

10 As Mainwaring (1990) and Linz (1990) have noted presidential systems lack the mechanisms to overcome crises such as the one faced by Siles in October–November 1984. The Bolivian Congress could have impeached Siles; however, the system was not likely to have survived. Ways out of these impasses were always innovative, but also inevitably

The July 1985 elections once again did not produce a government, as can be seen in Table 10.2, and for the third time since 1979, the task to elect a new president fell upon the National Congress. Although General Banzer's ADN won a slight plurality, a coalition between the MNR and MIR prevented his ascension to the presidency. At age 78, Victor Paz Estenssoro was elected to his fourth presidential term. A significant turning point came on August 6, when General Banzer accepted the outcome and pledged support to the democratic process.[11]

REESTABLISHING PRESIDENTIAL SUPREMACY: THE PACTO POR LA DEMOCRACIA

Reestablishing presidential supremacy entailed filling a power vacuum at the center of the Bolivian political system. Because Congress was again dominated by the opposition and organized labor was poised to prevent the imposition of harsh austerity measures, this was a difficult task. Nevertheless, Paz Estenssoro set in motion a pattern of governance that allowed his government to both impose economic stabilization and control opposition from Congress and labor. The relative success of Paz and the MNR suggests that Bolivia's hybrid presidential systems can produce the mechanisms to overcome crisis situations.

On August 29, 1985, through Decree No. 21060, the government introduced the Nueva Política Económica (NPE). Surprising the left and the groups that had supported his election in Congress, Paz Estenssoro announced a program that restructured the development strategy established 33 years earlier by the populist MNR. The NPE sought three basic objectives: the liberalization of the economy, the ascendance of the private sector as the central actor in economic development, and the recuperation of state control over key state enterprises that had been captured by factional cliques and labor groups. The NPE put forth a shock therapy of reducing fiscal deficits, freezing wages and salaries, devaluing the currency, and drastically cutting public-sector employment. The government also announced the privatization of state enterprises and other similar measures.[12]

unconstitutional. Consult Muller and Machicado (1987) for a transcript of the negotiations that led to the end of the Siles government.

11 However, Banzer had to control his supporters in ADN who had mobilized to take over the legislative palace to prevent the swearing in of Paz Estenssoro.

12 Public employment reductions, however, came mainly from firing mine workers, not

In one year the NPE was credited with reducing inflation to 10%. Government officials claimed that the foundations for economic recovery had been established. Internationally, Bolivia's NPE became a showcase as international financial institutions and foreign governments lavished extensive praise for the program. Bolivia's economic recovery, however, did not proceed rapidly. The collapse of the tin market in October 1985 and the decline in the price of natural gas – the country's only sources of hard currency – threatened to derail the NPE. In 1987, the economy finally showed signs of growth for the first time in the 1980s.

Considering the extreme crisis faced by the Paz Estenssoro government in 1985 and the structural weaknesses of Bolivian presidentialism, the success of the NPE must be explained in more detail. To neutralize labor, the MNR government declared a state of siege that banished hundreds of labor leaders, including COB leader Juan Lechín Oquendo, to remote jungle towns. It is worth recalling that the COB sabotaged every attempt by the Siles government to impose austerity. In the process, however, organized labor also eroded the effectiveness and legitimacy of strikes. Thus, when 23,000 mine workers were fired, the COB barely mustered enough support to call a general strike.

As in most presidential systems, in Bolivia the continuation of a state of siege depends on congressional approval.[13] Almost immediately, opposition groups in Congress set in motion interpellation maneuvers to counter the launching of the NPE and the state of siege. Owing to its association with Siles and the UDP and its humiliating defeat in the general elections, the left received little popular support for their congressional maneuvers. The only left-of-center party of significance was Jaime Paz Zamora's MIR, which had shrewdly abandoned the UDP and recast the party in more acceptable social democratic circles. In short, left-of-center groups in Congress lacked the votes to overturn the state of siege.

The only real threat in Congress came from General Banzer's ADN. Shortly after launching the NPE Paz Estenssoro moved to form a so-called Pacto por la Democracia, aimed mainly at securing congressional ratification for the state of siege. Beyond the patriotic gestures and democratic rhetoric, the pact provided legislative support for the NPE in exchange for an ADN share of state patronage. Because the MNR had seized upon many of the

---

middle-class bureaucrats. For an analysis of the privatization objectives of the NPE, consult Gamarra (1990).

13 See Article 111 of the Bolivian constitution. This is the main reason why Siles Zuazo was unable to launch a state of siege to control unrest between 1982 and 1985.

elements of ADN's economic stabilization program, Banzer was put into an untenable situation. He could either oppose the NPE for purely political reasons or support a program designed by members of his own economic team. A secret addendum (signed by the MNR and ADN in May 1988) provided for rotating the presidency between the two parties given that the MNR pledged to support Banzer's candidacy in the 1989 general elections. On a smaller scale, the Pacto por la Democracia introduced elements similar to those present in Colombia's governing pact between Liberals and Conservatives: a share in state patronage and a mechanism to ensure the rotation of the presidency between the MNR and ADN. In short, the pact was one of the most significant attempts at institutionalizing a governing arrangement between the government and the principal opposition party.

The Pacto por la Democracia revealed a basic reality about multiparty presidential systems. To govern presidents must be able to form and sustain coalitions in Congress to support their policy initiatives. Because the pact granted the executive a majority in Congress, decision-making authority was concentrated in the cabinet level of the executive branch.[14]

The pact allowed the president to overcome the severe conflict between weak executives and an opposition-controlled legislature. As was evident during the Siles Zuazo period, this tension made the parliamentary characteristics of the system more salient. Although this conflict was temporarily resolved by the Pacto, unless this contradiction is resolved through constitutional amendments or electoral reforms, every future president will be forced to replicate a version of the pact in order to govern. Paradoxically, this is both the principal strength and the main weakness of the system.

One of the most significant aspects about the pact was that it allowed Paz Estenssoro to overcome the problem of dual legitimacy that had plagued Siles Zuazo. Defenders of the arrangement argued that because the first- and second-place finishers in the 1985 elections entered into the pact, approximately 55% of the electorate was duly represented. That the MNR placed second was an important consideration in Paz Estenssoro's decision to enter into a governing pact with the winner of the elections.

In 1985 in Bolivia the key to forming and sustaining the pact rested mainly on the ability of Paz Estenssoro and General Bánzer to control their respective parties and maintain discipline in the coalition.[15] Owing largely

---

14 For a similar analysis see Conaghan, Malloy, and Abugattas (1990).

15 Throughout the three-year duration of the pact, members of ADN and the MNR complained about the alliance. MNR militants were upset by the loss of sources of patronage and the perceived loss of the party's traditional populist electorate. ADN members, in turn, did not trust the MNR's promises of support for Banzer's presidential bid in 1989.

to their stature, no faction could significantly challenge the grip of these two men over their respective parties. Thus, a crucial factor in the formation and maintenance of this pact was the role of statesmanship and old-fashioned caudillismo.

As some have argued (Malloy 1989) the pact resolved the institutional dilemmas of Bolivia's hybrid presidential system but ratified the significance of patronage. Paradoxically, the pact increased party patronage pressures on public employment despite the high-flown neoliberal rhetoric of reducing the size of the state. This logic also undermined the president's ability to assert authority over the state bureaucracy. The situation was made worse by the fact that the MNR had surrendered government posts to the MIR in return for its vote in Congress for Paz Estenssoro. After the signing of the pact the government was forced to generate patronage to feed the demands of three party organizations. In short, Paz Estenssoro's government faced Bolivia's most pressing problem: the need to provide employment to the dependent middle classes. As in other Latin American nations, in Bolivia *empleomanía* (the pursuit of patronage) drives the logic of political party competition and is crucial to the survival of presidents.

By emulating certain parliamentary features President Paz Estenssoro was also able to transcend the problems associated with job factionalism. To implement the NPE he established an economic cabinet team headed by Gonzalo Sanchez de Lozada, the "super" minister of planning, who became a de facto prime minister for economic affairs. Paz also established a political cabinet, headed by Foreign Affairs Minister Guillermo Bedregal, to control party discipline. In setting up two quasi–prime ministerial posts, Paz Estenssoro insulated himself from the day-to-day party squabbles and the battles constantly faced by the economic team. While this style proved successful for Paz Estenssoro, it would be difficult to replicate.[16]

From the perspective of institutionalizing this style of governing, the key was to reform the electoral mechanisms that had given birth to Bolivia's complex multiparty system. ADN and MNR strategists envisioned a two-party-dominant system. The opposition headed by Jaime Paz Zamora's MIR charged the two allies with attempting to establish a new "hegemonic" party; instead, the MIR proposed a new electoral court staffed by members of the top three vote getters in 1985. In a round of horse trading, the MIR's

Weekly meetings of representatives from each party resolved many of these issues. But in the main, the role and presence of both Bánzer and Paz Estenssoro prevented party discipline from breaking down earlier.

16 For a similar analysis, consult Malloy (1989).

electoral reform proposals were accepted in exchange for its support for a new tax code.

As some have noted (e.g., Mayorga 1989), the principal objective of the 1986 Electoral Law was to concentrate parliamentary representation in a few parties (ADN, MNR, MIR) through the revision of the allocation formula.[17] The authors of the new law believed the reforms could prevent the atomization of political parties and would make the National Congress into a more efficient legislative body. In short, these electoral reforms aimed to reestablish presidential supremacy through enhancing the advantage of the larger parties. Time would tell that the electoral reforms, especially the makeup of the national and departmental electoral courts, only added to the problems of electing presidents. Because Congress was given the authority to elect the members of the electoral court, the new law paradoxically positioned the ADN and MIR for a joint assault on the MNR during the 1989 general elections.

The May 1986 approval of the electoral reforms marked an important turning point for Bolivia's hybrid presidential system. Upon being signed into law by Paz Estenssoro, the MIR announced it would carry out a "constructive" opposition in Congress. This announcement could be interpreted as the MIR's official endorsement of the 1985 neoliberal reforms. For the next three years the Pacto por la Democracia and the MIR's mild opposition allowed Paz Estenssoro's presidency to impose two more congressionally sanctioned states of siege, delivering punishing blows from which organized labor has yet to recover.[18] The pact also allowed the imposition of NPE-related legislation, including the new tax code and three successive national budgets.

Although the Pacto por la Democracia demonstrated that formal congressional coalitions are essential to stability and effective government under presidential systems, it also revealed that governing pacts are seldom flexible enough to become viable electoral coalitions. Despite the pact's successes in forcing through the NPE and related legislation and the fact that popular support for the policy initiatives of the MNR government was quite high,

17 Under the previous (1956) law, even a party that had not obtained a "simple quota" of votes (defined as total valid votes divided by district magnitude) could participate in the allocation of seats remaining after allocation of quotas. Those seats were allocated by largest remainders, a procedure that tends to favor the smaller parties, when the quota is the simple quota. The 1986 law requires that a party receive a quota in order to be eligible for remainder seats.
18 The MIR's votes were not necessary to impose a state of siege; however, it is important to note that the MIR did not join any interpellation maneuvers, which could have threatened the government's attempt to defeat organized labor's strikes.

the MNR government could not survive the 1989 election campaign. At issue was the refusal of the MNR to live up to the terms of the secret May 1988 addendum that had ensured support for General Banzer's candidacy. Once again the patronage logic of the political parties destabilized the Bolivian political process. Despite the "modern" tone between 1985 and 1989, old ways of doing politics, specifically the determinant role of patronage and clientelism, survived as political parties revealed that they were interested more in controlling state patronage than in ruling effectively.

Based on the belief that popular support for the NPE could lead the MNR to an outright victory in the elections, the MNR named as its candidate Gonzalo Sánchez de Lozada, the "super" minister of planning and one of the principal architects of the 1985 stabilization measures. Sánchez de Lozada promptly broke the pact with ADN and conducted a bitter negative campaign that mimicked the worst of U.S. presidential campaigns.[19]

The MNR's campaign style and the decision to break the pact proved fateful. Although Sánchez de Lozada won a slight plurality, 23.07% to Banzer's 22.7% and Jaime Paz Zamora's 19.6%, neither the ADN nor the MIR would contemplate supporting the MNR's claim to the presidency. The insult of breaking the pact, compounded by the tone of the campaign, contributed to the MNR's isolation.[20] As a result, between May and August 1989, Bolivia lurched through three months of intense negotiations between the ADN and MIR and futile attempts by the MNR to strike a deal. As he ordered his party to support Paz Zamora's bid for the presidency on the eve of the convening of Congress to elect the next president, Banzer revealed that the least likely outcome had prevailed.

RETAINING PRESIDENTIAL SUPREMACY: THE ACUERDO PATRIÓTICO

Latin American presidential systems could draw many lessons from the Paz Estenssoro period. The most significant may be that the fundamental instrument required to govern when the president's party lacks a congressional

---

19 The role of Sawyer and Miller, a New York–based public relations firm, was crucial in the decision to break the pact. It was also responsible for the tone of the campaign. For an extension of this analysis, consult Gamarra and Malloy (1990).

20 The fact that together the MIR and ADN controlled the electoral court proved to be the key to the MNR's exclusion. Charges and countercharges of fraud were rampant. In the end the three parties pledged before the Catholic Church that the first priority of the new government would be to reform the electoral law once again.

majority is a ruling political pact between the ruling party and the principal opposition force in Congress. Apart from coordinating legislative actions with presidential initiatives, pacts provide decision-making capacity and efficiency to the executive branch. Pacts such as the Pacto por la Democracia also allow presidents to breach claims to legitimacy from Congress, thus providing the mechanisms to overcome crisis situations.

The ability to make and hold together coalitions that enabled (in the constitutional-legal sense) Paz Estenssoro to act decisively depended upon the institutional feature by which the Congress determines who occupies the top executive post. This parliamentary feature strengthened congressional control over the executive relative to what it would be with a president formally answerable only to the electorate. Thus, Bolivia's hybrid presidentialism was capable of overcoming the problem of dual legitimacies. While parties in Congress complained about the executive (and thereby gave an appearance of dual legitimacy), it was a congressional majority that supported every piece of legislation, especially those related to the NPE.

The Paz Estenssoro period also demonstrated how critical the congressional election of the president is for the balance of power between branches and for interparty relations. Congressional selection of the executive in a multiparty system suggested to every party that another two-party or multiparty coalition would be needed next term. Thus, collaboration among parties was extremely important. In 1989, Bolivian politicians appeared to have achieved an equilibrium that could not have existed were the system purely presidential, especially if the president were elected by a majority runoff.[21] This is not the case, for example, in Peru or Ecuador, where presidents are legitimated only via popular votes in a second-round runoff. In both cases, dual legitimacy constitutes a serious issue. Moreover, a second round has exacerbated tensions between the executive and legislative branches.

These lessons were partially learned by Jaime Paz Zamora, who ruled Bolivia between August 1989 and August 1993 with the support of General Banzer's ADN. Before assuming office Paz Zamora entered into the so-called Acuerdo Patriótico with General Banzer, claiming that they would not sign a document formalizing the arrangement because both leaders had pledged their word of honor.[22]

The new pact emulated many dimensions of the MNR–ADN pact. First and foremost, the coalition government's role was to push through Congress

---

21 I owe this idea to Matthew Shugart. For an expansion of his analysis, see Shugart and Carey (1992).

22 This was mainly a statement aimed at the MNR for its violation of the alternation addendum to the Pacto por la Democracia.

legislation designed to deepen NPE economic reforms. Under the Acuerdo Patriótico, the major problem was to find an "economic personality" that defined the new pact. Pushing through NPE-related legislation gave the new government no distinctive flavor to distinguish it from the MNR period. In January 1990, to overcome this situation Paz Zamora announced Decree No. 22407, intended to replace Decree No. 21060, which had introduced the NPE in 1985. Examined carefully, the new decree – apart from calling for a privatization law and new mining and hydrocarbon investment codes – was simply a ratification of the main premises of the political economy of the Paz Estenssoro government.

Taking a page from the Paz Estenssoro government, Paz Zamora also declared a state of siege to control organized labor's opposition to economic policy. In November 1989, under the Acuerdo Patriótico, hundreds of union leaders were arrested and banished to remote jungle towns. Unlike his predecessor, however, Paz Zamora could not seek congressional approval for his government's actions. Although the coalition controlled a majority in both houses of Congress, it did not command a two-thirds majority required to approve a state of siege.[23]

Using similar mechanisms the coalition also rolled over the opposition in the legislature for the approval of controversial policies, such as new investment laws that allowed for the privatization of hydrocarbon and mining industries. The MNR-led opposition charged the government with resorting to extraconstitutional measures to pass these laws. With no clout in Congress the opposition resorted to the Supreme Court, whose entire membership was named by supporters of the previous MNR government.[24] This is another key dimension that weakened and undermined the effectiveness of the Acuerdo Patriótico. The judiciary became the focus of political conflict as individuals and political groups pressed upon the Supreme Court to review not only all recent economic policy, but also political decisions of President Paz Zamora.[25] The conflict stemmed from a Supreme Court ruling declaring unconstitutional a tax on breweries. Claiming that the ruling was

23 Instead, the congressional leadership dominated by the ADN–MIR coalition declared a recess that lasted for most of the 90-day state of siege. Because the recess was approved without a quorum it correctly gave rise to charges of unconstitutionality.
24 Members of the Supreme Court are elected by the Chamber of Deputies for a 10-year term from a list submitted by the Senate. The MNR had won a majority of seats in the Senate in the 1985 elections (see Table 10.2).
25 Tensions with the Supreme Court began when Paz Zamora turned over to the U.S. Drug Enforcement Administration (DEA) – despite the absence of an extradition treaty – Colonel Luis Arce Gómez and Herlan Echevarría, two former officials of the García Meza government accused of drug trafficking. For an analysis of this conflict, consult Gamarra (1991).

the product of corruption, namely, the bribing of the justices by the two largest brewers in Bolivia, the executive refused to accept the Court's decision. Instead, the Acuerdo Patriótico's coalition initiated a malfeasance trial in the National Congress against eight Supreme Court justices. The MNR escalated the conflict by resubmitting a lawsuit demanding that the Court declare the 1989 elections null and void.

The impasse became one between a united Congress and executive, controlled by the coalition, and the judiciary, controlled by the opposition. As in the past, the preferred outcome was a short-term unconstitutional *salida*.[26] On February 5, 1991, a tentative agreement was reached with the opposition whereby the justices would be forced to step down in return for a new electoral law. When the government appeared to renege on its promises to reform the electoral law, the arrangement temporarily broke down.[27] Faced with declining popular support and accusations of deep-seated corruption, in mid-May 1991, the government allowed the eight suspended Supreme Court justices to return to their posts and a new electoral law was accepted.

Many of the problems facing the coalition had to do with the nature of the governing pact. In contrast to the Pacto por la Democracia, the Acuerdo was a pact between two parties exercising control over the executive branch. It did not constitute an arrangement between a ruling party and the principal opposition force, but rather one between two ruling parties to share power. The opposition was shut out of virtually all major decisions and posts, including membership in congressional committees or leadership posts. This was a key dimension that rendered President Paz Zamora's governing style ineffective.

Unlike the Pacto por la Democracia, the Acuerdo gave the presidency to the third-place finisher, thereby excluding the MNR, which won a plurality in May 1989. Although Banzer won the 1985 elections, the pact with the MNR and the resulting distribution of patronage ended contending claims to legitimacy from the legislature. Moreover, the subsequent informal entry of the MIR as a "loyal" opposition had much to do with the duration and stability of the three-year pact. In contrast, and to reiterate a

---

26 The term *salida* (way out) comes from an interview with a member of the National Congress in November 1984. When asked what the solution was to an impasse between the opposition-controlled legislature and Siles Zuazo's executive, the answer was, "in Bolivia there are no solutions, only *salidas*."

27 The government's bargaining leverage was undermined by the naming of retired colonel Faustino Rico Toro, whom the DEA suspected of ties to the narcotics industry, to head the Fuerzas Especiales de Lucha Contra el Narcotráfico, Bolivia's principal counternarcotics force. In the scandal that followed, the MNR spearheaded efforts to reduce Paz Zamora's term by calling for early elections.

point made earlier, the Acuerdo Patriótico excluded the MNR and most opposition parties from any patronage spoils.[28] The MNR, in turn, challenged the legitimacy of the ADN–MIR government, arguing that the MNR was deprived the presidency by virtue of electoral fraud.

The distribution of patronage among coalition members, however, ran deeper than was the case under the Pacto por la Democracia. While the government announced a new round of firings in the state mining corporation, the patronage requirements for the political class resulted in the establishment of 3 new ministries and 16 vice-ministerial posts.[29] Again the political needs of the pact ran counter to the neoliberal logic of reducing the size of the state. But the main political conflict had little to do with the economic logic of stabilization and everything to do with the exclusion of the MNR and other opposition parties from patronage spoils.

Along these lines the critical conflict was the coalition's refusal to live up to its promises to reform the electoral law by moving the second round of the presidential election from Congress to a direct popular vote and by creating an "apolitical" electoral court. Blocking the MNR's attempts to reform the law in the legislature, the ADN–MIR coalition crafted an alliance formula that aimed to elect General Banzer to the presidency in 1993. As proposed by the leadership of both ruling parties, the presidency would rotate back and forth between the ADN and MIR for the remainder of the 1990s. The opposition interpreted these maneuvers as attempts by the coalition to establish the facade of a two-party system disguising a de facto single-party structure.

As others have noted, locking the opposition out of the rotation of patronage does not bode well for the continuity of the democratic process (Linz 1994; Mainwaring 1993). In Bolivia, these maneuvers by the ruling alliance led to the discussion of scenarios where the opposition resorts to antidemocratic mechanisms to inject itself back into the power and patronage game. Whatever scenario plays itself out, Bolivian presidentialism must address the issue of patronage rotation among all sectors of the dependent middle-class.

As the situation stands in the mid-1990s, the principal political institutions in Bolivia have little or no public support (Gamarra and Malloy

---

28 The only party that has shared in the patronage distribution is Conciencia de Patria (CONDEPA), led by the populist radio and television station owner Carlos Palenque. CONDEPA's share came because it carried the department of La Paz in the 1989 elections.

29 According to one report the Acuerdo Patriótico government had increased the public payroll by 20,000 since August 1989. Comments delivered by Juan Cristóbal Soruco at the conference Democracia y Problemas de Gobernabilidad en Bolivia y América Latina, sponsored by Centro Boliviano de Estudios Multidisciplinarios (CEBEM) and Instituto Latinoamericano de Investigaciones Sociales (ILDIS), La Paz, Bolivia, May 16–18, 1991.

1996). Because political parties, Congress, and the judiciary have extremely low confidence ratings, nontraditional quasi-populist parties and leaders made their appearance in dramatic fashion toward the end of the 1980s. Max Fernández, a controversial brewery owner (Unión Cívica Solidaridad [UCS]) and Carlos Palenque, a radio and television station owner (Conciencia de Patria [CONDEPA]), became the front-runners in many public opinion polls.[30] Much of their support was based on appeals to race and class; however, their strategy is essentially patrimonial.

Fernández traveled extensively around the country building hospitals, sponsoring sporting events, and building patron–client networks. In the eyes of aspiring mestizo, or *cholo* entrepreneurial sectors, Fernández became Bolivia's Horatio Alger: He was a poor *cholo* man from Cochabamba who worked his way from delivering beer to owning the country's largest brewery. The emergence of *"cholo* capital" is quite significant because it represents a challenge to the traditional white, or K'ara, capital that has dominated Bolivian politics.[31]

Palenque, on the other hand, represents what could be termed *lumpen capital*, or the marginal sectors of the city of La Paz. He has become a powerful broker in national politics, although his power base is still La Paz. In many ways, Palenque's television and radio programs have become small-claims courts where La Paz's marginal but large Aymara-speaking population finds a quick resolution to the personal problems it cannot possibly hope to resolve in Bolivia's overburdened, corrupt, and discriminatory justice system.[32] In short, Fernández and Palenque positioned themselves to become powerful political contenders in the 1993 national elections.

PRESIDENTIAL AUTHORITY UNDER SIEGE: THE MNR'S RETURN TO OFFICE

The June 1993 elections brought Gonzalo Sánchez de Lozada into power. This time around the MNR's candidate garnered 34% of the vote, which translated into just short of a majority in the National Congress. The results,

---

30 For an excellent discussion of Carlos Palenque's rise to power and prominence, consult Joaquín Saravia and Godofredo Sandóval (1991).
31 This analysis draws heavily from a presentation delivered by Carlos Toranzo at a seminar entitled The Future of the Bolivian Left sponsored by ILDIS in La Paz, Bolivia, May 20, 1991. Accusing him of making his fortune from cocaine trafficking, the U.S. embassy has been the most nervous critic of Max Fernández. In 1991, however, the United States lifted proscriptions barring Fernández's beer from entering U.S. ports.
32 For an extension of this analysis, consult Gamarra (1991).

while not enough to win the presidency outright, were sufficient to prevent the Acuerdo Patriótico coalition – which came in second with less than 25% – or any other party from laying a claim to office. On August 6, Sánchez de Lozada won the congressional round and was sworn into office.

One of the most significant dimensions of the MNR's return to office was the electoral coalition with Víctor Hugo Cárdenas of the Movimiento Revolucionario Tupac Katari (MRTK), a party representing indigeneous people. During the campaign, Sánchez de Lozada and Cárdenas were portrayed as "children of the revolution" in a calculated attempt to tap into those social sectors that were once strongly identified with the MNR, such as the peasantry, but who had long before abandoned the party. As the first Aymara to achieve such high office, Cárdenas brought with him a great deal of expectations for the indigenous sectors of Bolivia. Cárdenas delivered a huge voting bloc of mainly rural Aymara campesinos to the MNR. Moreover, to prevent the growth of guerrilla-type movements that used ethnic symbols to mobilize support, Cárdenas represented the most important hope for bridging ethnic and linguistic cleavages and extending Bolivia's young democracy to the indigenous masses.[33]

Although Sánchez de Lozada and Cárdenas owned a majority in Congress, they still required coalitions to ensure smooth sailing for the implementation of the president's ambitious reform agenda. The key then, as before, was to build a coalition with opposition parties. In contrast to the coalitions that created the Pacto por la Democracia and the Acuerdo Patriótico, however, the MNR did not have to make a pact with the second- or third-place parties.

Sánchez de Lozada's search for a governing partner culminated in two surprises. On July 2, the MNR struck a deal, dubbing it the "Pacto por la Gobernabilidad" (Governability Pact), with Max Fernández, Bolivia's controversial beer baron and chief of the UCS. As in all previous pacts, the distribution of key government posts in exchange for the UCS's 21 seats in Congress sealed the agreement.[34] Moreover, Sánchez de Lozada brokered the

33 Since 1989 at least three such groups have made their appearance in Bolivia. The first, Zárate Wilka, has all but disappeared owing to the government's crackdown following the May 1989 assassination of two young U.S. Mormon missionaries, for which it was accused. A second group, the Ejército de Liberación Nacional–Nestor Paz Zamora, which boasted links to Peru's Tupac Amaru group, was dismantled after the kidnapping and subsequent assassination of Jorge Londsdale, a prominent businessman, for which it was accused. The third group, the Ejército Guerrillero Tupac Katari, has been more resilient; it has resorted only to occasional bombings of electric utility stations and the like.

34 Under the terms of the MNR–UCS pact, Fernández's followers secured one ministry, two undersecretary posts, two ambassadorships, the presidency of one regional development corporation, and the first-vice-presidency of both the Chamber of Deputies and the Senate.

first meeting between Fernández and the U.S. ambassador since accusations surfaced of his alleged ties to narcotics trafficking. The MNR's deal making did not end there. On July 7, Sánchez de Lozada signed the Pacto por el Cambio (Pact for Change), with the Movimiento Bolivia Libre (MBL, Free Bolivia Movement) doling out yet another set of government posts.[35]

A FRAGILE RULING COALITION

President Sánchez de Lozada made institutional reform the centerpiece of his government. The basic theme of the new government was that the process of reform initiated in the mid-1990s under the NPE had suffered a severe setback under the Acuerdo Patriótico government. Political institutions were not modernized and economic reforms were not consolidated.

Sánchez de Lozada put forth a so-called Plan de Todos, that promised a "social market economy" alternative to the rigid continuity of the NPE. The plan included seven "pillars": attracting investment, creating jobs, ensuring economic stability, improving health and education, encouraging popular participation, changing the role of government, and combating corruption. The key to the MNR's investment proposal rested on the "capitalization" of public enterprises, a significant departure from earlier privatization schemes. In February 1994, the MNR–MBL–UCS coalition in the Bolivian Congress approved a "capitalization law" that essentially authorizes a joint-venture association in which a state enterprise contributes its assets and a private investor contributes an equivalent amount in capital. In theory, this would double the original value of the enterprise. Once an enterprise is capitalized the investor would receive 50% of the company's stock and sole management control. The remaining stock would be distributed evenly among all Bolivians over the age of 18.[36] The government also claimed that this program would result in the creation of half a million new jobs.

The capitalization law also promised that revenue from the sale of state enterprises (expected to reach about U.S.$8 billion) would be employed in a pension fund for all Bolivians over the age of 18. Government economists argued that the capitalization of state enterprises would be equivalent to investing approximately 35% of Bolivia's GDP.

35 The MBL was promised one ministry, key congressional posts, and at least one embassy. Araníbar and the MBL extracted a high price considering this party won only 5% of the vote. Subsequently, Araníbar was named minister of foreign affairs.

36 In theory, these shares would be handled by pension fund administrators on behalf of these estimated 3.2 million Bolivians, who would then apply their shares toward a retirement fund. Constitutional reform of August 1994 lowered the voting age from 21 to 18.

While the premise of turning over the ownership of state assets to Bolivian citizens and workers and establishing a pension fund was an important shift from pure privatization, its implementation was extremely difficult. In 1995, the government successfully sold ENTEL (Empresa Nacional de Telecomunicaciones) (telecommunications), ENDE (Empresa Nacional de Electricidad, National Electricity [Power] Company) (electricity), and LAB (Lloyd Aéreo Boliviano) (airlines) to foreign investors. Nevertheless, the capitalization scheme stirred great passions – ranging from labor's claim that workers would be fired en masse to the ADN's claim that the government was giving away Bolivian assets to foreigners. Moreover, the government's private pension plan scheme was met with equal suspicion. Most controversial, however, was the attempted capitalization of YPFB (Yacimientos Petroliferos Fiscales de Bolivia, Bolivian Petroleum Company) (hydrocarbons) which was postponed until mid-1996 because of opposition from labor and others.

THE PLAN DE TODOS, GOVERNANCE, AND PRESIDENTIALISM

Implementing the government's reform agenda and governing Bolivia proved more difficult that Sánchez de Lozada anticipated. His problems in governing were rooted mainly in two significant factors: the fragility of his coalition and the timing of his reform attempts.

First, the ruling coalition faced difficulties controlling its ranks when both interparty and intraparty feuding proved destabilizing. A severe conflict between the president's party and the members of the cabinet was especially problematic. As in most presidential systems where a president controls the patronage in the cabinet, leaving control over the legislature to old party hacks, Sánchez de Lozada named an independent cabinet made up of technocrats and businessmen and left Congress in the hands of the MNR's old guard. A joke circulating among the opposition in the early months illustrates the problem. According to this version, Sánchez de Lozada forgot that to govern Bolivia one must always sign a pact with the MNR. These tensions eventually produced a cabinet crisis in March 1994, forcing Sánchez de Lozada to replace the most prominent private-sector ministers with members of the MNR. Another cabinet shift in September 1995 had similar characteristics.

The ruling coalition proved to be extremely unstable because of numerous outbursts from Max Fernández and the UCS.[37] In any given week unsubstantiated rumors abounded about a UCS departure from the cabinet. Fernández, who felt excluded from the decision-making process, lashed out against the MBL, and finally withdrew from the coalition in December 1994, only to rejoin and depart again in a huff in mid-1995. His party retained control over the Ministry of Defense and in September 1995 was granted the Ministry of Sustainable Development. The reality of the situation, however, was that beyond the specific and very limited role it played in the cabinet and the crucial votes it provided in the National Congress, the UCS was not very significant.

Max Fernández's untimely death on November 26, 1995, in an airplane accident may signal the end of the UCS. Without the caudillo this party will likely disappear, and its members will seek accomodation within the MNR or other larger parties. Because the UCS and CONDEPA shared a similar constituency, the latter alone is likely to sway the UCS followers, who are up for grabs.

By the same token, the MBL found itself in the difficult position of having to defend policies that it opposed over the preceding eight years, such as U.S.-designed counternarcotics programs and deepening neoliberal economic reforms. Only a national summit with Sánchez de Lozada in January 1994 cemented the MNR–MBL relationship. Antonio Araníbar, the MBL foreign minister, performed a crucial ceremonial role, and at least according to some opinion polls in early 1994, was the most popular member of the cabinet. A more accurate picture would reveal that the MNR engulfed both the MBL and UCS and that their fate rested entirely on Sánchez de Lozada's. Despite attempts by members of the MBL to retain their identity independently of the MNR, the fact remains that the future of this small band of well-intentioned leftists is tied intimately with the fortunes of the MNR government.

Concerning the second problem, the timing of reform attempts, the Sánchez de Lozada government raised numerous expectations that it would alleviate the social costs of economic reform and impose some sort of "social market" model. However, to prevent an economic crisis the government was forced to tighten austerity measures in its first two years. In contrast to the 1980s, though, social tolerance for austerity had decreased considerably. In the context of a fragile ruling coalition, the government was incapable

---

37 In March 1994, the UCS retained control over the Ministry of Defense when Sánchez de Lozada agreed to major changes in his cabinet. The outgoing UCS minister attempted in vain to break out of Max Fernández's control.

of pushing ahead without facing resistance from labor, students, regional groups, and opposition political parties.

President Sánchez de Lozada faced an all-out battle with opposition political parties from the very day he took office. In November 1993, for example, a few members of the two former ruling parties (ADN and MIR) called for his impeachment and/or the convocation of early elections. Then in December, when the MNR-controlled National Congress amended the electoral law, the opposition parties charged Sánchez with attempting to rig the rules of the game to favor his party.

But these moves were not significant since these parties faced severe internal crises and scandalous charges of corruption.[38] The unraveling of the opposition warrants more concern because it is intrinsically linked to the explosion of political corruption that plagued Bolivian democracy and has had serious repercussions for the governability of the country. Since leaving office in August 1993, the ADN became engulfed in tremendous internal political battles that forced General Banzer out of retirement. Banzer's return from early retirement confirmed the institutional weaknesses of the ADN, especially the inability to name a viable successor. No single individual other than Banzer appears capable of bringing the party together in time for the 1997 elections.

In many ways, ADN's internal crisis was fueled by speculation of widespread corruption during the 1989–93 term. Concern for corruption in office became the single most significant factor in the almost total collapse of the MIR. Since August 1993, former president Paz Zamora attempted to distance himself from his party and to pursue lofty international objectives that included possible stints at the Wilson Center in Washington, D.C., and serving on the International Peace Commission in Chiapas, Mexico. These goals, however, were dramatically altered with the March 1994 accusations by the Special Counternarcotics Force (Fuerza Especial de Lucha Contra el Narcotráfico [FELCN]) that widespread linkages between the MIR and narcotraffickers have existed since at least 1987.[39] These accusations extended to the entire leadership structure of the MIR and all but ended the party's quest for a return to political office at mid-decade. In a dramatic

---

38 Political parties were not the only ones facing egregious charges of corruption. Perhaps the most serious crisis concerned allegations of corruption against two members of the Supreme Court. The crisis began in mid-1993, when relatives of a member of the court solicited a bribe from Antonio Ibarra, a former official of the Nicaraguan government who was facing extradition procedures. With U.S. assistance, the Bolivian police recorded the conversation and proceeded to indict the Supreme Court justices. In June 1994, a Senate trial found the two justices guilty, sentenced them to two years in prison, and barred from ever holding public office.

39 The accusations detailed by the FELCN are reported in Gamarra (forthcoming).

sequence of events, drug traffickers outlined in painful detail before a congressional committee the manner in which Paz Zamora and the MIR had allegedly come to rely on the cocaine industry to finance their electoral campaign in 1989. The impact of these accusations was great. On March 25, 1994, Paz Zamora resigned from politics, claiming that "errors were made during his administration but no crimes occurred." In December, Oscar Eid Franco, the party's principal strategist, was arrested and as of this writing has not been released.

The MNR has not been exempt from charges of corruption. In September 1995, the government was rocked by allegations that several high-ranking members of the party had close relations with a trafficker who shipped four tons of cocaine in a DC-6 to Mexico from the country's principal airport. The planeload of cocaine was intercepted in Lima, Peru, only after DEA authorities in Bolivia alerted Peruvian police. Although the party dodged the accusations, few doubted that the *narcoavión* scandal, as it was named, would have a serious impact on the MNR's chances in 1997. Already there is talk that a few of the potential candidates for office have been tainted by the scandal. If this were to be the case, then the MNR could very well follow the MIR.

With the demise of the Acuerdo Patriótico, the troubled future of the ADN and MIR, and the implications of the *narcoavión* scandal, the main opposition appears to be CONDEPA, the populist party headed by Carlos Palenque, which in the December 1993 municipal election managed not only to expand its support outside of the department of La Paz, but to again win the mayor's office in the capital city. It is extremely unlikely, however, that CONDEPA will pose a serious challenge outside of La Paz. In this context, a return to the presidency by General Hugo Banzer in 1997 is not out of the question.

REFORMS TO BOLIVIA'S HYBRID PRESIDENTIALISM

Despite the weaknesses of the ruling coalition, the first twelve months of the Sánchez de Lozada government witnessed the congressional approval of five significant laws: the Cabinet Restructuring Law, the Capitalization Law, the Popular Participation Law, the Education Reform Law, and the Constitutional Amendments Law. As far as government officials were concerned this body of legislation provided a reform agenda as far reaching as Bolivia's 1952 National Revolution. But the difficulties in securing approval were numerous and revealed both the weakness of the coalition and the government's inability to sell its message.

In August 1994, 35 articles of the constitution were amended through the Constitutional Amendments Law, including: direct election of half of the members of the lower house of Congress from single-member districts; an increase in the length of terms for presidents, members of Congress, mayors, and municipal council members to five years, with general and municipal elections alternating every two and a half years; clear procedures favoring the direct election of the president and all mayors; a lowering of the voting age to 18; an increase in the powers to departmental prefects; and departmental assemblies composed of national representatives doing double duty as the only assembly members of the department from which they were chosen by the single-member-district procedure; the establishment of an independent human rights ombudsman; and the establishment of a constitutional tribunal.

These reforms are significant and warrant an extended discussion beyond the scope of this chapter. For our purposes the most significant reforms have to do with the way in which both presidents and members of the lower house will be elected beginning in 1997. Under the terms of the enacted reforms if no candidate achieves 50% of the vote, the congressional runoff will be decided between the top *two* candidates. This modification may prevent the impasses that characterized nearly all elections since the transition and ensure the quick election of a president.

The manner in which members of the lower house will be elected may force legislators to develop closer bonds with the districts they ostensibly represent. Representatives from single-member districts will be forced to campaign in their respective districts and may not be as tied to the party patronage structure as is currently the case. Charges abound, however, that two types of legislators have been created – those elected through single-member districts, who will see themselves as true representatives, and the rest, who will be seen as pure party hacks. Moreover, although its supporters claim that this new system will increase the chances of a congressional majority, there is no guarantee that this reform will foster coalition building, the only strength of the Bolivian system. The results of these reforms will not be felt until the end of the decade.

GOVERNABILITY UNDER THE NEW RULES

President Sánchez de Lozada's term has been marked by a series of confrontations with labor, students, coca growers, regional organizations, and the opposition. Throughout 1995, the government faced numerous strikes by the COB, a teachers' strike and various university student demonstrations demanding an end to educational reform, an incipient separatist movement from the southernmost department of Tarija, and a potential insurrection by coca-growing peasants in the Chapare Valley.

Two explanations may account for the resurgence of social conflict in Bolivia. First, the fragility of the ruling coalition has emboldened the op-position and the numerous groups that have challenged the government. Second, the economic strategy has done little for the Bolivian working class, which, after 10 years of neoliberalism, is expecting greater results. Whatever accounts for the resurgence of social conflict the result has been the same. The government resorted to the same mechanisms of the past 10 years to control labor and peasant unrest. Sánchez de Lozada declared a state of siege on April 18, 1995, for a 90-day period. In July it was extended for another 90 days. When the state of siege was finally lifted, social unrest continued, with students, coca growers, members of opposition parties, and others still on the warpath. The state-of-siege option may no longer be the one required to control unrest.

CONCLUSION

Bolivia's experience confirms the principal institutional problems faced by presidential systems in the context of democratization. Although the ex-tremity of the Bolivian case allows for the examination of trends obscured in other systems, it is still not prudent to generalize this national experience to other Latin American countries. Caution is warranted given the hybrid nature of Bolivia's presidentialism. Nevertheless, the Bolivian case provides a few conceptual lessons that could clarify the dilemmas faced by presiden-tial systems.

The Bolivian hybrid presidential system created mechanisms that ena-bled at least three presidents to overcome institutional crises. Ruling coa-litions have not been enough, however, to overcome constitutional and electoral mechanisms that give the Bolivian National Congress the power to elect the president when no candidate obtains a majority. As a result, in Bolivia three distinct types of coalitions have been formed: electoral coali-tions, which allow parties to establish a broad platform to appeal to wider segments of the electorate; congressional coalitions, which enable the elec-tion of a president; and a ruling coalition to govern the country. These principal characteristics anchor the entire system in the role and functioning of political parties and Congress. As long as this is the case Bolivia's system will not be strictly presidential, but a hybrid wherein the legislature plays a critical role.

One of the ways to overcome the dilemma of reconstituting alliances is to convert a ruling coalition into a viable electoral vehicle. As the breakdown of the Pacto por la Democracia revealed, ruling coalitions lack the flexibility to become viable electoral alliances because alternating positions in the executive branch between the members of the coalition entails recomposing client–patron networks and redistributing patronage. Moreover, to win elections political parties must form broad conjunctural alliances and propose populist platforms. By the same token, converting an electoral or congressional coalition into a viable governing coalition has proven extremely difficult.

One of the keys to institutionalizing the present system will be to form effective governing alliances that can fare well during electoral battles. Alliances must be able to transcend postelectoral bargaining. These objectives must take into consideration that in Bolivia the principal function of elections has been to allow competing leaders to restructure patronage networks periodically. In short, the recomposition of client–patron networks and redistribution of political patronage is the Achilles' heel of Bolivia's hybrid presidential system.

The critical issue raised by the Bolivian experience is the impact that the method of selecting the executive has had on policy outcomes. Owing to this fact, a recurrent need to form coalitions has paradoxically become both the strength and the weakness of the system. Coalitions – such as the Pacto por la Democracia, the Acuerdo Patriótico, and the Pacto por la Gobernabilidad – have enabled executives to overcome recalcitrant congressional opposition to imposing economic stabilization measures. By demonstrating a capacity to enter into long-term pacts, these coalitions have also revealed a degree of political maturity in Bolivia's political class. As recently as the mid-1980s it would have been improbable and even absurd to suggest the possibility of a coalition between ADN and MIR; this capacity to form coalitions gave the system a much needed dose of political stability. It is noteworthy, therefore, that Bolivia's hybrid presidential system does possess the capability to carry forth a democratization process while simultaneously implementing draconian austerity measures. The permanency of these trends, however, is still questionable, as events under the Sánchez de Lozada administration point out.

Coalitions have also served to shut out the opposition from the patronage spoils of the system and from the decision-making process. In domestic policy, the opposition has been excluded from participation in (or discussion of) the enactment of key legislation concerning the mining codes, investment laws, and the like. This situation has also revealed itself rather dramatically in the manner in which the government has negotiated foreign policy, especially counternarcotics agreements with the United States. Owing to this exclusionary style, Congress has demonstrated a lack of knowledge regarding the details of international agreements that it must approve and the technicalities of economic policy. This exclusionary pattern does not bode well for the future as opposition groups consider extrasystemic ways to influence policy making.

What can be learned from the recent Bolivian experience? First, we now know that imposing and sustaining market-oriented reforms in a small and poor country is a very difficult task indeed. A decade after the imposition of Decree No. 21060, Bolivia has reached a critical juncture. Although the country's economy has grown steadily – averaging 2.5% per year – this has not been enough to deal with declining socioeconomic conditions. Three democratically elected governments since 1985 have imposed states of exception to deal with labor and other social unrest. In the process, they have relied on the armed forces to engage in public security missions.

Second, the Bolivian experience suggests that decision making must be largely executive centered, with the Congress playing little or no legislative role other than approving executive initiatives. To achieve this, stable ruling coalitions are essential to avoid executive–legislative impasses. In some sense, however, this style of rule has resulted in a profound crisis within all major political institutions. Political parties are perhaps more disconnected from society in 1995 than at any time since the transition to democracy in 1982. Citizens are least confident in the legislature and the judicial branch. Third, the Bolivian case suggests that profound constitutional reforms are difficult to enact but even more difficult to implement. The Sánchez de Lozada administration's promise to resolve age-old problems of representation and administration of justice will take hold and have an impact only over time. Few in Bolivia, however, are willing to give the reforms a chance to succeed, given that short-term considerations are the only ones of significance in this country. Finally, it is clear that successive Bolivian governments have done quite a bit over the course of the past decade to fit into the neoliberal wave that has engulfed the Americas. Yet the relative insignificance of the country in regional affairs has resulted in little international interest or, more importantly, investment. Innovative ideas such as the capitalization initiative of the current government have received extensive praise at international financial institutions, but the program cannot survive on outside praise alone given a great deal of domestic political opposition.

11

CONCLUSION: PRESIDENTIALISM AND THE PARTY SYSTEM

Scott Mainwaring and Matthew Soberg Shugart

One of the fundamental arguments of this book has been that presidentialism has significant variations. Although this statement sounds intuitively sensible, little careful work has been done to conceptualize how presidentialism varies. In conjunction with Chapter 1, in this Conclusion we attempt to advance the efforts to develop such a conceptual map, oriented especially toward the Latin American cases. Here we analyze the party system characteristics on which Latin American countries vary and discuss how these features interact with the variations in legislative powers discussed in Chapter 1.

We argue that the nature of the party system, in particular the number of parties, makes a fundamental difference in how presidential systems function. The number of parties affects the likelihood of at least general compatibility between the assembly and the president. With a highly fragmented multiparty system, no party controls close to a majority. This situation can be problematic because the president typically has difficulties building reliable governing coalitions. The logical opposite situation, in which the president's party consistently has a majority, is not necessary or even desirable, but presidentialism usually works better if the president's party is a major party with a sizable legislative contingent. On this dimension there are marked contrasts among Latin American presidential systems. In some countries, presidents' parties consistently have at least 40% of the

Grace Ivana Deheza, Argelina Figueiredo, Mark Jones, and Jeff Weldon offered helpful criticisms of earlier drafts of this chapter.

seats in congress, whereas in others they usually hold a small minority of seats.

Presidentialism is also affected by how disciplined the political parties are. Disciplined parties afford a level of predictability and facilitate executive–legislative relations. However, extremely disciplined parties can actually obstruct presidential–assembly relations when the president does not have a majority and may obviate the advantages of presidentialism when he or she does. In terms of party discipline, the contrasts among Latin American democracies are striking, ranging from the disciplined legislative parties found in Venezuela and Mexico to the comparatively undisciplined parties that dominate electoral competition in Brazil and Colombia.

We then explore the ways in which party and electoral legislation shapes the number of parties and their degree of discipline. If the number of parties and the nature of party discipline conditions how presidentialism functions, it is meaningful to examine the institutional factors that shape these outcomes. We show that electoral rules and sequences have a powerful impact on the number of parties, on party discipline, and, therefore, ultimately on how presidentialism is likely to function.

The issues discussed in this chapter intersect with a president's legislative powers to affect how presidentialism functions. A president may have great formal powers, including the right to enact new legislation by decree, yet be stymied in effecting real change by a legislature in which his or her own party either holds a small minority of seats or, although holding a majority or large plurality, is deeply factionalized and undisciplined. The first situation describes Brazil, as Mainwaring's chapter shows, and the second one describes Colombia, as Archer and Shugart's chapter discusses. On the other hand, a president's formal powers may be limited, but if the president's party has a legislative majority and is highly disciplined, he or she may appear to be all-powerful, as Weldon indicates is the case in Mexico. The president's ability to enact policy reforms that he or she may have campaigned in favor of is therefore a product of the formal powers of the presidency interacting with the president's standing vis-à-vis the parties represented in congress.[1] In turn, the number of parties and their degree of internal cohesiveness is connected to the electoral system used for congressional and presidential elections.

---

1 Of course, nothing guarantees that a president's policies will succeed just because he or she is able to enact certain policies. Policies may be ill advised or designed, or the state may lack the bureaucratic capacity to implement them effectively.

MAJORITY GOVERNMENT UNDER PRESIDENTIALISM

One of the most important questions in executive–legislative relations in presidential systems is the relative size of the president's party. Just as is the case with parliamentary systems, the logic of presidential systems hinges on whether a majority party or a coalition of parties provides support for the president. Some analysts have observed that presidentialism is frequently prone to "minority government" situations in which the president's party lacks a majority of seats in congress (Abranches 1988; Jones forthcoming; Mainwaring 1993). If the president's party holds a distinct minority – say, under one-third of the seats – presidents may have a difficult time piecing together legislative coalitions.

There is a certain tension in whether majority government is the most desired situation in presidential systems. On the one hand, we can expect that executive–legislative relations will be smoother when a president has a majority than when he or she does not. On the other hand, a primary advantage of presidentialism is that it affords more of an opportunity for providing a check on executive power than Westminster parliamentary systems. Checks and balances are overridden to a considerable degree if the president and a *disciplined* majority of the same party have unified control over the government. Thus, although we argue that highly fragmented party systems tend to be problematic with presidentialism and that some degree of party discipline is desirable, the logical extreme of a disciplined single-party majority vitiates the advantage of independent branches of power separately elected to fixed terms.

Significant party system fragmentation is often a problem for presidentialism because it increases the likelihood of the executive having little legislative support, and therefore, of executive–legislative deadlock. With significant party system fragmentation, the president's party will not have anything close to a majority of seats in congress, so the president will be forced to rely on a coalition. Unfortunately, interparty coalitions tend to be more fragile in presidential systems for two reasons (Lijphart 1994; Mainwaring 1993).[2]

First and foremost, whereas party coalitions in parliamentary systems generally take place after the election and are binding, in presidential sys-

---

2 More research needs to be done on governing coalitions in presidential systems. Although there are reasons to believe that such coalitions tend to be more fragile than those in parliamentary systems, specific institutional factors affect the viability of coalitions in both parliamentary and presidential systems.

tems they often take place before the election and are not binding past election day. Executive power is not formed through postelection agreements among parties and is not divided among several parties that are co-responsible for governing, even though members of several parties often participate in cabinets. Governing coalitions in presidential systems can differ markedly from electoral coalitions. It is also common in multiparty parliamentary systems for legislative coalitions and governmental coalitions to differ somewhat, but usually only on peripheral policy matters. If a legislative majority opposes the cabinet on core areas of cabinet policy, a change of government is likely through the confidence vote procedure. Such an option does not exist in a presidential system.

Given the separation of powers, an agreement among parties may pertain only to congressional matters, with no binding implication for relations between the parties and the president. Several parties may support the same presidential candidate during the electoral campaign, but this does not ensure their support once the winner assumes office. Even though members of several parties often participate in cabinets, the parties as collectivities are not responsible for the government. Parties or individual legislators can join the opposition without bringing down the government, so presidents sometimes end their terms with little support in congress.

Second, in some presidential systems, the commitment of individual legislators to support an agreement negotiated by the party leadership is not secure. The extension of a cabinet portfolio does not necessarily imply disciplined party support for the president, as it does in most parliamentary systems. The commitment of individual legislators to vote the party line varies a great deal, for reasons mentioned later in this chapter, ranging from the extremely cohesive congressional parties in Venezuela to the comparatively undisciplined catchall parties in Brazil and Colombia. Weaker discipline reinforces the instability of congressional support for government policy. In contrast, in most parliamentary systems, individual legislators tend to support the government unless their party decides to drop out of the governmental alliance. Members of parliament risk bringing down a government and losing their seats in new elections if they fail to support the government.[3]

These problems in constructing stable interparty coalitions make the combination of fragmented multipartism and presidentialism problematic

[3] The key issue here is whether or not parties are disciplined, and nothing guarantees that they are in parliamentary systems. Nevertheless, the need to support the government serves as an incentive to party discipline in parliamentary systems that is absent in presidential systems. See Epstein (1964).

and help explain the paucity of long-established multiparty presidential democracies. At present, Ecuador, which has had a democracy only since 1979 – and a troubled one at that – is older than any other presidential democracy in the world with an effective number of parties in the legislature of at least 3.5.[4] Only one presidential system with a high number of parties, Chile, has ever sustained democracy for at least 25 consecutive years. There were at least 14 other multiparty presidential democracies before the present wave of democratization, but none lasted longer than the Brazilian regime of 1946–64 (Mainwaring 1993).

Where party system fragmentation is less pronounced, the need for interparty coalitions involving a large number of parties diminishes. The president may not enjoy a majority in congress, but his or her party is certain to be a major party that controls a significant share of the seats. Moreover, unless the president has no veto power, legislative coalitions will almost always need to take into account the preferences of the president and his or her party.[5] This situation should mitigate the problem of competing claims to legitimacy because many legislators have a stake in the success of the president. Conflicts between the legislature and the executive arise, but they tend to be less grave than when the overwhelming majority of legislators is pitted against the president. They may even be healthy for a fuller airing of issues than is sometimes possible in parliamentary systems with limited party system fragmentation, where intraparty or intracoalition disputes may mean the fall of the government.

The problems of the fixed term of office are also mitigated by limited party system fragmentation. The fixed term of office is particularly pernicious when the president's party is in a clear minority, making it difficult for the president to get a program accomplished. In a distinct minority situation, the specter of immobilism and ungovernability is often ubiquitous. It is probably no coincidence that the oldest and most established presidential democracies – the United States, Costa Rica, and Venezuela (between 1973 and 1993) – each has had just two major parties. There is no precise cutoff point below which presidentialism does not function well. In general, however, presidentialism is likely to function better if party system fragmentation is moderate (effective number of legislative parties up

---

4 The effective number of parties is a means of determining how many "serious" parties there are. Its derivation is explained later.
5 The constitutions of Nicaragua (1986) and Venezuela (1961) provide for very weak or nonexistent veto power. As a result, presidents who lacked working majorities sometimes have found themselves and their parties shut out of legislative coalitions. This situation can also occur in Costa Rica on the budget, although not on other types of legislation, as Carey's chapter discusses.

to about 3.5), such that presidents are likely to find a significant bloc of legislators to support their initiatives or sustain their vetoes so that presidents are not marginal to lawmaking.

If a president has legislative decree powers (see Chapter 1), he or she can partially offset a lack of congressional support, thereby averting the problem of immobilism. Indeed, as we suggest later on in this chapter, such strong presidential powers are most likely to be provided in constitutions precisely where parties are weak. A serious problem with presidential systems that permits the president to legislate by decree without prior congressional authorization is that they are more prone than other variants to what O'Donnell (1994) has called "delegative democracy" – a situation of weak institutional development and poor accountability. Moreover, as is argued in the chapters on Brazil and Colombia, even if a president has legislative decree powers, he or she is likely to need congressional support in order to sustain most policy initiatives. Thus, attention to party systems is crucial.

It is not only the number of parties and the share of seats of the president's party that matters. The ideological/policy proximity of parties also affects relations between the executive and the legislature. Following Sartori (1976) and Sani and Sartori (1983), we would expect that greater ideological distances among parties would make for more conflict in executive–legislative relations. If parties with close ideological positions on most key issues control a large share of seats, the need for the president's own party to control a large bloc of seats is reduced, since coalition building becomes easier. Conversely, suppose that the president's party controls a fairly large share of the seats, say 40%, but is isolated on the ideological spectrum and, further, that a majority vote can overturn the president's vetoes. In such a situation, governing is still likely to be difficult despite the substantial bloc of seats held by the president's party. On the other hand, if this same president's veto requires a two-thirds vote to override, then no legislation can be accomplished without the support of the president and his or her party. The result of the first scenario is likely to be a president who is bypassed in the process of making legislation – with resulting conflicts over the process of implementing the laws passed – while in the second scenario, the result might be either compromise or immobilism, depending on the electoral imperatives to make some kind of deal. Having support for a legislative agenda is only one of many factors that determine how successfully presidents govern, but being able to get some legislation accomplished is probably a necessary condition for a successful presidency.

Table 11.1 shows the mean share of congressional seats of the presidents' party and electoral coalition. We have included all the cases in this book,

Table 11.1. *Presidents' parties' mean share of congressional seats in Latin America (percentages)*

Country and period	Years	No. of elections	Presidents' party		Presidents' coalition	
			Lower chamber	Upper chamber	Lower chamber	Upper chamber
Argentina	1983–93	6	48.3	52.0	49.1	52.0
Bolivia	1980–93	4	33.9	47.2		
Brazil						
Ia	1945–50	3	34.8	44.0	52.2	48.6
Ib	1954–62	4	26.0	26.0	44.8	52.0
IIa	1985–90	4[a]	26.9	25.6	37.0	31.8
IIb	1994	1	12.1	13.6	35.4	42.0
Chile						
I	1932–73	18	23.3	20.8	41.6	41.2
II	1989–93	2	31.7	28.3[b]	58.3	46.3[b]
Colombia	1945–49, 1974–94	11	55.2	56.3	55.2	56.3
Costa Rica	1953–94	11	49.6	—	51.8	—
Dominican Republic	1962, 1966–90	8	55.6	69.1		
Ecuador	1978–94	7	22.0	—		
El Salvador						
I	1985–91	4	47.5	—		
II	1994	1	46.4	—		
Honduras	1981–93	4	54.2	—	54.2	
Mexico[c]	1982–91	4	65.8	95.8	65.8	95.8
Nicaragua[c]	1984–90	2	65.4	—		
Paraguay	1993	1	47.5	44.4	—	—

Peru	1980	1	54.4	43.3	54.4	42.2[a]
	1984–90, 1995	3	47.1	40.0[a]	47.1	43.3
Uruguay	1942–71, 1984–94	11	45.6	43.8		41.7[a]
Venezuela	1958–93	8	41.4	47.4	43.2	47.7

[a]Includes the indirect presidential election of 1985.

[b]For Chile II, appointed senators were included in calculating the president's share of Senate seats. If one takes only elected seats, the percentage increases to 34.2% for the presidents' party and 56.6% for the coalition.

[c]These cases are not included in those tables that analyze a relationship among variables (i.e., Tables 11.2, 11.3, and 11.4) because the elections are not sufficiently democratic.

[d]Does not apply to 1995; Peru moved to a unicameral legislature with the constitution of 1993.

Sources: For electoral data, Nohlen (1993); Mainwaring and Scully (1995); individual country studies in this volume. Countries for which we have only one observation (i.e., Paraguay) or that do not meet the criteria for democracy established in Chapter 1 (i.e., Mexico and Nicaragua) are excluded from those tables that explore relationships among variables (Tables 11.2, 11.3, and 11.4).

plus most other Latin American cases with some recent experience of democratic elections. The time period for specific countries in Table 11.1 reflects a basic continuity in electoral rules and sequences. For example, in Brazil, there was a shift from largely concurrent presidential and legislative elections (1945–50) to nonconcurrent ones (1954–62).[6] Conversely, although Uruguay suffered a democratic breakdown in 1973, its democratic elections since 1942 have occurred under roughly similar electoral rules and sequences, so we treat it as one case.

In the great majority of cases, determining the president's party was straightforward. A few presidents (Quadros in Brazil, Ibáñez and Alessandri in Chile; and Caldera [1993] in Venezuela) ran as independents. In such cases, we considered the president's party the largest of those that ran him as their presidential candidate.

In cases where not all the members of a chamber are elected at the same time, where possible we based figures on the composition of the entire chamber, not on the legislative results for that portion of the chamber that was elected in a given year. This includes the Argentine Chamber of Deputies (1985–95), the Argentine Senate (1989–95), the Brazilian Senate (1947–64, 1985–94), the Chilean Senate (1937–73), and the Ecuadoran unicameral legislature (in which, only part of the unicameral legislature is renewed every other election, that is, 1986, 1990, and 1994).

Determining the president's electoral coalition was no easy task because no single source lists this information. We consulted an array of sources and scholars and ultimately included the parties listed in the appendix to this chapter. We include this appendix partly to clarify methodological choices made in Table 11.1 and partly to bring this information together in one source. There are, however, occasional discrepancies among sources regarding what parties formed part of presidents' electoral coalitions.

The coalition figures reflect the legislative share of seats won by parties that formally supported the winning presidential candidate during his or her campaign. We did *not* attempt to account for situations in which (a) some parties defected from the electoral coalition after the elections or (b) other parties, despite not having supported the electoral coalition, subsequently joined the governing coalition. That is, our focus is exclusively on electoral coalitions and not governing coalitions. In cases where presidents are elected by majority runoff, we used the presidents' coalition in the first round. For nonelected presidents (e.g., Café Filho, Goulart, and Franco in Brazil), we did not compute a figure for the electoral coalition but did for

6 However, in 1947 there were nonconcurrent Senate elections.

the share of seats of the president's party, since this latter information is still relevant.

For nonconcurrent presidents, we entered a new figure for every election. For example, for the 1958–70 coalition figure in Chile, we took the share of seats that President Alessandri's (1958–64) coalition won in the 1957 legislative elections as the figure for 1958–61 and took that coalition's share of seats in the 1961 legislative elections as the figure for 1961–64. We then took the share of seats that President Frei's (1964–70) coalition (which consisted of only his own party) won in the 1961 legislative elections for 1964–65, his coalition's share of seats in the 1965 legislative elections for 1965–69, and his coalition's share of seats in the 1969 legislative elections for 1969–70. We took a simple mean of all these figures rather than a weighted mean, which would have given greater weight to longer time periods.

Is the figure for the president's party or coalition more meaningful? It is difficult to answer this question universally, and it is for this reason that we have provided both figures. In some cases – for example, in post-1989 Chile (see Siavelis, this volume) – parties of the electoral coalition have been faithful members of presidents' governing coalitions. Moreover, even allowing for the marked disjuncture between electoral coalitions and governing coalitions in some cases, we are confident that parties that form part of the electoral coalition are usually more likely to provide subsequent support for the president than those that do not.

However, in many cases parties of the electoral coalition have not been consistent legislative allies of the president. In Brazil, for example, parties of the electoral coalition have often defected from or remained less firmly within the governing coalition. In general, a president should be able to expect more concord with legislators elected under the same party name than under other party names, even those of the electoral coalition. For this reason we are inclined to think that the share of seats of the presidents' party is the more important information for most cases.[7]

Table 11.1 shows a wide variation in mean legislative support for presidents. The mean figures for presidents' parties in Bolivia, Brazil (for all four periods), Chile (for both periods), and Ecuador are strikingly lower than

---

7 The only case where this might be different would be in the event of joint preelection lists, as in Chile since 1989. The structuring of joint lists before an election, where the same parties are in the same coalition throughout the country, suggests a higher level of commitment to the coalition than do coalitions in which parties retain completely separate ballot identity. However, even joint lists imply that parties retain separate organizations and the option of leaving the coalition.

those for all the other countries. With the sole exception of the Bolivian Senate, in none of the houses in these legislatures has the president's party averaged as much as 35% of the seats. The gap between these four cases and the others narrows considerably when electoral coalitions are taken into account, but for reasons already given, a larger electoral coalition does not fully compensate for the weakness of the president's own party base.

At the other end of the range, not surprisingly, is Mexico, where since the 1980s presidents' parties have still averaged 66% of the lower chamber and 96% of the upper chamber seats. In several other countries (Argentina, Colombia, the Dominican Republic, Honduras) presidents have averaged at least 50% in at least one house of the legislature.

Do the Latin American cases confirm our hypothesis about the difficulties of multiparty presidentialism when presidents' parties hold only a distinctive minority of seats? The evidence is inconclusive but tends to support the hypothesis. In the 1980s, the three countries in which presidents consistently held a distinct minority of seats (Bolivia, Brazil, and Ecuador) presented some of the most dramatic problems of democratic governance in Latin America. Bolivia and Brazil experienced extremely high inflation rates, reaching 8,171% in Bolivia (1985) and 2,489% in Brazil (1993). All three countries experienced declining or stagnant per capita income and serious problems of democratic legitimacy and accountability. The causes of these problems were multiple and complex; it would be facile to attribute them exclusively or even principally to institutional arrangements. However, as Mainwaring's chapter on Brazil suggests, the search for answers to daunting political, economic, and social problems was obstructed by the institutional combination of minority presidentialism, a large number of parties, and relatively undisciplined catchall parties.[8] Conversely, virtually all of the cases of more continuous democracy in Latin America have involved less party system fragmentation.[9] These are also the cases with the greatest frequency of majorities.

On the other hand, Chile, which is the other case in which the president's party consistently has held a share of seats below 35%, since 1989 has been successful in most respects, and even the earlier Chilean democracy of 1932–73 recorded many achievements before breaking down. Thus, there are exceptions to the general tendency toward problematic democracies in cases of highly fragmented multiparty presidential systems. Faundez, in his

8　Jones (1995a) agrees that high fragmentation is problematic in presidential systems. González (1991) also suggests that increasing fragmentation contributed to problems of democratic governance in Uruguay before 1973. However, Nicolau (forthcoming) argues that high fragmentation did not contribute to problems of governability in Brazil after 1985.
9　Of course, the number of cases is small, and there is a possibility of spurious correlations.

chapter, suggests that the (mostly reactive) powers of the Chilean presidency helped moderate the pressures of a polarized multiparty system, until polarization got out of hand in the 1970s. Other fragmented party systems have tended to be associated with proactive presidencies (those with decree powers, as discussed in Chapter 1 and later in this chapter), a combination that may exacerbate the difficulties of extreme multipartism. As for post-1989 Chile, Siavelis (this volume) attributes its success to the consensual nature of the transition from authoritarianism and to the related willingness of parties to engage in joint lists as a result of a restrictive electoral system. He cautions, however, that the smoothness of multiparty presidentialism in this case may be temporary, especially given extremely high constitutional powers of the presidency.

INSTITUTIONAL ARRANGEMENTS AND THE NUMBER OF PARTIES

In this section we discuss the relationship between institutional arrangements and the number of parties. In order to examine this issue, we use the *effective* number of parties, N, a measure that allows each party to be weighted by its own size. The formula is $N = \Sigma(p_i^2)^{-1}$, where p_i is the share of votes or seats of the ith party (Laakso and Taagepera 1979). If there are three evenly sized parties (33.3%, 33.3%, 33.3%), $N = 3.0$. If one of the three becomes larger at the expense of one of the other parties (43.3%, 33.3%, 23.3%), N drops below 3.0 to 2.84. If instead one of the three splits in half (33.3%, 33.3%, 16.7%, 16.7%), N increases to 3.60. N can be measured in votes or seats; here, we focus on seats because of our concern with presidential–legislative relations.

As one would expect, as the share of seats of the president's party increases, the effective number of parties decreases. The correlation between the president's share of seats and the effective number of parties is a robust $-.85$ for lower houses and $-.86$ for upper.

If avoiding highly fragmented party systems is desirable with presidentialism, what are the factors that most influence the number of parties in Latin American democracies? Obviously, cleavage structures and historical and cultural factors play a role. However, there are very strong correlations between certain electoral rules and sequences, on the one hand, and the number of parties, on the other. It is possible that countries with certain cleavage structures or historical-cultural experiences are more likely to choose one rather than another set of electoral rules and sequences – and therefore have a given party system – but regardless of what explains the adoption of a set of institutions, once in place, institutions usually bind future politicians and therefore produce predictable outcomes.[10]

In Table 11.2 we group countries according to various institutional configurations to show the impact of electoral arrangements on the number of parties. Whereas Table 11.1 used countries as the unit of analysis, here we use the electoral system. According to Shugart and Carey (1992) and Jones (forthcoming), the timing of presidential and congressional elections in relation to one another – the electoral cycle – is a crucial variable in explaining the number of parties in presidential systems. If congressional elections are held concurrently with a presidential election and the president is elected by plurality rule, the party system is likely to be dominated by two large parties. The typical effect of plurality elections in producing two-party competition (Duverger 1954) is carried over to a considerable degree into the congressional elections, even though most Latin American congresses are elected by proportional representation (PR) and would therefore not – according to previous conventional wisdom on electoral systems – be expected to have just two large parties. Shugart and Carey (1992:293–300) develop a model that predicts the number of parties under this combination of a presidency elected by plurality and a congress elected by PR concurrently with the president. The prediction of their model is that the effective number of parties in congressional elections would fall between two and three even for those higher-magnitude electoral systems in which the effective number of parties would ordinarily be considerably greater than three if the system were parliamentary instead of presidential.

The arguments that we have just reviewed about the number of parties in presidential systems pertain to systems in which elections are concurrent and the president is elected by plurality. For other common institutional arrangements, Shugart and Carey (1992) argued that (1) where congressional elections are held nonconcurrently, the effective number of parties would be expected to be 3.0 or more, if a large district magnitude (i.e., the number of seats elected from an electoral district) is used, regardless of how the president is elected, and (2) where the president is elected by majority runoff, the effective number of parties would be 3.0 or more, again if a large district magnitude is used, regardless of the electoral cycle.

In considering electoral systems' propensity to support many or few parties, we use *effective* magnitude. If all legislators are elected in districts of the same size, the effective magnitude is simply equivalent to the magnitude of any one district. If magnitudes are of varying size, but all legis-

---

10 For a discussion of these themes, see Mainwaring (1991) and Shugart and Carey (1992: chap. 9).

Table 11.2. *Institutional configurations and effective number of congressional parties in Latin American countries*

Country (chamber)	Number of elections	Average effective magnitude	Average effective number of parties (standard deviation)
President elected by plurality, congress concurrent			
Dominican Republic (upper)	8	1[a]	1.70 (.30)
Brazil, 1945–50 (upper)	3	1 or 2[b]	2.71 (.47)
Dominican Republic (lower)	8	3.4	2.17 (.49)
Honduras	4	6.3	2.07 (.09)
Venezuela (upper)	8	6.5	2.76 (.80)
Peru, 1980 (lower)	1	7.0	2.47 (—)
Costa Rica	11	7.7	2.42 (.41)
Brazil, 1945–50 (lower)	2	6.5[c]	3.44 (.94)
Venezuela (lower)	8	25.8	3.31 (.97)
Uruguay (upper)	11	30	2.55 (.41)
Peru, 1980 (upper)	1	60	3.22 (—)
Uruguay (lower)	11	99	2.65 (.38)
Mean of all individual elections	76	—	2.53 (.68)
President elected by majority runoff, concurrent elections			
Brazil, 1994 (upper)	1	1 or 2[b]	6.08
Chile, 1989–93 (upper)[d]	2	2	4.51
Chile, 1989–93 (lower)	2	2	4.91 (.29)
Ecuador, 1979–94	7	3.0	5.95 (1.28)
El Salvador, 1994–present	1	5.3	3.06 (—)
Peru, 1985–90, 1995 (lower)	3	7.0	3.79 (1.82)
Brazil, 1994 (lower)	1	9.5[c]	8.13 (—)
Peru, 1985–90 (upper)	2	61.5	4.27 (1.80)
Mean of all individual elections	19	—	5.14 (1.61)
Congress and presidential elections nonconcurrent			
Brazil, 1986–90 (upper)	2	1 or 2[b]	3.91 (2.31)
Brazil, 1954–62 (upper)	3	1 or 2[b]	3.94 (.53)
El Salvador, 1985–91	3	4.4	2.51 (.32)
Chile, 1932–73 (upper)	9[e]	5	5.17 (.90)
Chile, 1932–73 (lower)	11	5.2	5.65 (1.63)
Brazil, 1954–62 (lower)	3	6.8[c]	4.55 (.05)
Brazil, 1986–90 (lower)	2	9.3[c]	5.74 (4.12)
Mean of all individual elections	33	—	4.88 (1.64)

Table 11.2. *(cont.)*

Country (chamber)	Number of elections	Average effective magnitude	Average effective number of parties (standard deviation)
Other cases			
Argentina (lower)	6	5.9	2.62 (.29)
Bolivia (upper)	4	3	2.64 (.72)
Bolivia (lower)	4	14.4	4.24 (.37)
Colombia, 1947, 1974–90 (upper)	6	5.0	2.15 (.18)
Colombia (lower)	10	7.7	2.22 (.37)
Colombia, 1991–94 (upper)	2	100	2.99 (.10)

Note: Systems are listed within each category in ascending order by district magnitude, except in "other cases" category.
[a]Where no decimal point is given, all districts are of the indicated magnitude.
[b]All districts have magnitude 1, then 2, in alternate elections.
[c]For Brazil 1950–62 and 1985–present, one could make a strong argument for adjusting the effective magnitude for the lower house because electoral rules allowed for the formation of coalitions of several parties in proportional elections. These coalitions rather than individual parties needed to reach the threshold. This provision reduces the threshold for a party by a factor of approximately three times when three parties run together, thus leading to a greater effective number of parties than one would expect on the basis of the average effective magnitude. The reason we did not make an adjustment for the coalition effect is that the rules regarding coalitions have changed frequently, making it difficult to determine how much one should adjust over a period of time.
[d]Excludes appointed senators.
[e]The total number of elections is 11, but data are incomplete for 1937 and 1957.

lators are elected from districts without complex districting (such as a nationwide pool of seats to compensate parties that are underrepresented in the districts) and without a threshold, then the effective magnitude is the average of all the individual district magnitudes. Where a threshold is applied in the districts, the magnitude is reduced and we use the formula devised by Taagepera and Shugart (1989) to determine effective magnitude in such cases.[11] We present averages of the effective values for each election considered, drawn from data in Jones (1995a) and Nohlen (1993).

---

11 Their formula is $M_{eff} = 50/T$, where M_{eff} is effective magnitude and T is the threshold, in percent. Argentina, Bolivia, and Brazil are the three countries that required adjust-

In Table 11.2, we group countries into four categories: (1) Congress is elected concurrently with a president elected by plurality;[12] (2) congress is elected concurrently with a president elected by majority runoff;[13] (3) congress and president are elected nonconcurrently, and (4) other cases. The final category includes three countries (Argentina, Bolivia, and Colombia) that do not fit any of the first three categories because of unique institutional configurations.[14]

Because our primary interest has shifted from the dynamics of executive–legislative relations (Table 11.1) to the impact of electoral laws and sequences (electoral cycles) on the number of parties (Table 11.2), the "num-

ments of this sort. In addition, for Venezuela's complex districting, we compute M_{eff} as the geometric average of the magnitude of the nationwide compensation district (90) and the district-level average magnitude (around 8). For a justification of these procedures, see Taagepera and Shugart (1989:chap. 12 and app. C5).

12 We include Brazil (1945–50), Costa Rica, and Peru (1980) in this category despite minor deviations. In Brazil congressional and presidential elections were concurrent in 1945 and 1950. In 1947, every state elected one senator, bringing the number of senators to three per state. But the number of legislators elected nonconcurrently in 1947 (one-third of the Senate and no deputies) pales in comparison to the number elected concurrently in 1945 (the entire legislature) and 1950 (the entire legislature except for one-third of the Senate). Therefore, the overall dynamic of this period was established by the concurrent elections. In Costa Rica, if no candidate obtains 40% of the votes, a runoff is held. Because the threshold in the first round is lower than a majority, this functions almost like the plurality rule. Similarly, in Peru in 1980, a runoff could have been averted if the leading candidate had won at least one-third of the vote.

13 We include Ecuador in this category despite some minor deviations. In Ecuador, the 1979 legislative elections coincided with the second round of the presidential election rather than the first (which was held in 1978, nine and one-half months earlier). Since 1984, presidents have held four-year terms and have always been elected concurrently with Congress. Most deputies (e.g., 65 of the 77 deputies in the 1994–96 legislature) have two-year terms, so every other time presidents and legistators are elected nonconcurrently. Twelve national deputies have four-year terms and are elected concurrently with the president.

14 In Argentina, besides the use of an electoral college to elect the president through 1995, some members of Congress are elected concurrently with the president, but others are elected during nonconcurrent elections held during the president's term. Deputies are elected to four-year terms with half the seats renewed at any one election. In addition, alone among upper houses in Latin America, the Argentine Senate is indirectly elected; moreover, it is not elected at exactly the same time as the president. (The constitutional reforms of 1994 have implemented a change to direct elections, but the change will not fully take effect until 2001.) In Bolivia, legislative elections coincide with the first round of presidential elections, but the Congress elects the president if there is no majority winner. This system is closest to our second category (concurrent elections with runoff), but the "runoff" is not conducted through popular election. In Colombia, Congress is elected about three months before the president. Thus, elections are literally nonconcurrent, but held within the presidential election campaign, and terms of office are concurrent. The 1991 election, called to replace the 1990 Congress when it was dissolved to implement the new constitution, was a one-time exception to this cycle.

ber of elections" refers to legislative elections only.[15] The averages of each group and, with a few exceptions, the results from individual countries support the expectations of the relation between institutional configuration and effective number of parties represented in congress. In the concurrent/ plurality group, the mean N is 2.53; two and a half parties are the norm here. Among these countries, only the Venezuelan lower chamber has an average N greater than 3.0, and then only in the lower house, with its large effective magnitude. Even that figure is exaggerated by three highly fragmented elections (1963, 1968, 1993), as can be seen from the very high standard deviation. From 1973 through 1988, the Congress was dominated by two large parties, with a high fragmentation of the rest of the Congress. That the electoral cycle and plurality rule for the presidency together significantly dampen the effect of magnitude on the number of parties is suggested by the Uruguayan case with magnitudes in its two chambers of 30 and 99, but with Ns not much higher than 2.5.[16] For those who favor proportional representation, the good news here is that PR need not produce high fragmentation in presidential systems.

In systems with nonconcurrent elections, the average N is 4.88, confirming expectations that party systems would tend to be more fragmented with this electoral cycle. The standard deviation is very large mainly because of sharp swings in the effective number of parties in Brazil since the return to democracy in 1985. Where the president is elected by majority runoff, even in concurrent elections, the number of parties is likewise high, 5.14 on average.

Table 11.3 shows the incidence of bicameral (or unicameral where there is only one chamber) majority legislative support according to different electoral arrangements. The data show that presidents elected by plurality, with congress elected at the same time, are far more likely to have majorities than are presidents under the other institutional formats. Fifty-four percent of the time (25 out of 46), presidents in such systems have held a majority in both chambers (or in the sole house of a unicameral chamber). Presidential

15 In Table 11.1 (and again in Table 11.3), in nonconcurrent cases (except Colombia), we determined data points for both legislative and presidential elections. For cases of staggered elections, the data indicate the composition of the full house after each partial renovation.

16 In recent elections, N has been increasing in Uruguay. Assuming the configuration of concurrent elections and plurality presidential elections does not completely override the effects of M, it would be expected that N would be higher in Uruguay than it generally has been. Even if it were around 4.0, however, it would still be low compared with other countries with such large magnitudes but without concurrently elected presidencies, such as Israel and the Netherlands. See Taagepera and Shugart (1993). As we suggest later, the requirement of straight party voting also contributes to limiting N in Uruguay.

majorities are much rarer in systems with nonconcurrent elections (3 of 31 observations) or when the congress is elected concurrently with a majority-runoff presidential election (2 of 13 observations).

In Table 11.3, we also consider the likelihood that presidents who have reactive powers will be able to sustain vetoes. Table 11.3 shows the frequency with which presidents' parties have a veto-sustaining share of seats in those cases in which they lack a majority. If a president can sustain vetoes, then he or she will be able to put a stamp on policy, even in the absence of a majority.[17] We used upper and lower houses since a president would need the support of only one chamber to sustain a veto. Presidents elected by plurality with concurrent congressional elections have had either a majority or a veto-sustaining share of seats over 70% of the time.

Presidents under the other institutional configurations are much less likely to have veto-sustaining seat shares for their own parties. We did not compute a separate figure for presidents' coalitions, because we are interested in how likely the president can escape being marginalized when he or she faces the second-worst situation imaginable in terms of partisan support: when only the president's own party remains supportive. (The worst possible situation is, of course, when not even the president's own party supports him or her.) If presidents in institutional configurations other than the concurrent/plurality format are rather unlikely to have veto-sustaining shares, they are nonetheless much more likely to be able to sustain vetoes than they are to have majorities, owing to the extraordinary majority override provisions in three of the cases that have very fragmented party systems: Bolivia, Brazil (1946–64), and Chile (pre-1973).

If presidents do not have enough partisan support to be able to sustain vetoes, they can more easily be marginalized in the legislative process, perhaps tempting them to act unconstitutionally. The data presented in Table 11.3 suggest that electing the congress concurrently with a plurality election for president is the format that best achieves this goal.

In sum, the party systems that have a very large effective number of parties and a concomitantly low likelihood that the president's party will have a majority of seats in the legislature are mainly those with nonconcurrent elections and/or majority-runoff election of the president: Bolivia, Brazil, Chile (pre-'73),[18] Ecuador, and Peru. These are the only cases in

---

17 For purposes of parsimony, we are assuming here that the president's party is united and that no other party supports him. In most countries, only rarely would these two conditions be met perfectly. But the share of seats of the president's party is still relevant to understanding how easy it is for the president to veto legislation successfully.

18 Post-Pinochet Chile has a low effective number of parties according to Table 11.2, despite using majority-runoff presidential elections. Some caveats are important here, however.

Table 11.3. *Congressional strength of presidents' parties*

Country	Number of elections	Number of times with majority in both houses[a]	% times with majority in both houses[a]	Number of times with veto-sustaining share but no majority[b]	% times with veto-sustaining share but no majority	% times either majority or veto-sustaining share
President elected by plurality, congress concurrent						
Brazil, 1945–50	3	2	66.7	0	0.0	66.7
Costa Rica	11	6	54.5	4	36.4	90.9
Dominican Republic	8	5	62.5	3	37.5	100.0
Honduras	4	4	100.0	0	0.0	100.0
Peru, 1980	1	0	0.0	1	100.0	100.0
Uruguay	11	5	45.5	0	0.0	45.5
Venezuela	8	3	37.5	0	0.0	37.5
Total	46	25	54.3	8	17.4	71.7
President elected by majority runoff, concurrent elections						
Brazil, 1994–	1	0	0.0	0	0.0	0.0
Chile, 1989–93	2	0[c]	0.0	2[d]	100.0	100.0
Ecuador, 1984–94[e]	6	0	0.0	1[f]	16.7	16.7
El Salvador, 1993	1	0	0.0	1	100.0	100.0
Peru, 1985–90, 1995	3	2	66.7	0	0.0	66.7
Total	13	2	15.4	4	30.8	46.2

Congress and presidential elections nonconcurrent

Brazil, 1954–64	4	0	0.0	2	50.0	50.0
Brazil, 1985–90	4[g]	1[b]	25.0	1[b]	25.0	50.0
Chile, 1932–73	18	0	0.0	2	11.1	11.1
Ecuador, 1978–79	1	0	0.0	1	100.0	100.0
El Salvador, 1985–91	4	2	50.0	2	50.0	100.0
Total	31	3	9.7	8	25.8	35.5
Other cases						
Argentina	6	0	0.0	6	100.0	100.0
Bolivia	4	0	0.0	3	75.0	75.0
Colombia	11	9	81.8	0	0.0	81.8

[a] Or in the sole chamber of a unicameral congress.

[b] Veto-sustaining seat share is a share of seats in one (or the sole) house that is sufficient to block an override of a veto, in the event that the president's party lacks a majority in both houses (or the sole house). Where veto override majorities differ by issue area, the one required for bills other than expenditures is used.

[c] Part of the Chilean Senate has been appointed. The Concertación would have had a majority without the appointed senators.

[d] Based on the Concertación, a preelection joint list, rather than on the president's own party alone.

[e] Some legislative elections in Ecuador are nonconcurrent.

[f] Based on veto override of two-thirds, which applies when the president returns a bill that he or she objects to only in part; however, the president may also reject a bill in its entirety, in which case the only way for Congress to attempt an override is to request a referendum on the issue.

[g] Includes the indirect presidential election of 1985.

[b] At the beginning of the 1987–90 legislature, the PMDB had a majority in both chambers, and we have consequently included this case as one of a presidential majority. However, defections from the party subsequently deprived the PMDB of this majority.

which the mean effective number of parties in at least one house of the legislature exceeds 4.0.

We now provide a statistical test of our hypotheses about the effects of various institutional configurations on the effective number of parties in presidential systems. The use of multiple regression analysis on a relatively small data set cannot be considered definitive, but if the results of the regressions match our hunches and our less formalized display of the data in Table 11.2, we will have reason to be more confident of our reasoning. We present regressions on the Latin American data and also on an expanded data set that includes the other two countries with extensive experience with presidential democracy, the Philippines and the United States. Table 11.4 displays the results.

We see from regressions 1 and 4 that our hypotheses about the effects of electing the president by plurality and concurrently with the congress are quite strong. This institutional configuration has the expected effect of reducing the number of parties and is significant. The result is essentially the same whether we use the Latin America data set (regression 1) or the expanded one (regression 4), which includes the United States, where half of all congressional elections are concurrent with presidential electors, who are chosen by plurality, and the Philippines. The expectation about majority runoff-presidential elections – that they would increase the number of parties – is also borne out in both specifications. We tried (but do not show) alternative codings on this variable. For example, coding Bolivia's unusual presidential election procedure as having majority runoff, even though the "runoff" is held in Congress rather than as a popular election, made no material difference in the result. However, the coding of those systems in which a runoff can be held, but in which the threshold for avoiding a runoff is lower than the usual 50% plus one member, made some difference. If such systems – all Costa Rican elections, Peru in 1980, and Argentina in 1995 – are coded as majority runoffs, this variable remains significant but is less robust. Thus, the statistical results reinforce our confidence in considering as effectively pluralities those two-round systems in which the first-round threshold for victory is considerably less than a majority.

Footnote 18 (cont.)

Our figure reflects preelection coalitions rather than separate party organizations. The coalescence of parties before elections may be traced to two primary factors. First, the district magnitude is low (2.0) for the congressional elections (which were concurrent with the presidential election in 1989 and 1993, but will not be in the future, because the presidential term has been lengthened to six years). Thus, the electoral rules have produced an artificial and possibly temporary reduction in the effective number of parties (coalitions). Second, the transition from dictatorship was quite consensual. As Siavelis's chapter notes, this low fragmentation cannot be expected to last.

Table 11.4. *Regressions of institutional variables and the effective number of parties in presidential systems*

Variable	1	2	3	4	5	6	7
Constant	3.701***	3.486***	2.136***	3.460***	2.898***	3.278***	2.065***
	(.388)	(.401)	(.272)	(.310)	(.326)	(.318)	(.167)
CONC/PLUR	-1.022***	-0.936***	—	-1.200***	-1.213***	-1.074***	—
	(.346)	(.345)		(.293)	(.275)	(.294)	
MAJRO	1.612***	1.681***	—	1.724***	1.385***	1.776***	—
	(.387)	(.384)		(.352)	(.342)	(.347)	
LOGMAG	.009	.021	.183*	.141	.088	.127	.205**
	(.160)	(.158)	(.092)	(.108)	(.117)	(.107)	(.063)
LIST	—	—	—	—	1.370***	—	—
					(.35)		
GOVLIST	—	.780*	—	—	—	.831**	—
		(.425)				(.394)	
Corrected R^2	.22	.24	.06	.28	.37	.31	.15
N	97	97	46	113	113	113	57

Note: Regressions are based on different data sets, as follows: 1, 2, all Latin American cases; 3, Latin American cases with concurrent elections and president elected by plurality only; 4, 5, 6, all Latin American cases, plus the Philippines and the United States; 7, Latin American cases with concurrent elections and president elected by plurality, plus the Philippines and the United States.

* $p \leq .10$

** $p \leq .05$

*** $p \leq .01$

Variables: CONC/PLUR, dummy variable, set to 1 when the president is elected by plurality, concurrent with the congresional election; MAJRO, dummy variable, set to 1 when the president is elected by majority runoff; LOGMAG, Effective magnitude, logged; LIST, dummy variable, set to 1 when the congress is elected by a party-list system; GOVLIST, dummy variable, set to 1 when provincial, state, or departmental governors are directly elected and the congress is elected by a list system.

We have also introduced two other variables in various regressions. One is the presence of a list system. All Latin American presidential systems except Colombia's use a party-list system for electing at least the lower house, although Mexico and (since recent reforms), Bolivia and Venezuela elect about half their deputies from single-member districts.[19] It is plausible that one reason for the much lower number of parties in Colombia, the Philippines, and the United States – even when compared with other systems that use plurality presidential elections and concurrent or near-concurrent elections – is the absence of party lists.

Without party lists – especially closed lists – it is easier for local chapters of a party or even individual candidates to tailor their campaigns to suit local concerns, while still acting within a party that can win the presidency. Thus, parties in non-party-list systems can be more internally diverse. Even with open lists, party leadership has control over the nominations that it would lack in systems that we have defined as not using lists (although, uniquely, this is not so concerning renominations of incumbents in Brazil). Therefore, the opportunity to express dissent within the party is reduced relative to a non-party-list system, even though it is probably greater under open than under closed lists. There is another reason why party lists enhance incentives to establish new parties: A defector, in setting up a rival list, can use his or her name appeal to help elect other members, given that votes are pooled within lists. Thus, the head of a new party list can potentially enhance his or her own power in congress; under non-party-list systems, this opportunity is unavailable.[20] For these reasons, party-list systems provide more incentives to set up new parties than do nonlist systems. Regression 5 tests this idea against the entire data set and finds it very plausible.[21] A list system increases the number of a parties, and the other variables that were significant in regression 4 remain so.

19 Given the absence of U.S.-style primaries or Philippine-style decentralized nominations procedures, even that half of the deputies elected from single-member districts may still be seen as effectively operating within a list system in which lists have only one name.

20 A partial exception is Colombia, but the expected result on incentives to form new parties is the same as described for other non-party-list systems. In Colombia there are multiple lists within parties, but votes are pooled only within the list and not within the party. Thus, given a lack of party control over nominations (discussed later), dissidents can set up their own lists, and votes cast for them will pool to other candidates on their lists. Thus, they may help elect other like-minded dissidents without helping elect rivals within the party (an option unavailable wherever there are party lists, whether open, closed, or, as in Uruguay, factional). The bottom line is that defectors do not need to register their lists under different party names; thus, there is reduced incentive to set up new parties, just as is the case in other non-party-list systems.

21 Because Colombia is the only system in Latin America that does not use party lists,

CONCLUSION 417

Another institutional variable that might be expected to increase the opportunities for local parties to establish themselves and hence increase the number of parties is the direct election of provincial, state, or departmental governors. We interact this variable with LIST because, for the same reason given earlier, the incentives to establish new parties around gubernatorial elections would be less in nonlist systems. Electing governors and other local officials makes either federalism or administrative decentralization more meaningful because it enhances the autonomy of subnational governments vis-à-vis the central government (Riker 1964). However, the way in which this enhanced autonomy plays out in terms of the national party system can be expected to vary with the electoral system used. If there are no party lists, electing local officials contributes to what Ordeshook (1995) terms "decentralized but vertically integrated parties" in which local chapters enjoy autonomy, but the local elections serve in part as a recruiting channel for national parties. However, list systems may inhibit the decentralization of parties and also create an opportunity for governors to establish local parties over whose lists they may wield a substantial amount of control.[22]

Thus, within party-list systems, separate local parties are more likely to grow up around local gubernatorial races. At the extreme, gubernatorial elections in party-list systems may contribute substantially to the fragmentation of a party system. The results of regressions 2 and, especially, 6 provide some support for this notion (without substantially affecting the other variables that were significant in regressions 1 and 4). That is, while the move toward decentralization and local democratization can be applauded, when coupled with the tendency to use party-list systems in Latin America, local elections may not assist the formation of the decentralized but vertically integrated party systems that may be essential to providing the twin desiderata of local autonomy and national integration.

One final observation about these regressions is the surprising insignificance of effective magnitude. Although magnitude has been termed the "decisive" factor in determining the number of parties (Taagepera and Shugart 1989; also Rae 1967; Lijphart 1994), the data sets on which such conclusions have been based have overwhelmingly consisted of parliamen-

running a regression on the Latin America data with LIST would be equivalent to using a dummy variable for Colombia and hence not theoretically interesting.
22 These statements would seem to apply even to the extremely decentralized open-list system of Brazil. Governors there wield greater control over nominations to open seats in their states' delegations to the National Congress than would be likely if there were no lists at all.

tary systems. In presidential systems, on the other hand, the importance of the presidency serves to reduce the number of parties, at least when the president is not elected by majority runoff and elections are concurrent. Thus, the special features of presidentialism override the impact of magnitude.[23] We did include two regressions (3 and 7) that take into account only the subset of cases that use the concurrent/plurality format, and we find that effective magnitude is indeed significant for this subset, especially when the non-Latin American cases are included (although the variance explained is very small). Thus, we would not characterize magnitude as irrelevant in presidential systems – just less important than the electoral cycle and the means of electing the president, and also less important than the presence or absence of party lists.

PRESIDENTIALISM AND PARTY DISCIPLINE

When we talk about party discipline, we have in mind a simple phenomenon: legislators of the same party voting together almost all the time. Even in undisciplined parties, legislators of the same party *usually* vote together, but this is because many legislative matters are relatively consensual across and within party lines. Even with comparatively undisciplined parties, it is important to avoid misleading stereotypes: under these circumstances, party labels are nonetheless meaningful indicators of most politicians' proclivities (Kinzo 1990). However, on issues that cleave the legislature as a whole, undisciplined parties are often divided. Defined in this fashion, a disciplined party need not be well organized, well institutionalized, or programmatic, although it is more likely to be so than is an undisciplined party. Having moderately disciplined parties facilitates the building of well-organized parties and an "institutionalized party system" (Mainwaring and Scully 1995), but it is not a sufficient condition.

The degree of party discipline affects the extent to which presidents can rely on party leaders to deliver the vote of their party or, conversely, the extent to which presidents need to secure the support of individual legislators and/or party factions. (The degree of discipline also affects the kind

---

23 Lijphart (1994:130–34) also finds that presidentialism with the concurrent/plurality format (i.e., Costa Rica and the United States) reduces the number of parties, even in a larger data set that includes parliamentary systems (and in which, therefore, magnitude is significant).

of representation that citizens enjoy, but this issue is less relevant for our purposes here.)

Linz (1994) and Sartori (1994a:189–94) properly argue that parliamentary systems function better with disciplined parties. We hypothesize that some measure of party discipline also facilitates the functioning of presidential systems. We cannot rigorously test this hypothesis here, but we do present our logic and believe that the case studies in this volume support it.

Parties in presidential systems need not be highly disciplined, but frequent indiscipline makes it more difficult to establish stable relationships between the government, the parties, and the legislature. Where discipline is weak, party leaders can negotiate a deal, only to have the party's legislative members back out of it. Presidents are forced to rely on ad hoc bases of support rather than on party leaders who can deliver the votes of their fellow legislators. This is a difficult situation for presidents, and it encourages the widespread use of clientelism and patronage to secure the support of individual legislators, as chapters by Archer and Shugart, Gamarra, and Mainwaring discuss. It can even tempt presidents to try to bypass congress through measures of questionable constitutionality or to flout the constitution, possibly with the military as an ally. Under these conditions, presidents may not be able minimally to accomplish their legislative agendas. Given the fixed nature of presidential terms, this situation can lead to protracted impasse, with deleterious consequences (Linz 1994). In this fashion, weak party discipline can contribute to the possibility of institutional deadlock.

With disciplined parties, the president does not have to negotiate a new ad hoc coalition for each legislative proposal, with the resulting need for the president to distribute patronage in order to win support. Although in Chapter 1 we suggested that an advantage of presidentialism is the possibility of sufficient legislative independence such that support for executive initiatives is not automatic, we nonetheless think it is desirable that there be a fairly large core of issues around which a party's support can be taken for granted. Presidents then can negotiate primarily with party leaders, thereby reducing the number of actors involved in negotiations and hence simplifying the process. They can count on party leaders usually being able to deliver the votes of most representatives of their parties, so there is greater predictability and transparency in the political process. Interparty agreements and coalitions in the legislature and cabinet are more likely to affect an entire set of issues than a single bill, and ad hoc bargaining over specific pieces of legislation would generally be required only on those proposals that would mark the greatest departures from the policy status quo.

Disciplined parties also help voters understand what different party labels and individual politicians stand for. With less disciplined parties, the ideological/policy differences among parties may be more opaque, hindering the process of accountability. It is certainly desirable for the party to be sufficiently cohesive that voters can have an expectation that a president and members of the legislature who share a party name will have a core set of policy concerns on which they are generally in accord.

The argument here should not be taken, however, to imply that *rigidly* disciplined parties are preferable with presidentialism, since there are potential perils of extremely tight discipline in presidential systems. We have already mentioned the subversion of checks and balances when presidents have a disciplined majority backing them. The congress may not function as an effective check on the president, but instead rubber-stamp all executive initiatives, if the president and the party leadership are in agreement. Mexico has such a situation, as Weldon's chapter shows, because even though most members are elected from single-member districts, the lack of reelection gives members no incentive to represent their supposed constituents. Thus, term limits, as well as the centralization of all ruling-party nominations in the hands of the president acting as party leader, reinforce the authoritarian dominance of the presidency over the congress.

If the president encounters a situation of "divided government," wherein a party or stable coalition opposed to the president holds a majority of seats in both houses (or the sole house) of congress, then extreme party discipline makes it difficult for the president to work out deals that cut across party lines. If the leadership of the dominant party seeks to be obstructionist, individual legislators must go along if they are subject to tight discipline. If, instead, individual members are free to break free from a leadership most interested in opposing the president, some may be coaxed to join with the president's party on certain legislative proposals.

Moreover, if the party leadership is at odds with its own president, rigid party discipline may make it difficult for the president to work with congress, even if the president's party is in the majority (Coppedge 1994a; Espinal 1991). Even in Costa Rica, as Carey's chapter shows, the combination of presidential primary elections and term limits means that presidents often have difficulty in dealing with their own parties once the next presidential candidate has been nominated, as this person, if victorious, will determine future appointive careers for the party's current congress members. If, on the other hand, party discipline is less rigid, it is unlikely that a president would ever be left without legislators willing to work with him or her even if the leadership had gone its own way.

Indeed, this possibility of cross-party alliances prevents U.S. presidentialism from being crisis-ridden during periods of divided government. Although divided government has led to numerous scholarly and popular critiques (e.g., Cutler 1980; Robinson 1985; Sundquist 1986), others have argued that the legislative process does not suffer at all under divided government (Fiorina 1992; Mayhew 1991)[24] or that voters even prefer it as a means to force compromise (Fiorina 1988; Ingberman and Villani 1993). Riggs (1988) goes so far as to argue that lack of discipline is preferable in presidentialism. Riggs overstates the degree of indiscipline in U.S. parties (see Cox and McCubbins 1993); however, U.S. parties clearly have loose enough discipline that cross-party legislative coalitions are common. This cross-party dealing facilitates governability in the United States under a divided government,[25] although it may detract from it under a unified government.

INSTITUTIONAL DETERMINANTS OF PARTY DISCIPLINE

The extent to which members of a given party's congressional delegation vote as a bloc or, on the other hand, vote independently of one another, can be expected to be strongly related to three basic features of the rules under which they become candidates and are elected. These three features – control of candidate selection, control of the order in which members are elected from a party list, and pooling of votes among a party's candidates – all strongly affect the degree of influence leaders have over the rank-and-file members.[26]

24 Consider one recent example of divided government in the United States. The 1992 presidential election was virtually dominated by cries of "gridlock" between the president and Congress. Yet Congress and the president under the Bush administration had accomplished several major pieces of legislation, including extensions of the clean air and voting rights acts and delegation of fast-track authority for negotiating free-trade agreements.

25 Divided government is most common in systems in which voters are likely to cast congressional votes on the basis of local issues or candidate characteristics rather than simply considering the national policy preferences that tend to dominate their presidential vote. Thus, the same feature of the electoral system that facilitates limited discipline – the electoral independence of legislators from party leaders – is also conducive to divided government because it encourages ticket splitting. See Shugart (1995a) for a fuller development and statistical test of this argument.

26 Congressional rules also affect party discipline. If the party leadership in congress controls resources that are important to other members of their delegation, this enhances party discipline (Cox and McCubbins 1993; Figueiredo and Limongi 1995). We do not have enough informtion on such congressional rules for Latin American countries to treat systematically this issue here. Although we focus here on party systems as the unit of

If party leaders control candidate selection, recalcitrant members cannot have the best of both worlds: deviation from the party line but continued use of the party's name in future elections. If the party leadership controls candidate selection, members who buck party wishes can be denied the right to be candidates with the party in the future.[27] When this is the case, potential candidates must be on good terms with the party leadership to win a place on the slate. The party has a powerful means of influencing politicians' behavior. An elementary feature of party cohesiveness is therefore the ability to determine who the party's candidates are. Party leaders in most of the industrialized democracies, as well as in most Latin American countries, have this power. However, the United States is a prominent example of a country where party leaders do not control who runs.

If party leaders control the order in which their members are elected, then they can selectively reward or punish rank-and-file members by moving them up or down on the party list (Carey and Shugart forthcoming). Members in such parties have little incentive to build personal reputations separate from those of their parties because voters do not vote for them as individuals, but rather for the whole party list. If, on the other hand, parties do not control the order of election, members have a powerful incentive to build their own reputations because their own ability to win personal votes can make the difference between victory and defeat. On this dimension, there is a continuum of possibilities, ranging from complete to no party control of the order in which candidates are elected.

If votes are pooled among all the candidates of a party, members' incentive to cultivate the collective reputation of their party is greater than if each candidate wins or loses solely on the basis of the personal votes he or she accrues. If the party does not control the order of election, being personally popular is one way to be elected, as noted earlier, but another way is to enter the congress on the coattails of some other popular member. This is possible with vote pooling because the first criterion in allocating seats is to determine the number of votes won by the party collectively in the district. Very popular individual candidates are thus an asset to less popular candidates, since their votes inflate the support of the party as a whole and

analysis, it is important to note that, within a given system, different parties sometimes differ markedly in discipline. In Brazil, for example, the leftist PT is very disciplined, while the centrist and rightist parties are comparatively undisciplined (Mainwaring and Pérez Liñán forthcoming).

27 Where there are bans on immediate congressional reelection, as in Costa Rica and Mexico, party leaders obviously lack the sanction of denying nomination in the next election. However, when the president comes from the same party, the provision or denial of future appointive positions offers a surrogate for the renomination sanction. See Carey's and Weldon's chapters.

thus help it win more seats. If, on the other hand, votes are not pooled, then a very popular candidate can be a liability. Because his or her votes cannot be shared with copartisans, votes beyond the number that candidate needed to win are "wasted" and cannot help elect other members. The best example of such a system is the single nontransferable vote used in Japan through 1993.

Table 11.5 reviews several Latin American electoral laws on each of these three provisions. For simplicity, we assume that each category is dichotomous, although one can imagine intermediate possibilities (Carey and Shugart forthcoming). We see from the table that closed-list systems are by far the most common in Latin America.[28] Included in this set are Argentina, Mexico, and Venezuela,[29] three countries in which parties are generally disciplined. Costa Rica is also a closed-list system, but there are primaries that are formally quite open; nonetheless, the importance of patronage gives presidential candidates de facto control (see Carey, this volume).

Closed-list systems give party organizations the greatest control over candidates. Of course, in order for control over a party label to be especially meaningful, there first must be a label to control. Electoral laws are only one factor in making a party label meaningful. Parties must earn the integrity of their labels among voters by providing public or private goods, creating a social base, and building a reputation for being worthy of public approbation. In some countries, such as Bolivia and Ecuador, party labels are less meaningful and the party systems are "inchoate" (Mainwaring and Scully 1995) in spite of leaders' authority over rank-and-file members of their parties. The weakness of public identification with parties makes it less costly for candidates dissatisfied with their ranking on a party list to defect and establish a new party. Where party labels are respected, a defector is more likely to find that he or she cannot bring many voters along, and thus the new party is more likely to fizzle. Such has been the case in Costa

---

28 This terminology may be somewhat confusing to readers from some Latin American countries. In Spanish, what the English-language literature calls "closed lists" are called *listas cerradas y bloqueadas* (closed and blocked lists). What we call "open lists" are called *listas cerradas y no bloqueadas* or *listas cerradas con voto preferencial* (closed lists with preferential voting), unless voters may vote for candidates from more than one list, in which case the term is *listas abiertas* or the French term *panachage*. Here, when we say "open list" we mean that voters may (or must) vote for one or more candidates, but only within one list.

29 In Mexico since 1993, in Venezuela, and beginning in 1997 in Bolivia, about half the members are/will be elected in single-member districts, while the rest are elected from multicandidate lists. Even in the single-member districts, party organizations in these countries determine nominations; thus, the electoral system for these seats is still one of closed party lists, where the "lists" each contain one name.

Table 11.5. *Electoral and party laws in Latin America: Provisions for party control over rank-and-file candidates (lower chamber)*

Provision for party control over candidates	Closed list	Mixed, closed list PR/single-member district	Closed list with primary	Factional list (sublemas)	Open list	Open list with "birthright candidate"	Personal list (effective single nontransferable vote)
Control candidate selection?	Yes	Yes	No	Yes	Yes	No	No
Control order of election?	Yes	Yes/NA[a]	Yes	No	No	No	No
Pool votes among party's candidates or lists within districts?	Yes	Yes/NA[a]	Yes	Yes	Yes	Yes	No
Examples in Latin America	Argentina Bolivia (to 1993) Dominican Republic Ecuador El Salvador Guatemala Honduras Nicaragua Panama Paraguay Venezuela (to 1988)	Bolivia, 1997 Mexico Venezuela, 1993	Costa Rica	Uruguay	Chile Peru	Brazil	Colombia

[a]For these systems, "yes" applies to the portion elected from party lists (about half of the total number of deputies). The order of election and vote pooling are not applicable for the seats elected from single-member districts.

Rica and, until the severe economic and political dislocations of the early 1990s, in Venezuela.

In an open-list electoral system, parties determine who their candidates are and pool votes among them, but do not control the order in which the candidates are elected. A citizen casts a vote for one candidate only,[30] but seats are first distributed between parties according to the total number of votes their candidates get and then within parties according to the number of individual votes. Even though the number of representatives is determined by party votes, whether or not a candidate is elected depends on his or her ability to obtain individual votes. This system provides a strong incentive for individualism in campaigns. There are variations among open-list systems, but Chile, Peru since 1985, and Brazil fit the basic type.

In Brazil, the personalism engendered by using open lists is reinforced by rules for candidate selection. Deputies cannot be denied future nomination by their parties, even if they have not submitted to party discipline during their tenure. The feature of the law that provides candidates with this degree of autonomy is known in Brazil as *candidato nato*, literally "birthright candidate" (Mainwaring 1991). Since a majority of incumbent deputies usually wins reelection, the effects of this provision are far reaching: Most deputies who win at any given election did not need the support of the party to appear on the ballot, although first-time candidates must receive party approbation at a state-level convention.

Uruguay is a sui generis case in terms of the three institutional issues we have identified as crucial to party discipline. Each of the major parties has several factional lists (known as *sublemas*), and each *sublema* has countless lists (*listas*) for deputies. Voters select one of these lists instead of a candidate directly. Votes for all such lists within a given party (*lema*) are summed first to determine the number of seats won by the party. The party's seats are then distributed proportionally to the *sublemas*, and the *sublema's* seats are proportionally distributed to the *listas*. The parties themselves have little control over the order of the ticket, but party factions have considerable influence because they order the *sublemas*. This system is listed in Table 11.5 between the closed-list and open-list systems because the incentives it generates are intermediate: more personalistic than in a closed-list system (due to intraparty voting) but less so than in open-list systems (because factional lists themselves are closed, and the party can theoretically determine how many factions can operate within the party).

---

30 It is possible for voters to be given the option of voting for more than one deputy, as in Switzerland and formerly in Italy; however, we know of no such systems in recent Latin American history at the national level.

In Colombia, parties cannot deny the use of the party label to candidates. Candidates actually run within lists, but multiple lists may use the same party name in any given district, and votes are not pooled from one list to another. If all the candidates of one party were to coalesce on one list, the system would be simply a closed-list system. However, given the lack of control over the label, lists are constructed by individual faction leaders and local bosses (see Archer and Shugart, this volume). A candidate who is unhappy with where a local faction boss would place the candidate on his list can negotiate with another boss or simply launch his or her own list. Most lists elect only one candidate each, so the system may be characterized as one of "personal lists." This tendency toward lists that are the electoral vehicles of individual candidates, coupled with the lack of pooling from one list to another, makes the system function essentially like the single nontransferable vote (SNTV) used in Japan (Cox and Shugart 1995).[31] Reforms of Party law since 1991 are moving in the direction of greater leadership control, but the practice of multiple lists continues (see Archer and Shugart, this volume).

In systems with limited party control over nominations, the order of the list, or both, candidates owe their election largely to their own efforts. Thus, they are not as beholden to the party as are candidates in closed-list systems. This arrangement promotes individualism in campaigning and fund raising, and successful candidates are less likely to be loyal legislators of a disciplined party when the latter did not secure their victory to begin with. Therefore, such systems contain strong incentives for individualism (as in Brazil) or factionalism (as in Colombia and Uruguay).

In all the variants of electoral systems shown in Table 11.5 except for closed lists, but especially in those in which the party leadership does not control the use of the label, rank-and-file members have the incentive to differentiate themselves from copartisans (Cain, Ferejohn, and Fiorina 1987; Carey and Shugart forthcoming). As the chapters by Mainwaring and by Archer and Shugart show, members secure their seats by building a reputation among a set of followers for being able to provide jobs, public works

31 However, the potential for one list to elect more than one member means that it is not a "pure" case of SNTV. That so many candidates present their own lists, yet do so under the label of one of Colombia's principal parties, is testament to the importance of the party label. If the label were not valuable, candidates who set up their own lists might be inclined to invent new party names for their lists. Thus, Colombia offers a mirror image of the Bolivian and Ecuadoran situations referred to earlier. In the latter two countries, parties control their labels, but the labels themselves are not valuable; thus, defectors must invent new names and are able to win votes under the auspices of a new party label. In Colombia, the situation is reversed: Defectors usually prefer to use a major party's name, and the party leadership cannot stop them.

projects, or outright graft to their followers (see also Ames 1995a, 1995b; Geddes and Ribeiro Neto 1992; Hagopian forthcoming). Such electoral laws therefore hamper the articulation of public policy alternatives and bias the party system in favor of those with money or, in many rural areas, with traditional power resources such as control over land. In addition, because members can (1) win office independently of party approbation and (2) win their office on the basis of personal services and not on promises of a policy-based nature, parties under these electoral systems tend to be factionalized and often undisciplined and clientelistic.

We have been considering the means by which parties control access to ballots for legislative candidates, but the issue also arises for presidential candidates. In the unusual circumstance that the party system is so inchoate that it is relatively easy for a new party to carve out a niche, the issue is less important. Both Fernando Collor de Mello in Brazil (1989) and Alberto Fujimori in Peru (1990) were able to win the presidency after they started new parties that were personal campaign vehicles.[32] Where party systems are more institutionalized such that presidents generally come from large established parties, it is important to consider how open or closed the presidential nomination process is. Until recently, nearly all Latin American parties nominated their presidential candidates in party conventions in which only dues-paying members – and sometimes only a relative handful of "bosses" – had any voice. Increasingly, however, for presidential nominations, Latin American countries are adopting primary systems that resemble those in the United States. In such a system, party leaders play a much smaller role in determining who party nominees will be. It is even possible for a candidate to be nominated over the manifest wishes of most party "insiders," as was the case with Jimmy Carter in the United States in 1976, Carlos Andrés Pérez in Venezuela in 1988, and Carlos Saul Menem in Argentina in 1989. Other countries now using some form of presidential primary in which voters who are not dues-paying activists may participate include Colombia and Costa Rica (see Carey, this volume).

The appeal of presidential primaries is obvious: If the president is the "people's" leader, then the people should participate in the earlier stages of choosing the president and not merely select from among the candidates chosen in the proverbial smoke-filled rooms. Even for party leaders, requir-

---

32 Their ability to be elected rested to no small degree on the majority-runoff system used to elect presidents in these two countries, which allows a relatively small share of the vote to be sufficient to qualify for the runoff. For example, Collor won 30.5% in the first round (and his runoff opponent won only 17%, but won the runoff by a close margin: 53 to 47%) and Fujimori won only 29.1% to Mario Vargas Llosa's 32.6% before defeating Vargas Llosa, 62.5 to 37.5% in the runoff.

ing presidential "pre-candidates" to earn a following in the electorate and to be in the public limelight long before the final campaign can help ensure that a popular nominee is chosen. On the other hand, if a party's own primary electorate is significantly different from the general electorate, the primary may produce an unelectable nominee.[33] Whatever the merits or problems with presidential primaries, it seems fair to say that they work best only with parties that are not rigidly disciplined. A situation of a president elected in a primary and a congressional party beholden to a small circle of leaders who do not support the president may exacerbate presidential–congressional tensions.

So, what kind of electoral system is preferable for presidentialism? If closed lists mean that members are overly responsive to party leaders and not to constituents, what about open lists? As we have suggested, the intraparty competition required in open-list (or SNTV) systems encourages members to be responsive to narrow groups within their broader electoral constituencies and to provide patronage as a means of winning votes. The result is often, as in Brazil and Colombia, comparatively low discipline.

Although we are not in a position to recommend an "ideal" electoral system for presidential systems – there probably is no such thing – we can sketch the outlines of what such a system should provide for. First of all, in order to give members of congress the incentive to be responsive to their broader constituents instead of to either party bosses or patron–client networks, intermediate systems between those using open and closed lists appear desirable. Such intermediate systems, in which neither party leaders' list rankings nor candidates' own vote-drawing ability is the *sole* criterion for determining the order of election, can be found in many European countries (Katz 1986). Systems drawn from the German example, in which about half the members are elected from closed PR lists and the rest in single-member districts, also have some promise. Systems of this sort are now in place in Bolivia, Mexico, and Venezuela and are frequently discussed in Brazil and elsewhere. In these systems the members elected from single-member districts would be expected to cater to local opinion (without having to compete with other candidates of their own party, as is done in open-list systems), but the PR component ensures that no one party dominates. If electoral reforms of these sorts continue to be enacted in Latin America, there is room for optimism that congresses may begin to provide more meaningful representation of their broader constituencies, rather than

---

33 The Colombian primary law helps guard against this possibility by permitting any voter to participate in a party's primary, whether or not the voter has any allegiance to the party at other levels. That is, Colombia uses an "open" primary. See Shugart (1992a).

of party bosses or narrow patron–client groups. If so, then congress would be in a better position to play an independent policy role, and thus its check on the president would be more meaningful. Interbranch disputes would then be more likely to be resolved through policy compromise, as is usually the case in the United States, than through the distribution of patronage.

RELATION BETWEEN CONSTITUTIONAL AND PARTISAN POWERS

We can now link our discussion of presidents' partisan powers – the main topic of this chapter – with our discussion of their constitutional powers over legislation, which we discussed in Chapter 1. We argue that there is a symbiotic relationship between presidents' constitutional and partisan powers; certain degrees of strength on one type of power have an "elective affinity" with certain levels of strength on the other. Before proceeding, however, we need an index of partisan powers. Such an index must give us a sense of not only how likely the president's party is to have a majority, but also how disciplined this party is.

The index takes the average percentage of seats held by the president's party in each case (Table 11.1) and weights it down for each "no" found in Table 11.5, which considered factors that would tend to reduce incentives for party discipline. The weighting factor on indiscipline is one that assumes that a party with poor discipline is about two-thirds as reliable as one that is fully disciplined.[34] Thus, if a country's electoral law scores a "no" three times in Table 11.5, the share of seats for that system is multiplied by two-thirds to arrive at its index of partisan powers. We then classify cases according to the following categories:

1. Very high: an adjusted score of at least 50 for both chambers (or for the only chamber in a unicameral system)
2. Medium high: an adjusted score of at least 40 for both chambers (or for

---

34 Although one could use other weightings, two-thirds is more appropriate than one-half, for example. Even very undisciplined parties have some core of issues on which their members agree. For instance, in work in progress, Mainwaring has found that even the Brazilian PMDB has a party discipline index of around 69% (after eliminating noncontroversial proposals from the set of congressional votes considered). The formula is to multiply the average value for each house from Table 11.1 by the factor $1 - 0.111N$, where N is the number of times the word *no* appears in Table 11.5 for the given case. The use of 0.111 allows the weighting factor to be 0.667 when there are three *no* scores.

the only chamber in a unicameral system), but under 50 for at least one chamber.

3 Low: an adjusted score of at least 30 for both chambers (or for the only chamber in a unicameral system), but under 40 for at least one chamber.

4 Very low: an adjusted score of under 30 for at least one chamber.

How would we expect partisan powers to be related to constitutional legislative powers? In some systems the party system exists first and a new constitution is adopted to manage the affairs of the country; we would expect that the framers of the constitution would adapt the configuration of presidential powers to the preexisting party format (and their expectations of the future). Elsewhere, the constitution is a preexisting reality to which politicians adjust in forming, combining, or splitting parties. Whichever came first – parties or the constitution – or whether both evolved simultaneously, we expect that certain combinations are more in "equilibrium" than others.

Recall from Chapter 1 that we divided constitutional powers over legislation into two basic categories, proactive and reactive. Proactive powers mean principally the ability to promulgate new laws by decree. Reactive powers include principally the veto, but also "gatekeeping" powers by which the president can defend the status quo against attempts by the congressional majority to change it. We identified four classifications of presidential powers over legislation (see Table 1.6): potentially dominant (both proactive and reactive powers, at least in some crucial policy areas), proactive, reactive, and potentially marginal (neither type of power, at least in some crucial policy areas). The following are a set of hypotheses about where cases will fall in a four-by-four matrix that combines our four levels of each type of power. We have no expectations regarding reactive presidencies, but we have hypotheses for each of the other three categories.

H.1. Potentially dominant presidencies will tend to occur with lower levels of partisan powers and only in constitutions with "presidentialist" origins.

The logic of this hypothesis – to take the second part of it first – is that constituent assemblies or congresses would not choose to give the presidency constitutional legislative powers that were so great that presidents might dominate the assembly/congress. Thus, potentially dominant presidencies would stem from constitution-drafting processes that were themselves dominated by the executive, as in a constitution that was drafted by a presidential commission without the participation of elected representatives and then ratified by a plebiscite. Such a dominant presidency is unlikely where the president expects to have disciplined majorities because a president needs very strong constitutional powers only where he or she lacks (or expects to lack) significant partisan powers, hence our expectation that none of these cases will appear in situations of medium to high partisan powers.

H.2. Proactive presidencies will tend to occur with lower levels of partisan powers and in constitutions drafted and ratified primarily by elected representatives.

The logic of this hypothesis is that endowing a presidency with decree powers – but allowing a congressional majority to overturn decrees – is a means of coping with bargaining problems that are likely to result from a fractious congress. That is, where sustaining policy-based majorities is likely to be difficult because of low party discipline and perhaps also a high number of parties, the executive will be granted proactive powers. The difference between this category and the potentially dominant category is that these congresses retain the means to rescind decrees or trump them with new legislation in the event that the president oversteps the bounds established by congress. In the category of potentially dominant presidencies, the congress lacks this ability, or it is difficult to carry out. This difference reflects the different origins hypothesized for the constitutions in these categories.

H.3. Potentially marginal presidencies will tend to occur at higher levels of partisan powers.

This hypothesis is based on two complementary logics. First, where a disciplined majority party exists when the constitution is drafted, the party can expect to dominate the legislative process from its control over the congress. It does not need a proactive presidency in order to accomplish a policy agenda, and endowing the president with reactive powers would risk marginalizing the party in the event of an opposition presidency in the future. Second, if a constitution along with a potentially marginal presidency were in place before a disciplined party had been formed, the very weakness of the presidency would be a powerful incentive for politicians to form a unified party that could endow a president of their choosing with partisan powers to compensate for the lack of constitutional legislative powers.

We confront these hypotheses with data in Table 11.6. Hypotheses 1 and 2 lead us to expect the two right-hand cells to be empty for both potentially dominant presidencies and for proactive presidencies. With the exception of one case, this expectation is borne out; six of seven presidencies in these categories have either medium low or very low partisan powers. Obviously the number of cases is too low for any firm generalizations to be made, but the results are suggestive that the logic of Hypotheses 1 and 2 is valid. Jumping to the bottom row, we find that, as expected, potentially marginal presidencies are found only in situations of medium high or very high partisan powers, as predicted in Hypothesis 3.

Among the potentially dominant presidencies, the Chilean and Ecu-

Table 11.6. *Relationship between presidents' constitutional and partisan powers in Latin America*

Constitutional powers over legislation	Presidents' partisan powers			
	Very low	Medium low	Medium high	Very high
Potentially dominant	Chile, 1989 Ecuador	Colombia, 1968	Argentina	
Proactive	Brazil, 1988	Colombia, 1991 Peru		
Reactive	Brazil, 1946 Chile, 1925	Bolivia	El Salvador Uruguay	Dominican Republic
Potentially marginal			Costa Rica Paraguay, 1991 Venezuela	Honduras Mexico Nicaragua

Note: Explanation of categories is found in text.

adoran constitutions are those that most clearly were the products of drafting processes in which elected representatives played no role.[35] Both constitutions were drafted at the service of military governments and were ratified by plebiscites conducted before the return to democratic rule. These two cases should fit Hypothesis 1 if any would.

The Argentine constitution of 1853 was not created in a presidentialist process; however, as Lutz (1994) notes, amending or replacing a constitution are only two ways of adapting the constitutional framework to contemporary needs. Especially where the existing constitution is difficult to amend – as is the case in Argentina – judicial reinterpretation is another way to adapt a constitution. The 1853 constitution made no provision for decree-laws, but as Jones's chapter discusses, President Menem succeeded in "packing" the Supreme Court with compliant judges through his party's control over the legislature, which confirms justices and sets the size of the Court. Thus, this de facto modification of the constitution may be termed presidentialist, as it did not come about through the normal constitutional amendment

---

35 Outside Latin America, there is at least one other constitution that conforms to the logic of Hypothesis 1: that of Russia. See Parrish (n.d.).

process. The new constitution of 1994 codifies the decree powers, while leaving the president with strong veto power; the drafting of this constitution occurred through the formal amendment process, but in the context of a president who had indicated his willingness to resort to unconstitutional means to change the constitution if the major opposition party did not "play ball" with him. Thus, Argentina is consistent with the second part of Hypothesis 1 – concerning the impact of the president in deciding what the constitutional allocation of powers would be – but not with the first. It is puzzling that President Menem should have felt a need for such dominant powers given that he enjoyed relatively high partisan powers,[36] although it could be noted that despite the "medium high" ranking, no election has produced a majority in both houses simultaneously for the president's party.

The Colombian case from 1968 to 1991 is our one nonpresidentialist constitution clearly in the potentially dominant category. Although President Lleras was the initiator of the reforms in 1968, they were approved through the sitting Congress according to established procedures. Therefore, the reforms cannot be termed *presidentialist*, as we used that term earlier. Thus, this case is somewhat anomalous. However, it is unique among the potentially dominant presidencies in having a majority (albeit factionalized) party as well as an "opposition" party that was at the time still very closely aligned with the majority party in a power-sharing agreement (the National Front). Hence, it was not as if the Congress was endowing a potentially "outsider" president with these enormous powers. Moreover, at the same time that the Congress increased the formal powers of the presidency, it reduced the majority needed to amend the constitution from two-thirds to an absolute majority. Hence, in the event of a future outsider president, the congressional majority was well positioned to clip the president's wings. The Colombian constitution is the only one of the potentially dominant cases in which the constitution is so easily amended. This is consistent with the spirit of the hypothesis concerning the relationship between presidential powers and who has control over the constitution itself.

There are two other cases of constitutions in this set that were drafted in what resemble presidentialist situations, Colombia (1991) and Peru (1993). In the Colombian case, the president initiated the process using emergency powers (see Archer and Shugart, this volume), but the president's own party fell short of a majority in the Constituent Assembly that actually drafted the constitution. The result of this process, in which all the parties

---

36 Perhaps part of the explanation lies in conjunctural factors – Menem's pursuit of neoliberal reforms that cut against the grain of his party, but we shall not delve into such matters here.

were poorly disciplined, was a proactive rather than a potentially dominant presidency, which is consistent with Hypothesis 2. In Peru in 1992–93, President Fujimori had shut down the previous Congress; while the new constitution was drafted in an elected assembly, the whole process was conducted under conditions that do not meet our criteria for being considered democratic. The assembly-based drafting process and the extremely low institutionalization of the president's political movement (which held a majority of seats) support Hypothesis 2, but the heavy shadow cast by the president's *autogolpe* means that a potentially dominant presidency would have been a plausible outcome. The result comes close to such an outcome, since the presidency was endowed with some new reactive powers (in the form of gatekeeping power – see Table 1.6), but the veto remains so weak that we do not classify it as potentially dominant. The other proactive presidency is Brazil II, where the constitution-drafting process supports Hypothesis 2, given the internal fragmentation of Brazilian parties.

The potentially marginal presidencies fall exactly as predicted by Hypothesis 3. In Venezuela, Costa Rica, and Honduras, a disciplined party controlled a majority or nearly so at the time of constitution drafting and presumably expected to remain a significant and disciplined party well into the future. In Mexico, as Weldon's chapter shows, presidents were in fact rather feckless until the presidency and the leadership of an "official" party were combined in the same person. Thus, the Mexican case supports not only the logic of Hypothesis 3, but also one of the major points of this book: What presidents lack in constitutional legislative powers they can make up for in partisan powers, even to the point of being "dominant."

This exercise in correlating constitutional powers with partisan powers has allowed us to confirm two basic generalizations that are suggestive for further research, albeit not definitive. First, potentially dominant presidencies are generally found in constitutions drafted with very strong presidential participation and, along with proactive presidencies, are associated with low partisan powers. Second, potentially marginal presidencies and high partisan powers go together.

FINAL REMARKS

The overall theme of this chapter has been that presidentialism is most fruitfully studied in relation to two key features of a party system. The first feature is the number of parties or the degree of party system fragmentation. With a highly fragmented party system or a very large number of parties, presidents are likely to be in a distinct minority situation in congress (and quite possibly in society as well). This situation can make it difficult for presidents to realize their agendas, can lead to impasse, and can encourage presidents to use patronage to win support and/or to circumvent congress and parties.

We have also emphasized that party discipline or the lack thereof affects how presidentialism functions. With weak party discipline, presidents' negotiations with individual legislators and/or regional party leaders become crucial; with tightly disciplined parties, presidents can negotiate primarily with national party leaders. As we have emphasized, under presidentialism there are problems both with relatively undisciplined parties and with extremely disciplined parties. We also showed that both the number of parties and the degree of party discipline are shaped by key features of electoral and party legislation. Finally, we argued that the interaction between presidents' partisan powers, discussed in this chapter, and their constitutional legislative powers, discussed in Chapter 1, fundamentally shapes their ability to get things done.

The importance of the interaction between presidentialism and the party system is not surprising in light of some comparative literature on related subjects. In writings on parliamentary systems, it has been apparent for some time now that there are very substantial differences between situations of majoritarian rule and situations of coalition or minority government (Lijphart 1984; Strom 1990). Moreover, a robust debate has emerged in the U.S. context on the impact of divided presidential government (Mayhew 1991; Fiorina 1992). Until quite recently, however, little attention has been paid to this question for presidential systems in Latin America. Moreover, in contrast to the wide recognition of the importance of party discipline in parliamentary systems, little has been done on party discipline in presidentialism.

In closing, let us emphasize two general conclusions of the book as a whole. First, we have argued that presidentialism has important variations. Much of the literature has treated presidentialism as a relatively homogeneous regime type. Yet a very strong claim can be made – and the previous chapters support this contention – that differences within the presidential regime type are quite important.

Presidential systems vary so greatly in the powers accorded to the president, the types of party and electoral systems with which they are associated, and the socioeconomic and historical context in which they were created that these differences are likely to be as important as the oft-assumed dichotomy between presidential and parliamentary systems. The way both presidential and parliamentary governments function, and ultimately the advantages and shortcomings of both, depend on the entire institutional context.

In Chapter 1 and this Conclusion, we have attempted to conceptualize the major institutional dimensions along which presidential systems vary, focusing on four key factors: (1) the degree to which they conform to or vary from "pure" presidentialism; (2) the legislative powers of the president; (3) the degree of party system fragmentation, which affects the prospects for general compatibility or conflict between the president and the assembly; and (4) the discipline or lack thereof of political parties. We dealt with the first two issues in Chapter 1 and the other two in this chapter.

Although we have focused on these institutional differences, we are aware that there are other very important factors in determining how presidentialism functions. The quality of leadership, the nature of social cleavages and political conflicts, the level of economic development, and the political culture strongly affect how democracy works. Nevertheless, institutional arrangements help or hinder democratic governments in their efforts to govern effectively.

The second major theme has been that these variations among presidential systems have consequences for how well they are apt to function. We believe that presidential systems tend to function better with limited executive powers over legislation, mainly because a weaker executive means that the congress has more opportunity for debating and logrolling on controversial matters. Having weaker executive powers also means that cases in which presidents lack reliable majorities are less likely to be crisis-ridden, since the president has fewer tools with which to try to do an end run around the congress. Finally, we have stressed that presidentialism usually functions better when presidents have at least a reasonably large bloc of reliable legislative seats. These desiderata would suggest the following institutional rules for presidential systems: Legislative elections should be concurrent with a presidential election that is based on a plurality or else on a runoff with a lower threshold than majority for first-round victory;[37] and an electoral system should offer some compromise on the usual dichotomy of open versus closed lists.

These conclusions should not be taken as firm, but rather as tentative. Much more research needs to be done on how institutions work in different

---

37 For instance, the rule in Costa Rica, where a candidate must obtain 40% in the first round to avoid a runoff, or a provision like the new one in Argentina that requires a minimum spread of votes, as discussed in Jones's chapter. See also Shugart and Taagepera (1994) for an analysis of runoff formats.

combinations and in different social, economic, and cultural contexts. It is in the spirit of furthering the analysis of institutional arrangements that we have compiled this study of presidential democracy in Latin America.

APPENDIX: PRESIDENTS' ELECTORAL COALITIONS

We list information only where a coalition in which at least two parties won legislative seats rather than a single party formally supported the winning presidential candidate. And we list only parties that won seats; in some cases, minor parties that did not win seats in the national congress also supported the winning presidential candidate.

John Carey, Brian Crisp, Mark Jones, Charles Kenney, and Michelle Taylor provided helpful information for this Appendix.

ARGENTINA

1989–95: Partido Justicialista, Partido Blanco de los Jubilados, Partido Intransigente, and the Partido Demócrata Cristiano.

1995–99: Partido Justicialista, Union del Centro Democrático, Partido Renovador de Salta, Movimiento Popular Jujeno, and Partido Bloquista.

BOLIVIA

We did not compute a figure for the president's coalition for 1982–85 because there were no popular elections in 1982. Siles Suazo was elected by Congress in 1982, but the congressional elections were held in 1980.

BRAZIL

1945–47 and 1947–50: Partido Social Democrático and Partido Trabalhista Brasileiro.

1950–54: Partido Trabalhista Brasileiro and Partido Social Progressista.

1955–58 and 1958–60: Partido Social Democrático and Partido Trabalhista Brasileiro.

1961: União Democrática Nacional, Partido Democrata Cristiano, Partido Libertador, and Partido Trabalhista Nacional.

1985 and 1986–89: Partido do Movimento Democrático Brasileiro and Partido da Frente Liberal.

1994: Partido Social Democrático Brasileiro, Partido da Frente Liberal, and Partido Trabalhista Brasileiro.

CHILE

For 1957–58 and 1958–61, we are missing data for the Senate. The mean for the Senate is therefore based on 16 elections.

Senate figures for 1937–45 are estimates. For these years, Nohlen (1993) gives information only on election results, not on Senate composition. For 1937–38 and 1938–41, we added the 1937 results (20 seats) to the 1932 results (45 seats). For 1941–42 and 1942–45, we added the 1941 results (20 seats) to the 1937 results.

1932–37 and 1937–38: Partido Liberal, Partido Liberal Unido, Partido Liberal Doctrinario, Partido Liberal Democrático, Partido Demo-crata, Partido Democrático, Partido Radical Socialista, Partido Social Republicano, and Partido Conservador.

1938–41 and 1941–42: Partido Radical, Partido Comunista Chileno, Partido Socialista, Partido Democrata, and Partido Radical Socialista.

1942–45 and 1945–46: Partido Radical, Partido Socialista, Partido Comunista Chileno, and Falange Nacional.

1946–49 and 1949–52: Partido Radical, Partido Comunista Chileno, and Partido Liberal.

1952–53, 1953–57, and 1957–58: Acción Renovadora, Partido Agrario, Partido del Trabajo, Partido Nacional, Partido Nacional Cristiano, Movimiento Republicano, Partido Agrario Laborista, Partido Demócrata, Partido Socialista Popular, and Movimiento Nacional Ibañista.

1958–61 and 1961–64: Partido Conservador, Partido Liberal, Movimiento Nacional del Pueblo, and Falange Nacional.

1970–73 and 1973: Partido Socialista, Partido Comunista Chileno, Partido Radical, Movimiento de Acción Popular Unitario, and Acción Popular Independiente.

1989–93: Democracia Cristiana, Partido por la Democracia, Partido Socialista, Partido Radical, Partido Humanista.

1993–present: Democracia Cristiana, Partido por la Democracia, Partido Socialista, Partido Radical. Senate figures for 1989–present include appointed senators.

COSTA RICA

1958–62: Partido Union Nacional and Partido de Unificación.

PERU

Peru switched to a unicameral Congress in 1992–93. (The Constitutional Congress of 1992 was unicameral, and the new constitution went into effect in 1993.)

> 1985–90: Alianza Popular Revolucionaria Americana, Democracia Cristiana, and Socidad y Democracia.

VENEZUELA

> 1978–83: Comité de Organación Político Electoral and Unión Republicana Democrática.
> 1983–88: Acción Democrática and Unión Republicana Democrática.
> 1993–present: Movimiento al Socialismo, Convergencia, Unión Republicana Democrática, Comité de Organización Político Electoral Independiente, and Movimiento de Integración Nacional.

APPENDIX: OUTLINES OF CONSTITUTIONAL POWERS IN LATIN AMERICA

Compiled by John M. Carey, Octávio Amorim Neto, and Matthew Soberg Shugart

INTRODUCTION

In this Appendix, we have compiled a summary of the provisions concerning executive–legislative relations from 23 constitutions in Latin America. We include not only the current constitutions of all the countries of this region that have popularly elected presidents, but also superseded ones in several cases in which the old constitutions are discussed in Chapter 1 or other chapters of this book. Thus, we include the superseded democratic constitutions of Argentina (1853), Brazil (1946), Chile (1925), Colombia (1886), and Peru (1979). For each of the current constitutions, the provisions summarized are those in effect as of late 1994, unless otherwise indicated. Dates of amended constitutions are noted only where they affect provisions listed in this Appendix. For the superseded constitutions, the provisions are those in effect as of the time the constitution was replaced, unless otherwise indicated. Most of the headings for provisions are self-explanatory, but a few require clarification.

Electoral cycle refers to the relative timing of elections for president and congress and may be either concurrent (when such elections are regularly held on the same day), nonconcurrent (when such elections are regularly held on separate days), or mixed (when terms are of different length, but

We are grateful to Mark Jones for his comments and assistance on this Appendix.

elections are held on the same day in those years when elections are held for both the executive and legislature).

Decree legislation refers to the authority of the president to issue new laws that do not require the consent of the legislature to have legal force. We do not, therefore, refer to the power held by most presidents to regulate existing laws or reorganize administrative functions. We have indicated where constitutions permit the president the right to emit legislative decrees on his own initiative, as well as where measures declared "urgent" by the president take the force of law in the absence of congressional action, and those provisions by which the congress may delegate legislative decree authority to the president temporarily.

Emergency powers refer to provisions granting the president the authority to suspend constitutional guarantees; these powers usually do not imply legislative decree authority unless so indicated.

The source for these constitutional provisions, unless otherwise indicated, is Blaustein and Flanz (1971–present). Article numbers from constitutional texts are given in parentheses. Where no article number is given, the shown provision is/was contained in law.

Argentina (1853; no longer in force)

Executive Election: By majority of the electoral college, each province and the capital sending double the number of electors as it has deputies and senators (81). The president and vice-president are chosen on separate ballots (81). Failing a majority, Congress in joint session elects both offices from between two top candidates in the first round (83).

Presidential Terms: 6 years for president and vice-president, with no immediate re-election (77).

Assembly Terms: Lower: 4, with half renewed every 2 years (42). Upper: 9, one-third renewed every 3 years (48).

Election Timing: Mixed.

Veto Override: By two-thirds vote in each chamber (72).

Exclusive Introduction of Legislation by Executive: No provision.

Decree Legislation: No provision.

Referendum/Popular Initiative: None.

Ministerial Appointments: The president appoints cabinet ministers without restrictions (86).

Dismissal of Ministers by Assembly: No provision.

Dissolution: None.

Impeachment: Of ministers or the president by two-thirds vote in both chambers (45, 51).

Emergency Powers: Foreign invasion, state of siege declared with consent of the Senate. Internal disturbance, only if Congress is not in session, until Congress reconvenes

(86:19). Suspension of the writ of habeas corpus but not legislative authority (86: 23).

Constitutional Amendments: By constitutional convention convoked after approval by two-thirds of members of each house (30).

Argentina (1994)

Executive Election: The president and vice-president are chosen on the same ticket by a two-round system, requiring 45% of the votes or else 40% with a margin of at least 10%, for first-round victory (94–98).

Presidential Terms: 4 years for president and vice-president, with one immediate reelection (90).

Assembly Terms: Lower: 4, with half renewed every 2 years (50). Upper: 6, one-third renewed every 2 years (56).

Election Timing: Mixed.

Veto Override: Two-thirds vote in each chamber (83). Partial veto and partial promulgation, if the approval of parts of the bill "does not alter the spirit or the unity of the bill as passed by Congress" (80).

Exclusive Introduction of Legislation by Executive: No provision.

Decree Legislation: With the exception of rules regulating penal, tax, or electoral matters or the system of political parties, the president may dictate decrees for reasons of "need and urgency," which must be countersigned by the appropriate minister and the chief of the Cabinet. Within 10 days, the measure must be submitted to Congress for discussion (99:3).

Referendum/Popular Initiative: At the initiative of the Chamber of Deputies, Congress may submit a bill to popular consultation. The law regarding this initiative may not be vetoed (40). Popular initiatives are established by 3% of the electorate. Congress must give them express treatment within 12 months (39).

Ministerial Appointments: The president alone appoints and removes the chief of the Cabinet of Ministers and other ministers (99:7).

Dismissal of Ministers by Assembly: The chief of the Cabinet of Ministers may be removed by absolute majority in each chamber (101).

Dissolution: No provision.

Impeachment: Of the president, chief of the Cabinet of Ministers, and ministers by two-thirds vote in both chambers (53, 59).

Emergency Powers: Foreign invasion, state of siege declared with consent of the Senate. Internal disturbance, only if Congress is in recess (99:16).

Constitutional Amendments: By constitutional convention convoked after approval by two-thirds of members of Congress (30).

Bolivia (1967)

Executive Election: In the absence of majority in popular vote, the president and vice-president are chosen, separately, by majority vote in both houses of Congress from among two leading candidates (three prior to 1994) in popular election (90).

Presidential Terms: 4 years, with no immediate reelection (86, 87).

Assembly Terms: 4 years (60, 65).

Election Timing: Concurrent. Assembly and presidential elections are fused.

Veto Override: By two-thirds vote in joint session (77).

Exclusive Introduction of Legislation by Executive: No provision.

Decree Legislation: No provision.

Referendum/Popular Initiative: No provision.

Ministerial Appointments: President appoints ministers without restriction (99).

Dismissal of Ministers by Assembly: No provision.

Dissolution: No provision.

Impeachment: Indictment by joint session of Congress (no extraordinary majority stipulated); decision by Supreme Court (68:12, 127:6).

Emergency Powers: Invasion, civil war, or internal disorder, for 90 days. If Congress is in session, continuation must be authorized by legislation (111). Increase size of armed forces, advance revenue collection, suspend writ of habeas corpus (112).

Constitutional Amendments: The constitution may be amended in parts by a two-thirds majority in each chamber (230).

Brazil (1946; no longer in force)

Note: Summary excludes the major revisions adopted in 1961, then rescinded in 1963.

Source: Campanhole and Campanhole (1971) and Senado Federal (1991).

Executive Election: President and vice-president by plurality, separate ballots for each office.

Presidential Terms: 5 years, with no immediate reelection (82).

Assembly Terms: 4 years for Chamber of Deputies (57). 8 years for Senate (60).

Election Timing: Mixed.

Veto Override: Package and partial; by two-thirds majority in joint session (70).

Exclusive Introduction of Legislation by Executive: Bills that would (1) increase salaries of public servants and create new jobs in existing public agencies and (2) modify the law establishing the size of the armed forces (67).

Decree Legislation: No provision.

Referendum/Popular Initiative: No provision.

Ministerial Appointments: The president has exclusive authority to appoint and dismiss cabinet ministers (87).

Dismissal of Ministers by Assembly: No provision.

Dissolution: No provision.

Impeachment: Charged by two-thirds of the Chamber, tried by the Supreme Court for common criminal offenses or by the Senate for criminal abuse of power (88).

Emergency Powers: State of siege decreed by the Congress. Congress must specify the constitutional guarantees that will still be in force during the state of siege. The state of siege must last 30 days and may not be extended for additional 30-day periods. In case of war, the state of siege may last as long as the war. During the recess of the legislature, the president may decree a state of siege. In this case, the Congress will be reconvened to approve/deny the state of siege (206–11).

Constitutional Amendments: Proposed by at least one-fourth of the members of either house or by more than half of the legislative assemblies of the states (provided that in each of them a majority of its members supports the proposal). Approval by absolute majority in each house. No amendments during state of siege (217).

Brazil (1988)

Executive Election: President and vice-president by majority runoff (77).
Presidential Terms: 4 years, with no immediate reelection (82).
Assembly Terms: 4 years for Chamber of Deputies (44). 8 years for Senate (46).
Election Timing: Concurrent (nonconcurrent before 1994).
Veto Override: Veto of an entire bill or any article, paragraph, subsection, or subpart. Override by absolute majority in joint session (66).
Exclusive Introduction of Legislation by Executive: Bills that deal with the size of the armed forces; creation of jobs, functions, and posts in public administration; salary increases for public servants; administrative and judicial organization; taxation and budgetary matters; careers of civil servants; administrative units of the territories; organization of the offices of the Government Attorney and the Public Defender of the Union, as well as general rules for the organization of the offices of Government Attorney and of the Public Defenders in the states, the federal district, and territories; creation and structure of ministries and other bodies of public administration (61). Bills declared "urgent" by the president must be voted on within 45 days, first in the Chamber, then in the Senate (64).
Decree Legislation: President may adopt "provisional measures" with the force of law, which must be submitted immediately to Congress. If these are not converted into law within 30 days, they lose effectiveness (62).
Referendum/Popular Initiative: Initiated by signatures of 1% of the electorate, distributed among at least five states, with not less than 0.3% of the voters in each (61).
Ministerial Appointments: The president appoints and dismisses cabinet ministers (84).
Dismissal of Ministers by Assembly: No provision.
Dissolution: No provision.
Impeachment: Upon being charged by two-thirds of the Chamber, tried by Supreme Court for common criminal offenses or by the Senate for criminal abuse of power (86).
Emergency Powers: Require consultation with the Council of the Republic and the National Defense Council and authorization by an absolute majority of the Congress (136–39).
Constitutional Amendments: Proposal by at least one-third of members of either house, by the president, by more than half the legislative assemblies of the federal units (provided that in each of them a relative majority of its members supports the proposal). Approval in two rounds by each house by three-fifths of the votes (60).

Chile (1925; no longer in force)

Source: Valencia Avaria (1986).
Executive Election: If no candidate receives a majority of valid votes, the Congress in

joint session, by majority vote in secret, selects the president between the two most voted candiates in the election (63–65).

Presidential Terms: 6 years, with no immediate reelection (62). In case of permanent vacancy, new election held within 60 days (69).

Assembly Terms: Lower: 4 (38). Upper: 8, renewed by half every 4 years (41).

Election Timing: Nonconcurrent.

Veto Override: By two-thirds vote in each chamber (53–54).

Exclusive Introduction of Legislation by Executive: Increase in expenditures established by the General Law of the Budget (45); bills involving modification of political or administrative divisions of the country; taxation; creation of public services; remuneration of civil servants; establishment of pensions and minimum wage of private-sector workers (Constitutional Reform, Law No. 17.284, January 23, 1970).

Decree Legislation: Congress may delegate decree authority (Constitutional Reform, Law No. 17.284, January 23, 1970).

Referendum/Popular Initiative: No provision.

Ministerial Appointments: The president appoints and dismisses cabinet ministers (72: 5).

Dismissal of Ministers by Assembly: No provision.

Dissolution: No provision.

Impeachment: Upon charge of one-half of the Chamber, upheld by two-thirds vote in the Senate (39, 42).

Emergency Powers: The president may declare in *estado de asamblea* one or more provinces invaded or threatened in case of foreign war, and a state of siege in one or more points of the republic in case of foreign attack. In the event of internal disturbance, only the Congress may declare a state of siege. But if the Congress is not convened, the president may do it for a certain period of time. Emergency powers do not imply legislative authority (72:17).

Constitutional Amendments: Approval by a majority of the members in each house and by a majority vote in a joint session in the presence of a majority of members. The president may propose modifications, subject to override by two-thirds of the members of each house. The president may then either promulgate the amendments as approved or convoke a plebiscite to decide on the points of disagreement between him or her and the Congress (108, 109).

From 1970 on, the president may also convoke a plebiscite when a constitutional amendment proposed by the president is rejected in its entirety by the Congress. No plebiscite may be convoked on any proposal to modify the procedures for convoking plebiscites (Law No. 17.284, January 23, 1970).

Chile (1980, including 1989 amendments)

Executive Election: By majority runoff (26). No vice-president.

Presidential Terms: 6 years (for president elected in 1989, 4 years), with no reelection (25). If the presidency is vacated, the Senate elects an interim president by vote of an absolute majority. The interim president serves until a new president is elected by direct election, concurrent with the next scheduled general election for Congress. The newly elected president serves only the remainder of the current term and cannot be reelected (29).

Assembly Terms: Lower: 4 (43). Upper: 8, renewed by half every 4 years (45). Ex-presidents who have served more than 6 years are senators for life. Also given Senate seats are two former ministers of the Supreme Court; a former comptroller general; former chiefs of the army, navy, air force, armed police; a former rector of the state university; and a former cabinet minister (45).

Election Timing: Mixed.

Veto Override: By two-thirds vote in both chambers (70). If a law of the president's initiative is rejected in the chamber to which it is first submitted, it may be resubmitted to the other chamber. If it passes this second chamber, it is resubmitted to the first and becomes law only if it is rejected here by a two-thirds majority (67).

Exclusive Introduction of Legislation by Executive: Bills that would reduce specific taxes; create new public services or employment in the state sector; contract loans to the state; establish or amend entitlement programs; establish procedures applicable to collective bargaining; establish or amend terms of social security (62). On the budget, Congress may amend proposed expenditures but not proposed revenues. Congress may not increase any expenditures without indicating where the funds shall come from. If the law is not passed by Congress within 60 days, the president's version takes effect (64).

Decree Legislation: The president may request, and the Congress authorize for up to one year, the delegation to the president of authority to order provisions with the force of law (61). With the signatures of all ministers, the president may decree payments not authorized by law to meet needs that cannot be ignored without "causing serious detriment to the country" (32:22).

Referendum/Popular Initiative: See Constitutional Amendments.

Ministerial Appointments: The president exclusively appoints cabinet ministers (32: 9).

Dismissal of Ministers by Assembly: No provision.

Dissolution: No provision.

Impeachment: By a majority of deputies, upheld by two-thirds vote in Senate (48, 49).

Emergency Powers: States of siege, exception, assembly, and emergency – all requiring the consent of Congress or the National Security Council – imply the suspension of individual rights but no unconstrained law-making power (39–41).

Constitutional Amendments: Proposed by president or any member of Congress. Preliminary approval by three-fifths of each house, unless amendment concerns such topics as constitutional rights and obligations, the armed forces, the Constitutional Court, the National Security Council, or amendment procedures, in which case two-thirds of each house is required (116). Sixty days afterwards, approval without debate by a joint session attended by a majority of all members. President may veto entire proposal, subject to override by two-thirds of the members of each chamber. President may veto parts of proposal, in which case the president's objections are deemed adopted by a supporting vote of three-fifths or two-thirds of the membership, in conformity with the majority required under Article 116. A two-thirds majority of the membership of each chamber may override the president's objections. The president may convoke a plebiscite to decide on the points of disagreement between him or her and the Congress (117).

Colombia (1886; no longer in effect)

Executive Election: The president is elected by plurality (114).

Presidential Terms: 4 years (114), with no immediate reelection (129). A *designado*, elected by Congress every 2 years, completes term in case of vacancy (124).

Assembly Terms: 4 years for senators and representatives (95,101).

Election Timing: Congressional elections precede presidential elections by 2 months.

Veto Override: By two-thirds majority in both chambers for all legislation related to legal codes; organic rules for the national budget; changes in territorial subdivisions; National Development Plan. Only an absolute majority in each chamber is needed for all other legislation (88). Partial veto (87) returns bill to committee, where only vetoed section of bill can be reconsidered; no partial promulgation. Package veto returns whole bill to chamber floors.

Exclusive Introduction of Legislation by Executive: Bills on organic rules for the national budget; public works; the structure of the executive ministries; salaries for public employees; general norms for foreign exchange, external trade, the national debt, and tariffs; laws decreeing public or private investment or creating new services; most tax exemptions (79).

Decree Legislation: Congress may temporarily vest in the president extraordinary powers "as necessity or the public good may counsel" (76:12). See also Emergency Powers, as these also imply legislative powers.

Referendum/Popular Initiative: No provision.

Ministerial Appointments: The president appoints and dismisses ministers, but must offer "an adequate and equitable share" to the second-largest party (120:1).

Dismissal of Ministers by Assembly: No provision.

Dissolution: No provision.

Impeachment: Initiated by House of Representatives (no extraordinary majority stipulated); must be upheld by two-thirds vote in Senate (102:4, 97).

Emergency Powers: With the consent of all the cabinet ministers, the president may declare a state of siege, under which existing laws may be suspended and new measures may be taken by decree to restore order. Such decrees lapse when the state of siege is lifted or at the end of the president's term (121). With the consent of all ministers, the president may declare a state of economic emergency and issue decrees pursuant thereto, subject to recission or amendment by Congress (122).

Constitutional Amendments: By absolute majorities of each house of Congress in two consecutive regular sessions (218).

Colombia (1991)

Executive Election: Majority runoff for president and vice-president (190).

Presidential Terms: 4 years (190), with no reeletion (197).

Assembly Terms: 4 years for senators and representatives (132).

Election Timing: Congressional elections precede presidential elections by 2 months, according to law; constitution requires elections to be nonconcurrent (262).

Veto Override: The government may totally or partially object to bills. Override requires absolute majorities of both chambers (166, 167, 200:1).

Exclusive Introduction of Legislation by Executive: Bills on the structure of the executive ministries; salaries of public employees; general norms for foreign exchange, external trade, the national debt, and tariffs; granting authority to executive to negotiate contracts and loans; establishment of revenues and expenses of administration and functions of the Central Bank (150).

Decree Legislation: On express request of government and by absolute majorities, Congress may delegate decree powers to the president for a period of up to 6 months (150:10). See also Emergency Powers.

Referendum/Popular Initiative: The president, with the approval of the ministers and the prior approval of the Senate, may call a binding referendum on a matter "of great national importance." Such consultation may not coincide with another election (103–106). See also Constitutional Amendments.

Ministerial Appointments: The president appoints and dismisses cabinet ministers freely (189:1).

Dismissal of Ministers by Assembly: On proposal of at least one-tenth of members of respective chamber, cabinet ministers may be dismissed by an absolute majority of each chamber (135:8, 9).

Dissolution: No provision.

Impeachment: Chamber of Representatives may charge the president before the Senate, which may dismiss the president by a two-thirds vote in public session (174, 175, 178).

Emergency Powers: The president, with the approval of all the ministers, may declare a state of internal disturbance in all or part of the country for a period no longer than 90 days, extendable for two similar periods, the second of which requires the consent of the Senate. The government can suspend laws incompatible with the state of disturbance. However, neither human rights nor fundamental freedoms may be suspended. In the case of events that disrupt the economic, social, or ecological order of the country or that constitute a grave public calamity, the president, with the signature of all ministers, may declare a state of emergency for periods up to 30 days in each case, which, in all, may not exceed 90 days. The president may, with the signature of all ministers, issue decrees with the force of law to restore order. During the year subsequent to the declaration of emergency, the Congress may repeal, amend, or add to the decrees. Executive may impose or amend taxes, but these measures lapse at the conclusion of the state of emergency (213–15).

Constitutional Amendments: The constitution may be reformed by the Congress, a constituent assembly, or by the people through referendum (374). The government, 10 Congress members, 20% of councilors or deputies, or 5% of voters may introduce an amendment proposal, subject to approval by a simple majority of each house, and to ratification by absolute majorites in second ordinary session (375). Congress, by absolute majority, may call a referendum to decide if a constituent assembly, with clear jurisdiction, term, and makeup, should be convened (376) or to vote on an amendment proposed by government or by 5% of voters (378). Amendments to rights guaranteed by the constitution must be submitted to a referendum (377).

Costa Rica (1949)

Executive Election: If no ticket receives 40% of popular votes, then a runoff is held between two top tickets (138). Two vice-presidents are elected on a single ticket with the president (138).

Presidential Terms: 4 years, with no immediate reelection (132, 134). If the presidency is permanently vacated, the vice-presidents succeed the president in the order of their nomination (135).

Assembly Terms: 4 years, with no immediate reelection (107).

Election Timing: Concurrent with first round of presidential election.

Veto Override: No veto on budget legislation (125). Override by two-thirds vote of the of Assembly on all other legislation (127).

Exclusive Introduction of Legislation by Executive: No provision.

Decree Legislation: No provision.

Referendum/Popular Initiative: No provision.

Ministerial Appointments: The president appoints cabinet as well as provincial governors without restriction (139).

Dismissal of Ministers by Assembly: No provision.

Dissolution: No provision.

Impeachment: By two-thirds vote in Assembly (121).

Emergency Powers: Suspension of rights by two-thirds vote in the Assembly (140:Sec. 4).

Constitutional Amendments: Partial amendment by two-thirds of Assembly (195). A general amendment of the constitution can be affected only by a constituent assembly convoked by two-thirds of the Assembly and does not require the approval of the executive (196, as amended by Law 4123, May 31, 1968).

Dominican Republic (1966)

Executive Election: By "direct vote" (49) jointly with the vice-president (51). Plurality rule.

Presidential Terms: 4 years (49).

Assembly Terms: 4 years for senators and deputies (21, 24).

Election Timing: Concurrent.

Veto Override: By two-thirds vote in each chamber. Failure to veto within 1 week (or within 3 days on legislation declared urgent) results in passage (41). Congress does not adjourn until the president has either promulgated or vetoed all passed legislation (42).

Exclusive Introduction of Legislation by Executive: No provision.

Decree Legislation: No provision.

Referendum/Popular Initiative: No provision.

Ministerial Appointments: The president appoints cabinet without restriction (55:1).

Dismissal of Ministers by Assembly: No provision.

Dissolution: No provision.

Impeachment: By three-quarters vote in both chambers (23).

Emergency Powers: Suspension of individual rights by the president is subject to approval by Congress, if it is in session (37:7, 8; 55:7).

Constitutional Amendments: Proposal by one-third of the members of either chamber or by the executive (116), approved by law not subject to presidential veto (117), ratified by two-thirds of the members present at a joint session with quorum of one-half of members (118).

Ecuador (1979)

Executive Election: President and vice-president are elected on same ticket, by majority runoff (74, 80).

Presidential Terms: 4 years; no reelection (73).

Assembly Terms: 4 years for members elected on national list; 2 years for those elected from provincial list; no immediate reelection (56–57). Unicameral.

Election Timing: Concurrent with first round of presidential election; also midterm election for members elected from provincial lists.

Veto Override: No veto on budget (70). On all other legislation, no override if president totally rejects the bill. However, Congress "may ask the President to submit [vetoed bills] to the voters by referendum." Moreover, if the president's objection relates only to a specific part of a bill, Congress may either rectify the section, effecting promulgation, or may override the veto by two-thirds vote (69).

Exclusive Introduction of Legislation by Executive: No provision.

Decree Legislation: The president may declare economic legislation urgent, in which case Congress must act on it within 15 days or it becomes law (65).

Referendum/Popular Initiative: The president may call referenda on questions "which, in his judgment, are of great importance to the state," in particular on constitutional amendments and on the ratification of international agreements that have been rejected by Congress (78). See also Veto Override. Popular initiative to amend the constitution and to amend and enact laws is recognized. The exercise of this right is regulated by law (65).

Ministerial Appointments: The president appoints and removes cabinet ministers without restriction (78, 85).

Dismissal of Ministers by Assembly: By majority of Congress "for violations commited in the fulfillment of their office." A minister censured by Congress may not serve in any other public role during the same presidential term (59:f, 87).

Dissolution: No provision.

Impeachment: "The president of the Republic can only be judged for treason to his Fatherland, bribery or any other infraction that would severely affect the national honor" (59). No extraordinary majority is stipulated.

Emergency Powers: The president may declare a state of emergency – which Congress may revoke but need not act to uphold – in case of foreign invasion or internal disturbance. The president may decree the advance collection of taxes, impose censorship, suspend constitutional guarantees (78:n).

Constitutional Amendments: Proposal by legislators, the president, the Supreme Court, or by referendum. Approval by two-thirds of deputies in two rounds. If the president totally or partially rejects an amendment approved by Congress, he may submit it to a referendum. The president may also call a referendum if an amendment proposed by him or her has been partially or totally rejected by the National Congress (143). See also Referendum/Popular Initiative.

El Salvador (1983)

Executive Election: Majority runoff (80).
Presidential Terms: 5 years, with no reelection (154).
Assembly Terms: 3 years, unicameral (124).
Election Timing: Mixed.
Veto Override: By two-thirds vote in the Assembly (137).
Exclusive Introduction of Legislation by Executive: No provision.
Decree Legislation: No provision.
Referendum/Popular Initiative: No provision.
Ministerial Appointments: The president appoints cabinet without restraint (162).
Dismissal of Ministers by Assembly: No provision, except in the form of recommendation (131:37).
Dissolution: No provision.
Impeachment: Assembly can remove the president for physical or mental incapacity based on two-thirds vote and unanimous finding of five physicians whom the Assembly appoints (131:20).
Emergency Powers: With the consent of all the cabinet ministers, and the Assembly if it is in session, the president may suspend constitutional guarantees and may authorize the disbursement of unappropriated funds to satisfy necessities arising out of any grave disturbance of order (167).
Constitutional Amendments: Proposal by at least 10 representatives, approved by two-thirds of the Legislative Assembly and ratified by two-thirds of the following Legislative Assembly. The articles concerning the form and system of government, the territory of the republic and the the principle of nonreelectibility of the president cannot be amended (248).

Guatemala (1985)

Executive Election: The president and vice-president are elected on the same ticket by majority runoff (184, 190).
Presidential Terms: 4 years (5 before 1994) (184). No person who has held the presidency by election, who has held the office for more than 2 years, or who has held the presidency unconstitutionally may be elected (186, 187).
Assembly Terms: 4 years (5 before 1994), unicameral (162).
Election Timing: Concurrent with first round of presidential elections. No midterm elections.
Veto Override: By two-thirds vote; no pocket or partial veto (178, 179).
Exclusive Introduction of Legislation by Executive: The president exclusively introduces the annual budget bill (183:j).
Decree Legislation: No provision.
Referendum/Popular Initiative: Either the president or Congress may request referenda on "political decisions of special significance." Referenda and popular initiatives are organized by the Supreme Electoral Court (173).
Ministerial Appointments: The president appoints and removes cabinet ministers (183:s).
Dismissal of Ministers by Assembly: Cabinet ministers can be interpellated at the

request of any deputy. A vote of no confidence against a minister (up to four at a time) can be petitioned by four or more deputies. Ministers can be dismissed by majority in a no-confidence vote. If the president appeals the no-confidence vote, a two-thirds majority is required to uphold the dismissal (166, 167).

Dissolution: No provision.

Impeachment: "The Congress has the power to declare, through the vote of two-thirds of the total number of deputies, the physical or mental disability of the president. The declaration must be based on the opinion beforehand of a committee of five physicians appointed by the Executive Board of the association following the request of Congress" (165:i).

Emergency Powers: The president dictates "provisions that may be necessary in cases of serious emergency or public catastrophe," and has the responsibility "to give account to Congress in its immediate sessions" (183:f).

Constitutional Amendments: Proposed by the president in the Council of Ministers, by 10 or more deputies, by the Court of Constitutionality, or by a petition of by no fewer than 5,000 citizens (277). In order to amend Article 277 on the guarantees of individual rights, the Congress by two-thirds vote must call a national consituent assembly (278). The Constituent Assembly and the Congress are able to function simultaneously, but it is not possible to be a deputy in both bodies simultaneously (279). For any other amendment, approval requires a two-thirds vote of Congress; ratification is by referendum (280). The principle of non-reelectibility of the president cannot be amended (281).

Honduras (1982)

Executive Election: The president and three designates on same ticket by plurality (236).

Presidential Terms: 4 years (237), with no reelection (239). If the presidency is vacated, Congress selects which of the designates will complete term (242).

Assembly Terms: 4 years, unicameral (196).

Election Timing: Concurrent with first round of presidential election. No midterm elections.

Veto Override: No veto on budget (218:6). Override on other bills by two-thirds vote (216). No pocket veto (217).

Exclusive Introduction of Legislation by Executive: No provision.

Decree Legislation: No provision.

Referendum/Popular Initiative: No provision.

Ministerial Appointments: The president appoints ministers without restriction (245: 5).

Dismissal of Ministers by Assembly: No provision.

Dissolution: No provision.

Impeachment: The Chamber of Deputies establishes whether there are grounds for impeachment of the president or cabinet ministers (205:15). No extraordinary majority is stipulated.

Emergency Powers: The president may "adopt special economic and financial measures when the national interest so requires," and must "give an account thereof to Congress" (245:20). Suspension of constitutional guarantees is by declaration of state of emergency by the president, on approval by the Council of Ministers (187).

Constitutional Amendments: Amendments of the constitution are decreed by the Congress with two-thirds of the votes of its members. The amendment decree must be ratified by the subsequent regular annual session, by the same number of votes (373). No amendment of provisions on eligibility for presidency (374).

Mexico (1917)

Executive Election: The president is elected directly (81). Plurality rule.

Presidential Terms: 6 years, with no reelection (83). If the presidency is vacated within the first 2 years of a term, Congress in joint session elects an interim president by absolute majority. The interim president serves for a period of 14 to 18 months, when a direct election is held to pick a president who fills the remainder of the original term. If the presidency is vacated in the last 4 years of a term, then the interim president elected by the joint session of Congress fills out the term (84).

Assembly Terms: 3 years for deputies (51), 6 years for senators (56). Neither deputies nor senators can be immediately reelected (59).

Election Timing: Concurrent, with midterm elections for Chamber and for half of Senate.

Veto Override: No veto on budget. Override on other bills by two-thirds vote in both chambers (72:C).

Exclusive Introduction of Legislation by Executive: The president and appropriate cabinet ministers introduce the budget and revenue bills at the start of each session. Budget is approved by Chamber of Deputies alone (74:IV).

Decree Legislation: No provision.

Referendum/Popular Initiative: No provision.

Ministerial Appointments: The president appoints cabinet freely (89:III).

Dismissal of Ministers by Assembly: No provision.

Dissolution: No provision.

Impeachment: Chamber can initiate impeachment of the president or cabinet ministers by majority vote. Senate must approve impeachment by two-thirds vote (110, 111).

Emergency Powers: In the event of invasion, serious disturbance of the public peace, or any other event that may place society in great danger or conflict, the president may suspend constitutional guarantees with consent of Congress or its Permanent Committee. Congress shall delegate authority it deems necessary to the president (29).

Constitutional Amendments: Approval by two-thirds vote of the members present, ratification by a majority of the legislatures of the states (135).

Nicaragua (1987)

Source: República de Nicaragua (August 1995).

Executive Election: The president and vice-president are elected on the same ticket; second round in event no ticket receives 45% of the votes (146, 147).

Presidential Terms: 5 years, with a two-term limit and no immediate reelection (no restriction before 1995) (147:a).

Assembly Terms: 5 years (6 before 1995), unicameral (136).

Election Timing: Concurrent.
Veto Override: By absolute majority (142, 143).
Exclusive Introduction of Legislation by Executive: No provision.
Decree Legislation: No provision.
Referendum/Popular Initiative: No provision.
Ministerial Appointments: The president appoints cabinet without restriction (150:6).
Dismissal of Ministers by Assembly: No provision.
Dissolution: No provision.
Impeachment: No provision.
Emergency Powers: The presidential decree of emergency must be forwarded to Assembly for ratification within a period of 45 days (150:9) and permits suspension, within part or all of the territory, of constitutional rights. However, individual rights, political rights, family rights, labor rights, and the rights of the communities of the Atlantic Coast may not be suspended. During a state of emergency, the president is authorized to approve the general budget and forward it to the National Assembly for its review (185, 186).
Constitutional Amendments: Partial reform proposed by president or one-third of the representatives of the National Assembly and ratified by three-fifths of representatives. Total reform requires proposal by absolute majority and ratification by two-thirds of representatives (191–94).

Panama (1972)

Executive Election: The president and vice-president are elected on the same ticket by majority (in effect, plurality) (157).
Presidential Terms: 6 years for both the president and the vice-president (157).
Assembly Terms: 6 years for the National Assembly (130). Municipal representatives to the National Legislative Council are elected for 2-year terms. Provincial and Indian District representatives are elected for 6-year terms (146:3).
Election Timing: Concurrent, with no midterm elections.
Veto Override: Package or item veto on legislation passed by National Legislative Council, subject to override by two-thirds vote (153).
Exclusive Introduction of Legislation by Executive: No provision.
Decree Legislation: No provision.
Referendum/Popular Initiative: No provision.
Ministerial Appointments: The president appoints cabinet without restriction (178).
Dismissal of Ministers by Assembly: No provision.
Dissolution: No provision.
Impeachment: Article 186 states that the president can be "held accountable" for exceeding constitutional powers or obstructing the National Assembly from exercising its functions or for any criminal offense, and that the penalty shall be removal from all public office. But there is no mention of the process, nor of who shall hold the president accountable.
Emergency Powers: In the event of foreign war or domestic disturbance, all or part of the republic may be declared to be in a state of siege, and civil rights, habeas corpus, and the right to private property may be temporarily suspended, wholly or in part

(51). The Cabinet Council must approve, under the collective responsibility of all its members and of the commander-in-chief of the National Guard, decrees that the president may issue concerning the suspension and restoration of guarantees (180:5).

Constitutional Amendments: Proposal by the National Assembly or by the Cabinet Council, ratification by absolute majority of the National Assembly that enters office in the following term (140).

Paraguay (1992)

Executive Election: The president and vice-president are elected jointly by a plurality of voters (230).

Presidential Terms: 5 years (229).

Assembly Terms: 5 years for senators and deputies (187). Former presidents who were democratically elected will be senators for life (189).

Election Timing: Concurrent (187).

Veto Override: By absolute majority in each house (208).

Exclusive Introduction of Legislation by Executive: No provision.

Decree Legislation: The president may issue decree, which, in order to be valid, must be countersigned by the respective minister (238:5). [From context, "decree" appears to refer to regulatory matters and not to new legislation; however, it is ambiguous – eds.]

Referendum/Popular Initiative: No provision.

Ministerial Appointments: The president appoints or removes freely cabinet ministers, the Government Special Attorney for Patrimonial Affairs, and other public officials whose appointment or tenure is not otherwise regulated by the constitution (238: sec. 6).

Dismissal of Ministers by Assembly: Each chamber, by an absolute majority, may individually summon and interpellate ministers and other senior administration officials (193). If a summoned official fails to appear before the respective chamber or if the chamber considers his or her briefing to be unsatisfactory, the two chambers, by a two-thirds absolute majority, will issue a vote of censure against him or her and will recommend that the president remove him or her (194).

Dissolution: No provision.

Impeachment: The Chamber of Deputies, by a two-thirds majority, may press charges for impeachment. The Senate may dismiss by a two-thirds majority (225).

Emergency Powers: Congress or the executive branch may declare a state of exception, in part or in all national territory, for a maximum of 60 days. A declaration of a state of emergency made by the executive branch has to be approved or rejected by the Congress within 48 hours. The 60-day deadline may be extended by successsive periods of 30 days by an absolute majority of the two houses. A decree or law declaring a state of exception must contain the rights that will be restricted. A state of exception does not disrupt the provisions of the constitution, particularly that concerning habeas corpus. By an absolute majority vote, Congress may at any time order the lifting of a state of exception (288).

Constitutional Amendments: Distinction between "reforms" and "amendments." The constitution may be reformed only 10 years after its promulgation. Proposal by one-quarter of the members of either chamber, by the president, or by 30,000 voters through a signed petition. Approval by two-thirds majorities, after which the Supreme Electoral Court will call election for a national constituent assembly within a period of 180 days. Such election may not coincide with any other scheduled election. The constitution may be amended 3 years after it has been promulgated, at the initiative of one-quarter of the members of either chamber, by the president, or by 30,000 voters through a signed petition. Approval by absolute majorities, then ratification via referendum. If an amendment has been approved by the two chambers of Congress, it is submitted to a referendum called by the Superior Electoral Court. The procedures established to reform the constitution, rather than those established for its amendment, will be followed with regard to those provisions affecting the election, composition, term in office, or powers of any of the branches of government or the provisions concerning basic principles and rights (289, 290).

Peru (1979; no longer in effect)

Executive Election: The president and two vice-presidents are elected by majority runoff (203).
Presidential Terms: 5 years, with no immediate reelection (205).
Assembly Terms: 5 years for senators, with former presidents of the republic automatically senators for life (166). 5 years for deputies, unless the Chamber is dissolved (167). If Chamber is dissolved, new deputies elected within 30 days fill out the remainder of the term (228).
Election Timing: Assembly concurrent with first round of presidential election.
Veto Override: By simple majority vote by each chamber (193).
Exclusive Introduction of Legislation by Executive: The president exclusively introduces the comprehensive budget bill annually (197).
Decree Legislation: The president may decree extraordinary measures in economic and financial matters (211:20). Congress may delegate to the president the authority to issue decrees with the force of law (188, 211:10). Such decrees are subject to approval by a majority vote in the Council of Ministers (218:2). If Congress does not pass the budget bill – amended or not – by December 15 each year, the president promulgates the budget by decree (198).
Referendum/Popular Initiative: No provision.
Ministerial Appointments: The president appoints the president of the Council of Ministers (prime minister) without restriction. He appoints individual ministers "upon the proposal and with the concurrence, respectively, of the president of the Council of Ministers" (216).
Dismissal of Ministers by Assembly: The Chamber of Deputies exclusively can censure individual members of the Council of Ministers (cabinet) or the entire Council. A vote of no confidence occurs only through ministerial initiative and "must be moved by no fewer than 25% of the legal number of Deputies." Approval of the no-confidence vote requires a simple majority (226). In the last year of the Chamber's term – during which time the president cannot dissolve the Chamber under any circumstances – a no-confidence vote requires a two-thirds majority (229).
Dissolution: The president can dissolve the Chamber of Deputies if it censures three or more councils of ministers. Elections for a new Chamber are held within 30 days

of dissolution. However, the president can use dissolution only once per term and not within 1 year of the end of a term or during a state of emergency (227–29).

Impeachment: The Chamber of Deputies can impeach the president or cabinet ministers (183). The Senate passes judgment on impeachment (184). No provision requiring extraordinary majorities.

Emergency Powers: With the approval of the Council of Ministers, the president may declare all or part of the nation in a state of exception, in the case of a disturbance of order. The president may also declare a state of siege, but this is subject to congressional approval. Under states of exception or siege, constitutional guarantees are suspended (231).

Constitutional Amendments: Proposal by the president, with the approval of the Council of Ministers, by senators and deputies, by the Supreme Court in judicial matters, or by 50,000 petitioning citizens. Approval by absolute majorities in two consecutive ordinary sessions (306).

Peru (1993)

Source: República de Peru, *Constitución, 1993*. Lima: Diario Oficial El Peruano.

Executive Election: The president and two vice-presidents are elected by majority runoff (111).

Presidential Terms: 5 years, with immediate reelection permitted (112).

Assembly Terms: 5 years (90). Unicameral (90).

Election Timing: Assembly concurrent with first round of presidential election.

Veto Override: By simple majority vote (108).

Exclusive Introduction of Legislation by Executive: The president exclusively introduces the comprehensive budget bill annually (78). Congress may neither increase amounts for items proposed by president nor create new items. Taxes must be initiated by the president. Only by a two-thirds majority vote may Congress establish selectively and temporally a special tax system for a specific region of the country (79).

Decree Legislation: The president may dictate extraordinary measures through urgency decrees with the force of law regarding economic and financial matters (117: 19). Congress may delegate to the president the authority to issue decrees with the force of law (104). All decrees are subject to approval by a majority vote in the Council of Ministers (125:2, 126). If Congress does not pass the budget bill by November 30 each year, the president promulgates budget by decree (80).

Referendum/Popular Initiative: No provision.

Ministerial Appointments: The president appoints the president of the Council of Ministers (prime minister) without restriction. He appoints individual ministers "upon the proposal and with the concurrence, respectively, of the President of the Council of Ministers" (121).

Dismissal of Ministers by Assembly: The Congress can censure individual members of the Council of Ministers (cabinet) or the entire Council. A vote of no confidence occurs only through ministerial initiative, and all motions of censure "must be presented by no fewer than 25% of the legal number of congress members." Approval of the no-confidence vote requires an absolute majority of the members of Congress (132).

Dissolution: The president can dissolve, after their censures, two cabinets, but may not dissolve any in the last year of his term or during a state of emergency. Elections for a new Congress are held within 4 months of dissolution; during the interregnum, the executive legislates by emergency decrees. The executive gives account of these decrees to the Permanent Committee of Congress, which submits them to the Congress when the latter reconvenes. If elections are not held within the designated period, the dissolved Congress reconvenes, recovers its prerogatives, and dismisses the Council of Ministers (134–36).

Impeachment: The Permanent Committee of Congress presses charges and Congress passes judgment on them (99, 100). No provision requiring extraordinary majority.

Emergency Powers: With the approval of the Council of Ministers, the president may declare all or part of the nation in a "state of exception," lasting 60 days, but renewable. The president may also declare a state of siege in the case of a foreign threat. However, under a state of siege, constitutional guarantees cannot be suspended. A state of siege may last for 45 days and its renewal requires the approval of Congress (137).

Constitutional Amendments: Proposal by the president, with the approval of the Council of Ministers, by congress members, or by petitioning citizens representing 0.3% of the voting population. Approval by absolute majority; ratified by a referendum or by two-thirds of members in two consecutive legislative sessions (206).

Uruguay (1966)

Source: Maestre Alfonso (1989).

Executive Election: By the system of double simultaneous vote for the president and vice-president, elected on the same ticket (151). The president is the first-ranked candidate on the list of the faction with the most votes within the party with the most votes. Same candidate may head list in more than one electoral district.

Presidential Terms: 5 years, with no immediate reelection (152).

Assembly Terms: 5 years for both House and Senate (89, 97).

Election Timing: Concurrent. Fused ticket for executive and legislative candidates.

Veto Override: Package or item, but subject to override by a majority of Congress in joint session (145). If the president objects to a bill or part of a bill, he or she may return it with modifications. The modifications may be adopted as law by majority in joint session. If no vote is held on a modified bill within 60 days of its return to Congress, the modified version becomes law (138, 139).

Exclusive Introduction of Legislation by Executive: Bills that would create tax exemptions or fix minimum wages or prices. Congress may not increase the tax exemptions or the minimum wages, nor may it lower the proposed maximum prices (133). The president also introduces the annual budget bill (168:19).

Decree Legislation: The president may declare legislation introduced by the executive urgent. If no vote has been taken on such a bill in Congress within 45 days, it becomes law, although if one house approves the bill in a different form the time period is extended by 20 days and the modified version becomes law if the other house does not act. The president may not send more than one "urgent" measure at a time or send additional urgent measures while one is still under consideration (168:7).

Referendum/Popular Initiative: One-quarter of all registered voters may petition for a referendum against any law (except tax laws and laws exclusively introduced by the executive) within one year of the law's passage (79).

Ministerial Appointments: "The President . . . shall allot the Ministries to citizens who, by virtue of their parliamentary support, are assured of remaining in office. Ministries shall cease to function by resolution of the President" (174).

Dismissal of Ministers by Assembly: Individual ministers or the whole cabinet may be censured by an absolute majority vote of the full membership of the General Assembly (joint session of Congress). If censure is voted by a majority of less than two-thirds, the president may veto it. If the General Assembly then maintains its censure by a majority of less than three-fifths, the president may dissolve both chambers, and new elections are held within 2 months. The newly elected General Assembly then must either maintain or revoke the vote of censure by an absolute majority. In the last year of a legislative and executive term, censure requires an original two-thirds majority, and Congress cannot subsequently be dissolved (147, 148).

Dissolution: See provisions for censure.

Impeachment: Impeachment of executive officials by majority vote of the House, subject to verdict by two-thirds vote in the Senate (93, 102).

Emergency Powers: The president may take prompt measures of security in grave crises, subject to report within 24 hours to the General Assembly, whose decision on such measures is final (168:17).

Constitutional Amendments: (1) Proposals initiated by one-tenth of registered voters or one-fifth of the General Assembly are submitted to a plebiscite in the following election. The General Assembly, in a joint session of both chambers, can propose substitute projects to be submitted to plebiscite, together with the popular initiative; ratified by a majority of voters. (2) Proposals initiated by senators, representatives, and the executive power must be approved by an absolute majority of the General Assembly, followed within 90 days by an election for a national constituent convention. The decisions of the Constituent Convention are made by an absolute majority of its members. The projects approved by the Convention must be ratified by the electorate. Ratification by plebiscite, provided at least 35% of registered voters approve. (3) Constitutional laws are approved by two-thirds of the members of each chamber and ratified by an absolute majority of voters. When amendment proposals referring to elective offices are submitted to a plebiscite that coincides with elections for the offices of the state, the offices will be simultaneously filled through the proposed system and by the previous one (331).

Venezuela (1961)

Executive Election: By plurality (183).

Presidential Terms: 5 years. Presidents who have held office for more than half a constitutional term cannot be reelected until 10 years have passed since they last held the office (185). If the presidency is vacated, Congress in joint session elects a replacement to serve as president for the remainder of the term (187).

Assembly Terms: 5 years for deputies and elected senators. Ex-presidents are senators for life, except while serving any subsequent term as president (148).

Election Timing: Concurrent.

Veto Override: The president may return a bill within 10 days with suggested changes. Override requires two-thirds vote by Congress in joint session. However, a simple majority returns the bill to the president, who may return it again within 5 days; but this time a simple majority promulgates legislation (173).

Exclusive Introduction of Legislation by Executive: No provision.

Decree Legislation: Congress may delegate to the president authority to issue decree-laws on appropriations, revenues, the creation or abolition of public services, and monetary policy, and to maintain order (190:8).

Referendum/Popular Initiative: No provision.

Ministerial Appointments: The president appoints cabinet without restriction (190:2).

Dismissal of Ministers by Assembly: Censure by two-thirds vote in the Chamber of Deputies (153).

Dissolution: No provision.

Impeachment: The president can be impeached by a majority vote in the Senate ruling that he or she should be subject to legal trial. The Senate votes on such a procedure only on the basis of a ruling by the Supreme Court that there are grounds (150:8).

Emergency Powers: The president may declare a state of emergency, which must be submitted to the Cabinet and to Congress within 10 days. It takes action by both the executive and a majority of each house of the legislature to end a state of emergency. The state of emergency implies suspension of constitutional guarantees, but not the power of legislative decree. Either the executive or the legislature may reinstate suspended or restricted constitutional guarantees (240–44).

Constitutional Amendments: Proposal by one-quarter of the members of one chamber, or by one-quarter of the legislative assemblies of the states, by decisions taken in not less than two discussions by an absolute majority of the members of each assembly. Approval by Congress by absolute majority, ratification by absolute majorities of state legislatures in two-thirds of states. "General reform" proposed by one-third of the members of Congress or by an absolute majority of the legislative assemblies by resolutions adopted in at least two discussions by an absolute majority of the members of each assembly. Approval by two-thirds of those present in a joint session of Congress. Ratification by referendum; proposal declared the new constitution if it is approved by a majority of the votes of the entire republic (245–49).

REFERENCES

Abranches Sérgio Henrique. 1988. "Presidencialismo de Coalizao: O. Dilema Institucional Brasileiro." *Dado*, 31, 1: 5–34.

Abrúcio, Fernando Luiz. 1994. "Os Barões da Federação." *Lua Nova*, no. 33, pp. 165–83.

Acuña, Carlos H. 1995. "Algunas notas sobre los juegos, las gallinas y la lógica política de los pactos constitucionales (Reflexiones a partir del pacto constitucional en la Argentina)." In Carlos H. Acuña, ed., *La nueva matriz política argentina* (pp. 115–50). Buenos Aires: Nueva Visión.

Acuña, Carlos H., and Catalina Smulovitz. 1995. "Militares en la transición argentina: Del gobierno a la subordinación constitucional." In Carlos H. Acuña, ed., *La nueva matriz política argentina* (pp. 153–200). Buenos Aires: Nueva Visión.

Adrogué, Gerardo. 1995. "El nuevo sistema partidario argentino." In Carlos H. Acuña, ed., *La nueva matriz política argentina* (pp. 27–70). Buenos Aires: Nueva Visión.

Aguílar Bulgarelli, Oscar. 1986. *La constitución de 1949: Antecedentes y proyecciones.* San José: Editorial Costa Rica.

Alvarado Mendoza, Arturo. 1990. "La fundación del PRI." In Instituto de Estudios Políticos, Económicos y Sociales, ed., *El partido en el poder* (pp. 15–85). Mexico City: El Día.

Alves, Maria Helena Moreira. 1985. *State and Opposition in Military Brazil.* Austin: University of Texas Press.

Ambito Financiero. 1992. "Hacia un nuevo federalismo fiscal en la Argentina," Suplemento Especial, August 28.

Ames, Barry. 1987. *Political Survival: Politicians and Public Policy in Latin America.* Berkeley: University of California Press.

Ames, Barry. 1995a. "Electoral Rules, Constituency Pressures, and Pork Barrel: Bases of Voting in the Brazilian Congress." *Journal of Politics* 57, 2 (May): 324–43.

Ames, Barry. 1995b. "Electoral Strategy under Open-List Proportional Representation." *American Journal of Political Science* 39, 2 (May):406–33.

Ames, Barry, and David Nixon. 1993. "Understanding New Legislatures? Observations and Evidence from the Brazilian Congress." Paper presented at the Annual Meeting of the American Political Science Association, Washington, D.C., September 2.

Amorim Neto, Octávio. 1995. "Cabinet Formation and Party Politics in Brazil." Paper presented at the Latin American Studies Association International Congress, Washington D.C., September 28–30.

Andrade Geywitz, Carlos. 1991. *Reforma de la constitución de la República de Chile de 1980*. Santiago: Editorial Jurídica de Chile.

Aramouni, Alberto, and Ariel Colombo. 1992. *Críticas al liberal-menemismo*. Buenos Aires: Fundación Proyectos para el Cambio.

Arboleda, Enrique. 1982. *La reforma constitucional de 1979: Su inexquibilidad*. Bogotá: Editorial Dintel.

Archer, Ronald P. 1990. "Paralysis of Reform: Political Stability and Social Conflict in Colombia." Ph.D. dissertation, University of California, Berkeley.

Archer, Ronald P., and Marc Chernick. 1989. "El presidente frente a las instituciones nacionales." In Patricia Vásquez de Urrutia, ed., *La democracia en blanco y negro: Colombia en los años ochenta* (pp. 31–79). Bogotá: Ediciones Uniandes.

Arriagada, Genaro. 1984. "El sistema político chileno (Una exploración del futuro)." *Colección Estudios CIEPLAN* 15:171– 202.

Asamblea Legislativa de Costa Rica. 1983–84. Ley de la moneda (Decreto no. 6,965, Exp. no. 9,736). San José: Archivo de la Asamblea Legislativa.

Asamblea Legislativa de Costa Rica. 1985a. *Actas de las Sesiones Plenarias*, no. 1, Asamblea Legislativa no. 18, May 1985, Tomo 405, pp. 1–41. San José: Archivo de la Asamblea Legislativa.

Asamblea Legislativa de Costa Rica. 1985b. *Mayo negro: Historia de una conjura*. San José: Documentos de la Asamblea Legislativa.

Asamblea Legislativa de Costa Rica. 1985–1988. Ley de inquilinato (Dec. no. 7,101, Exp. no. 10,180). San José: Archivo de la Asamblea Legislativa.

Asamblea Legislativa de Costa Rica. 1988. Modernización del sistema financiero de la República (Dec. no. 7,107, Exp. no. 10,523). San José: Archivo de la Asamblea Legislativa.

Asamblea Legislativa de Costa Rica. 1992. Interviews with deputies from the 1990–94 cohort. Coded as Int. 93-1 through Int. 93-57. The number 93 signifies that deputies serve in the 93rd Costa Rican Assembly. The 57 members are identified by number in order to maintain confidentiality.

Asamblea Nacional Constituyente de 1949. 1951. San José: Asamblea Legislativa.

Ayala, Susana. 1994. Interview (May 2). National deputy (1993–97) (PJ) from the province of Chaco.

Bagley, Bruce Michael. 1989. *The State and the Peasantry in Contemporary Colombia*. Latin American Issues: A Monograph Series on Contemporary Latin American and Caribbean Affairs, vol. 6. Meadville, Penn.: Allegheny College.

Baglini, Raúl. 1993. Interview (February 25). Former president of the UCR bloc in the Chamber and a national deputy (1983–93) from the province of Mendoza.

Barbera, Augusto. 1990. "Un' alternativa neo-parlamentare al presidenzialismo." *Democrazia e Diritto* Vol. 2.

Benevides, Maria Victória de Mesquita. 1976. *O Governo Kubitschek: Desenvolvimento Econômico e Estabilidade Política*. Rio de Janeiro: Paz e Terra.

Benevides, Maria Victória de Mesquita. 1981. *A UDN e o Udenismo*. Rio de Janeiro: Paz e Terra.

Benevides, Maria Victória de Mesquita. 1989. *O PTB e o Trabalhismo: Partido e Sindicato em São Paulo*. São Paulo: Brasiliense/CEDEC.

Berlín Valenzuela, Francisco. 1993. *Derecho parlamentario*. Mexico City: Fondo de Cultura Económica.

Berry, R. Albert, Ronald G. Hellman, and Mauricio Solaún, eds. 1980. *Politics of Compromise: Coalition Government in Colombia*. New Brunswick, N.J.: Transaction Books.

Bianchi, Alberto B. 1991. "La Corte Suprema ha establecido su tesis oficial sobre la emergencia económica." *La Ley (Jurisprudencia)* 41:141–91.

Blaustein, Albert P., and Gisbert H. Flanz, eds. 1971–present. *Constitutions of the Countries of the World*. Dobbs Ferry, N.Y.: Oceana.

Blondel, Jean, and Waldino Suárez. 1981. "Las limitaciones institucionales del sistema presidencialista." *Criteria* 1853–54 (February 26):57–70.

Bollen, Kenneth. 1979. "Political Democracy and the Timing of Development." *American Sociological Review* 44 (August): 572–87.

Brandenburg, Frank R. 1964. *The Making of Modern Mexico*. Englewood Cliffs, N.J.: Prentice-Hall.

Brewer-Carías, Allan R. 1980. *Evolución del régimen legal de la economía, 1939–1979*. Caracas: Editorial Jurídica Venezolana.

Brewer-Carías, Allan R. 1985. *Instituciones políticas y constitucionales*. Caracas: Universidad Católica del Táchira.

Cain, Bruce, John Ferejohn, and Morris Fiorina. 1987. *The Personal Vote: Constituency Service and Electoral Independence*. Cambridge, Mass.: Harvard University Press.

Campanhole, Adriano, and Hilton Lôbo Campanhole. 1971. *Todas as Constituições do Brasil*. São Paulo: Edtôra Atlas.

Carey, John M. 1996. *Term Limits and Legislative Representation*. Cambridge University Press.

Carey, John M., and Matthew S. Shugart. Forthcoming. "Executive Decree Authority: Calling Out the Tanks or Just Filling Out the Forms?" In Carey and Shugart, eds, *Executive Decree Authority: Calling Out the Tanks or Just Filling Out the Forms?* Cambridge University Press.

Carey, John M., and Matthew S. Shugart. Forthcoming. "Incentives to Cultivate a Personal Vote: A Rank Ordering of Electoral Formulas." *Electoral Studies*.

Carey, John M., and Matthew S. Shugart, eds. N.d. "Policy-Making by Decree." Typescript in preparation.

Carpizo, Jorge. 1978a. "México, poder ejecutivo: 1950–1975." In *Evolución de la organización político-constitucional en América Latina (1950–1975)*. Vol. 1, pp. 73–91. Mexico City: Universidad Nacional Autónoma de México.

Carpizo, Jorge. 1978b. *El presidencialismo mexicano*. Mexico City: Siglo XXI.

Carpizo, Jorge. 1988. *El sistema presidencial mexicano (algunas reflexiones)*. Mexico City:

Instituto de Investigaciones Jurídicas, Universidad Nacional Autónoma de México.

Carrillo Bedoya, Jaime. 1981. *Los paros cívicos en Colombia*. Bogotá: La Oveja Negra.

Casas Zamora, Kevin, and Olman Briceño Fallas. 1991. "Democracia representativa en Costa Rica? Análisis del sistema de elección de diputados en Costa Rica y sus perspectivas de cambio." Law School Thesis. San José: University of Costa Rica.

Catterberg, Edgardo. 1989. *Los argentinos frente a la política: Cultura política y opinión pública en la transición argentina a la democracia*. Buenos Aires: Planeta.

Catterberg, Edgardo. 1993. Interview (February 15). One of President Alfonsín's principal public opinion advisors, UCR pollster, and professor at the Universidad de San Andrés.

Ceaser, James. 1979. *Presidential Selection*. Princeton, N.J.: Princeton University Press.

Centeno, Miguel Angel. 1994. *Democracy within Reason: Technocratic Revolution in Mexico*. University Park: Pennsylvania State University Press.

Cepeda, E. Manuel José. 1985. "Las relaciones entre el Presidente y la Corte durante la emergencia económica: Un Semidiós enfrentando a un monstruo." In Manuel José Cepeda E., ed., *Estado de sitio y emergencia económica* (pp. 43-71). Bogotá: Contraloría General de la República.

Cepeda, E. Manuel José. N.d. *La Constituyente por dentro: Mitos y realidades*. Bogotá: Presidencia de la República, Consejería para el Desarrollo de la Constitución.

Christlieb Ibarrola, Adolfo. 1965. *Crónicas de la no-reelección*. Mexico City: Ediciones de Acción Nacional.

Clarín. Buenos Aires, Argentina (March 25, 1993).

Conaghan, Catherine, James M. Malloy, and Luis Abugattas. 1990. "Business and the Boys: The Origins of Neo-Liberalism in the Central Andes." *Latin American Research Review* 25: 3–30.

Congreso de Chile, 1994. *Proceso legislativo chileno: Un enfoque cuantitativo*. Valparaíso: Congress Nacional de Chile.

Coppedge, Michael. 1994. *Strong Parties and Lame Ducks: Presidential Partyarchy and Factionalism in Venezuela*. Stanford, Calif.: Stanford University Press.

Coral Quintero, Ignacio. 1988. *La lucha de masas y la reforma municipal*. Bogotá: Ediciones Suramérica.

Cornelius, Wayne A. 1973. "Nation Building, Participation, and Distribution: The Politics of Social Reform under Cárdenas." In Gabriel A. Almond, Scott C. Flanagan, and Robert J. Mundt, eds., *Crisis, Choice and Change: Historical Studies in Political Development* (pp. 392–498). Boston: Little, Brown.

Cornelius, Wayne A., Ann L. Craig, and Jonathan Fox, eds. 1994. *Tranforming State–Society Relations in Mexico: The National Solidarity Strategy*. La Jolla: Center for U.S.–Mexican Studies, University of California, San Diego.

Cosío Villegas, Daniel. 1975. *El estilo personal de gobernar*. Mexico City: Cuadernos de Joaquín Mortiz.

Cosío Villegas, Daniel. 1978. *El sistema político mexicano*. Mexico City: Cuadernos de Joaquín Mortiz.

Costeloe, Michael P. 1989. "Generals versus Politicians: Santa Anna and the 1842 Congressional Elections in Mexico." *Bulletin of Latin American Research* 8, 2:257–74.

Cox, Gary W. 1987. *The Efficient Secret: The Cabinet and the Development of Political Parties in Victorian England.* Cambridge University Press.

Cox, Gary W., and Mathew D. McCubbins. 1993. *Legislative Leviathan: Party Government in the House.* Berkeley: University of California Press.

Cox, Gary W., and Matthew S. Shugart. 1994. "Strategic Voting under Proportional Representation." Unpublished.

Cox, Gary W., and Matthew S. Shugart. 1995. "The Absence of Vote Pooling: Nomination and Vote Allocation Errors in Colombia." *Electoral Studies* 14, 4 (December):441–60.

Crisp, Brian F. 1994. "Limitations to Democracy in Developing Capitalist Societies: The Case of Venezuela." *World Development* 22 (October):1491–1509.

Crisp, Brian F. Forthcoming. "Presidential Decree Authority in Venezuela." In John M. Carey and Matthew S. Shugart, eds., *Executive Decree Authority: Calling Out the Tanks or Just Filling Out the Forms.* Cambridge University Press.

Crisp, Brian F., Daniel H. Levine, and Juan Carlos Rey. 1995. "The Legitimacy Problem." In Jennifer McCoy, William Smith, Andrés Stambouli, and Andrés Serbin, eds., *Venezuelan Democracy under Stress* (pp. 139–70). New Brunswick, N.J.: Transaction Books.

Cumberland, Charles C. 1972. *Mexican Revolution: The Constitutionalist Years.* Austin: University of Texas Press.

Cutler, Lloyd N. 1980. "To Form a Government." *Foreign Affairs* 59:126–43.

Dahl, Robert A. 1971. *Polyarchy: Participation and Opposition.* New Haven, Conn.: Yale University Press.

Dahl, Robert A., and Edward R. Tufte. 1973. *Size and Democracy.* Stanford, Calif.: Stanford University Press.

Dain, Sulamis. 1995. "Experiência Internacional e Especificidade Brasileira." In Rui de Britto Alvares Affonso and Pedro Luiz Barros Silva, eds., *Federalismo no Brasil: Reforma Tributária e Federação* (pp. 21–41). São Paulo: FUNDAP/ Editora da Universidade Estadual Paulista.

D'Araujo, Maria Celina Soares. 1982. *O Segundo Governo Vargas, 1951–1954.* Rio de Janeiro: Zahar.

de la Torre, Cristina, ed. 1985. *Reformas políticas: Apertura democrática.* Bogotá: Editorial Oveja Negra.

De Riz, Liliana. 1993. Interview (March 17). Research scholar at the Centro de Estudios de Estado y Sociedad (CEDES).

Diamond, Larry. 1989. "Introduction: Persistence, Erosion, Breakdown, and Renewal." In Larry Diamond, Juan J. Linz, and Seymour Martin Lipset, eds., *Democracy in Developing Countries: Asia* (pp. 1–52). Boulder, Colo.: Lynne Rienner.

Diario de Sesiones de la Cámara de Diputados. 1990. Buenos Aires: Imprenta del Congreso de la Nación.

Diario de Sesiones de la Cámara de Senadores. 1989. Buenos Aires: Imprenta del Congreso de la Nación.

Díaz Uribe, Eduardo. 1986. *El clientelismo en Colombia.* Bogotá: El Ancora Editores.

Diniz, Hindemburgo Pereira. 1984. *A Monarquia Presidencial.* Rio de Janeiro: Nova Fronteira.

Dirección Nacional Electoral. 1994. Data files of the Departamento de Estadísticas of the Dirección Nacional Electoral, Ministerio del Interior, República Argentina.

Dix, Robert H. 1967. *Colombia: The Political Dimensions of Change.* New Haven, Conn.: Yale University Press.

Dix, Robert H. 1987. *The Politics of Colombia.* New York: Praeger.

Dodd, Lawrence C. 1976. *Coalitions in Parliamentary Government.* Princeton, N.J.: Princeton University Press.

Dubnic, Vladimir Reisky de. 1968. *Political Trends in Brazil.* Washington, D.C.: Public Affairs Press.

Dugas, John, Angelica Ocampo, Luis Javier Orjuela, and German Ruiz. 1992. *Los caminos de la descentralización: Diversidad y retos de la transformación municipal.* Bogotá: Universidad de Los Andes.

Dulles, John W. F. 1961. *Yesterday in Mexico: A Chronicle of the Revolution, 1919– 1936.* Austin: University of Texas Press.

Dunkerley, James. 1988. *Power in the Isthmus: Political History of Modern Central America.* New York: Verso.

Durañona y Vedia, Francisco de. 1993. Interview (March 1). National deputy (1987–95) (UCeDé) from the province of Buenos Aires and former federal intervener in the province of Corrientes (1991–92).

Durrieu, Marcela. 1994. Interview (April 18). National deputy (1991–95) (PJ) from the province of Buenos Aires.

Duverger, Maurice. 1954. *Political Parties, Their Organization and Activity in the Modern State.* Translated by Barbara North and Robert North. New York: Wiley.

Duverger, Maurice. 1980. "A New Political System Model: Semipresidential Government." *European Journal of Political Research* 8:165–87.

Eckstein, Susan. 1977. *The Poverty of Revolution: The State and Urban Poor in Mexico.* Princeton, N.J.: Princeton University Press.

Edwards, Sebastian. 1995. *Crisis and Reform in Latin America: From Despair to Hope.* New York: Oxford University Press.

Enríquez Perea, Alberto. 1988. "Los sectores populares a la Cámara de Diputados: XXXVII Legislatura del Congreso de la Unión, 1937–1940." *Revista Mexicana de Ciencias Políticas y Sociales* 34, 134 (October–December):161–73.

Epstein, Leon D. 1964. "A Comparative Study of Canadian Parties." *American Political Science Review* 58, 1 (March):46–59.

Epstein, Leon D. 1967. *Political Parties in Western Democracies.* New York: Praeger.

Espinal, Rosario. 1991. "Presidencialismo vs. parlamentarismo: Análisis de un debate y consideraciones sobre el caso dominicano." In Dieter Nohlen and Mario Fernández, eds., *Presidencialismo vs. parlamentarismo: América Latina.* Caracas: Editorial Nueva Sociedad.

Espinosa-Saldaña Barrera, Eloy. 1995. "Algunas reflexiones sobre los decretos de necesidad y urgencia en el texto argentino reformado." In *Comentarios a la reforma constitucional* (pp. 153–66). Buenos Aires: Asociación Argentina de Derecho Constitucional.

Eulau, Heinz, and Kenneth Prewitt. 1973. *Labyrinths of Democracy.* Indianapolis, Ind.: Bobbs-Merrill.

Evans, Enrique. 1970a. *Relación de la constitución política de la Republica de Chile.* Santiago: Editorial Jurídica de Chile.

Evans, Enrique. 1970b. " La delegación de facultades legislativas." In Eduardo Frei et al. eds., *Reforma constitucional, 1970* (pp. 109–54). Santiago: Editorial Jurídica de Chile.

Faundez, Julio. 1980. " The Defeat of Politics: Chile under Allende." *Boletín de estudios latinoamericanos y del Caribe* 28 (June):59–75.

Faundez, Julio. 1988. *Marxism and Democracy in Chile.* New Haven, Conn: Yale University Press.

FBIS (Foreign Broadcast Information Service–Latin America). April 19, 1990), 17–18. "Raúl Alfonsín Interviewed on Political Parties."

Fernández, Eduardo. 1976. *La batalla de la oposición.* Caracas: Ediciones Nueva Política.

Ferreira Rubio, Delia. 1993. Interview (March 5). Researcher and expert on constitutional and electoral institutions.

Ferreira Rubio, Delia. 1995. Personal communication.

Ferreira Rubio, Delia, and Matteo Goretti. 1993. "The Emergency and the Relationship between the Executive and the Congress during President Menem's Administration in Argentina: Use and Misuse of Prerogative Powers." In Lawrence D. Longley, ed., *Working Papers on Comparative Legislative Studies* (pp. 133–48). Appleton, Wisc.: Research Committee of Legislative Specialists, International Political Science Association.

Ferreira Rubio, Delia, and Matteo Goretti. 1995. "La reforma constitucional argentina: Un presidente menos poderoso?" *Contribuciones* 12 (January–March): 60–89.

Ferreira Rubio, Delia, and Matteo Goretti. 1996. "Cuando el presidente gobierna solo: Menem y los decretos de necesidad y urgencia hasta la reforma constitucional (Julio 1989–Agosto 1994)." *Desarrollo Económico* 36:443–74.

Ferreira Rubio, Delia, and Matteo Goretti. Forthcoming. "Government by Decree in Argentina (1989–1993)," In John M. Carey and Mathew S. Shugart, eds., *Executive Decree Authority: Calling out the Tanks or Just Filling Out the Forms?* Cambridge University Press.

Figueiredo, Argelina Cheibub, and Fernando Limongi. 1994. "O Processo Legislativo e a Produção Legal no Congresso Pós-Constituinte." *Novos Estudos* 38 (March):24–37.

Figueiredo, Argelina Cheibub, and Fernando Limongi. 1995a. "Mudança Constitucional, Desempenho do Legislativo e Consolidação Institucional." *Revista Brasileira de Ciências Sociais* 10, 29 (October):175–200.

Figueiredo, Argelina Cheibub, and Fernando Limongi. 1995b. "Partidos Políticos na Câmara dos Deputados: 1989–1994." *Dados* 38, 3:497–524.

Findley, Roger W. 1980. "Presidential Intervention in the Economy and the Rule of Law in Colombia." *American Journal of Comparative Law* 28, 3 (Summer 1980):423–73.

Fiorina, Morris P. 1981. *Retrospective Voting in American National Elections.* New Haven, Conn.: Yale University Press.

Fiorina, Morris P. 1988. "The Reagan Years: Turning to the Right or Groping toward the Middle?" In Barry Cooper, Allan Kornberg, and William Mishler, eds., *The Resurgence of Conservatism in Anglo-American Democracies* (pp. 430–59). Durham, N.C.: Duke University Press.

Fiorina, Morris P. 1992. *Divided Government.* New York: Macmillan.

Fix-Zamudio, Hector. 1988. "El ejecutivo federal y el poder judicial." In *El sistema presidencial mexicano (algunas reflexiones)* (pp. 269–364). Mexico City: Instituto de Investigaciones Jurídicas, Universidad Nacional Autónoma de México.

Flynn, Peter. 1978. *Brazil: A Political Analysis*. Boulder, Colo.: Westview.

Fox, Jonathan. 1994. "The Difficult Transition from Clientelism to Citizenship." *World Politics* 46, 2 (January 1994):151–84.

Franco, Afonso Arinos de Melo. 1976. *A Câmara dos Deputados: Síntese Histórica*. Brasília: Centro de Documentação e Informação.

Freedom Review. 1985–95. Vol. 16–26. New York: Freedom House.

Frei, Eduardo, et al. 1970. *Reforma constitucional, 1970*. Santiago: Editorial Jurídica de Chile.

Frías, Pedro J. 1993. "Federalismo y reforma del estado en la Argentina." *Contribuciones* 10 (October–December):39–48.

Frías, Pedro J., et al. 1989. *Las nuevas constituciones provinciales*. Buenos Aires: Depalma

Gallón Giraoldo, Gustavo, ed. 1989. *Entre movimientos y caudillos: 50 años de bipartidismo, izquierda y alternativas populares en Colombia*. Bogotá: CINEP and CEREC.

Gamarra, Eduardo. 1987. "Political Stability, Democratization, and the Bolivian National Congress." Ph.D. dissertation, University of Pittsburgh.

Gamarra, Eduardo. 1990. "The Privatization Debate in Bolivia." In Dennis Gayle and Jonathan Goodrich, eds., *Privatization and Deregulation in Global Perspective* (pp. 198–212). New York: Quorum Books.

Gamarra, Eduardo. 1991. *The System of Justice in Bolivia: An Institutional Analysis*. Miami: Center for the Administration of Justice, Florida International University, Monograph Series.

Gamarra, Eduardo, and James M. Malloy. 1996. "The Patrimonial Dynamics of Party Politics in Bolivia." In Scott Mainwaring and Timothy Scully, eds. *Building Democratic Institutions: Party Systems in Latin America* (pp. 1–34, 477–82). Stanford, Calif.: Stanford University Press.

Garrido, Luis Javier. 1982. *El Partido de la Revolución Institucionalizada*. Mexico City: Siglo XXI.

Garrido, Luis Javier. 1989. "The Crisis of Presidencialismo." In Wayne A. Cornelius, Judith Gentleman, and Peter H. Smith, eds., *Mexico's Alternative Political Futures* (pp. 417–34). La Jolla: Center for U.S.–Mexican Studies, University of California, San Diego.

Garro, Alejandro, M. 1993. "Nine Years of Transition to Democracy in Argentina: Partial Failure or Qualified Success?" *Columbia Journal of Transnational Law* 31:1–102.

Gaxiola, Francisco Javier, Jr. 1938. *El Presidente Rodríguez*. Mexico City: Editorial Cultura.

Geddes, Barbara. 1986. "Economic Development as a Collective Action Problem: Individual Interests and Innovation in Brazil." Ph.D. dissertation, University of California at Berkeley.

Geddes, Barbara. 1994. *Politician's Dilemma: Building State Capacity in Latin America*. Berkeley: University of California Press.

Geddes, Barbara, and Arturo Ribeiro Neto. 1992. "Institutional Sources of Corruption in Brazil." *Third World Quarterly* 13, 4:641–61.

Gibson, William Marion. 1948. *The Constitutions of Colombia*. Durham, N.C.: Duke University Press.

Gillespie, Charles G., and Luis E. González. 1994. "Presidentialism and Democratic

Stability in Uruguay." In Linz and Valenzuela (1994), vol. 2, pp. 151–78.

Giraldo M., Luis Carlos, and Gustavo Gómez Velásquez. 1983. *La constitución política de la República de Colombia.* Bogotá: Colección Pequeño Foro.

Godoy, Oscar. 1994. "Elecciones presidenciales y parlamantarias de 1993." *Estudios Públicos* 54: 301–38.

Gómez, Hernando B. 1978. *Alfonso López Michelsen: Un exámen crítico de su pensamiento y de su obra de gobierno.* Bogotá: Tercer Mundo.

González, Luis Eduardo. 1991. *Political Structures and Democracy in Uruguay.* Notre Dame, Ind.: University of Notre Dame Press.

González Oropeza, Manuel. 1987a. *La intervención federal en la desaparición de poderes,* 2nd ed. Mexico City: Universidad Nacional Autónoma de México.

González Oropeza, Manuel. 1987b. *El Senado Mexicano: Por la razón de las leyes.* Vol. 2, part 2, ed. José Barragán Barragán, Jaime del Arenal Fenochio, and Manuel González Oropeza. Mexico City: Senado de la República.

Goodspeed, Stephen Spencer. 1947. "The Role of the Chief Executive in Mexico: Politics, Powers and Administration." Unpublished Ph.D. dissertation, University of California.

Gowland, María. 1993. Interview (March 12). President of the citizens' group Conciencia.

Gutiérrez Gutiérrez, Carlos José. 1984. "Sistema presidencialista y sistema parlamentario." In *El modelo político costarricense* (pp. 23–31). San José: Asociación Nacional de Fomento Económico.

Gutiérrez Saxe, Manuel, and Jorge Vargas Cullel. 1986. *Costa Rica es el nombre del juego.* San José: Asociación Nacional de Fomento Económico.

Hagopian, Frances. 1996. *Traditional Politics and Regime Change in Brazil.* Cambridge University Press.

Hartlyn, Jonathan. 1988. *The Politics of Coalition Rule in Colombia.* Cambridge University Press.

Hermens, Ferdinand A. 1941. *Democracy or Anarchy? A Study of Proportional Representation.* Notre Dame, Ind.: University of Notre Dame Press.

Hernández, Antonio María. 1993. Interview (April 15). National deputy (1991–95) from the province of Córdoba and UCR vice-presidential candidate for the 1995 presidential election.

Herrera y Lasso, Manuel. 1964. *Estudios constitucionales (segunda serie).* Mexico City: Editorial Jus.

Hippólito, Lúcia. 1985. *PSD: De Raposas e Reformistas.* Rio de Janeiro: Paz e Terra.

Hoskin, Gary. 1985. "The Democratic Opening in Colombia: How Do Party and Electoral Behavior Relate to It." Paper presented at the 45th annual meeting of the International Congress of Americanists, Bogotá, Colombia, July 1–7.

Huntington, Samuel P. 1991. *The Third Wave: Democratization in the Late Twentieth Century.* Norman: University of Oklahoma Press.

ICAP (Instituto de Capacitación Política). 1981. *Historia documental del Partido de la Revolución: PNR (1920–1932).* Vol. 1. Mexico City: Instituto de Capacitación Política.

IIJ (Instituto de Investigaciones Jurídicas), ed. 1985. *Constitución política de los Estados Unidos Mexicanos (comentada).* Mexico City: Instituto de Investigaciones Jurídicas, Universidad Nacional Autónoma de México.

Ingberman, Daniel, and John Villani. 1993. "An Institutional Theory of Divided Government and Party Polarization." *American Journal of Political Science* 37, 2 (May):429–71.

Instituto Libertad y Desarrollo. 1991. "Análisis cuantitativo del proceso legislativo." *Opinión sector político institucional*, series P19. Santiago, Chile.

Instituto Libertad y Desarrollo. 1992. "Trabajo parlamentario." *Temas públicos*, series 116:3–5. Santiago, Chile.

Insunza, Sergio. 1966. "Cómo escoger y utilizar las fuentes jurídicas." *Revista de Derecho y Jurisprudencia* 63 (June):98–99.

Jiménez Peña, Oscar. 1993. Interview (February 25). UCeDé legislative assistant and expert on provincial–center relations.

Jones, Mark. 1995a. *Electoral Laws and the Survival of Presidential Democracies.* Notre Dame, Ind.: University of Notre Dame Press.

Jones, Mark P. 1995b. "A Guide to the Electoral Systems of the Americas." *Electoral Studies* 14, 1:5–21.

Jones, Mark P. 1996a. "Increasing Women's Representation via Gender Quotas: The Argentine Ley de Cupos." *Women & Politics* (December).

Jones, Mark P. 1996b. "The Policy Consequences of Gender in Legislative Assemblies: A Comparative Study of Argentina, Costa Rica and the United States." Unpublished manuscript, Michigan State University.

Jones, Mark P. 1996c. "Assessing the Public's Understanding of Constitutional Reform: Evidence from Argentina," *Political Behavior* 18:25–49.

Karl, Terry. 1982. "The Political Economy of Petrodollars: Oil and Democracy." Ph.D. dissertation, Stanford University.

Katz, Richard S. 1986. "Intraparty Preference Voting." In Bernard Grofman and Arend Lijphart, eds., *Electoral Laws and Their Political Consequences* (pp. 85–103). New York: Agathon.

Kernell, Samuel. 1991. "Facing an Opposition Congress: The President's Strategic Circumstance." In Gary W. Cox and Samuel Kernell, eds., *The Politics of Divided Government* (pp. 87–112). Boulder, Colo.: Westview.

Kiewiet, Roderick, and Mathew D. McCubbins. 1988. "Presidential Influence on Congressional Appropriations Decisions." *American Journal of Political Science* 32, 3 (August):713–36.

Kiewiet, Roderick, and Mathew D. McCubbins. 1991. *The Logic of Delegation: Congressional Parties and the Appropriations Process.* Chicago: University of Chicago Press.

Kinzo, Maria D'Alva Gil. 1990. "O Quadro Partidário e a Constituinte." In Bolivar Lamounier, ed., *De Geisel a Collor: O Balanço da Transição* (pp. 105–34). São Paulo: Sumaré/IDESP.

Knapp, Frank A., Jr. 1953. "Parliamentary Government and the Mexican Constitution of 1857: A Forgotten Phase of Mexican Political History." *Hispanic American Historical Review* 33, 1:65–87.

Knight, Alan. 1990 [1986]. *The Mexican Revolution.* 2 vols. Reprinted. Lincoln: University of Nebraska Press.

Knight, Alan. 1992. "Mexico's Elite Settlement: Conjuncture and Consequences." In John Higley and Richard Gunther, eds., *Elites and Democratic Consolidation in Latin America and Southern Europe* (pp. 113–45). Cambridge University Press.

Kornblith, Miriam, and Thais Maingón. 1985. *Estado y gasto público en Venezuela: 1936–1980*. Caracas: Universidad Central de Venezuela.

Laakso, Markku, and Rein Taagepera. 1979. "Effective Number of Parties: A Measure with Application to Western Europe." *Comparative Political Studies* 12:3–27.

Lafer, Celso. 1970. "The Planning Process and the Political System in Brazil: A Study of Kubitschek's Target Plan." Ph.D. dissertation, Cornell University.

Lajous, Alejandra. 1979. *Los orígenes del partido único en México*. Mexico City: Universidad Nacional Autónoma de México.

Lambert, Jacques. 1969. *Latin America: Social Structure and Political Institutions*. Berkeley: University of California Press.

Lamounier, Bolivar. 1994. "Brazil: Toward Parliamentarism?" In Linz and Valenzuela (1994), 179–219.

Latorre, Mario. 1986. *Hechos y crítica polítca*. Bogotá: Universidad Nacional.

Leal Buitrago, Francisco, and Andrés Dávila Ladrón de Guevara. 1990. *Clientelismo: El sistema político y su expresión regional*. Bogotá: Tercer Mundo Editores.

Lerner de Sheinbaum, Bertha, and Susana Ralsky de Cimet. 1976. *El poder de los presidentes: Alcances y perspectivas (1910–1973)*. Mexico City: Instituto Mexicano de Estudios Políticos.

Levine, Daniel H. 1985. "The Transition to Democracy: Are There Lessons from Venezuela?" *Bulletin of Latin American Research* 4, 2:47–61.

Levine, Daniel H., and Brian F. Crisp. 1995. "Legitimacy, Governability, and Institutions in Venezuela." In Joseph S. Tulchin, Moisés Naím, Louis Goodman, and Johanna Mendelson-Forman, eds., *Lessons of the Venezuelan Experience* (pp. 223–51). Baltimore: Johns Hopkins University Press.

Libai, David, Uriel Lynn, Amnon Rubinstein, and Yoash Tsiddon. 1990. *Changing the System of Government in Israel – Proposed Basic Law: The Government*. Jerusalem: The Jerusalem Center for Public Affairs and the Public Committee for a Constitution for Israel.

Lijphart, Arend. 1984. *Democracies: Patterns of Majoritarian and Consensus Government in Twenty-One Countries*. New Haven, Conn.: Yale University Press.

Lijphart, Arend. 1994. "Presidentialism and Majoritarian Democracy: Theoretical Observations." In Linz and Valenzuela (1994), 91–105.

Lima, Olavo Brasil de. 1983. *Partidos Políticos Brasileiros: A Experiência Federal e Regional*. Rio de Janeiro: Graal.

Linz, Juan J. 1978. *The Breakdown of Democratic Regimes: Crisis, Breakdown, and Reequilibration*. Vol. 1 of Linz and Stepan (1978).

Linz, Juan J. 1990. "The Perils of Presidentialism." *Journal of Democracy* 1, 1:51–69.

Linz, Juan J. 1994. "Democracy, Presidential or Parliamentary: Does It Make a Difference?" in Linz and Valenzuela (1994), 3–87.

Linz, Juan, and Alfred Stepan. 1978. *The Breakdown of Democratic Regimes*. Baltimore: Johns Hopkins University Press.

Linz, Juan J., and Arturo Valenzuela, eds. 1994. *The Failure of Presidential Democracy: The Case of Latin America*. Baltimore: Johns Hopkins University Press.

Lipset, Seymour Martin. 1960. *Political Man: The Social Bases of Politics.* Garden City, N.Y.: Anchor.

Lipset, Seymour Martin. 1994. "The Social Requisites of Democracy Revisited." *American Sociological Review* 59:1–22.

Loaeza, Soledad. 1989. *El llamado de las urnas.* Mexico City: Cal y Arena.

López Villafañe, Víctor. 1986. *La formación del sistema político mexicano.* Mexico City: Siglo XXI.

Lowenstein, Karl. 1949. "The Presidency Outside the United States: A Study in Comparative Political Institutions." *Journal of Politics* 11, 3 (August):447–96.

Loyola Díaz, Rafael. 1980. *La crisis Obregón–Calles y el estado mexicano.* Mexico City: Siglo XXI.

Loyola Díaz, Rafael. 1990. "1938: El despliegue del corporativismo partidario." In Instituto de Estudios Políticos, Económicos y Sociales, ed., *El partido en el poder* (pp. 129–82). Mexico City: El Día.

Lutz, Donald S. 1994. "Toward a Theory of Constitutional Amendment." *American Political Science Review* 88, 2 (June):355–70.

Madrigal, Alvaro. 1992. Interview (March 11). Assistant to the Minister of the Presidency, 1992. San José.

Maestre Alfonso, Juan. 1989. *Constituciones y leyes políticas de América Latina, Filipinas y Guinea Ecuatorial.* Tomo II, Vol. I. Sevilla: Escuela de Estudios Hispano-Americanes de Sevilla.

Mainwaring, Scott. 1990. "Presidentialism in Latin America." *Latin American Research Review* 25:157–79.

Mainwaring, Scott. 1991. "Politicians, Parties, and Electoral Systems: Brazil in Comparative Perspective." *Comparative Politics* 24, 1 (October):21–43.

Mainwaring, Scott. 1993. "Presidentialism, Multipartism, and Democracy: The Difficult Combination." *Comparative Political Studies* 26, 2 (July):198–228.

Mainwaring, Scott. 1995. "Brazil: Weak Parties, Feckless Democracy." In Scott Mainwaring and Timothy R. Scully, eds., *Building Democratic Institutions: Party Systems in Latin America* (pp. 354–98). Stanford, Calif.: Stanford University Press.

Mainwaring, Scott, and Aníbal Pérez Liñán. Forthcoming. "Party Discipline in Multiparty Systems: A Methodological Note and an Analysis of the Brazilian Constitutional Congress."

Mainwaring, Scott, and Timothy R. Scully. 1995. "Party Systems in Latin America." In Scott Mainwaring and Timothy R. Scully, eds., *Building Democratic Institutions: Party Systems in Latin America* (pp. 1–34, 477–82). Stanford, Calif.: Stanford University Press.

Malloy, James M. 1989. "Democracy, Economic Crisis and the Problem of Governance: The Case of Bolivia." Paper presented at the 15th Annual Congress of the Latin American Studies Association, Miami, Florida, December 4–6.

Malloy, James M., and Eduardo Gamarra. 1988. *Revolution and Reaction: Bolivia, 1964–1985.* New Brunswick, N.J.: Transaction Books.

Manzetti, Luigi. 1993. *Institutions, Parties, and Coalitions in Argentine Politics.* Pittsburgh, Penn.: University of Pittsburgh Press.

Maqueda, Juan Carlos. 1993. Interview (April 21). National deputy (1991–95) (PJ) from the province of Córdoba.

Martz John. *Acción Democrática: Evolution of a Modern Political Party in Venezuela.* Princeton: Princeton University Press.

Mayhew, David R. 1974. *Congress: The Electoral Connection.* New Haven, Conn: Yale University Press.

Mayhew, David R. 1991. *Divided We Govern: Party Control, Lawmaking, and Investigations, 1946–1990.* New Haven, Conn: Yale University Press.

Mayorga, René A. 1989. "Tendencias y problemas de la consolidación de la democracia en Bolivia." Paper presented at the 15th Annual Congress of the Latin American Studies Association, Miami, Florida, December 4–6.

Medín, Tzvi. 1982. *El minimato presidencial: Historia política del maximato.* Mexico City: Era.

Mello e Souza, Nelson. 1968. "O Planejamento Econômico no Brasil." *Revista de Administração Pública,* no. 4.

Meyer, Lorenzo. 1977. "La etapa formativa del estado mexicano contemporáneo." In *Las crisis en el sistema político mexicano (1928–1977)* (pp. 5–30). Mexico City: Colegio de México.

Meyer, Lorenzo. 1978. *El conflicto social y los gobiernos del maximato.* Vol. 13 of *Historia de la revolución mexicana.* Mexico City: Colegio de México.

Meyer, Lorenzo. 1992. "Las presidencias fuertes: El caso de la mexicana." *Revista del Centro de Estudios Constitucionales* 13 (September–November): 55–71.

Meyer, Lorenzo, Rafael Segovia, and Alejandra Lajous. 1978. *Los inicios de la institucionalización: La política del maximato.* Vol. 12 of *Historia de la revolución mexicana.* Mexico City: Colegio de México.

Moe, Terry. 1984. "The New Economics of Organization." *American Journal of Political Science* 28:739–77.

Molinar Horcasitas, Juan. 1991. *El tiempo de la legitimidad: Elecciones, autoritarismo y democracia en México.* Mexico City: Cal y Arena.

Molinar Horcasitas, Juan. 1993. "Escuelas de interpretación del sistema político mexicano." *Revista Mexicana de Sociología* 55, 2: 3–56.

Molinar Horcasitas, Juan. 1994. "Reestructuración económica y realineamientos políticos en México." Unpublished manuscript.

Molinar Horcasitas, Juan, Arturo Sánchez Gutiérrez, and Jeffrey A. Weldon. 1994. "El año que votamos en más peligro." *Nexos* 200: 65–73.

Molinar Horcasitas, Juan, and Jeffrey A. Weldon. 1990. "Elecciones de 1988 en México: Crisis del autoritarismo." *Revista Mexicana de Sociología* 52, 4:229–62.

Molinar Horcasitas, Juan, and Jeffrey A. Weldon. 1994. "Programa nacional de solidaridad: Determinantes partidistas y consecuencias electorales." *Estudios Sociológicos* 12, 34:155–81.

Molinelli, N. Guillermo. 1991a. *Presidentes y congresos en Argentina: Mitos y realidades.* Buenos Aires: Grupo Editor Latinoamericano.

Molinelli, N. Guillermo. 1991b. *Clase política y reforma electoral.* Buenos Aires: Grupo Editor Latinoamericano.

Molinelli, N. Guillermo. 1993. Interview (February 16). Professor at the Universidad de Buenos Aires.

Molinelli, N. Guillermo. 1994. "Como funcionaría la nueva constitución." *La Ley,* March 24, pp. 1–3.

Molinelli, N. Guillermo. 1995a. "President–Congress Relations in Argentina, 1983–95: In the Context of the Past and with a Look into the Future." Paper presented at the 19th International Congress of the Latin American Studies Association, Washington, D.C.

Molinelli, N. Guillermo. 1995b. "Constitutional Reform in Argentina." Unpublished manuscript, Universidad de Buenos Aires.

Moreno Sánchez, Manuel. 1970. *Crisis política de México.* 4th ed. Mexico City: Editorial Extemporáneos.

Muller, Herbert, and Flavio Machicado, eds. 1987. *El diálogo para la democracia.* La Paz: Quipus.

Muñoz Quesada, Hugo Alfonso. (1981). *La Asamblea Legislativa en Costa Rica.* San José: Editorial Costa Rica.

Mustapic, Ana María. 1993. Interview (February 11). Professor at the Universidad Torcuato Di Tella.

Mustapic, Ana María, and Natalia Ferretti. 1995a. "El veto presidencial bajo Alfonsín y Menem (1983–1993)." Paper presented at the 19th International Congress of the Latin American Studies Association, Washington, D.C.

Mustapic, Ana María, and Natalia Ferretti. 1995b. "El veto presidencial bajo Alfonsín y Menem (1983–1993)." Working paper, Universidad Torcuato Di Tella.

Mustapic, Ana María, and Matteo Goretti. 1992. "Gobierno y oposición en el Congreso: La práctica de la cohabitación durante la presidencia de Alfonsín (1983–1989)." *Desarrollo Económico* 32:251–69.

Nación, La (Buenos Aires, Argentina). April 5, 1990.

Nagel, Jack. 1994. "Market Liberalization in New Zealand: The Interaction of Economic Reform and Political Institutions in a Pluralitarian Democracy." Paper prepared for the annual meeting of the American Political Science Association, New York, September 1–4.

Nava, N. Carmen. 1988. "La democracia interna del Partido de la Revolución Mexicana (PRM): El problema de la supresión de los consejos regionales." *Revista Mexicana de Sociología* 50, 3:157–66.

Neustadt, Richard. 1980. *Presidential Power: The Politics of Leadership from FDR to Carter.* New York: Macmillan.

Nicolau, Jairo Marconi. Forthcoming. "Presidencialismo, Multipartidarismo Fragmentado e Democracia."

Nino, Carlos Santiago. 1992. "Que reforma constitucional?" *Propuesta y Control* 21: 2307–35.

Nohlen, Dieter, ed. 1993. *Enciclopedia electoral de América Latina y el Caribe.* San José: Instituto Interamericano de Derechos Humanos.

Novaes, Carlos Alberto Marques. 1994. "Dinâmica Institucional da Representação: Individualismo e Partidos na Câmara dos Deputados." *Novos Estudos* 38 (March): 99–147.

Nunes, Edson de Oliveira. 1984. "Bureaucratic Insulation and Clientelism in Contemporary Brazil: Uneven State-Building and the Taming of Modernity." Ph.D. dissertation, University of California at Berkeley.

O'Donnell, Guillermo. 1992. "Transitions, Continuities, and Paradoxes." In Scott Mainwaring, Guillermo O'Donnell, and J. Samuel Valenzuela, eds., *Issues in Democratic Consolidation: The New South American Democracies in Comparative Perspective* (pp. 17–56). Notre Dame, Ind.: University of Notre Dame Press.

O'Donnell, Guillermo. 1994. "Delegative Democracy." *Journal of Democracy* 5, 1: 55–69.

Office of the Controller of Costa Rica. 1974–91. *Memoria Anual*, Tercera Parte, Cuadros 18 and 20.

Oliveira, Lúcia Lippi. 1973. "Partidos Políticos Brasileiros: O Partido Social Democrático." M.A. thesis, IUPERJ.

Olson, Mancur. 1965. *The Logic of Collective Action*. Cambridge, Mass: Harvard University Press.

Operations and Policy Research, Inc. 1963. *Venezuela Election Fact Book (Elections: 1963)*. Washington, D.C.: Institute for the Comparative Study of Political Systems.

Ordeshook, Peter. 1995. "If Hamilton and Madison Were Merely Lucky, What Hope is There for Russian Federalism?" Unpublished paper.

Orozco Henríquez, J. Jesús. 1988. "El sistema presidencial en el constituyente de Querétaro y su evolución posterior." In *El sistema presidencial mexicano (algunas reflexiones)* (pp. 1–148). Mexico City: Instituto de Investigaciones Jurídicas, Universidad Nacional Autónoma de México.

Osorio Marbán, Miguel. 1970. *El Partido de la Revolución Mexicana (ensayo)*. Vol. 1. Mexico City: ICSA.

Packenham, Robert. 1970. "Legislatures and Political Development." In Allan Kornberg and Lloyd Musolf, eds., *Legislatures in Developmental Perspective* (pp. 521–82). Durham, N.C.: Duke University Press.

Packenham, Robert. 1971. "Functions of the Brazilian National Congress." In Weston Agor, ed., *Latin American Legislatures: Their Role and Influence* (pp. 259–92). New York: Praeger.

Packenham, Robert. 1994. "The Politics of Economic Liberalization: Argentina and Brazil in Comparative Perspective." Kellogg Institute Working Paper no. 206, University of Notre Dame, April.

Palmer, Matthew S. R. 1995. "Toward an Economics of Comparative Political Organization: Examining Ministerial Responsibility." *Journal of Law, Economics, and Organization* 11, 1:164–88.

Parrish, Scott. Forthcoming. "Decree Power in Russia, 1991–95." In John M. Carey and Mathew S. Shugart, eds, *Executive Decree Authority: Calling Out the Tanks or Just Filling Out the Forms?* Cambridge University Press.

Participa. 1993a. *Resultados de las elecciones de 1993*. Santiago: Participa.

Participa. 1993b. "Estudio sobre la democracia y participación política: Informe Segunda Medición 1992." Santiago: Participa.

Pecaut, Daniel. 1988. *Crónica de dos décadas de política colombiana, 1968–1988*. Bogotá: Siglo Veintiuno Editores.

Pessanha, Charles. 1993. "Notas sobre as Relações entre Executivo e Legislativo no Brasil: 1964–1992." Paper presented at the 17th annual meeting of ANPOCS, Caxambu, Minas Gerais, October 22–25.

Petersen, Phyllis Jane. 1962. "Brazilian Political Parties: Formation, Organization, and Leadership, 1945–1959." Ph.D. dissertation, University of Michigan, Ann Arbor.

Piccato, Pablo. 1991. *Congreso y revolución.* Mexico City: Insituto Nacional de Estudios Históricos de la Revolución Mexicana.

Pinzón de Lewin, Patricia, and Dora Rothlisberger. 1991. "La participación electoral en 1990: Un nuevo tipo de votante." In Ruben Sánchez, ed., *Los nuevos retos electorales: Colombia 1990 – Antesala del cambio* (pp. 133–66). Bogotá: CEREC.

Pírez, Pedro. 1986. *Coparticipación federal y descentralización del estado.* Buenos Aires: Centro Editor de América Latina.

Political Risk Services. 1989. *IBC International Country Risk Guide.* Syracuse, N.Y.: Political Risk Services.

Political Risk Services. 1995. *IBC International Country Risk Guide.* Syracuse, N.Y.: Political Risk Services.

Pontussi, Ennio Pedro. 1993. Interview (April 1). President of the bloc of the Partido Renovador de Salta in the Salta provincial Senate (1989–93).

Powell, G. Bingham, Jr. 1982. *Contemporary Democracies: Participation, Stability, and Violence.* Cambridge, Mass: Harvard University Press.

Power, Timothy J. 1991. "Politicized Democracy: Competition, Institutions, and 'Civic Fatigue' in Brazil." *Journal of Interamerican Studies and World Affairs* 33, 3 (Fall 1991):75–111.

Power, Timothy J. 1994. "The Pen Is Mightier than the Congress: Presidential Decree Power in Brazil." Paper presented at the 18th International Congress of the Latin American Studies Association, Atlanta, March 10–12.

Power, Timothy. Forthcoming. "The Pen Is Mightier than the Congress: Presidential Decree Power in Brazil." In John M. Carey and Mathew S. Shugart, eds., *Executive Decree Authority: Calling Out the Tanks or Just Filling Out the Forms?* Cambridge University Press.

Prieto Laurens, Jorge. 1968. *Cincuenta años de política mexicana.* Mexico City: Editora Mexicana de Periódicos, Libros y Revistas.

Rabassa, Emilio. 1957. *La constitución y la dictadura.* 3rd ed. Mexico City: Porrúa.

Rae, Douglas W. 1967. *The Political Consequences of Electoral Laws.* New Haven, Conn: Yale University Press.

Ramos, Guerreiro. 1961. *A Crise de Poder no Brasil.* Rio de Janeiro: Zahar.

Rehren, Alfredo. 1992. "Organizing the Presidency for the Consolidation of Democracy in the Southern Cone." Paper presented at the 17th International Congress of the Latin American Studies Association, Los Angeles, September 24–27.

República de Bolivia. 1967. *Constitución política del estado.* La Paz: Ediciones Puerta del Sol.

República de Nicaragua. August 1995. *Constitución política: Con las reformas vigentes de 1995.* Managua: Documentación Parlamentaria de la Asemblea Nacional de Nicaragua, Segundo Edición Oficial.

República de Peru. 1993. *Constitución, 1993.* Lima: Diario de Oficial El Peruano.

Rey, Juan Carlos. 1993. "La crisis de legitimidad en Venezuela y el enjuiciamiento y remoción de Carlos Andrés Pérez de la Presidencia de la República." *Boletín Electoral Latinoamericano* 9 (January–June):67–112.

Rey, Juan Carlos. 1994. "Polarización electoral, economía del voto y voto castigo en Venezuela: 1958–1988." *Cuestiones Políticas* 12:3–95.

Riggs, Fred. 1988. "The Survival of Presidentialism in America: Para-Constitutional Practices." *International Political Science Review* 9, 4 (October):247–78.

Riker, William H. 1962. *The Theory of Political Coalitions.* New Haven, Conn.: Yale University Press.

Robinson, Donald L., ed. 1985. *Reforming American Government: The Bicentennial Papers of the Committee on the Constitutional System.* Boulder, Colo: Westview.

Rodríguez Sañudo, Hugo. 1993. Interview (March 4). National deputy (1991–95) (PJ) from the province of Santa Fe.

Romero Feris, José Antonio. 1993. Interview (March 15). National senator (PAL) from the province of Corrientes (1987–95) and governor of Corrientes (1983–87).

Rose, Richard. 1981. "Government against Sub-Governments: A European Perspective on Washington." In Richard Rose and Ezra Suleiman, eds., *Presidents and Prime Ministers* (pp. 284–347). Washington, D.C.: American Enterprise Institute.

Roverssi, Carlos. 1992a. "Distritales de PLN a Sala IV." *La República* (San José), p. 6A.

Roverssi, Carlos. 1992b. "Figuerismo hizo su fiesta." *La República* (San José), p. 2A.

Rueschmeyer, Dietrich, Evelyne Huber Stephens, and John D. Stephens. 1992. *Capitalist Development and Democracy.* Chicago: University of Chicago Press.

Sabsay, Daniel A., and José M. Onaindia. 1994. *La Constitución de los argentinos: Análisis de su texto luego de la reforma de 1994.* Buenos Aires: Errepar.

Salazar, Jorge Mario. 1981. *Política y reforma en Costa Rica: 1914–1958.* San José: Editorial Porvenir.

Sampietro, Darci. 1994. Interview (April 21). National deputy (1993–97) (PJ) from the province of Entre Rios.

Samuels, David J. Forthcoming. "Parties and Politicians: Collective and Individual Strategy under the Open List in Brazil."

Sani, Giacomo, and Giovanni Sartori. 1983. "Polarization, Fragmentation, and Competition in Western Democracies." In Hans Daalder and Peter Mair, eds., *Western European Party Systems* (pp. 307–40). Beverly Hills, Calif.: Sage.

Santamaría, Ricardo S., and Gabriel Silva. 1984. *Proceso político en Colombia: Del Frente Nacional a la apertura democrática.* Bogotá: CEREC.

Santos, Wanderley Guilherme dos. 1986. *Sessenta e Quatro: Anatomia da Crise.* São Paulo: Vértice.

Saravia, Joaquín, and Godofredo Sandóval. 1991. *Jach'a Uru: ¿La esperanza de un pueblo?* La Paz: ILDIS-CEP.

Sarles, Margaret J. 1982. "Maintaining Political Control through Parties: The Brazilian Strategy." *Comparative Politics* 15 (October): 41–72.

Sartori, Giovanni. 1966. "European Political Parties: The Case for Polarized Pluralism." In Joseph La Palombra and Myron Weiner, eds. *Political Parties and Political Development* (pp. 137–76). Princeton, N.J.: Princeton University Press.

Sartori, Giovanni. 1976. *Parties and Party Systems: A Framework for Analysis.* Cambridge University Press.

Sartori, Giovanni. 1994a. *Comparative Constitutional Engineering: An Inquiry into Structures, Incentives, and Outcomes.* New York: New York University Press.

Sartori, Giovanni. 1994b. "Neither Presidentialism nor Parliamentarism." In Linz and Valenzuela (1994), 106–18.

Schmidt, Gregory D. Forthcoming. "Presidential Decree Authority in Peru, 1980–1993: Passivity, Confrontation, and Compromise?" In John M. Carey and Mathew S. Shugart, eds., *Executive Decree Authority: Calling Out the Tanks or Just Filling Out the Forms.* Cambridge University Press.

Schneider, Ben Ross. 1992. "Privatization in the Collor Government: Triumph of Liberalism or Collapse of the Developmental State?" In Douglas Chalmers, Maria do Carmo Campello de Souza, and Atilio Borón, eds., *The Right and Democracy in Latin America* (pp. 225–38). New York: Praeger.

Scully, Timothy, and J. Samuel Valenzuela. 1993. "De la democracia a la democracia: Continuidad y variaciones en las preferencias del electorado y en el sistema de partidos en Chile." *Estudios Públicos* 51:195–228.

Segovia, Rafael. 1975. *La politización del niño mexicano.* Mexico City: Colegio de México.

Segovia, Rafael. 1987. "El fastidio electoral." In Soledad Loaeza and Rafael Segovia, eds., *La vida política mexicana en crisis* (pp. 13–23). Mexico City: Colegio de México.

Seligson, Mitchell. 1987. "Costa Rica and Jamaica." In Myron Weiner and Ergun Ozbudin, eds., *Competitive Elections in Developing Countries* (pp 147–98). Durham, N.C.: Duke University Press.

Shugart, Matthew S. 1988. "Duverger's Rule, District Magnitude, and Presidentialism." Ph.D. dissertation, University of California at Irvine.

Shugart, Matthew S. 1992a. "Leaders, Rank and File, and Constituents: Electoral Reform in Colombia and Venezuela." *Electoral Studies* 11, 1 (1992):21–45.

Shugart, Matthew S. 1992b. "Guerrillas and Elections: An Institutionalist Perspective on the Costs and Conflicts of Competition." *International Studies Quarterly* 36 (1992):121–52.

Shugart, Matthew S. 1995a. "The Electoral Cycle and Institutional Sources of Divided Presidential Government." *American Political Science Review* 89, 2 (June):327–43.

Shugart, Matthew S. 1995b. "Parliaments over Presidents?" *Journal of Democracy* 6, 2 (April):168–72.

Shugart, Matthew S. N.d. "The Inverse Relationship between Party Strength and Executive Strength: A Theory of Politicians' Constitutional Choices." Unpublished paper.

Shugart, Matthew S., and John M. Carey. 1992. *Presidents and Assemblies: Constitutional Design and Electoral Dynamics.* Cambridge University Press.

Shugart, Matthew S., and Daniel L. Nielson. 1994. "Liberalization through Institutional Reform: Economic Adjustment and Constitutional Change in Colombia." Unpublished paper.

Shugart, Matthew S., and Rein Taagepera. 1994. "Majority versus Plurality Election of Presidents: A Proposal for a Double Complement Rule." *Comparative Political Studies* 27, 3 (October):323–48.

Siavelis, Peter. 1993. "Nuevos argumentos y viejos supuestos: Simulaciones de sistemas electorales alternativos para las elecciones parlamentarias chilenas." *Estudios Públicos* 51:229–67.

Siavelis, Peter. 1995. "The Reductive Effect of Low District Magnitude in Multiparty Systems: Chile as a Case Study." Unpublished manuscript.

Skidmore, Thomas. 1967. *Politics in Brazil, 1930–1964: An Experiment in Democracy.* New York: Oxford University Press.

Smith, Donald Lee. 1974. "Pre-PRI: The Mexican Government Party." Unpublished Ph.D. dissertation, Texas Christian University.

Smulovitz, Catalina. 1993. Interview (February 18). Research scholar at the Centro de Estudios de Estado y Sociedad.

Smulovitz, Catalina. 1995. "Constitución y poder judicial en la nueva democracia argentina: La experiencia de las instituciones." In Carlos H. Acuña, ed., *La nueva matriz política argentina* (pp. 71–114). Buenos Aires: Nueva Visión.

Sojo Obando, Carlos. 1992. Interview (January 9). Researcher for the Facultad Latinoamericano de Ciencias Sociales.

Sordo Cedeño, Reynaldo. 1993. *El Congreso en la primera república centralista.* Mexico City: Colegio de México/Instituto Tecnológico Autónomo de México.

Souza, Maria do Carmo Campello de. 1976. *Estado e Partidos Políticos no Brasil (1930 a 1964).* São Paulo: Alfa-Omega.

Souza, Maria Tereza Sadek. 1986. "A Trajetória de Jânio Quadros." In Bolivar Lamounier, ed., *1985: O Voto em São Paulo* (pp. 66–88). São Paulo: IDESP.

Stepan, Alfred C. 1971. *The Military in Politics: Changing Patterns in Brazil.* Princeton, N.J.: Princeton University Press.

Stepan, Alfred C. 1978. "Political Leadership and Regime Breakdown: Brazil." In Linz and Stepan (1978), 110–37.

Stepan, Alfred C., and Cindy Skach. 1994. "Presidentialism and Parliamentarism in Comparative Perspective." In Linz and Valenzuela (1994), vol. 1, 119–36.

Strom, Kaare. 1990. *Minority Government and Majority Rule.* Cambridge University Press.

Suárez, Waldino. 1982. "El poder ejecutivo en América Latina: Su capacidad operativa bajo regímenes presidencialistas de gobierno." *Revista de Estudios Políticos* 29:109–44.

Sundquist, James L. 1986. *Constitutional Reform and Effective Government.* Washington D.C.: Brookings Institution.

Taagepera, Rein, and Matthew S. Shugart. 1989. *Seats and Votes: The Effects and Determinants of Electoral Systems.* New Haven, Conn.: Yale University Press.

Taagepera, Rein, and Matthew S. Shugart. 1993. "Predicting the Number of Parties: A Quantitative Model of Duverger's Mechanical Effect." *American Political Science Review* 87, 2:455–64.

Tamayo, Jaime. 1987. *En el interinato de Adolfo De la Huerta y el gobierno de Alvaro Obregón (1920–1924).* Vol. 7 of *La clase obrera en la historia de México.* Mexico City: Siglo XXI.

Tapia Valdés, Jorge. 1966. *La técnica legislativa*. Santiago: Editorial Jurídica de Chile.

Taylor, Michelle M. 1992. "Formal versus Informal Incentive Structures and Legislative Behavior: Evidence from Costa Rica." *Journal of Politics* 54, 4 (November):1055–73.

Tena Ramírez, Felipe. 1985. *Derecho constitucional mexicano*. 21st ed. Mexico City: Porrúa.

Tena Ramírez, Felipe. 1991. *Leyes fundamentales de México: 1808–1991*. 16th ed. Mexico City: Porrúa.

Tiempo, El. 1994a. "Quienes son los 'verdes' que aspiran al Congreso?" March 12, p. 13c.

Tiempo, El. 1994b. "Castigo a candidatos disidentes." October 24, p. 7A.

Tiempo, El. 1994c. "Liberalismo expulsó a César Pérez." December 16, pp. 1A, 8A.

Tribunal Supremo de Elecciones. 1989. *Código electoral y otras disposiciones conexas*. San José: Imprenta Nacional.

Tugwell, Franklin. 1975. *The Politics of Oil in Venezuela*. Stanford, Calif.: Stanford University Press.

Umaña Luna, Eduardo. 1985. *Hacia la paz*. Bogotá: Comité de Solidaridad con los Presos Políticos.

Urrutia, Miguel. 1991. "On the Absence of Economic Populism in Colombia." In Rudiger Dornbusch and Sebastian Edwards, eds., *Macroeconomic Populism in Latin America* (pp. 369–87). Chicago: University of Chicago Press.

Urzúa, Germán. 1968. *Los partidos políticos chilenos*. Santiago: Ed. Jurídica.

Valadés, Diego. 1978. "El poder legislativo en México (1950–1975)." In *Evolución de la organización político-constitucional en América Latina (1950–1975)* (vol. 1, pp. 49–71). Mexico City: Universidad Nacional Autónoma de México.

Valadés, Diego. 1988. "El control interorgánico entre los poderes legislativo y ejecutivo de México." In *El sistema presidencial mexicano (algunas reflexiones)* (pp. 245–68). Mexico City: Instituto de Investigaciones Jurídicas, Universidad Nacional Autónoma de México.

Valencia Avaria, Luis. 1986. *Anales de la república. Textos constitucionales de Chile y registro de los ciudadanos que han integrado los poderes ejecutivo y legistativo desde 1810*. Tomo I. Santiago de Chile: Editorial Andrés Bello.

Valenzuela, Arturo. 1977. *Political Brokers in Chile*. Durham, N.C.: Duke University Press.

Valenzuela, Arturo. 1978. *The Breakdown of Democratic Regimes: Chile*. Baltimore: Johns Hopkins University Press.

Valenzuela, Arturo. 1985. "Orígenes y características del sistema de partidos en Chile: Proposición para un gobierno parlamentario," *Estudios Políticos* 18 (Fall): 88–154.

Valenzuela, Arturo. 1990. "Partidos políticos y crisis presidencial en Chile: Proposición para un gobierno parlamentario." In Oscar Godoy, ed., *Hacia una democracia moderna: La opción parlamentaria* (pp. 129–80). Santiago: Ediciones Universidad Católica de Chile.

Valenzuela, Arturo. 1994. "Party Politics and the Crisis of Presidentialism in Chile: A Proposal for a Parliamentary Form of Government." In Linz and Valenzuela (1994), 91–150.

Valenzuela, Arturo, and Peter Siavelis. 1991. "Ley electoral y estabilidad democrática: Un ejercicio de simulación para el caso de Chile." *Estudios Públicos* 43:27–88.

Valenzuela, Arturo, and Alexander Wilde. 1979. "Presidential Politics and the Decline of the Chilean Congress." In Joel Smith and Lloyd Musolf, eds., *Legislatures in Development: Dynamics of Change in New and Old States* (pp. 189–215). Durham, N.C.: Duke University Press.

Valenzuela, Arturo, and Alexander Wilde. 1984. "El Congreso y la redemocratización en Chile." *Alternativas* 3:26–35.

Vanhanen, Tatu. 1990. *The Process of Democratization: A Comparative Study of 147 States, 1980–1988*. New York: Crane Russak.

Vanossi, Jorge Reinaldo. 1991. *Historia electoral argentina: 1853–1989*. Actualización 1975–89 por Fermín Pedro Ubertone. Buenos Aires: Lumiere.

Vargas, Getúlio. 1951. *A Campanha Presidencial*. Rio de Janeiro: José Olympio.

Vázquez Carrizosa, Alfredo. 1986. *El poder presidencial en Colombia: La crisis permanente del derecho constitucional*, 3rd ed. Bogotá: Ediciones Suramérica.

Velásquez, Ramón J. 1976. "Aspectos de la evolución política de Venezuela en el último medio siglo." In Ramón J. Velásquez, Arístides Calvani, Carlos Rafael Silva, and Juan Liscano, eds., *Venezuela moderna: Medio siglo de historia, 1926–1976* (pp. 1–385). Caracas: Fundación Eugenio Mendoza.

Ventura Robles, Manuel E. 1984. *La representación política*. San José: Editorial Juricentro.

Vidal Perdomo, Jaime. 1970. *La reforma constitucional de 1968 y sus alcances jurídicos*. Bogotá: Universidad Externado de Colombia.

Vidal Perdomo, Jaime, and Luis Carlos Sáchica. 1991. *Aproximación crítica de la constitución de 1991*. Bogotá: Cámara de Comercio de Bogotá.

Villa Aguilera, Manuel. 1987. *La institución presidencial: El poder de las instituciones y los espacios de la democracia*. Mexico City: Coordinación de Humanidades, Universidad Nacional Autónoma de México.

Villalobos, José Miguel. 1992. Interview (February 28). Secretary of the Costa Rican PLN Tribunal de Ética, 1986–87; assistant to PLN Assembly Caucus, 1982–89; assistant to José Miguel Corrales Bolaños, PLN presidential candidate, 1991–92. San José.

Villanueva Badilla, Jorge Luís. 1992. Interview (March 17). Costa Rican deputy for the PLN, 1966–70, 1982–86; president of the Legislative Assembly, 1983–84. Cartago.

Villegas Antillón, Rafael. 1992. Interview (January 6). Magistrate of the Costa Rican Tribunal Supremo de Elecciones. San José.

Volio Guevara, Julieta. 1988. "La organización del poder legislativo en Costa Rica." Law School thesis, Ciudad Universidad Rodrigo Facio, San José.

Weiner, Myron. 1987. "Empirical Democratic Theory." In Myron Weiner and Ergun Özbudun, eds., *Competitive Elections in Developing Countries* (pp. 3–34). Durham, N.C.: Duke University Press.

Weldon, Jeffrey A. 1994. "Congress, Political Machines, and the *Maximato*: The No-Reelection Reforms of 1933." Paper presented at meeting of the Latin American Studies Association, Atlanta.

Williamson, John. 1990. "The Progress of Policy Reform in Latin America." Washington, D.C.: Institute for International Economics, Paper no. 28 (January).

Williamson, John, and Stephan Haggard. 1994. "The Political Conditions for Economic Reform." In John Williamson, ed., *The Political Economy of Policy Reform* (pp. 527–96). Washington, D.C.: Institute for International Economics.

Williamson, Oliver. 1975. *Markets and Hierarchies, Analysis and Antitrust Implications: A Study in the Economics of Internal Organization.* New York: Free Press.

Williamson, Oliver. 1985. *The Economic Institutions of Capitalism: Firms, Markets, Relational Contracting.* New York : Free Press.

Wilson, Bruce M. 1994. "When Social Democrats Choose Neoliberal Economic Policies: The Case of Costa Rica." *Comparative Politics* 26:149–68.

World Bank. 1994. *World Development Report, 1994.* New York: Oxford University Press.

Zevada, Ricardo J. 1971. *Calles, el presidente.* Mexico City: Editorial Nuestro Tiempo.

Zuleta Puceiro, Enrique. 1993. Interview (February 18). President of the public opinion firm SOFRES-IBOPE and university professor.

INDEX